Cruel & Unusual

Also by John D. Bessler

Death in the Dark: Midnight Executions in America
Kiss of Death: America's Love Affair with the Death Penalty
Legacy of Violence: Lynch Mobs and Executions in Minnesota
Writing for Life: The Craft of Writing for Everyday Living

Cruel & Unusual

THE AMERICAN DEATH PENALTY AND THE
FOUNDERS' EIGHTH AMENDMENT

JOHN D. BESSLER

Northeastern University Press

BOSTON

NORTHEASTERN UNIVERSITY PRESS
An imprint of University Press of New England
www.upne.com
© 2012 Northeastern University
All rights reserved
Manufactured in the United States of America
Designed by Katherine B. Kimball
Typeset in Monticello by Keystone Typesetting, Inc.

University Press of New England is a member of the
Green Press Initiative. The paper used in this book meets
their minimum requirement for recycled paper.

For permission to reproduce any of the material in this book, contact
Permissions, University Press of New England, One Court Street,
Suite 250, Lebanon NH 03766; or visit www.upne.com

Library of Congress Cataloging-in-Publication Data
Bessler, John D.
Cruel and unusual : the American death penalty and the
founders' Eighth Amendment / John D. Bessler.
p. cm.
Includes bibliographical references and index.
ISBN 978-1-55553-716-6 (cloth : alk. paper)
ISBN 978-1-55553-717-3 (ebook)
1. Capital punishment—United States. I. Title.
KF9227.C2B478 2011
345.73'0773—dc23   2011034380

5 4 3 2 1

In memory of
Cesare Beccaria
and
Dr. Benjamin Rush

I am certainly not an advocate for frequent changes in laws and constitutions. But laws and institutions must go hand in hand with the progress of the human mind. As that becomes more developed, more enlightened, as new discoveries are made, new truths discovered and manners and opinions change, with the change of circumstances, institutions must advance also to keep pace with the times. We might as well require a man to wear still the coat which fitted him when a boy as civilized society to remain ever under the regimen of their barbarous ancestors.

—THOMAS JEFFERSON

Perhaps the whole business of the retention of the death penalty will seem to the next generation, as it seems to many even now, an anachronism too discordant to be suffered, mocking with grim reproach all our clamorous professions of the sanctity of life. —BENJAMIN CARDOZO

CONTENTS

Acknowledgments   xi

Introduction   1

1 | In Cold Blood   12

2 | On Crimes and Punishments   31

3 | The Abolitionists   66

4 | America's Founding Fathers   97

5 | The Eighth Amendment   162

6 | Capital Punishment in America   222

7 | The Road to Abolition   265

Conclusion   339

Notes   349

Bibliography   405

Index   417

ACKNOWLEDGMENTS

Writing a book is like hiking up a mountain—it's both exhilarating and exhausting. When you hike, you pick a trail, try to follow a few scattered markers, but occasionally wander off a not-so-worn path, getting momentarily lost in the forest as you wind your way to the top. The summit—above the tree line—often seems as if it will never come, but then, after climbing over boulders and logs, contending with pesky mosquitoes, crossing muddy streams, and taking narrow switchbacks through rocky, unfamiliar terrain, you suddenly find yourself with a clear view, from the peak, of all the valleys below. The writer E. L. Doctorow likens authoring a book to driving a car at night— and there's truth in what he says. "You can see as far as your headlights go," he relates, "but you can make the whole trip that way." For me, though, the hiking analogy is more apt. I've always found writing to be a slow, grueling process— and a car ride, even a long one through the dark, doesn't capture all the toil and sweat that goes into a book. There are the outlining and the research; the drafting of sentences and paragraphs, then whole chapters; and the endless revision—not to mention all the laborious proofreading of galleys, let alone the tedious preparation of the index. The publication process proceeds at a hiker's pace, and unlike a road trip, the task of writing a book means countless hours spent alone, away from family and friends.

This book—my fourth on the death penalty—is, in a way, the product of roughly two decades of work. Over the past twenty years, I've spent literally thousands of hours reflecting on capital punishment. For much of that time, I also practiced law full-time, making evenings and weekends—not exactly the most family-friendly times—my only available slots to research and write. I thus owe special thanks—at the very outset—to my wife and daughter, Amy and Abigail, for putting up with my writing life. They are the pride and joys of my life, and as talented writers themselves, they have indulged my odd-hours writing with a generosity of spirit I suspect few other spouses or kids would readily endure. I also owe a debt of gratitude to my friends and colleagues, whose support and encouragement allowed me to finish this book. The debts I owe, in fact, are too numerous to mention. Librarians located hard-to-find sources for me; the law students I've taught since 1998 have continually informed and shaped my views on capital punishment; and even random acts of kindness by fellow lawyers—perhaps nothing more than a forwarded link to a breaking news story—have helped me tremendously along the way. Law professor Victor Streib, at Ohio Northern University, graciously agreed to review the manuscript, as did Professor Paul Kaplan at San Diego State University. My parents, Bill and Marilyn Bessler, and three close friends—Bruce Beddow, Michael Handberg, and Rob Hendrickson—were also helpful as I wrote the book. I am especially grateful that Sister Helen Prejean—the author of *Dead Man Walking: An Eyewitness Account of the Death Penalty in the United States*—recommended Northeastern University Press as the publisher for my first book, getting me off to a good start on my trek.

The path to this book has been a long one. I grew up in Mankato, Minnesota, a wonderful town in the southern part of the state, but also the site of America's largest mass hanging. In 1862, in the midst of the Civil War, President Abraham Lincoln ordered the execution of thirty-eight Dakota Indians. A U.S. military commission sentenced more than three hundred Indians to die for participating in a violent uprising, but Lincoln, believing that number far too excessive, set aside all but thirty-eight of the death sentences. "Anxious to not act with so much clemency as to encourage another outbreak on the one hand, nor with so much severity as to be real cruelty on the other," Lincoln explained, "I caused a careful examination of the records of the trials to be made." That examination—revealing short trials bereft of due process—prompted Lincoln, the Illinois lawyer turned commander in chief, to temper his death warrant with a considerable show of mercy despite intense public opposition. Though Lincoln wrote out his order by hand and took precautions to ensure that only those he listed would die, at least one Dakota captive, Chaska, was executed by mistake. Acquitted for saving a woman's life, Chaska—also known as We-Chank-Wash-ta-don-pee—was confused with Chaskaydon, who had killed a pregnant woman and cut a fetus out of her womb. The lore of that mass execution, conducted on a large, wooden scaffold just a few blocks from where I grew up, gave me my first glimpse of the death penalty's long, sordid history.

In the 1980s, while in high school and college, I read a fair amount about capital punishment. But in truth, my eyes were not fully opened to the harsh reality of America's death penalty until I began studying and practicing law. As a law student at Indiana University in Bloomington, I took a death penalty course from Professor Joseph Hoffmann—a former law clerk for the late Chief Justice William Rehnquist. In that class, I read cases revealing the abysmal quality of counsel that death row inmates so often receive at their criminal trials. I also came to learn that juvenile offenders were then still subject to execution, and that race—then as now—routinely plays a decisive role in deciding who lives and who dies. After graduating from IU in 1991, I took the bar exam and went to work for Faegre & Benson, a large Minneapolis law firm where I worked on capital cases with Jim Volling, one of the firm's senior partners. Motivated by that experience, I wrote my first book, *Death in the Dark: Midnight Executions in America*, and began teaching a death penalty course at the University of Minnesota Law School. I later taught that seminar in Washington, D.C. at The George Washington University Law School and the Georgetown University Law Center. Two other books followed my first—one about the history of executions and extrajudicial killings in my home state, and another, a book-length essay, about the national, public policy debate surrounding capital punishment.

In *Cruel and Unusual: The American Death Penalty and the Founders' Eighth Amendment*, I now turn my attention to a different, much more focused question: does America's death penalty violate the U.S. Constitution's Eighth Amendment prohibition on "cruel and unusual punishments"? In my quest to answer that question, I gathered lots of materials and was aided by several top-flight research assistants: Michael Ansell, Jonathan Auerbach, Nyasha Griffith, Keith Hinder, Anne Marchessault, Bradley Sarnell, Mark Taticchi, John Tramazzo, and Laura Valden. These law students and recent graduates helped me gather valuable sources, and the book is a better one because of their efforts. I also need to thank the staff of the *Northwestern Journal of Law and Social Policy*. The staff's editing of my 2009 law review article, "Revisiting Beccaria's Vision: The Enlightenment, America's Death Penalty and the Abolition Movement," resulted in a much-improved manuscript. Special thanks, too, go to my colleagues at Georgetown and the University of Baltimore School of Law, especially Garrett Epps and C. J. Peters, who took the time to discuss this project with me. I'd also like to thank Fred Lawrence, president of Brandeis University and formerly dean of The George Washington University Law School, and Dean Phillip Closius at the University of Baltimore School of Law. A GWU summer research grant made my Northwestern law review article—and thus the origins of this book—possible, and additional summer research grants from UB allowed me to put the finishing touches on the manuscript.

I want to thank all of my many former students for taking my death penalty seminar and for their thoughtful in-class participation. The papers my students write every year always challenge and inspire me. I also need to thank the many guest speakers who spoke to my students and shared their own insights over the years: the late Hon. Donald P. Lay of the U.S. Court of Appeals for the Eighth Circuit; Sandra Babcock and Joseph Margulies at the Northwestern University School of Law; Robin Maher, Director of the American Bar Association's Death Penalty Representation Project; Richard Dieter, Executive Director of the Death Penalty Information Center; David Lillehaug, former U.S. Attorney for the District of Minnesota; Susan Karamanian, GWU's Associate Dean for International and Comparative Legal Studies; Hennepin County District Court Judge Bruce Peterson; and Amy Dillard, Tom Fraser, John Getsinger, Andre Hanson, Tom Johnson, Steven Kaplan, Greg Merz, Steve Pincus, Tim Rank, Jonathan Shapiro, Jim Volling, and Steve Wells—all lawyers who have handled capital cases. While studying international human rights law at Oxford University, I also had the privilege to take a class on international criminal law from Bill Schabas, the director of the Irish Centre for Human Rights and one of the world's leading experts on the death penalty. His first-rate scholarship on the abolition of the death penalty in international law has been a special inspiration to me.

Last but certainly not least, I want to thank everyone at the University Press of New England—the entity that acquires and edits, then markets and distributes, all of the books for Northeastern University Press. Richard Pult, my acquisitions editor, and Michael Burton, the director of the press, got behind this project from the start, and the press has done a masterful job of producing the book. I would especially like to thank the staff of the press, including freelance copyeditor David Chu, for all the editing and production assistance. Northeastern University Press has been publishing readable, high-quality books on capital punishment for decades now, and the commitment of the press to providing Americans with up-to-date information on this important topic is as commendable as the unparalleled assistance I received from the press through every stage of the publication process. As this book wound its way uphill, past the initial book proposal, through the writing and editorial phases, and finally, into galleys and proofs, the professionalism of everyone at the press really stood out. It is my sincere hope that this book—a view of capital punishment from the mountaintop, the vista I've reached after a long, arduous climb—will inject some new, much-needed clarity into America's contentious death penalty debate.

Cruel & Unusual

Introduction

In 1971, the U.S. Supreme Court agreed to hear the appeals of three black, indigent defendants—William Furman, Lucious Jackson, and Elmer Branch, all sentenced to death by Southern juries. The National Association for the Advancement of Colored People (NAACP) had launched a moratorium campaign against the death penalty in the 1960s, and the grant of certiorari in the three cases came at a time when, in America, more than six hundred inmates sat on death row. A racial disparity in the imposition of death sentences for rape had spurred lawyers at the NAACP's Legal Defense Fund to file legal challenges, especially after three U.S. Supreme Court Justices dissented in a 1963 case in which a black man had been sentenced to death for raping a white woman. The dissenters in *Rudolph v. Alabama*—Justices Arthur Goldberg, William Douglas, and William Brennan—raised questions about the death penalty's constitutionality under the Eighth and Fourteenth Amendments for rapists who did not kill their victims, citing a United Nations (UN) report detailing a worldwide trend against punishing rape by death. The dissenters specifically asked whether the death penalty's imposition for rape constituted "unnecessary cruelty" and violated the "evolving standards of decency" of a "maturing society"—the legal standard for evaluating Eighth Amendment claims; whether the taking of human life "to protect a value other than human life" was disproportionate to the crime; and whether permissible aims of punishment, such as deterrence, could be achieved just as effectively by punishing rape by life imprisonment.[1]

When the Supreme Court agreed to hear the claims of William Furman, Lucious Jackson, and Elmer Branch in 1971, no executions had taken place in the United States since 1967—and the death penalty's popularity, as reflected in public opinion polls, was declining. The NAACP's frontal assault on the death penalty, led by law professor Anthony Amsterdam, focused largely on the issues of race and whether death sentences were disproportionate to the crimes. Furman had been sentenced to die for killing—he claimed unintentionally—a white homeowner during a burglary, and Jackson and Branch had both been convicted of raping white women. In each man's case, the Court indicated its review would be limited to a single question: "Does the imposition and carrying out of the death penalty in this case constitute cruel and unusual punishment in violation of the Eighth and Fourteenth Amendments?" The Eighth Amendment bars "cruel and unusual punishments," while the Fourteenth Amendment—a post–Civil War amendment making the Eighth Amendment applicable to the States—reads: "No State shall make or enforce any law which shall abridge the privileges or immunities of citizens of the United States; nor shall any State deprive any person of life, liberty, or property, without due process of law; nor deny to any person within its jurisdiction the equal protection of the laws."[2]

The NAACP's amicus brief—joined by the National Urban League, the Southern Christian Leadership Conference, the Mexican-American Legal Defense and Educational Fund, and the National Council of Negro Women—highlighted the pattern of racial discrimination associated with lynchings and capital punishment. The NAACP had helped secure the passage of state anti-lynching laws after its formation in 1909, and the NAACP's brief recounted the history of slavery, lynchings, and vigilantism from 1882 to 1935, including the disparate punishment of minorities charged with rape. In making its case, the NAACP pointed to early American slave codes that—on their face—punished blacks more severely than whites and permitted "[t]he most brutal and inhumane forms of punishment—crucifixion, burning and starvation." In the era of slavery, the NAACP noted, every Southern state had laws defining felonies that carried capital punishment for slaves but lesser punishments for whites. Under those laws, slaves could receive the death penalty for murder or attempted murder, manslaughter, rape or attempted rape of a white woman, rebellion or attempted rebellion, poisoning, robbery, or arson. "This pervasive authorization of capital punishment," the NAACP argued, recalling the country's use of executions to achieve social order, "was, ironically, due to the fact that the slave trade was so thriving; often the masters of the slaves were so largely outnumbered that there was always the fear of violent rebellion." The first antislavery society was not formed until 1775 in Philadelphia; many of the Founding Fathers, including George Washington, James Madison, and Thomas Jefferson, owned slaves; and in 1791—the same year the Eighth Amendment was ratified—a bloody slave rebellion in St. Domingue (now Haiti) spurred dread among American slave owners that America, too, might witness a violent insurrection of its own.[3]

The NAACP's brief specifically sought to place the death penalty within "the full context of the struggle for racial justice." "The total history of the administration of capital punishment in America, both through formal authority, and informally," the NAACP argued, "is persuasive evidence, that racial discrimination was, and still is, an impermissible factor in the disproportionate imposition of the death penalty upon non-white American citizens." The NAACP made a strong statistical case: from 1882 to 1903, 1,985 blacks were killed by Southern lynch mobs, a number far higher than the figure for whites who met a similar fate; from 1903 to 1935, 1,015 blacks were also lynched, a number that did not even include "kangaroo court actions, unreported murders, or blacks killed in race riots"; and of the 3,334 persons executed for murder between 1930 and 1968, almost half, 1,630, were black, with 1,231 of those executions from one geographic region, the South. Of the 443 convicted rapists executed in the South from 1930 to 1968, an overwhelming number, 398, were black. Such social science data, the NAACP asserted, proved that "the death penalty is discriminatorily imposed in contravention to the Equal Protection Clause of the Fourteenth Amendment." "To take a life, without refutation of that impermissible factor," its brief argued, is "inconsistent" with the Eighth Amendment's Cruel and Unusual Punishments Clause.[4]

The NAACP next sought to put the information it presented into an even broader social context: "Slavery was exclusively a Southern phenomenon, lynching was primarily a Southern phenomenon, and the general data with respect to all crimes, and particularly the crime of rape, indicates that the South has been the prime contributor to the disproportionate application of the death penalty to blacks." "To vote to put a man to death," the NAACP asserted, "requires the juror to place some distance between himself and the defendant, and this process is facilitated if he can, because of some perception of the defendant, dehumanize him." Arguing that the petitioners "are engaged in a grim struggle for their lives," the NAACP invoked Martin Luther King Jr.'s commitment to nonviolence, noting that even Dr. King's assassination did not alter the Southern Christian Leadership Conference's anti–death penalty stance. After James Earl Ray's conviction, Dr. King's widow, Coretta Scott King, had spoken out against capital punishment on behalf of the civil rights organization her husband once led. "The death penalty for the man who pleaded guilty to the crime," she said, "would be contrary to the deeply held moral and religious convictions of my husband." "Retribution and vengeance," she added, "have no place in our beliefs." King himself—devastated by the brutal killing of fourteen-year-old Emmett Till in Mississippi—had once spoken out against extrajudicial violence, saying that "the law may not be able to make a man love me, but it can keep him from lynching me." Till, an African American boy from Chicago who reportedly whistled at a white woman, was beaten and had an eye gouged out—and was savagely attacked with a hatchet— before he was shot through the head and thrown into the Tallahatchie River.[5]

At oral argument in *Furman v. Georgia,* Anthony Amsterdam—William Furman's counsel—passionately argued that the Supreme Court should not hesitate "to strike down a rare and harsh punishment like capital punishment."

Instead of executing fifteen or twenty people every year, Amsterdam argued before the nation's highest court in January 1972, inmates should simply be imprisoned. Many countries had already abolished the death penalty, either in law or in practice, he noted, asserting that the factual record was sufficient to establish the death penalty as a "cruel and unusual punishment." American juries handed out only about one hundred death sentences each year, he argued, even though a far higher number of death-eligible murders and rapes were committed each year. And the small number of people who received death sentences, he emphasized, were disproportionately poor and minorities who got those sentences from "death-qualified" juries—a practice permitted by the U.S. Supreme Court whereby death penalty opponents are excluded from sitting in judgment in capital cases. The Eighth Amendment, Amsterdam argued, must be measured not only by "legislative disapproval," but by what judges, juries, and prosecutors do in practice. Amsterdam pointed out that while more than six hundred inmates had accumulated on American death rows over the years, executions themselves had fallen "into disuse." Executions—once so prevalent in American society—had dwindled, then ceased, though some juries, most often in the South, still occasionally handed out death sentences.[6]

For the State of Georgia in *Furman,* Assistant Attorney General Dorothy Beasley appeared at oral argument and said it would take a constitutional amendment to do away with capital punishment. Citing the Fourteenth Amendment, she argued that legislative enactments were entitled to a presumption of constitutionality and that a State may deprive someone of life so long as the deprivation is neither discriminatory nor violative of due process. Beasley refused to classify the death penalty as "uncivilized" or "torturous," noting that American juries were still imposing death sentences. After acknowledging that the meaning of "unusual" had not changed since the Eighth Amendment was written, she focused on the regime to be used to assess whether a punishment comports with "the evolving standards of decency that mark the progress of a maturing society"—the standard set out by the U.S. Supreme Court in the 1958 case of *Trop v. Dulles.* Arguing that the Court should defer to legislative enactments, Beasley contended that the petitioners failed to meet their burden of showing that the death penalty was a "cruel and unusual punishment." She believed that jurors' voices should be heard; that juries represent the conscience of the community; and that the Supreme Court should defer to prior judicial rulings upholding the death penalty's constitutionality. Just one year earlier, in *McGautha v. California,* the Supreme Court had rejected a Due Process Clause challenge to capital punishment, ruling that laws giving juries unbridled, standardless discretion to impose death sentences comported with due process. The Court, Beasley argued, should also refuse to classify the death penalty as an Eighth Amendment violation.[7]

On June 29, 1972, the U.S. Supreme Court handed down its landmark decision in *Furman v. Georgia.* All nine Justices filed separate opinions, and the majority's five-to-four decision—issued in a terse, six-sentence per curiam opinion—contained no legal analysis. After three sentences recounted the crimes for which the three petitioners had been sentenced to death, the per curiam opinion simply restated the legal issue before the Court: does the imposition of the death penalty constitute cruel and unusual punishment in violation of the Eighth and Fourteenth Amendments? Although the Justices' separate opinions gave assorted rationales for the Court's judgment, the substantive portion of the per curiam opinion was limited to the following two sentences: "The Court holds that the imposition and carrying out of the death penalty in these cases constitute cruel and unusual punishment in violation of the Eighth and Fourteenth Amendments. The judgment in each case is therefore reversed insofar as it leaves undisturbed the death sentence imposed, and the cases are remanded for further proceedings." The result of *Furman*— declaring unconstitutional all U.S. death penalty laws then in place—was to empty America's death rows, with prisoners' death sentences replaced by terms of life imprisonment.[8]

The public backlash against *Furman* was swift. In a virtual stampede, thirty-five states passed new death penalty statutes—laws designed to meet the concerns expressed in *Furman* about the arbitrary way in which the death penalty was being applied. In their concurring opinions in *Furman,* the five Justices who formed the majority worried about the "uncontrolled discretion of judges or juries"; the "selective and irregular use of penalties"; "discrimination"; "wholly arbitrary" punishments; and the "rarity," "infrequency," and "totally capricious selection of criminals for the punishment of death." Justice Potter Stewart called the death sentences at issue "cruel and unusual in the same way that being struck by lightning is cruel and unusual," as the petitioners were among "a capriciously selected random handful" of criminals sentenced to die. Bowing to public sentiment following the passage of those new death penalty laws, the U.S. Supreme Court—in *Gregg v. Georgia,* a 1976 case—then abruptly reversed course. In that case, the Court upheld the constitutionality of Georgia's new death penalty law in a case involving a convicted murderer. The Georgia law required jurors to weigh "aggravating" and "mitigating" circumstances, purportedly "guided" and "channeled" juror discretion, and narrowed the classes of death-eligible offenders. "We now hold that the punishment of death does not invariably violate the Constitution," the Court ruled.[9]

Since *Gregg,* the Supreme Court has upheld the constitutionality of capital punishment even as all other Western democracies have done away with it. For example, in 1987, in a five-to-four decision, the Court rejected an Eighth Amendment, race-based challenge to death sentences in *McCleskey v. Kemp.* There, a black man, convicted in Georgia of murdering a white police officer during a robbery, proffered a statistical study showing a clear disparity in the imposition of death sentences based on the murder victim's race and, to a lesser extent, the defendant's race. The so-called Baldus study showed that "after taking into account some 230 nonracial factors that might legitimately influence a sentence, the jury *more likely than not* would have spared McCleskey's life had his victim been black." The Court in *McCleskey,* however, found the risk of racial bias was not "constitutionally unacceptable," saying statistics "at most may show only a likelihood that a particular factor entered into some decisions." In 2008 in *Baze v. Rees,* the Court likewise rejected an attack on the constitutionality of Kentucky's three-drug lethal injection protocol. That much-awaited decision came on the heels of a national, seven-month de facto moratorium on executions, with the case focused on the risk of pain associated with lethal injections. "[I]t is clear that the Eighth Amendment does not prohibit the death penalty," Justice Clarence Thomas wrote in a concurring opinion, saying "[t]hat is evident both from the ubiquity of the death penalty in the founding era and from the Constitution's express provision for capital punishment." Justice Antonin Scalia, too, concurred, saying "the very text of the document recognizes that the death penalty is a permissible legislative choice."[10]

Such rulings—finding no Eighth Amendment bar to executions—have forced abolitionists to press their case before legislative bodies. In Illinois, where death row exonerations became more common than executions, state legislators passed a bill in 2011 to abolish capital punishment, and Governor Pat Quinn signed it. Anti–death penalty activists, seeking either abolition or a moratorium on executions, have thus had some success but more often than not have encountered substantial resistance. The death penalty is still popular among many elected officials, especially in the South, and legislators—much more than federal judges with life tenure—are susceptible to public pressure. In an era of Willie Horton ads and 24/7 cable news, politicians fear being labeled "soft on crime" and commonly express support for executions as an easy way to deflect that pejorative label. Because convicted killers are so reviled, politicians are often especially hostile to efforts to repeal death penalty laws. Having seen candidates and judges lose bids for elective office after pro–death penalty campaigns were waged against them, those eager to demonstrate their get-tough-on-crime credentials find that the path of least resistance is to express their unyielding support for capital punishment. Because modern-day executions are hidden from public view and occur only infrequently if at all in most locales, the vast majority of Americans, such politicians realize, will never actually see an execution anyway. Though the death penalty may come up from time to time in political debates, it is usually discussed only in the most abstract way, meaning Americans spend little if any time ever seriously considering the fate of specific death row inmates. With bans in place on the filming of executions, public apathy toward them has only grown, making it particularly difficult for anti–death penalty advocates to capture the public's attention, let alone the ear of legislators.[11]

While the Supreme Court to date has upheld the death penalty's constitutionality, the Cruel and Unusual Punishments Clause is still very much a part of America's capital punishment debate. Indeed, even as bills to abolish the death penalty have been sporadically introduced in recent years, the Eighth Amendment continues to be a major focus of U.S. death penalty litigation. Lawyers representing death row inmates, along with invoking the Constitution's Equal Protection and Due Process Clauses, among others, regularly raise Eighth Amendment claims on behalf of their clients. The courts routinely hear these claims, and at least some of them—along with a variety of miscarriage-of-justice and Sixth Amendment ineffective-assistance-of-counsel claims—have been successful. For its part, the U.S. Supreme Court itself has already issued a number of landmark rulings, all invoking the Eighth Amendment, to protect inmates from harm and to narrow the categories of death-eligible offenders. In *Ford v. Wainwright,* a 1986 case, the Eighth Amendment was held to prohibit the execution of insane prisoners. In 2002, the Court likewise invoked the Eighth Amendment in *Atkins v. Virginia* to bar the execution of mentally retarded offenders. And in 2005, the Court held in *Roper v. Simmons* that the Eighth Amendment prohibits the death penalty's imposition on offenders under the age of eighteen. Still other cases, in noncapital contexts, bar the use of excessive force against inmates. "When prison officials maliciously and sadistically use force to cause harm," the Supreme Court held in *Hudson v. McMillian* and *Wilkins v. Gaddy,* "contemporary standards of decency always are violated." Because the Court has made clear that its interpretation of the Eighth Amendment is not "static," but is tied to the "evolving standards of decency that mark the progress of a maturing society," a fundamental question recurs, and will continue to recur: does the death penalty itself violate the Eighth Amendment's Cruel and Unusual Punishments Clause?[12]

To answer that question, this book first explores the case of Christopher Simmons—the Missouri boy whose death sentence led the nation's highest court to rule that juvenile executions are unconstitutional. That case, which generated enormous controversy, including among the Justices themselves, sheds considerable light on the modern Eighth Amendment debate and puts in context the Supreme Court's role in interpreting the Cruel and Unusual Punishments Clause. The book then turns back the clock to America's founding era. The Founding Fathers—the group of revolutionaries who, in 1776, gave birth to the United States of America and who, in 1787, put in place our constitutional architecture—came of age at a time when corporal punishments and the death penalty were widely accepted as punishments for crime. Slaves were frequently whipped or executed, and criminals—if not hanged—might be exiled or put in stocks or pillories. The first American penitentiary was not even built until the late eighteenth century, and the idea of housing offenders in jails or state prisons for long periods of time was then a novel one. As one scholar writes: "Early American colonial experience was based upon the

European model: once convicted of a crime, corporal punishment, execution, or banishment were the accepted forms of punishment." Between 1706 and 1784, in Virginia alone, at least 555 slaves were condemned to die; between 1785 and 1865, 628 slaves were executed in that state; and between 1801 and 1865, Virginians ordered thousands of slaves to be whipped or given other corporal punishments.[13]

Still, after the 1764 publication of Cesare Beccaria's influential treatise *On Crimes and Punishments,* many Founding Fathers forcefully advocated penal reform. In Philadelphia, Dr. Benjamin Rush and Benjamin Franklin came to oppose executions—in Rush's case, for all crimes, and in Franklin's, for lower-level offenders such as thieves. Beginning in the late 1770s, the Quakers in Pennsylvania led a major reform effort that would lead to the elimination of corporal punishments and the curtailment of death sentences. Philadelphia's renovated Walnut Street Jail opened in 1790, and when that facility filled up, Pennsylvanians built the Western State Penitentiary near Pittsburgh in 1826 and the Eastern State Penitentiary outside of Philadelphia in 1829. Thomas Jefferson and James Madison, of Virginia, also sought to limit executions and to substitute terms of imprisonment in their state, though many of their contemporaries had fewer moral qualms about executing criminals. The Eighth Amendment, ratified in 1791 in the midst of such reform efforts, forbade any "cruel and unusual punishments," though the meaning of that verbiage—derived from the seventeenth-century English Bill of Rights, a product of the Glorious Revolution of 1688—has spawned endless debate. The Cruel and Unusual Punishments Clause, still part of the law of the land, thus continues to frame today's death penalty debate. Confusion over how the Framers intended future generations to interpret that clause is only complicated by the fact that the Eighth Amendment was not incorporated against the States until many decades later, following the Fourteenth Amendment's ratification.[14]

Cruel and Unusual: The American Death Penalty and the Founders' Eighth Amendment thoroughly examines the Eighth Amendment's history, meaning, and purpose, arguing that the Cruel and Unusual Punishments Clause should be read to bar executions. The Eighth Amendment broadly prohibits "cruel and unusual punishments," and the eighteenth-century debates surrounding the adoption of the U.S. Bill of Rights show that it was contemplated that later generations would interpret that language for themselves. The Framers of the Constitution established an independent federal judiciary to resolve all future disputes over the Constitution's meaning, and the historical record shows the Founding Fathers never sought to lock future generations into eighteenth-century mores. The Bill of Rights, ratified in 1791, safeguards individual rights, including the right to life, and such rights, it is plain, were to be protected by judges. When *Furman* was argued in 1971, American society looked nothing like it had in 1791, though opposition to the death penalty existed in both eras. This book argues that the Eighth Amendment, which nowhere exempts the death penalty from its operation, should not be interpreted as if today's Americans were still living in the distant past. Unlike in the eighteenth century, when prison escapes in places such as Philadelphia were relatively common, ultrasecure Supermax prisons now exist to house violent offenders, and life-without-parole sentences are the norm. As more and more of the world's nations abandon capital punishment, citing treaties and human rights principles, Americans—and the Justices of the U.S. Supreme Court—owe it to themselves to reevaluate the death penalty's use to punish crime.[15]

After considering the Founding Fathers' ambivalent views on capital punishment, this book examines the history of America's anti–death penalty movement, which traces its origins to the republic's founding. *Cruel and Unusual* then examines the present-day administration of the death penalty; recent legislative efforts to abolish capital punishment or to put a moratorium on executions; international human rights treaties, which increasingly restrict the death penalty's use; and the current state of the world's death penalty debate. In examining America's death penalty and the international trend toward abolition, it is particularly fitting to look back at the history of the abolitionist movement as the world approaches the 250th anniversary of the publication of Cesare Beccaria's influential treatise, *On Crimes and Punishments*. That book, read and admired by many of America's Founding Fathers, sparked a reexamination of long-held views on torture and executions and was the first Enlightenment text comprehensively to advocate the death penalty's total abolition. How long executions in America will continue is unknowable, yet examining the last two and a half centuries—and the tea leaves of history—provides a better understanding of America's death penalty and holds clues for how the Constitution should be read and what the future may hold for death as a punishment.

For decades, the Eighth Amendment has been an enigma. What does it mean? How should it be interpreted? There is scant legislative history behind its adoption, which has, of course, only fueled the controversy. Though scholars, lawyers, and judges continue to grapple with these questions, the historical record shows that the Eighth Amendment—like the rest of the Constitution—was framed by well-educated men who took extraordinary care with words. Thirty-four delegates at the Constitutional Convention were lawyers, and the Founding Fathers—who frequently revised what they wrote—paid special attention as they crafted the Constitution and the Bill of Rights. To be sure, many founders, such as John Adams and John Jay, saw capital punishment as a legitimate exercise of state power. But many leading patriots, such as Benjamin Franklin, Thomas Jefferson, James Madison, George Washington, and James Wilson, came to oppose executions, if not for all categories of offenders, then at least for many or some. In fact, history reveals that some early Americans, like Dr. Benjamin Rush, forcefully advocated the death penalty's complete abolition. In the end, the Eighth Amendment's text and history compel the conclusion that America's founders made the deliberate choice to leave to successive generations—and, in particular, to future judges—the task of determining whether any particular punishment, including the death penalty, qualifies as "cruel and unusual."[16]

The public backlash against *Furman* illustrates how controversial U.S. Supreme Court decisions can be. The public, certainly, has every right to be distrustful of power, including the exercise of judicial power. When judges strike down legislative enactments through judicial review, it is a big deal because the majority's will is thwarted. Indeed, the phrase "judicial activism" has long been part of public discourse, especially during confirmation battles, with Supreme Court decisions drawing the ire of conservatives and liberals alike. The label "activist judges" is thus routinely bandied about by political factions who dislike certain decisions or feel judges inject too much of their personal views into judicial opinions. As the ultimate guardians of the U.S. Constitution, federal judges are appointed, not elected, and therefore are not accountable to the public except through impeachment. Though this arrangement irritates some, that system, which gives the Supreme Court certain powers, is, like it or not, the one the Framers envisioned and put in place. As Alexander Hamilton elaborated in *The Federalist Papers:* "The interpretation of the laws is the proper and peculiar province of the courts." "A constitution," Hamilton wrote in *The Federalist No. 78,* "is, in fact, and must be regarded by the judges, as a fundamental law. It therefore belongs to them to ascertain its meaning." While Congress and state legislatures make the laws and executives enforce them, the judicial branch gets to decide if those laws are consistent with the U.S. Constitution.[17]

Though Americans live in a representative democracy, where majoritarian rule is the norm, it should never be forgotten that the Framers—first and foremost—set up a *constitutional* republic. The Constitution *restrains* majority power, giving federal judges with life tenure a special role—indeed, the constitutional obligation—to protect individual rights. When Congress in 1789 transmitted its proposed bill of rights to the states for ratification, its joint resolution clearly emphasized that "further declaratory and restrictive clauses should be added" to the Constitution in order to "prevent misconstruction" of its provisions or any "abuse of its powers." The Bill of Rights, as applied against the states through the Fourteenth Amendment, thus serves as an indispensable check on the abuse of government power—a check that has been used to desegregate schools and stop other forms of discrimination. The Eighth Amendment ban on "cruel and unusual punishments" is one crucial component of the Bill of Rights that serves to protect against such abuse.[18]

Whether death sentences, which are still applied in a discriminatory manner, violate the Eighth Amendment's Cruel and Unusual Punishments Clause is a question the Supreme Court has thus far answered in the negative. Though the Eighth Amendment has already been interpreted to bar odious corporal punishments such as whipping and the pillory, once considered by early American judges to be "usual" punishments, many "originalists" nonetheless continue to say that executions—an even more draconian form of punishment—are constitutional. Justice Scalia even told one interviewer in January 2011 that the question of the death penalty's constitutionality is so easy to resolve that "I don't even have to read the briefs, for Pete's sake." But so long as people reside on American death rows, and over three thousand men and women still do, the U.S. Supreme Court will have—as it has always had under the Founding Fathers' Constitution—the power to reassess its views and to decide the ultimate question: are executions unconstitutional?[19]

CHAPTER ONE

In Cold Blood

The Crime

On September 9, 1993, seventeen-year-old Christopher Simmons met his teenage friends, Charlie Benjamin and John Tessmer, at 2:00 a.m. at the mobile home of Brian Moomey, a convicted felon who allowed neighborhood teens to "hang out" at his trailer. Earlier that month, Simmons and his two friends—one fifteen and one sixteen—had discussed the possibility of committing a burglary and murdering someone. Simmons felt the best victim would be a "voodoo man" who lived nearby—a man rumored to own hotels and motels and to have lots of money despite his living in a trailer park. Simmons had assured his friends that their status as juveniles would allow them to "get away with it," and Simmons's plan was simple: find someone to burglarize, tie up the victim, and either leave the victim tied to a tree or push the victim off a bridge. Simmons spoke of stealing "a bunch of money" or a bank card. But after the three friends met at Moomey's house in the middle of the night, Tessmer got cold feet and refused to go along, returning home even as Simmons and Benjamin left to commit the crime. Tessmer later testified that Simmons had specifically asked Benjamin for help in killing somebody, that he saw ropes and gloves at Simmons's house, but that he didn't think Simmons would actually kill anybody because Simmons had no weapons or masks with him that night.[1]

In early September, Simmons had told Tessmer as many as five times about his plan to rob the "voodoo man," and Tessmer had seen Simmons cutting masks from old sweatshirts to use to hide their faces. Just five hours before the crime, Simmons had also told another friend, Christie Brooks, that he and two others were going to rob the man they had nicknamed "Voodoo." Simmons, Brooks testified later, had a ski mask, a dark button-up shirt with leather gloves, a small shotgun, and a large knife. But Simmons—who asked Brooks for a gun because three people were to be involved and he only had two weapons—changed his plans after the 2:00 a.m. rendezvous. After finding a window cracked open to accommodate a garden hose at the rear of Shirley Crook's home, the two teenagers opened that window, reached in, and unlocked and entered through the back door. Simmons switched on a hallway light, which woke up Mrs. Crook, who was all alone except for the intruders. "Who's there?" she asked, sitting up in bed. Simmons entered her bedroom and then suddenly recognized Mrs. Crook from a prior automobile accident. She recognized him, too, from their July 1992 traffic accident. At that point, Simmons—no doubt flustered—ordered Mrs. Crook to get out of bed. When she refused, Simmons and his accomplice forced Mrs. Crook to the floor. While Simmons located a roll of duct tape, Benjamin guarded Mrs. Crook—whose hands, once Simmons returned to the bedroom, were bound behind her back and whose eyes and mouth were taped shut.[2]

The two teenagers then forced Mrs. Crook into the back of her minivan, which Simmons drove to Castlewood State Park in St. Louis County, Missouri. After parking the van near a railroad trestle spanning the Meramec River, Simmons and Benjamin discovered that Mrs. Crook had freed her hands and managed to remove some of the duct tape from her face. They then tied up Mrs. Crook again using her purse strap, the belt from her bathrobe, and some electrical wire they spotted on the trestle. After restraining her hands and feet and covering her head with a towel and wrapping it with duct tape, Simmons pushed Mrs. Crook—hog-tied but still alive and conscious—off the railroad trestle into the river. Simmons and Benjamin then tossed Mrs. Crook's purse into the woods and drove the van back to the mobile home park across from Mrs. Crook's home. Brian Moomey—the convicted felon—testified later that, prior to the murder, Simmons and Benjamin had talked about robbing a house and killing a family, and that Simmons told Benjamin "they could do it and not get charged for it" because they were juveniles and "nobody would think that juveniles would do it."[3]

When Mrs. Crook's husband Steven, who worked for a carrier service, learned his wife had not reported for work, he returned home from his overnight trip. Once inside, he found their bedding in disarray, wads of duct tape on the floor, and the couple's dog, Chrissy, lying on the bed whimpering, its nose and legs tangled in duct tape. Mr. Crook immediately filed a missing person's report, though unbeknownst to him his wife was already dead; that very afternoon, two fishermen would find Mrs. Crook's body floating in the Meramec River, almost a mile downstream from the railroad trestle. That same day, again at Brian Moomey's house, Simmons had already bragged to Moomey about killing a woman "because the bitch seen my face." Moomey—who had spent time in prison for assault with a weapon, burglary, and stealing, and who drank heavily, passing out almost every night—was initially leery of giving testimony because of suspicions that he might also have been involved in Mrs. Crook's death. But after the medical examiner identified

Mrs. Crook's body from fingerprints—noting bruising and several fractured ribs, and specifying drowning as the cause of death—the police learned of Simmons's involvement in the murder. They arrested Simmons at his high school and took him to the Fenton Police Department in Jefferson County, Missouri, where Simmons was given a *Miranda* warning and waived his constitutional rights.[4]

After Simmons denied any involvement in the crime, the police detectives raised their voices, told Simmons he was lying, and suggested that his accomplice, Charlie Benjamin, might be confessing at that very moment. The interrogating detectives never touched Simmons or threatened him with physical harm, but they occasionally moved within a foot of Simmons's face. At one point during the interrogation, Lt. Edward Robertson—the head of the Greater St. Louis Major Case Squad—also entered the room and told Simmons that he was facing either the death penalty or life in prison. After two hours of questioning and being told it would be in his "best interest" to tell the truth, Simmons finally asked everyone in the room to leave except Detective Shane Knoll. He then confessed to the murder. Simmons also agreed to videotape his confession and to take part in a videotaped "reenactment" of the murder at the crime scene. After the police obtained the confession, Mrs. Crook's husband Steven indicated that his wife "was terrifically scared of height"—and that it terrified him to think of her blindfolded and thrown off a high spot, knowing how much pain she would have been in and how worried she must have been about her ill mother and the rest of her family.[5]

At trial, Mrs. Crook's husband, her two sisters, and her daughter gave gut-wrenching testimony about their now-deceased loved one and the impact of the crime. That evidence included Mrs. Crook's fear of heights, a prayer that one of Mrs. Crook's sisters read at the family's first Thanksgiving after the murder, and the recurring nightmares suffered by Mrs. Crook's daughter Kimberly Hawkins after the crime. "Like I said, I have dreams," Hawkins testified haltingly. "I dream about how she—how I imagine she felt during all of this, what she thought. I can't imagine what she went through, the terror that she felt. I just—I have a picture in my mind that she can't see, she can't speak, she can't scream out, she can't get her hands on anybody, she's tied up, she's naked." Hawkins continued: "I can imagine that she was being pushed over, and the freeness of the air. There's nothing below you, there's nothing holding you up. I can't imagine the terror that she's thinking, what's happening, what's going on, I can't see anything. Then I imagine her hitting the water. Does she know to take a breath? Does she know that's what was going to happen? Then you hit the water, and then you go in. And then if she had a breath that she held, how long could she hold it? Did it hurt? When the water came in, did it hurt?" At the penalty phase, Simmons's lawyers called an officer of the Missouri juvenile justice system, who said Simmons had no prior convictions, as well as members of Simmons's own family. Before the jurors, Simmons's mother pled for her son's life and testified to the responsibility Simmons once demonstrated in taking care of his two younger half brothers.[6]

The Punishment

After deliberating, the Missouri jury found Simmons guilty of first-degree murder and sentenced him to death. Simmons appealed the jury's verdict, raising a host of issues, including the introduction of the victim impact evidence, which Simmons challenged as a violation of his Eighth and Fourteenth Amendment rights. In addition, Simmons alleged a violation of his Sixth Amendment right to an impartial jury because the trial court had excluded "for cause" two venirepersons who expressed discomfort about the death penalty. Venire member Judith Fluegge indicated that her father was a minister who taught her "it's wrong to take someone's life," making her uncomfortable when contemplating the death penalty as a punishment. All she would say is that she would listen to the evidence—and, when pressed, that she could "possibly" consider imposing a death sentence. Venireperson Laura Hecht likewise expressed reservations about the death penalty, doubting her ability to concentrate on the evidence in the guilt/innocence phase of the trial with the penalty phase looming over her. On appeal, Simmons—looking for some way to overturn his conviction—also argued that his confession was given involuntarily, pointing to his age at the time of his interrogation, his low intelligence, and his lack of success as a high school student.[7]

Before Missouri's appellate court, Simmons further argued that he was falsely led to believe that his accomplice was making incriminating statements about him, and that his trial attorney rendered ineffective assistance of counsel by failing to present evidence of his childhood abuse during the penalty phase. The jury, he contended, never heard evidence that he was physically abused by his stepfather, suffered from mental illness and psychological abuse due to his parents' bitter divorce, smoked marijuana and drank alcohol, and that Brian Moomey threatened Simmons and his family after Simmons's arrest. After administering a battery of tests and interviewing members of Simmons's family and those familiar with his upbringing, a doctor diagnosed Simmons—once arrested as a suspect in a rape case—as having "borderline personality disorder" and a schizotypal personality disorder. Dr. Daniel Cuneo—who had been hired by defense counsel prior to trial—concluded that Simmons had an IQ of 88 but "was bright enough to do well in school if he had wanted." "It wouldn't have been easy," Dr. Cuneo said, "but he could have done it." Simmons—invoking a variety of constitutional rights, and seeking a sentence less than death—thus argued that his trial had been unfair.[8]

In 1997, the Missouri Supreme Court rejected all of his arguments and affirmed Simmons's conviction and death sentence. "When a prospective juror's views on the death penalty would 'prevent or substantially impair the performance of his duties as a juror in accordance with his instructions and oath,' the trial court may exclude the juror for cause," the Missouri Supreme Court ruled, citing the U.S. Supreme Court's controlling decision in *Wainwright v. Witt.* "We discover no abuse of the trial court's discretion in its decision to sustain the state's challenges for cause to these two venirepersons on the basis of their indecision," the Missouri Supreme Court ruled. In so holding, the Missouri Supreme Court gave its approval to the exclusion of Ms. Fluegge and Ms. Hecht—the two prospective jurors who had moral qualms or personal reservations about the death penalty's use. In upholding the voluntariness of Simmons's confession, the Missouri Supreme Court further noted: "Although Simmons was told he could face the death penalty, such a statement does not constitute a threat but is a permissible observation of the possible consequences of first degree murder." The federal courts also refused to grant Simmons any postconviction relief.[9]

In subsequent state habeas corpus proceedings, however, the death sentence was set aside—with the Missouri Supreme Court in 2003 reversing course and resentencing Simmons to life imprisonment without eligibility for parole. After Simmons argued it would be a cruel and unusual punishment to execute him, the Missouri Supreme Court—over a vigorous dissent—ruled that Simmons's Eighth and Fourteenth Amendment rights were violated because he was only seventeen when he killed Mrs. Crook. The Missouri court first noted that the U.S. Supreme Court had held in 1988, in *Thompson v. Oklahoma,* that it constituted cruel and unusual punishment to execute persons who were fifteen or younger at the time of their offenses. The Missouri court then emphasized that in *Atkins v. Virginia*—a 2002 case—the U.S. Supreme Court had found a "national consensus" against the execution of mentally retarded offenders. Finding that a "similar consensus" against the execution of juveniles aged sixteen and seventeen had developed since 1989, when the U.S. Supreme Court last addressed the issue, the Missouri Supreme Court opined that "a national consensus has developed against the execution of juvenile offenders." Among other things, the Missouri Supreme Court's majority opinion noted that "eighteen states now bar such executions for juveniles," that "twelve other states bar executions altogether," and that "the imposition of the juvenile death penalty has become truly unusual over the last decade."[10]

The three dissenters, in contrast, pointed to the U.S. Supreme Court's 1989 ruling in *Stanford v. Kentucky* as controlling precedent. In *Stanford,* a contentious, five-to-four decision, the U.S. Supreme Court ruled that there was not then a national consensus against the execution of sixteen- or seventeen-year-old offenders, and thus there was no bar to their execution. "Our constitutional form of government," Judge William Ray Price Jr. began the dissent, "allows for the will of the people to be expressed, for better or worse, through the laws enacted by their elected representatives." Noting that "[t]he role of the courts is merely to interpret such statutes and to rule upon their constitutionality, if necessary," Judge Price emphasized that Missouri had enacted a law providing that murderers over the age of sixteen were subject to the death penalty. Although he conceded that Missouri's statute "is subject to serious controversy," Judge Price called the law "the enacted will of the people of Missouri," contending it "must be enforced" unless it was found to be unconstitutional. Referring to the "solemn duty" of the Missouri courts to abide by U.S. Supreme Court decisions, Judge Price then invoked the principle of stare decisis—a legal doctrine cautioning adherence to precedent—and concluded that Simmons's writ of habeas corpus should have been denied.[11]

Roper v. Simmons

By the time his case reached the U.S. Supreme Court, Christopher Simmons was no longer seventeen; he was twenty-eight and had already spent a decade behind bars. In yet another five-to-four decision, the U.S. Supreme Court affirmed the decision of the Missouri Supreme Court, overruling *Stanford* and holding it unconstitutional under the Eighth and Fourteenth Amendments to execute offenders under the age of eighteen at the time of their crimes. In writing for the Court in its 2005 decision in *Roper v. Simmons,* Justice Anthony Kennedy first emphasized that Simmons "was still a junior in high school" when he committed the murder after discussing it in advance in "chilling, callous terms." In Justice Kennedy's lengthy opinion, joined by Justices John Paul Stevens, David Souter, Ruth Bader Ginsburg, and Stephen Breyer, a bare majority of the Court noted that "the Eighth Amendment guarantees individuals the right not to be subjected to excessive sanctions" and flows from the basic "precept of justice" that punishment for crime should be "graduated and proportioned" to the offense. "By protecting even those convicted of heinous crimes," Justice Kennedy wrote, "the Eighth Amendment reaffirms the duty of the government to respect the dignity of all persons." The concept of "human dignity," invoked in several prior U.S. Supreme Court opinions, has long been seen as one of the touchstones of the Eighth Amendment.[12]

Justice Kennedy's opinion outlined the majority's approach to evaluating Eighth Amendment claims. "The prohibition against 'cruel and unusual punishments,' like other expansive language in the Constitution," Kennedy wrote, "must be interpreted according to its text, by considering history, tradition, and precedent, and with due regard for its purpose and function in the constitutional design." "To implement this framework," he continued, "we have established the propriety and affirmed the necessity of referring to 'the evolving standards of decency that mark the progress of a maturing society' to determine which punishments are so disproportionate as to be cruel and unusual." The majority opinion then set forth a two-pronged approach. "The beginning point," Justice Kennedy held, after citing the Court's prior rulings in *Thompson, Stanford,* and *Atkins,* "is a review of objective indicia of consensus, as expressed in particular by the enactments of legislatures that have addressed the question." Such data, he noted, provide "essential instruction." The second step to be taken was more subjective, relying on the Justices' own views. "We then must determine, in the exercise of our own independent judgment, whether the death penalty is a disproportionate punishment for juveniles," the Court ruled.[13]

The focus on "consensus" and "evolving standards of decency"—words not found in the Eighth Amendment itself—led the Court in *Roper,* as it had done before in *Atkins* and other cases, to engage in a counting exercise. "The evidence of national consensus against the death penalty for juveniles is similar, and in some respects parallel, to the evidence *Atkins* held sufficient to demonstrate a national consensus against the death penalty for the mentally retarded," Justice Kennedy wrote for the Court in *Roper.* As Kennedy emphasized: "When *Atkins* was decided, 30 States prohibited the death penalty for the mentally retarded. This number comprised 12 that had abandoned the death penalty altogether, and 18 that maintained it but excluded the mentally retarded from its reach. By a similar calculation in this case, 30 States prohibit the juvenile death penalty, comprising 12 that have rejected the death penalty altogether and 18 that maintain it but, by express provision or judicial interpretation, exclude juveniles from its reach." "[E]ven in the 20 States without a formal prohibition on executing juveniles," Justice Kennedy wrote, emphasizing the unusualness of the punishment, "the practice is infrequent." Since *Stanford,* he noted, only six American states had executed persons for crimes committed as juveniles; and in the prior ten years, only three—Oklahoma, Texas, and Virginia—had done so. Justice Kennedy also pointed out that, in 2003, the Governor of Kentucky had spared Kevin Stanford's life, commuting that offender's sentence to one of life imprisonment without parole and declaring that "[w]e ought not to be executing people who, legally, were children."[14]

In analyzing Simmons's Eighth Amendment claim, the majority opinion in *Roper* also focused on "the rate of change"—another phrase not found in the Constitution. "Impressive in *Atkins,*" Justice Kennedy noted, was "the rate of abolition of the death penalty for the mentally retarded." "Sixteen States that permitted the execution of the mentally retarded at the time of *Penry,*" Justice Kennedy wrote, "had prohibited the practice by the time we heard *Atkins.*" In *Penry v. Lynaugh,* a 1989 case, the U.S. Supreme Court had ruled that it was not "cruel and unusual punishment" to execute the mentally retarded—a decision the Court in *Atkins* overruled just a decade and a half later. Justice Kennedy conceded in *Roper* that "the rate of change in reducing the incidence of the juvenile death penalty, or in taking specific steps to abolish it, has been slower." Only five States that allowed the juvenile death penalty at the time of *Stanford*—a case decided the same year as *Penry*—had abandoned it in the intervening fifteen years. Four had done so through legislative action and the fifth through judicial decision. "Though less dramatic than the change from

Penry to *Atkins,*" Justice Kennedy wrote for the majority in *Roper,* "we still consider the change from *Stanford* to this case to be significant."[15]

The "consistency of the direction of change"—yet another phrase absent from the Constitution itself—had been emphasized in *Atkins,* a theme repeated in *Roper.* With respect to the States that had abandoned executing the mentally retarded since *Penry,* the Court had noted in *Atkins,* "[i]t is not so much the number of these States that is significant, but the consistency of the direction of change." In applying that principle in *Roper,* Justice Kennedy wrote: "The number of States that have abandoned capital punishment for juvenile offenders since *Stanford* is smaller than the number of States that abandoned capital punishment for the mentally retarded after *Penry;* yet we think the same consistency of direction of change has been demonstrated." Kennedy, arguing by analogy, noted: "Since *Stanford,* no State that previously prohibited capital punishment for juveniles has reinstated it. This fact, coupled with the trend toward abolition of the juvenile death penalty, carries special force in light of the general popularity of anticrime legislation, and in light of the particular trend in recent years toward cracking down on juvenile crime in other respects." "Any difference between this case and *Atkins* with respect to the pace of abolition," Kennedy wrote in *Roper,* "is thus counterbalanced by the consistent direction of the change." In passing the Federal Death Penalty Act in 1994, Kennedy emphasized, Congress itself determined that the death penalty should not extend to juveniles. The majority opinion accordingly concluded that the "objective indicia of consensus"—said to encompass "the rejection of the juvenile death penalty in the majority of States; the infrequency of its use even where it remains on the books; and the consistency in the trend toward abolition"—provide "sufficient evidence that today our society views juveniles, in the words *Atkins* used respecting the mentally retarded, as 'categorically less culpable than the average criminal.'"[16]

The Court in *Roper* made clear that certain categories of offenders may not be executed "no matter how heinous the crime." "Because the death penalty is the most severe punishment," the Court ruled, "the Eighth Amendment applies to it with special force." Death sentences, Kennedy wrote, must be "limited to those offenders who commit 'a narrow category of the most serious crimes' and whose extreme culpability makes them 'the most deserving of execution.'" Referring to a series of cases holding that certain classes of offenders, such as the insane and the mentally retarded, may not be executed, the Court ruled: "There are a number of crimes that beyond question are severe in absolute terms, yet the death penalty may not be imposed for their commission." In *Roper,* the Court added juvenile offenders to that list. "A majority of States have rejected the imposition of the death penalty on juvenile offenders under 18," Justice Kennedy wrote, "and we now hold this is required by the Eighth Amendment." The Court emphasized that "juvenile offenders cannot with reliability be classified among the worst offenders"; that juveniles lack maturity, are susceptible to peer pressure, and often engage in irresponsible or reckless behavior; and that almost every State prohibits those under eighteen from voting, serving on juries, or marrying without parental consent.[17]

The majority opinion in *Roper* further concluded that the disproportionality of the death penalty for juvenile offenders "finds confirmation in the stark reality that the United States is the only country in the world that continues to give official sanction to the juvenile death penalty." Noting that "[t]his reality does not become controlling, for the task of interpreting the Eighth Amendment remains our responsibility," the majority nevertheless emphasized that, at least since 1958, the Court "has referred to the laws of other countries and to international authorities as instructive for its interpretation of the Eighth Amendment's prohibition of 'cruel and unusual punishments.'" In *Trop v. Dulles*—the 1958 case—the Court had noted that "[t]he civilized nations of the world are in virtual unanimity that statelessness is not to be imposed as punishment for crime." The Court in *Roper* noted that the UN Convention on the Rights of the Child, ratified by every country in the world except the United States and Somalia, contained an express prohibition on capital punishment for crimes committed by those under eighteen. The Court also pointed out that only seven countries other than the United States had executed juvenile offenders since 1990: Iran, Pakistan, Saudi Arabia, Yemen, Nigeria, the Democratic Republic of Congo, and China. "Since then," the Court reported, "each of these countries has either abolished capital punishment for juveniles or made public disavowal of the practice."[18]

Justice Kennedy specifically highlighted Great Britain's experience. "The United Kingdom's experience bears particular relevance here," he wrote, "in light of the historic ties between our countries and in light of the Eighth Amendment's own origins." Noting that the Eighth Amendment was modeled on a parallel provision in the English Bill of Rights of 1689, Kennedy recounted that England had abolished the death penalty in its entirety, and that decades before it took that step, Parliament had outlawed the execution of juvenile offenders. "In the 56 years that have passed since the United Kingdom abolished the juvenile death penalty," Justice Kennedy said, "the weight of authority against it there, and in the international community, has become well established." "It is proper," Justice Kennedy wrote, "that we acknowledge the overwhelming weight of international opinion against the juvenile death penalty, resting in large part on the understanding that the instability and emotional imbalance of young people may often be a factor in the crime." "The opinion of the world community, while not controlling our outcome," he said, "does provide respected and significant confirmation for our own conclusions."[19]

In *Roper*, Justice Stevens felt compelled to file a short concurrence, a one-paragraph opinion joined by Justice Ginsburg. "Perhaps even more important than our specific holding today," Justice Stevens wrote, "is our reaffirmation of the basic principle that informs the Court's interpretation of the Eighth Amendment." "If the meaning of that Amendment had been frozen when it was originally drafted," he wrote, referencing the common law at the time of the Eighth Amendment's adoption, "it would impose no impediment to the execution of 7-year-old children today." "The evolving standards of decency that have driven our construction of this critically important part of the Bill of Rights," he wrote, "foreclose any such reading of the Amendment." Speaking for himself and Justice Ginsburg, Stevens explained his reasoning: "In the best tradition of the common law, the pace of that evolution is a matter for continuing debate; but that our understanding of the Constitution does change from time to time has been settled since John Marshall breathed life into its text." In 1803, the famed jurist John Marshall—as the fourth Chief Justice of the U.S. Supreme Court—had authored the landmark opinion of *Marbury v. Madison,* confirming the Supreme Court's power, through judicial review, to strike down unconstitutional laws. "If great lawyers of his day—Alexander Hamilton, for example—were sitting with us today," Justice Stevens wrote, "I would expect them to join Justice Kennedy's opinion for the Court. In all events, I do so without hesitation."[20]

The Dissenters

The decision in *Roper,* however, was far from unanimous. Justice Sandra Day O'Connor—now retired—filed a dissenting opinion, which began pointedly: "The Court's decision today establishes a categorical rule forbidding the execution of any offender for any crime committed before his 18th birthday, no matter how deliberate, wanton, or cruel the offense. Neither the objective evidence of contemporary societal values, nor the Court's moral proportionality analysis, nor the two in tandem suffice to justify this ruling." Justice O'Connor wrote that the evidence before the Court simply failed to demonstrate conclusively the presence of "a genuine national consensus" against the execution of seventeen-year-olds. As O'Connor argued: "the rule decreed by the Court rests, ultimately, on its independent moral judgment that death is a disproportionately severe punishment for any 17-year-old offender." "I do not subscribe to this judgment," O'Connor said, explaining: "Adolescents *as a class* are undoubtedly less mature, and therefore less culpable for their conduct, than adults. But the Court has adduced no evidence impeaching the seemingly reasonable conclusion reached by many state legislatures: that at least some 17-year-old murderers are sufficiently mature to deserve the death penalty in an appropriate case." Rejecting the bright-line approach adopted by the majority, Justice O'Connor articulated her unwillingness to "substitute our judgment about the moral propriety of capital punishment for 17-year-old murderers for the judgments of the Nation's legislatures." "Rather," she wrote, "I would demand a clearer showing that our society truly has set its face against this practice before reading the Eighth Amendment categorically to forbid it." Justice O'Connor did note that, were she serving as a legislator instead of as a judge, she would support legislation to outlaw the execution of juvenile offenders.[21]

Because Justice O'Connor found no national consensus against the juvenile death penalty, seeing the evidence as "inconclusive," she assigned no "*confirmatory* role to the international consensus described by the Court" regarding what she called "a global trend in recent years towards abolishing capital punishment for under-18 offenders." "In short," she said, "the evidence of an international consensus does not alter my determination that the Eighth Amendment does not, at this time, forbid capital punishment of 17-year-old murderers in all cases." Justice O'Connor found that "a clear and durable national consensus against this practice may in time emerge." But, she wrote, "that day has yet to arrive," though she did take issue with Justice Antonin Scalia's view—as expressed in his dissent—that foreign and international law have no place at all in Eighth Amendment jurisprudence. "Over the course of nearly half a century," O'Connor wrote, "the Court has consistently referred to foreign and international law as relevant to its assessment of evolving standards of decency." "This inquiry," she said, "reflects the special character of the Eighth Amendment, which, as the Court has long held, draws its meaning directly from the maturing values of civilized society." "[T]his Nation's evolving understanding of human dignity," she wrote, "certainly is neither wholly isolated from, nor inherently at odds with, the values prevailing in other countries." "On the contrary," she emphasized, "we should not be surprised to find congruence between domestic and international values, especially where the international community has reached clear agreement—expressed in international law or in the domestic laws of individual countries—that a particular form of punishment is inconsistent with fundamental human rights."[22]

Justice Scalia's dissenting opinion in *Roper,* joined by Chief Justice William Rehnquist and Justice Clarence Thomas, railed against the majority opinion. Scalia called the Court's decision a "mockery" of Alexander Hamilton's vision, invoking *The Federalist No. 78,* in which Hamilton wrote that "[t]he judiciary . . . ha[s] neither FORCE nor WILL but merely judgment." Arguing that the majority adverted "not to the original meaning of the Eighth Amendment, but to 'the evolving standards of decency' of our national society," Scalia said the Court had, "on the flimsiest of grounds," found a nonexistent "national consensus" against juvenile executions. "Worse still," Scalia wrote, "the Court says in so many words that what our people's laws say about the issue does not, in the last analysis, matter." "The Court," he said, "proclaims itself sole arbiter of our Nation's moral standards—and in the course of discharging that awesome responsibility purports to take guidance from the views of foreign courts and legislatures." As Scalia wrote: "Because I do not believe that the meaning of our Eighth Amendment, any more than the meaning of other provisions of our Constitution, should be determined by the subjective views of five Members of this Court and like-minded foreigners, I dissent."[23]

After criticizing the "national consensus" standard, Justice Scalia chose to disregard the twelve states that then prohibited the death penalty altogether and engaged in a counting exercise of his own. Discounting the majority's inclusion of anti–death penalty states as part of the Eighth Amendment calculus, Scalia wrote: "*None* of our cases dealing with an alleged constitutional limitation upon the death penalty has counted, as States supporting a consensus in favor of that limitation, States that have eliminated the death penalty entirely. And with good reason." Scalia argued: "Consulting States that bar the death penalty concerning the necessity of making an exception to the penalty for offenders under 18 is rather like including old-order Amishmen in a consumer-preference poll on the electric car. Of *course* they don't like it, but that sheds no light whatever on the point at issue." "That 12 States favor *no* executions says something about consensus against the death penalty," Scalia wrote, "but nothing—absolutely nothing—about consensus that offenders under 18 deserve special immunity from such a penalty." "Words," he concluded, "have no meaning if the views of less than 50% of death penalty States can constitute a national consensus." In his dissent, Scalia further emphasized that "[o]ur previous cases have required overwhelming opposition to a challenged practice, generally over a long period of time."[24]

Justice Scalia also attacked what he called the real driving force behind the *Roper* decision: the Court's "own judgment" that "murderers younger than 18 can never be as morally culpable as older counterparts." Such an approach, Scalia said, "has no foundation in law or logic." "If the Eighth Amendment set forth an ordinary rule of law," he wrote, "it would indeed be the role of this Court to say what the law is." "But," he continued, "the Court having pronounced that the Eighth Amendment is an ever-changing reflection of 'evolving standards of decency' of our society, it makes no sense for the Justices then to *prescribe* those standards rather than discern them from the practices of our people." Scalia opined: "On the evolving-standards hypothesis, the only legitimate function of this Court is to identify a moral consensus of the American people. By what conceivable warrant can nine lawyers presume to be the authoritative conscience of the Nation?" "Today's opinion," he intoned, "provides a perfect example of why judges are ill equipped to make the type of legislative judgments the Court insists on making here."[25]

Justice Scalia's dissent took special aim at his pet peeve: the majority's citation of international and foreign law. "Though the views of our own citizens are essentially irrelevant to the Court's decision today," Scalia wrote, "the views of other countries and the so-called international community take center stage." Scalia noted that while all but two countries had ratified the UN Convention on the Rights of the Child, neither the United States nor Somalia had done so. Indeed, Scalia pointed out that the U.S. Senate ratified the International Covenant on Civil and Political Rights—a 1960s treaty barring the execution of juvenile offenders—only subject to a reservation reserving the right of the United States to impose capital punishment on offenders under eighteen years of age. "Unless the Court has added to its arsenal the power to join and ratify treaties on behalf of the United States," Scalia wrote, emphasizing the U.S. position on such treaties, "I cannot see how this evidence favors, rather than refutes, its position." "That the Senate and the President—those actors our Constitution empowers to enter into treaties—have declined to join and ratify treaties prohibiting execution of under-18 offenders can only suggest that *our country* has either not reached a national consensus on the question, or has reached a consensus contrary to what the Court announces." Scalia argued for the "primacy" of legislative judgments and also expressed skepticism that every other nation that said it no longer executed juvenile offenders actually adhered to that stated practice. "[T]he basic premise of the Court's argument—that American law should conform to the laws of the rest of the world—ought to be rejected out of hand," Scalia wrote. "To invoke alien law when it agrees with one's own thinking, and ignore it otherwise," he wrote, "is not reasoned decisionmaking, but sophistry."[26]

Justice Scalia lamented not only the citation of international and foreign law but also the Court's rejection decades earlier of a "purely originalist approach" to the Eighth Amendment. Foreign sources were consulted, Scalia said, "*not* to underscore our 'fidelity' to the Constitution," but "*to set aside* the centuries-old American practice—a practice still engaged in by a large majority of the relevant States—of letting a jury of 12 citizens decide whether, in the particular case, youth should be the basis for withholding the death penalty." For Scalia, even consulting international or foreign authorities for guidance was a cardinal sin. "What these foreign sources 'affirm,' rather than repudiate, is the Justices' own notion of how the world ought to be, and their diktat that it shall be so henceforth in America." As Scalia wrote: "The Court's parting attempt to downplay the significance of its extensive discussion of foreign law is unconvincing. 'Acknowledgment' of foreign approval has no place in the legal opinion of this Court *unless it is part of the basis for the Court's judgment*—which is surely what it parades as today." Scalia ridiculed Eighth Amendment decisionmaking as akin to "a show of hands on the current Justices' current personal views about penology," calling Eighth Amendment case law, at best, "a mirror of the passing and changing sentiment of American society" or "nothing more than a snapshot of American public opinion at a particular point in time."[27]

A Divided Court

The *Roper* case illustrates the Supreme Court's internal struggle as it grapples with capital cases in the Eighth Amendment context. While a bare majority of the Court found juvenile executions to be unconstitutional, other Justices vehemently opposed the majority's approach, finding it ill-advised and a usurpation of legislative power. How is it, some ask, that executions are found to be constitutional, yet juvenile executions—a subset of executions—can simultaneously be found to be an Eighth Amendment violation? If some offenders can be lawfully sentenced to death, Justices Scalia and Thomas would ask, just why exactly are other categories of offenders—whether juveniles or the mentally retarded—considered ineligible for execution? For example, Scalia points out that the Court has—using the Eighth Amendment—barred the death penalty as a "mandatory punishment for any crime," for "ordinary" murder, and for those committing felony murder absent a showing that the defendant possessed a sufficiently culpable state of mind. Dissenting in *Atkins v. Virginia,* which laid the foundation for *Roper,* Justices Scalia and Thomas decried the Court's ruling as "the pinnacle of our Eighth Amendment death-is-different jurisprudence." "Not only does it, like all of that jurisprudence, find no support in the text or history of the Eighth Amendment," they said, "it does not even have support in current social attitudes regarding the conditions that render an otherwise just death penalty inappropriate." "Seldom," Justice Scalia wrote for the dissenters, "has an opinion of this Court rested so obviously upon nothing but the personal views of its Members."[28]

While the majority in *Roper* made clear that the Justices' individual views can be determinative, the Supreme Court continues—almost reflexively—to adhere to the "evolving standards of decency" framework that has been in place for decades. Justice Oliver Wendell Holmes, in the 1920s, called judging a law's constitutionality "the gravest and most delicate duty" the Supreme Court is asked to perform, which explains, perhaps, why the Court so frequently invokes the doctrine of stare decisis in its opinions. That principle, derived from a Latin maxim and meant not to be an "inexorable command" but to encourage respect for precedent and the stability of the law, counsels against overturning a prior judgment unless the rationale for that decision no longer withstands careful analysis. If anything, however, the "evolving standards" test seems purposefully designed to deflect the focus of Eighth Amendment decision making from the Justices' own reasoned views regarding the Constitution's text to assessing the opinions of the public at large. By focusing on legislative activity and trends, the Court emphasizes societal opinions, whether informed or not, instead of parsing the Constitution's actual words. If the Court's "independent judgment" was, in and of itself, determinative, Eighth Amendment disputes would be resolved much differently. The Justices—under that scenario—would be forced to confront the concepts of cruelty and unusualness head-on and to make moral judgments on particular punishments. Clearly uncomfortable in that role, the Justices of the Court thus cling to the "evolving standards of decency" test, which sounds nice but totally ignores the Constitution's actual language in preference to taking the public's temperature before any decision is made as to the constitutionality of a given punishment.[29]

For Justice Scalia, who routinely looks to the founding era to see what punishments the Framers approved of, capital punishment is constitutional—and always will be. "[I]t is entirely clear," Scalia has written, "that capital punishment, which was widely in use in 1791, does not violate the abstract moral principle of the Eighth Amendment." As support for his originalist approach, Scalia cites the Fifth Amendment's language and a 1790 act of Congress providing that treason, murder, piracy, and other felonies "shall" be punishable by death. "For me," Scalia writes, "the constitutionality of the death penalty is not a difficult, soul-wrenching question. It was clearly permitted when the Eighth Amendment was adopted. . . . And so it is clearly permitted today." Instead, Scalia reads the Eighth Amendment—proposed and approved by the same Congress that passed the 1790 criminal code—to prohibit "only certain modes of punishment." "The Eighth Amendment," Scalia once wrote, "is addressed to always-and-everywhere 'cruel' punishments, such as the rack and the thumbscrew." And only if such a method of execution is "deliberately designed to inflict pain" would Scalia find an Eighth Amendment violation. In Scalia's view, the Eighth Amendment thus forbids neither lethal injection nor the execution of juvenile offenders or the mentally retarded, and the risk of executing innocent people is—in his judgment—outweighed by the people's belief in the deterrent value of capital punishment.[30]

Scalia, in fact, views decisions like *Roper* and *Atkins*—which carve out certain categories of offenders for less severe treatment—as imposing unwarranted impediments to the imposition of death sentences. Lamenting "the long list of substantive and procedural requirements" imposed by the Supreme Court under its "death-is-different jurisprudence," Scalia has argued that "[n]one of those requirements existed when the Eighth Amendment was adopted" and that "some of them were not even supported by current moral consensus." "There is something to be said for popular abolition of the death penalty; there is nothing to be said for its incremental abolition by this Court," Scalia wrote in *Atkins*. Indeed, Scalia has long sought to overturn a decades-old precedent—grounded in the Eighth Amendment—requiring individualized sentencing in capital cases. Since *Furman,* Scalia complains, the Court "has assumed the role of rulemaking body for the States' administration of capital sentencing—effectively requiring capital sentencing proceedings separate from the adjudication of guilt, dictating the type and extent of discretion the sentencer must and must not have, requiring that certain categories of evidence must and must not be admitted, undertaking minute inquiries into the wording of jury instructions to ensure that jurors understand their duties under our labyrinthine code of rules, and prescribing the procedural forms that sentencing decisions must follow."[31]

Locating a principled rationale for Eighth Amendment jurisprudence—particularly when it comes to death penalty cases—is not easy. In fact, it is impossible. The Supreme Court routinely seeks to identify a "national consensus" by doing a head count of legislative practices and, in some cases, surveying jury verdicts. Yet, the Court also refers to its ability to make an "independent judgment." Deference and independence, as concepts, however, are irreconcilable. The very notion of judicial independence—a principle that goes back to the founding era—is rooted in the idea that judges should *not* be subject or beholden to legislative or executive commands. James Madison, who pushed for the adoption of the Bill of Rights, spoke of "independent tribunals of justice" serving as the "guardians" of constitutional rights and being "an impenetrable bulwark against every assumption of power" by the legislative or executive branches. The Constitution was thus drafted—as the Court itself has held—to ensure the judiciary's independence from the control of those two branches. As President Thomas Jefferson wrote: "The leading principle of our Constitution is the independence of the Legislature, executive and judiciary of each other, and none are more jealous of this than the judiciary." By continually deferring to legislative judgments, the Supreme Court has—in effect—ceded its independence. In assessing the constitutionality of punishments, the Justices now essentially stick their fingers in the air to gauge public sentiment, applying tests and standards nowhere found in the Constitution itself. In the final analysis, Eighth Amendment case law is in such a state of disarray that locating a unifying set of principles in that body of law is like trying to solve a Rubik's Cube while blindfolded. It simply cannot be done.[32]

There are, of course, as many different and conflicting theories of constitutional interpretation as there are U.S. Supreme Court Justices. There is "original intent," a quest to divine the Founding Fathers' intentions; "original meaning," an attempt to figure out how words in the Constitution were originally understood; and what has been denoted the "living Constitution" approach. The last approach, as explained by Justice William Brennan, requires that we ask a simple, straightforward question: "What do the words of the text mean in our time?" "For the genius of the Constitution," Brennan said, "rests not in any static meaning it might have had in a world that is dead and gone, but in the adaptability of its great principles to cope with current problems and current needs." Former Chief Justice William Rehnquist—who occupied the opposite end of the ideological spectrum—grappled, too, with that very concept in a lecture he gave in 1976, saying "[a]t first blush it seems certain that a *living* Constitution is better than what must be its counterpart, a *dead* Constitution." But for Rehnquist, a "living Constitution" was susceptible of multiple meanings, with the conservative icon finding executions constitutional while Brennan found them to be just the opposite. While differing diametrically with Brennan on the death penalty's legality, even Rehnquist—it should be noted—found at least some common ground with his liberal colleague. "Where the framers of the Constitution have used general language," Rehnquist conceded, "they have given latitude to those who would later interpret the instrument to make that language applicable to cases that the framers might not have foreseen."[33]

The approaches to constitutional interpretation are almost endless because they are tied to the individual views of the Justices. Scholars themselves, in fact, are constantly wrestling with all the myriad possibilities. In his recent book *A Constitution of Many Minds: Why the Founding Document Doesn't Mean What It Meant Before,* Cass Sunstein explores at least three approaches: "traditionalism," "populism," and "cosmopolitanism." Traditionalism gives deference to the views of the drafters of the Constitution and the Bill of Rights; populism—as one commentator puts it—"comes into play when judges, in interpreting the Constitution, pay heed to the contemporary opinions of the American public"; and cosmopolitanism involves judges looking to the opinions of foreign jurists for guidance. Textualism is yet another prominent approach, while others favor some form of "living constitutionalism." Though pros and cons are regularly offered for every interpretive theory, for former Chief Justice William Rehnquist and many others, the fact that parts of the Constitution are—as Rehnquist put it—"couched in general phraseology" is key. As Rehnquist noted in commenting on what gives the Constitution its flexibility and life: "There is obviously wide room for honest difference of opinion over the meaning of general phrases in the Constitution; any particular Justice's decision when a question arises under one of these general phrases will depend to some extent on his own philosophy of constitutional law." "The genius of the U.S. Constitution," writes law professor David Strauss in *The Living Constitution,* "is precisely that it is specific where specificity is valuable and general where generality is valuable."[34]

For decades, judges and legal scholars have thus debated whether to follow a "textualist" or "originalist" approach; a "strict constructionist" methodology, which aims to strictly adhere to the Framers' intent; "precedentialism" or "structuralism"; or some variation of "living constitutionalism," what Justice Scalia derisively calls a "nonoriginalist" approach. Whatever approach or combination thereof one subscribes to, it is clear that many provisions of the Bill of Rights—including the Eighth Amendment—were written in general terms, giving much leeway to the Justices. "The framers of the Constitution," Rehnquist emphasized in his speech, "wisely spoke in general language and left to succeeding generations the task of applying that language to the unceasingly changing environment in which they would live." "Those who framed, adopted, and ratified the Civil War amendments to the Constitution," Rehnquist added, "likewise used what have been aptly described as 'majestic generalities' in composing the fourteenth amendment." The interplay between the Eighth and Fourteenth Amendments—the latter being designed to incorporate the Bill of Rights against the States and to ferret out racial discrimination—is one that certainly cannot be neglected in analyzing what, today, constitutes a "cruel and unusual" punishment. The Cruel and Unusual Punishments Clause, as originally conceived, restrained only the national government, but the Fourteenth Amendment—with its Due Process and Equal Protection Clauses—changed all that, transforming the scope of the Bill of Rights and the Eighth Amendment in particular.[35]

Given the Constitution's separation-of-powers architecture, the format of the Bill of Rights as an addition to the Framers' 1787 creation, and the Fourteenth Amendment's transformative properties, interpretive issues naturally arise regarding the Cruel and Unusual Punishments Clause: Should the Eighth Amendment be interpreted in isolation? Or should it be read in the broader context of the Constitution as a whole? Should it be read, for example, in conjunction with due process and equal protection guarantees? The Fifth and Fourteenth Amendments both provide that no person shall be deprived of life "without due process of law," and the Fourteenth Amendment—ratified more than seventy-five years after the Eighth Amendment—further guarantees "the equal protection of the laws." Can America's death penalty, rife as it is with factual and legal errors, racial bias, and instances of incompetent counsel and wrongful convictions, ever be administered in accordance with those additional constitutional safeguards? Or is it necessary to have a constitutional amendment to end state-sanctioned killing, the State's ultimate sanction? For some originalists, Professor Strauss writes in *The Living Constitution,* the fact that capital punishment was not understood to violate the Eighth Amendment in 1791 leads them to conclude that the death penalty "cannot ever be 'cruel and unusual.'" But is that theory of the Constitution— that brand of originalism—too simplistic? Indeed, might the Framers themselves have contemplated that a future generation might one day find executions unacceptable? Jefferson himself queried Madison about "whether one generation of men has a right to bind another," insisting "that the earth belongs . . . to the living."[36]

Each interpretive methodology has its adherents, and each may—especially in the Eighth Amendment context—lead to radically different results, just as Justice Kennedy's approach in *Roper* led to a much different conclusion than Justice Scalia's. At stake in this ongoing debate is how the Cruel and Unusual Punishments Clause will be read, and what approach to constitutional interpretation will win out. Who will decide what is "cruel" and what is "unusual"? Will it be judges or legislators? What qualifies as "cruel," as "unusual"? And what standards or benchmarks will be used to assess whether a particular punishment fits those descriptions? Will the Eighth Amendment be read in a manner that reflects a large measure of deference to the Founding Fathers' eighteenth-century views? To those of modern-day legislators? Or will the Eighth Amendment, as written, be seen as part of a vibrant, living Constitution—one that is to be read anew by each successive generation of Americans, with every new generation deciding for itself what constitutes "cruel and unusual" punishment? Most importantly, will the U.S. Supreme Court exercise independent judgment in evaluating the death penalty? Or will the Justices—who since the mid-1970s have frequently washed their hands of death penalty cases in preference to recognizing the finality of state-court judgments—continue largely to defer to legislatures? What can be fairly said now is that, more than two hundred years after the adoption of the Bill of Rights, the Supreme Court is still very much in search of a *principled* approach to the Eighth Amendment—one that may be hiding in plain sight, if only we follow the arc of history, logic, and human rights.

CHAPTER TWO

On Crimes and Punishments

Dei delitti e delle pene

In 1764, a short Italian treatise, *Dei delitti e delle pene,* was anonymously published in the Tuscan port of Leghorn and delivered for sale in Milan in mid-July. That treatise—destined to spark controversy and a worldwide movement to abolish capital punishment—was written by Cesare Beccaria, the twenty-six-year-old eldest son of an Italian nobleman. Translated into English three years later as *On Crimes and Punishments,* Beccaria's slender treatise—a little more than one hundred pages in length—would make its young author an instant celebrity after his identity was revealed. The book was quickly translated into several languages, including French, German, Dutch, Polish, and Spanish, with Russian and Greek translations to follow, and the Italian criminologist was soon a household name among European monarchs and intellectuals on both sides of the Atlantic. The first English translation of Beccaria's book became available in the United States in the 1770s, first in Philadelphia in 1776 and then the following year in Charleston, South Carolina, where a printer named David Bruce brought out the translation at his shop on Church Street. By the end of the century, approximately sixty editions of *On Crimes and Punishments* were in print, making the book an eighteenth-century bestseller.[1]

In his book, Beccaria argued that "there must be proportion between crimes and punishments." As the father of the abolitionist movement, Beccaria pointedly asked: "Is death really a *useful* or *necessary* punishment for the security or good order of society?" "By what right," he pondered, "can men presume to slaughter their fellows?" Railing against the barbarity of state-sanctioned executions, Beccaria saw these public spectacles as violative of natural law—a concept America's Founding Fathers embraced in crafting the Declaration of Independence. "It seems absurd to me," Beccaria wrote, "that the laws, which are the expression of the public will, and which execrate and punish homicide, should themselves commit one, and that to deter citizens from murder they should order a public murder." "[S]overeignty and the laws," he wrote, "are nothing but the sum of the smallest portions of the personal liberty of each individual; they represent the general will, which is the aggregate of particular wills." "Who has ever willingly given other men the authority to kill him?" he asked rhetorically, adding that "the death penalty is not a *right,* but the war of a nation against a citizen."[2]

For Beccaria, executions only brutalized societies. "If the passions or the necessities of war have taught us how to shed human blood," he wrote, "the laws, which moderate the conduct of men, should not augment that cruel example, which is all the more baleful when a legal killing is applied with deliberation and formality." To persuade skeptical readers, Beccaria posed a series of questions: "Can the cries of an unfortunate wretch rescue from time, which never reverses its course, deeds already perpetrated?" "When reading history, who does not shudder with horror at the barbaric and useless tortures that have been cold-bloodedly invented and practiced by men who considered themselves wise?" "What must men think when they see wise magistrates and solemn ministers of justice, who with tranquil indifference have a criminal dragged with slow precision to his death, and as a poor wretch writhes in his last agonies while awaiting the fatal blow, the judge goes on with cold insensitivity—and perhaps even with secret satisfaction at his own authority— to savour the comforts and pleasures of life?" Viewing life itself as "a natural right," Beccaria vehemently called for an end to executions. "[I]f I can demonstrate that the death penalty is neither useful nor necessary," the idealistic Beccaria proclaimed, "I will have won the cause of humanity."[3]

On Crimes and Punishments also spoke out against torture—a concept associated with the intentional infliction of pain. After criticizing the "time-honoured abuse" in many nations of "secret accusations," Beccaria called the pretrial torture of those accused of crimes a "cruelty condoned by custom in most nations." He pointed out that this practice was often employed to get a suspect "to confess a crime, to contradict himself, to discover his accomplices, or for some kind of metaphysical and incomprehensible purgation of infamy." Beccaria further contended that torture—which he likened to "the law of ancient and savage times, when ordeals by fire, by boiling water, and the uncertain fate of armed combat were called *judgments* of God"—is unlikely to produce truthful testimony and runs contrary to the principle that innocent people not be punished. "No man," Beccaria wrote, "can be considered *guilty* before the judge has reached a verdict, nor can society deprive him of public protection until it has been established that he has violated the pacts that granted him such protection." Beccaria especially decried the use of torture to punish infamy, writing that "a man judged infamous by the law" should not suffer "the dislocation of his bones." At common law, the conviction of an "infamous" crime—and there were many—affected a man's legal status, depriving him of honor and credit and rendering him incompetent as a witness and as a juror. "Torture itself," Beccaria emphasized, "causes real infamy to its victims."[4]

With executions and methods of torture such as the thumbscrew commonplace throughout Europe in the 1700s, the novelty of Beccaria's views was not lost on him. Indeed, Beccaria began his treatise with a quotation from Renaissance philosopher and English statesman Francis Bacon: "In all negociations of difficulty, a man may not look to sow and reap at once, but must prepare business, and so ripen it by degrees." Beccaria thus knew that change would not come easily, especially to any area of the law dealing with criminals and those accused of committing violent or infamous crimes—segments of the population with few advocates and little sympathy among the general public, let alone among Europe's iron-fisted monarchs. Medieval forms of torture were still in use, with tools like the Pear of Anguish, the rack, and the Judas Chair inspiring terror, and legal protections for criminal suspects still largely a distant reality. The Frenchman Baron de Montesquieu, invoking "the voice of nature crying out," attacked the use of torture by despotic governments in his widely read 1748 book *The Spirit of the Laws,* and Beccaria followed suit. "The only difference between torture and ordeals by fire or boiling water," Beccaria argued, seeking to do away with torture, "is that the outcome of the former seems to depend upon the will of the accused, while the outcome of the latter depends upon a purely physical and extrinsic fact."[5]

Although Beccaria and one of his early supporters, another Italian nobleman, Pietro Verri, argued for the abolition of torture, a practice now prohibited by international law, only limited reform on that front had taken place before Beccaria's rise to prominence. Sweden had outlawed torture for ordinary crimes in 1734, but would not do so for all purposes until 1772 after Gustavus III came to power. Also, Prussian king Frederick II—singled out by Beccaria as "one of the wisest monarchs of Europe" and who in turn became one of Beccaria's greatest admirers—had abolished torture prior to the publication of *On Crimes and Punishments.* Upon taking the throne in 1740, Frederick II (1712–1786) did away with judicial torture, except for cases involving treason and the murder of multiple victims. In 1747, Frederick the Great—as he became known—also outlawed the desecration of the corpses of those having committed suicide, then a common practice; and in 1754, he abolished torture altogether, calling it "gruesome" and "an uncertain means to discover the truth." In a 1777 letter to Voltaire, Frederick II lauded Beccaria, writing: "Beccaria has left nothing to glean after him; we need only to follow what he has so wisely indicated." Holy Roman Empress Maria Theresa of Austria (1717–1780), a powerful figure in the Habsburg royal family, was slower to act. She abolished torture only in 1776, in the midst of the American Revolution, mainly at the urging of Austrian law professor Joseph von Sonnenfels, a scholar inspired by Beccaria's work.[6]

In writing *On Crimes and Punishments,* Beccaria thus recognized that torture and executions—then firmly entrenched worldwide—would not disappear overnight. "Human sacrifices," Beccaria conceded, "were common among almost all nations." And he acknowledged that "only a few societies have refrained from use of the death penalty—and for only a brief period of time." Beccaria had read about Russia's penal system, and in his book he specifically referred to "the twenty-year reign of the Empress Elizabeth of Moscovy, during which," he commented on her anti–death penalty views, "she gave the leaders of all peoples an illustrious example worth at least as much as many conquests bought with the blood of her country's sons." Beccaria also noted that the death penalty's use through the centuries had never stopped crimes from being committed, thus negating any argument that executions deterred crime. That few nations had barred executions, he lamented, "is consistent with the fate of great truths, which last no longer than a flash of lightning in comparison with the long and dark night that envelopes mankind."[7]

Beccaria's Vision

Although a few early Christians opposed executions, Cesare Beccaria, a Milan native, was the first Enlightenment thinker to lay out a comprehensive case for the death penalty's abolition. A Roman Catholic, Beccaria was born in 1738 and attended a Jesuit school in Parma before attending the University of Pavia from 1754 to 1758. A voracious reader, Beccaria read—and was influenced by—Montesquieu's *Persian Letters,* Jean-Jacques Rousseau's *The Social Contract,* and the books of many other writers from France, England, and Scotland. After getting his law degree, he joined a social academy, the Academy of Fists, one of the many European salons and literary and reading societies of his time. Formed by his friend, Pietro Verri, a prominent writer and public intellectual, the Academy of Fists—which Beccaria joined in 1761 and which got its name from the pugilistic debates of its members—held reformist views that did not find favor elsewhere. The small group, which included Pietro's brother Alessandro and other men mostly in their twenties, sought to win over the Austrian rulers of Lombardy to a program of reform and was dedicated to contributing to the public good. The Habsburgs had governed Lombardy since 1707, but they only began reform efforts after the War of the Austrian Succession in 1748, to reduce a massive deficit created by the cost of the war. Though the Academy of Fists was short-lived, the ideas Beccaria produced as a result of his association with it made significant intellectual contributions, sparking the world's anti–death penalty movement.[8]

The members of the Academy of Fists wrote on an array of topics, ranging from political and economic to literary and scientific—though at that time contributors had to be wary of censors. Every ten days the group published a periodical, *Il Caffé,* the inaugural edition of which was aimed at accomplishing "what good we can for our country" through the distribution of "useful knowledge." Beccaria's own writings were quite diverse. After falling in love with the daughter of an army colonel, Beccaria published his first pamphlet, a study of currency problems in Milan, in 1762. In all, Beccaria wrote seven articles for the coffeehouse-inspired *Il Caffè*, and the topics ranged from the trivial and the whimsical (the statistical probabilities of winning a card game and an "Essay on Odors") to the literary (a "Fragment on Style") to the serious (an essay on smuggling operations). The weightiest product of his association, however, was the publication of his landmark treatise, *Dei delitti e delle pene*, first published anonymously due to fear of persecution and ecclesiastical censors. Beccaria had started work on his book in March 1763, with the first edition of it circulating in July 1764, first in Tuscany and then in Lombardy. "While writing my book," Beccaria later told his French translator, "I had before my eyes the examples of Galileo, Machiavelli, and Giannone," all of whom faced dire consequences—including imprisonment—for their actions or writings. In his book, Beccaria dealt with his subjects—crimes and punishments—in a methodical and philosophical manner, advocating trials by jury and condemning torture and the death penalty as antiquated practices.[9]

In discussing torture, Beccaria wrote that "[a] strange consequence" follows from the use of it: "the innocent individual is placed in a worse condition than the guilty; for if both are tortured, every outcome is stacked against him, because either he confesses to a crime and is convicted or he is declared innocent and has suffered an undeserved punishment." Viewing torture as "a cruelty," Beccaria believed only the guilty should be punished, and he worried considerably about false confessions. As Beccaria explained: "[T]he impression of pain may increase to such a degree that, filling the entire sensory capacity, it leaves the torture victim no liberty but to choose the shortest route to relieve his pain momentarily." "Under these circumstances," Beccaria concluded, "the statements made by the accused are as inevitable as the impressions made by fire and water." With regard to executions, Beccaria wrote that "[t]his futile excess of punishments, which have never made men better, has impelled me to consider whether the death penalty is really useful and just in a well-organized state." "The death penalty," he argued, "is not useful because of the example of cruelty that it gives to men." "If one were to raise the objection that in almost all ages and almost all nations the death penalty has been prescribed for some crimes," Beccaria wrote, "I would reply that this objection amounts to nothing in the face of the truth—against which there is no legal remedy—and that the history of mankind gives us the impression of a vast sea of errors, in which a few confused truths float about with large and distant gaps between them." If monarchs left "the ancient laws in place," Beccaria said, "it is because of the infinite difficulty in stripping the venerated rust of many centuries from so many errors."[10]

A decade and a half before *On Crimes and Punishments* was published, the

French jurist Baron de Montesquieu, who had inherited that title from his wealthy uncle, had also sought less severe punishments. "It is a misfortune in government," Montesquieu wrote, "when the magistracy sees itself thus constrained to make cruel laws." In discussing the history of Roman laws that punished slaves—even innocent ones—with death if their master was killed while traveling, Montesquieu remarked on the need to avoid cruelty. "A prudent legislator," he said, "avoids the misfortune of becoming a terrifying legislator." Montesquieu, who studied law at the University of Bordeaux, served as the commissioner of prisons and was, in the words of one historian, "one of the counsellors charged with overseeing the assignment of those condemned to the galleys, and could not have avoided participating in interrogations that relied upon torture." In *The Spirit of the Laws,* published in 1748, Montesquieu described how, in Japan, "almost all crimes are punished by death," and called Roman laws "very severe" and "full of very cruel provisions," citing an instance in which a man was pulled apart by two chariots.[11]

A believer in separation of powers, Montesquieu influenced James Madison's work on the Constitution, though Montesquieu, while calling for milder laws, did not himself oppose all executions or corporal punishments. "When in the last century laws were made making duels capital crimes," Montesquieu wrote, "perhaps it would have been enough to remove from one of the combatants his capacity to fight by the loss of a hand, as there is usually nothing sadder for a man than to survive the loss of his character." Montesquieu, however, was less than enthusiastic about capital punishment for theft, writing in his book: "The death penalty is the remedy, as it were, for a sick society. When one violates security with respect to goods there can be reasons for the penalty to be capital; but it would perhaps be preferable, and it would be more natural, if the penalty for crimes committed against the security of goods were punishable by the loss of goods." "And that ought to be so," Montesquieu added, "if fortunes were common or equal; but as those who have no goods more readily attack the goods of others, the corporal penalty has had to replace the pecuniary penalty." Montesquieu urged his readers: "A good legislator takes a middle way; he does not always order pecuniary penalties; he does not always inflict corporal penalties."[12]

In his own treatise, Beccaria found both torture and the death penalty to be cruel, articulating the plainspoken view that "the purpose of punishment is neither to torment and afflict a sentient being, nor to undo a crime already committed." For him, "perpetual penal servitude"—or life imprisonment, in today's parlance—was the best and most just way to deter others from committing violent acts. Echoing Montesquieu, Beccaria emphasized that "every act of authority of one man over another that does not derive from absolute necessity is tyrannical." "For a punishment to be just," Beccaria wrote, "it must have only that degree of intensity that suffices to deter men from crime." Viewing perpetual imprisonment as a viable alternative to death sentences, Beccaria—

who lived in an age of public executions—argued passionately in *On Crimes and Punishments*: "It is not the terrible but fleeting spectacle of a criminal's death that is the most powerful brake on crimes, but the long and arduous example of a man deprived of his liberty, who, having become a beast of burden, repays the society he has offended through his toils." "It is not the intensity of the punishment that has the greatest effect on the human mind," Beccaria reasoned, drawing upon his personal experience, "but its extension, for our sensibility is more easily and firmly affected by small but repeated impressions than by a strong but fleeting action." Thus, Beccaria saw executions not only as ineffective in fighting crime but also as counterproductive, writing: "With the death penalty, every example given to the nation requires a crime; with permanent penal servitude, a single crime provides many and lasting examples."[13]

In his book, Beccaria paid considerable homage to Montesquieu, calling him a "great" and "immortal" man. Born in 1689 to a wealthy Bordeaux family, Montesquieu spent nearly two decades writing *The Spirit of the Laws,* a study of legal customs throughout human history. "As the great Montesquieu says," Beccaria wrote, "every punishment that does not derive from absolute necessity is tyrannical." But Beccaria parted ways with Montesquieu on the death penalty, as Montesquieu approved of executions for homicide, attempted murder, and, at least in some cases, theft. "A man deserves death when he has violated the security of the subject so far as to deprive, or attempt to deprive, another man of his life," Montesquieu wrote. Beccaria, on the other hand, took the view that "no one" would "choose the total and permanent loss of his own liberty, no matter how advantageous a crime might be." Consequently, Beccaria believed that "the intensity of perpetual penal servitude, substituted for the death penalty, has all that is necessary to deter even the most determined mind." Beccaria expressed his preference for life imprisonment over capital punishment in this way: "To those who would say that permanent penal servitude is as painful as death, and therefore, equally cruel, I shall reply that, adding up all of the unhappy moments of slavery, it may very well be even more so, but these moments are drawn out over an entire lifetime, while death exerts the whole of its force in a single moment." "And this is the advantage of penal servitude, which frightens those who witness it more than those who suffer it," Beccaria wrote, "for the former consider the entire sum of unhappy moments, while the latter are distracted from future unhappiness by the unhappiness of the present moment."[14]

Beccaria recognized that serious crimes had to be punished severely, but he opined that "punishments and the methods of inflicting them must be chosen" so that, "in keeping with proportionality, they will make the most efficacious and lasting impression on the minds of men with the least torment to the body of the condemned." "The purpose of punishment," Beccaria wrote, "is none other than to prevent the criminal from doing fresh harm to fellow citizens and to deter others from doing the same." On the topic of executions, Beccaria, while writing that violations of a person's "right to security" must be assigned "some of the most severe punishments provided for by the law," thought a criminal's death justifiable only on two grounds: first, "in time of anarchy" to protect national security; and second, if the death penalty could be shown to deter crime. If someone "retains such connections and such power that he endangers the security of the nation even when deprived of his liberty," Beccaria wrote, that citizen's death "becomes necessary" because "his very existence can provoke a dangerous revolution in the established form of government." The "second reason" for believing "the death penalty could be just and necessary," Beccaria wrote, was for the sake of deterrence, though Beccaria emphasized that "centuries of experience" had taught that "the ultimate punishment has never deterred men determined to harm society." In other words, Beccaria did not believe executions would ever stop murderers from murdering or other criminals from committing crimes.[15]

Beccaria would repeat his anti–death penalty views—and add one more rationale for abolition, the irrevocability of capital punishment—in a government report he coauthored in 1792. That report, articulating a minority position of a committee charged with drafting a new penal code for Austrian Lombardy, was written by Beccaria, Francesco Gallarati Scotti, and Paolo Risi. Authored a year after the ratification of the U.S. Bill of Rights, the minority report favored "perpetual enslavement" and "forced labour" for the most serious crimes, saying "the death penalty should not be prescribed except in the case of absolute necessity." "[I]n the peaceful circumstances of our society, and with the regular administration of justice," the report's coauthors argued in the midst of one of the bloodiest of revolutions, the French Revolution, "we could not think of any case of absolute necessity other than the situation in which the accused, in plotting the subversion of the state, was capable, either through his external or internal relationships, of disturbing and endangering society even while imprisoned and closely watched." Citing Austrian and Tuscan anti–death penalty codes "received as models," Beccaria and his two colleagues felt compelled "to expose candidly and succinctly" their abolitionist views. "[W]e believe that the death penalty is not suitable," they wrote, "because it is not just, since it is not necessary"; "because it is less efficacious than perpetual punishment equipped with a good deal of continuous publicity"; and "because it cannot be undone."[16]

In *On Crimes and Punishments,* Beccaria laid out many of his ideas in great detail. "For the death penalty to be deemed necessary to serve as an example capable of discouraging the most serious crimes," Beccaria wrote, "it would be necessary to prove with facts, showing that where the death penalty has been most frequently employed, such crimes were far fewer in number than in places where the same death penalty was used less or not at all." Lacking such proof, Beccaria's reformist approach instead focused on punishing and preventing crime and educating the public. "[T]he surest but most difficult way to prevent crimes is to improve education," Beccaria wrote, saying crimes are "distributed across a scale that moves imperceptibly by diminishing degrees from the highest to the lowest" and that, "[i]f geometry were applicable to the infinite and obscure combinations of human actions, there would be a corresponding scale of punishments, descending from the most severe to the mildest." Swift, proportionate punishments, not barbaric ones, Beccaria believed, were "more just and useful." "Do you want to prevent crimes?" Beccaria wrote. "Then see to it that enlightenment accompanies liberty." Beccaria saw a better-educated populace as the key to crime prevention and viewed executions as totally ineffective, saying: "[W]hile the death penalty may be the most rapid way of getting rid of guilty people, it is not the most useful to deter crimes."[17]

Right from its publication, *On Crimes and Punishments*—as Beccaria no doubt expected—generated enormous controversy, drawing decidedly mixed reviews. The Venetian Inquisition blocked importation of the book into Venetian territory in August 1764; an Italian monk named Ferdinando Facchinei anonymously published a harsh rebuke of it in 1765; the Roman Inquisition banned it in February 1766, placing it on the Index of Forbidden Books; and in 1777 a Spanish translation was also banned in Spain. But the French writer and social activist Voltaire, who spent much of his life crusading on behalf of innocent persons, adored Beccaria's book, writing an extensive commentary on it in 1766—a commentary frequently reprinted with Beccaria's text and thus helping to promote it. "I was engrossed by a reading of *On Crimes and Punishments,*" Voltaire's passionate commentary begins. And in Milan, the reformer Count Carlo Firmian, the plenipotentiary of Austria's Empress Maria Theresa, defended Beccaria against charges of subversion and sacrilege. Indeed, Beccaria's book quickly garnered the attention of monarchs and led to calls for criminal law reform and the death penalty's abolition in Europe. For example, Maria Theresa Habsburg—the Holy Roman empress—and Grand Duke Leopold of Tuscany both expressed their admiration for Beccaria's ideas. The book even led Russian empress Catherine II to invite Beccaria to assist in the reform of Russia's penal code, an offer he considered for some time before turning it down.[18]

The reactions to Beccaria's ideas could not have been more divergent. In *Notes and Observations on the Book Entitled 'On Crimes and Punishments,'* Ferdinando Facchinei dismissed Beccaria's book, saying it had not proved "that the death penalty and torture are useless." The German philosopher Immanuel Kant, another big critic, said Beccaria's arguments amounted to "mere sophistry," arguing that murderers "must die." Voltaire, on the other hand, heaped endless praise on the young author, calling his book "*le code de l'humanité.*" "It was tyranny in particular," Voltaire declared, "that first decreed the death penalty for those who differed with the established Church on some dogmas." In both England and France, monarchs had long used executions to persecute religious minorities. For example, in England, the Catholic Queen Mary (1553–1558) and the Protestant Queen Elizabeth (1558–1603) both had religious dissenters put to death, with "Bloody Mary"—as Protestants called her—executing nearly three hundred people in just four years, many by burning. "It is clear," Voltaire added, "that twenty robust thieves, sentenced to labour on some public works for all of their lives, serve the state through their suffering, and that their deaths will only benefit the public executioner, who is paid to kill people in public." "The compassionate author of *On Crimes and Punishments*," Voltaire explained, "is more than justified to complain that punishment is too often excessive in relation to the crime, and that sometimes it is even detrimental to the state it was intended to benefit." Reciting the adage that "a hanged man is good for nothing," Voltaire urged his readers to "read and reread" *On Crimes and Punishments,* the work of "this lover of humanity."[19]

François-Marie Arouet, known as Voltaire to his readers, was born in Paris in 1694 and attended a Jesuit college with the intention of becoming a lawyer. After writing plays critical of the French government, Voltaire had been imprisoned in 1726 and then exiled to England. The Ordonnance Criminelle of 1670 set forth the code of penal laws in France in Voltaire's time, and that legal code made the death penalty and the mutilation of prisoners common punishments. Voltaire had criticized the Ordonnance as too harsh, saying, "Let the torments of criminals be useful. A hanged man is good for nothing, but a man condemned to public works still serves his country as a living lesson." Outraged at the execution of innocent persons, Voltaire—along with his fellow philosophers in Europe, who were then grappling in their writings with the societal justifications for executions—called the government's indiscriminate use of punishments "monstrous, irrational, and absurd." The English physician and philosopher John Locke, who lived from 1632 to 1704, had taken the position, by contrast, that an offender who had committed "some act that deserves death" had "by his fault forfeited his own life" and that "[e]ach transgression may be punished to that degree and with so much severity as will suffice to make it an ill bargain to the offender, give him cause to repent, and terrify others from doing the like." And in his work, Jean-Jacques Rousseau had similarly said that "every malefactor who attacks the social right becomes through his transgressions a rebel and a traitor to the homeland; in violating its laws, he ceases to be a member, and he even wages war with it." "In that case," Rousseau said, "the preservation of the state is incompatible with his own." In a chapter of *The Social Contract* titled "The Right of Life and Death," Rousseau emphasized, however, that while the guilty deserved to be punished, "there is not a single evil doer who could not be turned to some good." "[O]ne has the right to put to death, even as an example, only some who cannot be preserved without danger," Rousseau further clarified. In his *Discourse on*

Political Economy, Rousseau likewise stressed that while "any imbecile who is obeyed can, like anyone else, punish crimes . . . the true statesman knows how to prevent them." "In a well governed state," Rousseau declared, "there are few punishments, not because there are many pardons, but because criminals are rare."[20]

A well-known figure in America, Voltaire played a key role in shaping public discourse on penal reform, with his writings advertised and distributed by American booksellers as early as 1752. His books were popular among leading American revolutionaries such as George Washington, Thomas Jefferson, and Benjamin Rush, with John Adams admiring Voltaire's "vigor" and "fire" and speaking of his "fight for tolerance" and "his anger at the laws." James Madison's library contained most of Voltaire's major works; James Monroe's included, along with works by Rousseau, Montesquieu, and Montaigne, thirty volumes of Voltaire's writings; and John Adams, the lawyer turned diplomat, personally recorded a famous meeting between Voltaire and Benjamin Franklin at which the two men embraced and kissed one another. In Paris, Adams went to a "French Comedy" in 1778 and was seated "in the Front Box very near to Voltaire." As Adams recorded: "The Audience between the several Acts, called out, Voltaire! Voltaire! Voltaire! and clapped and applauded him during all the intervals."[21]

The irrepressible Voltaire spent many of his waking hours seeking to further the cause of justice and trying to right wrongful accusations and convictions. His pursuit of justice was infectious. According to Ben Ray Redman, a Voltaire scholar, Voltaire spent "three years to win a declaration of innocence for Calas, brutally executed on charges of having murdered a son because he wished to turn Catholic"; "nine years to obtain the exculpation of the Sirvens, accused of murdering a daughter for a similar reason"; and "twelve years to vindicate the Chevalier de La Barre, most horribly put to death for an offense against religion of which he had not been proved guilty!" The Sirvens were a Huguenot family whose youngest daughter was found drowned in a well, having suffered epileptic seizures that local nuns took as signs of her conversion to the "true faith." That family, which fled to Geneva, Switzerland, was later accused of murdering their daughter to prevent the conversion, though Voltaire's involvement later prompted French authorities to acquit the family, enabling them to return to France in 1771. The Chevalier Jean-François de La Barre—who was tortured and beheaded before his body was burned on a pyre and who, Voltaire felt, should not have been put to death—vandalized a crucifix and sang blasphemous songs, for which he was sentenced to be burned at the stake in 1766. The verdict against La Barre, a French nobleman, especially angered Voltaire, who told Beccaria that it was unjust. In his *Dictionnaire Philosophique,* Voltaire wrote: "When the chevalier de La Barre, the grandson of a lieutenant general of the army and a young man of much wit and great expectations, but with all the thoughtlessness of an unbridled youth, was convicted of singing impious songs, and even of passing a profession of priests without taking off his hat, the judges of Abbeville decreed not only should his tongue be cut out," but that La Barre should have "his hands cut off" and "his body burned in a slow fire." Pointing out that this happened in the eighteenth century, not in the thirteenth or fourteenth centuries, Voltaire lamented that though "[f]oreign nations judge France" by her plays, novels, and verses, "[t]hey do not know that there isn't a nation more cruel at the bottom, than the French."[22]

Voltaire's writings—and his crusading work, also well known to the Framers—inspired Americans to adopt hearsay rules in their legal codes that were specifically designed to exclude unreliable evidence. Most notoriously, in 1762 a French court in Toulouse had convicted Jean Calas, a sixty-four-year-old Protestant, of murdering his son to prevent his conversion to Catholicism. The son likely committed suicide, but his family attempted to conceal that fact so that the son's body would not be dragged through the streets and scandalously hanged in accordance with existing law. Calas, the father, was sentenced to death, but he protested his innocence even as he was judicially tortured, with his body broken on the wheel. Voltaire, who raised money for the Calas family after the brutal execution and who urged tolerance of religious views, represented Calas's wife and children after they, too, were placed on trial following the execution. Voltaire, who worried especially about the efficacy of torture, pointed out that much of the testimony was based on superstitions and hearsay. "It is as absurd to inflict torture to seek out the truth as it is to order a duel to assess who is the culprit," he wrote, adding: "[O]ften the robust and guilty one resists the ordeal, whereas the debilitated innocent succumbs to it." Voltaire denounced judicial torture in 1766, called for its actual abolition in 1778, and said that "atrocious old customs" should be rejected. Voltaire won banishment for Calas's family, avoiding death sentences, and after Jean Calas was posthumously cleared by authorities in 1765, the Calas family was allowed to return to France. Though Voltaire never came to oppose torture and executions in all cases, he and Beccaria shared concerns about the risk of condemning innocent persons to death and were in at least some respects kindred spirits. Voltaire himself wrote to Beccaria in 1768 to say "what an abominable jurisprudence is that which sustains religion only by means of the public executioner."[23]

Voltaire certainly did not agree with Beccaria in every respect. Whereas Beccaria opposed all torture, Voltaire thought it should be used as a last resort to discover the identities of accomplices of convicted regicides and parricides. Also, while Beccaria opposed all executions unless the state itself was endangered, Voltaire only believed in limiting the death penalty's application, opposing, for example, the execution of the mentally disturbed. In 1770, a French lawyer named Louis Philipon de la Madelaine sent Voltaire the text of a "Discourse on the Necessity and the Means of Suppressing Capital Punishment." Though Voltaire agreed capital punishment should be limited, he insisted that it be applied with the most extreme methods of execution in the case of the worst criminals. "Undoubtedly," Voltaire replied in his letter, "premeditated murders, parricides, incendiaries, deserve a death whose apparatus must be frightful." "I should without regret have condemned Ravaillac to be quartered," he wrote of the Frenchman who in 1610 stabbed to death King Henry IV of France, qualifying that "I should not have imposed the same torment on a man who had not wanted, nor been able, to kill his prince, and who must obviously have been mad." Unlike Beccaria, Voltaire thus saw only some executions and instances of torture as excessive, explaining in the very opening of his letter, however, why punishments must serve a legitimate purpose. "You have sent me a work dictated by humanity and eloquence," his response began. "It has never been better proved," he said, "that judges must start by being men, that the punishments of the evil-doers must be useful to society, and that a hanged man is no good to anyone."[24]

Philosophically, Beccaria favored incarceration over capital punishment and believed life sentences would deter crime just as effectively as death sentences. "Let us imagine two nations, each with a scale of punishments proportionate to crimes; in one, the maximum punishment is perpetual slavery and in the other it is breaking on the wheel. I maintain that there will be as much fear of the maximum punishment in the former as in the latter," Beccaria wrote. Indeed, the frontispiece to the third edition of *Dei delitti e delle pene,* published in 1765, was a copperplate engraving based on a sketch Beccaria provided. It depicts a figure, Justice, shunning an executioner who is carrying a sword and axe in his right hand and who is trying to hand Justice a cluster of severed heads with his outstretched left hand. Justice's gaze is instead transfixed on a pile of prisoner's shackles and worker's tools—the instruments symbolizing imprisonment and hard labor. "The happy epoch," the young Beccaria wrote, "has not yet arrived in which truth shall be—as error has heretofore been—in the hands of the greatest number." Now on a mission to do away with the death penalty itself, Beccaria declared he wanted prisons built to house offenders.[25]

Early Abolitionists

The list of prior abolitionist successes was extremely short in Beccaria's time. Beccaria, who read a lot but did not like to travel long distances, would not even have been aware of the bulk of that history, much of which had taken place in faraway lands in the Orient. Though Beccaria made a passing reference in his book to "the example of the citizens of Rome," a nearby and familiar locale, only a few early Buddhists, English Friends, and religious figures had opposed executions. For example, some Christians—frequently the victims of Roman executions, making the death penalty no theoretical matter for them—had argued that such killings were contrary to Christian ethics, with Pope Gregory I (590–604) and Pope Nicholas I (858–867) distancing themselves from executions or urging the abolition of capital punishment altogether. "Since I fear God," Gregory I said, "I shrink from having anything whatsoever to do with the death of anyone." "You should save from death not only the innocent but also criminals," Nicholas I wrote in a letter in 866, recommending the death penalty's abolition. While early Christians did not often go so far as to challenge the state's right to take life, some vigorously opposed the death penalty's use in certain circumstances, as John Chrysostom, archbishop of Constantinople, did in the fourth century, saying it is "not right to put a heretic to death."[26]

The only concrete abolitionist example Beccaria could provide in *On Crimes and Punishments* was the Empress Elizabeth Petrovna, Russia's ruler from 1741 to 1762. The Russian empress—the daughter of Peter the Great and Catherine I—pledged never to use capital punishment, and by all accounts, she kept her word. In her relatively calm and trouble-free reign, there were no serious rebellions or conspiracies, and while, on her ministers' advice, she never formally repealed death penalty laws, she suspended Russian executions, issuing decrees to that effect in the 1750s. She never once ordered a death sentence and commuted every capital sentence that came before her. When Peter Shuvalov, a Russian field marshal, presented her with his codification of Russian laws, which—as one academic notes—"bristled with cruel" and "vexatious" penalties, she refused to sign it, saying it was "written not with ink, but with blood." Though Beccaria praised the Russian empress for her actions, the "reality"—as another scholar, Franco Venturi, puts it—was that Russia's death penalty "was replaced by terribly cruel punishments which often resulted in the convict's death." Instead of being executed, convicts were exiled and often brutally tortured or worked to death in labor camps. As Venturi writes: "In fact, convicts were beaten with the *knut,* their nostrils were torn, and then their forehead and cheeks were branded with an iron. Many died and those who survived were usually deported to do forced labour in Siberia."[27]

Throughout Europe the story was much the same, with countless examples of torture and just a handful of places and rulers having ever experimented with the death penalty's abolition, even for a short time. In England, William the Conqueror—a rare exception—abolished the death penalty in 1066, long before Beccaria's seminal work, but that action hardly signaled a progressive victory or revolutionary change in social policy. The change was temporary, and William, known for his cruel treatment of criminals, only did so because he preferred terrible mutilations of the body, such as blinding and castration, over executions. Indeed, political opponents were still subject to execution during William the Conqueror's reign, as the trial and beheading of Earl Waltheof for treason in 1076 makes clear. Henry I ultimately reinstated the death penalty in 1108, and the death penalty was not abolished again in England until 1965, more than 850 years later. Napoleon did not abolish torture in Spain until 1808, and though the practice largely disappeared in Europe during the Revolutionary and Napoleonic wars, some Swiss cantons did not abolish torture until the mid-nineteenth century. Thus, at the time Beccaria wrote *On Crimes and Punishments,* executions and instruments of torture were still very much fixtures of European life.[28]

The only other examples of the death penalty's abolition came from outside Europe and were far apart in time and place. In the first century AD, Amandagamani, the Buddhist king of what is now Sri Lanka, abolished the death penalty during his reign, as did several successive kings of that tropical island nation. In AD 724, Japan's Emperor Shomu, a devout Buddhist, also forbade executions, as did some early Buddhist rulers in India who saw capital punishment and mutilation as at odds with the Buddhist philosophy of compassion. In the third century BC, for example, King Açoka, a devout Buddhist who ruled over nearly all of India, abolished capital punishment throughout his empire. Chinese pilgrims visiting India in the fifth century would take note of the fact that Indian kings ruled without resorting to executions. In AD 818 in Japan, Emperor Saga Tennô, following a period in which all executions were stayed, also joined the ranks of abolitionist rulers. He outlawed the death penalty for theft, then for robbery and other crimes, effectively abolishing capital punishment for more than three hundred years, until another execution took place in Japan in 1156. China, too, witnessed short periods of abolition, including during the Tang Dynasty, when Emperor Xuanzong abolished the death penalty in 747 for approximately ten years. In all of these places, of course, the death penalty would be brought back—often with a vengeance— after those periods of abolition.[29]

Prior to the publication of *On Crimes and Punishments,* executions, often carried out publicly and in the most horrific ways imaginable, were the norm for European and most other societies. In Nuremberg, Germany, a council treasurer was beheaded in the 1600s; the British Parliament did not forbid burning women at the stake until 1790; and the English did not abolish the gibbeting of murderers' corpses until 1834. Though executions for witchcraft in Bavaria took place mainly in the years 1560 to 1630, the last execution of a woman for witchcraft in that region took place as late as 1775. Between 1561 and 1670 alone, one researcher identified 3,229 witch burnings in southwestern Germany. "What constituted 'cruel' punishment," scholar Lynn Hunt explains, "clearly depended on cultural expectations." In 1757, nine years after the publication of Montesquieu's *The Spirit of the Laws,* a delusional man named François Damiens attacked Louis XV with a penknife. The king only suffered a scratch to his forearm, but Damiens had his hand melted off and his flesh peeled with red-hot pinchers. He then had boiling oil poured into his wounds and had horses tear off his limbs. As historian Jeremy Mercer writes: "By the mid-eighteenth century, there were 115 crimes punishable by death in France, including wearing armor without authorization, fighting a duel, smuggling salt or tobacco in groups of five or more armed men, and causing a leak in a ship."

"The methods of execution," Mercer explains, "ranged from being burned alive, broken on the wheel, hanged, beheaded, or drawn and quartered."[30]

Though Beccaria knew what he was up against, he remained optimistic, appealing to monarchs everywhere to rid society of capital punishment, promising the sweet vindication of history. "The voice of one philosopher," he admitted, "is too weak against the clamour and the cries of so many people who are guided by blind habit." But, calling upon "the few sages scattered across the face of the earth" to "echo" back to him, he countered: "if the truth should reach the throne of the monarch—despite the many obstacles that keep it at bay against his wishes—let him know that it arrives with the secret support of all mankind; and let him know that the bloody notoriety of conquerors will fall silent before him and that a just posterity will bestow him a pre-eminent place among the peaceful monuments of the Tituses, the Antonines, and the Trajans." Though Roman emperors had frequently ordered executions and overseen gladiators fighting to the death, Beccaria felt that a society without capital punishment would usher in a glorious new world order. Beccaria himself would harken back to rulers such as Antoninus Pius, who, once enthroned, refused to execute men previously slated for execution and who presided over a peaceful, prosperous period in Rome's history.[31]

In his own lifetime, Beccaria witnessed only modest success, dying alone in his house in 1794 in the midst of the bloody French Revolution, just a few years after the now-notorious French physician Dr. Guillotin conceived of a beheading machine to more painlessly kill the condemned. In 1786, persuaded by Beccaria's ideas, Grand Duke Peter Leopold of Tuscany did adopt a Tuscan penal code that totally eliminated the death penalty. Peter Leopold (or Leopold II, as he became known) also ordered the burning of instruments of torture and was apparently pleased with the results, reporting in 1789 that "mild laws together with a careful vigilance" had reduced common crimes and almost eliminated "the most atrocious" ones. And in 1787, Holy Roman Emperor Joseph II, Leopold's brother, followed suit, abolishing Austria's death penalty save for crimes of revolt against the state. When Leopold published his "Reform of the Criminal Law of Tuscany" on November 30, 1786, he proscribed not only death as a punishment but also mutilation, branding, infamy, and torture. In lieu of the death penalty, Leopold made the maximum penalty forced labor for life in double chains—with a special uniform and placard to be worn on the convict's breast reading "Extreme Penalty" ("ultimo supplizio"). Joseph II of Lombardy, by contrast, retained branding and infamy—though Beccaria was later appointed to a commission to reexamine the laws of Lombardy, a commission that began its work in 1791 but that led to little more than drawn-out discussions among its participants. In 1790, Grand Duke Leopold reestablished the death penalty for incitement to rebellion—and later for murder and attempts to destroy the religion of the state. In the end, it was only the translation of Beccaria's ideas into other languages that breathed life into them over time.[32]

In October 1774, the Continental Congress approved a Declaration of Rights pronounced on the basis of "the immutable laws of nature, the principles of the English constitution, and the several charters or compacts" of the colonies. The Declaration's first resolution proclaimed, using the language of John Locke, that the inhabitants of the English colonies in North America "are entitled to life, liberty and property." Later that month, Congress issued a "Letter to the Inhabitants of Quebec" as a piece of propaganda targeted at Canadians, who had also been subjected to English tyranny. In that open letter, drafted by Richard Henry Lee, Congress quoted Cesare Beccaria and Baron de Montesquieu: "'In every human society,' says the celebrated Marquis Beccaria, 'there is an effort, continually tending to confer on one part of the heighth of power and happiness, and to reduce the other to the extreme of weakness and misery. The intent of good laws is to oppose this effort, and to diffuse their influence universally and equally.'" "Rulers stimulated by this pernicious 'effort,' and subjects animated by the just 'intent of opposing good laws against it,'" the letter of Congress continued in remarking on America's "mild system" of laws, "have occasioned that vast variety of efforts, that fill the histories of so many nations." Citing the rights to habeas corpus and to trial by jury before any deprivation of life, liberty, or property, the letter of Congress concluded that histories "demonstrate the truth of this simple position, that to live by the will of one man, or sett of men, is the production of misery to all men."[33]

Beccaria's influence on Anglo-American law—and on the death penalty debate—is demonstrated by the sheer number of times his name comes up. According to historian Mary-Margaret Barr, *On Crimes and Punishments* "was known in America immediately after its first appearance in France" largely because of Voltaire's famous commentary that accompanied it. Popular in lending libraries, it also sold quickly in bookstores because of the public's interest in revolutionary ideas. In 1786, in Connecticut, it was even serialized in a New Haven newspaper, with the Yale senior class—just two years earlier—having vigorously debated whether the death penalty was "too severe & rigorous in the United States for the present Stage of Society." Like Montesquieu's *The Spirit of the Laws,* which was widely celebrated by the Founding Fathers, *On Crimes and Punishments* also ended up being closely read and admired by many of those men. Beccaria was "well known" in America, two U.S. Supreme Court Justices once wrote, pointing out that he "was the main voice against the use of infamy"—calling its use as a punishment a "civil stain." "Beccaria seems to have been principally introduced to America by Voltaire," the Justices said, noting that the U.S. Constitution's Fifth Amendment "was designed to protect against infamy." "No person shall be held to answer for a capital, or otherwise infamous crime, unless on a presentment or indictment of a Grand Jury," the Fifth Amendment guarantees in no uncertain terms. The

Fifth Amendment right against self-incrimination itself originated out of a desire to stop courts of criminal jurisdiction from exacting incriminatory admissions through means of interrogation that might involve torture. One of its predecessors, a decree by Virginia's General Assembly in 1677, had long before established the principle that "noe law can compel a man to sweare against himselfe in any matter wherein he is lyable to corporall punishment."[34]

On Crimes and Punishments, though not translated and distributed everywhere all at once, would shape countless Enlightenment thinkers, including advocates of prison reform. In Europe, William Eden, a Beccaria disciple, authored *Principles of Penal Law* in 1771; Voltaire, taken with Beccaria's book, wrote his famous commentary on it that was then commonly reprinted with it; and in 1791, Maximilien Robespierre advocated the death penalty's abolition in France. Beccaria's writings also heavily influenced John Howard, a vocal opponent of capital and corporal punishments. Voltaire especially helped publicize *On Crimes and Punishments.* After reading Beccaria's book, Voltaire called Beccaria "a brother" and "a beneficent genius whose excellent book has educated Europe." Voltaire had successfully campaigned to exonerate a wrongfully condemned man in 1763, wrote extensively on the need for criminal law reform, and had direct contact with Benjamin Franklin and Dr. Benjamin Rush. The execution of Jean Calas, in particular, had inspired Voltaire to take up the cause of the death penalty. Though relentlessly tortured, Calas had refused to name any accomplices, telling his torturers: "Where there is no crime, there cannot be any accomplices." With Calas's son Marc-Antoine most likely having committed suicide, Voltaire's tireless campaign led French authorities to set aside sentences against Marc-Antoine's mother and brother, both of whom had been arrested in what became known as the "Calas affair."[35]

In admiring Beccaria's book Voltaire was not alone. English legal scholars, including Jeremy Bentham and William Blackstone, were also intrigued and moved by Beccaria's writings. Bentham wrote that a punishment is "to induce a man to choose always the least mischievous of two offences." An English philosopher and social reformer, Bentham began reading *On Crimes and Punishments* around the time he was admitted to the bar in 1769, and he was so taken with the book that he wrote of Beccaria: "Oh, my master, first evangelist of Reason . . . you who have made so many useful excursions into the path of utility, what is there left for us to do?" Bentham, who freely acknowledged Beccaria's influence, was a vocal critic of capital punishment, objecting to its "irremissibility." Blackstone's *Commentaries on the Laws of England*—another heavy influence on American lawyers—also explicitly referred to Beccaria. The Oxford scholar whose writings were frequently cited by colonial lawyers, Blackstone called Beccaria "an ingenious writer, who seems to have well studied the springs of human action, that crimes are more effectually prevented by the certainty, than by the severity, of punishment." Criticizing the infliction of harsh punishments, Blackstone said it is "absurd and impolitic to apply the same punishment to crimes of different magnitude." While remaining supportive of executions and corporal punishments such as the cutting off of noses and ears, Blackstone favored death sentences only in limited circumstances. Indeed, he recounted the "melancholy truth" that English law made approximately 160 different crimes death-eligible.[36]

The legendary William Blackstone assumed the Vinerian Chair at Oxford in 1758, and the first volume of his *Commentaries on the Laws of England*—a huge success in the American colonies—was published in 1765. The fourth book, which dealt with "Public Wrongs, or Crimes and Misdemeanors," was published in 1769, after the release of Beccaria's book. In it, Blackstone expressed the view that a punishment "ought always to be proportioned to the particular purpose it is meant to serve, and by no means exceed it." For example, Blackstone wrote: "[T]he pains of death, and perpetual disability by exile, slavery, or imprisonment, ought never to be inflicted, but when the offender appears *incorrigible:* which may be collected either from a repetition of minuter offenses; or from the perpetration of some one crime of deep malignity, which of itself demonstrates a disposition without hope or probability of amendment and in such cases it would be cruelty to the public, to defer the punishment of such a criminal, till he had an opportunity of repeating perhaps the worst of villainies." In England, monarchs had long used executions to inspire terror, with horrendous punishments—however perverse—often tied in some way to the nature of the crimes. For instance, in 1190 Richard I had issued an order making crusaders subject to execution for military offenses. "Whoever shall slay a man on ship board, he shall be bound to the dead man and thrown into the sea," read one ordinance. "If he shall slay him on land he shall be bound to the dead man and buried in the earth," read another.[37]

In his *Commentaries,* Blackstone expressed the belief that executions should be avoided where "the evil to be prevented is not adequate to the violence of the preventative." As Blackstone wrote: "A multitude of sanguinary laws (besides the doubt that may be entertained concerning the right of making them) do likewise prove a manifest defect either in the wisdom of the legislature, or the strength of executive power." "It is a kind of quackery in government, and argues a want of solid skill," Blackstone argued, "to apply the same universal remedy, the *ultimum supplicium,* to every case of difficulty." "It is, it must be owned," Blackstone wrote, "much *easier* to extirpate than to amend mankind: yet that magistrate must be esteemed both a weak and a cruel surgeon, who cuts off every limb, which through ignorance or indolence he will not attempt to cure." The word "sanguinary," a term commonly used during the founding era, has long been defined as "bloody," "cruel," or "murderous." According to Sir William Holdsworth, "it was Beccaria's book which helped Blackstone to crystallize his ideas, and it was Beccaria's influence which helped to give a more critical tone to his treatment of the English criminal law than to his treatment of any other part of English law."[38]

Beccaria's influence was also felt keenly—and quickly—in the American colonies, a landscape already bursting at the seams with revolutionary ideas and impulses. Thomas Jefferson and George Washington both bought copies of Beccaria's book, most likely in 1769, and by the 1770s it was clear that Beccaria had made a splash across the Atlantic. Indeed, in 1770, the American patriot and lawyer John Adams famously defended the British soldiers accused of murder in the Boston Massacre, showing close familiarity, even then, with the reform-minded Italian criminologist. In taking on this unpopular cause, Adams—though a death penalty supporter—eloquently invoked Beccaria in his opening statement: "I am for the prisoners at the bar and shall apologize for it only in the words of the Marquis Beccaria: 'If by supporting the rights of mankind, and of invincible truth, I shall contribute to save from the agonies of death one unfortunate victim of tyranny, or ignorance, equally fatal, his blessings and years of transport shall be sufficient consolation to me for the contempt of all mankind.'" Adams, who owned an Italian edition of Beccaria's book, had copied Beccaria's words into his diary before recording his own thoughts: "The Sovereign Power is constituted, to defend Individuals against the Tyranny of others. Crimes are acts of Tyranny of one or more on another or more. A Murderer, a Thief, a Robber, a Burglar, is a Tyrant." John Quincy Adams himself later remarked on the "electric effect" Beccaria's words, as spoken by his father, had on jurors. In 1786, John Adams, who also gave a copy of *On Crimes and Punishments* to his son Thomas in 1800, copied yet another quotation from Beccaria into his diary, first in English, then in the original Italian: "Every Act of Authority, of one Man over another for which there is not an absolute Necessity, is tyrannical."[39]

Aaron Burr, who served as the third Vice President of the United States under Thomas Jefferson, also invoked Beccaria's writings in his own. As a student at Princeton, Burr had become a convert of Beccaria and his utilitarian philosophy, and Burr later befriended and lodged with Jeremy Bentham at Bentham's London residence. Bentham and Burr discussed prison reform, among many other issues, and as New York's Attorney General, Burr prepared a report of "Observations" in 1791 that New York Governor George Clinton brought to the attention of the state legislature. At that time, New York still punished counterfeiting and forgery as capital crimes, a practice Burr opposed using Beccaria's ideas. "An unprejudiced mind," Burr said, "will not readily admit the justice or policy of sentencing to death him who forges an order for three crowns or for a pair of boots (cases which have actually come under judicial cognizance), when he who steals a thousand pounds is sentenced to be whipped." "Punishments," Burr wrote, "should be proportioned to the dangerous tendency of the crime, the degree of depravity which it denotes, the incentives to the perpetration, the facility of detection or escape, or perhaps to the result of a combined view of all these circumstances." "Gradations in crimes," he determined, "require corresponding gradations in punishments."[40]

As the state's attorney general, Burr prosecuted cases involving murder, theft, counterfeiting, forgery, and rape, putting him in close proximity with offenders. This gave Burr a special interest in criminal justice issues. In 1787, Burr's friend Jeremy Bentham, who had also given the matter considerable thought, conceived of a prison—in his words, an "inspection-house"—in which all the prisoners could be viewed at any time without their actually knowing when or whether they were being watched. Burr was drawn to Bentham's plan for penitentiary reform, called "the Panopticon"—a new prison design that would keep inmates under constant surveillance, with a central observation tower placed in the middle of a circular institution. In his legislative report, Burr favored less draconian sentences, writing: "Indiscriminate severity renders the law odious, occasions frequent convictions and frequent pardons, leads jurors to consider the consequences of their verdict, perhaps to the disregard of the facts proven, and the oaths they have taken. Thus the public sympathy is excited against public administration, and the terror of death is diminished by the hope of favor from jurors, or mercy from the chief magistrate." "Despite his liberal plea," Burr's biographer Nancy Isenberg writes, "Burr's fellow legislators ignored his reform agenda, suggesting that his view was perhaps too 'unprejudiced'—or, one might say, ahead of its time." As a reward for Burr's service as the state's attorney general, Governor Clinton backed Burr in his election, helping make Burr the next U.S. Senator from New York.[41]

James Wilson, a leading founder, was also enamored of Beccaria's ideas and regularly referred to Beccaria's treatise in his own writings and law lectures. A Pennsylvania native who opposed slavery, Wilson served in the Second Continental Congress, was the Federalists' chief spokesman in Pennsylvania, played a leading role in the U.S. Constitution's ratification, and was only one of six men to sign both the Declaration of Independence and the Constitution. He served as the College of Philadelphia's first law professor, was given the honor of presenting an oration in Philadelphia on July 4, 1788, in front of more than seventeen thousand people in celebration of America's independence, and became an Associate Justice of the U.S. Supreme Court in 1789. When he gave his inaugural "Lecture on Law" at the College of Philadelphia in December 1790, the attendees included George and Martha Washington, Vice President John Adams, and numerous federal and state legislators. In his writings, Wilson openly expressed reservations about capital punishment, called the prior English practice of not affording counsel to those accused of capital crimes "unreasonable and severe," and argued that false confessions had been made, noting that one man had shown up alive after three people were hanged for his supposed murder. In one case that Wilson handled as a new lawyer, his client was on trial for murder. In his final summation to the jury, Wilson, then a novice lawyer who had yet to rise to the top of his profession, confessed himself "unknown and inexperienced at the bar," but passionately pled for his client's life. "Upon you," Wilson told the jurors, "will depend whether the prisoner at the bar shall be remanded to the place from whence he came, and from thence to be carried to the place of execution, there to hang between heaven and earth as if unworthy of either; or whether, acquitted by your verdict, he shall be released from his confinement and restored with joy and safety to his friends and country." "I hope and pray, in his behalf," Wilson urged, that the latter "may be the case."[42]

Wilson in fact took great pride in how few American crimes were punished by death. In charging a Virginia grand jury in 1791, the year the Bill of Rights was ratified, Wilson began by giving two directives: "To prevent crimes is the noblest end and aim of criminal jurisprudence." "To punish them is one of the means necessary for the accomplishment of this noble end and aim." Anglo-American traditions not only attached importance to citizen participation at trials in the adjudication of guilt or innocence, but grand juries—composed of a large number of citizens, usually more than twenty—sat with courts of general jurisdiction and took part in the process of charging their fellow citizens. In effect, grand jurors, who had to approve indictments, served as a check on prosecutors. During the course of his remarks to Virginia grand jurors, Wilson cited Beccaria, calling him "eloquent and benevolent," and echoed Beccaria's reformist approach, saying, "Let the punishment be proportioned—let it be analogous—to the crime." Wilson also expressed pride at the difference between English and American laws: "How few are the crimes—how few are the capital crimes, known to the laws of the United States, compared with those known to the laws of England!"[43]

Wilson, whose house had been viciously attacked in 1779 by an armed mob after he defended Tories in Philadelphia accused of treason, despised "cruel punishments" that served only to inflict gratuitous suffering. In the deadly melee that was later nicknamed the battle of Fort Wilson, the boisterous mob of disgruntled militiamen had marched against those believed to be Tory sympathizers, laying siege to Wilson's three-story brick house on the corner of Third and Walnut. With Wilson and more than two dozen others, including merchants Robert Morris and Thomas Mifflin, trapped inside, a firefight broke out that claimed several lives and left many others wounded. Wilson, who survived that brush with death, told grand jurors in 1791 that an "accurate and unbiased examination" exposed the fallacy that "the number of crimes is diminished by the severity of punishments." The "unwieldy size" and "en-sanguined hue" of "the criminal codes," he said, showed the "general and prevalent" opinion in favor of severe punishments, though Wilson favored the "imitation" of criminal laws that "inflicted very few capital punishments." In his remarks, Wilson contrasted "moderate and mild" sentences with more severe sanctions, noting how "one degree of severity opens and smooths the way for another, till, at length, under the specious appearance of necessary justice, a system of cruelty is established by law." Adding that "cruelty" is the "parent of *slavery*" and is "always attended by cowardice," Wilson called "cruel" punishments "dastardly and contemptible." Grand juries, Wilson recognized, served as valuable checks on prosecutorial discretion, a role played by such citizen bodies since their formative stages in England when they protected subjects against the power of the Crown.[44]

Wilson, whose ambition was to be America's Blackstone, saw little purpose in killing citizens convicted of crimes. "It is the opinion of some writers, highly respected for their good sense, as well as for their humanity," Wilson noted, no doubt alluding once more to Beccaria, "that capital punishments are, in no case, necessary." "It is an opinion," Wilson said, "which I am certainly well warranted in offering—that nothing but the most absolute necessity can authorize them." Although Wilson favored speedy punishments and noted that "if a capital punishment ought to be inflicted for any crimes," it would be for premeditated murders, he said that for death sentences, the punishment should be delayed so that the interval would "render the language of political expediency consonant to the language of religion." Decrying any "tyrant" who gave "standing instructions to his executioners" to "protract the expiring moments of the tortured criminal" and to "manage the butchering business with such studied and slow barbarity" as to prolong the pain, Wilson further remarked, speaking this time of executions themselves: "Another opinion I am equally warranted in offering—that they should not be aggravated by any sufferings, except those which are inseparably attached to a violent death." In one of his lectures, Wilson also emphasized that, while the term "felony" had long been "very strongly connected with capital punishment," it was no longer accurate, as not every felony was then a death-eligible offense.[45]

Dr. Benjamin Rush, who served in the Continental Congress, signed the Declaration of Independence, and, most famously, got John Adams and Thomas Jefferson to reconcile after a painful parting of the ways, revered Beccaria too. Indeed, Rush invoked Beccaria's name at a reading about the negative effects of public punishments that he gave at the house of Benjamin Franklin—yet another Beccaria admirer—in March 1787. "I have said nothing upon the manner of inflicting death as a punishment for crimes, because I consider it as an improper punishment for any crime," Rush explained, holding up the Italian criminologist and citing the death penalty's abolition in Tuscany, a development often invoked by American death penalty opponents. A humanitarian and devout Christian, Rush regularly expressed his faith and his anti–death penalty views in his correspondence, citing Beccaria in his writings multiple times. As one legal scholar has written: "Rush challenged the widely held view that the executioner was God's servant, labeling it sacrilegious for public officials to claim that they shared with God the right to punish by death. Rush urged incarceration, with the possibility of rehabilitation, in lieu of execution."[46]

John Hancock, another signer of the Declaration of Independence, also studied Beccaria's writings, as did other early American patriots such as William Bradford and Thomas Paine. A former Pennsylvania Attorney General and later the country's second Attorney General, Bradford, who was James Madison's close friend and college classmate, conducted "An Enquiry How Far the Punishment of Death is Necessary in Pennsylvania" in 1793. He questioned the necessity of capital punishment and argued for the elimination of it for all offenses except high treason and murder until more information could be obtained. Paine—oftentimes referred to as "The Father of the American Revolution"—was, like Rush, an ardent abolitionist. He opposed Louis XVI's execution, regretted the French Assembly's vote to impose a death sentence (as Thomas Jefferson did, if less vocally), and ended up risking his own life in the process of trying to save the French king from execution. In 1793, in a speech before a joint session of the legislature, Massachusetts governor John Hancock—most famous now for his flamboyant signature—asked legislators to follow Beccaria's call for less discretion in sentencing. In January of that year, Hancock further called for an end to the punishments of "cropping and branding, as well as that of the Public Whipping Post," which he called "an indignity to human nature." In their place, Hancock suggested that "a sentence to hard labor will perhaps have a more salutary effect than mutilating or lacerating the human body." In calling for an end to capital punishment for burglary, Hancock proclaimed: "Degrees of guilt demand degrees of Punishment in order to maintain the equity of the Government."[47]

Thomas Jefferson, the principal drafter of the Declaration of Independence, was especially fascinated by Beccaria's ideas. Between 1774 and 1776, Jefferson, the plantation owner and future President, copied out by hand into his commonplace book twenty-six different passages from Beccaria's text. Jefferson also drafted three proposals for Virginia's constitution that would have curtailed the death penalty's use, and the Declaration of Independence that he penned famously recites the "inalienable" right to "Life." While Jefferson was part of a committee that, in the 1770s, advised the Continental Congress to expand the death penalty's availability in wartime, he also drafted a bill for consideration by Virginia's legislature calling for proportionate punishments. In a 1790 letter, Jefferson even recommended Beccaria—a clear favorite—to his cousin John Garland Jefferson, an aspiring lawyer. Indeed, as President, the well-read Jefferson—who sold his breathtaking collection of 6,487 books to the Library of Congress to reconstitute it after British troops burned down the U.S. Capitol in 1814—continued to show genuine and sustained affection for Beccaria's book. In an 1807 letter, Jefferson recommended that its recipient, John Norvell, who later worked in the newspaper business with Benjamin Franklin's grandson, read "Beccaria on crimes & punishments." One of only a handful of books Jefferson recommended Norvell read on the principles of government, Jefferson told Norvell to read the book "because of the demonstrative manner" in which Beccaria "has treated that branch of the subject." Because Jefferson singled out *On Crimes and Punishments,* it is clear he especially treasured Beccaria's treatise.[48]

Beccaria's Legacy

The young Italian philosopher Cesare Beccaria identified or anticipated nearly all of the problems that have plagued—and continue to plague—capital punishment. He identified what many people consider to be the barbaric example that executions set, arguing that death sentences do not deter crime any better than life imprisonment. "[T]he strongest impediment to crimes is not the terrible and fleeting spectacle of death of a wretch," Beccaria believed, "but the long and repeated example of a man deprived of his liberty." He saw and condemned the arbitrariness and unfettered discretion that are so often present in the law—something the U.S. Supreme Court itself pointed to in *Furman v. Georgia* in at least temporarily striking down death penalty laws as unconstitutional as applied. Beccaria also railed against the inequalities in the law's treatment of rich and poor, prejudices associated with corporal and capital punishments for centuries and that today still manifest themselves in the death penalty's close association with poverty and race. And long before the advent of DNA evidence and sophisticated studies on mistaken eyewitness identifications, he recognized the death penalty's "irreparability," the ever-present possibility of human error, and thus the continual risk of condemning or executing the innocent. As Beccaria and his two colleagues wrote in their 1792 report on the reform of the criminal justice system in Austrian Lombardy: "In almost all nations, it is not unheard of to find examples in which the apparently guilty were sentenced to death because they were shown to be so according to these supposedly incontrovertible proofs. Nor do we intend to attribute this to the incompetence, negligence, or bad will of the judges, but to the necessary imperfection of the law."[49]

In *On Crimes and Punishments,* Beccaria—like Montesquieu—frequently spoke of "cruelty," the concept that lies at the very heart of the Eighth Amendment. In the introduction to his treatise, Beccaria emphasized that "very few have studied and fought against the cruelty of punishments and the irregularities of criminal procedures, an area of legislation so fundamental yet so neglected almost everywhere in Europe." "As punishments become more cruel," Beccaria wrote, "the minds of men, which like fluids always adjust to the level of the objects that surround them, become hardened, and the ever lively force of passions is such that after a hundred years of cruel punishments, breaking on the wheel causes no more fear than imprisonment previously did." "For a punishment to achieve its objective," Beccaria opined, "it is only necessary that the harm that it inflicts outweighs the benefit that derives from the crime, and into this calculation ought to be factored the certainty of punishments and the loss of the good that the commission of the crime would produce." "Everything beyond this," Beccaria concluded, "is superfluous and, therefore, tyrannical." "The death penalty is not useful because of the example of cruelty that it gives to men," Beccaria wrote elsewhere, as he helped set off a worldwide movement to end torture and capital punishment.[50]

Beccaria's influence on American thought is undeniable, with one commentator calling *On Crimes and Punishments* "more influential than any other single book" in America's revolutionary period. James Madison studied Beccaria's ideas and included Beccaria's works in a list of recommended books for use by the Continental Congress. Other founders and early American jurists also turned to Beccaria for guidance. One study reveals that America's founders, in their writings and speeches, invoked Beccaria so much that Beccaria ranks seventh overall in frequency of citation—only St. Paul, Montesquieu, Sir William Blackstone, John Locke, David Hume, and Plutarch rank higher. More than one third of all libraries in the period from 1777 to 1790 contained a copy of *On Crimes and Punishments,* and Beccaria accounted for about one percent of citations to published writers in the 1770s and three percent in the 1780s. Though not embracing all of his ideas, many founders plainly shared Beccaria's antipathy toward torture and the frequency with which death sentences were meted out. Writing in 1729, before Beccaria was born, Benjamin Franklin railed against innocent men being "dragg'd into noisome Dungeons, tortured with cruel Irons, and even unmercifully *starv'd* to Death." And in *Notes on the State of Virginia,* written in 1781 and first published in Paris in 1784, Thomas Jefferson also showed his disdain for torture, comparing the torture of slaves under Roman law with Virginia's practice of not resorting to slaves for evidence.[51]

Many of America's founders did not oppose executions, which were then public spectacles for all to see. John Adams, who served with Jefferson on the committee that recommended expanding the death penalty's availability during wartime, thought the death penalty necessary for certain crimes and, as commander in chief, signed death warrants for military deserters. Patrick Henry—of "Give me liberty or give me death" fame—likewise helped draft a bill that gave Virginia's governor broad powers to arrest those opposing American independence, to hold them without recourse to bail or a writ of habeas corpus, and to forcibly remove behind enemy lines those refusing Virginia's oath of allegiance, with the ability to order death for those refusing to go. John Jay, the first president of the Continental Congress and the country's first Chief Justice, was specifically asked whether he thought the death penalty violated the commandment against taking life. Jay replied it did not, saying: "As to murderers, I think it not only lawful for government, but that it is the duty of government, to put them to death." Jay believed that "[t]he moral or natural law was given by the Sovereign of the universe to all mankind," and that the death penalty "must of necessity be consistent with the moral law." In line with that view, the First Congress, which met in New York, then

Philadelphia, made several crimes punishable by hanging, including treason, murder on federal land, forgery, uttering forged securities, counterfeiting, and piracy on the high seas.[52]

At the same time, however, many Americans—heavily influenced by Beccaria's book—were deeply troubled by capital punishment for other classes of offenders. New York governor John Jay, for instance, opposed capital punishment for lower-level offenders, arguing that "establishments for confining, employing and reforming criminals" were "indispensible." Even during the Revolutionary War, Jay described "trying criminals" as "the most disagreeable part" of his duty. "Punishments," Jay wrote Gouverneur Morris in 1778, complaining about the frequency of robberies, "must of course become certain, and mercy dormant—a harsh system, repugnant to my feelings, but nevertheless necessary." Saying robberies gave Tories food and that the woods afforded criminals shelter, Jay told Morris that "lenity would be cruelty," and that "severity is found on the side of humanity." Virginia governor Patrick Henry also reformed the death penalty, which was imposed for many felonies and even minor offenses. "This was a practice that Henry felt was both unjust and cruel," notes Henry biographer David Vaughan, who writes that Henry "developed a plan of granting pardons, after hard labor, for lesser crimes." In a directive to Charles Pearson, the man responsible for pardoned prisoners, Henry commanded him "to observe such a degree of humanity towards these people as their condition will permit, in everything that relates to them." They were to be kept "warm and comfortable" and to have "plenty of wholesome food." In a 1785 letter to the mayor of Richmond, Governor Henry expressed dissatisfaction with the death penalty's disproportionality for certain cases. Edmund Randolph—a fellow Virginian—would remark that the state's executive had "at last" been "persuaded of their power to make the Beccarian experiment on the condemned."[53]

James Wilson, the Scottish-born lawyer who admired many of Beccaria's ideas, also expressed the view that America's criminal law "greatly needs reformation." Along with his friend Dr. Benjamin Rush, Wilson played a pivotal role in Pennsylvania politics and in shaping that state's law, and Rush, in turn, later urged John Adams to use his influence to get Wilson appointed to the U.S. Supreme Court. Wilson said that "the seeds of reformation are sown" but cautioned that "[t]hose seeds, and the tender plants which from some of them are now beginning to spring, let it be our care to discover and to cultivate." After calling English law "defective to a degree both gross and cruel" and citing Sabacos, who in Egypt replaced capital punishment with life sentences to be carried out "in the publick works," Wilson called for proportionate punishments. He also expressed the view that "[p]unishments ought unquestionably to be moderate and mild." Wilson supported the passage of a Pennsylvania law limiting the death penalty to first-degree murder while acknowledging that premeditated murder was itself still commonly punished by death. As Wilson wrote: "In England, in the United States, in Pennsylvania, and almost universally throughout the world, the crime of wilful and premeditated murder is and has been punished with death. Indeed it seems by all, that, if a capital punishment ought to be inflicted for any crimes, this is unquestionably a crime for which it ought to be inflicted." In a reflection of the changing times, though, Wilson's son Bird, a lawyer trained by his own father, later resigned his Pennsylvania judgeship because of his opposition to capital punishment. As a judge of the Court of Common Pleas, Bird had condemned a man to die, then left the bench to pursue a calling as a minister and theologian. When his niece and a friend were at his bedside toward the end of his life, Bird exclaimed in a bitter tone: "He was launched into eternity unprepared; but, O God! impute it not to me!"[54]

Even southern Founding Fathers such as Charles Pinckney and Pierce Butler of South Carolina opposed capital punishment for certain categories of offenders—at least when it came to punishing whites. Pierce Butler, one of South Carolina's four delegates to the 1787 Constitutional Convention, actually wrote a letter in 1791 to his quick-tempered friend Colonel James Gunn, in which he advised against capital punishment for a man alleged to have had an affair with the colonel's wife. As Butler wrote: "The chastising of a bad Man, or still worse, putting him to death will not restore to You the domestic happiness You have lost." Another southerner, William Few of Georgia, also no doubt felt deeply ambivalent about capital punishment. Few, a signer of the U.S. Constitution who became a Georgia superior court judge, sentenced a murderer and a horse thief to death—sentences that were later set aside. Few's elder brother James had been a Regulator in North Carolina during a time of rampant mob violence and was executed. Between 1766 and 1771, some two to three thousand untrained North Carolina residents known as Regulators had waged a fight against corrupt county officials appointed by the royal governor, but the Tory governor William Tryon had crushed the rebellion. On one day alone, June 19, 1771, six Regulators were publicly hanged in Hillsborough before a crowd that contained the condemned men's own children and wives. Although Tryon wished to spare the life of William Few's brother and twice urged the taking of an oath in lieu of a hanging, the young James Few refused. On May 17, 1771, James Few, who had participated in riots and was considered an outlaw, was thus hanged in front of the army, leaving behind a wife and twins born just months earlier. As far as William Few's own views are concerned, his biographer notes that Few himself often called for sentences that he handed down to be remitted. Such judicial behavior—however inexplicable at first blush—was in line with the views of many Americans of the time, with instances of jury nullification quite common, and mandatory death sentences often seen as too harsh.[55]

Other American leaders, both before and after the 1770s, likewise called for reform of death penalty laws or engaged in individual acts of mercy. For example, early American presidents, who often used or threatened military force or called out the militia to put down rebellious activities, frequently made use of the clemency powers granted by Article II of the Constitution. George Washington, using his constitutional power, pardoned leaders of the Whiskey Rebellion in 1795; John Adams, over protests from his cabinet, pardoned three leaders of a Pennsylvania insurrection known as "Fries's Rebellion" that occurred between 1799 and 1800; Thomas Jefferson granted clemency to persons convicted under the Alien and Sedition Acts; and James Madison pardoned deserters to fill up army ranks during the War of 1812 and, after the war, issued a pardon to Jean Lafitte's Baratarian Pirates who fought to defend New Orleans in 1815. John Fries, who led a tax revolt among Pennsylvania farmers, was pardoned by Adams even though Fries had been sentenced to die by Samuel Chase, a fellow signer of the Declaration of Independence. Fries had been sentenced to death for his role in the rebellion in which many homeowners refused to pay taxes and were incarcerated, with Fries himself having led a mob of approximately 150 men to free tax evaders. Washington, as commander of the Continental Army, sometimes pardoned capital offenders; Madison set aside the death sentence of a career burglar who had broken into a store, pardoned "a certain Negro lad" named Nathan who had been sentenced to death after breaking into a house in the District of Columbia, and remitted the death sentence of Brigadier General William Hull after he had been sentenced to be shot; and Jefferson set aside the death sentence of burglar Samuel Miller and also pardoned a slave convicted of having "burglariously broken and entered" a home. After a mutiny in Pennsylvania in 1783 that reflected widespread postwar dissatisfaction among army veterans, Congress itself—at the urging of Dr. Benjamin Rush—pardoned men who had been condemned to death by a court-martial or who had been ordered to be punished corporally.[56]

Such pardons or reprieves were handed out in spite of the precarious state of affairs in the country and in spite of a long-standing tradition of using the death penalty to punish rebels. The Whiskey Rebellion, one of the more serious threats, had begun in the fall of 1791 when gangs with blackened faces on the western frontier started viciously attacking federal tax collectors, resorting to horsewhipping and tarring and feathering government officials. Even those complying with the U.S. government's new tax on hard liquor were subjected to threats and intimidation, with rebels burning the barns or crops of civilian collaborators or those who registered their stills. President Washington raised thirteen thousand troops and then led them over the Appalachians to quash the "treasonable opposition" and to enforce the first tax ever levied on a domestic product, distilled liquor. Of twelve cases that eventually went to trial, only two rebels, Philip Wigle and John Mitchell, were sentenced to death, but President Washington pardoned both condemned men after the crisis was averted. During the Revolutionary War itself, Thomas Jefferson—as Virginia's governor from 1779 to 1781—pardoned felons convicted of capital crimes on the condition that they work for a term of years on public works projects, including in lead mines that produced bullets. Because of the need for ammunition and the high cost of labor, the humane practice of granting conditional pardons was followed by successive governors until 1785, when the Virginia Court of Appeals declared that conditions attached to the pardons were unconstitutional.[57]

Even John Adams was no zealot when it came to executions. For example, though War Department papers contain an unsigned presidential endorsement of capital punishment for Andrew Anderson, a soldier court-martialed for deserting his post and assisting two prisoners to escape from confinement, Adams signaled his intent to pardon him at the last minute in a letter he sent to Secretary of War James McHenry dated September 18, 1799. "I have ruminated so long upon the case of Andrew Anderson, that I am under some apprehension that my feelings have grown too strong, and produced a result that will not appear to you perfectly right," Adams began his letter. "In announcing the pardon inclosed," Adams concluded, "you may order what solemnities you think fit. He may receive his pardon at the gallows, where it may be announced that it will be the last time such a crime will be pardoned." Likewise, Adams wrote to McHenry about another court-martialed soldier, Richard Hunt. In his letter of June 5, 1799, Adams wrote: "The discipline of the army will require the punishment of death for desertion in many cases, and none perhaps will deserve it more than that of Richard Hunt; and I should not hesitate to sign the warrant for his execution, serious as is the act of depriving a fellow of his life, but I wish to know, whether the officers who composed the court-martial were commissioned, and if not, what evidence we shall rely upon of the appointments, in case the legality of this business should be examined by a grand jury." The inquiry into the legality of the sentence later morphed into a commutation of Sergeant Hunt's death sentence. In still another case, that of artilleryman Samuel Ewing, court-martialed for desertion and sentenced to be shot, Adams acknowledged receipt of a letter suggesting that the condemned soldier might have been insane at the time of his offense and cancelled Ewing's death warrant pending a further report.[58]

Also, when writing about some letters of his that were intercepted by a British ship and reprinted by the enemy, Adams noted in his autobiography that there were only "a few Expressions which hurt me." As Adams wrote: "The Expressions were Will your judiciary Whip and hang without Scruple. This they construed to mean to excite Cruelty against the Tories, and get some of them punished with Severity." "Nothing was farther from my Thoughts. I had no reference to Tories in this," Adams explained. "[M]y Question," he said, "meant no more than 'Will your judges have fortitude enough to inflict the severe punishments when necessary as Death upon Murderers and other capital Criminals, and flaggellation upon such as deserve it.'" Adams emphasized: "Nothing could be more false and injurious to me, than the imputation of any sanguinary Zeal against the Tories, for I can truly declare that through the whole Revolution and from that time to this I never committed one Act of Severity against the Tories." "On the contrary," he protested, "I was a constant Advocate for all the Mercy and Indulgence consistent with our Safety."[59]

John Adams was certainly no proponent of cruelty. In one of his letters to his wife Abigail, sent from Baltimore in 1777, Adams spoke of the "cruel times" that would make him "melancholy" and of his disgust for the way in which the British had treated Americans. As Adams wrote in his letter, "I, who would not hurt the hair of the head of any animal, I, who am always made miserable by the misery of every susceptible being that comes to my knowledge, am obliged to hear continual accounts of the barbarities, the cruel murders in cold blood even by the most tormented ways of starving and freezing, committed by our enemies, and continued accounts of the deaths and diseases contracted by their own imprudence." "These accounts," Adams wrote, "harrow me beyond description." "I know of no policy, God is my witness," he said, "but this, piety, humanity, and honesty are the best policy." "Blasphemy, cruelty, and villainy have prevailed and may again. But they won't prevail against America in this contest," he wrote, "because I find the more of them are employed the less they succeed." Abigail herself wrote in 1781 to her husband, "My Dearest Friend," that "[h]e who, as an individual, is cruel, unjust, and immoral, will not be likely to possess the virtues necessary in a general or statesman." Like George Washington, who in 1774 complained that the Crown was not protecting Virginians from "cruel and bloodthirsty" Indians in the backwoods, John Adams plainly loathed acts of cruelty.[60]

Before the Revolutionary War, John Adams even expressed the view that "Man" is "distinguished from other Animals, his Fellow-Inhabitants of this Planet, by a Capacity of acquiring Knowledge and Civility." In a "Savage State," Adams wrote, "[e]ach Individual is his own Sovereign, accountable to no other upon Earth, and punishable by none." "Each one then," Adams mused, "must be his own Avenger." "Hence arises the Idea of an Avenger of Blood," and "thus the Notions of Revenge," Adams said, adding, "Nature has implanted in the human Heart, a Disposition to resent an Injury when offered." "And this Disposition is so strong," Adams thought, "that even the Horse treading by Accident on a gouty Toe, or a Brick-batt falling on the Shoulders, in the first Twinges of Pain, seem to excite the angry Passions, and we feel an Inclination to kill the Horse and break the Brick-batt." Adams wrote that "the Man feels the sweetest, highest Gratification when he inflicts the Punishment himself," but that there exists an "obstinate Disposition in barbarous Nations to continue barbarous" behavior, noting "the extreme Difficulty of introducing Civility and Christianity among them." "[T]he great Distinction between Savage Nations and polite ones, lies in this, that among the former, every Individual is his own Judge and his own Executioner; but among the latter, all Pretensions to Judgment and Punishment, are resigned to

Tribunals erected by the Public." "To exterminate, from among Mankind, such revengeful Sentiments and Tempers," Adams concluded, "is one of the highest and most important Strains, of civil and humane Policy."[61]

Though John Adams did not express moral qualms about capital punishment for murderers, the writings of his wife, who saw prison life as harsh and recoiled at the idea of executing all lower-level offenders, show that early Americans at least contemplated that the death penalty might one day be abolished. In a letter dated March 31, 1797, Abigail—living in a time of great upheaval—wrote her husband just after he ascended to the presidency, fearing what might happen if executions were outlawed: "We are suffering under the same apprehensions which have afflicted other places. The attempts to destroy Boston by fire are daily, or rather Nightly repeated. Patroles are constantly kept. They have detected but few. The vile wretches have got into the Country. At Milton they keep a Nightly watch. It is really a distressing calamity, but we shall be infested with more vagabonds, if the states go on to abolish capital punishment." Just six days earlier, Abigail had written her "Dearest Friend": "Poor Pennsylvania keeps no gallows, but she keeps Rogues and villans who deserve one, and she will find to her cost that she has not reachd the Millenium." In another letter, written in 1794, the year after Marie Antoinette was pulled from her cell, paraded through the streets of Paris on a cart, and beheaded, Abigail also wrote to her husband: "In France they have at length added the Murder of [the] unfortunate Queen to the measure of their Inequality." "Whilst Humanity sickens at the recital of their crimes," she said, "her death is less horrible than the cruel imprisonment and indignities she has sustaind."[62]

The ambivalence felt by John and Abigail Adams toward indiscriminate executions is illustrated by yet another event that occurred as a result of their foreign travels. Once, outside London, a coach carrying Abigail Adams entered the Blackheath forest, a locale crawling with robbers, when her party got a dire warning: "A robbery, a robbery!" "We were not a little alarmed," Abigail wrote, "and everyone was concealing their money." "The robber," she recorded, "was pursued and taken in about two miles and we saw the poor wretch, ghostly and horrible, brought along on foot." "He looked like a youth of twenty only, attempted to lift his hat," but looked of "despair," she wrote, adding: "You can form some idea of my feelings when they told him: Ay, you have but a short time; the assize sits next month; and then my lad, you swing." "Though every robber may deserve death," she said, "yet to exult over the wretched is what our country is not accustomed to. Long may it be free from such villanies, and long may it preserve a commiseration for the wretched." In a letter to her niece Elizabeth Cranch, Abigail wrote from England: "what can be said of the wretched victims who are weekly Sacrified upon the Gallows, in numbers Sufficient to astonish a civilized people?" After John Adams and George Washington received a guided tour of the Pennsylvania Hospital from

Dr. William Shippen, Adams himself noted: "We saw in the lower rooms underground the cells of the lunatics . . . some furious, some merry, some melancholy." The death penalty, no doubt, was something passionately discussed and mulled over at length, on more than one occasion, in the Adams family and other households of that era.[63]

Indeed, John Quincy Adams, the sixth President of the United States, took a special interest in death penalty issues throughout his life. He studied law in the late 1780s and was admitted to the bar in 1790. His diary reveals that even before he became a lawyer he was spending time thinking about capital punishment. "At nine o'clock this morning," he recorded in his diary on February 13, 1787, "the Class read a forensic disputation" that he wrote while on vacation on the following issue: "Whether the infliction of capital punishments, except in cases of murder be consistent with equity?" "Sovereigns," he wrote for the declamation exercise, "have attempted to abolish capital punishments entirely, but this scheme, like many others, which appear to great advantage in theory have been found impracticable, because it has been attended with consequences very injurious to society." Quoting Montesquieu and Shakespeare, the soon-to-be lawyer grappled with the issue on a theoretical level, concluding at the time that "if mildness in punishments instead of deterring men from the commission of crimes, encourages them to it, the innocent, and virtuous part of the community, who have surely the greatest claim to the benevolence of a legislator, would be the greatest sufferers." Other students of the age were equally engaged with the issue. Of Yale's commencement in 1788, another young man—Jeremiah Mason—made this admission in his diary regarding his own disputation on "whether capital punishment was in any case lawful": "I stole most of my arguments from the treatise of Marquis Beccaria."[64]

John Quincy Adams's views, however, would evolve over his lifetime, as would the views of other early Americans. In a letter to his father John Adams, written from The Hague in 1795, the still-young John Quincy Adams was more circumspect and less sure of himself. In that letter, John Quincy Adams commented on the "rigorous" army discipline he saw in Europe, saying "[t]he only complaint I have heard against it is its being too severe." "The examples of capital punishment, which have been inflicted in more than one of the cities upon soldiers guilty of the most trifling thefts," he wrote, now speaking in a much more experiential context, "are painful to a people among whom the penalty of death is very seldom executed, and reserved for the most enormous crimes." In 1825, as America's new President, John Quincy Adams also refused to approve a deserter's death sentence. As he wrote in his diary: "I told the General that I could not approve this sentence. Death was too severe a punishment for desertion in time of peace." And in yet another diary entry, made in 1831, John Quincy Adams wrote about Jefferson's and Madison's efforts to pass penal reform. "With regard to the criminal law," he wrote, "the committee substituted for some capital punishments the lex talionis, which, on further reflection, Mr. Jefferson justly disapproves."[65]

To date, Beccaria's vision of a world without torture and the death penalty, in which life imprisonment would be the ultimate sanction, has not yet been realized, not by a long shot. Acts of torture still occur around the globe, and fifty-eight countries, including the United States of America, still authorize capital punishment for what are classified as ordinary crimes, that is, criminal acts committed during peacetime and not under the auspices of military law. But a growing number of nations—139 at last count—have outlawed executions either by law or in practice. This means that fewer countries carry out executions than ever before; the ones that do are now in a distinct, ever-dwindling minority. Of the countries that retain capital punishment for ordinary crimes—among them Afghanistan, China, Cuba, the Democratic Republic of Congo, Iran, Iraq, Libya, Malaysia, North Korea, Pakistan, Saudi Arabia, Somalia, Uganda, and Yemen—autocratic or totalitarian regimes with abysmal human rights records are commonplace; in that list, only Japan and the United States stand out as highly industrialized countries. And Japan, which in prior years carried out its executions with the utmost secrecy and only released information on its hangings on execution day, is now in the midst of a national debate over whether to abolish capital punishment. Keiko Chiba, the country's justice minister from 2009 to 2010, specifically called for such a debate, and only two executions took place under her tenure.[66]

The progress made by the world's abolitionist movement is thus striking, especially when one considers the sheer number of executions carried out in the Middle Ages and in the Enlightenment era. During the reign of Henry VIII, king of England from 1509 until his death in 1547, an estimated seventy-two thousand executions—or about two thousand executions per year, on average—were carried out in that country alone. And in the early 1790s, during the French Revolution's infamous Reign of Terror, approximately seventeen thousand executions of presumed enemies of the state took place. Today, by contrast, Europe is a death penalty–free zone; America's closest neighbors, Canada and Mexico, are abolitionist; American death sentences and executions are declining in number; and a growing number of poor and developing countries, such as Albania, Angola, Cambodia, Columbia, Haiti, Nicaragua, Rwanda, and Azerbaijan, have totally barred executions. Even South Africa, once the home of a brutal apartheid regime that made frequent use of executions, no longer authorizes them. In that locale, the country's Constitutional Court declared them unconstitutional more than a decade ago. In its 1995 decision, South Africa's highest court ruled that the death penalty constitutes "cruel, inhuman or degrading treatment or punishment" and thus declared the practice unlawful.[67]

In the United States, where convicted killers now frequently receive life-without-parole sentences for their crimes, the U.S. Constitution's Eighth

Amendment—broadly prohibiting "cruel and unusual punishments"—has for decades taken center stage in America's death penalty debate. Given the similarity between South Africa's Constitution and the text of the Eighth Amendment, one wonders whether the U.S. Supreme Court will ever declare the death penalty unconstitutional, too. The death penalty is now largely seen as a human rights violation in other parts of the world, so it is not all that far-fetched to believe that one day America might also put an end to the death penalty. Though the Supreme Court has thus far declined to find the death penalty itself unconstitutional, the Court has already used the Eighth Amendment to strike down death sentences for various categories of offenders. Already, corporal punishments such as flogging, which George Washington and others in the founding era once regularly ordered to be imposed, are no longer tolerated in America's criminal justice system. With America's legal, social, and political climates still rapidly evolving, worthy and important questions will and should recur: Will the U.S. Supreme Court, by judicial order, ever use the Eighth Amendment to outlaw capital punishment for all offenders? Could the nation's highest court ever do so given language in the Constitution that contemplates capital prosecutions and death sentences? And will American executions, whether by legislative or judicial decision, ever go the way of the stocks, the pillory, and the whipping post and be abolished for all time?[68]

CHAPTER THREE

The Abolitionists

Dr. Benjamin Rush

In the same year that the Constitutional Convention met in Philadelphia to forge the U.S. Constitution, Dr. Benjamin Rush, a prominent Pennsylvania physician, penned an important essay on penal reform. Educated at the College of New Jersey (now Princeton University), Rush graduated in 1760 with a Bachelor of Arts degree at the age of fifteen and then studied medicine in Philadelphia. Having gone on to earn a medical degree at the University of Edinburgh, Dr. Rush returned to Philadelphia in 1769 to open a medical practice and to become a chemistry professor at the College of Philadelphia. Active in the Sons of Liberty, Rush befriended and advised leading revolutionary figures, including Thomas Paine, and represented Pennsylvania in the Continental Congress in 1776 and 1777. A prolific writer, Dr. Rush also published books on chemistry, psychiatry, and medical education, and joined the ranks of the American Philosophical Society, an organization of well-known scientists including luminaries such as Benjamin Franklin and Thomas Jefferson. As a doctor and a leading opponent of slavery, Rush was extremely active in civic affairs. He served as surgeon general of the Continental Army during the Revolutionary War. President John Adams selected him to be the U.S. Mint's treasurer, and he was the president of the Philadelphia Medical Society and a founding member of the Philadelphia Bible Society. A product of the Enlightenment, Rush studied French, Italian, and Spanish while in Europe, avidly read Cesare Beccaria's *On Crimes and Punishments,* and forcefully advocated criminal justice reform.[1]

A founding member of the Philadelphia Society for Alleviating the Miseries of Public Prisons, Dr. Rush became one of the first Americans to call for the death penalty's total abolition. As part of his work with the prison society, Rush had been tasked to "visit prisons" and "give advice." He came to believe that many prisoners could be rehabilitated, especially first-time offenders who had committed a single crime in "a sudden gust of passion," and he saw the society's humanitarian work as promoting virtue. "A prison," Rush wrote a friend, "sometimes supplies the place of a church and out-preaches the preacher in conveying useful instruction to the heart." Philadelphia's Walnut Street Jail, built in accordance with a 1773 Pennsylvania law, was close to Rush's house, and its prisoners—if not executed, as some were—were often mistreated or abused. From 1750 to 1775, no less than thirty-six people, including two women, were hanged in Philadelphia for various crimes. Almost two thirds were executed for property crimes, mainly burglary, with nearly 20 percent executed for murder. Acts such as counterfeiting, desertion, highway robbery, and infanticide also led to executions. Between 1776 and 1783, yet another forty-one men were hanged in Philadelphia, making executions a familiar scene during the Revolutionary War. Of those executions, twenty-five, or more than 60 percent of the total, were also for property crimes. When Dr. Rush first published his views on capital punishment in 1787, executions in Philadelphia thus remained a grim fact of life, even for crimes in which no murder took place. In the ten years preceding 1787, twenty-six people were put to death for burglary, twenty-three for robbery, and four for rape. Fervently believing "a faithful imitation of the example of our Savior" and a "general obedience" to the Gospel could bring about social change, Rush—ever the evangelist—opposed executions, insisting that "improvement consists in obeying the doctrines and obeying the precepts of the Christian religion."[2]

Early English and American jails were dirty, disease-ridden institutions. While local jails existed in the colonies, they were, as one commentator puts it, "crude, unimpressive buildings," with incarceration mainly used to pressure debtors. In 1771, Thomas Jefferson, along with two other men, put out a "Notice of Bidding for the Erection of a Prison" in Charlottesville, though the earliest known jail there was built in 1785. The solicitation to bid called for "[t]he building of a prison of brick, with two rooms below, and two above stairs." In 1787, a Philadelphia grand jury concerned about prostitution and general conditions at the local jail denounced the "general intercourse between criminals of the different sexes" at the facility, with Quakers preferring silence so inmates would, in the words of one scholar, "retreat inward to find the Light of God in their consciences." In 1776, the Philadelphia Society for Relieving Distressed Prisoners had been formed to address the dire situation, but it began at an inopportune time and was dissolved the next year. After the Revolutionary War, though, prison and penal reform once again got back on the American agenda. In 1796, for example, Robert Turnbull published *A Visit to the Philadelphia Prison,* an essay in which he decried the "cruel and immoderate punishments" once meted out by Roman kings, as well as the "deplorable" effects of "cruel punishments" dished out locally in his own time. After invoking Dr. Rush and his "remarkable proof of the impropriety of the punishment of death," Turnbull called for the punishment of death to be abolished even for the crime of murder. After noting that, by then, the Philadelphia prison had "wise and humane regulations," Turnbull reiterated his call for abolition by saying that "[t]he despotic soil of Italy gave birth to the projector of the plan, a humane Beccaria."[3]

In the late eighteenth century, in fact, prison reform captivated civic leaders in both England and America. In 1777, John Howard, an English prison reformer, published a detailed account of the terrible conditions of British prisons and called for changes in prisoners' treatment. In his writings, he decried the filth of prisons and the neglect of their overseers, arguing that day-and-night solitary confinement was too harsh. English prisons, used to house offenders awaiting transportation to American or Australian penal colonies, often kept prisoners in irons. Colonial jails were grim places, too, used to hold debtors, suspects pending trial, convicts awaiting punishment, or to assure the testimony of key witnesses. State prisons in America were not built until the eighteenth century's last decades, and when they were, they did not resemble prisons in any modern sense. As legal historian Lawrence Friedman explains: "In Connecticut, a prison was improvised in 1773 out of certain copper mines at Simsbury. Called 'Newgate' after the English prison, it became the state prison of Connecticut in 1790." "This was, by all accounts," Friedman writes, "a horrendous dungeon, a dark cave of 'horrid gloom.'" The first real U.S. prison, on Walnut Street in Philadelphia, was originally built in 1773 as a local jail, then converted into a "penitentiary house" in 1790. Quakers, who sought to reform offenders while providing humane treatment, favored the use of hard labor and lengthy periods of solitary confinement. The birth of America's prison system, which only later blossomed into a series of maximum-security penitentiaries, thus did not occur until around the time that the Constitution and Bill of Rights were ratified.[4]

During the mid-1780s and the following decade, law professor Steven Wilf explains in his new book *Law's Imagined Republic: Popular Politics and Criminal Justice in Revolutionary America,* "Americans launched a polemic attack upon English criminal codes." By 1776, nearly two hundred crimes in England were punishable by death, leading Americans to derogatorily call English criminal law the "Bloody Code." "Criticism of the Bloody Code became commonplace in American writings of the 1780s and 1790s," writes Wilf. "It was found everywhere: newspapers, periodicals, letters, charges to grand juries, and political pamphlets." As one example, Wilf cites the following charge to a Philadelphia grand jury: "In England where they boast of the equity and mildness of their legal institutions, and where they allege that neither racks, tortures, nor extorted confessions were ever acknowledged to be any part of their laws, yet their books are crowded with penal statutes which appear to have resulted from the barbarous dictates of revenge . . . to inflict the punishment of death alike on persons guilty of murder . . . or stealing a trifle." In

England, wrote Nathaniel Chipman, a Yale-educated U.S. Senator from Vermont and that state's chief justice, the "multitude are restrained by fear" and "laws, like those of Draco, may emphatically be said *to be written in blood*." "They string up monthly numbers of their fellow mortals," lamented another writer in a newspaper in 1784, and Pennsylvanians, including Dr. Benjamin Rush, were obsessed with recording the sheer number of English executions.[5]

Dr. Rush first publicly spoke out against the death penalty for murderers at the end of a paper advocating private punishments. That paper was read at Benjamin Franklin's house on March 9, 1787. Rush's essay, *An Enquiry into the Effects of Public Punishments upon Criminals, and upon Society*, began by reciting the purposes of punishment: to "reform" offenders, to "prevent" crimes, and to "remove" from society those persons shown to be "unfit to live in it." Acknowledging that "in every age and country (with only a few exceptions) legislators have thought that punishments should be *public*," Rush took the view that "all *public* punishments tend to make bad men worse" and only serve to increase crimes "by their influence upon society." The "infamy" of public punishments, Rush contended, destroys offenders' "sense of shame" and increases "propensities to crimes." "A man who has lost his character at a whipping-post," Rush wrote, "has nothing valuable left to lose in society." Public punishments are "arbitrary acts of cruelty," he argued, asserting that "the secret voice of God himself, speaking in the human heart," decries "the folly and cruelty of public punishments." The English law that "punishes the shooting of a swan with death," Rush wrote, has "produced a thousand murders," adding that spectators seeing "blows" inflicted upon criminals "in cold blood" removes "the natural obstacles to violence and murder in the human mind." "Laws can only be respected, and obeyed," Rush believed, harkening back to Beccaria, if they bear "an exact proportion to crimes."[6]

Under Pennsylvania law, convicts—known as "wheelbarrow men"—labored in public, on chain gangs, on roads and other building projects. Objecting to employing criminals "on the high-ways and streets," Rush railed against public punishments by posing a series of rhetorical questions: "What has been the operation of the seventy thousand executions, that have taken place in Great-Britain from the year 1688, to the present day, upon the morals and manners of the inhabitants of that island?" "Has not every prison door that has been opened, to conduct criminals to public shame and punishment, unlocked, at the same time, the bars of moral obligation upon the minds of ten times the number of people?" "How often do we find pockets picked under a gallows, and highway-robberies committed within sight of a gibbet?" "Why is the public executioner of the law an object of such general detestation?" "Let it not be supposed, from any thing that has been said, that I wish to abolish punishments," Rush clarified. "Far from it—I wish only to change the *place* and *manner* of inflicting them, so as to render them effectual for the reformation of criminals, and beneficial to society," he said. Rush wanted a prison with iron doors constructed "in a remote part of the state." "Let a guard constantly attend at a gate that shall lead to this place of punishment, to prevent strangers from entering it," he wrote. Lamenting the "indifference and levity with which some men suffer the punishment of hanging," Rush also called for fixed punishments in an "abode of discipline and misery" free of "any signs of mirth." "If public punishments are injurious to criminals and to society, it follows," Rush emphasized, "that crimes should be punished in private, or not punished at all."[7]

Though Dr. Rush's essay focused on the infamy of public punishments, he also made clear his opposition to capital punishment. "I have said nothing upon the manner of inflicting death as a punishment for crime," Rush wrote, "because I consider it as an improper punishment for *any* crime." "Even murder itself is propagated by the punishment of death for murder," he said, pointing to Tuscany's abolition of capital punishment. "Of this we have a remarkable proof in Italy," Rush wrote, explaining to his readers that "[t]he Duke of Tuscany, soon after the publication of the Marquis of Beccaria's excellent treatise upon this subject, abolished death as a punishment for murder." A trained scientist, Dr. Rush was constantly gathering information. "A gentleman, who resided five years at Pisa, informed me, that only five murders had been perpetrated in his dominions in twenty years," Rush wrote, comparing that figure with another as his essay continued: "The same gentleman added, that after his residence in Tuscany, he spent three months in Rome, where death is still the punishment of murder, and where executions, according to Doctor Moore, are conducted with peculiar circumstances of public parade. During this short period, there were sixty murders committed in the precincts of that city." Rush thus saw the death penalty's abolition as the key to Tuscany's low crime rate. "The abolition of death alone, as a punishment for murder, produced this difference in the moral character of the two nations," Rush concluded.[8]

Dr. Rush's activism against public executions was part of a much broader reform effort to repeal death penalty laws, especially ones aimed at lower-level offenders. In England, theologian William Paley's book, *Principles of Moral and Political Philosophy,* was published in 1785. "The proper end of human punishment is not the satisfaction of justice, but the prevention of crimes," Paley wrote, complaining of the "defect" of English law in not providing for "any other punishments than that of death" for certain crimes. Though Paley was generally supportive of England's enactment of a wide array of capital punishment laws, he opposed the use of death sentences to punish thieves. Jeremy Bentham's *Principles of Penal Law,* published in 1775, likewise lamented that "sanguinary executions" were causing a "deep-rooted antipathy" against the laws and those administering those laws. "All beyond simple death," Bentham wrote, citing Montaigne, "appears to me to be cruelty." Bentham, pointing to the risk of false testimony and a variety of "melancholy errors," drew special attention to the death penalty's finality in the face of a fallible system of justice. "The objection arising from the irremissibility of the punishment of death applies to all cases," Bentham explained, "and can be removed only by its complete abolition." "This punishment," he added, "is far from being popular; and it becomes less and less so every day, in proportion as mankind become more enlightened, and their manners more softened." The only instance Bentham identified as being popular regarding capital punishment was the case of murder. Finding the death penalty unnecessary in ordinary cases, and favoring "perpetual imprisonment," Bentham concluded: "In fine, I can see but one case in which it can be necessary, and that only occasionally." That instance was rebellion, with Bentham specifically making reference to Beccaria's views.[9]

Of God and Country

Benjamin Rush was one of Pennsylvania's leading reformers. A devout Christian, Dr. Rush packed his writings with religious references. In one letter from the Revolutionary War period, Rush wrote: "I long to see the image of God restored to the human mind." "I long," he said, "to see an asylum prepared for the persecuted and oppressed of all countries, and a door opened for the progress of knowledge, literature, the arts, and the gospel of Jesus Christ to the ends of the earth." In another letter, to the trustees of Dickinson College, he wrote: "It has pleased God to call us into existence at an important era." "Let us show ourselves worthy of our present stations in this country," he wrote, "and thank God for the opportunity he has afforded us of imitating the example of the Saviour of the world by fresh acts of self-denial and benevolence." With his usual evangelical fervor, Rush railed against "the mischievous effects" of hard liquor and the "licentiousness of the press," labeling horseracing and cockfighting "unfriendly amusements to morals" and calling for "[t]hese vulgar sports" to be "forbidden by law in all Christian and republican countries." Rush even solicited Thomas Jefferson's "religious creed," prompting Jefferson to send one to Rush in the strictest of confidence. Jefferson titled his creed "Syllabus of an Estimate of the Merit of the Doctrines of Jesus, compared with those of others," and in it, he set forth his views on Christianity. "I am a Christian," Jefferson told Rush in an accompanying letter, adding that his views were "the result of a life of inquiry and reflection" and "very different from that anti-Christian system imputed to me by those who know nothing of my opinions."[10]

For Dr. Rush, the death penalty—tied up with whether man, or only the divine, had the right to take human life—was inseparable from religion. In his essay *An Enquiry into the Effects of Public Punishments upon Criminals, and upon Society,* Rush quoted biblical passages and anticipated a major argument in favor of capital punishment from readers of the Bible. "I suspect the attachment to death, as a punishment for murder, in minds otherwise enlightened," Rush's essay explained, "arises from a false interpretation of a passage contained in the old testament, and that is, 'he that sheds the blood of man, by man shall his blood be shed.'" That passage, Rush wrote, "has been supposed to imply, that blood could only be expiated by blood." "But I am disposed to believe," Rush said, citing the Reverend William Turner, "that it is rather a *prediction,* than a *law.*" The scriptural language, Rush argued, "is simply, that such will be the depravity and folly of man, that murder, in every age, shall beget murder." "Laws, therefore, which inflict death for murder," Rush contended, "are, in my opinion, as unchristian as those which justify or tolerate revenge; for the obligations of Christianity upon individuals, to promote repentance, to forgive injuries, and to discharge the duties of universal benevolence, are equally binding upon states." "The power over human life," he said, "is the solitary prerogative of HIM who gave it." "If society can be secured from violence, by confining the murderer," Rush wrote, "the end of extirpation will be answered." Appealing to virtue, Rush thus implored his fellow citizens to abolish capital punishment: "Whatever is humane, is wise—whatever is wise, is just—and whatever is wise, just, and humane, will be found to be the true interest of states, whether criminals or foreign enemies are the objects of their legislation."[11]

Dr. Rush came fervently to oppose what he called the "wheelbarrow law," the Pennsylvania law passed in 1786 requiring convicts to do public works. Prisoners were chained to wheelbarrows, built, cleaned, and repaired streets and roads, and had their heads shaved as a mark of infamy. Public shaming was intended to get offenders to change their ways, though the law proved to be very controversial. To help instigate reform, Rush distributed a pamphlet against public punishments to friends such as John Dickinson, an eminent lawyer from Philadelphia and Wilmington, Delaware, and a future signer of the U.S. Constitution. On April 5, 1787, Rush wrote to Dickinson, his Quaker friend, enclosing a copy of his essay *An Enquiry into the Effects of Public Punishments upon Criminals, and upon Society.* Rush's letter explained: "The enclosed pamphlet, written with a design to procure *further* alterations in our penal law, humbly solicits your acceptance. It has made many converts in our city from the assistance it has derived from the miserable spectacle which is daily before our eyes." Rush's opposition to the law is also reflected in a letter he sent his wife Julia in August 1787, and in the sentiments of another letter, sent by Susanna Dillwyn to her father William Dillwyn in May 1787, that read: "I stept out to a booksellers & got two or three pamphlets, which I thought might be acceptable to thee." "The enquiry into the effects of Public punishments," she wrote, "was occasion'd by the method they have lately adopted of making criminals clean the streets—dig vaults & cellars for public buildings—& do other work of that kind with great irons around them—to the end of which a monstrous ball of iron is fast'ned to prevent their running away—it is a painful sight and in other respects I believe they find more disadvantages than was expected from it." Repealed at Rush's urging in 1789, the wheelbarrow law and its resulting chain gangs were replaced by "hard labor in private" and "solitary imprisonment."[12]

Rush's letter to his wife, written from Philadelphia, was particularly poignant. It described a scene "before our doors" in which one of the "wheelbarrow men (who were all at work in cleaning our street) asked me for a penny." As the doctor related to his wife: "I told him I had none but asked him if a draught of molasses beer would not be more acceptable to him. He answered in the affirmative." After Dr. Rush had someone fetch some beer from the cellar, the dozen or so members of the chain gang drank three jugs of beer out of a quart mug while "[t]he keeper of the poor fellows stood by and in a good-natured way indulged them in a little rest while they drank their beer." As a crowd gathered, one of the prisoners made a lasting impression on Dr. Rush, as he relayed to his wife Julia: "One of them struck me above the rest. He took a large dog in his arms and played with him in the most affectionate manner. 'This dog,' said he 'came from England with me and has been my companion ever since.'" As Rush the devoted husband explained to his wife: "A heart is not wholly corrupted and offers at least one string by which it might be led back to virtue that is capable of so much steady affection even for a dog. The conduct of the dog excited my admiration and conveyed a faint idea by his fidelity of that infinite love which follows the human species however much reduced by distress, debased by crimes, or degraded by the punishments of a prison, of ignominy, or of pain." Just as John Dickinson made charitable contributions to aid in the care of prisoners, Rush, too, did his part, giving prisoners turkey dinners on Christmas or sending gifts of vegetables or watermelons to the jail to what he called his "other class of friends."[13]

As an early American doctor, Rush regularly used bloodletting to treat his patients and saw suffering and death up close. He lived through deadly bouts of yellow fever, dark days when carts piled with cadavers made their way through the streets. He also treated wounded soldiers during the Revolutionary War, with his letters discussing bayonet stabbings and deaths. As a father, Dr. Rush bore witness—in a deeply personal way—to the human cost of killing. His eldest son John, a navy lieutenant, killed a fellow naval officer in a duel in New Orleans in 1807. He was promptly arrested, though he was later adjudged insane and placed in the Marine Hospital. After trying to kill himself, John Rush was brought home in 1810 and committed to the Pennsylvania Hospital where he remained until his death in 1837. Dr. Rush wrote to both John Adams and Thomas Jefferson about this painful family episode. His son "intended to waste his fire," Rush told Adams, "but was led to do otherwise by being assured his antagonist intended 'to kill or be killed.'" "Could the advocates for duelling and the idolaters of the late General Hamilton peep into the cell of my poor boy," Dr. Rush wrote Adams, "they would blush for their folly and madness in defending a practice and palliating a crime which has rendered a promising young man wretched for life and involved in his misery a whole family that loved him." When his son came back, Rush reported, he was in "a state of deep melancholy and considerable derangement," had dirty skin, ragged clothes, long, uncombed hair, and would not speak. "[H]is long nails and beard," Rush noted, "rendered him an object of horror to his afflicted parents and family." "Could he have been seen, in the state I have described him . . . by the Assembly of your state when they deliberated upon the punishment for duelling," Dr. Rush wrote Jefferson, "they would have classed it with the first of crimes and decreed a long, long season of confinement and labor to expiate it."[14]

The Push for Reform

Dr. Rush elaborated further on his anti–death penalty views in a July 1788 essay titled "Considerations on the Injustice and Impolicy of Punishing Murder by Death." Published in the *American Museum* magazine, Rush's essay was later expanded and separately published in Philadelphia and London. In it, Rush laid out why he had taken an anti–death penalty stance and sought to "answer all the objections" raised against that viewpoint. Rush divided his essay into three sections, with three corresponding Roman numeral headings. His first rationale: "Every man possesses an absolute power over his own liberty and property, but not over his own life." Rush argued that because a person "has no right to dispose of his life, he cannot commit the power over it to any body of men." His second point: "The punishment of murder by death, is contrary to reason, and to the order and happiness of society." Executions, he contended, "multiply murders" and lessen "the horror of taking away human life." The "experiments of some of the wisest legislators in Europe," he noted, pointing to the "empress of Russia, the king of Sweden, and the duke of Tuscany," had "nearly extirpated murder from their dominions." Third, Rush argued that "[t]he punishment of murder by death, is contrary to divine revelation." "A religion which commands us to forgive and even to do good to our enemies," he said, "can never authorize the punishment of murder by death." For Rush, it made no difference that *the state* was taking life, as opposed to an individual member of society. As Rush explained: "It is to no purpose to say here, that this vengeance is taken out of the hands of the individual, and directed against the criminal by the hand of government." It is a usurpation of "the prerogative of heaven," Rush said, "whether it be inflicted by a single person, or by a whole community."[15]

In his essay, Dr. Rush felt compelled to address head-on those biblical passages frequently cited in support of the death penalty. Executions are "contrary to the will of God," Rush wrote, explaining away one scriptural passage—known as "the law of Moses"—before turning once more to the Old Testament verse reading that "whoso sheddeth man's blood, by man shall his blood be shed." Here Rush turned again to the Reverend William Turner, who once wrote: "I hope that I shall not offend any one, by taking the liberty to put my own sense upon this celebrated passage, and to enquire, why it should be deemed a precept at all. To me, I confess, it appears to contain nothing more than a declaration of what will generally happen; and in this view, to stand exactly upon the same ground with such passages as the following: 'He that leadeth into captivity shall go into captivity.' 'He that taketh up the sword, shall perish by the sword.'" "The form of expression," Rush argued, construing the language, "is exactly the same in each of the texts; why, then, may they not all be interpreted in the same manner, and considered, not as commands, but as denunciations?" "[L]et the murderer live," Rush said, "to suffer the re-proaches of a guilty conscience," "to make compensation to society for the injury he has done it," "to maintain the family of the man whom he has mur-dered," "that murder may be extirpated from the list of human crimes!"[16]

Rush urgently appealed to judges, attorneys, witnesses, juries, and sher-iffs—the actors in the criminal justice system—to stop using capital punish-ment. "I beseech you to pause, and listen to the voice of reason and religion, before you convict or execute another fellow-creature for murder!" Rush im-plored. But like Beccaria, Rush sensed what he was up against, writing, "I despair of making such an impression upon the present citizens of the united states, as shall abolish the absurd and unchristian practice." Predicting "it will probably descend to posterity," Rush appealed to future readers: "To you, therefore, the unborn generations of the next century, I consecrate this humble tribute to justice. You will enjoy in point of knowledge, the meridian of a day, of which we only perceive the twilight. You will often review with equal con-tempt and horror, the indolence, ignorance and cruelty of your ancestors. The grossest crimes shall not exclude the perpetrators of them from your pity. You will *fully* comprehend the extent of the discoveries and precepts of the gospel, and you will be actuated, I hope, by its gentle and forgiving spirit." Rush continued: "You will see many modern opinions in religion and government turned upside downwards, and many new connexions established between cause and effect. From the importance and destiny of every human soul, you will acquire new ideas of the dignity of human nature, and of the infinite value of every act of benevolence that has for its object, the bodies, the souls, and the lives of your fellow-creatures." "You will love the whole human race," Rush concluded, "for you will perceive that you have a common Father, and you will learn to imitate him by converting those punishments to which their folly or wickedness have exposed them, into the means of their reformation and happiness."[17]

The new essay, Rush explained in a 1788 letter to his London literary agent, the Quaker physician and philanthropist John Coakley Lettsom, was "in-tended as an appendix to the essay on public punishments." "If you approve of the 'Inquiry,' " Rush wrote, "I take it for granted that you will procure a place for it in one of your periodical papers." In May 1787, Rush had written another letter to Lettsom about the Philadelphia Society for Alleviating the Miseries of Public Prisons, an organization that would distribute anti–capital punishment literature and serve, in the words of one scholar, "as the center of a web of transatlantic correspondence about Pennsylvania's experiment." In that letter, Rush explained that the new institution had grown out of John Howard's "excellent history of Prisons, aided in a small degree by the pamphlet lately published in this city upon the effects of public punishments upon criminals and society." The organization, Rush explained, "consists chiefly" of Quakers, though Rush was a Presbyterian. William White, an Episcopal bishop and Robert Morris's brother-in-law, was the Society's first president, and from May 1787 to the spring of 1788 the membership grew rapidly, expanding from thirty-seven Philadelphians—among them physicians, merchants, ministers, lawyers, and artisans—to 175 members. Rush asked Lettsom to share materials about the Philadelphia Society with John Howard, the renowned prison reformer Rush so admired. Indeed, Dr. Rush personally invited Howard to come to the United States to lecture, an invitation that Howard never received, as he died in Russia in January 1790 shortly after Rush posted his letter. "Upon the subject of criminal jurisprudence and the treatment of prisoners," Rush had written in his invitation, "the waters are troubled in every part of America." "Come then, dear sir," he wrote Howard, "and direct them into their proper channel." In his letter, Rush not only thanked Howard for "the acceptable presents conveyed to me through the hands of Dr. Lettsom," but praised Howard "for the immense services" he had provided "to humanity and science" by way of his histories of prisons. Howard had sent Rush a copy of the Duke of Tuscany's new penal code, which abolished capital punishment, along with a copy of his *Account of Lazarettos and Hospitals*—a work Rush called "excellent" and said contained "[i]nnumerable facts" proving "that solitude and labor reclaim the worst of criminals." Howard himself had edited and published the *Edict of the Grand Duke of Tuscany, for the Reform of the Criminal Law in His Dominions*.[18]

Dr. Rush's fervor for abolition was clearly reflected in his 1789 invitation to John Howard and in a letter he wrote the day before to the Reverend Jeremy Belknap in Boston. "To me," Rush wrote Howard, "there is no truth in mathematics or even morals more self-evident than that solitude and labor might be so applied for all crimes as to make the punishment of death and public disgrace forever altogether unnecessary." "In Pennsylvania," he wrote Howard, "you may command the friendship and services of thousands, especially of the people called Quakers." As Rush wrote: "Remember, my dear sir, that we are at present in a *forming* state. We have as yet but few habits of any kind, and *good* ones may be acquired and fixed by a good example and proper instruction as easily as *bad* ones without the benefit of either." The Duke of Tuscany, Rush told

Belknap, had reported that crimes of all kinds had become less frequent. "I am not more satisfied of the truth of any proposition in Euclid than I am of the truth of this declaration," Rush wrote Belknap, saying: "*Murder is propagated by hanging for murder.* How disgraceful to our republics that the monarchs of Europe should take the lead of us in extending the empire of reason and humanity in this interesting part of government!" The year before, Rush had sent another letter to Belknap, enclosing his anti–death penalty essay and calling it "the boldest attack I have ever made upon a public opinion or a general practice." Rush sought to have Belknap republish it, saying his essay had mistakenly been ascribed to Benjamin Franklin but that "[i]t has already made some converts and staggered many Old Testament saints and legislators."[19]

Dr. Rush's views subjected him to much criticism. Shortly after his essay was published in the *American Museum,* a reply to it, under the signature of "Philochoras," appeared in the *Pennsylvania Mercury.* The reply came from Robert Annan, a Scottish-born Associate Reformed Presbyterian minister who was, ironically, Reverend Belknap's predecessor at the Federal Street Church in Boston. Called to preach at the Old Scots Church in Philadelphia, where he served until 1801, Annan took aim at Rush's essay, which prompted Rush to pen an answer and to complain to Belknap about the way in which Annan had treated him. "My essay upon the punishment of murder by death has been attacked in our newspapers by the Reverend Mr. Annan," Rush wrote Belknap on October 7, 1788. "He rants in a most furious manner," Rush wrote of Annan, adding that "so far from treating me with the meekness of a Christian, he has not even treated me like a gentleman." "His arguments are flimsy and such as would apply better to the 15th than the 18th century," Rush said, adding, "They all appear to flow from his severe Calvanistical principles." As Rush wrote Belknap in his letter: "It is impossible to advance human happiness while we believe the Supreme Being to possess the passions of weak or wicked men and govern our conduct by such opinions. 'The Son of Man came not to destroy men's *lives,* but to *save* them,' is a passage that at once refutes all the arguments that ever were offered in favor of slavery, war, and capital punishments."[20]

Rush's rejoinder to Philochoras sought to refute what Rush called an attempt "to justify public and capital punishments, as well as war, by the precepts of the gospel." While acknowledging that his critic was a minister and "a man of a worthy private as well as public character," Rush sought to refute Annan's points one by one, likening an execution in a republic to a "human sacrifice in religion" and "an offering to monarchy." "I believe in the doctrine of atonement," Rush wrote at the beginning of his reply, invoking Beccaria for the proposition that "in a perfect human government there should be *no pardoning power.*" Citing reason and experience, Rush contended that the arguments against capital punishment stood on "immoveable foundations" and referenced anecdotal evidence from Europe. Rush cited a favorable passage from the instructions to the commissioners appointed by Catharine II, the Russian empress, to frame a new code of laws for the Russian empire; a British review of a new German penal code; and information from an Italian nobleman and a Swedish naval captain about the abolition of capital punishment in Tuscany and Sweden. "It is true," Rush conceded, "this happy revolution in favour of justice and humanity, in the instances that have been mentioned, did not originate in a convocation or a synod." But, Rush argued, "reason and religion have the same objects." Invoking Voltaire and Beccaria, Rush said the death penalty's abolition would further public order and lead to a happier society. The satisfaction of using "imprisonment and labour," Rush contended, "would far exceed that which is derived from the punishment of death."[21]

Meticulous in his approach to any issue, Rush believed both reason and the Bible supported his position. "[E]xperience has taught us," Rush argued, "that where *certainty* has taken the place of *severity* of punishment, crimes have evidently and rapidly diminished in every country." Executions, Rush opined, "are the natural offspring of monarchical governments," constitute "private revenge," and are not in accord with "the principles of republican governments," which "teach us the absurdity of the divine origin of kingly power." "Kings," he noted, "believe that they possess their crowns by a divine right: no wonder, therefore, they assume the divine power of taking away human life." "Kings," he stressed, "consider their subjects as their property: no wonder, therefore, they shed their blood with as little emotion as men shed the blood of their sheep or cattle." By contrast, Dr. Rush argued, republics "appreciate human life, and increase public and private obligations to preserve it." As the source of many of Rush's arguments, Beccaria himself had argued that "[a]s punishments become milder, clemency and pardons become less necessary."[22]

For Rush, solitude—not death—was the worst possible punishment. As Rush wrote in 1789: "Too much cannot be said in favor of SOLITUDE as a means of reformation, which should be the *only* end of *all* punishment. Men are wicked only from not *thinking*." "A wheelbarrow, a whipping post, nay even a gibbet," Rush told Enos Hitchcock, a Rhode Island minister, "are all light punishments compared with letting a man's conscience loose upon him in solitude." "Company, conversation, and even business are the opiates of the Spirit of God in the human heart," Rush reasoned. "For this reason," Rush concluded, "a bad man should be left for some time without anything to employ his hands in his confinement. Every *thought* should recoil wholly upon *himself*." Reverend Hitchcock was preparing a manuscript on domestic education for publication, and at Hitchcock's urging Rush offered his own thoughts on the subject. "I have discovered that all corporal corrections for children above three or four years old are highly improper," Rush wrote, "and that *solitude* is the most effective punishment that can be contrived for them." Rush then recounted his use of solitude to rear his own children: "I have used it for many years in my family with the greatest success. My eldest son, who is now near 12 years old, has more than once begged me to flog him in preference to confining him." Rush added: "The duration of the confinement and the disagreeable circumstances that are connected with it are proportioned to the faults that are committed. I have in one instance confined my two eldest sons in separate rooms for two days. The impression which this punishment has left upon them I believe will never wear away, nor do I think it will ever require to be repeated."[23]

Activism and Pamphleteering

As Rush distributed his anti–death penalty essays, America's abolitionist campaign, focused initially in New York and Pennsylvania, took off, soon to be joined and invigorated by other abolitionist leaders. Rush's Pennsylvania counterparts—men such as George Clymer, a fellow signer of the Declaration of Independence, a state legislator, and a member of the Continental Congress who opposed capital punishment—were already receptive to reform. After Rush's essays were published, Pennsylvania attorney general William Bradford took up many of the reforms Dr. Rush had advocated. Bradford's father, an important figure in his own right who fought in the American Revolution, was the publisher of the *Pennsylvania Journal* and the official printer for the Continental Congress. Due in part to Dr. Rush's and William Bradford's advocacy, in 1794, the year of Beccaria's death, Pennsylvania took the novel step of dividing murder into degrees and restricted capital punishment to instances of first-degree murder. Yet Rush, who wanted to see the total abolition of capital punishment, remained unsatisfied. This led to his publication, in 1797, of *An Inquiry into the Consistency of the Punishment of Murder by Death, with Reason and Revelation.* Rush began that essay with a heading: "The Punishment of Murder by Death, is contrary to *reason,* and to the order and happiness of society." That work, however, received an icy reception. "I met with but three persons in Philadelphia who agreed with me," Rush lamented.[24]

Still, Rush's 1797 essay showcased his rationality and intellect. Under his first Roman numeral, Rush listed his reasons for opposing capital punishment: "1. It lessens the horror of taking away human life, and thereby tends to multiply murders." "2. It produces murder by its influence upon people who are tired of life, and who, from a supposition that murder is a less crime than suicide, destroy a life (and often that of a near connection) and afterwards deliver themselves up to the laws of their country, that they may escape from their misery by means of a halter." "3. The punishment of murder by death multiples murders, from the difficulty it creates of convicting persons who are guilty of it." "Humanity, revolting at the idea of the severity and certainty of a capital punishment," Rush noted, often collects "evidence in favour of a murderer" or "palliates his crime into manslaughter." In all, Rush articulated five reasons for opposing capital punishment before moving on to his next heading: "The punishment of murder by death is contrary to *divine revelation*." "A religion which commands us to forgive, and even to do good to, our enemies," Rush wrote, "can never authorise the punishment of murder by death."[25]

Like most early abolitionists, Rush was constantly wrestling with biblical verses, grounding his opposition in interpretations of scriptural passages. Rush first referenced "the law of Moses": "he that killeth a man shall be put to death." Arguing that this biblical passage did not warrant the infliction of capital punishment, Rush wrote: "Forgive, indulgent heaven! the ignorance and cruelty of man, which, by the misapplication of this text of scripture, has so long and so often stained the religion of Jesus Christ with folly and revenge." Rush then proceeded to list six points, the first two being that the death penalty cannot be agreeable "to the will of God" because the death penalty "is contrary to reason" and "destroys" order and societal happiness. As to the familiar biblical verse that "whoso sheddeth man's blood, by man shall his blood be shed," Rush once again explained it away by saying: "soon after the flood, the infancy and weakness of society rendered it impossible to punish murder by confinement." "It pleased God, in this condition of the world," Rush said, to temporarily delegate "his exclusive power over human life" to "an infant society" for "the safety and preservation" of that society, "which might otherwise have perished."[26]

In his essay, Dr. Rush pleaded again that capital punishment be abolished. "[L]et us not counteract the government of God in the human breast: let the murderer live," Rush wrote. Rush wanted every murderer "to suffer the reproaches of a guilty conscience" and "to make compensation to society for the injury he has done it, by robbing it of a citizen." "[T]he heart," Rush argued, "may retain a sound part after committing murder," saying that "even murderers, after repentance, may be the vehicles of great temporal and spiritual blessings to mankind." Human life was "extremely cheap" under Roman law, Rush emphasized, adding, "Of this we need no further proof than the head of John the Baptist forming a part of a royal entertainment." Explaining that imprisonment and hard labor would result in more frequent murder convictions and end the possibility of "impunity" for murderous acts, Rush once more made religious appeals. "The conduct and discourses of our Saviour," he said, "should outweigh every argument that has been or can be offered in favour of capital punishment for any crime." "When the woman caught in adultery was brought to him, he evaded inflicting the bloody sentence of the Jewish law upon her," Rush explained. "He forgave the crime of murder, on his cross; and after his resurrection," Rush continued, "he commanded his disciples to preach the gospels of forgiveness, first at Jerusalem, where he well knew his murderers still resided."[27]

Like Beccaria, Rush advocated a "scale of punishments," believing a system could "easily be contrived" to differentiate "the different degrees of atrocity in murder." For first-degree murder, Rush advocated solitary confinement in darkness and "a total *want* of employment." For second-degree murder, Rush thought "solitude and labour, with the benefit of light" most appropriate, whereas for third-degree murder, he pushed for "confinement and labour." The duration of these punishments, Rush said, should be tied to "the atrocity of the murder, and by the signs of contrition and amendment in the criminal." Saying every nation had a duty "to preserve, restore, or prolong human life," Rush argued in opposition to war and capital punishment, both of which, he said, have as their objects the "unprofitable destruction of the lives of men." "Pause, Legislators," he implored, "when you give your votes for inflicting the punishment of death for any crime." His argument: "You frustrate in one instance, the design of the mission of the Son of God into the world, and thereby either deny his appearance in the flesh, or reject the truth of his gospel." "It is only because I view murder with such superlative horror," Rush said, "that I wish to deprive our laws of the power of perpetuating and encouraging it."[28]

Dr. Rush thought incessantly about social progress, describing in his essay how societies had witnessed a decline in violence and oppression over the previous two centuries. "The world has certainly undergone a material change for the better within the last two hundred years," he wrote. Saying the change had been "produced chiefly" by "the secret and unacknowledged influence of Christianity upon the hearts of men," Dr. Rush looked to the historical record, writing: "It is agreeable to trace the effects of the Christian religion in the extirpation of slavery—in the diminution of the number of capital punishments, and in the mitigation of the horrors of war." Civic leaders in Philadelphia had been at the center of efforts to abolish the slave trade, and Rush believed then that the arc of history would vindicate his anti–death penalty views. "There was a time," Rush wrote, "when torture was part of the punishment of death, and when the number of capital crimes in Great Britain, amounted to one hundred and sixty-one." "Christianity," he said, "has abolished the former, and reduced the latter to not more than six or seven." And, Rush added, "[i]t has confined, in some instances, capital punishments to the crime of murder— and in some countries it has abolished it altogether."[29]

In a postscript to his 1797 essay, published later as part of a larger collection of his writings, Dr. Rush expressed immense pleasure at seeing "his principles reduced to practice in the State of Pennsylvania." There, the death penalty had been abolished for all crimes except first-degree murder, and private punishments had been substituted for public ones. "The effects of this reformation," Rush wrote, had been "a remarkable diminution of crimes of all kinds," coupled with an increase in convictions. "The Author is happy in adding," he said, "that a reformation in the penal laws of the states of New York and New Jersey has taken place, nearly similar to that which has been mentioned, in Pennsylvania." In particular, Rush credited two men with effectuating such momentous penal reforms. "It would be an act of injustice," Rush said, "not to acknowledge that the principles contained in the foregoing essays, would probably have never been realized, had they not been supported and enforced by the eloquence of the late William Bradford Esq. and the zeal of Caleb Lownes." "To both these gentlemen," Rush said, "humanity and reason owe great obligations." Lownes, through his philanthropy and "plans for employing, and reforming his unfortunate fellow creatures in the Philadelphia prison," Rush emphasized, had shown particular "ingenuity and benevolence." A Philadelphia merchant and prison reformer, Caleb Lownes was a Quaker ironmonger and a charter member of the Philadelphia Society for Alleviating the Miseries of Public Prisons. In 1792, Lownes published the influential work *An Account of the Alteration and Present State of the Penal Laws of Pennsylvania.*[30]

At first, Rush remained optimistic about the possibility of penal reform, actively campaigning for the death penalty's total abolition. Though Rush told a friend in late 1789 that he had "taken leave of public life and public pursuits" and lived only "for the benefit of my family and my patients," he still found time away from his busy medical practice to press his cause. Along with his work in Pennsylvania, Rush wrote the Humane Society of Massachusetts in 1793 to rejoice in their successful endeavors "to disseminate knowledge upon the important subject of preserving human life." That same year, Rush also predicted—overly optimistically, it turned out—that "humanity and reason are likely to prevail so far in our legislature that a law will probably pass in a few weeks to abolish capital punishments in *all cases* whatever." But over time, Rush grew weary and disillusioned. "Tired out, and distressed with the unsuccessful issue of all my public labors for the benefit of my fellow citizens," Rush told Thomas Eddy in 1803, "I have for some years past limited my studies and duties wholly to my profession." Eddy, another Beccaria disciple and a leading penal reformer in his own right, had Quaker roots, made a fortune in New York, and then devoted himself to philanthropic causes. Inspired by Philadelphia's Walnut Street Jail, Eddy—with the backing of Alexander Hamilton's father-in-law, General Philip Schuyler—built a penitentiary in New York in the 1790s. In 1816, New York built its Auburn Prison, which limited the use of solitary confinement to the most dangerous criminals. In 1801, Eddy, who stayed in touch with his Quaker friends in Philadelphia as he pursued reform, also wrote *An Account of the State Prison or Penitentiary House in the City of New York.* Eddy wanted Rush, who by then had an international reputation, to write a history of Pennsylvania's penal laws, but Rush declined, suggesting another writer, Charles Brown, and saying: "I must be excused from undertaking the work you have suggested to me."[31]

Though Dr. Rush was too busy to undertake the project, his 1803 response to Thomas Eddy reflected Rush's concern over the state of penal reform—and his fear of legislative backsliding. "I wish the history of our prison," Rush wrote, "may not some years hence end with an account of the restoration of our old laws for whipping, cropping, burning in the hand, and taking away life." "Many of our citizens wish for it," Rush told Eddy in his letter, "and I am sorry to say the manner in which our mild penal code has of late years been executed has furnished too much reason for retrograde opinions upon this important subject." Rush had frequently visited the Walnut Street Prison and believed in its ability to "triumph over vice," though he complained of "the imperfect manner" in which prison officials had carried out its mission by allowing more than one criminal to sleep in the same cell. After giving Eddy his opinions on the use of "solitary beds and rooms" within prisons, as well as his recommendations for prisoners' diets, Rush expressed the view that "there never was a soul so completely shipwrecked by vice that something divine was not saved from its wreck." Expressing "great respect" for Eddy's "zeal and industry in advancing the interests of humanity and justice," Rush closed his letter on a hopeful note. "I shall never think our penal code perfect till we deprive our laws of the power of taking away life for *any* crime. It is in my opinion murder to punish murder by death," Rush wrote.[32]

Nearly a decade later, the energetic Dr. Rush repeated that absolutist view in his new treatise *Medical Inquiries and Observations upon the Diseases of the Mind*. Published in 1812, Rush's book explored the causes of "madness" and "derangement." In it, Rush recounted a host of circumstances causing mental diseases and advised physicians to avoid all "acts of cruelty." Among the many causes of madness that Rush described were "remorse of conscience in consequence of killing a friend in a duel" and "the cruel or unjust conduct of schoolmasters and guardians to the persons who were the subjects of their power and care." Suicidal thoughts, Rush added, often caused those afflicted to commit murder, which, in turn, would "provoke death from the hands of the government"—the very thing desired by the suicidal person. In his book, Rush also urged "[t]he abolition of the punishment of death, and of cropping, branding, and public whipping," asserting that "substituting" for them "confinement, labour, simple diet, cleanliness, and affectionate treatment" had produced "moral effects in the jail of Philadelphia." "May this christian system of criminal jurisprudence be spread, without any of its imperfections, throughout the world!" Rush wrote. "[A]nd," he continued, "may the rulers of nations learn from it, that the reformation of criminals, as well as the prevention of crimes, should be objects of all punishments, and that the latter can be effected much better by living than by dead examples!"[33]

In 1810, in the lead-up to his book's publication, Dr. Rush also gave an impassioned lecture on the subject of "medical jurisprudence" to a group of University of Pennsylvania medical students. In his lecture, Rush spoke of murder and madness and of the role of doctors in the legal system, citing his role in examining a man condemned to die for treason for participating in the 1794 Whiskey Rebellion in western Pennsylvania. After the man "was said to have lost his reason after sentence of death had been pronounced upon him," a physician declared his madness to be feigned, whereupon Dr. Rush, Dr. William Shippen, and Dr. Samuel P. Griffitts were appointed to assess the claim at President George Washington's direction. The panel ultimately concluded the man was mad, with Dr. Rush emphasizing that the man's pulse was "more than 20 beats above what it would be in health." The man's execution—as well as that of his compatriot, who had also been sentenced to death—was postponed for two months, during which time, Rush noted, "the popular clamor for their lives so far subsided, that they were both pardoned by the executive of the United States." In his lecture, Rush also described and tried to make sense of murder-suicides, a baby killer, the killing of a little boy named Ira Lane by a New Yorker "with uncommon circumstances of cruelty," and the "shocking" 1804 execution of a man "upon the rack."[34]

Reflecting on the "insanity" and "derangement in the will" associated with murderers, Rush argued that "all the light and knowledge of our science should be employed to oppose the usual punishment inflicted upon them." "It is equally absurd, and far more cruel," Rush said, "to inflict the punishment of death upon a fellow creature, for taking away a life under the influence of a deranged state of the will." In making a final appeal to his audience, Rush sought the abolition of capital punishment "in all cases whatever," even "for the crime of deliberate murder itself." "Yes. I say again, for the crime of deliberate murder itself," Rush appealed to his listeners. "It is to be lamented," Rush said, "that the most palpable contradictions exist in the principles and conduct of mankind upon this subject." Rush explained: "We bestow much study and great labour in restoring the wandering reason of our fellow creatures; but we neglect their erring hearts. We erect splendid and commodious buildings to confine persons, whom intellectual derangement has rendered dangerous to society, and we employ our skill and humanity to relieve them; but with an unmerciful impatience, we consign persons, whom moral derangement has rendered mischievous, to the exterminating ax and halter. We believe that no man possesses a property in his own life; and yet we convey that property to our governments." Only by eliminating capital punishment, Rush offered, would "the original harmony between the virtues" of humanity and justice be restored, thus enhancing "the reputation of our courts" and "the order and happiness of society."[35]

William Bradford

Dr. Rush's writings persuaded William Bradford of the Pennsylvania Supreme Court to rethink his position on capital punishment. A prominent Philadelphia lawyer and judge, Bradford was a lifelong friend of James Madison; their friendship developed during their days together at Princeton. After graduating in 1772, Bradford read law in Philadelphia before volunteering in the Pennsylvania militia. He served as Pennsylvania's attorney general from 1780 to 1791 and was appointed to the Pennsylvania Supreme Court in 1791. In 1794, President Washington then tapped Bradford to replace Virginia's Edmund Randolph as the United States Attorney General, a position Bradford served in until his untimely death in 1795. In one of his many letters to John Adams, Dr. Rush cited penal reform in Pennsylvania as an example "to illustrate the injustice and error that take place with respect to opinions and events." Writing to Adams, Rush specifically invoked Bradford's change of heart on the issue. Inspired by Dr. Rush's work and asked by Pennsylvania governor Thomas Mifflin to advise the state legislature on the issue of capital punishment, William Bradford wrote an influential pamphlet titled *An Enquiry How Far the Punishment of Death Is Necessary in Pennsylvania*. "When a proposal for mitigating the severity of our penal laws was first published in Pennsylvania, and solitary labor was recommended as a substitute for whipping, cropping, and hanging," Rush told John Adams in 1806, "the late worthy Judge Bradford treated that proposal with good-humored ridicule." "A few years afterwards," Rush reported, Bradford "adopted all the ideas he had ridiculed, and defended them in a learned and eloquent pamphlet." Saying that Bradford "is now revered as one of the authors of our new system of penal laws," Rush added that Benjamin Franklin "shares with him in that honor," even though Franklin, to Rush's knowledge, "never wrote a line nor uttered a statement in favor of it."[36]

William Bradford and Dr. Rush, his personal physician, were close friends. They collaborated on prison reform, and their reputations blossomed alongside of one another. By 1787, historian Peter Okun explains, "the influence of local reformers Ben Franklin, Dr. Benjamin Rush, and Justice William Bradford had widened considerably, and their prison society meetings were, quite literally, confluent and concurrent with" the Constitutional Convention hosted in Philadelphia. When Bradford died in 1795, Rush painfully recorded in his diary: "This evening, Sunday, died my excellent friend William Bradford, Esquire. Never did I labor more to save a life." On his deathbed, Bradford even bequeathed Rush a thousand dollars to use for charitable purposes—and to be bequeathed by Rush, at his death, either for charitable purposes or to his children. So involved was he in his friend's affairs that Rush even got embroiled in a litigated dispute involving Bradford's estate. As Rush told John Adams in 1808: "About two weeks ago I was summonsed a second time to give my testimony in favor of the late Wm. Bradford, attorney general of the U. States, having died intestate (after destroying a will in which he had left most of his estate to his wife) and of his having performed, after making this declaration, certain acts in my presence which indicated a sound mind." On his deathbed, Bradford had torn up his will and made a dying declaration to Rush that "the law"—not his will—"should divide his estate."[37]

Bradford's own essay, *An Enquiry How Far the Punishment of Death Is Necessary in Pennsylvania,* showed Dr. Rush's influence, a fact that should hardly be surprising, especially considering how well they knew each other. Published in 1793, Bradford's essay began by invoking Beccaria and Montesquieu and then articulated three principles said to have attained "the force of axioms": first, that the prevention of crimes is "*the sole end of punishment*"; second, that every punishment "*which is not absolutely necessary for that purpose is a cruel and tyrannical act*"; and third, that every penalty "*should be proportioned to the offence.*" "These principles," Bradford said, "serve to protect the rights of humanity," "to prevent the abuses of government," and "are so important that they deserve a place among the *fundamental* laws of every free country." Advertised as a "memoir" written at the request of Pennsylvania's governor, Bradford's essay called the punishment of death "the highest act of power that man exercises over man." The essay's objective was, in Bradford's words, "to review the crimes which are still capital in Pennsylvania" to determine "whether the punishment of death be, in any case, necessary."[38]

In *An Enquiry How Far the Punishment of Death Is Necessary in Pennsylvania,* Bradford argued that legislators "feel themselves elevated above the commission of crimes which the laws proscribe, and they have too little personal interest in a system of punishments to be critically exact in restraining its severity." "Hence," Bradford concluded, "sanguinary punishments, contrived in despotic and barbarous ages, have been continued when the progress of freedom, science, and morals renders them unnecessary and mischievous." In Pennsylvania, Bradford noted a year before becoming the country's chief law enforcement officer, some capital crimes had already been abolished, with Bradford predicting that "the Legislature would resume the benevolent talk." Pennsylvania legislators, he wrote, had acted with "caution" in reforming "an ancient system," but he expressed the hope that "they have not abandoned the work." A viable substitute, "perpetual imprisonment," he argued, could prevent offenders from reoffending, and Bradford advocated "solitary imprisonment, hard labor, or stripes" in the death penalty's place. After grappling with anecdotal evidence on the issue of deterrence, Bradford concluded that "the opinion of many of the most enlightened men in America" favored "greatly" reducing death sentences or "totally" abolishing them. Bradford specifically mentioned "Mr. Jefferson, Mr. Wythe and Mr. Pendleton of Virginia," who, as a committee, had recommended the abolition of capital punishments in their state in all cases except treason and murder. "[U]nfortunately for the interests of humanity," Bradford wrote, the Virginia proposal, drafted by Thomas Jefferson and carried in the state assembly by James Madison, "was rejected in the Legislature by a single vote."[39]

In his essay, Bradford surveyed a variety of state constitutional provisions dealing with the punishment of criminals. He quoted from New Hampshire's constitution, declaring "[t]hat all penalties should be proportioned to the nature of the offence, and that a multitude of sanguinary punishments is impolitic and unjust, the true design of all punishments being to reform, and not to exterminate, mankind." He also cited provisions from the state constitutions of Maryland and Vermont, and quoted from Pennsylvania's 1776 constitution, which directed future legislators "to reform the penal laws—to make punishments less sanguinary, and, in some cases, more proportioned to the offences." After highlighting Maryland's constitution, which, like Pennsylvania's, called for avoiding "sanguinary punishments," Bradford emphasized that "[t]he other constitutions which touch on this subject content themselves with generally declaring, 'That cruel punishments ought not to be inflicted.'" "But," Bradford pointed out in discussing such provisions, "does not this involve the same principle, and implicitly prohibit every penalty which is not evidently necessary?" "One would think, that, in a nation jealous of its liberty," Bradford wrote, "that the infliction of death" would "seldom be prescribed where its necessity was doubtful."[40]

Bradford then expressed support for the direction of penal reform in his home state. "Happily for Pennsylvania," he wrote, "the examination and reform of the penal laws have been considered by the Legislature as one of its most important duties." As Bradford explained: "Much attention has been paid to this subject since the revolution. Capital punishments have, in several instances, been abolished; and, in others, the penalty has been better proportioned to the offence." Bradford saw "perpetual imprisonment" not only "as effectual as death" but also as having several advantages, among them "that punishment may follow quick upon the heels of the offence, without violating the sentiments of humanity or religion." Citing prevention of crime as the object of punishment, Bradford conceded that "[i]t is more difficult to determine what effects are produced on the mind by the *terror* of capital punishments." Pondering aloud whether executions "be absolutely necessary to deter the wicked from the commission of atrocious crimes," Bradford nonetheless concluded—based on his observations—that offenders rarely "deliberately count the cost," making capital punishment of "doubtful" utility.[41]

Bradford's lengthy essay specifically traced the history of Pennsylvania's criminal laws. "It was the policy of Great Britain to keep the laws of the Colonies in unison with those of the mother country," Bradford explained, noting that the royal charter to William Penn directed that Pennsylvania's laws "respecting felonies, should be the same with those of England, until altered by the acts of the future Legislature." The "natural tendency" of that policy, Bradford wrote, "was to overwhelm an infant colony, thinly inhabited, with a mass of sanguinary punishments hardly endurable in an old, corrupted and populous country." "But the Founder of the province," Bradford emphasized, speaking of William Penn, who had studied law for a year in England before converting from Puritanism to the Quaker faith, "was a philosopher whose elevated mind rose above the errors and prejudices of his age, like a mountain, whose summit is enlightened by the first beams of the sun, while the plains are still covered with mists and darkness." Under Penn's leadership, only "willful and premeditated" murder, a crime said to be a violation of "the law of God," was punishable by death. "Robbery, burglary, arson, rape, the crime against nature, forgery, levying war against the Governor, conspiring his death, and other crimes," Bradford explained, "were declared to be no longer capital." Penn, Bradford reported, was "a leader of a sect"—the Quakers—who saw "the wickedness of exterminating where it was possible to reform; and the folly of capital punishments in a country where he hoped to establish purity of morals and innocence of manners."[42]

But Pennsylvania's Quaker-inspired reforms, Bradford went on, did not sit well with the Crown. After the new laws were transmitted to England, as required by the colony's charter, they were repealed by Queen Anne, only to be immediately reenacted by Pennsylvania legislators in a colonial-monarchical tug of war. The progressive laws, Bradford noted, were in force until 1718, "and might," he wrote in his 1793 essay, "have remained to this day had not high handed measures driven our ancestors into an adoption of the sanguinary statutes of the Mother Country." Fearful of "political annihilation," Bradford relayed, the Quakers sought "to secure the favor of their Sovereign" by adopting harsh English penal laws. Pennsylvania's colonial chief justice David Lloyd thus drafted an act authorizing more death-eligible offenses— an act, accompanied by a petition to the Crown, which passed in just a few days. "By this act," Bradford noted, treason, murder, robbery, burglary, rape, sodomy, buggery, malicious maiming, manslaughter, witchcraft, arson, and "every other felony (except larceny) on a second conviction" were declared capital offenses. To this list—"already too large," Bradford editorialized— "were added, at subsequent periods, counterfeiting and uttering counterfeit bills of credit." Thus ended what Bradford called a "humane experiment in legislation."[43]

An Enquiry How Far the Punishment of Death Is Necessary in Pennsylvania sought to reframe the debate. "We perceive, by this detail," Bradford wrote of his history of Pennsylvania law, "that the severity of our criminal law is an exotic plant and not the native growth of Pennsylvania." "It has been endured, but, I believe, has never been a favorite," Bradford explained, adding that "many of our citizens" opposed capital punishment on religious grounds and that "as soon as the principles of Beccaria were disseminated, they found a soil that was prepared to receive them." Bradford specifically distinguished between the pre– and post–Revolutionary War era in discussing Pennsylvania's penal laws. Many offenses, Bradford wrote, were capital crimes at the outset of the war, with no reform attempted during the colony's "connection with Great Britain." "[B]ut," Bradford added, "as soon as we separated from her, the public sentiment disclosed itself, and this benevolent undertaking was enjoined by the constitution." "This," Bradford wrote, "was one of the first fruits of liberty, and confirms the remark of Montesquieu, 'That, as freedom advances, the severity of the penal law decreases.'" Noting that Pennsylvania's assembly had in 1786 substituted "hard labor" for the formerly capital offenses of "the crime against nature, robbery and burglary," Bradford's essay sought to answer the question "whether this punishment has been less efficacious in preventing these crimes than the punishment of death."[44]

In the section of his essay titled "Of the Crime Against Nature," Bradford, a product of the eighteenth century, argued that "[i]n a country where marriages take place so early, and the intercourse between the sexes is not difficult, there can be no reason for severe penalties to restrain this abuse." "This crime, to which there is so little temptation," Bradford wrote, "is, in America, as rare as it is detestable." Bradford pointed out that in the six years preceding the new law, during which the punishment was capital, there were only two recorded offenders, whereas in the same period of time since the law there was "*but one*." From this anecdotal evidence, Bradford argued that "the mildness of the punishment" had not increased the incidences of "the offence," emphasizing that the one offender apprehended after the change in law could not have been "seduced by the mildness of the punishment, because at the time, and long after his arrest, he believed it to be a capital crime." "These facts prove," Bradford asserted, "that to punish this crime with death would be a useless severity." Taking a swipe at "capital punishments formerly inflicted on adultery and witch-craft," Bradford called it "dangerous" to "rashly" adopt the "Mosaical institutions." "Laws," he said, "might have been proper for a tribe of ardent barbarians wandering through the sands of Arabia which are wholly unfit for an enlightened people of civilized and gentle manners."[45]

In another section of his essay, Bradford argued that the "salutary effects" of Pennsylvania's change in law "are not so evident in the cases of robbery and burglary as in that of the crime against nature." But Bradford pointed out that in a large city such as Philadelphia "there is always a class of men, sometimes greater and sometimes less, who live by dishonest means." "It so happened, that about the time of passing the act for amending the penal laws," Bradford reported, "there was accumulated in the gaol of the city and county of Philadelphia a great number of persons who had been convicted of theft and other infamous crimes, and were either pardoned by the mercy of the government, or had undergone the punishment (and some of them the *repeated* punishment) of the pillory and whipping-post." Bradford then explained his view that these "wretches, hardened by the nature of the punishment they had sustained" and "corrupted by each other," had, upon their discharge, immediately "returned to their old vocation." "Pardons, so destructive to every mild system of penal laws," Bradford wrote, "were granted with a profusion as unaccountable as it was mischievous." After noting that "solitary confinement and coarse fare" had not been imposed as a "*necessary* part of the punishment" on many of the offenders, Bradford saw the need to impose harsher penalties on "the more hardened offenders." "I understood from the nephew of the Marquis Beccaria, while he was in America," Bradford wrote, that "beneficial effects" had resulted from distinguishing between criminals "armed with dangerous and mortal weapons" and those without any "violent intentions." "It is evident," Bradford concluded, "that the principle of the new system, properly modified, coincides with the public safety as much as with the dictates of humanity," and that "there is little to apprehend" from extending the "experiment" to "other crimes."[46]

In his essay, Bradford went on to discuss Pennsylvania's then-prevailing capital crimes: counterfeiting, rape, arson, malicious mayhem, manslaughter, murder, and treason. "[T]here does not appear to be any necessity for so violent a remedy," Bradford wrote first of counterfeiting coins, asking whether it was just to punish a counterfeiter the same way as someone guilty of "deliberate murder." For rapists and arsonists, Bradford also thought the death penalty excessive. In discussing the crime of rape, he emphasized that William Penn considered "imprisonment, stripes and hard labour as punishment adequate to this crime and sufficient to check the commission of it." For anyone who thought a prison sentence too lenient, Bradford suggested a visit "to the penitentiary house lately erected as part of the gaol of Philadelphia." As Bradford explained: "When he looks into the narrow cells prepared for the more atrocious offenders—When he realizes what it is to subsist on coarse fare—to languish in the solitude of a prison—to wear out his tedious days and long nights in feverish anxiety—to be cut off from his family—from his friends—from society—from all that makes life dear to the heart—When he realizes this he will no longer think the punishment inadequate to the offence." For arsonists, Bradford wrote, solitude and hard labor would be "as efficacious" as death, with Bradford arguing that noncapital sentences allowed the offender to be reformed. Again, Bradford held up "the laws of William Penn" as a model of moderation.[47]

As to the crime of murder, Bradford treaded more carefully. He first acknowledged that "whether it be lawful, in *any* case, to take away the life of the criminal" had "divided the philosophers of Europe." But Bradford, who knew the legal and political landscape as well as anyone, was unwilling to go as far as his friend Dr. Rush. "Murder, in its highest degree," Bradford wrote, "has generally been punished with death, and it is for deliberate assassination, if in any case, that this punishment will be justifiable and useful." "The life of the deliberate assassin," he offered, "can be of little worth to society, and it were better that ten such atrocious criminals should suffer the penalty of the present system, than that one worthy citizen should perish by its abolition." For Bradford, though, life was sacred—a principle he knew was inconsistent with the death penalty's use. "Existence is the first blessing of Heaven," he wrote, "because all others depend upon it." "Its protection," he insisted, "is the great object of civil society and governments are bound to adopt every measure which is, in any degree, essential to its preservation." Indeed, Bradford found himself grappling with the inherent conflict between executions and the sacredness of human life toward the end of his essay.[48]

In analyzing the death penalty's legitimacy for different categories of murder, Bradford at first took a utilitarian tack, pondering "whether it be *necessary* to the peace, order, and happiness of society." For the moment, Bradford was willing to let executions proceed for the worst offenders. "If we seek a punishment capable of impressing a strong and lasting terror," Bradford wrote, "we shall find it in an execution *rarely* occurring—*solemnly* conducted—and inflicted in a case, where the feelings of mankind *acquiesce in its justice* and do not revolt at its severity." Bradford, however, was also more than willing to contemplate a future devoid of executions. "But while I contend that this is the most powerful curb of human governments," Bradford said of state-sanctioned killing, "I do not affirm that it is *absolutely* necessary, or that a milder one will be insufficient." On the contrary, Bradford wrote that "the further diffusion of knowledge and melioration of manners, may render capital punishments unnecessary in all cases." Bradford just wanted, in his words, "to tread with caution on such delicate ground, and to proceed step by step in so great a work." Bradford, whose essay included a table of offenders for various years for purposes of evaluating deterrence, thought "more experience" would help clarify the issue. "A few years experience," he wrote, "is often of more real use than all the theory and rhetoric in the world."[49]

Dr. Rush's Influence

Benjamin Rush was a prolific writer who stayed in close touch with many leading American patriots and men of letters. In his correspondence, Rush deplored executions and what he called "mobocracy," once referring to the "cruelty of the mob," how men were "sacrificed" by a mob in Amsterdam, and how advocates of Holland's independence were executed. Rush was especially vocal about the execution of the king of France, calling it "unjust, unconstitutional, illegal, impolitic, and cruel in the highest degree." The guillotining of Louis XVI on January 21, 1793, in a public square in Paris, had in fact caused many Americans to grieve. Fighting the British Empire had been no easy task, and the French government, led by Louis XVI, had supported and helped finance the American Revolution. "From the private history of his life and the public history of his death," Rush wrote of the king, who had taken the throne in 1774, "I am disposed to believe that he was the best king in Europe and the honestest man in the French nation." "Ninety-nine of our citizens out of a hundred," Rush wrote, "have dropped a tear to his memory. He was the father of the freedom and independence of the United States."[50]

As a confidant of John Adams, James Madison, and Thomas Jefferson, Dr. Rush was an influential figure. Indeed, Dr. Rush maintained lifelong friendships with many of America's leading founders, dining with the likes of Benjamin Franklin. He wrote to Patrick Henry, recollecting with pleasure Henry's influence on America's independence and that Henry had "first taught us to shake off our idolatrous attachment to royalty." He wrote to John Dickinson to congratulate him on the adoption of the U.S. Constitution; to say that Dickinson's letters had "added to the seeds of liberties" planted in France by writers such as Montesquieu and Voltaire; and to remind his "dear friend" that "none liveth to himself" and that "'To do good' is the business of *life.*'" To Thomas Jefferson, he complained of a "cruel and absurd system of penal laws" and extended "[t]he wishes and prayers of thousands" that Jefferson would "live to realize" the ideals behind the Declaration of Independence. To Adams, one of his most frequent correspondents, he spoke of meeting Alexander Cruden, the author of *A Complete Concordance to the Holy Scriptures of the Old and New Testaments,* and remembering, nearly forty years later, what Cruden had told him: "God punishes some crimes in this world to teach us there is a Providence, and permits others to escape with impunity to teach us there is a future judgment." And to James Madison, Rush wrote to sing the praises of his son Richard, who was admitted to the bar in 1800; to express his view that "mankind are growing wiser upon the subject of penal laws"; and to advocate peaceful resolution of conflicts, arguing for a body of "umpires" to decide "national disputes without appealing to arms."[51]

Benjamin Rush's second-eldest son Richard, a successful lawyer, would himself enter the political arena at the highest levels of government, also becoming a presidential confidant. Appointed Pennsylvania's attorney general in 1811, Richard Rush went on to work for four U.S. Presidents. He was the comptroller of the treasury and the United States Attorney General during James Madison's administration, serving as one of Madison's closest advisors; he became the secretary of the treasury under John Quincy Adams; and he also served as the minister to Britain and the minister to France. In 1828, Richard Rush even ran unsuccessfully as a vice presidential candidate on John Quincy Adams's reelection ticket. As John Powell, Richard Rush's biographer, explains, Dr. Rush's son Richard studied law in a Philadelphia law office before being admitted to the bar and opening his own office. As the country's attorney general, Richard Rush edited the Laws of the United States, a codification of all federal statutes enacted between 1789 and 1815, and said the "common law of England" contained a "dark catalogue of crimes and punishments." And as a diplomat in England, Rush called that country's criminal code "sanguinary," noting, "Whether the life of their King or the lowest subject be struck at, let the law have its course is the cry in England."[52]

Benjamin Rush regularly wrote letters to John Adams and Thomas Jefferson, and his pivotal role in reigniting the friendship of the two ex-Presidents is legendary. Viewing the two men as "the North and South Poles of the American Revolution," Rush successfully encouraged them to reconcile. Rush's letters, though, did much more than just get Adams and Jefferson to correspond with one another; they also brought to their attention what Rush called "the cause of humanity," with specific references to his advocacy of penal reform.

"Your correspondent," Rush wrote Adams, "has lived in a constant succession of contests with ignorance, prejudice, and vice, in all which his only objects were to lessen the miseries and promote the happiness of his fellow men." Rush told Adams he was fighting "in the cause of truth, humanity, and justice in the present world," and frequently sang the praises of Frederick II of Prussia, who, Rush said, possessed "*the talent to forgive.*" Adams himself kept two editions of Beccaria's book in his personal library, and Adams and Jefferson both admired Dr. Rush. Jefferson once told Rush, "I read with delight every thing which comes from your pen," and after learning of Rush's death, Jefferson wrote to John Adams: "Another of our friends of seventy-six is gone, my dear Sir, another of the co-signers of the Independence of our country. And a better man than Rush could not have left us, more benevolent, more learned, of finer genius, or more honest." A grief-stricken Adams replied, "I know of no Character living or dead, who has done more real good in America."[53]

Ironically, when a federal bill of rights was proposed, Dr. Rush vehemently opposed the idea. An early supporter of a strong central government, Rush told Pennsylvania's ratifying convention that he "considered it an honor to the late convention that this system has not been disgraced with a bill of rights." "Would it not be absurd to frame a formal declaration that our natural rights are acquired from ourselves?" he said. Though Rush rejoiced at state ratifications of the newly proposed Constitution in 1788, he thought a bill of rights unnecessary, even misguided. "The objections which have been urged against the federal Constitution, from its wanting a bill of rights," Rush wrote, "have been reasoned and ridiculed out of credit in every state that has adopted it." "There can be only two securities for liberty in any government, viz., representation and checks," Rush wrote his friend David Ramsay, a fellow graduate of the College of New Jersey, a South Carolina legislator, and the author of an important book, *History of the American Revolution.* "Without them," Rush argued, "a volume of rights would avail nothing; and with them, a declaration of rights is absurd and unnecessary; for the people, where their liberties are committed to an equal representation and to a compound legislature such as we observe in the new government, will always be the sovereigns of their rulers and hold all their rights in their own hands." "To hold them at the mercy of their servants," Rush added, "is disgraceful to the dignity of freeman." Rush placed his trust in the principles of self-government. "Men who call for a bill of rights," he said, "have not recovered from the habits they acquired under the monarchical government of Great Britain."[54]

The English had a tradition of using written instruments to safeguard their rights and liberties, though Parliament could freely alter them. The Magna Carta, the Petition of Right of 1628, the Habeas Corpus Act of 1679, and the English Bill of Rights of 1689 were all venerated examples, the last having been put in place as a result of the Glorious Revolution of 1688. The Glorious Revolution involved the overthrow of James II by an invading army led by the

Dutch stadtholder William III of Orange-Nassau, also known as William of Orange. A Catholic, James II had assumed the throne in 1685 after the death of Charles II and attempted to reinstitute Catholicism in the realm. In July 1685, James II had crushed an armed rebellion by his Protestant nephew the Duke of Monmouth at the Battle of Sedgemoor. He then oversaw, along with his chief legal advisor Lord Chief Justice George Jeffreys, the execution of hundreds of inhabitants of the English West Country in what came to be known as the Bloody Assizes. Many of the executed rebels claimed to be martyrs for the Protestant faith, with the ruthless Lord Chief Justice Jeffreys, himself a Protestant, responsible for many of the executions after Monmouth's failed rebellion. The Duke of Monmouth, the bastard son of Charles II, was himself executed in the Tower of London on July 15, 1685, and other rebels and religious dissenters such as the Quakers were persecuted and imprisoned. James II's regime, it has been noted, "seemed to delight in blood." William III and his wife Mary II, the successors of James II, were Protestants and agreed to accept a declaration of rights before assuming their roles as king and queen in February 1689. "Throughout the eighteenth century," writes historian Harry Dickinson, "no major debate involving any discussion of fundamental political principles took place without the events of 1688–89 being used as a source of inspiration or guidance."[55]

The English Declaration of Rights described William of Orange's call that the Commons and Lords meet at Westminster on January 22, 1689, to establish a government so that "their Religion Lawes and Libertyes might not againe be in danger of being subverted." The Declaration enumerated in detail the wrongs committed by James II's regime and laid out the rights of British subjects and the limits of royal authority. The Declaration specifically listed thirteen "undoubted Rights and Liberties," among them that "excessive Bayle ought not to be required nor excessive fynes imposed nor cruell and unusuall Punishments inflicted." After expressing the popular sentiment that William of Orange would "preserve them from the violation of their rights which they have asserted," the Declaration resolved that William and Mary should be declared king and queen of England. After William accepted the Declaration and promised to "doe all that is in My Power to advance the Welfare and Glory of the Nation," the crown was placed in his hands. The Declaration of Rights was later enacted as a statute commonly known as the Bill of Rights of 1689. William's ascension to the throne marked a new beginning for England, which had seen much turbulence in its governance. In 1649, the House of Commons had established a special court to try Charles I for attempting "to subvert the ancient and fundamental laws and liberties of this nation" and introducing "an arbitrary and tyrannical government." Charles I was executed in 1649 and, for a time, the monarchy was abolished, with a short-lived "Commonwealth"—led by Oliver Cromwell, with power exercised by "the representatives of the people in Parliament"—taking its place. "[I]n the late eighteenth century," Yale law professor Akhil Amar notes, "every schoolboy in America knew that the English Bill of Rights' 1689 ban on excessive bail, excessive fines, and cruel and unusual punishment—a ban repeated virtually verbatim in the Eighth Amendment—arose as a response to the gross behavior of the infamous Judge Jeffreys."[56]

While seeing a federal bill of rights as unnecessary, Dr. Rush, who feared the misuse of power in whatever hands in which it might be placed, had no illusions about the capacity of rulers, legislators, and citizens alike to engage in vile acts. "But are we to consider men entrusted with power as the receptacles of all the depravity of human nature?" Rush asked. "By no means," he answered. "The people," he said, "do not part with their full proportions of it." Echoing Madison's view that men are not angels, Rush wrote: "Reason and revelation both deceive us if they are all wise and virtuous. Is not history as full of the vices of the people as it is of the crimes of the kings?" The "present moral character of the citizens of the United States," Rush explained, "proves too plainly that the people are as much disposed to vice as their rulers, and that nothing but a vigorous and efficient government can prevent their degenerating into savages or devouring each other like beasts of prey." But Rush, a champion of public education, looked forward to "the expansion and dignity the American mind" would acquire under the new federal government, telling David Ramsay: "To look up to a government that establishes justice, insures order, cherishes virtue, secures property, and protects from every species of violence, affords a pleasure that can only be exceeded by looking up, in all circumstances, to an overruling providence. Such a pleasure I hope is before us and our posterity under the influence of the new government."[57]

Dr. Rush was not alone in thinking a federal bill of rights unnecessary. Thomas Paine, for example, saw no need for a bill of rights either. Paine, who sailed for Europe in the spring of 1787, believed that a "bill of rights is more properly a bill of wrongs, and of insult," for he took the view that the people themselves had "natural rights." "Natural rights," Paine explained, "are those which appertain to man in right of his existence." Paine called the English Bill of Rights "but a bargain." Also, Alexander Hamilton thought the "constitution is itself, in every rational sense, and to every useful purpose, a Bill of Rights." The sections of the Constitution "in favour of particular privileges and rights," Hamilton said, adopted the "common and statute law of Great Britain, by which many other rights, not expressed, are equally secured." An American reluctance to import English common-law rules on a wholesale basis, however, is clearly evident in the colonial and postcolonial periods. As U.S. Supreme Court Justices have themselves explained: "For a variety of reasons, including the absence of trained lawyers and judges, the dearth of law books, the religious and ideological commitments of the early settlers, and the novel conditions of the New World, the colonists turned to a variety of other sources in addition to principles of common law." American hostility to the

English often manifested itself in the outright rejection of English common-law principles, with places such as Pennsylvania and New Jersey for a time proscribing by statute the citation of English decisions in their courts.[58]

The U.S. Bill of Rights, of course, was ultimately approved, largely through James Madison's perseverance. Madison, who initially saw a bill of rights as unnecessary, eventually warmed to the idea and promised to work for the passage of one following the U.S. Constitution's adoption. Thomas Jefferson, who supported Madison's efforts to secure passage of a federal bill of rights, had felt the assertion of such rights was essential to the new republic. "A bill of rights," Jefferson believed, "is what the people are entitled to against every government on earth, general or particular, & what no just government should refuse or rest on inference." In the irony of all ironies, the Eighth Amendment—a constitutional amendment Dr. Rush thought unnecessary, though he opposed cruelty—now sits at the very center of America's death penalty debate. The Cruel and Unusual Punishments Clause, which, following the Fourteenth Amendment's ratification, bars all government officials from engaging in acts of cruelty in the administration of justice, thus now stands as the one and only clause of the Constitution that, on its face, might plausibly be read to bar the punishment of death, a cause Dr. Rush fought for his entire adult life.[59]

CHAPTER FOUR

America's Founding Fathers

The American Revolution

The United States of America was forged through revolution. The Stamp Act of 1765, requiring the purchase of revenue stamps for acts of official business, was widely seen by colonists, including the fiery orator Patrick Henry, as unconstitutional. Colonists, who saw themselves as Englishmen, viewed Parliament's acts as an affront to their right not to be taxed by people other than their elected representatives. In protest, mobs in Boston led by the Sons of Liberty took to the streets, destroying houses owned by government officials and hanging in effigy Andrew Oliver, the Massachusetts stamp commissioner. After beheading and burning the straw effigy, the crowd of waterfront laborers called for a hangman's rope, broke into Oliver's mansion and destroyed his property. Other effigies were hanged in Maryland, New York, Pennsylvania, and Virginia, with Richard Henry Lee—later a delegate to the Continental Congress—dressing as a hangman and dispatching effigies of George Grenville, the British exchequer, and George Mercer, the Virginia stamp distributor. In 1776, Lee, a Virginian and one of the signers of the Declaration of Independence, personally offered the motion declaring "that these United Colonies are, and of right ought to be, free and independent states." A mob in Newport, Rhode Island, built a gallows for the stamp collector, forcing him to flee to a British warship, and as rioting spread, stamp officers resigned in Connecticut, Maryland, New Jersey, New York, North Carolina, Pennsylvania, South Carolina, and Virginia. Though the Stamp Act was repealed in 1766, Parliament simultaneously asserted its right to legislate for the colonies "in all cases whatsoever," further alienating the colonists. The Boston Massacre in 1770 and the Boston Tea Party three years later, along with Parliament's passage of the "Intolerable Acts" in 1774, galvanized opposition to Parliament and the English Crown and set the colonists on a path to a protracted war with the mother country. Out of anger and frustration,

American revolutionaries even resorted to tarring and feathering British loyalists or, as a form of intimidation, brought them to the gallows without actually hanging them.[1]

The thirteen American colonies struggled mightily—and at times, it seemed, against all odds—to forge a new nation. The First Continental Congress convened in Philadelphia in 1774, the same year Thomas Jefferson wrote *A Summary View of the Rights of British America,* and issued a declaration that "the inhabitants of the English colonies in North America, by the immutable laws of nature," have certain "Rights"—among them "life, liberty and property." The Second Continental Congress, in 1775, appointed George Washington to command the Continental Army, and the colonists—at Lexington and Concord and later at the Battle of Bunker Hill—began their long fight for independence, a fight that only intensified after George III refused to receive Congress's Olive Branch Petition. By 1776, any hope of a peaceful, amicable resolution had evaporated, with the colonists determined to sever ties with the English monarchy. Thomas Paine's *Common Sense,* first published anonymously in January 1776, made a powerful case for independence from British rule; the Continental Congress authorized the framing of new state constitutions later that year; and on July 4, 1776, Congress formally declared American independence. The first wave of state constitution-making began in Virginia in 1776, and the Articles of Confederation, first proposed in 1777, took effect in 1781 after Maryland, the last holdout, finally ratified them. The Articles of Confederation established "The United States of America," what it called a "perpetual Union," though each state retained "its sovereignty, freedom, and independence, and every power, jurisdiction, and right" not "expressly delegated to the United States." Thus, Congress had only limited powers, with the Articles of Confederation merely establishing "a firm league of friendship" among the states for the purposes of "their common defense, the security of their liberties, and their mutual and general welfare."[2]

Severing ties with the British Empire was in and of itself an audacious act fraught with grave risk. The American spy Nathan Hale, forced to carry his own coffin to his execution on September 22, 1776, was condemned to die by British general William Howe without a trial, leading to Hale's famous last words, "I only regret that I have but one life to lose for my country." Not only did the colonists undertake to fight a powerful military foe, but while at war they had to confront deep divisions within their society and build governmental infrastructure from scratch. "In Virginia," Richard Henry Lee wrote Patrick Henry in April 1776, "we have certainly no Magistrate lawfully qualified to hang a murderer, or any other villain offending ever so atrociously against the state." Born in Virginia but educated in England, Lee had been appointed a justice of the peace in 1757 and went on to chair the judiciary committee of Virginia's House of Burgesses before taking his seat in the Continental Congress. "We cannot," Lee explained in his letter, "be Rebels excluded from the King's protection and Magistrates acting under his authority at the same time." "This proves the indispensable necessity of our taking up government immediately, for the preservation of Society," he said. "Division among ourselves, and the precipice on which we stand with our paper money," Lee wrote again to Patrick Henry in 1778, "are, I verily believe, the sources of their hope," a reference to the enemy. Calling "forgeries of our currency" both "mischievous" and "seriously dangerous," Lee, who told Samuel Adams in 1775 that "Traitors to their Country shall all hang" from a tree, sought swiftly to curtail criminality. "[T]hese Miscreants who forge our money," Lee wrote Henry, "are as much more criminal than most other offenders, as parricide exceeds murder." As Lee explained: "The mildness of our law will not deter from this tempting vice. Certain death on conviction seems the least punishment that can be supposed to answer the purpose." "I believe most nations have agreed in considering and punishing the contamination of money as the highest crimes against Society," he wrote, asking, "Cannot the Assembly be prevailed on to amend the law on this point, and by means of light horse to secure the arrest, and punishment of these Offenders"? In the Carolinas, a number of Tories were hanged as an incentive for others to disavow their ties to Great Britain and accept service in the Continental Army.[3]

Samuel Adams and others held similar views, advocating for severe punishments while the nation was at war and struggling to establish itself. In 1777, Adams wrote harshly of "the Tories in Boston & Massachusetts Bay," calling them "the most dangerous Enemies of America," and asked for the passage of a law swiftly to punish those doing "Injury to our Cause." As Sam Adams wrote to John Pitts: "I cannot conceive why a Law is not made declaratory of Treason & other Crimes & properly to punish those who are guilty of them. If to conspire the Death of a King is Treason and worthy of Death, surely a Conspiracy to ruin a State deserves no less a Punishment." To his wife Betsy, Adams also wrote from Philadelphia on April 1, 1777, to report: "Yesterday an unhappy Man was executed here for attempting to entice some of the Pilots to enter into the Service of Lord Howe. He was first examined by the Board of War, and afterwards tried by a Court Martial and condemned." Adams reported to Betsy that the man had been confined to the gaol; that before his execution "the whole Proceedings of the Court were laid before Congress," which approved the judgment; and that the evidence against the man "was full and clear, but not more so than his own Confession." As Adams reported: "He said that he had been at New York about a Month before he was detected, and that Mr. Galloway, a Man of Fortune & a noted Tory in this State, who last Winter went over to the Enemy, was his Advisor there." "No Doubt there were others here who secretly abetted & supported him," Adams wrote, adding that some persons had disappeared since the man's detection after he attempted to bribe the pilots. In his biography *The Life of George Washington,* Chief Justice John Marshall also noted that Rhode Island's assembly passed an act for inflicting capital punishment on those convicted of supplying the English army or navy with provisions or of holding any traitorous correspondence with Great Britain or any of its agents.[4]

The divisions within American society were intense and real, with major differences of opinion over how best to proceed to secure independence. In March 1782, North Carolina governor Thomas Burke, a member of the Continental Congress from 1777 to 1781, wrote to South Carolina governor John Mathews to say his goal was "to deprive the enemy of the advantages they derive" from having a body of disaffected men "in the heart of the Country," with Burke desiring to make them "either Continental soldiers or prisoners of War." For many, executions were thought necessary to punish British loyalists and to maintain order. Writing to a prior South Carolina governor, John Rutledge, in February 1782, Burke emphasized that "we have executed some Traitors and Felons at Hillsborough, and have some Prospect of recruits from our disaffected." Even while at war, however, there was a major concern about using executions too frequently. For example, inhabitants of the Hillsborough District petitioned the state legislature in one case, that of Thomas Estridge, then "under Sentence of Death for High Treason," to pardon him as well as those "unhappy Citizens who have been deluded by the Artifices of the Enemy." The petitioners called for "Humane Treatment" and noted that Estridge had a "Wife and a Number of Small Children" who could not be supported if the condemned man were hanged. General Nathanael Greene, the commander of military efforts in the Southern Department from December 1780 until the end of the Revolutionary War, also urged moderation, saying "it has ever been my wish to avoid cruelty and the dignity of our cause requires that it should be marked with humanity, justice and moderation." Greene, who supported capital punishment to end "plundering" but opposed policies rooted in "revenge and Persecution," advised his subordinates to end what he termed "private murders," that is, the killing of Tories outside the confines of legitimate warfare. Through his example, Greene hoped to convince loyalists to abandon their support for the British, with Greene seeking "to soften the malignity and deadly resentments subsisting between the Whigs and the tories" and trying to "put a stop as much as possible to that cruel custom of putting people to death after they have surrendered themselves prisoners." "Cruelty," Greene said, "always marks the authors with disgrace and is generally attended with disadvantage." Governor Burke himself advised one of his military officers that, except for the "very mischievous and atrocious," "I wish to see very few submitted to the Executioner."[5]

In the American Revolution, not only did Americans fight the redcoats and vehemently oppose British policies and loyalists, but in the lead-up to it, they had long expressed antipathy for the British judiciary's use of "transportation." Convicts had been sent to the American colonies from England since the seventeenth century, and colonial legislatures and newspapers had railed against this practice and the "cruel murders" committed by such convicts. As the *Pennsylvania Gazette* editorialized in 1751: "When we see our papers filled continually with accounts of the most audacious robberies, the most cruel murders, and infinite other villainies perpetrated by convicts transported from Europe, what melancholy, what terrible reflections it must occasion! What will become of our posterity! These are some of thy favours, Britain! Thou art called our Mother Country; but what good mother ever sent thieves and villains to accompany her children; to corrupt them with their infectious vices, and murder the rest?" With his ever-sharp pen, Benjamin Franklin even suggested that, in exchange for convicts, Pennsylvanians send England rattlesnakes, with Franklin proposing "to have them carefully distributed in St. James's Park, in the Spring Gardens and other places of pleasure about London; in the gardens of all the nobility and gentry throughout the nation; but particularly in the gardens of the Prime Ministers, the Lords of Trade and Members of Parliament; for to them we are most particularly obliged." Rattlesnakes, Franklin said, "seem the most suitable returns for the human serpents sent us by our Mother Country."[6]

Because of the Revolutionary War's high stakes, the Founding Fathers, who had to worry continually about being hanged for treason, longed for the day when Great Britain would recognize America's independence. As Richard Henry Lee wrote Thomas Jefferson in 1779: "It is certain that they begin in England seriously to debate about treating with us as Independent Sovereign States—They are in great distress & confusion—God grant these may increase, until they learn to substitute reason justice & humanity for madness, pride, & cruelty." Conversely, the popular hostility toward opponents of the American Revolution generated a series of treason trials. Between September 1778 and April 1779, twenty-three men were tried in Philadelphia for high treason against Pennsylvania for assisting in the British occupation. Spurred by a Patriotic Society formed to ferret out those "disaffected to the American cause," the identification of traitors only more deeply divided Pennsylvania society as the Supreme Executive Council published the names of 139 suspected collaborators. Though only forty-five accusations of treason were brought to the grand jury, less than half that number proceeded to trial, with James Wilson playing the role of lead defense counsel. Trained by John Dickinson, Wilson was largely successful, with juries acquitting all but four of the accused traitors. Only two of those convicted, Abraham Carlyle and John Roberts, both Quakers, were sentenced to death for aiding the royal cause. Thomas McKean, a signer of the Declaration of Independence who served as the second president of the Continental Congress, served as chief justice of the Pennsylvania Supreme Court while those trials were taking place. In that role, he presided over the case in which Roberts, a miller, was sentenced to die. After the sentencing, McKean preached the Gospel to Roberts, urging him to accept Christ before his execution. "You will probably have but a short time to live,"

McKean said, advising Roberts "to repent," "to be incessant in prayers to the great and merciful God to forgive your manifold transgressions and sins," and "to seek the fellowship, advice and prayers of pious and good men." "Before you launch into eternity," McKean said, "it behooves you to improve the time that may be allowed you in this world." When the executions were carried out in 1778, they were memorialized by a fellow Quaker, diarist Elizabeth Drinker: "They have actually put to death, Hanged on ye Commons, John Roberts and Abraham Carlyle. An awful day it has been."[7]

The Declaration of Independence, drafted principally by Thomas Jefferson, had drawn a line in the sand, capturing the revolutionary zeal of the time. As the thirteen colonies unanimously declared: "We hold these Truths to be self-evident, that all Men are created equal, that they are endowed by their Creator with certain unalienable Rights, that among these are Life, Liberty, and the Pursuit of Happiness." "[T]o secure these Rights," the Declaration of Independence proclaimed, "Governments are instituted among Men, deriving their just Powers from the Consent of the Governed." "[W]henever any Form of Government becomes destructive of these Ends," it added, "it is the Right of the People to alter or to abolish it, and to institute new Government, laying its Foundation on such Principles, and organizing its Powers in such Form, as to them shall seem most likely to effect their Safety and Happiness." In short, the colonists believed they had a natural, God-given right to self-governance, a notion reflected in their long list of grievances. The king, they said, in what resembled a criminal indictment, "has refused his Assent to Laws, the most wholesome and necessary for the public Good"; "has obstructed the Administration of Justice, by refusing his Assent to Laws for establishing Judiciary Powers"; and "has made Judges dependent on his Will alone, for the tenure of their offices, and the amount and payment of their salaries." The Declaration of Independence, Dr. Benjamin Rush said, "produced a new era," causing the state militia "to be actuated with a spirit more than Roman." "The cry of them all is for BATTLE," Rush told Charles Lee, a Virginia planter turned Continental Army general.[8]

Every signer of the Declaration of Independence certainly knew what was at stake—and how much peril they were placing themselves in—by affixing their names. After a Fourth of July celebration in 1811, Dr. Rush wrote John Adams to lament, "Scarcely a word was said of the solicitude and labors and fears and sorrows and sleepless nights of the men who projected, proposed, defended, and subscribed the Declaration of Independence." "Do you recollect your memorable speech upon the day on which the vote was taken?" Rush reminisced twenty-five years after its issuance. "Do you recollect the pensive and awful silence which pervaded the house when we were called up, one after another, to the table of the President of Congress to subscribe what was believed by many at that time to be our own death warrants?" "The silence and gloom of the morning were interrupted," Rush recalled, "only for a moment by

Colonel Harrison of Virginia, who said to Mr. Gerry at the table: 'I shall have a great advantage over you, Mr. Gerry, when we are all hung for what we are now doing. From the size and weight of my body I shall die in a few minutes, but from the lightness of your body you will dance in the air an hour or two before you are dead.'" "This speech procured a transient smile," Rush remembered of the exchange between the rotund Virginia planter Benjamin Harrison and the slender Massachusetts merchant Elbridge Gerry, "but it was soon succeeded by the solemnity with which the whole business was conducted."[9]

The Declaration of Independence proclaimed that it was necessary "for one People to dissolve the Political Bands which have connected them with another" and laid out "the causes which impel them to the Separation." "The History of the present King of Great-Britain," it declared in one grievance, "is a History of repeated Injuries and Usurpations, all having in direct Object the Establishment of an absolute Tyranny over these States." "He has abdicated Government here," it continued, "by declaring us out of his Protection and waging War against us." "He has plundered our Seas, ravaged our Coasts, burnt our Towns, and destroyed the Lives of our People," it said elsewhere, also noting that the king "is, at this Time, transporting large Armies of foreign Mercenaries to compleat the Works of Death, Desolation, and Tyranny, already begun with circumstances of Cruelty and Perfidy, scarcely paralleled in the most barbarous Ages, and totally unworthy the Head of a civilized Nation." John Hancock, the president of the Second Continental Congress, wanted Congress to make the vote on the declaration unanimous, fully aware of the icy reception it would receive in England. "There must be no pulling different ways," Hancock said. "We must all hang together." In response, Benjamin Franklin reportedly rejoined, "Yes, we must indeed all hang together, or most assuredly we shall all hang separately." As historian Edith Gelles aptly notes: "Every man who signed this document did so knowing that his signature confirmed his status as a traitor to England."[10]

In drafting the Declaration of Independence, the Founding Fathers chose their words carefully. Following Richard Henry Lee's resolution for the states to be "absolved from all allegiance to the British Crown," Congress appointed a five-member committee to draft a declaration that could be issued if Congress decided to pursue independence. That committee, which had several meetings, consisted of Thomas Jefferson, the soft-spoken Virginia lawyer known as a talented draftsman; John Adams, the Massachusetts lawyer whose influential *Thoughts on Government* was published in 1776; Benjamin Franklin, the renowned Philadelphia inventor, printer, and statesman; Connecticut's Roger Sherman, another respected lawyer; and New York's Robert Livingston, the first chancellor of New York, then the highest judicial officer in the state. Because of his reputation as a superb writer, Jefferson was selected to produce the first draft, a draft Adams and Franklin edited before passing it along to Sherman and Livingston. Inspired by Enlightenment ideas and

George Mason's draft Virginia Declaration of Rights, Jefferson's preliminary draft sought to recognize "inherent & inalienable rights," language that later morphed into "certain unalienable rights." As early as 1625, the Dutch jurist Hugo Grotius had spoken of the "natural rights" of mankind; his German disciple Samuel Pufendorf had publicized and further refined those natural law teachings; and Swiss natural law theorist Jacques Burlamaqui had published *The Principles of Natural Law* in 1747. Jefferson, familiar with such writings, took a decidedly natural law approach in crafting the Declaration of Independence, with the preamble making reference to "Nature's God" and "the Laws of Nature."[11]

The drafting process for the Declaration of Independence involved small edits and major revisions, evidencing how carefully the founders picked their words. After Jefferson wrote the first draft, he showed the language to Franklin, who had spent decades as a writer and editor. "Will Doctor Franklin be so good as to peruse it and suggest such alterations as his more enlarged view of the subject will dictate?" Jefferson wrote in a cover note. Franklin made only modest changes, tinkering with Jefferson's language, but most memorably crossing out the last three words of Jefferson's phrase "We hold these truths to be sacred and undeniable." Influenced less by one of Jefferson's favorite philosophers, John Locke, and more by David Hume's empiricism and Isaac Newton's scientific determinism, Franklin changed the phrase to "We hold these truths to be self-evident." Congress itself treated Jefferson's draft much less gently, deleting whole passages and sentences. This infuriated Jefferson, who felt his language was better. "I was sitting by Dr. Franklin, who perceived that I was not insensible to these mutilations," Jefferson recalled later. "I have made it a rule whenever in my power," Franklin consoled him, "to avoid becoming the draughtsman of papers to be reviewed by a public body." Franklin then told the story of when he was a journeyman printer and an apprentice hatter came to him with plans to open his own shop. The hatter had composed an inscription for a sign, "John Thompson, Hatter, makes and sells hats for ready money," along with a figure of a hat. But after showing it to his friends, the word "Hatter" was struck out as redundant; "makes" was cut out as his customers, he was told, would not care who made the hats; and "for ready money" was struck out as useless because it was not customary to sell on credit. Franklin joked that, in the end, the inscription was reduced to nothing more than "John Thompson" with a figure of a hat.[12]

The Father of the Revolution

It was the writings of Thomas Paine that set the stage for the Declaration of Independence. The son of Joseph Pain, a Quaker corsetmaker, and Frances Cocke, the daughter of an Anglican lawyer, Thomas Paine was born in Norfolk, England and reared as a Quaker. Criminal cases were heard every March in Thetford, and during that time thieves and lower-class offenders were frequently executed. Gallows Hill itself could be seen from the Paine home, making a lasting impression on young Tom, who came to despise capital punishment. Paine had met Benjamin Franklin, a mentor, in London, and Franklin helped Paine immigrate to America, where the ambitious Paine hoped to make a name for himself. Franklin encouraged his own son-in-law Richard Bache to help Paine find employment and also sent a letter of introduction to his friend Dr. Benjamin Rush. Rush first met Paine in a Philadelphia bookshop in mid-March 1775, and Rush and Paine—who shared a hatred of slavery, with Paine calling that institution a "savage practice"—soon began meeting regularly. After the Battle of Lexington, in which eight militiamen lost their lives and several others were injured, Paine took up the cause of independence and wrote the essay "Thoughts on Defensive War" for the July 1775 issue of *The Pennsylvania Magazine.* Signed "A Lover of Peace," Paine's essay wrestled with whether violent means could be legitimately used to defend human liberty, a question Paine resolved by writing: "I am thus far a Quaker, that I would gladly agree with all the world to lay aside the use of arms, and settle matters by negotiation; but unless the whole world will, the matter ends, and I take up my musket and thank heaven he has put it in my power." After the Continental Congress declared independence, Paine was true to his word. He enlisted in Pennsylvania's military, served as an aide-de-camp to General Nathanael Greene, and fought for American independence.[13]

Benjamin Rush himself suggested that Paine write what would become his runaway bestseller, *Common Sense.* As Dr. Rush wrote to James Cheetham, Paine's biographer: "I called upon Mr. Paine and suggested to him the propriety of preparing our citizens for a perpetual separation of our country from Great Britain by means of a work of such length as would obviate all the objections to it. He seized the idea with avidity and immediately began his famous pamphlet in favor of that measure." After composing a first draft of the opening section of the manuscript, Paine brought the pages to Rush's house and read them aloud, line by line, editing the text along the way. When the manuscript was completed, Rush told Paine to put it into the hands of Benjamin Franklin, Samuel Adams, and James Wilson for their review. Rush also put Paine in touch with Robert Bell, a Scottish-born Philadelphia publisher who had published William Blackstone's *Commentaries* in 1772. Bell, a supporter of independence, agreed to run the risk of printing the radical pamphlet, with Rush suggesting the pamphlet's title. Paine had originally called his pamphlet *Plain Truth,* but Rush suggested *Common Sense,* a title Paine—in Rush's words—"instantly adopted." The pamphlet, priced at two shillings, sold an astounding 120,000 copies by year's end and was read aloud in public, discussed at length in schools and clubs, and reprinted in newspapers.[14]

In *Common Sense,* Paine wrote that "[t]he cause of America is in a great measure the cause of all mankind." "The laying a country desolate with fire and sword, declaring war against the natural rights of all mankind, and extirpating the defenders thereof from the face of the earth," he wrote, "is the concern of every man to whom nature hath given the power of feeling." In discussing "the English constitution" and "the cruel disposition of the British Court," Paine saw only "Monarchical tyranny," saying that royal hereditary succession had only laid "the world in blood and ashes." Seeing reconciliation with England as a "fallacious dream," Paine actively encouraged the taking up of arms, writing that "[a] government of our own is our natural right." To his Quaker friends, Paine argued: "We fight neither for revenge nor conquest; neither from pride nor passion; we are not insulting the world with our fleets and armies, nor ravaging the globe for plunder." "Beneath the shade of our own vines," Paine wrote, "are we attacked; in our own houses, and on our own lands, is the violence committed against us." "We view our enemies," he added, "in the characters of Highwaymen and Housebreakers, and having no defence for ourselves in the civil law, are obliged to punish them by the military one, and apply the sword, in the very case, where you have before now, applied the halter." "If the bearing of arms be sinful," Paine explained, "the first going to war must be more so, by all the difference between wilful attack and unavoidable defence."15

At the end of 1776, Paine wrote that "[t]hese are the times that try men's souls," a reflection of the everyday hardships faced by American soldiers and patriots. Only after the Revolutionary War ended in 1783 did Paine say those trying times "are over" and proclaim that "the greatest and completest revolution that the world ever knew" had been "gloriously and happily accomplished." With independence and what he called "an inheritance for posterity" achieved, Paine urged Americans in April 1783 to recalibrate their "senses" and "pass from the extremes of danger to safety—from the tumult of war to the tranquility of peace." As Paine wrote: "To see it in our power to make a world happy—to teach mankind the art of being so—to exhibit, on the theatre of the universe a character hitherto unknown—and to have, as it were, a new creation intrusted to our hands, are honors that command reflection, and can neither be too highly estimated, nor too gratefully received." While Paine, who detested the use of paper currency, suggested three years later, in 1786, that any legislator even proposing such a system ought to be punished by death, Paine later advocated the death penalty's abolition, even for treason against the state. "When, in countries that are called civilized, we see age going to the workhouse and youth to the gallows," Paine wrote in *Rights of Man,* "something must be wrong in the system of government." "Civil government does not exist in executions," Paine wrote, "but in making such provision for the instruction of youth and the support of age, as to exclude, as much as possible, profligacy from the one and despair from the other."16

England's Glorious Revolution of 1688, a revolt led by Englishmen tired of the Crown's interference with their rights, had led to a constitutional monarchy and to the English Bill of Rights that Paine would have studied as a young man. In *Rights of Man,* published in 1791 as a response to Edmund Burke's *Reflections on the Revolution in France,* Paine expressed admiration for what the English Parliament of 1688 had done for the English people, though he took issue with "binding and controlling posterity to the end of time." "Every age and generation," Paine wrote, "must be as free to act for itself *in all cases* as the age and generations which preceded it." "The vanity and presumption of governing beyond the grave," Paine argued, "is the most ridiculous and insolent of all tyrannies." As Paine explained in *Rights of Man:* "Every generation is, and must be, competent to all the purposes which its occasions require. It is the living, and not the dead, that are to be accommodated. When man ceases to be, his power and his wants cease with him; and having no longer any participation in the concerns of this world, he has no longer any authority in directing who shall be its governors, or how its government shall be organised, or how administered." "I am contending for the rights of the *living,*" Paine emphasized, saying that no parliament or "any generation of men" ever possessed "the right or the power of binding and controuling posterity to the 'end of time'" or of making "clauses, acts or declarations" that attempted to do so. "It requires but a very small glance of thought," Paine wrote, "to perceive that altho' laws made in one generation often continue in force through succeeding generations, yet they continue to derive their force from the consent of the living."[17]

Paine's worldview thus became clear. "Every place has its Bastille, and every Bastille its despot," Paine inveighed in *Rights of Man,* expressing the view that every generation has the right to control its own destiny. As Paine wrote: "The circumstances of the world are continually changing, and the opinions of men change also; and as government is for the living, and not for the dead, it is the living only that has any right in it. That which may be thought right and found convenient in one age may be thought wrong and found inconvenient in another." "In such cases," Paine asked rhetorically, "who is to decide, the living or the dead?" After invoking the storming of the Bastille, the royal prison seized by the Parisian crowd on July 14, 1789, Paine defended the French Revolution and all the chaos of the crowd that ensued. "Whom has the National Assembly brought to the scaffold?" he asked. "None," he answered, saying that "but four or five persons," including the governor of the Bastille, were seized by the populace and instantly put to death. "Their heads were struck upon spikes, and carried about the city," Paine wrote, noting that "it is upon this mode of punishment that Mr. Burke"—a reference to the British statesman Edmund Burke—"builds a great part of his tragic scene." "Let us therefore examine," Paine wrote in countering Burke's *Reflections on the Revolution in France*, "how men came by the idea of punishing in this manner." "They learn it," he said, "from the governments they live under; and retaliate the punishments they have been accustomed to behold." As Paine explained:

"The heads stuck upon spikes, which remained for years upon Temple Bar, differed nothing in the horror of the scene from those carried about upon spikes at Paris; yet this was done by the English Government." Temple Bar, demarcated by a stone gateway designed by Christopher Wren, divided London from Westminster, and in the eighteenth century the heads of traitors were exhibited on the roof of that structure. "It may perhaps be said," Paine added in his book, "that it signifies nothing to a man what is done to him after he is dead; but it signifies much to the living; it either tortures their feelings or hardens their hearts, and in either case it instructs them how to punish when power falls into their hands."[18]

For Paine, executions were "barbarous" and "cruel spectacles" to be done away with. "Lay then the axe to the root, and teach governments humanity. It is their sanguinary punishments which corrupt mankind," Paine wrote in 1791, the same year the U.S. Bill of Rights was ratified. As Paine wrote in *Rights of Man*:

> In England the punishment in certain cases is by hanging, drawing and quartering; the heart of the sufferer is cut out and held up to the view of the populace. In France, under the former Government, the punishments were not less barbarous. Who does not remember the execution of Damien, torn to pieces by horses? The effect of those cruel spectacles exhibited to the populace is to destroy tenderness or excite revenge; and by the base and false idea of governing men by terror, instead of reason, they become precedents. It is over the lowest class of mankind that government by terror is intended to operate, and it is on them that it operates to the worst effect. They have sense enough to feel they are the objects aimed at; and they inflict in their turn the examples of terror they have been instructed to practise.

Comparing the Parisians who carried heads on iron spikes to the English mobs who committed "the burnings and devastations in London in 1780," Paine tried to explain the crowd's behavior in carrying out summary executions "on the spot." "These outrages," Paine wrote, "were not the effect of the principles of the Revolution, but of the degraded mind that existed before the Revolution, and which the Revolution is calculated to reform." "I detest everything that is cruel," Paine wrote three years later in *The Age of Reason,* specifically referring to "cruel and torturous executions."[19]

The French Revolution sought to secure people's natural rights, though it played out much differently than the American Revolution. On July 11, 1789, the Marquis de Lafayette had presented a declaration of rights to France's National Assembly. Jefferson, then in France, had reviewed a draft of that declaration, even forwarding a copy to Madison, telling him that everyone in France "is trying their hands at forming declarations of rights." While in Paris, Jefferson sent official reports and also wrote Paine to describe the rapidly unfolding events, reporting that the National Assembly considered its first task to be the drafting of "a Declaration of the natural and imprescriptible rights of man." Lafayette's presentation was followed on July 14, 1789, with the storming of the Bastille, the prison fortress in Paris holding common criminals and others imprisoned for printing forbidden ideas. "The Governour and Lt. Governour were put to death and their heads elevated upon long poles, which were carried through the principal streets and exhibited in Palais Royal (which Mr. Govr. Morris very properly calls the Liberty pole of France) before six o'clock this evening," wrote Major Elnathon Haskell, an American then living in Paris. "They took all the arms, discharged the prisoners," and "cut off" the heads of the governor and lieutenant governor at "the Grève," "the place of public execution," Jefferson wrote of the siege of the royal prison, noting that "[t]he decapitation of M. de Launai, the Governor of the Bastille, worked powerfully through the night on the whole aristocratical party."[20]

Over time, Jefferson stood by the French revolutionaries even as they resorted to indiscriminate violence. In the midst of the upheaval, his reform-minded friend the Duc de La Rochefoucauld was actually pulled from his coach and killed in front of his own wife and mother. Jefferson saw the French Revolution as having been "awakened" by America's revolution, and he told Lafayette that one did not travel "from despotism to liberty in a feather-bed." In 1793, Jefferson thus justified the use of violence as he wrote of the French Revolution: "The liberty of the whole earth was depending on the issue of the contest, and was ever such a prize won with so little innocent blood? My own affections have been deeply wounded by some of the martyrs to this cause, but rather than it should fail, I would have seen half the earth desolated." In an autobiographical statement written in 1821, Jefferson still expressed understanding for the French people's zealous desire for a "fixed constitution, not subject to changes at the will of the King." "Nor should we wonder at this pressure," Jefferson wrote, "when we consider the monstrous abuses of power under which this people were ground to powder, when we pass in review . . . the cruelty of the criminal code generally, the atrocities of the Rack, the venality of judges, and their partialities to the rich." "Surely under such a mass of misrule and oppression," Jefferson concluded, "a people might justly press for a thoro' reformation."[21]

On the day when the Bastille fell, however, both Jefferson and Gouverneur Morris were more circumspect, even shocked by what was happening before their eyes. When Morris saw the heads on display, he changed his tune. After seeing a mutilated seventy-five-year-old victim—his head on a spike and his body dragged naked on the ground—and describing another man "put to death and cut to Pieces, the Populace carrying about the mangled Fragments with a Savage Joy," Morris recorded in his diary: "Gracious God what a People!" After a sleepless night, Morris wrote to his wife: "I was never till now fully apprized of the mildness of American character." "I have seen my countrymen enraged and threatening," he wrote. "But," he continued, "we know not what it is to slay the defenseless Victim who is in our Power. We cannot parade the Heads of our fellow Citizens and drag the mangled Carcasses through the streets. We cannot feast our Eyes on such Spectacles." "That these People were tyrannical I shall agree tho I do not know it," he wrote Mrs. Morris, adding, "But to be executed without Trial without being heard and then with such a horrid Spectacle." When Morris and Jefferson had tea a day after what happened, Jefferson wrote that very day to John Jay to lament the people's "bloodthirsty spirit."[22]

Paine's fervent anti–death penalty stance is clear from his floor speeches. On January 15, 1793, in France's National Assembly, Paine invoked Maximilien Robespierre's earlier call to abolish the death penalty in pleading that Louis XVI's life be spared. "It has already been proposed to abolish the punishment of death," Paine said, "and it is with infinite satisfaction that I recollect the humane and excellent oration pronounced by Robespierre on that subject in the Constituent Assembly." "This cause," he urged, "must find its advocates in every corner where enlightened politicians and lovers of humanity exist, and it ought above all to find them in this assembly." As Paine explained: "Monarchical governments have trained the human race, and inured it to the sanguinary arts and refinements of punishment; and it is exactly the same punishment which has so long shocked the sight and tormented the patience of the people, that now, in their turn, they practice in revenge upon their oppressors." "But it becomes us," he added, "to be strictly on our guard against the abomination and perversity of monarchical examples: as France has been the first of European nations to abolish royalty, let her also be the first to abolish the punishment of death, and to find out a milder and more effectual substitute."[23]

On January 19, 1793, a determined Paine, who became an honorary delegate in the French assembly because of his role in the American Revolution, expressed regret over the National Assembly's vote to sentence Louis XVI to death. The National Convention voted 387 to 334 in favor of a death sentence, which Paine protested: "I voted against it from both moral motives and motives of public policy." In his speech to his fellow delegates, Paine was twice interrupted by the Jacobin journalist Jean-Paul Marat, who questioned the translation of Paine's words and said Paine was "incompetent" to vote on the question because he was a Quaker whose "religious principles" were "opposed to capital punishment." Still, Paine persisted in his oration:

> I know that the public mind of France, and particularly that of Paris, has been heated and irritated by the dangers to which they have been exposed; but could we carry our thoughts into the future, when the dangers are ended and the irritations forgotten, what to-day seems an act of justice may then appear an act of vengeance. [*Murmurs.*] My anxiety for the cause of France has become for the moment concern for her honor. If,

on my return to America, I should employ myself on a history of the French Revolution, I had rather record a thousand errors on the side of mercy, than be obliged to tell one act of severe justice. . . .

France has but one ally—the United States of America. That is the only nation that can furnish France with naval provisions, for the kingdoms of northern Europe are, or soon will be, at war with her. It unfortunately happens that the person now under discussion is considered by the Americans as having been the friend of their revolution. His execution will be an affliction to them, and it is in your power not to wound the feelings of your ally. Could I speak the French language I would descend to your bar, and in their name become your petitioner to respite the execution of the sentence on Louis.

Paine—a spiritual person, though dismissive of organized religion and Quaker pacifism—came to categorically oppose state-sanctioned executions. He himself had once been assaulted at a dinner party at the Palais Égalité by a Captain Grimstone, an assault that could have carried the penalty of death. Some of Paine's friends favored Grimstone's prosecution, but Paine, the deist with an aversion to executions, arranged a passport for Grimstone to travel out of the country, even paying his attacker's traveling expenses.[24]

Despite Paine's pleas, Louis Capet, the French monarch now stripped of his royal title, was guillotined on January 21, 1793, in a public square renamed "Place de la Révolution," for plotting against the French Revolution. When the news reached America in late March 1793, the reaction—not surprisingly—was mixed. George Washington and Alexander Hamilton were aghast at all the bloodshed in France, and John Adams decried Robespierre, Marat, and company as "furies." Hamilton singled out Marat and Robespierre as "assassins still reeking with the blood of murdered fellow citizens," and condemned "the horrid and disgusting scenes" playing out in France. "Dragon's teeth have been sown in France and come up monsters," Adams said, having special reason to despair. The English-speaking Duc de La Rochefoucauld, the grandson of a famous French moralist, befriended Adams in Paris and translated the American Declaration of Independence. He was stoned to death by a mob, which led Adams ruefully to tell his wife Abigail: "The whole drama of the world is such tragedy that I am weary of the spectacle." Adams said he had no heart for "king-killing" and was appalled by toasts drunk to Robespierre and Marat. Though Adams, like Washington, said nothing publicly, Adams told a correspondent in England: "Mankind will in time discover that unbridled majorities are as tyrannical and cruel as unlimited despots." Hamilton noted that all the violence had "cured" him of his "goodwill for the French Revolution," explaining that a struggle for liberty "sullied by crimes and extravagancies" loses its respectability. He called the events in France a "state of things the most cruel, sanguinary, and violent that ever stained the annals of mankind." On the other hand, Jefferson, who once called Louis XVI "a good man" and "an honest man," privately observed that monarchs were now "amenable to punishment like other criminals." In a letter written in May 1794, as executions in Paris reached nearly eight hundred a month, Jefferson wrote Tench Coxe, the assistant secretary of the treasury under Alexander Hamilton, to say that he awaited the day when "kings, nobles, and priests" would be brought "to the scaffolds which they have been so long deluging with human blood." While Madison expressed qualms about "the follies and barbarities" in Paris, he, too, continued to admire the French Revolution, describing it as "wonderful in its progress." If the king was a traitor, Madison said, "he ought to be punished as well as another man."[25]

In the end, Paine's revolutionary zeal—in particular, his meddling in French politics—nearly cost him his life. By 1792, the French king Louis XVI was jailed, and Paine—charged with seditious libel in England for attacking hereditary monarchy in *Rights of Man* but tipped off by the poet William Blake that authorities planned to arrest him—fled Britain for the continuing tumult of France. After taking a boat from Dover to Calais, Paine, a refugee whose book was banned in England, became an honorary French citizen and a delegate to France's National Convention. In Paris, a guillotine, which came to symbolize the French Revolution, would be erected near the Tuileries, with 1,400 political prisoners killed in France in the September Massacres. "Let the blood of traitors flow," Jean-Paul Marat, one of the French Revolution's leaders, said approvingly, a sentiment echoed by his Jacobin compatriot Maximilien Robespierre, who likewise favored Louis XVI's execution. Paine—never afraid to speak his mind, even after his likeness was burned in effigy and the English found him guilty of libel in absentia—soon got caught up in the intrigue of French politics and the Reign of Terror led by Robespierre. After war broke out between England and France and he alienated Robespierre by pleading in the Convention that Louis XVI's life be spared, the English-speaking Paine was arrested in 1793 as an enemy of France. In November 1793, Robespierre had called for action against "foreign conspirators" in France, and on Christmas Eve the police had arrested Paine.[26]

The author of *Common Sense*, suddenly unwelcome in both England and France, was condemned to die and taken to Luxembourg Prison with another foreigner, Anacharsis Cloots, a Prussian participant in the French Revolution. As time wore on, the Reign of Terror escalated. The Jacobins guillotined scores of political opponents, with 2,600 people executed the following summer in Paris alone, and Paine barely escaped that fate, avoiding execution only through a stroke of luck. As Paine reported years later, 168 people were taken from the Luxembourg Prison in one night, with 160 people guillotined the next day. A guard had walked through the prison, putting chalk marks on the cell doors of condemned prisoners, but Paine's door was open at the time. When the door was closed, the mark on it was hidden from view, fortuitously saving Paine from the executioner. Though the public prosecutor on July 24 had scheduled Paine for execution, Paine had collapsed that month with a fever that nearly killed him. The fact that Paine's cellmates had asked permission to keep their cell door open so that a breeze might enter to ease Paine's fever led to his accidental reprieve. After ten months in prison and the overthrow of Robespierre, Paine was finally freed on November 5, 1794, through the efforts of James Monroe, an admirer of the pamphleteer and then America's minister to France. Monroe's fearless wife Elizabeth, who traveled with her husband to France, herself braved Parisian mobs during the Reign of Terror to go by coach to the notorious Plessis prison near the Sorbonne to save the Marquis de Lafayette's wife Adrienne from the guillotine. After Lafayette had been wounded at the Battle of Brandywine near Philadelphia in 1777, then-Lieutenant James Monroe, a war hero who rose to become President of the country he fought to establish, had tended to Lafayette's wounds through the night, making the men life-long friends. Robespierre—who once opposed the death penalty, but then condemned others to die—was, ironically, himself executed in 1794.[27]

The U.S. Constitution

The Treaty of Paris, signed in 1783, ended America's hard-fought War of Independence, but the Articles of Confederation conferred too little power on the federal government. While providing for the conduct of war and diplomacy, the Articles of Confederation failed to create a federal judiciary and made Congress impotent. Instead, each state retained the exclusive power to handle and prosecute offenders, even those accused of the most serious crimes. According to Article IV of the Articles of Confederation: "If any person guilty of, or charged with, treason, felony, or other high misdemeanor in any State, shall flee from justice, and be found in any of the United States, he shall, upon demand of the Governor or executive power of the State from which he fled, be delivered up and removed to the State having jurisdiction of his offense." "Full faith and credit shall be given in each of these States to the records, acts, and judicial proceedings of the courts and magistrates of every other State," Article IV proclaimed, making clear that states—through comity, not federal judges—would enforce state-court judgments. The Articles of Confederation, addressing matters of foreign relations and giving Benjamin Franklin, John Adams, and John Jay the necessary authority to negotiate the end of hostilities with British diplomats, made the national government, in terms of domestic policy, extremely vulnerable and weak. Shays's Rebellion, a tumultuous armed uprising in western Massachusetts to halt farm foreclosures, would, just a few years after the Treaty of Paris was signed, show the need for a much stronger national government.[28]

A veteran of the Revolutionary War, Daniel Shays led a rebellion in 1786 and early 1787 that closed the state courts and prevented the prosecution of debtors. Two thousand farmers—some donning their old Continental Army uniforms—had risen up to protest taxes that had either bankrupted or impoverished them. After shutting down the state supreme court, the angry farmers had marched to a federal arsenal, intent on seizing arms, artillery, and ammunition. Alarmed, the governor of Massachusetts organized a private militia of four thousand men, and Congress dispatched General Henry Knox to raise a federal army to put down the rebels. The rebellion, quashed in February 1787, was short-lived, but the threat of anarchy was real. Benjamin Franklin called the rebellion the work of "disorderly people," while Abigail Adams, who closely followed public events, wrote Thomas Jefferson to tell him it was the work of "desperadoes, without conscience" and "a deluded multitude." Her husband John had a different take, though, telling Jefferson not to be alarmed "at the late Turbulence in New England," what the fiery Adams called a "Commotion" that "will terminate in additional Strength to Government." From Paris, Jefferson responded coolly, telling Abigail: "I like a little rebellion now and then. It is like a storm in the Atmosphere." To Madison, he said much the same thing: "I hold it that a little rebellion now and then is a good thing, and as necessary in the political world as storms in the physical." To Colonel William Smith, the Adamses' son-in-law, Jefferson famously wrote: "The tree of liberty must be refreshed from time to time with the blood of patriots and . tyrants." Shays's Rebellion more than anything else risked the country's descent into lawlessness, sparking the need for the 1787 Constitutional Convention in Philadelphia.[29]

The Constitutional Convention, working in secret, set out to deal with the crisis of confidence provoked by Shays's Rebellion. A committee composed of Alexander Hamilton, George Wythe, and Charles Pinckney drew up the rules and procedures for the convention, and under those rules, "nothing spoken in the House" could "be printed, or otherwise published, or communicated without leave." Journalists and other spectators were forbidden from attending the proceedings; delegates were sworn to secrecy, with George Washington reprimanding delegates after proposed resolutions were mislaid, threatening public disclosure; and after completing their daily business, delegates had to hold their tongues even as they ran the gauntlet of newspaper reporters and beggars awaiting them outside. Outside the walls of the state house, the prisoners at the Walnut Street Jail—in close proximity to the Convention proceedings, and cursing anyone who ignored them—thrust long poles with cloth caps on the ends through the prison's barred windows, seeking alms. Meanwhile, inside the Convention, James Madison, intent on recording the proceedings for posterity's sake, sat in the front row so he could take minutes. Madison's copious notes of the secret proceedings were not published until decades later, demonstrating the Framers' intent to let the Constitution's words—the product of deliberation and compromise—speak for themselves. To polish those words, a five-member Committee of Style and Arrangement, chaired by William Samuel Johnson, was appointed to craft the final work product. That committee, also made up of Alexander Hamilton, Rufus King, James Madison, and Gouverneur Morris, called upon the flamboyant Morris—who had a wooden leg—to do much of its work. The victim of a carriage accident, Morris feared mob rule, once advising that a few mutinous seamen be hanged at each port as examples. Morris carefully arranged the articles of the Constitution, honing and revising its prose and adding his own rhetorical flourishes. "As its chief draftsman," historian Ron Chernow writes, "Morris shrank the original twenty-three articles to seven and wrote the great preamble with its ringing opening, 'We the People of the United States.'" Madison himself paid tribute to Morris's drafting skills, writing, "The *finish* given to the style and arrangement fairly belongs to the pen of Mr. Morris."[30]

The punishment of crime is a core function of government, but the Constitutional Convention, at which thirty-four of the fifty-five participating delegates were lawyers or had at least studied law, debated criminal law issues only a modest amount. Piracy, a crime then universally punishable by death, was raised in connection with a provision giving Congress the authority "[t]o define and punish Piracies and Felonies committed on the high Seas, and Offences against the Law of Nations." As the scholar Timothy Goodman explains: "Given the substantial threat against American interests on the high seas, piracy was a key concern at the 1787 Constitutional Convention at Philadelphia. Concerns over the threat of piracy prompted the Founding Fathers to include in Article I, Section 8 of the Constitution the power of Congress to define and punish piracy." Dealing with pirates—including those from Algiers, Tripoli, and Tunis, North Africa's "Barbary" states—would remain a serious challenge for the new American government to face. Counterfeiting, too, came up at the Convention, with the same section of the Constitution authorizing Congress "[t]o provide for the Punishment of counterfeiting the Securities, and current Coin of the United States." That authority "was necessary," writes the scholar Brandon Bigelow, "because the Constitution rejected the common law conception of treason—of which counterfeiting was a part—in favor of a more restrictive definition." In *The Federalist No. 42,* James Madison emphasized that "[t]he punishment of counterfeiting the public securities, as well as the current coin, is submitted of course to that authority which is to secure the value of both."[31]

At the Convention, limited discussion of the death penalty did occur, but it was mainly in connection with the Bankruptcy Clause and the Treason Clause. The Bankruptcy Clause was adopted on September 3, 1787, with Roger Sherman of Connecticut the sole vote against it. "Mr. Sherman," the record reveals, "observed that Bankruptcies were in some cases punishable with death by the laws of England & He did not chuse to grant a power by which that might be done here." Before the vote, Gouverneur Morris of Pennsylvania, as one of many influential delegates, had attempted to reassure Roger Sherman. As it was reported: "Mr. GOVR, MORRIS said this was an extensive & delicate subject. He would agree to it because he saw no danger of abuse of the power by the Legislature of the U.S." The debate over the Treason Clause centered largely on how treason should be defined and whether it could be committed against a state (as opposed to the United States). "This Country must be united. If persuasion does not unite it, the sword will," Gouverneur Morris urged his colleagues, adding that "[t]he stronger party . . . will make traytors of the weaker; and the Gallows & Halter will finish the work of the sword." After the Framers debated the scope of the Treason Clause and settled on a narrow definition of treason, the First Congress passed a law making treason punishable by death, though at the Convention itself the Framers did not mandate the punishment of death and rejected an attempt to exclude "cases of treason" from the President's pardoning power.[32]

Indeed, at Virginia's ratifying convention, James Madison expressly defended vesting the pardoning power in the President, saying it would have been "extremely improper to vest it in the House of Representatives, and not much less so to place it in the Senate" because "numerous bodies were actuated more or less by passion, and might in the moment of vengeance forget humanity." In his debate with George Mason, Madison argued: "It was an established practice in Massachusetts for the Legislature to determine in such cases." "It was found," Madison said, "that two different sessions, before each of which the question came, with respect to pardoning the delinquents of the rebellion, were governed precisely by different sentiments—the one would execute with universal vengeance, and the other would extend general mercy." George Mason—in one of his "Objections to the Constitution," which were widely distributed throughout the states—had argued that the President ought not to have the power of pardoning, because he might pardon crimes he might himself instigate. Mason also said that Congress, using the Necessary and Proper Clause, might "constitute new crimes, inflict unusual and severe punishment, and extend their power as far as they shall think proper; so that the State Legislatures have no security for the powers now presumed to remain to them; or the people for their rights."[33]

The U.S. Constitution, as originally conceived, adopted, and then ratified, contains several protections for those accused or convicted of crimes. Article I, Section 9 provides that "[t]he Privilege of the Writ of Habeas Corpus shall not be suspended, unless when in Cases of Rebellion or Invasion the public Safety may require it." That section also provides that "[n]o Bill of Attainder or ex post facto Law shall be passed," with parallel language in Article I, Section 10 providing that "[n]o State shall . . . pass any Bill of Attainder" or "ex post facto Law." Bills of attainder and ex post facto laws, Madison wrote in *The Federalist No. 44*, "are contrary to the first principles of the social compact, and to every principle of sound legislation." "Treason against the United States," Article III also provides, "shall consist only in levying War against them, or in adhering to their Enemies, giving them Aid and Comfort." And the right to trial by jury, which the founders saw as a fundamental check on government power, was also explicitly recognized in the original text of the Constitution. Thus, Article III, Section 2 states: "The Trial of all Crimes, except in Cases of Impeachment, shall be by Jury; and such Trial shall be held in the State where the said Crimes shall have been committed." John Adams called jury trials "the heart and lungs of liberty," and Thomas Jefferson considered them "the only anchor ever yet imagined by man" to hold a government "to the principles of its constitution." "Trial by jury," Jefferson said, "is part of that bright constellation which has gone before us and guided our steps through an age of revolution and reformation."[34]

The protections included in the Constitution to protect individual rights were significant, though hardly comprehensive. The writ of habeas corpus, a procedural device for subjecting restraints on liberty to judicial review, had originated in England and soon became a symbol—and a powerful guardian—of individual liberty. Ex post facto laws, unequivocally outlawed by America's Founding Fathers at both the federal and state levels, were laws that imposed punishment for acts not punishable when they were committed or that added punishment to acts already prohibited by law. Bills of attainder, used for centuries in England and once legally permitted in America, were legislative acts deciding an individual's fate in the absence of a jury. In essence, a legislative body would sit in judgment, taking the place of normal courtroom procedures. James Iredell, a Justice of the U.S. Supreme Court from 1790 until 1799, called bills of attainder, which the Constitution explicitly bars, "outrageous" and "despotic." Thomas Jefferson, who once drafted one, found them appropriate if used in a proper context, though his views represented a minority position. Responding to what he called a critic's "diatribe" against them, Jefferson once wrote: "The occasion and proper office of a bill of attainder is this: When a person charged with a crime withdraws from justice, or resists it by force, either in his own or a foreign country, no other means of bringing him to trial or punishment being practicable, a special act is passed by the legislature adapted to the particular case." The U.S. Supreme Court later explicitly held that the Bill of Attainder Clauses "reflected the Framers' belief that the Legislative Branch is not so well suited as politically independent judges and juries to the task of ruling upon the blameworthiness of, and levying appropriate punishment upon, specific persons."[35]

The Constitution the country's leaders adopted in 1787 also contains, as originally conceived, a few other important safeguards for criminals and criminal suspects. Article II, Section 2 gives the President the "Power to grant Reprieves and Pardons for Offenses against the United States, except in Cases of Impeachment." This power, derived by the Framers from the British monarch's power to alter or reduce punishments, confers an almost unreviewable authority to reduce a sentence imposed by a court. The President, the Supreme

Court has held, can even commute a prisoner's sentence of death to life imprisonment subject to the condition that the prisoner not be eligible for parole. The power to "reprieve," in fact, has long been associated with the suspension or commutation of a death sentence. For treason cases, which had been common during the Revolutionary War and in the period thereafter, as exemplified by the prosecution of Aaron Burr, Article III, Section 3 conferred special evidentiary protections. "No Person shall be convicted of Treason unless on the Testimony of two Witnesses to the same overt Act, or on Confession in open Court," reads a key provision. At the Constitutional Convention, Benjamin Franklin, worried about wrongful convictions, successfully advocated requiring two witnesses instead of one to an overt act of treason. John Marshall, who in 1807 sat in judgment as the trial judge in Burr's sensational case, would himself conclude that insufficient evidence of treason had been proffered to prove the alleged conspiracy. Article IV, Section 2 of the Constitution further provides that "[t]he Citizens of each State shall be entitled to all Privileges and Immunities of Citizens in the several States." The concept of privileges and immunities had also been included in the Articles of Confederation, and, as Yale law professor Akhil Amar puts it, the "simple idea" behind the Article IV clause "was that in the domain of civil rights—'Privileges and Immunities'—no state should discriminate against a sister-state citizen as such."[36]

Congress and the Northwest Ordinance

Although the Constitution as originally approved did not include a prohibition on cruel and unusual punishments, the Continental Congress, meeting in New York City, passed the Northwest Ordinance on July 13, 1787, just weeks before the Constitutional Convention finished its work in Philadelphia. That law, titled "An Ordinance for the government of the territory of the United States northwest of the river Ohio," read in part: "All persons shall be bailable, unless for capital offences, where the proof shall be evident or the presumption great. All fines shall be moderate; and no cruel or unusual punishments shall be inflicted." Drafted by Massachusetts lawyer Nathan Dane, the Northwest Ordinance established governance for the territory that became Illinois, Indiana, Michigan, Ohio, Wisconsin, and parts of Minnesota. It was adopted under the auspices of the Articles of Confederation, and its sixth article further provided: "There shall be neither slavery nor involuntary servitude in the said territory, otherwise than in the punishment of crimes whereof the party shall have been duly convicted." That language was derived from a 1784 proposal made by Thomas Jefferson—the slave owner who, in *Notes on the State of Virginia,* expressed hostility toward slavery—as part of a committee examining governance issues for western lands. "The whole commerce between master and slave," Jefferson wrote in the early 1780s, "is a perpetual exercise of the most boisterous passions, the most unremitting despotism on the one part, and degrading submissions on the other." The carving out of "the punishment of crimes" in the Northwest Ordinance left officials unambiguously free to require hard labor for those convicted of crimes.[37]

The Northwest Ordinance of 1787 was historic, landmark legislation. It barred slavery in the new territories, and—unlike Virginia's Declaration of Rights barring "cruel and unusual punishments"—it prohibited "cruel or unusual punishments." The governance of western lands was then a hot topic of debate, though the difference in wording between Virginia's declaration and the language of the Northwest Ordinance attracted no attention. On July 14, 1789, following the U.S. Constitution's ratification, the First Congress took up the Northwest Ordinance again when another committee was appointed to create a bill to "provide for the government of the Western Territory." After examining the issue, Congress reenacted the Northwest Ordinance, again prohibiting "cruel *or* unusual punishments." It did so, of course, in close proximity to Madison's introduction of the Bill of Rights and its Eighth Amendment barring "cruel *and* unusual punishments." Madison introduced his proposed amendments to the Constitution on June 8, 1789, and a letter he sent to Thomas Jefferson makes clear that, in drafting his proposed amendments, he was trying to avoid controversy. "Every thing of a controvertible nature that might endanger the concurrence of two-thirds of each House and three-fourths of the States was studiously avoided," Madison told Jefferson in 1789, enclosing a draft of his proposed amendments. Because the First Congress accepted the "cruel or unusual" language and the "cruel and unusual" language in close proximity to one another in the same legislative session, congressmen, to the extent they even paid attention to the difference, likely saw little significance in the textual discrepancy. Congress agreed to the language of the Eighth Amendment by a "considerable majority," and the Northwest Ordinance was adopted "without issue."[38]

Though the Constitution outlaws "cruel *and* unusual punishments," language from the Northwest Ordinance, including its prohibition on "cruel *or* unusual punishments," later was incorporated elsewhere, perpetuating that particular verbiage. For example, the State of Michigan, the first English-speaking jurisdiction in the world to abolish capital punishment for murder, included a prohibition on "cruel or unusual punishments" in its 1850 constitution. While Michigan's 1835 constitution provided that "cruel and unjust punishments shall not be imposed," the 1850 Michigan constitution returned to the "cruel or unusual" phraseology of the Northwest Ordinance. Notably, the U.S. Constitution's Thirteenth Amendment, ratified in 1865, also made use of the "slavery" and "involuntary servitude" language derived from Jefferson's original proposal for the governance of western lands. Though the Framers carefully avoided the actual use of the word "slavery" in the Constitution as originally drafted, the Thirteenth Amendment put slavery out of its misery, declaring as a matter of law: "Neither slavery nor involuntary servitude, except as a punishment for crime whereof the party shall have been duly convicted, shall exist within the United States, or any place subject to their jurisdiction." With Virginia slaveholders in the founding era able, by law, to abuse or even kill slaves for misbehavior without legal repercussions, historian Ron Chernow explains, "virtually all of the founders, despite their dislike of slavery," took part in what Chernow calls a "conspiracy of silence," taking "the convenient path of deferring action" on the slavery issue "to a later generation."[39]

Most eighteenth-century citizens did not see slavery or death sentences, let alone corporal punishments, as either "cruel and unusual" or "cruel or unusual" punishments. Not only was the slave trade still in operation, but capital and corporal punishments were then still common. Thus, in 1787, explains law professor Rory Little, the Framers—unsurprisingly, perhaps—gave "little attention to the death penalty" in their debates. Pelatiah Webster, a Federalist and a Yale-educated Pennsylvania merchant who wrote *A Dissertation on the Political Union and Constitution of the Thirteen United States of North America* in 1783, would, for example, say this of America's penal system four years later: "Were we to view only the gaols and dungeons, the gallows and pillories, the chains and wheel-barrows, of any state, we might be induced to think the government severe; but when we turn our attention to the murders and parricides, and robberies and burglaries, the piracies and thefts, which merit these punishments, our idea of cruelty vanishes at once, and we admire the justice, and perhaps clemency, of that government which before shocked us as too severe."[40]

The concept of cruelty, however, was all in the eye of the beholder—as it remains today. In 1801, a certain Giuseppe Caracciolo di Brienza, part of a noble family from Naples, sent Thomas Jefferson a letter in Italian from Baltimore. "It would be too long to recount my sad story, and I would never dare to give you a report that would certainly be boring to you," it read in translation. "It suffices you to know," the letter continued, "that, after the king of the Two Sicilies sacrificed my relatives on the gallows, far from being sated by having shed the blood of so many victims, he wanted to exercise his cruelty on me as well; even if, at that point, my age protected me, yet all this would have not rescued me from his fury, had I not been lucky enough to save myself by taking flight." "After having suffered more than any man can bear," the letter writer said, "I arrived in this city, one month ago, where I teach the Italian language." One of the man's relatives, an admiral, had been hanged from the yardarm of a ship he had formerly commanded, one of more than a hundred people to be hanged in that part of the world after a change in regimes.[41]

Even before the Revolutionary War, John Adams—in "A Dissertation on the Canon and the Feudal Law," published in the *Boston Gazette* in 1765—had spoken of the cruel treatment of Americans and their ancestors. "We have been afraid to think," Adams wrote, saying that there had been a reluctance to examine "the grounds of our privileges, and the extent in which we have an indisputable right to demand them against all the power and authority, on earth." "The cause of this timidity," he explained, "is perhaps hereditary and to be traced back in history, as far as the cruel treatment the first settlers of this country received, before their embarkation for America, from the government at Home." He noted that "our fathers" had been the "objects of the persecutions" and that their "modesty, humanity or fear"—and "human nature itself"—had made them reluctant to "a manly assertion" of their rights. "We have been told," he wrote, that "the word 'Rights' is an offensive expression," that the king and Parliament " 'will not endure to hear Americans talk of their Rights.'" Invoking the concept of liberty and "the same great spirit" that "severed the head of Charles the first from his body" and "drove James the second from his kingdom," Adams urged his readers to "study the law of nature" and "search into the spirit of the British constitution." "Set before us," he pled, "the conduct of our own British ancestors, who have defended for us, the inherent rights of mankind, against foreign and domestic tyrants and usurpers, against arbitrary kings and cruel priests, in short against the gates of earth and hell." "Let us dare to read, think, speak and write," Adams urged, decrying once more "the cruelty of that oppression" that drove their ancestors from their homes.[42]

In organizing the new federal government, the Founding Fathers did have to appoint judges and set up, from scratch, the federal judiciary, a system that would impose death sentences. In 1789, the First Congress—of which Madison was a member, having been elected to serve in the House of Representatives—formally established the federal courts, setting up thirteen district courts and three circuit courts. In the Judiciary Act of 1789, a landmark piece of legislation drafted principally by Senator Oliver Ellsworth of Connecticut, Congress also decided that the U.S. Supreme Court would consist of a Chief Justice and five Associate Justices, a number only later increased to nine. Those Justices would need to "ride circuit" twice a year, traveling country roads and staying in backwater inns to perform their duties. The Judiciary Act—following the Constitution's ratification—laid out the jurisdiction of the federal courts themselves. "[T]he district courts," that law provided, "shall have, exclusively of the courts of the several States, cognizance of all crimes and offences that shall be cognizable under the authority of the United States, committed within their respective districts, or upon the high seas; where no other punishment than whipping, not exceeding thirty stripes, a fine not exceeding one hundred dollars, or a term of imprisonment not exceeding six months, is to be inflicted." "[I]n cases punishable with death," another section read, reflecting the realities of sentencing practices in that era, "the trial shall be had in the county where the offence was committed, or where that cannot be done without great inconvenience, twelve petit jurors at least shall be summoned from thence." "[U]pon all arrests in criminal cases," yet another provision provided, "bail shall be admitted, except where the punishment may be death."[43]

After setting up the federal judiciary and providing for how criminal trials and bail determinations would be handled, Congress took up defining the scope of federal crimes the next year. In 1790, Congress, whose members largely took capital and corporal punishments for granted, thus moved beyond structural and procedural issues, specifying a list of capital crimes and authorizing the use of the pillory and public whipping. In April of that year, Congress passed a law mandating the death penalty for those convicted of treason, murder, piracy, counterfeiting, forgery, and rescuing from the gallows any person convicted of a capital crime. The method of execution was to be "hanging the person convicted by the neck until dead," and the common-law doctrine of benefit of clergy, allowing first-time offenders to receive more lenient sentences, was abolished by statute. Congress at the same time provided for the appointment of counsel "learned in the law"—"not exceeding two," the statute read—in capital cases, and guaranteed that lawyers would have "free access" to their clients "at all seasonable hours."[44]

In the U.S. Senate and House of Representatives, the death penalty provisions generated the only recorded debate in either body regarding the crime bill. When the Senate took up its bill in January 1790, it added a provision allowing judges to order executed prisoners' bodies to be delivered "to a surgeon for dissection." But when the House considered the bill in April of that year, a motion was made to strike that provision, as it "was wounding the feelings of the living, and could do no good." The motion generated heated discussion. "It was said, in answer," it was reported, "that it was only following a mode adopted by some of the wisest nations," and "was making those who had injured society to contribute to its advantage by furnishing subjects of experimental surgery." "[I]mportant improvements," it was noted, "had been made in surgery from experiments." "It was attended with salutary effects," one unidentified member argued, "as it certainly increased the dread of punishment, when it is contemplated with this attendant circumstance." In the debate, Representative Michael Stone of Maryland spoke against allowing dissection, saying "it was contrary" to "the practice of several States" and that "it was making punishment wear the appearance of cruelty, which had a tendency to harden the public mind." James Madison, however, spoke in favor of the new clause, saying "We ought to proportion the terror of punishment to the degree of offense."[45]

In another part of the debate, over whether counterfeiters and those uttering forged instruments should be punished by being hanged, the "degrees of criminality" were discussed by Connecticut's Roger Sherman. Massachusetts congressman Theodore Sedgwick, remarking on "the pernicious consequences of counterfeiting," observed that he thought "the degrees of punishment ought to be proportioned to the malignity of the offence," and he went on to say he considered it "as a crime against the most important interests of society, and of a peculiarly malignant tendency in the present and probable situation of the United States." "Persons addicted to forgery," he added, "are seldom, if ever, reclaimed—the security of the society, therefore, appears to depend on a capital punishment." Thomas Fitzsimons of Pennsylvania agreed that the motion for a "less punishment" for certain types of "uttering or passing" should not be agreed to, with Fitzsimons raising "the injurious and fatal consequences to credit which result from forgery." "Hence the inexorable rigor" of Great Britain's laws "in cases of forgery," Fitzsimons said, with the legislative reporter further recording the congressman's views: "He could not see so clearly, as some gentlemen appear to see, the difference between forging, and simply uttering what is known to be counterfeit—the mischief is not completed till the forgery is uttered. He enlarged on the idea of guarding public paper by every possible expedient." For his part, Representative Alexander White of Virginia disagreed with the legislative report, observing "that he was opposed in general to inflicting death, except for murder, or crimes which might terminate in murder." "[I]n the present case," it was reported, "he thought there were degrees of guilt, and the punishment ought to be proportioned." "[H]e was," it was stated, "opposed to a capital punishment in this case, as he conceived it would tend to prevent convictions." Roger Sherman added that he "had known persons who had been convicted of this crime, that had afterwards reformed."[46]

The Senior Statesman

The debates in the First Congress did not occur in a vacuum. Following the publication of *On Crimes and Punishments,* many people, including prominent Philadelphians, advocated outlawing death sentences for theft and other lower-level offenses, though they still favored capital punishment for murderers. Benjamin Franklin—one of those citizens—favored eliminating capital punishment for all crimes other than mutiny and murder. Condemning the disproportion between crimes and punishments in England, Franklin wrote in 1785:

> If we really believe, as we profess to believe, that the law of Moses was the law of God, the dictates of divine wisdom, infinitely superior to human; on what principles do we ordain death as the punishment of an offence which, according to that law, was only to be punished by a restitution of fourfold? To put a man to death for an offence which does not deserve death, is it not murder? . . .
>
> I read, in the last newspaper from London, that a woman is capitally convicted at the Old Bailey, for privately stealing out of a shop some gauze, value fourteen shillings and threepence; is there any proportion between the injury done by the theft, value fourteen shillings and threepence, and the punishment of a human creature, by death, on a gibbet?

Might not that woman, by her labor, have made the reparation ordained by God, in paying fourfold? Is not all punishment inflicted beyond the merit of the offence, so much punishment of innocence? . . .

If I think it right that the crime of murder should be punished with death, not only as an equal punishment of the crime, but to prevent other murders, does it follow that I must approve of inflicting the same punishments for a little invasion of my property by theft? If I am not myself so barbarous, so bloody-minded and revengeful, as to kill a fellow-creature for stealing from me fourteen shillings and threepence, how can I approve of a law that does it?

In the year after Franklin wrote those lines, Pennsylvania passed a law outlawing the death penalty for robbery, burglary, and sodomy.[47]

A community leader and a man of the world, Benjamin Franklin had known Benjamin Rush since 1766, when the two men began corresponding. Not only did they share a close friendship, but they were united in their opposition to slavery and other forms of cruelty. For instance, Franklin had spoken out forcefully against a mob's murder of a group of peaceful Indians in 1763 near Lancaster, Pennsylvania. When Franklin learned of the massacre and lynching of Conestoga Indians by frontiersmen, he wrote a pamphlet entitled *A Narrative of the Late Massacres in Lancaster County, of a Number of Indians, Friends of this Province*. "These poor defenceless creatures," Franklin wrote of the six Indians who were initially massacred, "were immediately fired upon, stabbed and hatcheted to death!" Of the mob that lynched fourteen other Indians taken into protective custody, Franklin wrote:

Those cruel men again assembled themselves, and hearing that the remaining fourteen Indians were in the work-house at Lancaster, they suddenly appeared in that town, on the 27th of December. Fifty of them, armed as before, dismounting, went directly to the work-house, and by violence broke open the door and entered, with the utmost fury in their countenances. When the poor wretches saw they had no protection nigh, nor could possibly escape, and being without the least weapon for defence, they divided into their little families, the children clinging to the parents. They fell on their knees, protested their innocence, declared their love to the English, and that, in their whole lives, they had never done them injury; and in this posture they all received the hatchet! Women and little children—were every one inhumanly murdered!—in cold blood!

"But the wickedness cannot be covered," Franklin wrote. "The guilt," he said, "will lie on the whole land till justice is done on the murderers. THE BLOOD OF THE INNOCENT WILL CRY TO HEAVEN FOR VENGEANCE."[48]

Franklin was in regular contact with many people who advocated penal reform. In 1785, the year before Pennsylvania reformed its laws, Franklin had written to his friend Benjamin Vaughan on the subject of crime and punishment. In his letter, Franklin contrasted the severe approach taken by an English author, who advocated "hanging *all* thieves" to deter theft, with that of a Frenchman who argued "for proportioning punishments to offences." Franklin, as he was so apt to do, then told a story as he proceeded to critique the English author's approach:

> I have read, indeed, of a cruel Turk in Barbary, who, whenever he bought a new Christian slave, ordered him immediately to be hung up by the legs, and to receive a hundred blows of a cudgel on the soles of his feet, that the severe sense of the punishment, and fear of incurring it thereafter, might prevent the faults that should merit it. Our author, himself, would hardly approve entirely of this Turk's conduct in the government of slaves; and yet he appears to recommend something like it for the government of English subjects, when he applauds (p. 105) the reply of Judge Burnet to the convict horse-stealer, who, being asked what he had to say why judgment of death should not pass against him, and answering, that it was hard to hang a man for *only* stealing a horse, and was told by the judge: "Man, thou are not to be hanged only for stealing a horse, but that horses may not be stolen."
>
> The man's answer, if candidly examined, will, I imagine, appear reasonable, as being founded on the eternal principle of justice and equity, that punishments should be proportioned to offences; and the judge's reply brutal and unreasonable, though the writer "wishes all judges to carry it with them whenever they go the circuit, and to bear it in their minds as containing a wise reason for all the penal statutes which they are called upon to put in execution. It at once illustrates," says he, "the true grounds and reasons of all capital punishments whatsoever, namely, that every man's property, as well as his life, may be held sacred and inviolate."

Quoting Montesquieu and French legal maxims, Franklin pondered: "Is there then no difference in value between property and life?" "I ask you if we could not diminish the number of offenses by making punishments more shameful and less cruel," Voltaire himself wrote Franklin, whose own papers make several mentions of Voltaire. Franklin even proposed erecting a statue of Voltaire in Philadelphia after the French philosopher's death, to recognize his contributions to the nation's laws. "That it is better a hundred guilty persons should escape than one innocent person should suffer," Franklin emphasized elsewhere, "is a maxim that has been long and generally approved; never, that I know of, controverted."[49]

At the Constitutional Convention of 1787, Franklin, the president of Pennsylvania, played the dual role of host and senior statesman. Though he suffered from gout, Franklin arrived at the Convention in a sedan chair he brought from Paris, a one-of-a-kind vehicle carried by four prisoners from the Walnut Street Jail through the yard of the Philadelphia State House. Franklin had known tragedy and lived abroad in London for many years, so he had seen the justice systems on both sides of the Atlantic. In 1737, acquaintances of Franklin had actually been charged with murder after a mentally impaired apprentice named Daniel Rees was splashed with flaming spirits, causing his clothes to catch fire. After the apprentice's death two days later, Franklin, in the role of a witness, testified at the trial of Rees's master and two others, a case focusing on whether the death was accidental or intentional. Two of the accused were convicted, albeit of the lesser charge of manslaughter, while the third man was acquitted. John Rice, an English stockbroker whom Franklin knew, had also gotten into trouble with the law and been jailed, convicted, and then hanged for embezzlement and forgery. The latter event motivated Franklin to pen *The Art of Virtue,* in which he set out his reform-minded objective: "Many people lead bad lives that would gladly lead good ones, but know not *how* to make the change." Among the cardinal virtues Franklin formulated were "Justice— Wrong none, by doing injuries or omitting the benefits that are your duty," and "Humility—Imitate Jesus and Socrates." In London, Franklin, the candle-maker turned printer, no doubt saw prisoners in the pillory, and he long shared Dr. Rush's aversion to cruelty. He opposed torture and, as early as 1735, called the right against self-incrimination one of the "common Rights of Mankind."[50]

George Washington

George Washington, a military man who oversaw the Articles of War and many cases of desertion throughout his career, frequently ordered military commanders to use executions. As the commander in chief of the Virginia Regiment in the 1750s, Washington vowed to "terrify the soldiers" from desertions and had deserters chained, flogged, and executed for disciplinary purposes. In 1755, he wrote one captain to ask him to tell his men "that if any Soldier deserts, altho' he return *himself,* he shall be hanged." In 1756, he likewise decreed that one Henry Campbell, described by Washington as "a most atrocious villain" who "richly merits an ignominious death," be put to death. Not only had Campbell deserted, but he had encouraged seven others to do the same. In ordering the execution, Washington followed the British army's standard practice. And in 1757, as a British officer, Washington had complained to another British soldier, John Stanwix, about insubordinate militia. "Militia," he wrote, "will never answer your expectation," noting that over a fourth of his men had deserted, leading him to take "the most vigorous measures to apprehend those fellows." "I have a Gallows near 40 feet high erected (which has terrified the rest exceedingly)," Washington explained, adding, "I am determined, if I can be justified in the proceeding, to hang two or three on it, as an example to others." Two weeks later, Washington told Stanwix that he had done just that, noting, "we have been able to apprehend 22; two of whom were hanged on thursday last." Although Washington had originally decided to hang fourteen of the deserters, he eventually settled on just two repeat offenders, reprieving the others. In explaining his actions to Robert Dinwiddie, a British colonial administrator who served as Virginia's lieutenant governor in the 1750s, Washington reported: "I send Your Honor a copy of the proceedings of a General Court martial. Two of those condemned, namely, Ignatious Edwards, and Wm Smith, were hanged on thursday last, just before the companies marched for their respective posts." Washington apologized for hanging the men instead of shooting them, but felt "[i]t conveyed much more terror to others; and it was for example sake, we did it." Washington emphasized that Edwards "had deserted twice before" and that Smith "was accounted one of the greatest villains upon the continent."[51]

In that era, military executions were relatively common, employed to maintain discipline and stop desertions. The British themselves used executions to try to force the colonists to capitulate and submit to British rule. After Washington took command of the Continental Army, the Continental Congress appointed a committee headed by Benjamin Franklin to help mold the colonial militia into an effective fighting force. That committee met with Washington and his staff for seven days, with discipline being a central focus of their discussions. Not only did the committee resolve that sentries caught sleeping on duty would receive anywhere from twenty to thirty-nine lashes, but the group authorized the death penalty for mutiny and incitement thereto. Washington felt strongly that executions deterred crime and preserved order, so he freely permitted his commanders to use capital punishment. To Brigadier General William Heath of Massachusetts Washington wrote that he had the "discretion" to execute such prisoners under sentence of death as were "proper objects for Capital punishment." And in 1775, Washington urged Colonel Benedict Arnold, at the time still loyal to Washington and on a mission to capture Quebec, to "check by every Motive of Duty, and Fear of Punishment every Attempt to Plunder or insult any of the Inhabitants of Canada." Should any American soldier attempt to injure any Canadian or Indian, Washington advised, "I do most earnestly enjoin you to bring him to such severe & exemplary Punishment as the Enormity of the Crime may require." "Should it extend to Death itself," Washington wrote, "it will not be disproportionate to its Guilt at such a Time and in such a Cause."[52]

Like many of his contemporaries, though, Washington felt that executions were too frequently employed, and he saw executions as a last resort. This seems particularly clear from a communication Washington sent to the Continental Congress just days after the signing of the Declaration of Independence. When discussing the capture, plunder, and murder of some American colonists by Indians, Washington expressed only a reluctant willingness to resort indiscriminately to capital punishment to punish those posing a challenge to the young nation's security. "The Inhuman Treatment to the whole, and Murder of part of our People after their Surrender and Capitulation," Washington wrote, "was certainly a flagrant violation of that Faith which ought to be held sacred by all civilized nations, and founded in the most Savage barbarity. It highly deserved the severest reprobation, and I trust the Spirited Measures Congress have adopted upon the Occasion, will prevent the like in future." "But if they should not, and the claims of humanity are disregarded," Washington added, "Justice and Policy will require recourse to be had to the Law of retaliation, however abhorrent and disagreeable to our natures in cases of Torture and Capital Punishments." Regarding the treatment of captured Hessian troops, Washington gave unambiguous instructions: "Treat them with humanity, and Let them have no reason to Complain of our Copying the brutal example of the British Army in their Treatment of our unfortunate brethren who have fallen into their hands." Washington himself sometimes set aside soldiers' death sentences, seeing such punishments as too draconian. For example, he wrote a letter in April 1778 to express his preference for "detention and confinement" over "capital punishment" for an enlisted soldier. He also penned a clemency order in February 1780 remitting the death sentence for another soldier, Thomas Warren, "on account of the frequency of capital punishments" and because his general represented it was Warren's first offense. In Washington's 1780 letter, his merciful act for the prisoner was tempered by the fact that he sought to ensure the prisoner's "future good conduct" by authorizing the letter's recipient to keep the pardon secret "for a few days" before letting the prisoner know his life had been spared.[53]

The concept and claimed legitimacy of "Retaliation," in light of wartime atrocities and all the bad blood between British and American citizens, was hotly debated during the Revolutionary War. In a 1778 letter to George Washington, British general William Howe—writing that many British subjects "have suffered Death, from Tortures inflicted by the unrelenting Populace" and asserting some were "dragged to Trial for their Loyalty, and in cruel Mockery of Law, condemned and executed"—said "the savage Principle of indiscriminate Retaliation" was "unsupported by the Rules of War, abhorred by every civilized Country, and solemnly condemned by the Law of Nature." "It is in America only," he wrote angrily, "where a Set of Men are to be found, who affecting the Character of Legislators, retaliate upon the Innocent." "God forbid that I should be provoked to follow so horrid an Example," Howe threatened, with his letter stating: "The common Soldier, taken in Arms against his King, guilty as he is of the Crime of Rebellion, shall not become the Object of a retaliating Punishment. It is only against the Authors of Cruelty that Retaliation can be made consonant with Justice."[54]

On the American side, James Madison favored retaliating during the war as a way to protect American property, to stop British acts of cruelty, and to safeguard the lives of American prisoners of war. In 1781, Madison himself authored a report in response to British soldiers "burning our towns & villages, desolating our Country & sporting with the lives of our captive Citizens." That report resolved that "the Department of War is hereby ordered to cause all the Officers in the service of the King of G. B. now in their custody, to be duly-secured, and on the first authentic notice of the burning of any Town or Village in any one of the U. States unauthorized by the laws of war, to cause such & so many of the said Officers as they shall judge expedient, to be put to instant death." In that same year, Madison also made a "Motion for Reprisal" against Great Britain's detention of Henry Laurens, a South Carolina merchant who served as the president of the Second Continental Congress. Charged with treason after the British navy intercepted his ship on a voyage to Holland, Laurens was transported to England and imprisoned in the Tower of London until his release on December 31, 1781, in exchange for General Lord Cornwallis. Madison's motion resolved that the secretary of war immediately imprison British soldiers "in the Mines at Simsbury in Connecticut" and treat them "in such manner as will make their situation correspond as near as may be to that of the Citizens of the U.S." imprisoned in Great Britain. Madison's motion further resolved that such treatment "continue in force" until "authentic information shall be received by Congress that H. Laurens Esqr. and the other Citizens" were "duly exchanged, or discharged from their commitment." Madison's motion—though never adopted because of George Washington's dislike of a retaliatory policy—sought to relieve American prisoners "from their present sufferings" and to ensure them "the treatment to which as prisoners of war they are entitled by the established usage of civilized nations." Washington believed that, "of all Laws," "Retaliation" was "the most difficult to execute, where you have not the transgressor himself in your possession." "Humanity," he said, "will ever interfere and plead strongly against the sacrifice of an innocent person for the guilt of another."[55]

As a military commander, Washington vacillated between extending mercy to individual soldiers and using threats and harsh measures to motivate and steel his men as a fighting force. Washington endorsed death sentences for men who looted property, and made "examples" of other men, too, by ordering their deaths. When Anthony Wayne, one of his officers, ordered the firing squad deaths of a dozen men involved in a mutiny, Washington later approved the tactic. "Sudden and exemplary punishments," Washington said, "were certainly necessary upon the new appearance of that daring and mutinous spirit which convulsed the line last winter." In another instance, though, Washington regretted that an execution had been carried out by one of his generals without any authorization. "With respect to the Tory, who was tried and executed by your order," Washington wrote Brigadier General Preudhomme de Borre, "though his crime was heinous enough to deserve the fate he met with, and though I am convinced you acted in the affair with a good intention, yet I cannot but wish it had not happened." After a Connecticut soldier named Ebenezer Leffingwell was found guilty of cowardice at the Battle of Harlem Heights in 1776, Washington personally decided to spare him, though only at the last possible moment. The popular Sergeant Leffingwell had left the ranks—he said to procure more ammunition—and was on his knees, preparing to be shot, when Washington issued the reprieve. Granted on the same day that the British executed Nathan Hale in Manhattan, Leffingwell's pardon generated sustained cheers from American soldiers. On his instructions, Washington also allowed his subordinates to reprieve men just before they were to be hanged on gallows. Still, as to war profiteers who deprived his men of critical supplies, Washington, who lived through the misery at Valley Forge, angrily expressed his frustrations: "I would to God that one of the most atrocious of each state was hung in gibbets upon a gallows five times as high as the one prepared by Haman."[56]

Indeed, in 1778, Washington called for more proportionate punishments and the curtailment of death sentences. On January 29, 1778, Washington wrote to the Continental Congress to propose more proportionate sanctions to reform army discipline:

> Several new regulations will, I imagine, be found useful in the articles of war; which the Judge Advocate, from his official experience of the deficiency, can more accurately indicate. One thing, we have suffered much from, is the want of a proper gradation of punishments: the interval between a hundred lashes and death is too great and requires to be filled by some intermediate stages. Capital crimes in the army are frequent, particularly in the instance of desertion: actually to inflict capital punishment upon every deserter or other heinous offender, would incur the imputation of cruelty, and by the familiarity of the example, destroy its efficacy; on the other hand to give only a hundred lashes to such criminals is a burlesque on their crimes rather than a serious correction, and affords encouragement to obstinacy and imitation.

Washington—seeking to avoid that "imputation of cruelty"—then lamented the fact that the law did not provide more flexibility to judges in meting out punishments:

> The Courts are often in a manner compelled by the enormity of the facts, to pass sentences of death, which I am as often obliged to remit, on account of the number in the same circumstances, and let the offenders pass wholly unpunished. This would be avoided, if there were other punishments short of the destruction of life, in some degree adequate to the crime; and which might be with propriety substituted. Crimes too are so various in their complexions and degrees, that to preserve the just rule of proportion, there ought to be a gradual scale of punishments; in

order to which, whipping should be extended to any number at discretion, or by no means, limited lower than five hundred lashes.[57]

Having read Beccaria's views on proportionate punishments and having been advised by Lafayette that courts-martial punishments were too harsh, George Washington wrote to the Continental Congress on August 31, 1778, saying this about the use of capital punishment:

> The frequent condemnations to capital punishment, for want of some intermediate one between that and a Hundred lashes (the next highest under our present military articles) and the necessity of frequent pardons in consequence, induced me a few days ago, to lay the matter before a Board of Officers for them to consider, whether some mode might not be devised of equal or greater efficacy for preventing crimes and punishing Delinquents when they had happened, less shocking to humanity and more advantageous to the States, than that of Capital execution. The inclosed paper No. 3, contains the opinion of the Board upon the subject, which with all deference I submit to the consideration of Congress and doubt not but they will adopt the expedient suggested, if it shall appear in anywise calculated to promote the service. I will only observe before I conclude upon this occasion, that when I call the Board to consult upon the point, there were Eleven prisoners under sentence of death, and probably many more for trial, in the different guards on charges that would effect their lives.

The enclosure, Paper No. 3, was a copy of the proceedings of the Council of General Officers dated August 20, 1778. That document noted that "his Excellency" had requested the Council's sentiments on "the expediency of punishment by hard and severe labor, instead of death," and in it, the Council reported that it was unanimously decided that "severe hard labour be recommended . . . to be the intermediate punishment between one hundred Lashes, and Death."[58]

After the Constitution's ratification, President Washington also had to decide the fate of men who petitioned him for clemency. "Permit a stranger to inform your Excellency," read one, "that about twelve months since, I was apprehended & committed" to a gaol in Portland, Maine, "charged with the murder of Capt. John Connor, of the Sloop Mary, upon the Coast of Africa." "That yesterday I was tried & found guilty of the Crime, & that the District Judge, a few hours since pronounced the fatal sentence, that still rings in my Ears & harrows up my soul, the sentence of Death, which is to be Executed upon me on the 25 day of June Inst.," it continued. "The time is short Great Washington," Thomas Bird pleaded, "too short, for a wretch harden'd in Crimes to prepare for that Country," with the condemned man entreating Washington "to grant him a Pardon or Commute the punishment to something, to any thing, short of

Death," or at least to grant him "a Reprieve for a few months longer." "It is usual for Kings and Emperors, at the Commencement of their Reign to grant such indulgences," Bird said, begging for mercy. On June 5, 1790, U.S. District Court Judge David Sewall wrote Washington with further details on the case, and Washington himself consulted with John Jay about it, asking "would there be prudence, justice or policy in extending mercy to the Convict mentioned in the enclosed Papers?" "There does not appear to be a single Circumstance in the Case of the Murderer in question," Jay responded on June 13, "to recommend a Pardon—His own Petition contains no averment of Innocence, no Palliative for Guilt, no complaint of Court Jury or witnesses, nor of the want of witnesses." Following Jay's advice, Washington wrote back to Judge Sewall on June 28, explaining: "No palliating circumstance appeared in the case of this unhappy man to recommend him to mercy for which he applied: I could not therefore have justified it to the laws of my Country, had I, in this instance, exercised that pardoning power which the Constitution vests in the President of the United States."[59]

Years later, in his seventh annual message to Congress, President Washington urged milder punishments, however. Delivered in Philadelphia on December 8, 1795, Washington's message had this to say regarding the pardoning of capital offenders involved in the Whiskey Rebellion:

> It is a valuable ingredient in the general estimate of our welfare that the part of our country which was lately the scene of disorder and insurrection now enjoys the blessings of quiet and order. The misled have abandoned their errors, and pay the respect to our Constitution and laws which is due from good citizens to the public authorities of the society. These circumstances have induced me to pardon generally the offenders here referred to, and to extend forgiveness to those who had been adjudged to capital punishment. For though I shall always think it a sacred duty to exercise with firmness and energy the constitutional powers with which I am vested, yet it appears to me no less consistent with the public good than it is with my personal feelings to mingle in the operations of Government every degree of moderation and tenderness which the national justice, dignity, and safety may permit.

Washington, who came of age before America's prison system was developed, thus viewed executions as a necessity but also as a last resort, to be used only if he felt them absolutely necessary. "I always hear of capital executions with concern, and regret that there should occur so many instances in which they are necessary," he wrote during the Revolutionary War. In the case of Washington's July 1795 pardon of those involved in the Whiskey Rebellion, his advisor Alexander Hamilton noted that "few offenders of any consequence remained subject to prosecution" and that only "[t]wo poor wretches" had been sentenced to die, "one of them little short of an idiot, the other a miserable follower in the hindmost train of rebellion, both being so insignificant in all respects, that after the lenity shown to the chiefs, justice would have worn the mien of ferocity, if she had raised her arm against them." "The sentiment that their punishment ought to be remitted," Hamilton said, "was universal; and the President, yielding to the special considerations, granted them pardons."[60]

Alexander Hamilton

Alexander Hamilton, who joined George Washington's staff in 1777 and became the country's first treasury secretary, himself made clear before the century's end that he too felt death sentences could be too harsh in some instances. A defender of the presidential pardoning power, Hamilton did not hesitate to support the use of capital punishment if he felt it would be effective. As Washington's aide-de-camp and an army general under President John Adams, Hamilton advocated using executions to prevent desertions. "I have heretofore spoken to you of the frequency of desertion, and of the necessity of repressing it by severe punishment," he wrote to Lieutenant Colonel Josias Carvel Hall, a soldier who reported that "[i]n European Armies Desertion is punished with Death," that "[t]o American Habits of thinking this appears inadequate" as death should be reserved for desertion cases with aggravating circumstances, and that "branding" deserters "on some conspicuous Part of the Face" with a "hot Iron" might be a better option. "It is not my wish to influence opinion in any particular case," Hamilton told Hall, "but I believe that a few examples of capital punishment, perhaps one in each regiment, will be found indispensable." In 1776, while still a young man, Hamilton had himself joined nearly twenty thousand spectators in a meadow to watch a Continental Army soldier, Thomas Hickey, swing from the gallows. A member of Washington's personal guard, Hickey was implicated in a scheme to sabotage the Continental Army that was reportedly coordinated by royal governor William Tryon. George Washington had decided to make an example of Hickey, who was court-martialed and convicted of mutiny and sedition and of holding "treacherous" correspondence with the enemy. Hamilton saw death sentences as part of the fabric of the law, and he applauded Hickey's execution, which Washington had ordered every brigade to watch when it took place on June 28, 1776, on a gallows in a field near New York's Bowery. "It is hoped the remainder of those miscreants now in our possession will meet with a punishment adequate to their crimes," Hamilton wrote of the hanging.[61]

Born in the West Indies, Hamilton became a lawyer in the 1780s after studying at King's College and reading influential legal treatises, including William Blackstone's *Commentaries* and the writings of Sir Edward Coke. The author of the much-studied *Institutes of the Laws of England*, Coke inventoried English law and its frequent use of death sentences. The third part of

Coke's series, first published in 1644, contained sections on, among other things, "High Treason," "Petit Treason," "Heresie," and "Felony by Conjuration, Witchcraft, Sorcery, or Inchantment." After defining high treason, Coke said "the principall end of punishment is, That others by his example may feare to offend." "But such punishment," Coke qualified, "can be no example to Mad-men, or Infants that are not of the age of Discretion." "And God forbid," Coke added, "that in Cases so penal, the Law should not be certaine; if it be certaine in case of Murder and Felony, *á fortiori*, it ought to be certaine in case of Treason." Coke, invoking the French legal concept *de non sane memorie*, noted that if a man convicted of treason or a felony should become of unsound mind, "he shall not be executed, for it cannot be an example to others." "Petit Treason," said to encompass "when a servant slayeth his Master, or a wife her husband, or when a man secular or religious slayeth his Prelate to whom he oweth faith and obedience," could result, Coke recorded, in death by hanging or being burned to death. As Queen Elizabeth's attorney general, Coke famously prosecuted Sir Walter Raleigh and the Gunpowder Plot conspirators for treason, and his legal writings on the common law were once considered classic texts. After defining a "Conjurer," a "Witch," an "Inchanter," and a "sorcerer," Coke cited the Biblical passage, "Thou shalt not suffer a Witch to live" and said "the Holy Ghost hath compared the great offense of rebellion to the sinne of Witchcraft." "[I]t appeareth by our ancient books," Coke wrote, "that these horrible and devilish offenders, which left the everliving God, and sacrificed to the Devill, and thereby committed Idolatry, in seeking advice and aide of him, were punished by death."[62]

Though Hamilton studied Coke's writings, he lived in a much different era. Though Coke looked, as Hamilton did, to the divine, Coke had served as the Chief Justice of the Court of Common Pleas, and later, as the Lord Chief Justice of the King's Bench, all long before Hamilton was even born. Hamilton, a product of a different century who defended some accused criminals in his law practice, thought in terms of natural rights. "The sacred rights of mankind are not to be rummaged for among old parchments or musty records," Hamilton wrote. "They are written, as with a sunbeam, in the whole *volume* of human nature by the hand of the divinity itself and can never be erased or obscured by mortal power." As a lawyer, Hamilton, like John Adams, had taken on unpopular causes and some high-profile criminal cases. In 1786, for example, he represented George Turner, indicted as a "dueller, fighter, and disturber of the peace." In plying his trade, Hamilton advocated the doctrine of judicial review and relied upon a wide array of legal sources, including English and Roman law, Spanish, Dutch, and French writers, and "the law of nations." After the years-long Revolutionary War, Hamilton—at a great distance from the time of Coke, and having read works in French by Molière and Voltaire—had even courageously preached restraint toward disloyal Tories. In 1784, when New York City saw a new series of Tories being tarred and feathered,

Hamilton appealed to the public for tolerance, saying that he had "too deep a share in the common exertions of this revolution to be willing to see its fruits blasted by the violence of rash or unprincipled men, without at least protesting against their designs." "The world has its eye upon America," Hamilton wrote, adding, "The noble struggle we have made in the cause of liberty has occasioned a kind of revolution in human sentiment."[63]

Hamilton thought executions necessary, but he, like others in early America, recognized that "[t]he temper of our country, is not a little opposed to the frequency of capital punishment." In *The Federalist No. 74,* for instance, Hamilton defended the presidential pardoning power, saying it was necessary, in part to avoid "sanguinary" or "cruel" results. As Hamilton wrote:

> Humanity and good policy conspire to dictate, that the benign prerogative of pardoning should be as little as possible fettered or embarrassed. The criminal code of every country partakes so much of necessary severity, that without an easy access to exceptions in favor of unfortunate guilt, justice would wear a countenance too sanguinary and cruel. As the sense of responsibility is always strongest, in proportion as it is undivided, it may be inferred that a single man would be most ready to attend to the force of those motives which might plead for a mitigation of the rigor of the law, and least apt to yield to considerations which were calculated to shelter a fit object of its vengeance.[64]

For the honor-obsessed Hamilton, even the method of execution, often used to signify the gravity of one's crime, was worth arguing about. In 1780, Major General Benedict Arnold, at one time among George Washington's most trusted commanders, entered into a secret pact with the British to seize the garrison at West Point, which the disgruntled Arnold had requested he be allowed to command. After the arrest of his collaborator Major John André, adjunct general of the British army and, more notoriously, Arnold's contact, Washington had to decide whether André would be shot like a gentleman, or— if adjudged a spy—be hanged from the gallows as a common criminal. Traveling under a pseudonym, André had been caught carrying intelligence from Arnold about West Point's artillery and troop strength, as well as minutes of a war council sent by Washington himself. Hamilton argued André should be shot, but Washington, who felt bitterly betrayed by Arnold's treasonous conduct, disagreed. "Arnold has betrayed us!" Washington had angrily exclaimed, unsure of which officers he could really trust in the wake of such treachery. With Arnold having escaped to the British man-of-war *Vulture,* Washington turned his wrath on the cultivated and handsome André, a skilled artist who had been educated in Switzerland but who had used a fake name and shed his uniform in the course of dealing with the turncoat Arnold. After Hamilton visited André at the tavern in Tappan, New York, where André was being held captive, Hamilton became an admirer even as Washington received a threat from Arnold himself that the British would "retaliate" against members of Washington's army if André should be executed. After a board of officers found André should be treated as a spy, André was hanged on October 2, 1780, after Washington was unable to negotiate a swap of prisoners. "I am reconciled to my fate, but not to the mode," a stoic André said in his final minutes. "The death of André could not have been dispensed with," Hamilton lamented two years after the fact, "but it must still be viewed at a distance as an act of *rigid justice*."[65]

Like President Washington, Hamilton could be merciful. In 1799, Hamilton specifically reminded New York City lawyer Washington Morton, a judge advocate in the court-martial of Sergeant Richard Hunt, that the Articles of War "require that two thirds shall agree in cases where death is inflicted," and eventually recommended that Sergeant Hunt's life be spared. In that case, after John Adams—the country's second President—received word of Hunt's death sentence, he questioned the legitimacy of the court-martial process and sent a series of letters about the deserter's case to James McHenry, the secretary of war. "I return the proceedings of the court-martial in the cases of the deserters," Adams wrote McHenry on June 19, 1799, saying: "The absolute necessity of examples in such cases as that of Richard Hunt, is very deeply impressed on my mind, and I should not dare to pardon him, if the proceedings are all regular." After mentioning Sergeant Hunt's case again on July 13, 1799, Adams wrote to McHenry about the case six days later. After telling McHenry, "I wish that courtsmartial may be advised to be as cautious as possible, in all their proceedings, especially in cases of life," Adams wrote on July 19 that "the crime of Richard Hunt is of so deep a die, that I have not seen my way clear to avoid the signature of the warrant for his execution, which is here returned." "Yet," Adams qualified, "if you and General Hamilton, think that one example, may suffice, for the purposes of public justice, the execution of Hunt or Pierce may yet be respited."[66]

Upon receiving Sergeant Hunt's death warrant, Hamilton in turn wrote to McHenry, a signer of the U.S. Constitution and an army surgeon who studied medicine under Dr. Benjamin Rush in Philadelphia. In that letter, Hamilton laid out his view that the death penalty should be used sparingly, arguing that public opinion "is not wholly to be disregarded" and that there must be "some caution not to render our military system odious by giving it the appearance of being sanguinary." "The idea of cruelty," Hamilton wrote, "inspires disgust, and ultimately is not much more favourable to authority than the excess of lenity." Though McHenry had previously been convinced that the death penalty's use was necessary to curtail rampant desertions, Hamilton now advised using executions less frequently. "To disseminate the examples of executions so far as they shall be indispensable," Hamilton emphasized, "will serve to render them more efficacious." Hamilton ended his letter by urging mercy for the soldier:

Under these impressions, if I hear nothing to the contrary from you by the return of the post, I shall issue an order to the following effect: "That, though the President has fully approved the sentence of Sergeant Hunt, and, from the heinous nature of his conduct, considers him a very fit subject for punishment; yet, being unwilling to multiply examples of severity, however just, beyond what experience may show to be indispensable, and hoping that the good faith and patriotism of the soldiery will spare him the painful necessity of frequently resorting to them, he has thought fit to authorize a remission of the punishment; directing, nevertheless, that Sergeant Hunt be degraded from his station."

President Adams went along with Hamilton's proposal.[67]

Hamilton also opposed the execution of Captain Charles Asgill of the First British Regiment of Foot, once slated to be executed in retaliation for the murder of another man, Joshua Huddy. Huddy, a New Jersey militia artillery captain who boasted of personally hanging Tories, had been captured by the British in April 1782 and then turned over to a group of Tory civilians who placed him in the custody of Captain Richard Lippincott. Huddy was later hanged to avenge the "Cruel murders of our Brethren," including one Phillip White, a British loyalist who had been executed around the same time Huddy was taken into custody. Huddy's body, with a note fastened to the chest reading "Up Goes Huddy for Philip White," was left swinging from a tree as a warning to rebels. George Washington said of Huddy's killing that "this instance of Barbarity . . . calls loudly for Retaliation," with Washington calling Huddy's death "the most wanton, unprecedented and unhuman Murder that has ever disgraced the arms of a civilized people." Patriot tempers flared to new heights after a British court-martial acquitted Captain Lippincott, the man who actually hanged Huddy on April 12, 1782. Lippincott, it was found in the adjudication, had simply been following orders, orders that had come from none other than Governor William Franklin, the estranged son of Benjamin Franklin who had sided with the British. Vexed that Lippincott had been cleared of wrongdoing and would not be punished, Washington ordered that one of his own brigadier generals, Moses Hazen, choose by lot a British officer to be executed.[68]

Captain Asgill, a seventeen-year-old British officer captured at Yorktown and the son of a London alderman, was selected at random to be the sacrificial lamb. Although it looked for a time as if Asgill would be executed, Alexander Hamilton spoke up, saying that executing Asgill "will be derogatory to the national character." "A sacrifice of this sort," Hamilton said, "is entirely repugnant to the genius of the age we live in and is without example in modern history nor can it fail to be considered in Europe as wanton and unnecessary." To make matters worse, Washington in the articles of capitulation had guaranteed the safety of prisoners taken captive at Yorktown. "[S]o Solemn and deliberate a sacrifice of the innocent for the guilty," Hamilton said, "must be condemned on the present received notions of humanity, and encourage an opinion that we are in . . . a state [of] barbarism." Henry Knox, one of George Washington's favorite officers, agreed. "My sentiments on frequent executions at this or any other period," he told Hamilton, "are very similar to yours." "I am persuaded," Knox said, that "dispassionate and enlightened minds" would be convinced "that executions have been too frequent, under the color of the Laws of the different states and they hereafter will be recited to sully the purity of our cause." After Captain Lippincott's acquittal, James Madison told Edmund Randolph that, with regard to "selecting" an "innocent" officer, Washington "seems to *lean to the side of compassion* but *asks the direction of Congress.*" "What that will be," Madison said, had yet to be determined. Negotiations over Asgill's fate continued until the fall of 1782, when at Washington's urging Congress decided to release Asgill, who had become a cause célèbre after his mother, Lady Asgill, pled for her son's life. Washington said that, under the circumstances, "humanity dictates a fear for the unfortunate offering and inclines me to say that I most devoutly wish his life may be saved." While Washington initially felt "duty" bound to make a decisive decision and insisted that Asgill's fate lay in the hands of "the British commander-in-chief," when Louis XVI's foreign minister requested mercy for Asgill after his mother's desperate plea at the court of Versailles, it gave Washington an excuse to order Asgill's release. Despite his notorious temper, Hamilton, who weighed in on Asgill's behalf, thus justly earned a deserved reputation for treating enemy soldiers with dignity. Indeed, when some of his men clamored for revenge in another case, Hamilton interceded, even stopping a captain from running a British officer through the chest with a bayonet. Hamilton later reported proudly: "Incapable of imitating examples of barbarity and forgetting recent provocations, the soldiers spared every man who ceased to resist."[69]

In an age when many elites used duels to resolve insults, Hamilton was famously killed in one by Vice President Aaron Burr. Hamilton had much experience with duels, having agreed for example to serve as the designated "second" in a duel in early December 1778, what his biographer Ron Chernow calls "the first of many such 'affairs of honor' in which he participated." Hamilton's eldest son Philip had actually been killed in a duel, causing Hamilton to fall into a deep depression. Philip's death, he confessed to Benjamin Rush, was "beyond comparison the most afflicting of my life." Though Benjamin Franklin thought dueling a "murderous practice," and men such as Thomas Jefferson, Thomas Paine, John Adams, and Rufus King all opposed dueling, Hamilton—the military man known for his hot temper—feared being branded a coward if he avoided a duel. This was so even though Hamilton himself had come to oppose dueling and New York law outlawed the practice. Before his duel with Burr, Hamilton, who likely threw away his shot at Burr, had written his wife Eliza to say that "[t]he scruples of a Christian have determined me to expose my own life to any extent, rather than subject myself to the guilt of taking the life of another." In the early morning hours of July 11, 1804, Hamilton and Burr rowed across the Hudson River to Weehawken, a popular dueling ground in New Jersey, where the punishment for dueling was not as severe. There, after ten paces were marked off, the men exchanged fire, with Burr, an expert marksman, mortally wounding his foe. Ironically, in one of the last major speeches of his career, Hamilton had denounced dueling "on the principle of natural justice that no man shall be the avenger of his own wrongs, especially by a deed alike interdicted by the laws of God and man."[70]

Thomas Jefferson

Thomas Jefferson thought long and hard about executions, the power of the state, and the criminal law. As a leading advocate of the American Revolution, Jefferson was at the very center of the storm, risking his life in the name of liberty. Trained as a lawyer, Jefferson had a way with words, a skill he put to use for his country during the war and thereafter. John Adams, who professed "a great Opinion of the Elegance" of Jefferson's pen, enlisted Jefferson in June 1776 to draft the Declaration of Independence, and Jefferson also used his formidable legislative drafting skills to press for criminal law reform in his home state. In a letter he sent in 1786 to an Englishwoman named Maria Cosway, with whom he had fallen in love, Jefferson even used the literary device of alternating voices—a "dialogue" between "my Head" and "my Heart"—to describe his innermost feelings, and his love of America, after he dropped her off at her carriage. In the course of that dialogue, Jefferson, then the minister to France, ruminated on America and spoke of London's "lying newspapers," lamenting that "all Europe is made to believe we are a lawless banditti, in a state of absolute anarchy, cutting one anothers throats, & plundering without distinction." "But you & I know that all this is false," Jefferson then wrote back to himself, saying "that there is not a country on earth where there is greater tranquillity, where the law's are milder, or better obeyed." Americans, he wrote, were occupied in constructing canals and roads, building schools and academies, erecting busts and statues of great men, and "abolishing sanguinary punishments." "The art of life is the art of avoiding pain," Jefferson wrote, adding rhetorically, "If our country, when pressed with wrongs at the point of the bayonet, had been governed by its heads instead of its hearts, where should we have been now? Hanging on a gallows as high as Hamans."[71]

Jefferson's efforts to reform the criminal law began in the very midst of the American Revolution. On December 4, 1775, the Continental Congress resolved that if Virginians "shall find it necessary to establish a form of government in that Colony," they should take that step in such a manner "as in their judgment will best produce the happiness of the people." After the Continental Congress—at the urging of John Adams—also recommended that the "United Colonies" adopt new forms of government, Jefferson, then attending Congress in Philadelphia, took it upon himself in late May and early June of 1776 to draft a proposed constitution for Virginia. Jefferson's draft sought to establish, in his words, "Fundamental principles," and Jefferson gave his draft to his long-time mentor George Wythe, who was returning from Congress to Williamsburg, Virginia, in the company of Richard Henry Lee. Wythe, who signed the Declaration of Independence, had been admitted to the bar at age twenty, had been a clerk of the House of Burgesses, and had built a successful law practice. His most illustrious client was George Washington, and he later became a law professor at the College of William and Mary after Thomas Jefferson in 1779 engineered a reorganization of the faculty to create a Chair of Law and Police. Lee, Wythe's traveling companion and another prominent figure in Virginia politics, had blown off the fingers of one of his hands in a hunting accident and made for a memorable sight, as his hand was wrapped in a black silk handkerchief.[72]

Jefferson's proposed constitution for Virginia never came to fruition. When Wythe and Lee got back to Virginia, the Virginia delegates had already debated a plan of government and, though receptive to a few changes, were in no mood to consider a whole new scheme. As Wythe wrote to Jefferson on July 27, 1776: "When I came here the plan of government had been committed to the whole house. To those who had the chief hand in forming it the one you put into my hands was shewn. Two or three parts of this were, with little alteration, inserted in that." "[B]ut such was the impatience of sitting long enough to discuss several important points in which they differ, and so many other matters were necessary to be dispatched before the adjournment," Wythe added, "that I was persuaded the revision of a subject the members seemed tired of would at that time have been unsuccessfully proposed." In fact, Jefferson realized his draft might never be adopted but felt compelled to make the effort anyway. As Jefferson wrote after the fact: "I was then at Philadelphia with Congress; and knowing that the Convention of Virginia was engaged in forming a plan of government, I turned my mind to the same subject, and drew a sketch or outline of a Constitution, with a preamble, which I sent to Mr. Pendleton, president of the convention, on the mere possibility that it might suggest something worth incorporation into that before the Convention." Edmund Pendleton, a Virginia lawyer, elder statesman, and member of the House of Burgesses, had been licensed to practice law in 1741 and had been a delegate to the Continental Congress in 1774.[73]

Jefferson's draft constitution recited a number of "fundamental laws & principles of government," which, Jefferson proposed, "shall henceforth be established." "The Legislative, Executive, & Judicial offices," read one, "shall be kept for ever separate, & no person exercising the one shall be capable of appointment to the others or to either of them." The draft constitution also sought to alter radically Virginia's criminal justice system, something Jefferson thought might be possible. "The General assembly," one provision stated, "shall have no power to pass any law inflicting death for any crime excepting murder & excepting also those offenses in the military service for which they shall think punishment of death absolutely necessary; and all capital punishments in other cases are hereby abolished." "[N]or shall they have power to prescribe torture in any case whatever," read another, with Jefferson explicitly attempting to outlaw without exception the power of legislators to authorize acts of torture. In 1776, an engaged Edmund Pendleton had himself written Jefferson on the subject of penal reform. "Our Criminal System of Law," Pendleton said, "has hitherto been too Sanguinary, punishing too many crimes with death, I confess." Though Pendleton said he "could wish to see that change for some other mode of Punishment in most cases," he warned Jefferson not to go too far, saying, "if you mean to relax all Punishments and rely on Virtue and the Public good as sufficient to prompt Obedience to the Laws, you must find a new race of men to be the subjects of it."[74]

Though Jefferson's draft constitution pushed the envelope too far, at least for Virginians in 1776, Jefferson's efforts to curtail executions did not stop there. Between 1776 and 1779, Jefferson absorbed *On Crimes and Punishments,* intensely studying Beccaria's book as he drafted a bill calling for more proportionate punishments in Virginia. Jefferson's bill, inspired by Beccaria's treatise, called for "a corresponding gradation of punishments" in relation to the seriousness of the offense. Along with Edmund Pendleton, Thomas Lee, George Mason, and George Wythe, Jefferson served on the Committee of Revisors, a committee charged shortly after independence with drafting revisions to Virginia's laws to be submitted to the state legislature for approval. "I have strictly observed the scale of punishments settled by the Committee, without being entirely satisfied with it," Jefferson wrote Wythe after drafting his bill, asking his mentor, a senior member of the bar, "scrupulously to examine and correct it, that it may be presented to our committee, with as few defects as possible." A member of the Continental Congress, Wythe had trained Jefferson as he read law and Wythe himself would later become a distinguished jurist. Under Wythe's tutelage, Jefferson studied ethics and philosophy and read works by Blackstone, Coke, Hume, Locke, and Montesquieu. While Jefferson's bill footnoted Beccaria's treatise four times, it also extensively cited medieval, far less progressive, sources, something that Jefferson felt obliged to do but that made him uncomfortable. "The 'Lex talionis,'" Jefferson told Wythe of the doctrine he felt constrained by tradition to include in his bill, "will be revolting to the humanized feelings of modern times." "An eye for an eye, and a hand for a hand," Jefferson wrote, "will exhibit spectacles in execution, whose moral effect would be questionable."[75]

The legislation that Jefferson ultimately drafted and that Wythe reviewed did not seek to abolish capital punishment entirely. Though it sought to curtail the death penalty's use, it called for mandatory death sentences for treason and murder, including for cases where a family member was murdered. In essence,

Jefferson's proposed code followed in many ways what one of Jefferson's biographers called "the Roman lex talionis, the law of the claw, and the Mosaic law, an 'eye for an eye and a tooth for a tooth,' as he put it." The proposed code provided for death by poison for those who killed by poisoning, the hanging and gibbeting of any challenger who killed someone in a duel, castration for male rapists and men committing sodomy, and, for acts of maiming, similar disfigurement. "Whosoever on purpose," Jefferson's bill stated, "shall disfigure another, by cutting out or disabling the tongue, slitting or cutting off a nose, lip, or ear, branding, or otherwise, shall be maimed, or disfigured in like sort." If an offender lacked the body part to be maimed or disfigured, the bill provided that "some other part of at least equal value and estimation, in the opinion of a jury," was to be taken. Indeed, Jefferson, who wrote his legislation in the midst of the Revolutionary War, later conceded that in drafting the bill he "thought it material not to vary the diction of the antient statutes by modernizing it, nor to give rise to new questions by new expressions." The speed with which executions were to be carried out under the bill showed Jefferson's belief in swift punishments, another idea advanced by Beccaria. Jefferson's bill provided that executions were to be carried out almost immediately—literally within days of sentencing—for those convicted of treason or murder. "Whenever sentence of death shall have been pronounced against any person for treason or murder," Jefferson's bill read, "execution thereof shall be done on the next day but one, after such sentence, unless it be Sunday, and then on the Monday following."[76]

Years later, in making observations on a manuscript written for the *Encyclopédie Politique,* Jefferson explained that "[i]n forming a scale of crimes & punishments, two considerations have principal weight": "1. The atrocity of the crime." "2. The peculiar circumstances of a country which furnish greater temptations to commit it, or greater facilities for escaping detection. The punishment must be heavier to counterbalance this." To Jefferson, like Beccaria, the state of the nation itself was thus of critical importance in assessing the propriety of a given punishment. "Was the first the only consideration," Jefferson wrote, "all nations would form the same scale." "But as the circumstances of a country have influence on the punishment, and no two countries exist precisely under the same circumstances," Jefferson added, "no two countries will form the same scale of crimes & punishments." As Jefferson noted on the proofs of Monsieur de Meusnier's manuscript: "[I]n America, the inhabitants let their horses go at large in the uninclosed lands which are so extensive as to maintain them altogether. It is easy therefore to steal them & easy to escape. Therefore the laws are obliged to oppose these temptations with a heavier degree of punishment. For this reason the stealing of a horse in America is punished more severely than stealing the same value in any other form." Saying that different arrangements for crimes and punishments would be found in Italy, Turkey, and China, Jefferson contrasted America's circumstances with those of Europe. "In Europe," Jefferson said, "where horses are confined so securely that it is impossible to steal them, that species of theft need not be punished more severely than any other." "In some countries of Europe," Jefferson wrote, "stealing fruit from trees is punished capitally." "The reason," Jefferson said, "is that it being impossible to lock fruit trees up in coffers, as we do our money, it is impossible to oppose physical bars to this species of theft." "This to an unreflecting American," Jefferson added, "appears the most enormous of all the abuses of power; because he has been used to see fruits hanging in such quantities that if not taken by men they would rot; he has been used to consider it therefore as of no value, as not furnishing materials for the commission of a crime." "This must," Jefferson concluded, "serve as an apology for the arrangements of crimes & punishments in the scale under our consideration."[77]

Jefferson's proposed legislation, "A Bill for Proportioning Crimes and Punishments in Cases Heretofore Capital," contained controversial and draconian provisions. Not only did it call for castration of males committing polygamy, sodomy, or rape, but under the legislation, a female committing rape or a homosexual act was to be punished "by boring through the cartilage of her nose a hole of one half inch in diameter at the least." One of the authorities quoted in a note to that section of the bill defined "sodomitry" as "carnal copulation against nature, to wit of man or woman in the same sex, or of either of them with beasts." In Jefferson's time, homosexuality was a crime and had long been treated as a felony. In 1776, male homosexuality was universally punishable by death in the thirteen American colonies, and in earlier times, in at least one colony, lesbians were also subject to the same punishment for relations with other women. Not until 1786, when reform began sweeping the country, did Pennsylvania change its penal laws so that anyone committing "robbery, burglary, sodomy, or buggary" would suffer not death, but instead the forfeiture of all his lands and goods and servitude for a term "not exceeding ten years." Only after Jefferson's rape provision came under attack in Europe did Jefferson recant his support for it. As Jefferson wrote James Madison from Paris: "I shall be glad when the revisal shall be got thro.' In the criminal law, the principle of retaliation is much criticised here, particularly in the case of Rape. They think the punishment indecent & unjustifiable. I should be for altering it, but for a different reason: that is on account of the temptation women would be under to make it the instrument of vengeance against an inconstant lord, & of disappointment to a rival."[78]

Despite its harsh provisions, Jefferson's bill was still quite progressive for the age. It greatly restricted the categories of death-eligible offenses and proclaimed that offenders committing "an inferior injury" are, after suffering proportionate punishments, entitled to the protection of the law. In Connecticut, by contrast, a draconian law, modeled on a two thousand–year-old Hebrew law stating that "[i]f any man lyeth with mankinde as he lyeth with a woman, both of them have committed abhomimation, they both shall surely be put to death," remained on the books until forty-six years after the Declaration of Independence. Jefferson's bill, which sought to moderate punishments, described capital punishment as "the last melancholy resource" against those whose existence has become "inconsistent with the safety of their fellow citizens." In his handwritten outline of the bill, prepared in 1777, Jefferson divided crimes into three categories: (1) death-eligible offenses, in Jefferson's notation, "Crimes whose punishmt. Extends to *Life*"; (2) "Crimes whose punishment goes to *Limb*," such as castration for rapists; and (3) "Crimes punishable by *Labor* &c." In limiting the death penalty to treason and murder, Jefferson thus categorically rejected executions for the one hundred–plus felonies that England's criminal code made death-eligible. In the bill itself, Jefferson specifically emphasized that "cruel and sanguinary laws defeat their own purpose." As he wrote to Edmund Pendleton in August 1776, Jefferson believed in "strict and inflexible punishments," but in ones that were "proportioned to the crime," "proportioned to the offense."[79]

The first section of Jefferson's bill gives a sense of Jefferson's approach to the criminal law at the time he drafted it. "Whereas it frequently happens that wicked and dissolute men, resigning themselves to the dominion of inordinate passions, commit violations on the lives, liberties, and property of others," Jefferson explained, "government would be defective in its principal purpose, were it not to restrain such criminal acts by inflicting due punishments on those who perpetrate them." "[B]ut it appears at the same time," Jefferson wrote, that a member of society "committing an inferior injury, does not wholly forfeit the protection of his fellow citizens, but after suffering a punishment in proportion to his offence, is entitled to their protection from all greater pain, so that it becomes a duty in the Legislature to arrange in a proper scale the crimes which it may be necessary for them to repress, and to adjust there a corresponding gradation of punishments." Under Jefferson's scale of punishments, some crimes were to be punished corporally or by transportation out of the country. For example, section 29 of his bill read: "All attempts to delude the people, or to abuse their understanding by exercise of the pretended arts of witchcraft, conjuration, enchantment, or sorcery, or by pretended prophecies, shall be punished by ducking and whipping, at the discretion of a jury, not exceeding fifteen stripes." "Slaves guilty of any offence punishable in others by labour in the public works," the bill read, "shall be transported to such parts in the West-Indies, South-America, or Africa, as the Governor shall direct, there to be continued in slavery." In a subsequent footnote to his bill, Jefferson added: "It is not only vain, but wicked, in a legislator to frame laws in opposition to the laws of nature, and to arm them with the terrors of death. This is truly creating crimes in order to punish them."[80]

Other sections of Jefferson's bill also laid out the gradation of punishments Jefferson then had in mind. Section 2 read that "no crime shall be henceforth punished by the deprivation of life or limb, except those herein after ordained to be so punished." In another footnote, Jefferson explained: "This takes away the punishment of cutting off the hand of a person striking another, or drawing his sword in one of the superior courts of justice." "In an earlier stage of the Common law," Jefferson added, "it was death." Section 3 laid out death by hanging as the punishment for treason, with "death by burying alive," considered in an earlier outline, having been rejected for that offense. Section 4 likewise provided: "If any person commit petty treason, or a husband murder his wife, a parent, his child, or a child his parent, he shall suffer death, by hanging, and his body be delivered to Anatomists to be dissected." For cases of manslaughter, Jefferson's bill provided that the guilty "shall, for the first offence, be condemned to hard labour for seven years in the public works," and that "[t]he second offence shall be deemed murder." "Manslaughter is punishable at law, by burning in the hands, and forfeiture of chattels," Jefferson recorded in another footnote. Counterfeiting, another crime that elsewhere was punishable by death or "cutting off the hand," was proposed to be punished under Jefferson's bill by six years of "hard labour" in the "public works," along with a forfeiture of all lands and goods to the commonwealth. Jefferson proposed that burglary—punishable by death at common law—be punished instead with four years of "hard labour . . . in the public works," along with "double reparation to the persons injured," and that "horse-stealing" be punished by three years' "hard labour . . . in the public works" with "reparation to the person injured." "The offence of Horse-stealing," Jefferson explained in one of his many footnotes, "seems properly distinguishable from other larcenies, here, where these animals generally run at large, the temptation being so great and frequent, and the facility of commission so remarkable."[81]

Jefferson's bill ultimately failed to pass by a single vote, but it undeniably marked an attempt by Jefferson drastically to scale back death sentences. One commentator writing in 1887 praised the bill for attempting to remove the death penalty for twenty-seven felonies at a time far earlier than when such legislative efforts were made in England. In a draft autobiography written in the twilight of his life, Jefferson himself reflected on the bill's narrow defeat even as he explicitly rejected the doctrine of lex talionis. "On the subject of the Criminall law," Jefferson wrote of his bill, "all were agreed that the punishment of death should be abolished, except for treason and murder; and that, for other felonies should be substituted hard labor in the public works, and in some cases, the Lex talionis." "How this last revolting principle came to obtain our approbation," Jefferson remarked, "I do not remember." In his autobiographical statement, Jefferson specifically credited Beccaria's book for being the catalyst for his anti–death penalty stance. As Jefferson wrote: "Beccaria and other writers on crimes and punishments had satisfied the reasonable world of the unrightfulness and inefficacy of the punishment of crimes by death." Noting that "hard labor on roads, canals and other public works, had been suggested as a proper substitute," Jefferson pointed out that "[t]he Revisors had adopted these opinions; but the general idea of our country had not yet advanced to that point." Only many years after it was first introduced did a different version of Jefferson's bill seeking more proportionate punishments gain passage in Virginia.[82]

Many Founding Fathers were highly ambivalent about capital punishment, and Jefferson, it is clear, was no exception. During the Revolutionary War, Jefferson saw executions as warranted to maintain order and discipline during wartime. Indeed, he helped to revise the Articles of War in 1776, expanding the number of death-eligible offenses in them. On June 17, 1776, Jefferson himself joined a committee report to Congress dealing with the mistreatment of prisoners of war. The report recounted that, after several hundred Continental Army soldiers surrendered at a garrison at The Cedars, a strategic locale west of Montreal, enemy forces made up of British and Indian combatants stripped the men of their clothes and turned the captive prisoners over to Indians who "murdered two of them, butchering the one with tomahawks & drowning the other." Others, the report said, were left "exposed in an island naked & perishing with cold & famine." When Continental Army reinforcements arrived at the garrison, an enemy captain named George Forster reportedly notified Brigadier General Benedict Arnold that if an attack occurred all five hundred prisoners would be put to death. "Arnold," the report said, "was extremely averse to entering on any agreement of that kind, & was at length induced to do it by no other motive than that of saving the prisoners from cruel & inhuman death, threatened in such terms as left no doubt it was to be perpetrated." The agreement reached on May 27, 1776, called for a prisoner exchange, but the report stated that the enemy captain had "detained a considerable number of the prisoners he had thus stipulated to deliver, & sent them into the Indian countries for purposes unknown." The report, in Jefferson's handwriting, offered up a number of resolutions, one of which said "the murder of two of the prisoners of war was a gross and barbarous violation of the laws of nature & nations." "Resolved," read another, "that it is the opinion of this committee that if the enemy shall put to death, torture, or otherwise ill treat any of the hostages in their hands . . . recourse must be had to retaliation as the sole means of stopping the progress of human butchery, & that for that purpose punishments of the same kind & degree be inflicted on an equal number of their subjects taken by us, till they shall be taught due respect to the violated rights of nations."[83]

In 1778, Jefferson—concerned about lawlessness—even helped draft a bill of attainder against Josiah Philips, an "outlaw" charged with "committing murders, burning houses, wasting farms," and confederating with others to levy war against the Commonwealth of Virginia. A Tory, Philips had a British commission and was using it, as historian Leonard Levy puts it, "as a shield for plundering and terrorizing the Virginia countryside." Governor Patrick

Henry had offered a five-hundred-dollar reward for the capture of Philips, dead or alive, and placed the matter before Virginia's assembly. Jefferson and Henry decided a bill of attainder would be the best mechanism to deal with Philips, and the assembly promptly adopted a bill of attainder written by Jefferson. It provided that "the usual forms and procedures of the courts of law" would leave citizens exposed to further crimes, stating that if Philips and his confederates did not surrender in one month, they "shall stand and be convicted and attainted of high treason, and shall suffer the pains of death." "[B]e it further enacted," the bill read, "that from and after the passing of this act, it shall be lawful for any person, with or without orders, to pursue and slay the said Josiah Philips and any others who have been his associates or confederates." Once apprehended, Philips was indicted for highway robbery for stealing twenty-eight men's felt hats (worth twenty shillings apiece) and a ball of twine (valued at five shillings) from James Hargrove. In 1815, long after Philips's capture and execution, Jefferson commented on his bill of attainder, which was not actually used to justify the execution of Philips, when marking up proof sheets for a book on Virginia history. "No one doubted," Jefferson wrote, speaking of his use of a bill of attainder thirty-seven years earlier, "that society had a right to erase from the roll of its members any one who rendered his existence inconsistent with theirs; to withdraw from him the protection of laws, and to remove him from among them by exile, or even by death if necessary." Though Jefferson himself had proposed a new constitution for Virginia in 1783 that denied the legislature any power "to pass any bill of attainder" or "other law declaring any person guilty" of "treason or felony," Jefferson noted long after the fact that, in 1778, he was "thoroughly persuaded of the correctness of this proceeding, and am more and more convinced by reflection."[84]

While recognizing the necessity of punishments, even harsh ones, Jefferson saw proportionality above all else as the touchstone of the law and often saw death as an inappropriate criminal sanction. For example, in the aftermath of the French Revolution, Jefferson felt conflicted and remorseful over the execution of the French king and queen, seeing death as unnecessary. In his draft autobiography, written in 1821, Jefferson laid out his feelings:

The deed which closed the mortal course of these sovereigns, I shall neither approve nor condemn. I am not prepared to say that the first magistrate of a nation cannot commit treason against his country, or is unamenable to it's punishment: nor yet that where there is no written law, no regulated tribunal, there is not a law in our hearts, and a power in our hands, given for righteous employment in maintaining right, and redressing wrong. Of those who judged the king, many thought him wilfully criminal, many that his existence would keep the nation in perpetual conflict with the horde of kings, who would war against a regeneration which might come home to themselves, and that it were better that one should die than all. I should not have voted with this portion of the legislature. I should have shut up the Queen in a Convent, putting harm out of her power, and placed the king in his station, investing him with limited powers, which I verily believe he would have honestly exercised, according to the measure of his understanding.

To Albert Gallatin, his secretary of the treasury, Jefferson also wrote in 1808 of smugglers violating an embargo on shipments: "If all these people are convicted, there will be too many to be punished with death." "My hope is that they will send me full statements of every man's case, that the most guilty may be marked as examples, and the less so suffer long imprisonment under reprieves from time to time."[85]

While in France, Jefferson regularly visited with Thomas Paine, the committed abolitionist; and upon Paine's return home to America in 1802, Jefferson hosted him at Monticello and the White House, once remarking: "No writer has exceeded Paine in ease and familiarity of style, in perspicuity of expression, happiness of elucidation, and in simple and unassuming language." Just weeks before dying, Jefferson—himself an extraordinary writer—wrote Washington, D.C.'s mayor in 1826, recalling Richard Rumbold's last words. In his final speech, made on the scaffold, Rumbold, an English colonel executed for treason in 1685, said he was "sure there was no Man born marked of God above another; for none comes into the World with a Saddle on his Back, neither any Booted and Spurr'd to Ride him." To Mayor Roger Weightman, preparing to celebrate the fiftieth anniversary of the Declaration of Independence, Jefferson similarly wrote: "All eyes are opened, or opening, to the rights of man. The general spread of the light of science has already laid open to every view the palpable truth, that the mass of mankind has not been born with saddles on their backs, nor a favored few booted and spurred, ready to ride them legitimately, by the grace of God." In his letter, the last of his life, Jefferson described the Declaration of Independence as a kind of beacon for mankind, though he recognized its principles had yet to be fully realized. "May it be to the world," Jefferson wrote, "what I believe it will be, (to some parts sooner, to others later, but finally to all,) the signal of arousing men to burst the chains under which monkish ignorance and superstition had persuaded them to bind themselves, and to assume the blessings and security of self-government."[86]

A pragmatist, Jefferson believed in punishment but thought the punishments of his age too harsh. In his letter to Edmund Pendleton in August 1776, Jefferson, when discussing his bill to revise Virginia's laws, laid out his early views on capital punishment in no uncertain terms: "The fantastical idea of virtue and the public good being a sufficient security to the state against the commission of crimes, which you say you have heard insisted on by some, I assure you was never mine. It is only the sanguinary hue of our penal laws which I meant to object to. Punishments I know are necessary, and I would provide them, strict and inflexible, but proportioned to the crime." "Death," Jefferson wrote, worried that the crime of treason might be construed too expansively, "might be inflicted for murther and perhaps for treason if you would take out of the description of treason all crimes which are not such in their nature." For rape and "buggery," Jefferson told Pendleton, "punish by castration." "All other crimes," Jefferson added, "by working on high roads, rivers, gallies &c. a certain time proportioned to the offence." "Laws thus proportionate and mild," Jefferson said, "should never be dispensed with." "Let mercy be the character of the law-giver," he added, "but let the judge be a mere machine." In other words, Jefferson preferred that society be governed by laws, not men, and that those laws dictate the criminal sanctions, not the whim or the discretion of judges. As Jefferson wrote: "The mercies of the law will be dispensed equally and impartially to every description of men; those of the judge or of the executive power," he warned, "will be the eccentric impulses of whimsical, capricious designing man."[87]

Jefferson himself certainly paid close attention to penal reform in Pennsylvania, where he had spent some time and where his friend Dr. Benjamin Rush had very publicly advocated change. In 1821, in the twilight of his life, Jefferson explained that after his bill for proportioning crimes and punishments failed by a single vote, "the public opinion was ripening, by time, by reflection, and by the example of Pennsylvania." Philadelphia and its Quakers had been at the epicenter of penal reform, and Jefferson specifically noted that in 1796, just two years after Pennsylvania divided murder into degrees, "our legislature resumed the subject, and passed the law for amending the penal laws of the Commonwealth." By then, Jefferson had shown his clear and increasing distaste for the death penalty, including in his private correspondence. In 1816, Jefferson penned a letter to William Wirt, Patrick Henry's biographer and Jefferson's choice to be the prosecutor in Aaron Burr's treason trial. In that letter, Jefferson stated with obvious satisfaction that Virginia "justly prides itself on having gone thro' the revolution without a single example of capital punishment connected with that." And in that respect, Jefferson was hardly alone among his contemporaries. His friend the Marquis de Lafayette, the Revolutionary War general who served in the Continental Army under George Washington, also opposed executions. Lafayette, who drafted the French Declaration of the Rights of Man and of the Citizen with Jefferson's assistance, spoke out forcefully against executions, saying that "the abolition of capital punishment" had been "advocated by the most eminent statesmen," including America's Edward Livingston. "I shall ask for the abolition of the punishment of death," Lafayette famously said, "until I have the infallibility of human judgment demonstrated to me." The French Declaration of 1789 itself proclaimed that "[o]nly strictly and obviously necessary punishments may be established by the law."[88]

After Virginia's penal code was finally changed, Jefferson himself commented on the passage of the bill reforming Virginia's laws. That reform effort had been led by George Keith Taylor, who implored Virginians to "imitate and adopt" Pennsylvania's approach. In 1796, the Virginia legislature abolished the death penalty for all crimes committed by free persons except for first-degree murder, thus ending the death penalty for such crimes as counterfeiting "tobacco notes," negotiable certificates recording the weight of a crop, which could be used in the payment of taxes. Even treason was no longer declared a capital crime. As part of the reform measure, Virginia's governor was directed to buy land for a penitentiary, and thirty thousand dollars was appropriated to build one large enough to hold two hundred inmates. Taylor, Jefferson wrote, avoided "the adoption of any part of the diction of mine, the text of which had been studiously drawn in the technical terms of the law, so as to give no occasion for new questions by new expressions." "When I drew mine," Jefferson said, "public labor was thought the best punishment to be substituted for death." "But, while I was in France," Jefferson added, "I heard of a society in England, who had successfully introduced solitary confinement, and saw the drawing of a prison at Lyons, in France, formed on the idea of solitary confinement." Jefferson then explained what he did next: "[B]eing applied to by the Governor of Virginia for the plan of a Capitol and Prison, I sent him the Lyons plan, accompanying it with a drawing on a smaller scale, better adapted to our use. This was in June, 1786." "Mr. Taylor very judiciously adopted this idea," Jefferson said, noting that the idea had already "been acted on in Philadelphia, probably from the English model." Taylor, Jefferson emphasized, "substituted labor in confinement" for the "public labor" originally proposed by the Committee of Revisors. As Jefferson recalled: "The public mind was ripe for this in 1796, when Mr. Taylor proposed it, and ripened chiefly by the experiment in Philadelphia; whereas, in 1785, when it had been proposed to our assembly, they were not quite ripe for it."[89]

In a letter written in 1809 from Monticello, Jefferson also commented on his role in Virginia's revisal project and the passage of Taylor's bill. As to the revisal, Jefferson explained that "Col. Mason declined undertaking the execution of any part of it, as not being sufficiently read in the law," and that the distribution of committee work led him to assume responsibility for "the laws concerning crimes and punishments." "The digest of that act," Jefferson explained, "employed me longer than I believe all the rest of the work, for it rendered it necessary for me to go with great care over Bracton, Britton, the Saxon statutes, and the works of authority on criminal law; and it gave me great satisfaction to find that in general I had only to reduce the law to its ancient Saxon condition, stripping it of all the innovations and rigorisms of subsequent times, to make it what it should be." After the committee members completed their work separately, Jefferson noted of his handling of the common law: "Mr. Wythe, Mr. Pendleton and myself" met in Williamsburg and held "a long session" spent "weighing and correcting every word" of their work. "Experience has convinced me," Jefferson wrote in his letter, "that the change in the style of the laws was for the better, and it has sensibly reformed the style of our laws from that time downwards, insomuch that they have obtained, in that respect, the approbation of men of consideration on both sides of the Atlantic." "Whether the change in the style and form of the criminal law, as introduced by Mr. Taylor, was for the better," Jefferson added, "is not for me to judge." "The substitution of the penitentiary, instead of labor on the high road and of some other punishments truly objectionable," Jefferson emphasized, "is a just merit to be ascribed to Mr. Taylor's law." "When our report was made," Jefferson said of his work many years earlier, in 1779, "the idea of a penitentiary had never been suggested, the happy experiment of Pennsylvania we had not then the benefit of." Plainly, Jefferson, like Philadelphia's pioneering reformers, had come to embrace the concept of prisons as a way to handle and house offenders.[90]

Jefferson's waning interest in capital prosecutions is further reflected in his correspondence with James Monroe. Monroe, a Virginia governor destined to become the fifth President of the United States, had sought Jefferson's advice as to how rebellious slaves should be punished. It all began after a twenty-four-year-old blacksmith named Gabriel, a literate slave on Thomas Prosser's plantation six miles outside of Richmond, was caught stealing a pig from a white overseer in 1799. Prosser treated his slaves with great barbarity, as Jefferson would learn, and Gabriel bit off the pig owner's ear in the ensuing melee and was branded on the left hand for his crime. Jailed a second time for attacking a white man, Gabriel, whether inspired by the French Revolution, efforts in Virginia to abolish slavery, or a successful slave rebellion in the Caribbean, thereafter concocted a plot to win freedom for himself and other slaves in southeastern Virginia. During the spring and summer of 1800, he forged swords and made five hundred bullets and enlisted others, including two whites, in his plan, crafting a flag reading "Death or Liberty." "It is unquestionably the most serious and formidable conspiracy we have ever known of this kind," Governor Monroe told Jefferson after the plot, involving five surrounding counties, was exposed. The slaves, it was later revealed, planned to kill Gabriel's tormentors, seize some guns from a tavern and the penitentiary, then march on Richmond, setting fires and capturing the state capital, the armory, the treasury building, and the governor's residence. Gabriel harbored hopes that he and his compatriots might obtain a ship to escape the United States, or that Governor Monroe, who had served as America's ambassador in Paris, would emancipate him. When the plot to take the capital and hold Monroe hostage was foiled at the end of August, however, Monroe did nothing of the sort; instead, he called out the state militia and Virginia soldiers began rounding up slaves thought to have joined the conspiracy.[91]

In the wake of the plot, which had long been rumored, a number of slaves—some twenty-six in all—were hanged in Richmond and on the outskirts of town. Monroe kept Jefferson apprised of what was happening and, in letters, sought his advice on what to do. "There has been great alarm here of late at the prospect of an insurrection of the Negroes in this city and its neighborhood," Monroe wrote Jefferson on September 9, 1800, noting that "[a]bout thirty are in prison who are to be tried on Thursday, and others are daily discovered and apprehended in the vicinity of the city." "We have had much trouble with the negroes here," Monroe reiterated to Jefferson six days later, explaining that the "plan of an insurrection" had been "clearly proved." The plot, Monroe wrote, had been "of considerable extent," relaying to Jefferson that conspirators had already been "condemned & executed." The trials of the slaves, conducted in a hurried manner, attracted considerable public attention, with guilty verdicts followed quickly by sentences of death.[92]

Under Virginia law, slaves were not tried in the same courts as whites. Instead, accused slaves appeared before a special five-judge court, all of whom had to agree on the punishment for death to be imposed. Unless the governor pardoned an offender, the court's decision was final, with the judges possessing the power to order public hangings. "It is the opinion of the magistrates who examined those committed that the whole, very few excepted, will be condemned," Monroe apprised Jefferson. On its first day of proceedings, convening less than two weeks after the first arrests, the court sentenced six defendants to die at dawn or noon of the next day. The following week, even more slaves were hanged, with troops protecting the scaffold so that hostile citizens—in the mood for lynchings—would not get to the slaves first. "[W]hen it became indispensably necessary to resort to strong measures with a view to protect the town, the public arms, the treasury, and the jail," Monroe said, "a display" was made "to intimidate those people." Monroe, it appears, feared a repeat in Virginia of the kind of violent slave rebellion that had occurred in Santo Domingo. "It is hardly to be presumed," Monroe told Jefferson, that "a rebel who avows it was his intention to assassinate his master" will, if pardoned, "ever become a useful servant." By mid-September, however, Monroe began questioning the wisdom of further reprisals. Telling Jefferson on September 15 that the state, which by then had already executed ten conspirators, had "made a display of force," Monroe predicted that up to forty more slaves would hang unless he intervened. Unsure "whether mercy or severity is the better policy in this case," Monroe nonetheless expressed the view that "when there is cause for doubt it is best to incline to the former." "When to arrest the hand of the executioner is a question of great importance," Monroe wrote Jefferson, adding, "I shall be happy to have your opinion on these points."[93]

In his response to Monroe, Jefferson agreed: "Where to stay the hand of the executioner is an important question." "Those who have escaped from the immediate danger," Jefferson wrote back, "must have feelings which would dispose them to extend the executions." "Even here, where every thing has been perfectly tranquil, but where a familiarity with slavery, and a possibility of danger from that quarter prepare the general mind for some severities," Jefferson noted, writing from Monticello, "there is a strong sentiment that there has been hanging enough." The proprietor of Monticello, on which more than a hundred slaves raised crops, tended livestock, and made everything from clothes to nails to carriages, feared a backlash if the executions continued unabated. "The other states & the world at large will forever condemn us if we indulge in a principle of revenge, or go one step beyond absolute necessity," Jefferson said. "Our situation is indeed a difficult one," Jefferson added, saying that "I doubt whether these people can ever be permitted to go at large among us with safety." "To reprieve them and keep them in prison till the meeting of the legislature," Jefferson offered, would only "encourage efforts for their release." In lieu of executions, Jefferson sought alternative measures, writing: "Is there no fort or garrison of the State or of the Union, where they could be confined, and where the presence of the garrison would preclude all ideas of attempting a rescue? Surely the Legislature would pass a law for the exportation, the proper measure on this and all similar occasions." "I hazard these thoughts for your own consideration only," Jefferson said, "as I should be unwilling to be quoted in the case." After Jefferson's letter arrived, Monroe, who commuted to transportation many death sentences imposed by county courts, recommended leniency for many of the slaves. While some convicted conspirators received pardons or were "reprieved for transportation" to Spanish Louisiana, in the end twenty-six slaves were hanged for their role in the conspiracy, including Gabriel, who was located in hiding after a three-hundred-dollar reward was placed on his head. After his arrest, Gabriel had been transported to Richmond in irons on September 27, tried nine days later, and then quickly sentenced to die, a sentence that was carried out in early October along with those of other coconspirators.[94]

James Madison

James Madison, who saw the Revolutionary War as a fight for "the rights of human nature," considered military force necessary to preserve order. In addressing Virginia's constitutional convention, Madison implored his colleagues: "Can any government be established, that will answer any purpose whatever, unless force be provided for executing its laws?" "The militia ought to be called for to suppress smugglers," Madison said, emphasizing that the proposed constitution empowered Congress to set up courts "to try felonies and piracies committed on the high seas." Richard Henry Lee, his fellow Virginian, had in 1781 specifically advocated the use of capital punishment to combat pirating and the raiding of America's coastline. Madison was deeply concerned with preserving order. "If riots should happen, the militia are proper to quell it, to prevent a resort to another mode," Madison said. "As to the infliction of ignominious punishments," though, Madison pointed out in his discussion of the militia that "we have no ground for alarm, if we consider the circumstances of the people at large." As Madison sparred with George Mason over whether "severe," "ignominious," or "grievous" punishments would be inflicted on state militia members as a pretence for establishing a standing army, Madison concluded: "There will be no punishments so ignominious as have been inflicted already. The militia law of every state to the north of Maryland, is less rigorous than the particular law of this state." "I think that the people of those states," he observed, "would not agree to be subjected to a more harsh punishment than their own militia laws inflict." The state's militia, Madison said, would still be able to "suppress insurrections" and "quell riots" when "they were not in the actual service of the United States."[95]

As a young man, Madison had seen the power of the law—and the potential for its abuse—in his native Virginia. Baptist ministers there lived under continual threat of persecution and punishment, with whips stuck down the throats of Baptist preachers. According to John Leland, a Baptist leader, some thirty Baptist preachers were imprisoned in Virginia between 1768 and 1775, with Madison and others coming to despise the corruption of the Anglican Church, England's official denomination. One indictment, for example, charged that the evangelical Baptists "can not meet a man upon the road, but they must ram a text of scripture down his throat!" This state of affairs prompted Madison, who wanted greater religious tolerance, to pen a letter in January 1774 to his closest friend William Bradford. In 1773, Madison had protested the imprisonment of unlicensed Baptist preachers. To Bradford, Madison wrote of the "diabolical, hell-conceived principle" allowing "well-meaning men" to be imprisoned "in close jail for publishing their religious sentiments, which in the main are very orthodox." The sympathetic Bradford quickly wrote back, lauding the religious freedom in Pennsylvania. "I am sorry to hear that Persecution has got so much footing among you," he wrote to his Virginia friend. "Persecution is a weed that grows not in our happy soil," Bradford explained, writing that Madison's description of Virginia—what Bradford called "your Country"—"makes me more in love with mine." In Virginia, the death penalty itself could be imposed for certain religious offenses. In 1788, in line with a statute of King James I applicable to England and Wales, the state legislature made bigamy and polygamy capital crimes. In colonial times, Virginia's "Dade Code," promulgated in 1610, had authorized the punishment of death for anyone who spoke "impiously or maliciously" of the "Holy and Blessed Trinity" or "against the known articles of Christian faith."[96]

After graduating from the College of New Jersey in 1771, Madison, who had Anglican roots but had studied at Princeton under John Witherspoon, a Presbyterian minister, had seriously contemplated becoming a lawyer. He never traveled to England to attend the Inns of Court, as some young men did, but he told his college classmate William Bradford in 1773 that he intended "to read Law occasionally and have procured books for that purpose." Madison also corresponded with Bradford about his friend's decision to take up the study of law, once asking Bradford to send him a draft of Pennsylvania's constitution so he could learn more about "religious Toleration." In the course of their correspondence, Madison urged Bradford to become a "fervent Advocate in the cause of Christ," advised him to "always keep the Ministry obliquely in View whatever your profession be." "This will lead you," he told Bradford, "to cultivate an acquaintance occasionally with the most sublime of all Sciences and will qualify you for a change of public character if you should hereafter desire it." Bradford had decided to study law in Philadelphia with Edward Shippen, and Madison asked Bradford to send him a reading list. Bradford later told his friend that he was reading Blackstone's *Commentaries*, a title Bradford said "I am most pleased with & find but little of that disagreeable dryness I was taught to expect."[97]

Following the Revolutionary War, Madison, despite never having practiced law, readily joined Jefferson, his more experienced Virginia colleague, in seeking to prohibit cruelty and reform the country's penal laws. As the primary architect of the U.S. Constitution, Madison was responsible for defending that document in his home state, and he ultimately embraced the prohibition against "cruel and unusual punishments." Unlike Virginia, which had a written declaration of rights, the proposed federal constitution initially lacked one—something Madison could hardly ignore when he returned home. In fact, Virginia's ratification convention only begrudgingly endorsed the Constitution in 1788, appending to its approval a list of proposed amendments, collectively described as "a declaration or bill of rights." Thirteenth on the list was language copied from Virginia's own declaration: "That excessive bail ought not to be required, nor excessive fines imposed, nor cruel and unusual punishments inflicted." Delegates from state ratifying conventions in New York, North Carolina, Rhode Island, and Pennsylvania also wanted language resembling that of Section 10 of the English Bill of Rights. That section, as originally drafted and introduced in the House of Commons, had read: "The requiring excessive Bail of Persons committed in criminal Cases, and imposing excessive Fines, and illegal Punishments, to be prevented." But Parliament changed that draft language, so the final version of Section 10 of the English Bill of Rights, as adopted, read as Virginia's would later: "That excessive Bail ought not to be required, nor excessive Fines imposed; nor cruel and unusual Punishments inflicted." When drafting amendments for presentation to the First Congress in 1789, Madison naturally looked to Virginia's declaration and liked the prohibition on cruelty, making only one modification. To strengthen the text, he substituted the mandatory declarative "shall not" for the more hortatory "ought not," leading to what is today the language of the Eighth Amendment.[98]

By seeking the adoption of the Cruel and Unusual Punishments Clause, Madison demonstrated his commitment—a long-term one at that, as it would be in the Constitution itself—to safeguarding prisoners' human rights. Indeed, Article V of the Constitution makes amending it extremely difficult, as "two thirds of both Houses" or "two thirds of the several States" must concur, followed by the ratification "by the Legislatures of three fourths of the several States." Madison himself had grown up in a slaveholding culture in which the death penalty was a grim reality, especially for blacks. In 1748, just three years before Madison was born, Thomas Crew, the sheriff of Orange County, executed a slave named Eve accused of poisoning her master. Crew lived in the house closest to the Madisons' estate, and Eve's execution was brutal: she was burned at the stake. Despite hailing from a locality also known to have exhibited the head of an executed slave on a pole, Madison told Dr. Benjamin Rush that he favored penal reform. Dr. Rush and Madison actually carried on an active correspondence in 1790, including one letter sent by Rush on February 18 in which Rush commented on how "theft & murder are contrary to the divine commands." And that letter was by no means the only one to mention the criminal law. On February 27, 1790, Rush also wrote Madison, this time adding to his letter a long postscript that began by noting that "extracts contained in the enclosed pamphlet show that mankind are growing wiser upon the subject of penal laws." The pamphlet had recommended the abandonment of the gallows, and Madison replied two weeks later, ending his letter with the following statement: "I must add my thanks for the little pamphlet covered by your last. I have for some time been a thorough believer in the doctrine which it exemplifies. I am not unapprized of the obligation which in common with other proselytes, I am under to the lessons of your pen." According to one historian, Madison, the man who played a central role in framing the Bill of Rights, "favored abandoning capital punishment altogether," though Madison himself wrote little on the subject and, as a later letter makes clear, may not in fact have opposed executions for every category of offender.[99]

In his native Virginia, Madison actively worked alongside Jefferson for penal reform. As a member of the Virginia House of Delegates, Madison took the lead in attempting to pass Jefferson's bill seeking more proportionate punishments. Although the committee Jefferson chaired to revise Virginia's laws met in early 1777, it was not until late 1778 that a busy Jefferson had the bill drafted. The bill was submitted by the Committee of Revisors in 1779 but was tabled, and it was not until 1785 that the bill was introduced in the Virginia legislature. By then, Jefferson was serving as America's ambassador in Paris, so it fell to James Madison to present the bill in Jefferson's absence. Madison, who came to believe Virginia's revisors "were unfortunately misled into some of the specious errors of Beccaria, then in the zenith of his fame," did his best to secure the bill's passage, though he told James Monroe in December 1785 that the bill was "assailed on all sides" and that "Mr. Mercer has proclaimed unceasing hostility against it." After the bill's defeat, Madison, who once predicted to Monroe that, despite changes to the bill, "I think the main principle of it will finally triumph over all opposition," wrote that the bill's fate was sealed by "[t]he rage against Horse stealers." *On Crimes and Punishments* had addressed a wide range of topics, with Beccaria's arguments against torture and the death penalty forming only part of his treatise. In 1787, Madison, who favored more proportionate punishments, ruefully informed Jefferson that the bill, "after being altered so as to remove most of the objections," "was lost by a single vote." Madison expressed disappointment in the bill's narrow defeat, with Jefferson nonetheless later expressing deep gratitude to "the unwearied exertions of Mr. Madison" in wrestling with the legislature "in opposition to the endless quibbles, chicaneries, perversions, vexations and delays of lawyers and demilawyers." Apparently, Virginians found unsatisfactory the provision in the bill targeted at horse thieves. "Whosoever shall be guilty of horse-stealing," that provision read, "shall be condemned to hard labour three years in the public works, and shall make reparation to the person injured." Virginia's legislature had repeatedly made efforts to curb the theft of horses, with the death penalty extended to accessories to that crime in 1792 and horse thievery made ineligible for "benefit of clergy" in 1789.[100]

After Jefferson's bill failed by a single vote in 1785, Madison—who liked to win—expressed his frustrations to his closest friends. To James Monroe, Madison wrote in December 1785: "Our progress in the Revisal has been stopped by the waste of time produced by the inveterate and prolix opposition of its adversaries, & the approach of Christmas. The Bill proportioning crimes & punishments was the one at which we stuck after wading thro' the most difficult parts of it." To Jefferson, Madison lamented on February 15, 1787, that, because of the bill's defeat, "our old bloody code is by this event fully restored." Madison had also written Jefferson a year earlier, in 1786, to describe the difficulties he had repeatedly encountered in the legislative process to enact a revised code: "We have never been without opponents who contest at least every innovation inch by inch. The bill proportioning crimes & punishments on which we were wrecked last year, has after undergoing a number of alterations, got thro' a Committee of the whole; but it has not yet been reported to the House, where it will meet with the most vigorous attack." In 1788, Madison—concerned about the severity of executions, yet maybe still unsure of where he himself stood on the issue—made these remarks on a draft Virginia constitution prepared by Thomas Jefferson:

It is at least questionable whether death ought to be confined to "Treason and murder." It would not therefore be prudent to tie the hands of Government in the manner here proposed. The prohibition of pardon, however specious in theory would have practical consequences which render it inadmissible. A single instance is a sufficient proof. The crime of treason is generally shared by a number, and often a very great number. It would be politically if not morally wrong to take away the lives of all even if every individual were equally guilty. What name would be given to a severity which made no distinction between the legal & the moral offence—between the deluded multitude and their wicked leaders. A second trial would not avoid the difficulty; because the oaths of the jury would not permit them to hearken to any voice but the inexorable voice of the law.[101]

People's views, of course, constantly evolve, and Madison was no exception. In 1816, President Madison, who regularly followed developments in the nation's laws, called as commander in chief for a liberalization of the country's criminal laws. As Madison said in his annual congressional message that year: "I submit to the wisdom of Congress whether a more enlarged revisal of the criminal code be not expedient for the purpose of mitigating in certain cases penalties which were adopted into it antecedent to experiment and examples which justify and recommend a more lenient policy." Perhaps the best articulation of Madison's views on capital punishment itself, however, was expressed privately to someone he barely knew. After he finished his presidential term, Madison wrote a letter to a war veteran who had solicited his views on the death penalty, which Madison once called "one of the most solemn acts of sovereign authority." In 1823, G. F. H. Crockett, a Kentuckian, wrote to Madison, enclosing a copy of Crockett's address to the Kentucky legislature on the abolition of capital punishment. Madison wrote back later that year, acknowledging receipt of Crockett's letter and his legislative address.[102]

Madison's letter in reply to Crockett said that "enlightened opinions are as yet much at variance" on the subject, noting that "[n]othing will probably reconcile them but actual and fair experiments." Adding that "no where can such be made with less prejudice or less inconvenience than in the United States," Madison offered that "innovations" can be brought about by "the Legislative power" of "each confederated member"—a reference to federalism and the power of the states. Madison emphasized that only "partial evil" would result "if they fail" but that there was the potential of "a ready extension" of such policies "to the whole if found to be improvements." Madison then commented:

> I should not regret a fair and full trial of the entire abolition of capital punishments by any State willing to make it: tho' I do not see the injustice of such punishments in one case at least. But it is not my purpose to enter into the important discussion; nor do I know that I could furnish you with any new ideas or hints such as you ask, if there were time for the task. You seem to have consulted some of the sources where they were most likely to be found.

By 1823, the subject of capital punishment was one that the aging Madison, who then had little more than a decade to live, preferred to leave to others.[103]

What Madison told Crockett was in line with what he told a much more prominent correspondent, Edward Livingston, the year before. Although efforts to abolish the death penalty in the South were never as pronounced as they were in New England, a notable exception was Edward Livingston of Louisiana, who joined that state's assembly in 1820 and was appointed to draft a penal code for the state. Elected to the U.S. House of Representatives in 1822, Livingston pushed for the abolition of capital punishment in legislative reports he submitted in 1822 and 1824, and he corresponded with Madison on the subject of penal reform. "I was favored some days ago with your letter of May 19, accompanied by a copy of your Report to the Legislature of the State on the subject of penal Code," Madison wrote Livingston on July 10, 1822. "I should commit a tacit injustice if I did not say that the Report does great honor to the talents and sentiments of the Author," Madison said, commenting that the report "abounds with ideas of conspicuous value and presents them in a manner not less elegant than persuasive." Madison remarked that "if compleat success" did not follow from Livingston's labors, "there is ample room for improvements in the criminal jurisprudence of Louisiana as elsewhere which are well worthy the exertion of your best powers" and which "will furnish useful examples to other members of the Union." "Among the advantages distinguishing our compound Govt.," Madison wrote, "it is not the least that it affords so many opportunities and chances in the local Legislatures, for salutary innovations by some, which may be adopted by others; or for important experiments, which, if unsuccessful, will be of limited injury, and may even prove salutary as beacons to others."[104]

Indeed, Madison remained an active correspondent in his later years, taking a continuing interest in penal reform issues even after retiring from public service. In 1827, he thanked Roberts Vaux, a reform-minded, Pennsylvania-born Quaker from a prominent family, for sending him a copy of a letter "so judiciously and seasonably interposed in behalf of the Penitentiary System, an experiment so deeply interesting to the cause of Humanity." The next year, Madison also replied to another letter—this one from a Philadelphia lawyer named Thomas J. Wharton—after being sent a "Report on the Penal Code." The governor of Pennsylvania had appointed Wharton to a three-member board "to revise the Penal Code of this commonwealth, to suggest what additions, alterations and changes should take place in the system, and to report a bill to the next Legislature, *adapted to, and modelled on the principle of labour and solitary confinement,* together with such suggestions and observations as may be necessary to a proper determination on the subject." Writing from Montpellier, Madison acknowledged Wharton's letter and said he was "sorry" that he had not been able to give the whole report "the careful perusal" that "it well merits." "My attention," Madison said, "was most attracted to what relates to the penitentiary discipline as a substitute for the cruel inflictions so disgraceful to penal codes, and I cannot withhold the praise due to the ability with which the subject is examined and presented." "The lights collected and added by the Report, give it a great Legislative value everywhere," he said, adding that "the questions incident to solitary confinement" are "peculiarly interesting." As Madison wrote: "The plan preferred in the report, of combining a discriminating proportion of the solitary arrangement with joint and silent labour, under the eye of a superintendent, if this can be enforced with the success anticipated, seems to involve all the desiderata better than any yet suggested." "No apology, certainly, could have been necessary," Madison concluded, "for a freedom of remarks on the late proceedings of the Virginia Legislature; some of which will not, I am persuaded, be reviewed with complacency by the more enlightened members, when the political fervor which produced them shall have cooled down to the ordinary temperature."[105]

Less than a year earlier, Madison had written another letter to Thomas Wharton after Wharton—in a Fourth of July speech—ascribed to Madison the making of "the first public proposal for the meeting of the Convention to which we are indebted for our present Constitution." After receiving a copy of Wharton's oration, Madison replied that "it may be proper to state in a few words the part I had in bringing about that event." "Having witnessed, as a member of the Revolutionary Congress, the inadequacy of the Powers conferred by the 'Articles of Confederation,' and having become, after the expiration of my term of service there, a member of the Legislature of Virginia, I felt it to be my duty to spare no efforts to impress on that Body the alarming condition of the U.S. proceeding from that cause, and the evils threatened by delay, in applying a remedy." Though Madison said nothing to Wharton about how the Constitution's Cruel and Unusual Punishments Clause might someday bear upon the death penalty, he specifically used the word "cruel" in relation to aspects of the existing penal code and certainly knew that, after his death, subsequent generations would continue to wrestle with the legitimacy of capital punishment, especially once a viable alternative to it could be found.[106]

In the years before his death, Madison actually continued to send and receive correspondence on the subject of penal reform, though his energy was fading. For example, in 1830 Madison received a letter from Howard Malcom in Boston that read: "Knowing the deep interest you continue to take in topics such as are treated in the accompanying reports of the prison aid Society I take the liberty of forwarding you a copy." Likewise, on September 14, 1831, a prominent New York legislator named Silas Stilwell sent Madison a legislative report about what would become known as the Stilwell Act, a New York law that abolished imprisonment for debtors. Prior to its passage in 1831, a "Gaol," or debtors' prison, was used to imprison those who owed debts. In his letter, Stilwell solicited Madison's views on the subject, and Madison responded two weeks later, saying his "great age" and the "crippled state" of his health prevented him from "examining the subject in all its principles & provisions."

"I must content myself," Madison wrote, "with saying that I have read the Report with pleasure and instruction, and that the statute appears to have been prepared with much care and practical information." "[T]he law in its actual form," Madison added, "affords a meritorious example, and I wish it may lead to successful revisions of the Debt code."[107]

Madison's willingness to respond to Stilwell's letter actually led the New Yorker to send another letter to Madison the following year. "I am emboldened again to trouble you, in consequence of having met with so kind and flattering a reception on a recent occasion," Stilwell wrote Madison in 1832, telling him that the law outlawing the imprisonment of debtors had taken effect. Along with his new letter, Stilwell sent Madison "a report and Bill on the subject of capital punishment," with Stilwell inquiring: "Your opinion, my dear sir, will be invaluable on this subject, and as I am desirous to concentrate the opinion of the wisest and best men of our Country shall feel myself peculiarly obliged and gratified by the receipt of your opinion." Stilwell, the chairman of a select committee, had been appointed "to inquire into the Expediency of a Total Abolition of Capital Punishment." "The American People," Stilwell noted in his letter, "have for so long a time been accustomed to look upon your views and opinions with reverential respect that it cannot on this occasion fail to produce the most salutary effect." While Madison, the revered Founding Father, apparently never found the time to respond to this letter, the Constitution's prohibition of "cruel and unusual punishments"—language Madison himself chose for the Bill of Rights—makes twenty-first-century views, not eighteenth- or nineteenth-century ones, dispositive. Judicial decisions, of course, must be made by *living* judges in cases as they arise, so Madison's choice to use common, everyday words in the Eighth Amendment was particularly inspired. What is "cruel" and what is "unusual" will change as society changes and can be reassessed over time, making the Constitution's language relevant not just to a single generation, but to all future ones. With Madison's solid eighteenth-century foundation still in place, twenty-first-century judges are free to make their own judgments about what so qualifies. Thus, living American judges—not men who died many decades ago—get to gauge for themselves whether executions are still necessary or have become anachronisms in an age of maximum-security penitentiaries and life-without-parole sentences.[108]

CHAPTER FIVE

The Eighth Amendment

The Bill of Rights

The U.S. Constitution was approved in Philadelphia in September 1787, but ratification was still necessary and both Patrick Henry and George Mason felt strongly that a bill of rights was needed. "If you intend to reserve your unalienable rights," Henry said, invoking Virginia's cruel and unusual punishments clause, "you must have the most express stipulation." Mason, an Anti-Federalist and George Washington's friend and neighboring plantation owner, feared Congress would use the Constitution's Necessary and Proper Clause to create "new Crimes" or "inflict unusual and severe Punishments." Samuel Bryan, another Anti-Federalist, wrote in Philadelphia's *Freeman's Journal* on October 24, 1787, that although the new plan "does propose to secure the people of the benefit of personal liberty by the *habeas corpus;* and trial by jury for all crimes," it failed to contain a provision "that the requiring of excessive bail, imposing of excessive fines and cruel and unusual punishments be forbidden." "The injunction of secrecy imposed on members of the late Convention," Bryan complained, "was obviously dictated by the genius of Aristocracy." "The authors of the new plan, conscious that it would not stand the test of enlightened patriotism," Bryan wrote as "Centinel," "tyrannically endeavored to preclude all investigation." As Bryan wrote: "Whatever specious reasons may be assigned for secrecy during the framing of the plan, no good one can exist, for leading the people blindfolded into the implicit adoption of it. Such an attempt does not augur the public good—It carries on the face of it an intention to juggle the people out of their liberties."[1]

Indeed, after the Constitutional Convention, several men, often using pseudonyms, spoke of the need to prohibit cruel and unusual punishments. "For the security of liberty," one "Brutus" wrote in Thomas Greenleaf's *New York Journal* in November 1787, "it has been declared, 'that excessive bail should not be required, nor excessive fines imposed, nor cruel or unusual punishments inflicted.'" Likewise, "Philadelphiensis" wrote: "To such lengths have these bold conspirators carried their scheme of despotism, that your most sacred rights and privileges are surrendered at discretion. When government thinks proper, under the pretence of writing a libel, &c. it may imprison, inflict the most cruel and unusual punishment, seize property, carry on prosecutions, &c. and the unfortunate citizen has no *magna charta,* no *bill of rights,* to protect him." In March 1788 in the *Virginia Independent Chronicle,* the "Impartial Examiner" also railed against the ability of Congress to make laws "repugnant" and "totally derogatory" to Virginia's constitution. "How will your bill of rights avail you any thing?" he asked. Saying the proposed federal constitution was "without any kind of stipulation" for "natural rights," the Impartial Examiner said "it is evident that the most flagrant acts of oppression may be inflicted; yet, still there will be no apparent object injured: there will be no unconstitutional infringement." The Impartial Examiner then posed a hypothetical: "For instance, if Congress should pass a law that persons charged with capital crimes shall not have a *right to demand the cause or nature of the accusation,* shall not be *confronted with the accusers or witnesses, or call for evidence in their own favor;* and a question should arise respecting their authority therein,—can it be said that they have exceeded the limits of their jurisdiction, when *that* has no limits; when no provision has been made for such a right?" "The same observation," he said, "may be made on any arbitrary or capricious imprisonments *contrary to the law of the land.*" "The same," he added, "may be made, if *excessive bail should be required;* if *excessive fines should be imposed;* if *cruel and unusual punishments should be inflicted.*"[2]

Many Americans, though, saw a national bill of rights as redundant because state constitutions already guaranteed rights. Others also felt that a prohibition on "cruel and unusual punishments" would be useless. For example, in the campaign for ratification, James Iredell, one of the original Justices of the U.S. Supreme Court, argued that the inclusion of a protection against "cruel and unusual" punishments, as was already in place in England and Virginia, would be meaningless. An ardent Federalist writing under the alias of "Marcus," Iredell, appointed by George Washington in 1790 to serve on the nation's highest court, replied to George Mason's concern, trying to meet it. "The expressions 'unusual and severe' or 'cruel and unusual,'" he said, "surely would have been too vague to have been of any consequence, since they admit of no clear and precise signification." "If to guard against punishments being too severe, the Convention had enumerated a vast variety of cruel punishments, and prohibited the use of any of them, let the number have been ever so great," Iredell mused, "an inexhaustible fund must have been unmentioned, and if our government had been disposed to be cruel their invention would only have been put to a little more trouble." A listing in the Constitution of "what punishments should not be exercised" or "what punishments should," Iredell wrote in the *Norfolk and Portsmouth Journal* on March 12, 1788, would have led to "a labyrinth of detail" that "would have appeared perfectly ridiculous, and not left a room for such changes according to circumstances, as must be in the power of every Legislature that is rationally formed." Iredell, who had emigrated from Great Britain as a teenager, thus saw the "cruel and unusual" language as ill-advised. "Let us also remember," Iredell said, "that as those who are to make those laws must themselves be subject to them, their own interest and feelings will dictate to them not to make them unnecessarily severe; and that in the case of treason, which usually in every country exposes men most to the avarice and rapacity of government, care is taken that the innocent family of the offender shall not suffer for the treason of their relation."[3]

The arguments over the U.S. Bill of Rights, and, in particular, whether to include one, were intense. Initially, many Federalists argued that a bill of rights was not needed and would even be "dangerous," as it would contain "various exceptions to powers not granted." "For why declare that things shall not be done which there is no power to do?" asked Alexander Hamilton in one of his *Federalist* papers. "Why, for instance, should it be said," he asked, writing as "Publius," "that the liberty of the press shall not be restrained when no power is given by which restrictions may be imposed?" "Why not?" pondered Patrick Henry, taking the opposite view, adding: "Is it because it will consume too much paper?" Henry labeled the rights enshrined in Article I, Section 9 of the new Constitution—prohibiting ex post facto laws and bills of attainder and guaranteeing "[t]he Privilege of the Writ of Habeas Corpus"— as too "feeble and few." Patrick Henry felt Congress had to make "substantial amendments," saying that the "American union depends on the success of amendments." "I trust," Henry said, "that gentlemen, on this occasion, will see the great objects of religion, liberty of the press, trial by jury, interdiction of cruel and unusual punishments, and every other sacred right, secured, before they agree to that paper." Mason, too, thought a bill of rights of critical importance. "It would give great quiet to the people; and with the aid of the State declarations, a bill might be prepared in a few hours," Mason had said to no avail on September 12, 1787, as the Convention was wrapping up its work.[4]

Finding the Constitution unpalatable, especially because it lacked a bill of rights, Mason and another Virginian, Governor Edmund Randolph, refused to add their names to it. Randolph wanted explicit protection for individual rights, but thought a prohibition on cruel punishment unnecessary. Most dramatically, Mason announced during the Philadelphia Convention's final weeks that he would "sooner chop off his right hand than put it to the Constitution as it now stands." Just five days before adjournment, Mason, who left the Convention in what Madison called "exceeding ill humour," proclaimed that he "wished the plan had been prefaced with a Bill of Rights." When Connecticut's Roger Sherman, who opposed the idea, argued that state constitutional protections "are sufficient," Mason responded by noting that the "Laws of the U.S.

are to be paramount to State Bills of Rights." The Constitution's Supremacy Clause, to which Mason alluded, declares in no uncertain terms that the U.S. Constitution, federal statutes, and U.S. treaties are "the supreme Law of the Land" and that "the Judges in every State shall be bound thereby." In the end, the fatigued Convention delegates in Philadelphia, voting in blocks for their states and anxious to return to their families, unanimously rejected Mason's plea for a federal bill of rights. Thus, the arguments over whether to adopt a bill of rights would continue well beyond the Constitutional Convention.[5]

James Madison, who acknowledged that some Americans "wish for further guards to public liberty & individual rights," at first offered only lukewarm support for a national bill of rights. As he explained to Thomas Jefferson: "My own opinion has always been in favor of a bill of rights; provided that it be so framed as not to imply powers not meant to be included in the enumeration. At the same time I have never thought the omission a material defect, nor been anxious to supply it by *subsequent* amendment, for any other reason than that it is anxiously desired by others. I have favored it because I supposed it might be of use, and if properly executed could not be of disservice." Among the reasons Madison listed for why he had "not viewed it in an important light" was his view that majorities—in his experience—had never been deterred from violating declarations of rights. "Repeated violations of these parchment barriers," Madison wrote Jefferson, "have been committed by overbearing majorities in every State." "In Virginia," Madison emphasized, "I have seen the bill of rights violated in every instance where it has been opposed to a popular current." In discussing the prospect of a federal bill of rights, he told Jefferson in 1788: "The restrictions however strongly marked on paper will never be regarded when opposed to the decided sense of the public; and after repeated violations in extraordinary cases, they will lose even their ordinary efficacy."[6]

But the pressure to add a bill of rights was substantial, with Robert Morris, the financier of the American Revolution, noting that "[p]oor Madison got so cursedly frightened in Virginia" during that state's ratification convention "that I believe he has dreamed of amendments ever since." Eventually, the Federalists did change their tactics, acknowledging the need for amendments but insisting they be made subsequent to ratification. Madison, who teamed up with Alexander Hamilton and John Jay to write *The Federalist Papers*, himself concluded that constitutional amendments would be beneficial. "[A]mendments, if pursued with a proper moderation and in a proper mode," he said, "will be not only safe, but may serve the double purpose of satisfying the minds of well meaning opponents, and of providing additional guards in favour of liberty." As Madison, the Virginia politician who had to court voters, wrote to a Baptist minister in a letter intended for public circulation: "It is my sincere opinion that the Constitution ought to be revised, and that the first Congress . . . ought to prepare and recommend to the States . . . the most satisfactory provisions for all essential rights." Among others, Thomas Jefferson, who felt "essential amendments" would be obtained, persuaded Madison to favor the adoption of a federal bill of rights. Indeed, Madison, a proponent of judicial independence, ultimately concluded that something akin to the English Bill of Rights—which was freely alterable by Parliament—would be insufficient because it could be overridden at will by a legislative act. A bill of rights might be "less necessary in a republic, than a Monarchy," Madison told Richard Peters, the Speaker of Pennsylvania's General Assembly. But a bill of rights was, he said, "in some degree rational in every Govt., since in every Govt. power may oppress." If amendments to the Constitution were approved, Madison added, "it will kill the opposition every where," putting "an end to the disaffection to the Govt. itself."[7]

One of the amendments that Madison, as well as Richard Henry Lee, felt was necessary protected against cruel and unusual punishments. On October 2, 1787, shortly after the Constitutional Convention adjourned, Richard Henry Lee, then in New York, wrote to Dr. William Shippen. "I have considered the new Constitution," Lee wrote, with "all the attention and candor that the thing and the times render necessary, & I find it impossible for me to doubt, that in its present State, unamended, the adoption of it will put Civil Liberty and the happiness of the people at the mercy of Rulers who may possess the great unguarded powers given." "The necessary alterations," Lee wrote, "will by no means interfere with the general nature of the plan, or limit the power of doing good; but they will restrain from oppression the wicked & tyrannic." "If all men were wise and good," he said, "there would be no necessity for government or law." "But," he noted, "the folly & the vice of human nature renders government & laws necessary for the Many, and restraints indispensable to prevent oppression from those who are entrusted with the administration of one & the dispensation of the other." "You will see herewith the amendments that appeared to me necessary," Lee wrote, adding that "[p]erhaps they may be submitted to the world at large." Among the amendments Lee thought necessary for the "Social Compact" was "[t]hat excessive Bail, excessive Fines, or cruel and unusual punishments should not be demanded or inflicted." The preceding amendment Lee proposed read simply: "That the right administration of justice should be secured by the freedom and independency of the Judges."[8]

At Virginia's ratifying convention, Madison assured the wavering delegates that if the convention ratified the Constitution without requiring prior amendments, he and other supporters of it would remain at the convention and vote on recommended amendments. Madison was true to his word. After the delegates approved the Constitution by a narrow margin of eighty-nine to seventy-nine, the delegates thus took up the issue of recommended amendments. George Wythe was appointed to head up a committee to prepare a list to accompany the ratification resolution, and Patrick Henry, James Madison, George Mason, and John Marshall were added to the twenty-person committee. Two days later, on June 27, 1788, the Wythe committee presented its report, setting forth those amendments "deemed necessary to be recommended to the consideration of Congress." Many of the amendments were derived from those proposed by an informal committee chaired by George Mason that had met earlier to discuss changes its members wanted to see. Among the recommended amendments listed in Wythe's report was: "That, in all criminal and capital prosecutions, a man hath a right to demand the cause and nature of his accusation, to be confronted with the accusers and witnesses, to call for evidence, and be allowed counsel in his favor." Another said "[t]hat excessive bail ought not to be required, nor excessive fines imposed, nor cruel and unusual punishments inflicted," while another stated that "no freeman ought to be . . . deprived of his life, liberty, or property, but by the law of the land."[9]

During the ratification debate over the Constitution, the states proposed numerous amendments to the document produced in Philadelphia. When Madison learned that Massachusetts had ratified the Constitution, he saw amendments proposed by that state as "a blemish," though his views would soon change. In Virginia, Wythe, who had served in Virginia's legislature since 1758 and whose pupils included Henry Clay and James Monroe, asked his fellow Virginians to ratify the Constitution for the sake of unity. Though Wythe saw the "propriety" of amendments, he recognized "the extreme danger of dissolving the Union" made it advisable to defer changes until the new system of government went into effect. And changes would ultimately be made. After the First Congress began meeting in New York City in the spring of 1789, Madison himself took up the task of sifting through and drafting proposed amendments, a task for which he was well suited, having been a member of the committee that framed the 1776 Virginia Declaration of Rights, someone familiar with the bill of rights in the 1787 Northwest Ordinance, and a delegate to both the Constitutional Convention and Virginia's ratifying convention. The Northwest Ordinance of 1787, enacted under the auspices of the Articles of Confederation by a body without proper authority to pass such a bill, was drafted by Massachusetts lawyer Nathan Dane. Though Madison said the Northwest Ordinance was passed "without the least color of constitutional authority," it contained a limited bill of rights for Western lands, the first bill of rights enacted by the federal government. Among the protections that the Northwest Ordinance provided would "forever remain unalterable" were the rights to habeas corpus, trial by jury, and freedom from "cruel or unusual punishments." The Northwest Ordinance—adopted on July 13, 1787, by the Continental Congress, then sitting in New York—was framed, Dane said, "mainly" from the laws of Massachusetts, which explains why it prohibits "cruel or unusual" instead of "cruel and unusual" punishments. Dane himself later took credit for the guarantees of individual rights set forth in Article II of the Ordinance. Unlike Virginia's Declaration of Rights prohibiting "cruel and unusual punishments," the 1780 Massachusetts Constitution bars "cruel or unusual punishments," the language chosen for the Northwest Ordinance in New York City while the Constitutional Convention met in Philadelphia.[10]

After the Constitution was delivered to the Continental Congress in New York City on September 20, 1787, Richard Henry Lee proposed a federal bill of rights in that forum. It was modeled on George Mason's 1776 Virginia Declaration of Rights. One of the amendments Lee proposed, as he recorded in a letter to Mason himself, provided that "excessive Bail, excessive Fines, or cruel and unusual punishments should not be demanded or inflicted." Another read "[t]hat the trial by Jury in Criminal and Civil cases, and the modes prescribed by the Common Law for safety of Life in criminal prosecutions shall be held sacred." "Universal experience," Lee argued, showed "the most express declarations and reservations are necessary to protect the just rights and liberty of Mankind from the Silent, powerful, and ever active conspiracy of those who govern." "[I]t appearing to be the sense of the good people of America by the various Bills or Declarations of Rights whereon the Governments of the greater number of the States are founded," Lee said, "such precautions are proper to restrain and regulate the exercise of the great powers necessarily given to Rulers." "[T]he new Constitution," Lee contended, should therefore "be bottomed upon a declaration, or Bill of Rights, clearly and precisely stating the principles upon which the Social Compact is founded." Lee's proposed amendments, however, were rejected in their entirety and without debate. The failure of the Continental Congress to adopt Lee's proposed amendments meant that it would fall to the First Congress to decide whether to adopt a federal bill of rights along the lines to be proposed by James Madison. Lee himself was to circulate his list of proposed amendments to Samuel Adams, George Mason, Elbridge Gerry, Edmund Randolph, and William Shippen Jr., his brother-in-law in Philadelphia. Above all else, Lee, who said that chains were still chains, "whether made of gold or of iron," wanted to "restrain from oppression the wicked and Tyrannic."[11]

In all, Madison, who heard constant agitation for amendments, reviewed nearly two hundred recommendations made by state ratifying conventions. The Massachusetts convention, for example, proposed a series of amendments on February 6, 1788, including one reading "[t]hat no person shall be tried for any Crime by which he may incur an infamous punishment or loss of life until he be first indicted by a Grand Jury." On June 21, 1788, the New Hampshire convention also proposed a similarly worded amendment: "That no Person shall be Tryed for any Crime by which he may incur an Infamous Punishment, or loss of Life, untill he first be indicted by a Grand Jury." The Virginia convention, which offered its proposed amendments six days later, wanted "a Declaration or Bill of Rights asserting and securing from encroachment the essential and unalienable Rights of the People," including the "natural" right to the "enjoyment of life and liberty," and—"THIRTEENTH" on its list—"That excessive Bail ought not to be required, nor excessive fines imposed, nor cruel and unusual punishments inflicted." The New York convention, making its proposals on July 26, 1788, wanted "every Government" to "respect and preserve" the "enjoyment of Life, Liberty and the pursuit of Happiness" as "essential" rights, and sought additional amendments that "no Person ought to be taken imprisoned . . . or deprived of his Privileges, Franchises, Life, Liberty or Property, but by due process of Law," that "no Person ought to be put twice in Jeopardy of Life or Limb for one and the same Offence," and "[t]hat excessive Bail ought not to be required; nor excessive Fines imposed; nor Cruel or unusual Punishments inflicted." Such suggestions shaped Madison's thinking as he prepared for the First Congress and the debate to come.[12]

In picking and choosing, Madison limited himself to those amendments he regarded as "important in the eyes of many," "most called for by the opponents of the Government," and "least objectionable to its friends" or "objectionable in those of none." "The applications for amendments come from a very respectable number of our constituents," Madison said, adding that "it is certainly proper" for Congress to take up the subject "in order to quiet that anxiety which prevails in the public mind." Taking notice that many constituents were still "dissatisfied" with the Constitution, Madison opined: "We ought not to disregard their inclination, but, on principles of amity and moderation, conform to their wishes, and expressly declare the great rights of mankind secured under this Constitution." Madison, who thought the public would be alarmed if amendments were not approved by Congress in its first session, also pointed out that some states have "no bills of rights" or "very defective ones." Though eleven states had constitutions protecting certain rights, only seven states— Delaware, Maryland, Massachusetts, New Hampshire, North Carolina, Pennsylvania, and Virginia—had formal bills or declarations of rights. Madison said he concurred with "those gentlemen" who at Virginia's convention had fought for "some security" for "those great and essential rights which they had been taught to believe were in danger." "It will be a desirable thing," Madison added, "to extinguish from the bosom of every member of the community any apprehensions, that there are those among his countrymen who wish to deprive them of the liberty for which they valiantly fought and honorably bled."[13]

Worried about "ambiguities" as to how amendments would relate to the Constitution, Madison wanted the amendments incorporated into the text. "I conceive," Madison argued, "that there is a propriety in incorporating the amendments in the Constitution itself, in the several places to which they belong—the system will in that case be uniform and entire." "If these amendments are added to the Constitution by way of supplement, it will embarrass the people," Madison said, noting, "It will be difficult for them to determine to what parts of the system they particularly refer." "[T]here is a neatness and propriety in incorporating the amendments into the Constitution itself," Madison emphasized, arguing that "if they are supplementary," the meaning could only be ascertained "by a comparison of the two instruments." Madison, as well as a House Select Committee of which he was a member, thus recommended in 1789 that the "cruel and unusual punishments" prohibition be added to the Constitution in Article I, Section 9. That section already prohibited ex post facto laws and bills of attainder, protections Madison called "wise and proper restrictions." The full House and Senate, however, wanted the amendments listed separately, just as the states had done in promulgating declarations of rights. Madison, who said "form is of some consequence," but conceded it was less important than "substance," ultimately lost his battle to integrate amendments into the Constitution's text. After the congressional debate, the amendments—initially covering nineteen points, but later condensed and put into a separate Bill of Rights—were jointly approved by the House and Senate on September 25, 1789, and submitted to the states for ratification.[14]

The debate in Congress took time, and it was contentious. After making a campaign pledge to work to safeguard "all those essential rights" thought to be "in danger," Madison introduced his proposed constitutional amendments in the First Congress in June 1789. "I will state my reasons why I think it proper to propose amendments, and state the amendments themselves," Madison said at that time, telling fellow legislators that if Congress "will devote but one day to this subject" it would have "a salutary influence" on the public. "It appears to me," Madison said, "that this House is bound by every motive of prudence, not to let the first session pass over without proposing to the State Legislatures, some things to be incorporated into the Constitution, that will render it as acceptable to the whole people of the United States, as it has been found acceptable to a majority of them." "[I]f all power is subject to abuse," Madison acknowledged, "then it is possible the abuse of the powers of the General Government may be guarded against in a more secure manner than is now done." "We have in this way," he said, "something to gain, and, if we proceed with caution, nothing to lose." Madison then introduced "those provisions for the security of rights" to which he believed "no serious objection has been made by any class of our constituents" and which "would be likely to meet with the concurrence of two-thirds of both Houses, and the approbation of three-fourths of the State Legislatures." Madison added that "a declaration of the rights of the people" was "proper" and "highly politic" for "the tranquility of the public mind" as well as "the stability of the government." Madison admitted "paper barriers" might sometimes be insufficient to protect individuals, but he believed the rights listed in his amendments would have a "tendency to impress some degree of respect for them, to establish the public opinion in their favor, and rouse the attention of the whole community."[15]

Before introducing the proposed amendments, Madison showed them to President Washington. "I see nothing exceptionable in the proposed amendments," Washington responded, adding: "Some of them, in my opinion, are importantly necessary, others, though of themselves (in my conception) not very essential, are necessary to quiet the fears of some respectable characters and well-meaning men." "Upon the whole, therefore, not foreseeing any evil consequences that can result from their adoption," Washington replied, "they have my wishes for a favorable reception in both houses." Madison was to use the President's letter to persuade his colleagues that they should support the amendments. Because of "dilatory" tactics and "the diversity of opinions and fancies" of congressmen, however, it took considerable time to win over fellow legislators. Madison called the work "extremely wearisome" and "extremely difficult and fatiguing." To his colleagues, Madison, who felt duty-bound to take up the issue of amendments, was apologetic for taking up their time. In outlining the proposed amendments, Madison explained to his fellow congressmen: "I am sorry to be accessory to the loss of a single moment of time by the house." Madison added: "The people of many states, have thought it necessary to raise barriers against power in all forms and departments of government, and I am inclined to believe, if once bills of rights are established in all the states as well as the federal constitution, we shall find that altho' some of them are rather unimportant, yet, upon the whole, they will have a salutary tendency." "[I]n every Govt. power may oppress," Madison would also write by way of explanation to Federalist lawyer and speaker of the Pennsylvania Assembly Richard Peters, noting that "declarations on paper, tho' not an effectual restraint, are not without some influence."[16]

Don't Be Cruel

The idea of not inflicting draconian fines or punishments is a simple one and has been around in one form or another for centuries. The Magna Carta of 1215 guaranteed proportionate fines, tying "amercements" to the "gravity," "degree," or "manner" of the offense; the 1682 Frame of Government of Pennsylvania provided that "all fines shall be moderate"; and the English Bill of Rights of 1689—the Eighth Amendment's predecessor—forbade "excessive Baile," "excessive Fines," and "cruell and unusuall Punishments." Thus, the Eighth Amendment has many antecedents, the English Bill of Rights and the Virginia Declaration of Rights simply being the most historically significant. Even before the English Bill of Rights came into existence, in fact, the Englishman Sir Robert Beale had invoked the Magna Carta in the late sixteenth century to question the monarchy's power to inflict "cruel" punishments. Beale, an Oxford-educated lawyer and member of Parliament, had written a manuscript in 1583 that attacked the English crown's right to punish persons for ecclesiastical offenses and its High Commission's use of torture. The High Commission, which could make use of the rack and a dungeon to extract information if witnesses were uncooperative, was a court set up to try certain types of ecclesiastical offenses. The Clerk of the Privy Council, Beale wrote the official record of the execution of Mary, Queen of Scots, which he personally witnessed. He was a Puritan who became the first person to object to torture even when it was "authorized by the royal prerogative," and he represented Puritan ministers deprived of their benefices. Beale argued in vain that the use of torture to extract confessions violated the Magna Carta, and in 1592, after serving as a member of the High Commission but resigning because of its inquisitorial methods, he was banished from the royal court. Because of his actions, the Archbishop of Canterbury John Whitgift even had a "Schedule of Misdemeanors" drawn up against Beale, admonishing him that he had "condemneth (without exception of any cause) the racking of grievous offenders as being cruel, barbarous, contrary to law, and unto the liberty of English subjects." Not until 1688 was the High Commission dissolved, with the English Bill of Rights specifically prohibiting the reinstitution of ecclesiastical courts.[17]

In England, where the Eighth Amendment language originates, convicted criminals were traditionally punished in horrific ways. William Blackstone, in his *Commentaries on the Laws of England,* wrote that capital offenders were usually "hanged by the neck till dead," though he said that "in very atrocious crimes other circumstances of terror, pain, or disgrace are superadded." For "treasons of all kinds," Blackstone wrote, the prescribed punishment was "being drawn or dragged to the place of execution"; for "high treason affecting the king's person or government, embowelling alive, beheading, and quartering"; and for murder, "a public dissection." Women committing treason, Blackstone recorded, received a judgment "to be burned alive," though English authorities often mitigated the harshness of death sentences by rendering the condemned unconscious before carrying out such sentences. As Blackstone wrote: "[T]he humanity of the English nation has authorized, by a tacit consent, an almost general mitigation of such part of these judgments as savour of torture or cruelty: a sledge or hurdle being usually allowed to such traitors as are condemned to be drawn; and there being very few instances (and those accidental or by negligence) of any person's being embowelled or burned, till previously deprived of sensation by strangling." Corporal punishments, Blackstone noted, were still inflicted, though he again took pains to point out that other countries used such methods more frequently. "Some, though rarely," he wrote of English subjects, "occasion a mutilation or dismembering, by cutting off the hand or ears: others fix a lasting stigma on the offender, by slitting the nostrils, or branding in the hand or face." Others, Blackstone reported, suffer "ignominy" and "some degree of corporal pain," such as "whipping, hard labour in the house of correction, the pillory, the stocks, and the ducking-stool." "Disgusting as this catalogue may seem," Blackstone added, "it will afford pleasure to an English reader, and do honour to the English law, to compare it with that shocking apparatus of death and torment, to be met with in the criminal codes of almost every other nation in Europe."[18]

In his *Commentaries,* Blackstone emphasized that in England a judge's power was restrained by the law. Calling it "one of the glories of our English law" that "the nature, though not always the quantity or degree, of punishment," is "*ascertained* for every offence," Blackstone wrote that "it is not left in the breast of any judge, nor even of a jury, to alter that judgment, which the law has beforehand ordained." Discretionary fines and terms of imprisonment were an established part of English law, but mandatory—not discretionary—death sentences were the norm. A death sentence, what Blackstone called "the most terrible and highest judgment" in English law, would even result in a common-law "*attainder.*" As Blackstone explained that concept: "For when it is now clear beyond all dispute, that the criminal is no longer fit to live upon the earth, but is to be exterminated as a monster and a bane to human society, the law sets a note of infamy upon him, puts him out of it's protection, and takes no farther care of him than barely to see him executed. He is then called attaint, *attinctus,* stained, or blackened." Stripped of his reputation, Blackstone said, "he cannot be a witness in any court" and is treated as if "he is already dead in law." As to fines and prison sentences, Blackstone said that "the duration and quantity" of such fines or terms of imprisonment were properly left to judges. "[H]owever unlimited the power of the court may seem," Blackstone wrote of those instances, "it is far from being wholly arbitrary," for, he emphasized, the judge's "discretion is regulated by law." "For the bill of rights has particularly declared," he wrote, "that excessive fines ought not to be imposed, nor cruel and unusual punishments inflicted." As to that clause, Blackstone pointed to "some unprecedented proceedings in the court of king's bench, in the reign of king James the second."[19]

The prohibition on "cruel" punishments first came into American law through the Reverend Nathaniel Ward, a Puritan preacher, long before the English Bill of Rights itself came into force. Born in England, the Cambridge-educated Ward studied law and became an English barrister before following in his father's footsteps and entering the ministry. In England, he was excommunicated, so he made his way to New England in 1634, settling in Ipswich, Massachusetts. In his new home, he drafted a legal code known as "The Body of Liberties" during a period of political unrest. Adopted by the General Court of Massachusetts in December 1641, that code, which listed several capital offenses based on biblical passages, was distributed throughout the Massachusetts Bay Colony and sought to restrain the discretion of magistrates. Among the capital crimes listed were rebellion, witchcraft, blasphemy, murder, bestiality, adultery, and bearing false witness, though the code also provided certain safeguards to those facing criminal charges. The first clause read that no man's life "shall be taken away," nor any man dismembered, unless the General Court adjudged "it be by vertue or equitie of some expresse law" that was "sufficiently published, or in case of the defect of a law in any parteculer case by the word of God." Another clause limited beatings to "40 stripes" and prohibited a "gentleman" from being whipped unless "his crime be very shamefull," while another forbade putting a man to death within four days after his condemnation. "No man shall be forced by Torture to confesse any Crime against himselfe nor any other unlesse it be in some Capitall case, where he is first fullie convicted by cleare and suffitient evidence to be guilty," read another, though it was also provided that if it were "very apparent there be other conspiratours, or confederates with him," he "may be tortured, yet not with such Tortures as be Barbarous and inhumane." Clause 46, the one bearing on the concept of cruelty, provided simply that "For bodilie punishments we allow amongst us none that are inhumane, barbarous or cruel."[20]

The English Bill of Rights of 1689, which the Eighth Amendment and several similar state constitutional provisions were modeled on, was enacted after England's monarch James II fled to France. William of Orange had informally called for elections, and on February 12, 1689, the newly elected Parliament, sitting as a "convention," adopted a Declaration of Rights, which its members presented the next day to William and Mary, who became the country's new king and queen. After William ascended the throne, the declaration was revised, and Parliament reenacted what became the Bill of Rights on December 16, 1689. That law, "An Act Declaring the Rights and Liberties of the Subject and Settling the Succession of the Crown," contained a number of *whereas* clauses, including ones reciting that "excessive bail hath been required of persons committed in criminal cases to elude the benefit of the laws made for the liberty of the subject"; that "excessive fines have been imposed"; and that "illegal and cruel punishments" have been "inflicted." After making those recitals, the English Bill of Rights then provided "[t]hat excessive bail ought not to be required, nor excessive fines imposed, nor cruel and unusual punishments inflicted." The driving force behind it was to curb the excesses of English judges under James II, to wit, abuses by Lord Chief Justice George Jeffreys of the King's Bench. Jeffreys, who reputedly sold pardons and arbitrarily and capriciously sentenced people to die, presided over the Bloody Assizes after the Duke of Monmouth's rebellion in 1685. The term "Bloody Assizes" refers to the treason trials that took place after King James II of the Stuart dynasty defeated his nephew the Duke of Monmouth at the Battle of Sedgemoor. A commission that Jeffreys led tried, convicted, and oversaw the execution of hundreds of suspected rebels, many of whom were executed by horrific means such as disembowelment, beheading, drawing and quartering, and burning for female offenders. Jeffreys himself sent 292 prisoners to their deaths. Among those executed was a deaf widow in her seventies.[21]

More than a century before the Eighth Amendment's ratification, Jeffreys's arbitrary use of power became the focus of a public controversy in the case of Titus Oates. A Protestant cleric, Oates had been convicted of two counts of perjury in 1685. Horrifically, Oates had made false allegations in 1678, causing the execution of fifteen Catholics, including the leader of the Jesuit order in

England, for allegedly organizing the "Popish Plot," a fictitious conspiracy to kill the king. The "infamous Popish Plot," historian Leonard Levy explains, was "an accusation that English Catholics, led by Jesuit priests, intended to assassinate Charles II." In the anti-Catholic hysteria that ensued, those ordered executed included Oliver Plunkett, the chief Catholic prelate of Ireland, and Edward Coleman, James Stuart's secretary. As punishment, Oates was fined, ordered to be imprisoned for life, and stripped of his clerical position. In addition, the English court ordered that Oates "stand upon the Pillory, and in the Pillory" at the gate at Westminster for an hour's time on the next Monday, with a paper over his head declaring his crime. He was further ordered to be pilloried on Tuesday at the Royal Exchange in London with the same inscription; to be "whipped from Aldgate to Newgate," the site of London's prison, on Wednesday; and, on Friday, to be "whipped from Newgate to Tyburn, by the hands of the common hangman." For the rest of his life, Oates was also ordered to stand in the pillory "at Tyburn, just opposite to the gallows, for the space of an hour on April 24th of every year." Tyburn was the notorious village that for centuries was used to execute English criminals. Finally, Oates was ordered, on an annual basis, to be pilloried at Westminster on August 9, at Charing Cross on August 10, at Temple Gate on August 11, and at the Royal Exchange on September 2. When Oates first appeared in the pillory in 1685, he was jeered and pelted with eggs while the crowd yelled "cut off his ears" and "hanging is too good for him."[22]

At the sentencing, Jeffreys complained that death was no longer available as a penalty for the cleric's perjury, lamenting that "a proportionate punishment of that crime can scarce by our law, as it now stands, be inflicted upon him." Though his sentence was harsh, Oates did not die—as some no doubt expected he might—from the severe corporal punishments inflicted on him. Instead, after the adoption of the English Bill of Rights, which referred to "ancient rights and liberties" established by English law, Oates petitioned both houses of Parliament to set aside his sentence as illegal. The fate of Titus Oates, who became a symbol of all the excesses and abuses during James II's reign, would be decided by Parliament, and the issue was one of first impression: whether the sentence he received constituted "cruel and unusual punishment." Initially, the House of Lords, finding Oates to be "so ill a Man," affirmed the judgment rendered against him. However, a minority of the Lords dissented. They called Oates's punishment "barbarous, inhuman, and unchristian" and "contrary to" the English Bill of Rights, adding that "there is no Precedent to warrant the Punishments of whipping and committing to Prison for Life, for the Crime of Perjury." The dissenters saw the King's Bench judgment, which divested Oates of "his canonical and priestly Habit," as "a Matter wholly out of their Power, belonging to the Ecclesiastical Courts only." "Unless this Judgment be reversed," the dissenters intoned, "cruel, barbarous and illegal Judgments" would be encouraged, with the dissenters pointing to the command in the Bill of Rights "whereby it doth appear, that excessive bail ought not to be required, nor excessive fines imposed, nor cruel nor unusual punishments inflicted." The House of Commons, after conducting its own review, passed a bill to annul Oates's sentence, and Oates was released in 1689. The House of Commons specifically invoked England's new "cruel and unusual" punishments clause, calling Oates's punishment "barbarous," an "ill Example to future Ages," and "unusual" in that "an Englishman should be exposed upon a Pillory, so many times a Year, during his Life."[23]

Historians have shown that the English Bill of Rights was not promulgated as a result of the vile methods of execution ordered as part of the Bloody Assizes. Indeed, such brutal methods of execution as beheading and drawing and quartering traitors—not repealed until the 1800s—remained legal in England long after the English Bill of Rights went into effect. Instead, it was Jeffreys's imposition of unprecedented penalties in the Oates case that drew the attention of England's Parliament. The House of Commons itself emphasized that it had "a particular Regard" for Oates's sentence, among others, when it drafted the prohibition against cruel and unusual punishments. It is doubtful that most Americans, in debating the U.S. Bill of Rights a century later, fully understood the precise origins of the English Bill of Rights. The Americans who voted to ratify the U.S. Bill of Rights were not all lawyers, and, lacking access to the full panoply of English legal resources, even the Framers themselves were not experts on the development of English law. More likely, the vast majority of Americans—including America's founders—paid relatively little attention to the precise origins of the "cruel and unusual punishments" prohibition. As law professor Akhil Amar writes: "In 1789 the right as written had relatively little judicially enforceable bite against Congress; a congressionally authorized penalty might be 'cruel,' but would it be both cruel 'and unusual'?" "At most," Amar explains in his book *The Bill of Rights: Creation and Reconstruction,* "the clause seemed to disfavor the oddball statute, wholly out of sync with other congressional criminal laws." After all, the English Bill of Rights "was not designed," Amar recounts, "to create judicially enforceable rights against the legislature; on the contrary, that 1689 clause was written to restrain lawless and bloody judges like George Jeffreys." States such as New York and Virginia in fact already had similar provisions in place by the time the Constitution was ratified, so a prohibition on cruelty was only needed, if at all, to guard against oppression from the national government. Indeed, Markus Dubber, a New York law professor, writes that the prohibition against "cruel and unusual punishments" was merely seen as "constitutional boilerplate" that had been adopted "in state constitution after state constitution."[24]

What is clear beyond any doubt is that the U.S. Constitution's Eighth Amendment, added to assuage the concerns of Anti-Federalists about abuses of power by the national government, was derived from the English Bill of

Rights and its American counterpart, the Virginia Declaration of Rights. Like the English Bill of Rights, the Virginia Declaration—authored principally by George Mason, the man Jefferson regarded as "the wisest man of his generation"—explicitly prohibited "cruel and unusual punishments." A plantation owner from Fairfax County, Mason, who had been orphaned as a child, had no formal training in law, though he had come under the tutelage of an uncle, the lawyer John Mercer, who had an extensive library. In drafting Virginia's historic declaration, Mason, who had studied the natural rights philosophy of the English Whig John Locke, simply adopted verbatim the language of the English Bill of Rights, most likely intending to ensure that Americans would enjoy the same rights as Englishmen. "Every British subject born on the continent of America," the Boston jurist James Otis once insisted, "is entitled to all the natural, essential, inherent and inseparable rights of our fellow subjects in Great Britain." Indeed, as early as 1766, Mason himself had asserted that American colonists "claim Nothing but the Liberty & Privileges of Englishmen, in the same degree, as if we had still continued among our Brethren in Great Britain." In 1774, just two years before being called upon to draft the Virginia Declaration, Mason had further emphasized that colonists were entitled to all the "Privileges, Immunities and Advantages" of English law. In other words, if Englishmen were protected against "cruel and unusual punishments," then Mason felt Virginians should enjoy the same protection. "We have received the ancient constitutional and common-law rights of Englishmen from our Ancestors," Mason said, noting that "with God's Leave, we will transmit them, unimpaired to our Posterity."[25]

The Virginia Declaration of Rights, adopted by Virginia's Constitutional Convention on June 12, 1776, served as an influential model for other state legislatures as they wrote their own constitutions and defined the scope of their citizens' rights. Benjamin Franklin used the text in drafting the Pennsylvania Constitution in August of 1776; John Adams used it as an outline for the Massachusetts Constitution of 1780; and it also foreshadowed the natural law philosophy charted in the Declaration of Independence. In drafting the latter document, Thomas Jefferson had actually seen a draft of Virginia's Declaration of Rights, prepared by George Mason, as it appeared on June 12, 1776, in the *Pennsylvania Gazette*. Calling natural law "the decree of the divine will discernible by the light of nature," the philosopher John Locke had written in the late 1600s that governments were formed to protect the natural rights of man. Locke, whose writings were familiar to the Founding Fathers, identified the trinity of natural rights as "life, liberty, and property": the last, being alienable, became "the pursuit of Happiness" in the Declaration of Independence. Because Jean-Jacques Rousseau's influential *Social Contract* of 1762 had used the phrases "rights of man" and "rights of humanity" and Blackstone himself had described the "rights of man" as "the natural liberty of mankind," the Founding Fathers felt especially comfortable in embracing a natural law philosophy. In 1776, George Mason and Thomas Jefferson simply became pioneers in delineating, for Americans, what those natural, God-given rights actually were.[26]

The preamble to Mason's Virginia Declaration spoke of rights pertaining to "the good people of Virginia" and "their posterity," and its very first section—like the Declaration of Independence—invoked the concept of natural rights, declaring: "That all men are by nature equally free and independent and have certain inherent rights, of which, when they enter into a state of society, they cannot, by any compact, deprive or divest their posterity; namely, the enjoyment of life and liberty, with the means of acquiring and possessing property, and pursuing and obtaining happiness and safety." Another section of the Virginia Declaration spoke of "the duty which we owe to our Creator," asserting "it is the mutual duty of all to practise Christian forbearance, love, and charity toward each other." Section 9 cribbed directly from the English Bill of Rights, adopting its language verbatim: "That excessive bail ought not to be required, nor excessive fines imposed, nor cruel and unusual punishments inflicted." The way in which that language was incorporated into Virginia's declaration has led yet another scholar, Laurence Claus, to conclude that the language—especially to a nonlawyer such as George Mason—may have been seen as nothing more than constitutional boilerplate. Indeed, Thomas Jefferson pointed out later that when it came time to reform Virginia's laws, Mason withdrew from the task, seeing himself as unqualified. What is crystal clear, however, is that Mason—as patriotic as they came, and familiar with much English history and law—felt it necessary to include the "cruel and unusual punishments" language in a declaration that contained only sixteen short sections.[27]

The Virginia Declaration of Rights, the first of its kind in America, set off a chain reaction across the country. After the Declaration of Independence was issued on July 4, 1776, the states asserted their sovereignty and passed new constitutions and, in many cases, declarations of rights. On August 14, 1776, just weeks after the Declaration of Independence was promulgated, Maryland delegates approved a declaration proclaiming that Maryland inhabitants were entitled to "the benefit of such of the English statutes, as existed at the time of their first emigration." Two clauses of that declaration specifically addressed cruel acts. Clause 14 read: "That sanguinary laws ought to be avoided, as far as is consistent with the safety of the State: and no law, to inflict cruel and unusual pains and penalties, ought to be made in any case, or at any time hereafter." And Clause 22 provided: "That excessive bail ought not to be required, nor excessive fines imposed, nor cruel or unusual punishments inflicted, by the courts of law." Delaware, too, promulgated a declaration of rights on September 11, 1776, providing "[t]hat every member of society hath a right to be protected in the enjoyment of life, liberty and property," and "[t]hat excessive bail ought not to be required, nor excessive fines imposed, nor cruel or unusual punishments inflicted." The fact that Maryland's 1776 Declaration of Rights spoke out against "cruel *and* unusual pains and penalties" and "cruel *or* unusual punishments" in the same document may indicate that the drafters paid little if any attention to whether "and" or "or" was used between the words "cruel" and "unusual."[28]

In late September 1776, Pennsylvania also enacted a new constitution under the direction of Benjamin Franklin so that its citizens, as it recited, could "enjoy their natural rights, and the other blessings which the Author of existence has bestowed upon man." The preamble referenced "a most cruel and unjust war" being waged by the king of Great Britain, and its declaration of rights—at the very beginning of the constitution—proclaimed that "all men are born equally free and independent, and have certain natural, inherent and inalienable rights, amongst which are, the enjoying and defending life and liberty, acquiring, possessing and protecting property, and pursuing and obtaining happiness and safety." One provision of Pennsylvania's constitution stated that "every member of society hath a right to be protected in the enjoyment of life, liberty and property," while another expressly forbade "[e]xcessive bail" for "bailable offenses" and provided that "all fines shall be moderate." Sections 38 and 39, influenced by Quaker sentiments, also dealt with punishments and the treatment of criminals, though neither provision spoke of "cruel" or "unusual" punishments. "The penal laws as heretofore used," Section 38 read, "shall be reformed by the legislature of this state, as soon as may be, and punishments made in some cases less sanguinary, and in general more proportionate to the crimes." "To deter more effectually from the commission of crimes, by continued visible punishments of long duration, and to make sanguinary punishments less necessary," Section 39 declared, "houses ought to be provided for punishing by hard labour, those who shall be convicted of crimes not capital; wherein the criminals shall be imployed for the benefit of the public, or for reparation of injuries done to private persons."[29]

Other states soon followed suit in terms of protecting citizens' rights through written declarations. In December 1776, North Carolina delegates approved a declaration of rights providing "[t]hat excessive bail should not be required, nor excessive fines imposed, nor cruel or unusual punishments inflicted." In 1778, South Carolina established a constitution that provided that "the penal laws, as heretofore used, shall be reformed, and punishments made in some cases less sanguinary, and in general more proportionate to the crime." And in Massachusetts, John Adams, a fierce proponent of an independent judiciary, drafted a constitution for his home state containing a similar guarantee. That constitution, ratified in 1780, called for "a government of laws and not of men," and required a complete separation of legislative, executive, and judicial powers. "It is the right of every citizen to be tried by judges as free, impartial and independent as the lot of humanity will admit," the document asserted. The Massachusetts Constitution, read aloud by Samuel Adams at Faneuil Hall in Boston, made explicit reference to "natural rights," "the goodness of the Great

Legislator of the Universe," and "the blessings of life." "All men are born free and equal, and have certain natural, essential, and unalienable rights; among which may be reckoned the right of enjoying and defending their lives and liberties," Article 1 began. Consistent with other provisions being put in place around the country, some of which were specifically targeted at restraining the abuses of courts, Article 26 of the Massachusetts Constitution read: "No magistrate or court of law shall demand excessive bail or sureties, impose excessive fines, or inflict cruel or unusual punishments." Adams's declaration of rights borrowed heavily from earlier examples, as Adams noted in a letter he sent to Benjamin Rush around the time he assumed the role of principal drafter. Adams told Rush he was happy "of having a share in this great Work," but that it was "impossible for Us to acquire any Honour, as so many fine Examples" had already come before.[30]

New Hampshire and New York also got into the act. A new constitution for New Hampshire, which took effect on June 2, 1784, and which was modeled largely on the approach taken by Massachusetts, contained a number of criminal law protections. "[N]o subject," Clause 15 read, "shall be arrested, imprisoned, despoiled, or deprived of his property, immunities, or privileges, put out of the protection of the law, exiled or deprived of his life, liberty, or estate, but by the judgment of his peers or the law of the land." "All penalties ought to be proportioned to the nature of the offence," Clause 18 provided, adding: "No wise legislature will affix the same punishments to the crimes of theft, forgery and the like, which they do to those of murder and treason" because "where the same undistinguished severity is exerted against all offences" the people "are led to forget the real distinction in the crimes themselves." Clause 18 continued: "For the same reason a multitude of sanguinary laws is both impolitic and unjust. The true design of all punishments being to reform, not to exterminate, mankind." "No magistrate or court of law," Clause 33 read, borrowing from the language of John Adams's Massachusetts Constitution, "shall demand excessive bail or sureties, impose excessive fines, or inflict cruel or unusual punishments." A New York Bill of Rights, passed on January 26, 1787, also provided "[t]hat excessive bail ought not to be required, nor excessive fines imposed, nor cruel and unusual punishments inflicted."[31]

There is some evidence that the Framers of the English Bill of Rights and the Eighth Amendment may have understood the concept of "cruel and unusual" punishments as a unitary concept of inhumane or cruel punishment. Some state constitutional provisions enacted shortly before and after the Eighth Amendment's ratification simply prohibited "cruel punishments," dropping any reference to the term "unusual." For example, Kentucky's first constitution, of 1792, states "[t]hat excessive bail shall not be required, nor excessive fines imposed, nor cruel punishments inflicted." This suggests, perhaps, that some legislators viewed the "unusual" language as mere surplusage. In 1850, the Reverend Charles Elliott, in his book *Sinfulness of American Slavery*, went so far as to say that "*cruel* or *unusual* mean precisely the same thing, and will be so construed by the court." Elliott's comment was directed not at the Eighth Amendment itself, but at a Mississippi law that forbade inflicting any "cruel or unusual punishment" on any slave within the state. The clergyman was quick to point out, though, that "without the testimony of the slave, a law of this nature is nugatory." In that era, American laws did in fact expressly prohibit blacks from giving any testimony against whites.[32]

Over time, the various language variants—"cruel or unusual," "cruel and unusual," and "cruel"—all persisted, even finding their way into various federal and state laws. By 1790, nine states had constitutional provisions barring "cruel and unusual," "cruel or unusual," or "cruel" punishments. And by 1868, when the Fourteenth Amendment was adopted, the states themselves were fairly evenly divided between the "cruel and unusual" versus "cruel or unusual" language. By then, seventeen state constitutions banned cruel *and* unusual punishments, fourteen state constitutions banned cruel *or* unusual punishments, and four state constitutions banned "cruel" punishments without any reference to the "unusual" terminology. Today, twenty-two states bar "cruel and unusual" punishments, nineteen states prohibit "cruel or unusual" punishments, and six states prohibit "cruel" punishments and omit the "unusual" element. Though state constitutions still vary, what the Eighth Amendment says, of course, is "cruel *and* unusual punishments," so that, ultimately, is the language the U.S. Supreme Court must interpret.[33]

The words "cruel" and "unusual," certainly, were familiar ones to the Founding Fathers, who used those words in a wide variety of contexts and social interactions. Benjamin Franklin, for instance, called it "unjust and cruel" to punish a man on account of the guilt of another, and he referred to "cruel, unjust and barbarous Tempers." He also penned phrases such as "cruel Animosities," "cruel Captivity," and "cruel treatment," and even referred to a "cruel Mother-in-Law." In his writings, he also used the phrases "cruel Murders," "that cruel Disease," and "that cruel Gout," and made reference to "unusual Treatment," "unusual Quantities of Ice," and "unusual Words in the Pamphlet." After spending eight months in France, Gouverneur Morris expressed the view that Paris was "perhaps as wicked a Spot as exists" and, in his list of detailed complaints, grouped "Cruelty" with killing and other criminal acts: "Incest, Murder, Bestiality, Fraud, Rapine, Oppression, Baseness, Cruelty." In a 1796 American case report, a solicitor general likewise refers to a "beating" as being "cruel or unusual," another indication that early Americans may have seen the "cruel and unusual punishments" terminology as reflecting, perhaps, a unitary prohibition against cruel or inhumane treatment. There is, after all, something inherently unusual in inflicting any cruel punishment, making a finding of cruelty influential in determining a punishment's unusualness.[34]

In the 1796 case, the "cruel or unusual" phrase was actually used in a North Carolina murder trial in a discussion about whether a slaying was to be classified as murder or manslaughter. "The grand distinction between murder and manslaughter," the solicitor general argued, is that "murder is accompanied with the circumstances of malice aforethought—and manslaughter is not." "The true legal idea of malice, as applied to the case of killing," it was urged, had to do with whether the circumstances showed "the slayer to have a cruel and diabolical temper and disposition, above what is ordinarily found amongst mankind." As the solicitor general argued, "It is the cruelty of the action, and the malignity of heart the action discovers, to which the law attributes the crime of murder; and which causes the killing to be considered as unfit to be reduced to any species of homicide inferior in denomination and punishment to that of murder. This cruelty and malignity of heart is discoverable from the action itself, and the causes that lead to it."

The case involved a stabbing that took place after two men got into a fight—with each calling the other "a damned liar." Saying the crime was done "in a cruel and unusual manner," the solicitor general asserted that the facts showed "the heart of the slayer to have been more than ordinarily cruel." As the solicitor general argued just five years after the Eighth Amendment's ratification: "[O]ne who has behaved himself with so much obduracy and perverseness, should no longer be regarded as entitled to that compassion which the frailties of human nature may justly claim. He has acted not from the frailty of his nature, but from the unfeeling ferocity of a savage heart; and this circumstance causes the law to impute to him the crime of murder." "Whenever this excess of cruelty appears," the solicitor general said, alluding to "a heart excessively cruel and turned to inhuman revenge," the homicide "amounts to murder."[35]

For the solicitor general, the circumstances of the killing showed its excessive cruelty, prompting him to use the "cruel or unusual" terminology in his argument. The solicitor general first posed a question: "What can be more cruel, more indicative of a malignant heart, than this deed of the prisoner?" "He quarrels with another and is beaten," the solicitor general spoke of the accused, noting how the defendant had then sought out a deadly weapon before returning to kill his antagonist. Would other men placed in this "every day" situation have been so "cruel" by "seeking so deadly a revenge?" the solicitor general asked. He answered himself: "I think they would not; and it seems to me the act can appear no otherwise that as the effect of a cruel disposition, not of human weakness deserving of our compassion; and if it be the effect of cruelty it amounts to murder." Emphasizing that the defendant on trial had gone eighty or a hundred yards before returning to stab his victim, the solicitor general argued that "there are but few men in the world who in all this time, would not have persuaded themselves to abandon the inhuman design—but very few who would not have been awakened and alarmed by the workings of so black a spirit within them, and have shrunk from its suggestions." Contending that "the cruelty of the act" was displayed "in its most heightened colours," the solicitor general argued that the case exceeded that of the typical manslaughter case where "the blood is heated," "the passions boil," and "rage dictates" the conduct. "That," the solicitor general offered, "is not like the case before us; here the combatants were separated, and the fatal blow not given till three or four minutes afterwards." "Any circumstance of deliberation accompanying the fact of killing," the solicitor general said, "will cause the slayer to fall under the imputation of murder." "I submit the fate of this unhappy man to the decision of the court and jury," the solicitor general concluded.[36]

In answering the solicitor general's charge that the beating had been done in a "cruel or unusual manner," the defendant's counsel commented on the evidence at great length, arguing that the crime amounted to manslaughter, not murder. In particular, defense counsel cited legal precedents in which deaths occurred through "the influence of violent anger" or as a result of "the heat of passion and resentment." If "passions have not had time to subside and cool," it was argued, "it is manslaughter only." In one case—described as "Rowley's case"—counsel emphasized that it was adjudged to be manslaughter "where two boys fought, one beat the other and drew blood from his nose" and where one of the boys "ran three quarters of a mile to his father, who came with a staff and struck the other boy" with a lethal blow. Noting that the death in Rowley's case was "owing to the heat of the passions at the time the blow was given," defense counsel pled for his own client's life. After instructing the jury on the difference between manslaughter and murder—manslaughter, one judge said, "is committed under the operation of furious anger, that suspends for a time the proper exercise of reason and reflection"—the jury acquitted the defendant on the murder charge but convicted him of manslaughter. In reaching that verdict, the jury thus rejected the views of another judge who had instructed the jury in this suggestive manner: "I cannot think it an excuse to reduce the offence to manslaughter, where two persons quarrel and fight, and one goes some distance, gets a knife, returns and kills the other with it— such disputes happen every day." "Did not this show a murderous intent, and that his heart was bent upon cruelty?" that judge had asked in the jury's presence. The defendant, the record reflects, avoided a death sentence and was ultimately "burnt in the hand and discharged" following the manslaughter conviction.[37]

James Madison, who urged the adoption of the Bill of Rights, himself regularly used the words "cruel" and "unusual," employing them in everyday, ordinary ways. "[I]t would be cruel to sacrifice to possible dangers the feelings of a public servant," Madison wrote to Henry Lee in 1786. "Mr. Wythe I suppose will not decline any duty which may be imposed on him, but it seems almost cruel to tax his patriotic zeal any farther," Madison wrote to Thomas Jefferson in 1786, again employing the word in an informal, almost colloquial way. Madison also used the phrases "cruel war," "cruel sufferings," "cruel instruments," and "cruel invaders" in messages to Congress, and he spoke of "cruel abuses" and the "sometimes cruel" will of an officer in 1804 correspondence with James Monroe. When making notes of others' remarks at the Constitutional Convention, Madison describes a plan pronounced to be "cruel to individuals," used "unjust & cruel" in the context of "discrimination," and also jotted down the word when Gouverneur Morris said "how cruel" it would be to keep someone under "a temporary disability & disfranchisement." On August 8, 1787, in transcribing the substance of another speech by Gouverneur Morris, Madison recorded Morris's phrase "cruel bondages" as Morris attacked the institution of slavery. And in the First Congress, Madison, in discussing duties on imported articles and workers who might be injured by a change, said that "it would be cruel to neglect them." Most significantly, when crafting the absolute bar on "cruel and unusual punishments" without tacking on any qualifier, Madison chose to make the prohibition applicable to more than just courts and magistrates, in contrast to what Massachusetts and New Hampshire had chosen to do with their language. Thus, Congress, the President, and the rest of the executive branch, in addition to judges themselves, would be constrained by the Cruel and Unusual Punishments Clause.[38]

In the ratification debates over the Constitution, the Founding Fathers' aversion to cruelty became crystal clear. At Virginia's convention, George Mason worried about the establishment of "odious" and "cruel martial regulations" that would subject people to "unnecessary severity of discipline in time of peace," with Patrick Henry also worrying about "the most cruel and ignominious punishments on the militia." Indeed, Henry included the "interdiction of cruel punishments" as part of his discussion of "sacred" and "most important human rights." His colleague Edmund Pendleton also emphasized that "the most respectable writers," including Baron de Montesquieu and Locke, "properly discard from their system, all the severity of cruel punishments, such as tortures, inquisitions, and the like." Such oratory, in fact, was fully consistent with how the Founding Fathers commonly expressed their dislike of cruel punishments prior to the ratification of the Constitution itself. Even before the Continental Congress issued its Declaration of Independence, John Adams had referred to "cruel whippings."[39]

At the Virginia ratifying convention, the state's governor, Edmund Randolph, spoke of the bar against "cruel and unusual punishments" as being so elementary that it did not even require inclusion in the Constitution. "As to the exclusion of excessive bails and fines, and cruel and unusual punishments," Governor Randolph stated on June 15, 1788, in response to Patrick Henry's expressed concerns, "this would follow of itself, without a bill of rights." Randolph felt that the "number" of representatives would be "the highest security" and that "we must presume corruption in the House of Representatives, Senate, and President, before we can suppose that excessive fines can be imposed or cruel punishments inflicted." "Before these cruel punishments can be inflicted," Randolph continued, "laws must be passed, and judges must judge contrary to justice." "This," he said, "would excite universal discontent and detestation of the members of the government." As Randolph explained: "They might involve their friends in the calamities resulting from it, and could be removed from office. I never desire a greater security than this, which I believe to be absolutely sufficient."[40]

Needless to say, George Mason and Patrick Henry won the argument about the need for a U.S. Bill of Rights, and, with Madison's help and perseverance, the Eighth Amendment's Cruel and Unusual Punishments Clause was added to the Constitution in 1791. What Governor Randolph said in 1788 about bills of rights in general, however, is noteworthy. "Why is the bill of rights distinct from the constitution?" Randolph asked, speaking of Virginia's own constitution and bill of rights. "I consider bills of rights in this view," he answered, "that the government should use them when there is a departure from fundamental principles, in order to restore them." "This is the true sense of a bill of rights," he emphasized. The Eighth Amendment's prohibition on "cruel" punishment, properly understood, thus articulates a *fundamental principle*, not some archaic code word—soon to be rendered a nullity by the passage of time—that captures only what the founders themselves thought to be cruel in their lives and times. As an enduring principle, the prohibition on cruel punishments does not ever become obsolete but remains viable and relevant to every generation of Americans.[41]

The word "unusual"—the second half of the Eighth Amendment equation—actually appears in the Declaration of Independence in one of the lines indicting the king of England: "He has called together Legislative Bodies at Places unusual, uncomfortable, and distant from the Depositories of their public Records, for the sole Purpose of fatiguing them into Compliance with his Measures." In his letters and speeches, Madison himself spoke of "unusual forbearance," "unusual size," "unusual colors," an "unusual disaster," "unusual means to raise funds," "unusual questions of morality," and an "unusual degree of health." He spoke elsewhere of "adverse weather of unusual violence and continuance," "unusual attention," "unusual licentiousness," "unusual process," and "unusual backwardness to all the preparations for the ensuing crops." On at least one occasion, Madison even used the everyday word "unusual" in close proximity to the concept of cruelty. In a letter to William Bradford Jr., Madison made a reference to "the unusual cruelty of the Indians." Though none of these references pertain to the Eighth Amendment itself, they do show how the words "cruel" and "unusual" were regularly employed and commonly understood in Madison's day. Both "cruel" and "unusual" were flexible words capable of conveying a broad array of ideas, and nobody, whether lawyer or nonlawyer, had any trouble using those words in daily life.[42]

The Legislative History and Early Perspectives

Although the Framers—men such as James Madison, the principal drafter of the Constitution, and James Wilson, a gifted lawyer and legal scholar—despised governmental abuses of power and excessive punishments, very little legislative history regarding the Eighth Amendment actually exists. The only recorded material in the debates of the First Congress on the Bill of Rights are two comments about the vagueness of the provision by opponents of it. This is all that appears:

> Mr. Smith, of South Carolina, objected to the words "nor cruel and unusual punishments;" the import of them being too indefinite.
>
> Mr. Livermore [of New Hampshire]: "The clause seems to express a great deal of humanity, on which account I have no objection to it; but as it seems to have no meaning in it, I do not think it necessary. What is meant by the terms excessive bail? Who are to be the judges? What is understood by excessive fines? It lies with the court to determine. No cruel and unusual punishment is to be inflicted; it is sometimes necessary to hang a man, villains often deserve whipping, and perhaps having their ears cut off; but are we in future to be prevented from inflicting these punishments because they are cruel? If a more lenient mode of correcting vice and deterring others from the commission of it could be invented, it would be very prudent in the Legislature to adopt it; but until we have some security that this will be done, we ought not to be restrained from making necessary laws by any declaration of this kind."

The record reveals that after these brief comments were made, the Eighth Amendment "was agreed to by a considerable majority."[43]

Also, the absence of such a restraint in the Constitution as originally conceived was mentioned in only two of the state ratifying conventions. At the Massachusetts convention, Abraham Holmes spoke out against the possibility of barbaric punishments. An Anti-Federalist and one of 364 delegates to the Massachusetts ratifying convention, Holmes expressed concern that the "diabolical institution" of the Spanish Inquisition—what he called "the disgrace of Christendom"—might be replicated in America. Holmes protested:

> What gives an additional glare of horror to these gloomy circumstances is the consideration, that Congress have to ascertain, point out, and determine, what kinds of punishments shall be inflicted on persons convicted of crimes. They are nowhere restraining from inventing the most cruel and unheard-of punishments, and annexing them to crimes; and there is no constitutional check on them, but that racks and gibbets may be amongst the most mild instruments of their discipline.[44]

At Virginia's convention, Patrick Henry, who had become familiar with Montesquieu's *The Spirit of the Laws*, also expressed the fear that Congress would have unlimited power to prescribe punishments. Henry vehemently objected to the lack of a bill of rights, fearing "tortures" and "cruel and barbarous" punishments. "There is no principle to guide the legislature to restrain them from inflicting the utmost severity of punishment," he said, emphasizing: "What has distinguished our ancestors? That they would not admit of tortures, or cruel and barbarous punishment." For example, Henry worried that Congress might "introduce the practice of France, Spain, and Germany—of torturing, to extort a confession of the crime." He also said Congress "may introduce the practice of the civil law"—with its penchant for ex parte communications, instead of live, face-to-face testimony, as evidence against the accused—"in preference to that of the common law." "They will say," he said of members of Congress, "that they might as well draw examples from those countries as from Great-Britain; and they will tell you, that there is such a necessity of strengthening the arm of Government, that they must have a criminal equity, and extort confession by torture, in order to punish with still more relentless severity." "We are then lost and undone," he said. Henry also discussed the proposed power of Congress to raise armies, noting with equal concern:

> Your men who go to Congress are not restrained by a bill of rights. They are not restrained from inflicting unusual and severe punishments, though the bill of rights of Virginia forbids it. What will be the consequence? They may inflict the most cruel and ignominious punishments on the militia, and they will tell you that it is necessary for their discipline.

"[W]hen we come to punishments," Henry said, "no latitude ought to be left, nor dependence put on the virtue of representatives." Emphasizing that Virginia barred "cruel and unusual punishments," Henry passionately pled his case: "Are you not, therefore, now calling on those gentlemen who are to compose Congress, to . . . define punishments without this control?" Henry would vehemently rail against "the tyranny of Philadelphia" and even went so far as to compare the new charter to "the tyranny of George III."[45]

Though the legislative history is scant and, in many ways, the text of the Cruel and Unusual Punishments Clause speaks for itself, at least a few clues provide evidence of what was on the Framers' minds when they adopted the Eighth Amendment. In Virginia's ratification debate, for instance, George Mason expressed the view that "there were few clauses in the Constitution so dangerous as that which gave Congress exclusive power of legislation within ten miles square." The District of Columbia, he said, "may, like the custom of the superstitious days of our ancestors, become the sanctuary of the blackest crimes." "Now, sir," Mason argued, "if an attempt should be made to establish tyranny over the people, here are ten miles square where the greatest offender may meet protection." One delegate, George Nicholas, questioned whether a bill of rights would effectively prevent torture. "If we had no security against torture but our declaration of rights," Nicholas stated, "we might be tortured to-morrow; for it has been repeatedly infringed and disregarded." "A bill of rights," he said, "is only an acknowledgment of the preexisting claim to rights in the people." Mason replied that "the worthy gentleman was mistaken in his assertion that the bill of rights did not prohibit torture," saying that a "clause of the bill of rights provided that no cruel and unusual punishments shall be inflicted; therefore, torture was included in the prohibition." Mason also pointed out that another clause provided that "no man can give evidence against himself" and that "the worthy Gentleman must know, that in those countries where torture is used, evidence was extorted from the criminal himself." Though Nicholas quickly "acknowledged the Bill of Rights to contain that prohibition," saying "the Gentleman was right with respect to the practice of extorting confession from the criminal in those countries where torture is used," he still "saw no security" from the prohibition because it was "but a paper check" and "had been frequently violated with impunity."[46]

In reality, many early Americans, including an array of lawyers and jurists, came to view the Eighth Amendment as barring vile *methods* of punishment— something the English Bill of Rights was never intended to do. This conception of the Eighth Amendment is revealed by a review of early American legal sources. For example, an 1801 case report from North Carolina cites a lawyer's argument that the common-law punishment of *peine forte et dure*, or "pressing to death," could not be imposed because it would violate the state constitution's "cruel and unusual punishments" clause. "You need not argue that; it is clear it cannot," the judge said in response to the lawyer's argument in that horse-stealing case, no doubt aware that England itself had officially abolished the practice in 1772. An 1824 decision of the Virginia Supreme Court, which interpreted that state's cruel and unusual punishments clause, likewise opined that the provision was "merely applicable to the modes of punishment." In that case, John Aldridge was indicted as "a free man of color" for the larceny of bank notes valued at one hundred and fifty dollars. Convicted of the crime, Aldridge was sentenced by the jury to be inflicted with thirty-nine "stripes." On appeal, the court ruled that "the best heads and hearts of the land of our ancestors, had long and loudly declaimed against the wanton cruelty of many of the punishments practised in other countries," declaring the clause "was framed effectually to exclude these, so that no future Legislature, in a moment perhaps of great and general excitement, should be tempted to disgrace our Code by the introduction of any of those odious modes of punishment." Finding that Virginia's provision "denouncing cruel and unusual punishments" had no "bearing" on the case, the Virginia Supreme Court, writing in the wake of Gabriel's Rebellion and at a time when slaves were still being frequently executed or brutally whipped as a form of discipline, held that the provision "was never designed to control the Legislative right to determine *ad libitum* upon the *adequacy* of punishment, but is merely applicable to the modes of punishment." Despite "the general terms used in the Bill of Rights," the court ruled, reflecting the overt racial prejudice of that time, "it is undeniable that it never was contemplated, or considered, to extend to the whole population of the State." "Can it be doubted, that it not only was not intended to apply to our slave population, but that the free blacks and mulattoes were also not comprehended in it?" the court noted rhetorically.[47]

Historically, the Virginia courts—which still permit executions—have long deferred to legislative judgments and focused on the modes of punishments. For example, in *Hart v. Commonwealth*, Virginia's Supreme Court of Appeals held in 1921 that the "cruel and unusual punishments" provision of Virginia's constitution "must be construed to impose no limitation upon the legislative right to determine and prescribe by statute the quantum of punishments deemed adequate by the Legislature." "[T]he only limitation so imposed," it ruled, "is upon the mode of punishments, such punishments only being prohibited by such constitutional provision as were regarded as cruel and unusual when such provision of the Constitution was adopted in 1776, namely, such bodily punishments as involve torture or lingering death—such as are inhumane and barbarous—as, for example, punishment by the rack, by drawing and quartering, leaving the body hung in chains, or on the gibbet, exposed to public view, and the like." "However," the court in *Hart* noted, "there has been for a long while a difference of judicial opinion on the subject under consideration." "[W]hile a large majority of the American courts have taken the same view of the subject as that of the Virginia court," the judges clarified, "a minority of them have held that the constitutional provision in question imposes a limitation, not alone upon the legislative right to determine and prescribe by statute the mode of punishments, but also upon the quantum of punishments, upon the theory that punishment should be proportional to the gravity of the offense, and that punishment may by its length, or other severity, be so disproportioned to the offense as to constitute cruel and unusual punishment within the meaning of the constitutional prohibition." In fact, in their new book *Proportionality Principles in American Law*, professors Thomas Sullivan and Richard Frase make clear that modern courts "often emphasize the 'unnecessary' or 'gratuitous' use of force or discipline" in their judicial decisions, but that "proportionality principles are almost always implicit."[48]

After the Eighth Amendment's ratification, the influential constitutional scholar Joseph Story, whom James Madison appointed to serve on the U.S. Supreme Court in 1811, himself expressed the view that it only targeted modes of punishments. While riding circuit in 1814, Justice Story gave his own views on the death penalty when instructing a Massachusetts jury in a capital murder trial involving a mariner. "Homicide is either justifiable, excusable, or felonious," he said, explaining: "It is justifiable when the act is done from some unavoidable necessity, or for the advancement of public justice, or for the prevention of some atrocious crime; such as the execution of a criminal convict, and the killing of a person who attempts to rob, murder, or commit some other atrocious felony upon the person or property of another." "[T]he true legal notion of malice," he charged the jury, "extends to all cases of homicide perpetrated under such circumstances of wanton cruelty and implacable revenge" such that if, "upon a sudden provocation of a slight nature one beat another in a cruel and unusual manner so that he dies, though he did not intend to kill him, it is murder by express malice." The case concerned George Travers, a seaman who got involved in a snowball fight at a navy yard and who was accused of unfairly concealing a brickbat in a ball of snow. After denying the accusation, a fight ensued, the participants were ordered to report to the guard house, but Travers refused and later shot two men with a musket who were trying to detain him. The question, once again, was whether the deaths constituted murder or manslaughter. The jury found Travers guilty of manslaughter—the less serious offense—after Justice Story concluded his instructions to the jurors by saying: "Your duty to your country and to the prisoner requires you to act with caution, and in giving your verdict to consult the honest dictates of your consciences."[49]

Though Justice Story asserted that society had the right to inflict the punishment of death, he nonetheless opposed "cruel" punishments and opined that the death penalty should be reserved for the worst offenders. In his treatise *Commentaries on the Constitution of the United States*, Story editorialized: "The laws of the Roman kings, and the twelve tables of the Decemviri, were full of cruel punishments; the Porcian law, which exempted all citizens from the punishment of death, silently abrogated them all. In this period the republic flourished. Under the emperors severe laws were revived, and then the empire fell." Story—noting Beccaria's work in another source, *Encyclopedia Americana*—also wrote that the right to inflict the death penalty "has been doubted by some distinguished persons; and the doubt is often the accompaniment of a highly cultivated mind, inclined to the indulgence of a romantic sensibility, and believing in human perfectibility." "When the right of society is once admitted to punish for offences," Story emphasized, "it seems difficult to assign any limits to the exercise of that right, short of what the exigencies of society require." Story, however, went on to say: "Certainly, punishments ought not to be inflicted, which are utterly disproportionate to the offense, and beyond the exigencies of society. No government has a right to punish cruelly and wantonly, and from mere revenge." The death penalty, he qualified, should be reserved for "a crime of great atrocity and danger to society," with the legal scholar saying "[a] man who has committed murder deliberately, has proved himself unfit for society." "As a general rule," Story wrote, "humanity forbids such punishments to be applied to any but crimes of very great enormity, and danger to individuals or the state." As to the manner of inflicting punishments, Story reported: "Barbarous nations are generally inclined to severe and vindictive punishments, and, where they punish with death, to aggravate it by prolonging the sufferings of the victim with ingenious devices in cruelty." "In modern times," he wrote, "the public opinion is strongly disposed to discountenance the punishment of death by any but simple means; and the infliction of torture is almost universally reprobated." "In the U. States of America," Story added, "hanging is the universal mode of capital punishment," with Story then pointing to the Eighth Amendment language prohibiting "cruel and unusual punishments."[50]

Nathan Dane, the Massachusetts legislator who drafted the Northwest Ordinance, also wrote a comprehensive treatise on American law in which he focused on changes in American law and the shifting modes of punishment. "When our country was first settled," Dane noted, "there were many more capital and infamous punishments, than exist at present; probably because our ancestors came from a country in which these were very numerous." "Infamous punishments," he explained, included "gallows, pillory, state prison, branding, hard labour, and whipping, and some imprisonments." Dane added that corporal punishments in the U.S. Army had been abolished, and that "punishments have been varied in other respects; the pillory, gallows, whipping, and branding have almost disappeared, and solitary imprisonment, and hard labour in state prisons" had been "generally substituted in their place, as also much in the place of capital punishments." He emphasized: "we have many felonies, not one punished with forfeiture of estate, and but a very few with death." Dane's treatise also included a series of "MAXIMS," one of which came from Beccaria. "Servitude for life," it read, "has a better effect on spectators, than death; ... servitude is a perpetual warning,—death occasional; death is pernicious, from the example of barbarity it affords." Dane then editorialized: "Very sensible writers differ on this subject, and upon it public opinion has several times changed." "[T]his opinion of Beccaria, as to capital punishment," Dane said, "has been adopted but partially; the better opinion has been otherwise, as to treason, murder, rape, and very atrocious crimes; so his opinion, that servitude has a better effect on spectators than death, as a punishment for crimes, may be questioned; certainly if he means a greater effect." "So," Dane explained, "is our experience: when, in this State, a man indicted for burglary, was tried for his life, his trial attracted attention far and near, and his execution brought thousands to see it from great distances. Now such a criminal is only punished in the State prison,—his trial attrracks [sic] no attention at all; his case is scarcely distinguished from that of a common thief, or that of any other criminal condemned to that prison." Dane noted that the common law authorized death by hanging and that death by shooting was employed in some military cases, though he pointed out that Beccaria, "and others of his good and humane disposition, admit that punishments must be made to conform not only to the nature of the crime, but also to times and existing circumstances." Dane was especially proud of the fact that in his time, in his home state of Massachusetts, counsel was routinely appointed for those accused of capital crimes. He compared the "value and excellency" of Massachusetts procedure with the "severity, or rather cruelty of the English law" denying the accused the right to counsel.[51]

Some scholars and jurists, while then seeing the death penalty as a necessary part of the criminal justice system, nonetheless saw reform over the horizon. James Kent, the chancellor of New York, wrote in *Commentaries on American Law* that the Cruel and Unusual Punishments Clause serves as "a further guard against abuse and oppression in criminal proceedings." Writing in the early nineteenth century, Kent remarked that the death penalty "ought to be confined to the few cases of the most atrocious character, for it is only in such cases that public opinion will warrant the measure, or the peace and safety require it." "[W]hile cruel and unusual punishments are universally condemned," he added, "[t]he punishment of death is, doubtless, the most dreadful and the most impressive spectacle of public justice; and it is not possible to adopt any other punishment equally powerful by its example." "Civil society," Kent explained, "has an undoubted right to use the means requisite for its preservation; and the punishment of murder with death, accords with the judgment and practice of mankind, because the intensity and the violence of the malignity that will commit the crime, require to be counteracted by the strongest motives which can be presented to the human mind." Kent noted, though, that "some theorists have proposed the entire abolition of the punishment of death, and have considered it to be an unnecessary waste of power, if not altogether unjust and unwarrantable." He also pointed out that "[t]hough the penitentiary system has not been able sufficiently to answer the expectations of the public, either in the reformation of offenders, or as an example to deter others," new state prisons, including one at Sing Sing in New York, "afford encouraging expectations that they will be able to redeem the credit of the system, and recommend the punishment of solitary imprisonment and hard labour, instead of capital and other sanguinary punishments to the universal approbation of the civilized world."[52]

Early nineteenth-century judicial decisions also give at least some sense of how the Eighth Amendment was understood in the early days of the republic. For example, in 1825 in *James v. Commonwealth,* the Pennsylvania Supreme Court struck down the punishment of Nancy James. Adjudged "a common scold" in 1824, James had been sentenced "to be placed in a certain engine of correction, called a cucking or ducking-stool . . . and being so placed therein, to be plunged three times into the water." In colonial and early America, a chair-like device known as the "ducking stool" was sometimes used to dunk offenders under water. In striking down the punishment, the Pennsylvania Supreme Court did not rely on constitutional grounds but noted: "The object of the framers of the act of 1790, was the abolition of all infamous, disgraceful, public punishments—all cruel and unnatural punishments—for all the classes of minor offences and misdemeanors, to which they had been before applied." James's sentence, the court declared, "has created much ferment and excitement in the public mind; it is considered as a cruel, unusual, unnatural and ludicrous judgment," though the court noted that "whatever prejudices may exist against it, still, if it be the law of the land, the court must pronounce judgment for it." After reciting the history of the punishment under English law and noting that "this customary ancient punishment for ducking scolds" was "never adopted, and therefore, is not the common law of Pennsylvania," the court noted:

> In coming to the conclusion, that the ducking-stool is not the punishment of scolds, I do not take into consideration the humane provisions of the constitutions of the United States and of this state, as to cruel and unusual punishments, further than they show the sense of the whole community. If the reformation of the culprit, and prevention of the crime, be the just foundation and object of all punishments, nothing could be further removed from these salutary ends, than the infliction in question. It destroys all personal respect; the women thus punished would scold on for life, and the exhibition would be far from being beneficial to the spectators. What a spectacle would it exhibit!

An 1832 assault case noted that Pennsylvania's 1790 law had made various offenses, including assault and battery, not capital, with the court reporting: "It was not usual in Pennsylvania, (nor ever, it is believed, exercised before the act for reforming the penal laws,) to inflict whipping, the pillory, or imprisonment for life, or other ignominious corporal punishments, for any assault, whatever the intention might be, unless committed with very atrocious designs on the person, as with intention to murder, ravish, or commit the unnatural crime."[53]

The Eighth Amendment

The U.S. Constitution's Eighth Amendment contains just sixteen words: "Excessive bail shall not be required, nor excessive fines imposed, nor cruel and unusual punishments inflicted." That language, however, has generated endless controversy, and the lack of particularity in just what the Eighth Amendment prohibits has fueled much litigation. "The Eighth Amendment," law professor Ronald Dworkin points out, "forbids 'cruel and unusual punishment,' but it does not indicate whether any particular methods of executing criminals—hanging or electrocution, for example—are cruel or, indeed, whether the death penalty is itself cruel no matter what method of execution is used." Indeed, on its face, the text says neither how large fines or bail amounts can be before they become "excessive" nor what specific punishments are "cruel and unusual." Thus, the U.S. Supreme Court, which is obligated to decide what those terms mean, has had to decide how to interpret the Eighth Amendment and what conduct or practices violate or are consistent with those words. In a series of cases handed down since the ratification of the Bill of Rights, all three of the Eighth Amendment's clauses—the Bail Clause, the Excessive Fines Clause, and the Cruel and Unusual Punishments Clause—have been interpreted by the nation's highest court.[54]

In interpreting the Eighth Amendment, the Supreme Court has held that the amendment—addressed as it is to bail, fines, and punishments—applies principally to criminal prosecutions and punishments. "The purpose of the Eighth Amendment, putting the Bail Clause to one side," the Court ruled in *Austin v. United States,* "was to limit the government's power to punish." As the Court explained in *Ingraham v. Wright:* "Bail, fines, and punishment traditionally have been associated with the criminal process, and by subjecting the three to parallel limitations the text of the Amendment suggests an intention to limit the power of those entrusted with the criminal-law function of government." "An examination of the history of the Amendment and the decisions of this Court construing the proscription against cruel and unusual punishment," the Court said, "confirms that it was designed to protect those convicted of crimes." Thus, the Eighth Amendment, invoked frequently in both state and federal courts and restraining not just courts but any governmental act, has formed the basis for legal challenges over the years to corporal punishments, "status" crimes, conditions of confinement, lengthy sentences of incarceration, and—of course—death sentences.[55]

On their face, the Bail and Excessive Fines Clauses bar "excessive" sanctions, and the common, everyday term "excessive" plainly has a subjective quality to it. What is excessive to one may not be excessive to another—and what is considered excessive will naturally vary from one generation to the next. In a draft of considerations for a convention with Spain for the rendition of "Fugitives from Justice," written in a clerk's hand but signed by Thomas Jefferson on March 22, 1792, a reference is found to "Excessive punishment," though not in the context of bail or fines. The notes read: "All Excess of punishment is a Crime. To remit a fugitive to Excessive punishment, is to be accessary to the crime." "In England, and probably in Canada," the notes read, "to steal a Hare, is death the 1st. offence: to steal above the value of 12d. death the 2d. offence." "Exile, in some countries, has been the Highest punishment allowed by the laws," the notes state elsewhere, adding: "To most minds it is next to death: to many beyond it." "We should not wish then to give up to the Executioner the Patriot who fails, and flies to us," another notation read, with the draft considerations also stating that, for "Crimes against Property," "[t]he punishment, in most countries" is "immensely disproportionate to the crime."[56]

The Eighth Amendment does not define "excessive," let alone attempt to provide examples or illustrations of what qualifies, leaving that matter entirely to the courts. As New Hampshire's Superior Court of Judicature, quoting William Blackstone, ruled in 1819: "[T]he determination of 'what bail shall be called excessive must be left to the courts on considering the circumstances of the case.'" Often, judges quite appropriately determine that offenders are not entitled to bail at all. In *United States v. Salerno,* the U.S. Supreme Court itself ruled—in accord with Blackstone's views and, indeed, with common sense—that serious offenders, such as murderers, can be held without bail. In *Stack v. Boyle,* conversely, the Supreme Court held that bail is "excessive" for other, less serious offenders if bail is set "at a figure higher than an amount reasonably calculated" to secure a defendant's presence at trial. What amount is reasonable, or whether any amount would be sufficient, is, under American law, left to judges to decide on a case-by-case basis. Indeed, in *Austin,* which applied the Excessive Fines Clause to civil forfeiture proceedings, one of the few cases to apply the Eighth Amendment in a noncriminal context, the Court explicitly refused to adopt a rigid definition of "excessive." In that case, the Court declined to adopt a multifactor test for determining when a forfeiture is constitutionally excessive. In *United States v. Bajakajian,* the Court instead emphasized that "[t]he touchstone of the constitutional inquiry under the Excessive Fines Clause is the principle of proportionality." "The amount of the forfeiture," the Court held, "must bear some relationship to the gravity of the offense that it is designed to punish." "[A] punitive forfeiture," the Court ruled, "violates the Excessive Fines Clause if it is grossly disproportional to the gravity of a defendant's offense."[57]

Court rulings interpreting the Cruel and Unusual Punishments Clause have proven to be the most controversial by far. "The feeling that modern Eighth Amendment jurisprudence has gone off the rails," notes one commentator, "has arisen, at least in part, from the wildly inconsistent rulings that have emanated from the Supreme Court over the past few decades, particularly regarding proportionality in sentencing and the death penalty." Part of this feeling no doubt stems from the Supreme Court's frequent reversals in relatively short spans of time when faced with important Eighth Amendment questions. *Penry v. Lynaugh,* a 1989 case, found that executing mentally retarded offenders did not violate the Eighth Amendment, a ruling the Court overturned in 2002 in *Atkins v. Virginia.* In 2005, in *Roper v. Simmons,* the Court likewise held it was unconstitutional to inflict death sentences on any offenders younger than eighteen, a decision overturning the result of another 1989 case, *Stanford v. Kentucky.* In 1987 and 1989, the Supreme Court ruled and then reaffirmed that the Eighth Amendment bars the admission of "victim impact" evidence. Yet in 1991 in *Payne v. Tennessee,* the Court—after two Justices were replaced—did an about-face, finding that the Eighth Amendment did *not* bar the admission of such testimony. The Court in *Payne* thus disregarded its prior rulings in *Booth v. Maryland* and *South Carolina v. Gathers.* The reversal of precedents is always sure to generate controversy, but when the Court sets aside precedents of recent vintage, Americans are especially certain to sit up and take notice.[58]

Anyone in search of a principled approach to the Eighth Amendment—one rooted in its text—has thus been bitterly disappointed by the Supreme Court's decisions. How can it be that the Court rules one way on the Cruel and Unusual Punishments Clause in one decade, then the exact opposite way in the next decade? Or one way, then another, in a span of just two years? The overturning of so many precedents in such a short time raises eyebrows and has caused judges, lawyers, and academics alike to look anew at the Court's rulings, spilling gallons of ink desperately trying to make sense of them. "Power, not reason, is the new currency of this Court's decisionmaking," Justice Thurgood Marshall wrote in dissent in *Payne,* noting that "[n]either the law nor the facts supporting *Booth* and *Gathers* underwent any change in the last four years." "Only the personnel of this Court did," Marshall wrote, arguing that the principle of *stare decisis* should have been followed "because fidelity to precedent is part and parcel of a conception of 'the judiciary as a source of impersonal and reasoned judgments.'" In a 2008 case, the Court itself acknowledged that another aspect of its Eighth Amendment jurisprudence "is still in search of a unifying principle." The seemingly unending search for how to interpret the Eighth Amendment properly thus continues unabated, as it has for decades.[59]

The U.S. Supreme Court first thoroughly examined the Eighth Amendment's history in *Weems v. United States.* In that 1910 case, the Court held that a fifteen-year sentence in irons and shackles for falsifying a document was excessive. "[I]t is a precept of justice," the Court ruled, echoing back to Beccaria, "that punishment for crime should be graduated and proportioned" to the offense. After citing the legal scholar Joseph Story for the proposition that the Eighth Amendment was " 'adopted as an admonition to all departments of the national government, to warn them against such violent proceedings as had taken place in England in the arbitrary reigns of some of the Stuarts,' " the Court held that "a principle, to be vital, must be capable of wider application than the mischief which gave it birth." The Court in *Weems* found that the Eighth Amendment was originally motivated by a distrust of power, a distrust deeply felt by Patrick Henry and others. "[I]t was believed," the Court explained, "that power might be tempted to cruelty." In fact, as Virginia's governor, Patrick Henry himself had advocated reform of the state's death penalty laws. In a 1785 letter to Richmond's mayor, Henry had ordered the mayor to halt blanket executions and to build a prison for perpetrators of lesser offenses. "With respect to some of them," he wrote, "the punishment of death seems disproportionate to the crime." As one of Henry's biographers has written: "As governor, Henry attempted to reform a number of British laws he considered harsh. The death penalty, for example, was imposed for many felonies, regardless of the severity of the crime. This was a practice that Henry felt was both unjust and cruel. He thus developed a plan of granting pardons, after hard labor, for lesser crimes."[60]

At issue in *Weems* was not an American criminal sanction, but an outlandish sentence imposed in the Philippines. As Chief Justice Warren Burger later explained: "In *Weems,* the Court had struck down as cruel and unusual punishment a sentence of cadena temporal imposed by a Philippine Court. This bizarre penalty, which was unknown to Anglo-Saxon law, entailed a minimum of 12 years' imprisonment chained day and night at the wrists and ankles, hard and painful labor while so chained, and a number of 'accessories' including lifetime civil disabilities." After noting the Founding Fathers' distrust of power, the Court in *Weems*, in the context of applying the Eighth Amendment to the dispute, offered its own interpretive guidance: "Legislation, both statutory and constitutional, is enacted, it is true, from an experience of evils but its general language should not, therefore, be necessarily confined to the form that evil had theretofore taken." "This is peculiarly true of constitutions," the Court explained, adding: "They are not ephemeral enactments, designed to meet passing occasions. They are, to use the words of Chief Justice Marshall, 'designed to approach immortality as nearly as human institutions can approach it.'" In other words, though the Filipino practice at issue in *Weems* was foreign both to modern and eighteenth-century America (when harsh corporal punishments were themselves still regularly applied), the Cruel and Unusual Punishments Clause, because of the broad way in which it was drafted by the Framers, effectively barred that cruel, unfamiliar punishment.[61]

The Court in *Weems* thus rejected a rigid interpretation of the Eighth Amendment. Indeed, in drafting the Constitution, the Framers—who could not have foreseen every social or technological advance, let alone a future with automobiles, the Internet, and jet airplanes—clearly chose "general language" in many places so that the Constitution would be relevant to future generations. Instead of trying to set in stone eighteenth-century practices, the Constitution and the Bill of Rights articulated, in general terms, certain fundamental principles and values, such as the need for "due process" and the legislators' collective aversion to "cruel and unusual punishments." Had the Framers wanted to codify eighteenth-century norms in the Constitution, they certainly could have done so—and said so. They did not, of course, and what the Court in *Weems* seemed to say, in its first crack at examining the Eighth Amendment's history and purpose, is that the Constitution and the Eighth Amendment as written are adaptable, and were intended to be adaptable, to modern circumstances and future disputes. In short, the Constitution—as a matter of logic and common sense, and as purposefully designed by the Founding Fathers—must be viewed as a vibrant, living document, not an antiquated catalog of eighteenth-century thought.[62]

Since *Weems,* the Supreme Court has stuck with that approach and has interpreted and applied the Eighth Amendment in a variety of contexts. For example, in *Trop v. Dulles,* a U.S. Army private was court-martialed, convicted of desertion, given a dishonorable discharge, stripped of his American citizenship, and sentenced to "three years at hard labor" with "forfeiture of all pay and allowances." Finding an Eighth Amendment violation, the Court held in 1958 that "the total destruction of the individual's status in organized society" is "a form of punishment more primitive than torture." "[T]he expatriate has lost the right to have rights," the Court ruled, striking down the imposition of a punishment causing statelessness. The scope of the Eighth Amendment, the Court emphasized, "is not static," with the Court noting that "[t]he basic concept underlying the Eighth Amendment is nothing less than the dignity of man." "While the State has the power to punish," the Court held, "the Amendment stands to assure that this power be exercised within the limits of civilized standards." The Court also credited the fact that "[t]he civilized nations of the world are in virtual unanimity that statelessness is not to be imposed as punishment for crime." The Framers themselves, of course, also frequently looked to the laws and practices of other nations for guidance, as the Eighth Amendment's English origins make clear. *The Federalist Papers* alone include references to more than fifty foreign sources, including countries in Africa, Asia, and Europe. Indeed, the Constitution itself references "the Law of Nations."[63]

In modern times, the U.S. Supreme Court has interpreted the Eighth Amendment to do much more than bar odious modes of execution. In the noncapital context, for example, *Robinson v. California* struck down a misdemeanor sentence for the crime of addiction to a controlled substance. The Court held that while "imprisonment for ninety days is not, in the abstract, a punishment which is either cruel or unusual," it may not be imposed for the "status" of being "addicted to the use of narcotics." As Justice Potter Stewart explained in *Robinson*: "Even one day in prison would be a cruel and unusual punishment for the 'crime' of having a common cold." In *Solem v. Helm,* the Court also held that the Eighth Amendment prohibited the imposition of a life-without-parole sentence upon a repeat offender for uttering a one-hundred-dollar, no-account check. "Incarcerating him for life without possibility of parole," the Court ruled, "is unlikely to advance the goals of our criminal justice system in any substantial way" and was found to be "disproportionate" and "therefore prohibited by the Eighth Amendment." In contrast, the Court has upheld other lengthy sentences, such as the ones imposed in *Ewing v. California* and *Harmelin v. Michigan.* In *Ewing,* a repeat offender in California was sentenced to life imprisonment without the possibility of parole for the theft of twelve hundred dollars' worth of golf clubs, under the state's "Three Strikes and You're Out" law. The Court found no Eighth Amendment violation there or in *Harmelin,* in which the Court upheld another life-without-parole sentence for possession of cocaine even though the offender had no prior criminal record.[64]

In capital cases since *Furman v. Georgia*, the U.S. Supreme Court has declined to find the death penalty unconstitutional even as it has frequently used the Eighth Amendment to restrict the categories of death-eligible offenders. *Ford v. Wainwright* barred the execution of the insane. *Atkins v. Virginia,* citing a "dramatic shift in the state legislative landscape," outlawed the execution of the mentally retarded. *Roper v. Simmons* categorically barred the execution of offenders who were under the age of eighteen at the time of their crimes, and *Enmund v. Florida* forbade the execution of a defendant who did not take life, attempt to kill, or intend that lethal force be used in the commission of the crime. The defendant in the latter case, Earl Enmund, was a getaway driver in a car on the side of the road when a robbery turned into a double murder at a nearby farmhouse. The Court, using the Eighth Amendment, rejected the death penalty's imposition for accomplice liability, finding that Enmund, who aided and abetted a robbery, never intended to kill anyone. The thread running through these cases is that the offender possessed—as the Court itself has declared—"a diminished personal responsibility for the crime." "For purposes of imposing the death penalty," the Court ruled in *Enmund,* a defendant's "criminal culpability" must be limited to his participation in the crime, and a defendant's punishment "must be tailored to his personal responsibility and moral guilt." As far back as 1799, Virginia's Supreme Court of Appeals held that the Eighth Amendment language was designed to ensure that no offender was punished "beyond the real measure of his own offence."[65]

In the context of nonhomicidal rape, the U.S. Supreme Court has also struck down death sentences as Eighth Amendment violations. In *Coker v. Georgia,* the Supreme Court held that a death sentence was "grossly disproportionate and excessive punishment" for the rape of an "adult woman." Emphasizing that Georgia, where the rape took place, was the sole U.S. jurisdiction authorizing a sentence of death for that crime, the Court held that the sentence violated the Cruel and Unusual Punishments Clause. "We have the abiding conviction," the Court ruled, "that the death penalty, which 'is unique in its severity and irrevocability,' is an excessive penalty for the rapist who, as such, does not take human life." As the Court emphasized: "The murderer kills; the rapist, if no more than that, does not. Life is over for the victim of the murderer; for the rape victim, life may not be nearly so happy as it was, but it is not over and normally is not beyond repair." And in 2008 in *Kennedy v. Louisiana,* a ruling roundly criticized by both John McCain and Barack Obama in the midst of that year's heated presidential campaign, the *Coker* ruling was extended to acts of child rape. The Court held that, at least with respect to "crimes against individuals," the death penalty would not be permitted for nonhomicidal acts. "We do not address," the Court simultaneously clarified, however, "crimes defining and punishing treason, espionage, terrorism, and drug kingpin activity, which are offenses against the State."[66]

The Supreme Court has also used the Eighth Amendment to, in its words, "ensure consistency in determining who receives a death sentence." To guarantee "restraint and moderation in use of capital punishment," the Supreme Court thus insists on judging the "character and record of the individual offender and the circumstances of the particular offense as a constitutionally indispensable part of the process of inflicting the penalty of death." Thus, in *Lockett v. Ohio,* the Court held in 1978 that Ohio's death penalty statute did not permit the type of individualized consideration of mitigating factors required by the Eighth and Fourteenth Amendments in capital cases. A defendant in a capital trial consequently has the right to raise as a mitigating factor any aspect of his or her character or record and any circumstances of the offense that might be a basis for a sentence less than death. The inherent conflict between two competing constitutional principles—that defendants be treated alike, so as to comport with equal protection and avoid racial bias, and also that they be treated as individuals, in recognition of their humanity and their unique characteristics—actually led Justice Harry Blackmun, near the end of his judicial career, to conclude that the death penalty itself is unconstitutional. "It is virtually self evident to me now that no combination of procedural rules or substantive regulations ever can save the death penalty from its inherent constitutional deficiencies," Blackmun dissented in *Callins v. Collins.* In 1985, in *Caldwell v. Mississippi,* a majority of the Court also held that it is constitutionally impermissible under the Eighth Amendment to rest a death sentence on a determination made by a jury led to believe that the responsibility for determining the appropriateness of that sentence rested elsewhere—for example, with an appellate tribunal.[67]

Though Justices William Brennan and Thurgood Marshall, while on the Court, frequently wrote dissents opining that executions per se constitute "cruel and unusual punishments," the majority of the Justices have long disagreed. The Court in fact has upheld the constitutionality of more than one method of execution. In 1878, in *Wilkerson v. Utah,* the Court approved the use of a firing squad, finding that execution by shooting or hanging was a customary military practice. In 1890, in *In re Kemmler,* the Court also rejected an Eighth Amendment challenge to the use of the electric chair, though decades later it granted certiorari in a Florida case to reconsider that ruling. The latter case was eventually dismissed as moot after the Florida legislature adopted a lethal injection protocol. *Holden v. Minnesota,* another 1890 case, likewise approved a Minnesota law requiring private, nighttime executions, though that decision was not rooted in the Eighth Amendment but came in the context of an ex post facto challenge. State legislatures had begun passing laws mandating private executions in the 1830s and nighttime executions in the 1880s, laws that often forbade journalists from attending or even so much as reporting on executions. By giving approval to such laws, the Court's ruling in *Holden* actually accelerated the passage of such censorship laws in other states. An

Eighth Amendment challenge to a New York law requiring solitary confinement of convicted murderers prior to their execution was also rejected in 1891 in *McElvaine v. Brush*. And in 1947, in a particularly bizarre case, *Louisiana ex rel. Francis v. Resweber,* the Court further held that it was not "cruel and unusual punishment" to carry out an inmate's execution—that of Willie Francis—after the first attempt to electrocute him failed to kill him. Most recently, in *Baze v. Rees,* the Supreme Court turned aside yet another Eighth Amendment challenge by upholding the constitutionality of Kentucky's three-drug lethal injection protocol.[68]

The death penalty itself has been upheld too. After the Supreme Court's highly contentious, five-to-four decision in *Furman,* the Court upheld three state death penalty statutes by seven-to-two votes in *Gregg v. Georgia, Jurek v. Texas,* and *Proffitt v. Florida.* Those rulings, coming in 1976, just four years after the Court's ruling in *Furman,* were premised on the notion that the passage of new death penalty statutes by thirty-five states had undercut the rationale of *Furman.* That legislative activity, the Court ruled in *Gregg,* made it "evident" that "a large proportion of American society" continued to view capital punishment "as an appropriate and necessary criminal sanction." Citing considerations of federalism and respect for a legislature's ability to evaluate the death penalty's morality and "social utility," the Court held that the Georgia, Texas, and Florida laws suitably directed and limited juror discretion so as to minimize the risk of wholly arbitrary and capricious sentencing decisions. But even then, the Supreme Court saw limits to what state legislatures could do and once again used the Eighth Amendment to say so. Thus, in *Roberts v. Louisiana* and *Woodson v. North Carolina,* two other 1976 cases, the Court moderated its stance, striking down as unconstitutional two statutes calling for mandatory death sentences. The failure to allow consideration of mitigating factors or a defendant's individual circumstances, the Court ruled, violated the Constitution's Eighth and Fourteenth Amendments. Though early American laws imposed mandatory death sentences and the common-law approach once automatically imposed death sentences on convicted murderers, the nation's highest court in its 1976 decisions rejected mandatory death sentences as "unduly harsh and unworkably rigid."[69]

In still other cases, though, the Supreme Court has simultaneously interpreted the Eighth Amendment to regulate various aspects of capital prosecutions, all the way down to scrutinizing the precise wording of particular jury instructions given at trial. In 1980, in *Godfrey v. Georgia,* the Supreme Court struck down the imposition of a death sentence because a statutory "aggravating circumstance" was construed so broadly that it might involve *any* murder. In that case, the Georgia Supreme Court had affirmed a death sentence based on nothing more than the finding that the offense was "outrageously or wantonly vile, horrible and inhuman." In *Maynard v. Cartwright,* a 1988 case, the Supreme Court likewise held that the language of an Oklahoma aggravating circumstance—"especially heinous, atrocious, or cruel"—gave no more guidance than the aggravating circumstance at issue in *Godfrey*. "Claims of vagueness directed at aggravating circumstances defined in capital punishment statutes," the Court held, "are analyzed under the Eighth Amendment." Such claims, the Court said, "characteristically assert that the challenged provision fails adequately to inform juries what they must find to impose the death penalty and as a result leaves them and appellate courts with the kind of open-ended discretion which was held invalid in *Furman*." In 1993, in *Arave v. Creech*, by contrast, the Court held that one of Idaho's aggravating factors— that "by the murder, or circumstances surrounding its commission, the defendant exhibited utter disregard for human life"—did not, at least as construed by the Idaho Supreme Court, run afoul of the Eighth and Fourteenth Amendments. While the majority noted that a limiting construction limited its reach to a "cold-blooded, pitiless slayer," the dissent argued that, "in everyday parlance," the term "cold-blooded" is routinely used to describe "*all* murders."[70]

Along with striking down death sentences for certain categories of offenders and regulating capital trials to ensure their fairness, the Supreme Court has indicated, often in dicta, that the Eighth Amendment bars certain antiquated modes of punishment. For example, in *In re Kemmler*, which upheld the constitutionality of the electric chair, the Court noted that "burning at the stake, crucifixion, breaking on the wheel, or the like" would fall within the ambit of "cruel and unusual" punishments. "Punishments are cruel when they involve torture or a lingering death," the Court ruled. "[P]unishments of torture," the Court had ruled more than a decade earlier in *Wilkerson v. Utah*, "are forbidden." In 2010, in *Graham v. Florida*, the Court—in its most recent articulation of this principle—put it this way as it struck down a juvenile's life-without-parole sentence for a burglary: "The Cruel and Unusual Punishments Clause prohibits the imposition of inherently barbaric punishments under all circumstances." The Court in *Wilkerson* and in *In re Kemmler*, of course, had let a shooting by firing squad and an electrocution go forward, with language in *In re Kemmler* quick to clarify the Court's position on the death penalty generally: "[T]he punishment of death is not cruel within the meaning of that word as used in the constitution. It implies there something inhuman and barbarous, something more than the mere extinguishment of life."[71]

As construed by the Supreme Court, the Eighth Amendment bars not only "barbaric" punishments but also those deemed "excessive" or "disproportionate" to the crime. "The concept of proportionality," the Court said in *Graham*, "is central to the Eighth Amendment." A punishment is "excessive" if it is "grossly out of proportion to the severity of the crime" and "makes no measurable contribution to acceptable goals of punishment and hence is nothing more than the purposeless and needless infliction of pain and suffering." The legitimate goals of punishment, the Court has held, include retribution, deterrence, incapacitation, and rehabilitation. Whether a death sentence is "disproportionate" to the crime committed, the Court notes, depends on societal standards and the individual views of the Justices themselves. In addition to looking at "legislative enactments and state practice," the Court says that it looks to the text, history, meaning, and purpose of the Eighth Amendment; to "the standards elaborated by controlling precedents"; and to "its own independent judgment whether the punishment in question violates the Constitution." A state's power to punish must, it has been held more than once, "be exercised within the limits of civilized standards." In other words, while history informs the Court's decisions, it does not control them.[72]

In *Graham*, the Supreme Court held that the Eighth Amendment prohibits the imposition of a life-without-parole sentence on a juvenile offender who did not commit a homicide. In so ruling, the Court divided its prior precedents addressing the proportionality of sentences into two categories: those involving challenges to the length of term-of-years sentences, and those imposing "categorical restrictions on the death penalty." The Court noted that, in the first category, it "considers all of the circumstances of the case to determine whether the sentence is unconstitutionally excessive." "A court," it ruled, "must begin by comparing the gravity of the offense and the severity of the sentence." In the "rare case" leading to an inference of "gross disproportionality," a court then compares the defendant's sentence "with the sentences received by other offenders in the same jurisdiction and with the sentences imposed for the same crime in other jurisdictions." In the second category, the Court noted its use of "categorical rules to define Eighth Amendment standards," as in its cases outlawing the death penalty for nonhomicidal rape or for juveniles. In that second grouping, the Court classified two distinct subsets of cases: one considering *the nature of the offense,* and the other considering *the characteristics of the offender.* "In the cases adopting categorical rules," the Court said, it considered "objective indicia of society's standards" to determine whether a "national consensus" against a practice existed, before turning to "its own independent judgment."[73]

The Fourteenth Amendment

The Civil War, which claimed hundreds of thousands of lives, forced Americans to confront head-on the institution of slavery, an evil, barbaric practice. Slavery had long pitted the North against the South, and in the lead-up to the war tensions had only been exacerbated by the Supreme Court's horrendous 1857 decision in the *Dred Scott* case, which held that a slave had no right to sue for his freedom. The post–Civil War Reconstruction Amendments, however, radically altered the federal government's relationship with the states. The Thirteenth Amendment, ratified in 1865, barred "slavery" and "involuntary servitude" except "as a punishment for crime"; the Fourteenth Amendment, ratified in 1868, overruled *Dred Scott* and conferred citizenship; and the

Fifteenth Amendment, ratified in 1870, gave all citizens the right to vote regardless of color or race. In terms of the Eighth Amendment's future, the Fourteenth Amendment explicitly provided that "[n]o State shall make or enforce any law which shall abridge the privileges or immunities of citizens of the United States" and that no state shall "deprive" any person of "life, liberty, or property, without due process of law." In 1789, James Madison had tried but failed to have certain protections of the U.S. Bill of Rights—in particular, the rights to jury trial and freedom of speech and the press—apply to the states. The Fourteenth Amendment, ratified on July 9, 1868, did that and much more, ultimately making a whole panoply of protections, including that of the Eighth Amendment, applicable to the states.[74]

The Fourteenth Amendment, which also gave minorities "the equal protection of the laws," was intended to make the first eight amendments of the Bill of Rights applicable to the states. Before the Civil War broke out, Republican congressman Cydnor Tompkins of Ohio had railed against the "barbarity and cruelty" of slavery, and in the thirty-ninth Congress, Representative John Bingham, the primary author of Section 1 of the Fourteenth Amendment, stated on at least two occasions that Section 1 would bar cruel and unusual punishments. Bingham—who once described Lord Chief Justice George Jeffreys as a "judicial monster" whose "judicial crimes" included "a judicial massacre of three hundred and twenty victims"—described the Fourteenth Amendment's Privileges or Immunities Clause as encompassing "the bill of rights," saying "the privileges and immunities of citizens of the United States" are "chiefly defined in the first eight amendments to the Constitution of the United States." The Fourteenth Amendment, he said, would stop "cruel and unusual punishments" that had been inflicted under State laws and allow enforcement of "the bill of rights as it stands in the Constitution today." While Bingham wanted constitutional amendments so that Congress could enforce "every one of those limitations so essential to justice and humanity," still others condemned "the lash and the scourge," "laceration of the body," and other forms of "cruel or unusual punishment." Appalled by degrading punishments in former slave states, Representative John Kasson of Iowa introduced a bill in 1867—the year before the Fourteenth Amendment's ratification—to bar cruel and unusual punishments through legislation. It was the duty of Congress, he said, "to take early action to prevent what is now both cruel and unusual from becoming simply cruel and usual." His bill, he said, "protects both whites and blacks" and would apply "to all the States of the Union." Senator Jacob Howard—the Fourteenth Amendment's U.S. Senate sponsor and the man who spoke on behalf of the Joint Committee on Reconstruction—would also describe "privileges and immunities" as encompassing the right to be free from cruel and unusual punishments. As Howard argued: "To these privileges and immunities, whatever they may be—for they are not and cannot be fully defined in their entire extent and precise nature—to these should be added the personal rights guarantied and secured by the first eight amendments of the Constitution."[75]

Prior to the Fourteenth Amendment's adoption, the Eighth Amendment was held to be applicable only to the federal government. In 1833, in the landmark case of *Barron v. Baltimore,* the Supreme Court held that the Fifth Amendment was inapplicable to the states. In doing so, the Court emphasized that the provisions in the Bill of Rights "contain no expression indicating an intention to apply them to the state governments." In 1866, in *Pervear v. Commonwealth,* the Supreme Court cited and reaffirmed *Barron,* holding that the Eighth Amendment "does not apply to State but to National legislation." In that case, the Court found "nothing excessive, or cruel, or unusual" in a fifty-dollar fine and three months of imprisonment "at hard labor in the house of correction" for the illegal sale and storage of alcohol. Thus, until the Fourteenth Amendment was held to apply provisions of the Bill of Rights to restrain state action, criminals and criminal suspects facing state charges were protected only by their respective state constitutions. As the Court ruled in *Barron:* "The constitution was ordained and established by the people of the United States for themselves, for their own government, and not for the government of the individual states. Each state established a constitution for itself, and in that constitution, provided such limitations and restrictions on the powers of its particular government, as its judgment dictated."[76]

The Fourteenth Amendment specifically guaranteed "due process of law." That concept—drawn from the Fifth Amendment, but appearing in English law since 1354 as a safeguard when one's life or property was on the line—is a centuries-old principle. The words "due process," Alexander Hamilton declared in the eighteenth century, "have a precise technical import and are only applicable to the process and proceedings of the courts of justice; they can never be referred to an act of legislature." The "due process" protection, however, has long been understood by the Supreme Court to constrain not only judges but "arbitrary" legislative and executive actions too. The Court's view of "due process" has thus evolved over time, just as its view of what constitutes a "cruel and unusual" punishment has changed over the years. "The most familiar office" of the Fourteenth Amendment's Due Process Clause, the Court holds, "is to provide a guarantee of fair procedure in connection with any deprivation of life, liberty, or property by a State." But the Court also now speaks of "substantive" due process rights, with the nonprocedural component of due process protecting unenumerated liberties and guarding against "certain government actions regardless of the procedures used to implement them." "It is now the settled doctrine of this Court," Justice Felix Frankfurter wrote in 1950, "that the Due Process Clause embodies a system of rights based on moral principles so deeply imbedded in the traditions and feelings of our people as to be deemed fundamental to a civilized society as conceived by our whole history." "Due Process," he wrote, "is that which comports with the deepest notions of what is fair and right and just." Accordingly, due process is violated if a practice or rule "offends some principle of justice so rooted in the traditions and conscience of our people as to be ranked as fundamental." Today, the concept of "due process of law" thus encompasses far more than just a fair trial before an impartial judge, once thought to be the principal purpose of that protection.[77]

Oddly enough, despite the Fourteenth Amendment's wording and the drafters' intent, the Eighth Amendment was not immediately applied against the states after the Fourteenth Amendment's ratification. Indeed, though U.S. Senator Jacob Howard of Michigan explained in 1866 that the Fourteenth Amendment "prohibits the hanging of a black man for a crime for which the white man is not to be hanged," the scourge of racial prejudice in the death penalty context continues unabated, though in more subtle ways than in the era of slavery. In *Slaughter-House Cases*, an 1873 decision almost universally condemned as being wrongly decided, the U.S. Supreme Court held that the Fourteenth Amendment only protected the "privileges and immunities" of *U.S.* citizens and did not confer on *state* citizens "any additional protections." In that case, involving challenges to a Louisiana law permitting the creation of a state-sanctioned monopoly on the butchering of animals within the city of New Orleans, Justice Samuel Miller wrote for the Court that the Privileges or Immunities Clause protects only those rights "which owe their existence to the Federal government, its National character, its Constitution, or its laws."[78]

That peculiar interpretation of the Constitution proved to be long lasting. In *In re Kemmler* and *McElvaine v. Brush,* two death penalty cases, the Supreme Court likewise held that the Fourteenth Amendment's Privileges or Immunities Clause did not aid the petitioners in those cases. In short, the protections of the U.S. Bill of Rights were held to be inapplicable to the states, en bloc, via the Privileges or Immunities Clause. In line with that approach, in the 1892 case of *O'Neil v. Vermont,* the Supreme Court—over vigorous dissents—continued to downplay the Fourteenth Amendment's significance, stubbornly clinging to the notion that the Eighth Amendment did not apply to the states. Citing *Pervear,* the Court in *O'Neil* emphasized that "it has always been ruled that the 8th Amendment to the Constitution of the United States does not apply to the States." Only later did the Supreme Court, initially reluctant to alter the *Pervear* rule, articulate its "selective incorporation" doctrine and hold the Eighth Amendment to be applicable to the states through its use. That doctrine, first articulated in 1897, would be used to apply a whole host of protections of the U.S. Bill of Rights against the states, one by one, via the Fourteenth Amendment's Due Process Clause.[79]

Because the Eighth Amendment originally applied only against the national government, only a handful of Eighth Amendment precedents exist from the earliest days of the republic. While the U.S. Supreme Court eventually held that the Eighth Amendment applied against the states, that legal development took considerable time. What is more, it was not done, as might have been expected, through the Fourteenth Amendment's Privileges or Immunities Clause, but through the Fourteenth Amendment's Due Process Clause. In *Resweber,* a 1947 case, the Supreme Court assumed, without deciding, that the Cruel and Unusual Punishments Clause applied to the states via the Fourteenth Amendment's Due Process Clause. But not until 1962, in *Robinson v. California,* did the Court finally make the Eighth Amendment applicable to the states.[80]

The notion of "substantive due process," as one federal district court puts it, is "a shorthand term for those substantive rights that the Supreme Court has interpreted the due process clause of the Fourteenth Amendment to confer." While the Eighth Amendment's Cruel and Unusual Punishments Clause, in the post-*Robinson* world, plainly confers substantive rights on state prisoners, the Court itself analyzes Eighth Amendment claims and "substantive due process" claims differently. For example, in a 1989 case, *Graham v. Connor,* the Supreme Court held that if a constitutional claim is covered by a specific constitutional provision, such as the Eighth Amendment, the claim must be analyzed under the standard appropriate to that particular provision, not under the generic rubric of "substantive due process." While the Court currently evaluates Eighth Amendment claims using its "evolving standards of decency test," to succeed on a "substantive due process" claim a litigant must establish that a law is operating in an "arbitrary and irrational" manner. "The touchstone of due process is protection of the individual against arbitrary action of government," the Court has ruled.[81]

This distinction in evaluating inmates' claims does not mean, of course, that the Supreme Court can disregard "due process" or "equal protection" violations in the context of capital cases. All prisoners plainly have those Fourteenth Amendment rights, as the Court's own decisions make clear. For example, in *Deck v. Missouri,* the Court held in 2005 that the "due process of law" guaranteed by the Constitution's Fifth and Fourteenth Amendments forbids the use of visible shackles during the penalty phase of a capital trial unless their use is justified by an "essential state interest" such as courtroom security specific to the defendant on trial. The Equal Protection Clause, the Court has held, "embodies a general rule that States must treat like cases alike but may treat unlike cases accordingly." *Batson v. Kentucky,* a 1986 case involving a black man convicted by an all-white jury, held that the provision forbids a prosecutor from striking jurors "solely on account of their race or on the assumption that black jurors as a group will be unable impartially to consider the State's case against a black defendant." While the Supreme Court to date has never relied on the Privileges or Immunities Clause to make the Eighth Amendment applicable to the states, the Fourteenth Amendment's Due Process Clause has been used for that precise purpose, thus expanding the Eighth Amendment's scope far beyond what it did as of 1791.[82]

The 1868 ratification of the Fourteenth Amendment—what has been called the country's "second Constitution"—represented a major step forward in protecting individual rights. Prior to the adoption of the Fourteenth Amendment, the Constitution's Cruel and Unusual Punishments Clause only restricted the practices of the federal government, which was tiny at America's founding. For example, in *Barker v. People,* the New York Supreme Court explicitly held in 1824 that the state's antidueling law did not contravene the Eighth Amendment. "The provision in the constitution of the United States, that cruel and unusual punishments shall not be inflicted," the Court ruled, "is a restriction upon the government of the United States only; and not upon the government of any state." In its 1962 decision in *Robinson,* on the other hand, the U.S. Supreme Court struck down a state law making the status of narcotics addiction a criminal offense, finding the law inflicted a "cruel and unusual punishment" in violation of the Eighth and Fourteenth Amendments. The majority opinion thus invalidated a state law requiring the imposition of at least a ninety-day sentence for its violation. Before the Fourteenth Amendment's ratification, such a ruling invalidating a state's criminal statute on that ground would have been inconceivable.[83]

Post-Reconstruction Cases

Though it was not until 1962 that the U.S. Supreme Court finally held the Eighth Amendment to be applicable to the states, a wave of cases decided after the Fourteenth Amendment's ratification do show how nineteenth-century jurists viewed the Eighth Amendment or its state law counterparts. For instance, in the 1872 case of *Whitten v. Georgia,* the Georgia Supreme Court heard the appeal of a defendant who quarreled with a farmer and then knifed and clubbed him over the head with a piece of rail. Found guilty of assault and battery, the defendant was sentenced to six months of imprisonment, whereupon he appealed, asserting that his sentence constituted a cruel and unusual punishment. After noting that "the Legislature has given the Judge discretion," and that the sentencing judge "acted within the limits fixed by law," the Georgia Supreme Court held that the Cruel and Unusual Punishments Clause "was, doubtless, intended to prohibit the barbarities of quartering, hanging in chains, castration, etc." "When adopted by the framers of the Constitution of the United States," the court ruled in an opinion authored by Judge Henry McCay, "larceny was generally punished by hanging; forgeries, burglaries, etc., in the same way, for, be it remembered, penitentiaries are of modern origin, and I doubt if it ever entered into the mind of men of that day, that a crime such as this witness makes the defendant guilty of deserved a less penalty than the Judge has inflicted." "It would be an interference with matters left by the Constitution to the legislative department of the government," the court held, "for us to undertake to weigh the propriety of this or that penalty fixed by the Legislature for specific offenses." As the court ruled: "So long as they do not provide cruel and unusual punishments, such as disgraced the civilization of former ages, and make one shudder with horror to read of them, as drawing, quartering, burning, etc., the Constitution does not put any limit upon legislative discretion."[84]

Another Georgia case, *In re Birdsong,* also articulated the view that the Eighth Amendment served only to restrict barbarous modes of punishment. In that case, a federal district court investigated a prisoner's treatment after a local paper reported that a county jailer had disciplined Joe Warren, the prisoner, by chaining his neck to the grating of his cell. After finding the facts to be as stated in the newspaper, the court, without mincing any words, found the conduct to be "at best, an ignominious, cruel, and unusual punishment," and issued its ruling in 1889: "The arbitrary power in a prison-keeper to iron a prisoner, or indeed, to select at his pleasure a penalty which he thinks adequate as a disciplinary measure for real or fancied misconduct, is intolerable among a free and enlightened people. It has no place among English-speaking nations." "[N]either this court, nor, indeed, the highest court in the land," the court ruled, "would assume, even after full hearing, to exercise the power to chain up by the neck a prisoner for disorderly conduct, even the most atrocious, and even though committed in the actual presence of the court." "Had any judge of America done with the most degraded convict what this jailer admits he did with the person of this prisoner," the court said, "his impeachment would be inevitable." "At common law," the court emphasized, citing Sir Edward Coke, "it was not lawful to hamper a prisoner with irons, except to prevent an escape."[85]

In *In re Birdsong,* the prisoner, left alone in a painful standing position, had been chained for more than three hours, with two physicians—worried about strangulation—testifying that the prisoner's punishment might have been fatal. "The constitution forbids a cruel or unusual punishment," the court ruled in the case involving a federal prisoner being held in a local county jail, noting that "in this day of Christian civilization" even disciplined prisoners were treated with "humanity." "[T]o chain a prisoner around the neck with a trace chain and padlock, in a position where he can neither lie down nor sit down, and thus to leave him chained in solitude, in the night, in the darkness of his cell, for more than three hours," the court held, "is to inflict a degree of torture which has no warrant in the law, either state or federal, and to expose him to danger to health and to life, from which it is the duty of society to protect him." The court called the jailer's conduct "repugnant" to the laws of Georgia and the United States, emphasizing that the pillory, akin to what the prisoner was subjected to, had been outlawed in France in 1832, in England in 1837, and in America in 1839. "It was, in fact," the court held, "punishment by the pillory, but a pillory where the links of the trace chain and padlock encircling the bare neck of the prisoner were substituted for the wooden frame." "Not even may a judge or jury assume a power so uncertain and so dangerous," the court said, ruling that the jailer's conduct is "as worthy of condemnation in the light of the state and federal constitution, as in the benignant and merciful spirit of Christian civilization."[86]

The emphasis on prohibiting antiquated or barbaric punishments, as well as looking at what had been permissible under the common law, played out in other cases too. In *In re McDonald*, the Wyoming Supreme Court speculated in 1893 that "[t]he constitutional provisions aimed at cruel and unusual punishments were probably intended to prevent the imposition of obsolete, painful and degrading punishments, such as the whipping post, the pillory, and such as making capital a grade of offenses like larceny, forgery and the like." The court also quoted Thomas Cooley's *A Treatise on the Constitutional Limitations,* which offered: "Probably any punishment declared by statute for an offense which was punishable in the same way at the common law could not be regarded as cruel or unusual, in the constitutional sense." After citing another case, *People v. Morris,* which held that a lengthy prison term for horse stealing was not a cruel and unusual punishment, *In re McDonald* opined that a prison term arising out of a failure to pay a fine was neither cruel nor unusual. *Minnesota v. Borgstrom* also held in 1897 that "fine and imprisonment are not ordinarily cruel and unusual punishments." In that case, the Minnesota Supreme Court emphasized that barbaric punishments—the rack, torture, drowning, disembowelment, burning, cutting off the hands or ears, boiling in oil, and putting someone in the pillory—qualified as "cruel" and thus were "prohibited by our constitution." "[H]appily," the court ruled, "the more humane spirit of this nation does not permit such punishments to be inflicted upon criminals."[87]

Other courts in the late nineteenth century and around the turn of the century also gave considerable, almost total, deference to legislative determinations. In the lower court in *In re Kemmler,* the New York County Court for Cayuga County—in considering the constitutionality of the state's new electric chair—described the question as "one largely of fact," but then held that as to every legislative act "there attaches a presumption of constitutionality." Saying "the burden of showing it to be unconstitutional is upon him who assails it," the New York court found the testimony "to be conflicting, and, of necessity, in great degree speculative and hypothetical, for on no person has the experiment yet been tried, and no endeavor to take human life by means of electricity has been made." Even as the court emphasized in 1889 that "our own state fundamental law is so benignant that not even he who cruelly murders can be cruelly punished," it noted that courts had "rarely been called upon to construe" the phrase "cruel and unusual punishments." Despite its "history of 200 years," the court said, harkening back to its English origins, "it is not an easy task to define it." But after citing Blackstone and the Cooley treatise, which afforded broad deference to common-law practices, the New York court held that no constitutional violation had been shown. "Death," the court emphasized, "was the penalty for murder at the common law."[88]

Once again, the lower court in *In re Kemmler* focused on barbarous *modes* of executions, though the Eighth Amendment itself does not refer to "modes" or "methods" and instead prohibits any "cruel and unusual punishments," of whatever nature. "Beyond doubt," the court wrote, "many of the methods used for the infliction of the death penalty in other times and countries would to-day and in our land be held illegal." "As among these," the court said, "may be mentioned crucifixion, boiling in water, oil, or lead, blowing from cannon's mouth, burning, breaking on the wheel, dismemberment, burying alive." As late as 1531 can be found an Act of Parliament authorizing that a person be thrown into boiling water and be boiled to death for the offense of poisoning a bishop's family, though such barbaric forms of execution—including impalement, starvation, crushing beneath the feet of animals, and piercing with javelins—have long since fallen into disuse. Citing the U.S. Supreme Court's decision in *Wilkerson* that approved a firing squad execution in Utah, the *In re Kemmler* court nonetheless wrote: "But not death itself is a cruel and unusual punishment, nor is death by gunshot or by hanging, though there seems to be an element of cruelty inseparable from any taking of human life as punishment for crime; but it is clearly not against this that the constitutional prohibition is directed." The challenged New York law, the court wrote, "but changed the means whereby to produce death." As the judge ruled in summarily rejecting William Kemmler's claim: "Before the statute can rightfully be abrogated, there should be judicial knowledge that the punishment therein provided is cruel and unusual. There is no such knowledge, and his contention fails."[89]

In construing South Dakota's prohibition on "cruel punishments" in *State v. Becker*, the South Dakota Supreme Court also said in 1892 that "it devolves upon the legislature to fix the punishment for crime, and that in the exercise of their judgment great latitude must be allowed." "[T]he courts," it said, "can reasonably interfere only when the punishment is so excessive or so cruel as to meet the disapproval and condemnation of the conscience and reason of men generally." "It is a very noticeable fact that this question has seldom been presented to the courts," it stated, "and we take this fact to signify that it has been the common understanding of all that courts would not be justified in interfering with the discretion and judgment of the legislature, except in very extreme cases, where the punishment proposed is so severe and out of proportion to the offense as to shock public sentiment and violate the judgment of reasonable people." In upholding a law prescribing a punishment for keeping and maintaining a common nuisance, the court ruled: "We feel sure we should go quite beyond reason or precedent if we should hold this law invalid on this account."[90]

Likewise, in 1900, in *State v. Stubblefield*, the Missouri Supreme Court held that "[p]unishment is not to be regarded as either cruel or unusual because never inflicted before on a certain class of criminals." "The Legislature is not necessarily restricted in inflicting the death penalty, because such legislation is newly enacted," the court stated. In upholding the law at issue and affirming a conviction and ten-year sentence for stopping a train with intent to rob it, the court ruled: "The primary object of such a law is its deterrent effect, and the Legislature has the right to so increase the punishment of crimes, as to strike terror into the hearts of those who but for such intimidation, might be more strongly tempted to commit them." In *Hobbs v. State,* the Indiana Supreme Court, deciding the 1893 appeal of two defendants convicted of riotous conspiracy and sentenced to two years in prison, also dismissed a "cruel and unusual punishment" claim. The defendants' position, the court ruled, "seems to be without authority to support it," with the court noting: "We have been unable to find but a single instance in which this provision of the Constitution has been in question before this court, and then the question was regarded as possessing no merit, and was disposed of without serious consideration." The word "cruel," the court held, "when considered in relation to the time when it found place in the bill of rights, meant not a fine or imprisonment, or both, but such as that inflicted at the whipping-post, in the pillory, burning at the stake, breaking on the wheel, etc." "The word, according to modern interpretation," the court said, "does not affect legislation providing imprisonment for life or for years, or the death penalty by hanging or electrocution." "Neither is punishment by fine or imprisonment 'unusual,'" the court said.[91]

In another case, *In the Matter of Bayard,* the New York Supreme Court in 1881 heard the appeal of Isadore Bayard, convicted of larceny in the city of Cohoes and sentenced to be imprisoned for one year. Arguing that elsewhere in the state the punishment was only six months, Bayard alleged his sentence constituted cruel and unusual punishment. The court ruled against Bayard, explaining that the punishment "cannot fairly be said to be either cruel or unusual," though candidly acknowledging that "[t]he courts have rarely had occasion to construe the meaning of the phrase 'cruel and unusual punishment.'" "[S]ince no punishment can be inflicted until authorized by the legislature which is often elected, and represents the general moral idea of the people," the court said, "it is not likely that they will often be called on to construe it." Citing a number of treatises, the court referred back to the English Bill of Rights, noting that "[t]he punishments complained of were the pillories, slittings, and mutilations which the corrupt judges of King James had inflicted without warrant of law." The English Bill of Rights, it declared, "was intended to forbid the imposition of a punishment of a kind not known to the law, or not warranted by the law" and "did not then refer to the degree of punishment, for the criminal law of England was at that time disgraced by the infliction of the very gravest punishment for slight offenses, even petit larceny being then punishable with death." "The text writers," the court explained, summarizing commentary on the clause, "have discussed it to some extent, and they seem to understand it as prohibiting any cruel or degrading punishment not known to the common law, and probably also, those degrading punishments which in any state had become obsolete when its existing constitution was adopted, and punishments so disproportioned to the offense as to shock the sense of the community." "Laws may be inexpedient, oppressive, even cruel," the court held, "but unless they infringe upon some constitutional restrictions, the remedy is with the electors and not with the courts."[92]

In sharp contrast, other nineteenth-century judges took the position that the Cruel and Unusual Punishments Clause constrained state actors in a much less deferential way. For example, in the 1878 case of *State v. Driver,* the North Carolina Supreme Court took up the claim of a man who pled guilty to beating his wife. While drinking, he kicked and whipped his wife with a switch, hitting her with such force as to leave marks on her arms and shoulders for two or three weeks. After receiving a five-year sentence to be served in the county jail, Giles Driver, the husband, argued that the sentence, which also required him to post a five-hundred-dollar bond to "keep the peace" toward his wife, constituted a "cruel and unusual punishment." In an era when domestic violence was not taken as seriously as it is today, the appellate court agreed, thus reversing Driver's sentence. Though the court acknowledged that Driver "is a bad man, and not likely to have much of the public sympathy," it held that "it appears both by precedent, and by reason of the thing, and by express constitutional provision, that there is a limit to the power of the Judge to punish, even when it is expressly left to his discretion." Analogizing to an "excessive pecuniary fine" of thirty thousand pounds imposed upon a lord by the Court of King's Bench in 1689, the *Driver* court found the punishment inflicted in Driver's case not only "cruel" and "unusual" but also "unheard of," saying that "[i]t is therefore in violation of the Constitution."[93]

In making its ruling, the *Driver* court, like the *Bayard* court, noted the dearth of Eighth Amendment precedents. "[W]e find very little authority about it," the court said, "which is probably owing to the fact that the administration of our criminal law is so uniformly humane that there is seldom occasion for complaint." The court then looked to Joseph Story's influential treatise for guidance, quoting at length from a section of it about the Eighth Amendment:

The provision would seem to be wholly unnecessary in a free government, since it is scarcely possible that any department of such a government should authorize or justify such atrocious conduct. It was however adopted as an admonition to all Departments of the National Government to warn them against such violent proceedings as had taken place in England in the arbitrary reigns of the Stuarts. In those times a demand of excessive bail was often made against persons who were odious to the Court and its favorites, and on failure to procure it, they were committed to prison. Enormous fines and amercements were also sometimes imposed, and cruel and vindictive punishments inflicted. Upon this subject Mr. Justice Blackstone has wisely remarked, that sanguinary laws are a bad symptom of the distemper of any State, or at least of its weak Constitution.

"It is true," the *Driver* court said, "that there has never been anything in our government, State or National, to provoke such provision, yet it was thought to be so appropriate, that it was adopted into our Bill of Rights, and has ever been preserved in our fundamental law, as a 'warning.'" "Nor was it intended to warn against merely erratic modes of punishments or torture," the court opined, "but applied expressly to 'bail,' 'fines,' and 'punishments.'"[94]

The California case of *Kow v. Nunan* from 1879 illustrates yet another interpretive approach. In that case, a Chinese plaintiff sued to recover damages for alleged maltreatment by San Francisco's sheriff. "The maltreatment," noted the federal circuit court, "consisted of having wantonly and maliciously cut off the queue of the plaintiff, a queue being worn by all Chinamen, and its deprivation being regarded by them as degrading and as entailing future suffering." The plaintiff alleged that "it is the custom of Chinamen to shave the hair from the front of the head and to wear the remainder of it braided into a queue"; that the defendant knew of this custom and the Chinese religious faith, which viewed the deprivation of the queue as bringing "misfortune and suffering after death"; and that "in disregard of his rights," the sheriff cut off the plaintiff's queue, causing the plaintiff to be "ostracized from association from his countrymen." While the sheriff asserted he was merely enforcing a San Francisco ordinance directing that every male imprisoned in the county jail immediately have their hair "cut or clipped" to a "uniform length of one inch from the scalp thereof," the plaintiff asserted the ordinance was "special legislation" imposing a "degrading and cruel punishment" upon a class of people entitled to "the equal protection of the laws."[95]

In its opinion, the federal circuit court agreed with the plaintiff, finding his assertions "well taken." The court found that the act had no disciplinary purpose and that the notion that the law was put in place to promote health was a mere pretence. "A treatment to which disgrace is attached, and which is not adopted as a means of security, but merely to aggravate the severity of his confinement," the court ruled, "can only be regarded as a punishment additional to that fixed by the sentence." Finding the government exceeded its powers in ordering the plaintiff's hair clipped, the circuit court also held that the ordinance, which targeted the Chinese, violated the principle of equal protection. As the court ruled: "It is not creditable to the humanity and civilization of our people, much less to their Christianity, that an ordinance of this character was possible." Concluding that the "Queue Ordinance" operated with "special severity upon Chinese prisoners," the federal court, citing the

Fourteenth Amendment in a place still rampant with racial prejudice, held that "[u]pon the Chinese prisoners its enforcement operates as 'a cruel and unusual punishment.'" Saying the Constitution prohibits punishments "of a cruel and unusual nature," the court held that the ordinance, which imposed a punishment that only a certain class of people felt, had violated the plaintiff's constitutional rights.[96]

The Dynamic Duo

The Eighth and Fourteenth Amendments, however interpreted, operate together to prohibit arbitrary or discriminatory punishments and set a constitutional floor beneath which neither federal nor state officials can traverse. The scholar Laurence Claus has even referred to the Eighth Amendment itself as an "antidiscrimination" amendment, calling it "a forerunner to the sweeping generality of the Fourteenth Amendment's Equal Protection Clause." Arguing that "unusual" was a synonym for "illegal" when the English Bill of Rights of 1689 came into force, Claus asserts that "[t]he principle that lies behind the Eighth Amendment is nondiscrimination." As evidence, he contrasts a clause in the English Declaration's litany of wrongs against James II—recounting the "illegal and cruel punishments inflicted"—with the "cruel and unusual punishments" language elsewhere in that document. The "core concern" of the English counterpart to the Eighth Amendment, Claus argues, was thus "violation of the common law or of existing statutes," to ensure that no offender would be singled out for a greater punishment than was "customarily imposed." The "tentativeness" of the use of the word "ought" in the English Declaration, Claus contends, "suggested that the common law was understood to be the source" of the asserted rights to be free from excessive fines, excessive bail, and cruel and unusual punishments. "[H]ad existing statutes clearly established them," Claus observes, "greater certitude would have been appropriate."[97]

To further bolster his argument that the Eighth Amendment was itself designed to prohibit discriminatory punishment, Claus cites an early American case, *Ely v. Thompson*. That 1820 decision construed the prohibition on "cruel punishments" in the Kentucky Constitution of 1792. In particular, the Kentucky Court of Appeals took up the case of Rhody Ely, "a free person of color" whom state officials had ordered to be subjected to thirty lashes under a state statute. "If any negro or mulatto, or Indian, bond or free, shall, at any time, lift his or her hand in opposition to any person not being a negro, mulatto or Indian," the statute read, "he or she, so offending, shall, for every such offence, proved by the oath of the party, before a justice of the peace of the county where such offence shall be committed, receive thirty lashes on his or her back, well laid on by order of such justice." The oath of the complaining party was to be conclusive, forcing the justice of the peace to inflict the odious punishment even if the proof was not credible. After Ely brought an action of trespass and assault and battery against the justice of the peace and a constable, the justice of the peace claimed Ely's punishment was lawful because Ely had "lifted his hand in opposition to a white man." The constable likewise justified the infliction of stripes because of the sentence imposed by the justice of the peace. Ely, however, asserted that the state statute was contrary to the state's constitution and therefore void, forcing the Kentucky Court of Appeals to address—in its words—"the disagreeable necessity of deciding upon its constitutionality, so far as it operates on free persons of color." Ultimately, that court found that the state statute "is unconstitutional in so far as it subjects the free person of color to corporal punishment for raising his hand in opposition to a white person, if it be done in self defense." Invoking the state constitution's prohibition against "cruel punishments," the court ruled: "If a justice of the peace, or any other tribunal, should, under this act, inflict the stripes against a free person of color, who lifted his hand to save him or herself from death or severe bodily harm, all men must pronounce the punishment cruel indeed." "Although free persons of color are not parties to our social compact," the court noted in that era of rampant discrimination and continual appeals to natural rights, "yet they have many privileges secured thereby, and have a right to its protection."[98]

That the Eighth Amendment itself has long served to prohibit unfair and disparate treatment is, certainly, not an outlier view, or one that has never been expressed before. In a concurring opinion in *Furman,* no less a figure than U.S. Supreme Court Justice William O. Douglas specifically equated "unusual" with "discriminatory," adding: "There is evidence that the provision of the English Bill of Rights of 1689, from which the language of the Eighth Amendment was taken, was concerned primarily with selective or irregular application of harsh penalties and that its aim was to forbid arbitrary and discriminatory penalties of a severe nature." As Justice Douglas argued: "It would seem to be incontestable that the death penalty inflicted on one defendant is 'unusual' if it discriminates against him by reason of his race, religion, wealth, social position, or class, or if it is imposed under a procedure that gives room for the play of such prejudices." Even in *In re Kemmler,* the nineteenth-century case that approved the use of the electric chair, the Supreme Court recognized the broad implications of the Fourteenth Amendment, saying that its language "[u]ndoubtedly . . . forbids any arbitrary deprivation of life, liberty, or property, and secures equal protection to all under like circumstances in the enjoyment of their rights; and, in the administration of criminal justice, requires that no different or higher punishment shall be imposed upon one than is imposed upon all for like offenses."[99]

Historically, the concept of "cruel and unusual" punishment is closely associated with slavery. In 1829, North Carolina chief justice Thomas Ruffin wrote that "[t]he power of the master must be absolute, to render the submission of the slave perfect." Even before the adoption of the Virginia Declaration of Rights and the Eighth Amendment, however, prohibitions on the cruel treatment of slaves—while enforced laxly—began to appear. A South Carolina law—denominated "the negro Act of 1740" and once called a "time-honored," "fundamental code"—contained a clause reading as follows: "If any person shall, on a sudden heat or passion, or by undue correction, kill his own slave, or the slave of any other person, he shall forfeit the sum of three hundred and fifty pounds, current money." That law also expressly prohibited certain forms of cruelty—in particular, "cruel punishment"—toward slaves in this chillingly worded clause: "[I]n case any person or persons shall willfully cut out the tongue, put out the eye, castrate, or cruelly scald, burn, or deprive any slave of any limb, or member, or shall inflict any other cruel punishment, other than by whipping, or beating with a horse-whip, cow-skin, switch, or small stick, or by putting irons on, or confining, or imprisoning such slave; every such person shall, for every such offence, forfeit the sum of one hundred pounds, current money." To beat a slave over the head with a pistol "may emphatically be denominated a cruel punishment," a South Carolina court ruled in 1840 when interpreting that law, then one hundred years old. "The Act of Assembly," the court emphasized in rejecting the appeal of a man who, while intoxicated and without provocation, viciously beat and disabled a slave, "designates the horse-whip, cow-skin, switch, or small stick" as the only "instruments proper to be used for the correction of slaves."[100]

The 1740 prohibition on "cruel punishment" then morphed into slave-related proscriptions on "cruel or unusual" punishments. Ten Southern penal codes eventually made mistreatment of slaves a crime, though the provisions varied somewhat from state to state. Alabama's statute prohibited the infliction of "cruel or unusual punishment" on any slave, making any offense punishable by a fine of fifty to one thousand dollars. Mississippi's 1822 law also prohibited the "cruel or unusual punishment" of a slave, though in that state the fine could not exceed five hundred dollars. While a Texas statute, also enforced by fine, allowed masters "to inflict any punishment upon the slave, not affecting life or limb," so long as the punishment did not come "within the definition of cruel treatment, or unreasonable abuse," Louisiana's law used an "unusual rigor" standard. "The slave," Louisiana's statute read, "is entirely subject to the will of his master, who may correct and chastise him, though not with unusual rigor, nor so as to maim or mutilate him, or to expose him to the danger of loss of life, or to cause his death." Such antebellum statutes, writes law professor Scott Howe, "seemed designed to legitimize the use of commonly accepted, though brutal, methods of slave chastisement—such as whipping—as much as to prohibit more barbaric and unusual methods."[101]

In early American judicial opinions, one thus finds multiple references to the phrases "cruel or unusual" or "cruel and unusual" in the context of slavery. In *Mann v. Trabue*, the Missouri Supreme Court wrote in 1827 that a slave's death was brought about by "cruel and unusual treatment." In 1834 in *State v.*

Maner, the South Carolina Court of Appeals, construing the state's "Act of 1740" prohibiting "cruel punishment" other than by "whipping" or other specified means, said the Act "makes any unusual and cruel treatment of a slave an indictable offence." "I think, under this act," the appellate court judge wrote tentatively of an assault and battery on a slave named Phil, "the shooting" of the slave with an intent to murder "might be indicted as a cruel punishment." In 1844, addressing Mississippi's statutory bar on the "cruel or unusual punishment" of a slave, Mississippi's High Court of Errors and Appeals held in *Kelly v. State* that "what is cruel and unusual punishment" is "a question of fact for a jury, who most generally are slave owners." In that case, which reversed the manslaughter conviction of two men convicted of killing a slave, the Mississippi court noted: "It is not contended that a greater degree of punishment may not be inflicted here by the master upon his slave, than by the master upon the servant at Common Law, because such here may be usual from necessity." In 1853, that same Mississippi court wrote of the whipping of a female slave in "a very cruel manner." The court described the runaway slave as "being in a delicate situation incident to females," reported she had been whipped in a "cruel and unusual manner," and variously described her as receiving "cruel treatment," "ill treatment," "cruel and unusual treatment," "cruel and unjustifiable treatment," and "cruel punishment."[102]

By the 1850s and early 1860s, the "cruel or unusual" or "cruel and unusual" terminology had become a standard usage to articulate the prevailing legal duty with regard to the treatment of slaves. In 1856, the Florida Supreme Court cited *Thompson's Digest* for the proposition "that no cruel or unusual punishment shall be inflicted upon a slave by any master, employer or owner." That same year, Mississippi's High Court of Errors and Appeals described the state's statutory bar on "cruel or unusual punishment" as making "it criminal for any one to inflict cruel punishment on a slave within this State." And in 1860, that Mississippi appellate court, in two separate cases, assessed the validity of jury instructions on the "cruel and unusual manner" of a slave's treatment. In the first case, the plaintiff's slave had required medical attention and had to be confined to bed for seven weeks after being severely whipped by two men "for the purpose of extorting from him" information on a runaway slave. On those facts, the Mississippi court approved a jury instruction "that if the defendants whipped the slave in a cruel and unusual manner without the master's consent, and the injuries sustained by him resulted from said whipping and the exposure the slave was subject to in getting back to his master," "the defendants are liable for damages." In the second case, the court considered an instruction "[t]hat when a man kills another in the heat of passion, without malice, in a cruel and unusual manner, and not in necessary self-defence, the law reduces the crime from murder to manslaughter." In that case, the Mississippi court set aside the manslaughter conviction of a slaveowner who killed a slave for not shelling corn fast enough. The slaveowner contended that the deceased, one John, was "a violent, turbulent, and rebellious slave" who "had been guilty, on the day before, of an act of disobedience, which was usually punished on the plantation by whipping." In its ruling, the court emphasized that "whether the blow inflicted on the negro slave was or not necessary to overcome the resistance of the slave to the lawful authority of the master" was a "material" issue. "Unconditional submission and obedience to the lawful commands and authority of the master," the court ruled, "is the imperative duty of the slave, as well as the undoubted right of the master."[103]

While the Civil War ended slavery, America's judicial system still tolerates the death penalty's discriminatory infliction, largely in the same Southern states where slavery once predominated. Though executions continue, the Eighth Amendment—as construed by the U.S. Supreme Court itself—has been held simultaneously to shield state and federal prisoners from harm, mistreatment, and abusive conditions of confinement. For example, in *Rhodes v. Chapman,* the Court emphasized that the Cruel and Unusual Punishments Clause guards against "serious deprivations of basic human needs." Thus, when someone is imprisoned, the Court has held, the Constitution imposes "a corresponding duty" on the government "to assume some responsibility" for that inmate's "safety and general well being." In another case, *Farmer v. Brennan,* the Court explicitly held that prison officials have a duty under the Eighth Amendment to provide humane conditions of confinement. The Eighth Amendment, it ruled, ensures that inmates "receive adequate food, clothing, shelter, and medical care." Addressing a claim that prison officials failed to protect a transsexual inmate from a prison rape, the Court held that the Eighth Amendment requires that prison officials "take reasonable measures to guarantee the safety of inmates." In *Rhodes,* a 1981 case, Justice Brennan further emphasized in his concurring opinion that "individual prisons or entire prison systems in at least 24 States have been declared unconstitutional under the Eighth and Fourteenth Amendments." "No one familiar with litigation in this area," Brennan wrote, "could suggest that the courts have been overeager to usurp the task of running prisons." While legislators and prison officials are entrusted with running them, Brennan noted, "courts have emerged as a critical force behind efforts to ameliorate inhumane conditions."[104]

The Constitution, certainly, does not mandate "comfortable prisons," as the Court ruled in 1994 in *Farmer,* "but neither," it added, "does it permit" an "inhumane one." Prisoners are not entitled to the best diet or the highest-quality health care, but two types of prisoner civil rights claims have been recognized as legitimate under the auspices of the Eighth Amendment: those regarding intolerable conditions of confinement and those involving the use of excessive force. "[E]xtreme deprivations are required to make out a conditions-of-confinement claim," the Supreme Court has made clear. "Because routine discomfort is 'part of the penalty that criminal offenders pay for their offenses against society,'" the Court held in *Hudson v. McMillian,* only those deprivations denying "the minimal civilized measure of life's necessities" are "sufficiently grave to form the basis of an Eighth Amendment violation." Restricting a prisoner's diet is not an Eighth Amendment violation, it has been held, unless the inmate can show starvation or adverse health effects caused by the condition of the food. In the 1980s and early 1990s, federal appellate courts held that serving inmates cold food or only two meals a day is permissible, though the Fifth Circuit emphasized that "the Constitution does not tolerate" a "gulag-type of death by incremental starvation." "Because society does not expect that prisoners will have unqualified access to health care," the Court noted in *Hudson,* "deliberate indifference to medical needs amounts to an Eighth Amendment violation only if those needs are 'serious.'" The Eighth Amendment has even been used for failures to protect prisoners from harm from other prisoners, suicide risk, severe disciplinary measures, or for failures to ensure periodic out-of-cell exercise. "[T]he lower courts have learned from repeated investigation and bitter experience," Justice Brennan wrote in *Rhodes,* "that judicial intervention is indispensable if constitutional dictates—not to mention considerations of basic humanity—are to be observed in the prisons."[105]

The U.S. Supreme Court has, through its decisions, frequently stood up for prisoners' rights. For example, in *Hudson*, a 1992 case, a Louisiana prisoner named Keith Hudson brought a federal civil rights suit alleging his Eighth Amendment rights were violated by a beating that he received in prison. Hudson testified that, while he was handcuffed and shackled, two prison guards punched him in the mouth, eyes, chest, and stomach, and kicked and punched him from behind. As a result of the incident, the inmate said, he received minor bruises, facial swelling, loosened teeth, and a cracked dental plate. A supervisor, the inmate alleged, watched the beating take place but merely advised the officers "not to have too much fun." In that case, the Court explicitly held that excessive physical force against a prisoner may constitute cruel and unusual punishment even though the prisoner does not suffer serious injury. "[W]e hold that whenever prison officials stand accused of using excessive physical force in violation of the Cruel and Unusual Punishments Clause," the Court ruled, "the core judicial inquiry is . . . whether force was applied in a good-faith effort to maintain or restore discipline, or maliciously and sadistically to cause harm." As the Court explained: "When prison officials maliciously and sadistically use force to cause harm, contemporary standards of decency always are violated. This is true whether or not significant injury is evident. Otherwise, the Eighth Amendment would permit any physical punishment, no matter how diabolic or inhuman."[106]

Ironically, the Supreme Court's Eighth Amendment jurisprudence thus *protects* inmates from physical harm yet *permits* their execution. For example, in *Farmer,* the conditions-of-confinement case involving the transsexual prisoner allegedly beaten and raped by a cellmate after being placed in the general prison population, the Supreme Court held that a prison official's "deliberate indifference" to "a substantial risk of serious harm to an inmate" violates the Eighth Amendment. In articulating that standard, the Court said that "deliberate indifference" requires a showing that the official was "subjectively aware" of the risk. A prison official, the Court ruled, "may be held liable under the Eighth Amendment for denying humane conditions of confinement only if he knows that inmates face a substantial risk of serious harm and disregards that risk by failing to take reasonable measures to abate it." The standard for excessive force claims is different, but that line of cases also protects prisoners from physical harm. In excessive force cases, prison officials are not held to a "deliberate indifference" standard, but to the less intrusive standard announced in *Whitley v. Albers*. The *Whitley* standard asks whether force was applied "maliciously and sadistically," with only "unnecessary and wanton infliction of pain" forbidden by the Eighth Amendment. Regardless of what standard is used, though, the *Rhodes, Hudson, Farmer,* and *Whitley* cases all make clear that intentionally harming prisoners when it is unnecessary to do so—exactly what executions do—is not permitted under the Eighth Amendment.[107]

CHAPTER SIX

Capital Punishment in America

Where We Stand

Though the Eighth Amendment unequivocally bars "cruel and unusual punishments," Americans are split over the propriety of capital punishment. Sixteen states and the District of Columbia have abolished capital punishment, but thirty-four states, plus the federal government and the U.S. military, still authorize death sentences. The majority of states—at least on the books—continue to make first-degree murder a capital crime, and Congress has made approximately sixty offenses death-eligible. Everything from genocide and using weapons of mass destruction to murdering a federal egg, meat, or poultry inspector is a capital crime. For example, the United States Code makes treason and espionage, as well as various homicidal acts and drug-related crimes, punishable by death. A murder-for-hire, a retaliatory killing of a witness or informant, or a murder by a drug kingpin or a federal prisoner can bring a death sentence, as can killings related to the smuggling of aliens, murders committed in a federal facility or an international airport, or killings committed as part of a carjacking or drive-by shooting. Aviation-, maritime-, and train-related deaths, as well as civil rights violations resulting in death, are also capital offenses, as are those acts causing deaths through kidnapping, hostage-taking, the transportation of explosives, or the destruction of government property. Federal law specifically makes the murder of a high-level government official, a correctional officer, or a federal law enforcement officer death-eligible. Thus, it is a capital crime to kill the President, the Vice President, a Supreme Court Justice, a member of Congress, an executive branch official, a foreign official, a federal judge or law enforcement officer, or a court officer or juror. As with typical state law provisions, federal jurors, for whatever offense, must weigh "aggravating" versus "mitigating" factors before deciding whether to impose a death sentence, with federal law providing that a jury cannot impose a death sentence unless the vote is unanimous.[1]

In America, where the morality of executions is increasingly questioned, statistics show a clear divide between jurisdictions that authorize executions but rarely carry them out, and those that still actively, if capriciously, use state-sanctioned killings. While federal law, for instance, makes dozens of crimes death-eligible, federal executions only rarely occur. Sixty federal prisoners now sit on death row, but the U.S. government, since 1976, has executed only three inmates—most memorably, Oklahoma City bomber Timothy McVeigh. Indeed, of all death penalty jurisdictions, only a few Southern states—mainly Texas—regularly execute offenders. Of the more than twelve hundred American executions carried out since 1976, the State of Texas, with more than 460 executions, accounts for more than one third of the total, making it far and away the nation's execution capital. The Commonwealth of Virginia, with 108 executions since 1976, is a distant second in terms of executions, followed, in terms of the numbers, by seven other Southern states: Oklahoma, Florida, Missouri, Georgia, Alabama, North Carolina, and South Carolina. Kansas, New Hampshire, and the U.S. military, all of which still authorize executions, have not had one in more than three decades; five death penalty states—Connecticut, Idaho, Colorado, Wyoming, and South Dakota—have had only one execution each in the last thirty-five years; and nine other death penalty states—Tennessee, Utah, Maryland, Washington, Nebraska, Pennsylvania, Kentucky, Montana, and Oregon—have all seen fewer than eight executions apiece in that time frame.[2]

Executions have become rare, and they are heavily and increasingly concentrated in the same geographic area—the South—that once spawned scores of extrajudicial lynchings. Though annual U.S. executions peaked at ninety-eight in 1999, they have trailed off since then, in part because so many American states rarely or never use them. There were 85 executions in 2000; 71 in 2002; 59 in 2004; and 53 in 2006. But that number declined to 42 in 2007 and fell even further, to 37, in 2008, as executions were put on hold while the U.S. Supreme Court, in *Baze v. Rees,* considered an Eighth Amendment challenge to lethal injection. Between 1950 and 1964, approximately 60 percent of American executions took place in the South, a percentage that has since risen substantially. In the last two decades of the twentieth century, the South's share of executions rose to more than 80 percent. Even within the South, executions are principally concentrated in just a few locales. Of the 42 executions in 2007, Texas alone accounted for 26, or more than 60 percent of the total, and no other state that year saw more than three inmates executed. Even in Texas, just a handful of counties, where local prosecutors have prioritized capital cases, account for the majority of Texas executions. Just one, Harris County, which includes Houston, itself accounts for more than 25 percent of all Texas executions. And just four of Texas's 254 counties—Bexar, Dallas, Harris, and Tarrant—account for approximately half of all of that state's executions.[3]

In the United States, more than thirty-two hundred inmates, predominantly men, live on death row, often spending years or decades in prison before execution, exoneration, or death by natural causes. As of January 1, 2010, there were sixty-one women on death row, constituting less than 2 percent of the total population. The size of death rows varies considerably, often depending on whether the jurisdiction is active or inactive when it comes to death sentences and executions. California, with 697 death row inmates, has by far the biggest death row population, followed by Florida with 398 inmates. The state of Texas, with 337 inmates and its much more aggressive policy of pursuing executions, has only the third-largest total, followed by Pennsylvania and Alabama, which both house more than two hundred inmates. The death row populations of Ohio, North Carolina, Arizona, and Georgia—the places with the next-largest concentrations—each consist of more than one hundred inmates, but most states have far fewer, sometimes just a handful, incarcerated. As of January 1, 2010, Tennessee had 90; Louisiana, 85; Oklahoma, 84; Nevada, 77; South Carolina, 63; Mississippi and Missouri, 61 each; Arkansas, 42; Kentucky, 35, and Oregon, 32. As of that date, seventeen states had fewer than twenty death row inmates apiece, and of those places, eleven states—plus the U.S. military—had ten or fewer.[4]

The racial composition of death row inmates is evenly split between blacks and whites, though the defendant's race or the victim's race often plays a decisive role in deciding who lives or dies. A study of Philadelphia prosecutions found the odds of receiving a death sentence is nearly four times higher if the defendant is black, and a study of twenty-four hundred cases in Georgia found that defendants whose victims were white were 4.3 times more likely to receive a death sentence than similarly situated killers of blacks. Overall, 44 percent of death row inmates are white, 42 percent are black, and 12 percent are Latino. But again, studies done across the country, as the one in Georgia confirms, consistently find the odds of receiving a death sentence is exponentially higher if the murder victim is white. A 1990 report of the General Accounting Office found that in 82 percent of all post-*Furman* studies on race and the death penalty, the victim's race was found to influence the likelihood of being charged with capital murder or receiving a death sentence. Though nationally only 50 percent of murder victims are white, 77 percent of murder victims in cases resulting in executions were white. In fact, African Americans, especially in the Deep South, are often targeted for exclusion from capital juries themselves. In the 2005 case of *Miller-El v. Dretke,* for example, the Supreme Court found Dallas County prosecutors unlawfully struck jurors in a racially discriminatory fashion. Prosecutors used peremptory strikes against ten of eleven qualified black venirepersons during jury selection, and out of twenty black members on the original, 108-member venire, only one served.[5]

Because many American states so rarely execute offenders, those sent to death row frequently die there, not in execution chambers, but in prison infirmaries. Condemned inmates, suffering from bouts of depression, often take their own lives or, while awaiting execution, die of old age or disease before their execution dates arrive. One Florida study showed that 35 percent of death row inmates in that state attempted suicide and that 42 percent considered suicide. From 1977 to 2008 in North Carolina, nineteen inmates died of natural causes or suicide, compared to a grand total of forty-four executions during that same time frame. One Arizona inmate named Leroy Nash died of natural causes in 2010 at age ninety-four after spending more than twenty-five years on death row, and since 1978, no less than forty-three California death row inmates died of natural causes, another sixteen having committed suicide. A recent report on California's death penalty issued in 2008 found that 30 persons had been on California's death row for more than 25 years; 119 for more than 20 years; and 240 for more than 15 years. California, which is not nearly as proactive as Texas in pushing for executions, has carried out only thirteen executions since 1976, meaning the chance of a California death row inmate dying of natural causes is more than three times greater than that of dying by execution. Whereas the national average between the pronouncement of a death sentence and an execution is approximately twelve years, in California the average lapse of time is more than seventeen years. In short, in most states, even those sentenced to death are rarely put to death, with the passage of time instead of lethal injection needles frequently claiming inmates' lives.[6]

Many death row inmates, known as "volunteers," actually waive their appeals while in the depths of despair and choose to die, resulting in a bizarre form of state-assisted suicide. From 1972 to 2007 in the United States, 128 inmates dropped their appeals and asked to be executed, and since 1976, volunteers have comprised roughly 12 percent of executions. Gary Gilmore, shot through the heart by an anonymous, five-member Utah firing squad, is just but one example of suicide-prone murderers. In another case, in 2002 in Kentucky, Marco Chapman committed a rape and then murdered the woman's seven-year-old daughter and her six-year-old brother, leaving for dead their ten-year-old sister and their mother after stabbing them multiple times. On being arrested in West Virginia, the deranged Chapman asked a police officer to do him a favor and "put a bullet in my forehead." Competency evaluations later revealed Chapman's mental health issues, but Chapman was executed in 2008 after he fired his lawyers, pled guilty to the murders, and requested a death sentence. Chapman's stated desire was to commit "suicide by court." As a general matter, suicide victims almost uniformly suffer from diagnosable mental disorders, and the same is true, not surprisingly, of death row volunteers. Among such inmates, 88 percent were found to have suffered from mental illness, severe substance abuse disorders, or both. In many instances, those who volunteer for execution are schizophrenic or have attempted suicide either before or during their incarceration.[7]

For those who linger on death row and maintain their appeals, prolonged stays have led to serious Eighth Amendment challenges—claims rooted in the mental and physical toll exacted by the isolation of death row. In 1891, the U.S. Supreme Court itself took up the case of convicted murderer Charles McElvaine, who was sentenced to death in the state of New York and ordered to be kept in solitary confinement until his execution at the Sing Sing prison. "It is contended," the Court reported, "that the solitary confinement thus provided for constitutes cruel and unusual punishment and brings the statute within the inhibition of the eighth amendment to the federal constitution." Although the Court sidestepped the issue by noting that the Bill of Rights as then interpreted was not intended to limit state power, the isolation of death row confinement, even for a short time, was considered a serious issue. Indeed, in 1890, the Supreme Court had considered the case of another man under sentence of death in the state of Colorado who had been ordered to be kept in solitary confinement until his execution. Though that opinion focused on the Ex Post Facto Clause, not the Eighth Amendment, the Court emphasized that the matter of "solitary confinement" itself is not "a mere unimportant regulation as to the safe-keeping of the prisoner." In that case, the Court noted that while solitary confinement had first been used in 1703 at the Hospital San Michele in Rome, not much was known about its adverse effects until "the experiment in Walnut-Street Penitentiary, in Philadelphia, in 1787" and the adoption of other solitary confinement arrangements in other states. "[E]xperience demonstrated that there were serious objections to it," the Court ruled in 1890, noting: "A considerable number of the prisoners fell, after even a short confinement, into a semi-fatuous condition, from which it was next to impossible to arouse them, and others became violently insane; others still, committed suicide; while those who stood the ordeal better were not generally reformed, and in most cases did not recover sufficient mental activity to be of any subsequent service to the community."[8]

A death sentence all by itself is a traumatic experience, but living for years or even decades under a sentence of death amounts to what capital defendants describe as a "living death." Executions in colonial times and early America were carried out in a matter of months, weeks, or even days; in the mid-1700s, executions occurred two days after sentencing or, if a death sentence was imposed on a Friday, then on the following Monday. Even when contested legal issues arose, most capital cases through the early 1800s were resolved within six months of the conviction. By the end of the 1960s, however, the average time spent on death row had grown to almost three years, with much longer delays still to come. Today's lengthy periods of preexecution confinement, coupled with harsh prison conditions and the routine delays associated with capital litigation, have served to intensify prisoners' suffering, especially since death row inmates are routinely confined to their six-by-nine-foot cells for twenty-three hours each day. Mental anguish and mental breakdowns inevitably result from such isolation, with one U.S. Supreme Court Justice—in line with the experience of prison wardens—remarking as long ago as 1950 that "onset of insanity while awaiting execution of a death sentence is not a rare phenomenon." Clinton Duffy, the former warden of California's San Quentin death row facility, observed decades ago, when the average time spent on death row was far less, that "[o]ne night on death row is too long." "[T]he length of time spent there" by inmates, he noted, "constitutes cruelty that defies the imagination." "It has always been a source of wonder to me," he said, "that they didn't all go stark, raving mad." Recalling the case of Henry Arsenault, who suffered recurring nightmares, urinated uncontrollably, and wet his pants while confined on death row, one Massachusetts judge writing in 1980 specifically concluded that "the ordeal" imposed on condemned inmates is "cruel" or "unusual" punishment. That judge, interpreting the Massachusetts prohibition on "cruel or unusual punishments," noted that "[t]he raw terror and unabating stress that Henry Arsenault experienced was torture." In his concurring opinion to a judicial ruling striking down Massachusetts's death penalty as impermissibly "cruel," the judge wrote that "[t]wo months—or for that matter one day—of torture offends the Constitution."[9]

Though U.S. courts have yet to recognize the "death row phenomenon," a concept associated with the extreme emotional distress experienced by death row inmates during their confinement, many other courts and countries have already done so. In 1989, in *Soering v. United Kingdom,* the European Court of Human Rights specifically took notice of the phenomenon, finding that exposing a person to such treatment would violate the European Convention for the Protection of Human Rights and Fundamental Freedoms. Article 3 of that convention, invoked in the case, states that "[n]o one shall be subjected to torture or to inhuman or degrading treatment or punishment." Because of the "real risk of treatment going beyond the threshold set by Article 3," the court ruled that it would be unlawful for the British government to extradite a man to Virginia because, if convicted and sentenced to death, he would be exposed to the "death row phenomenon." In a later case, *Chahal v. United Kingdom,* the same court held that deporting a terrorism suspect to India, where he faced a risk of ill treatment at the hands of Indian security forces, also constituted an Article 3 violation. Foreign tribunals as diverse as the United Kingdom's Privy Council, the Ugandan Supreme Court, and the Zimbabwe Supreme Court have found it would constitute "torture" or "inhuman and degrading punishment" to execute inmates who have been confined on death row for long periods of time. In 1993, the Judicial Committee of the Privy Council, the court of last resort for member countries of the British Commonwealth, concluded that it was an "inhuman act to keep a man facing the agony of execution over a long extended period of time," finding the delay of fourteen years in a Jamaican case to be "shocking." In 2009, the Ugandan court ruled that a delay of more than three years between confirmation of a prisoner's death sentence on appeal and execution was unlawful. The Supreme Court of India has held that a condemned prisoner may ask whether it is "just and fair" to permit execution in instances of prolonged delay, commuting death sentences to life terms when such lapses of time have occurred. The Supreme Court of Zimbabwe in its ruling concluded that delays of five to six years were "inordinate" and constituted "torture" or "inhuman or degrading punishment or other such treatment."[10]

In fact, Justice Stephen Breyer wants the U.S. Supreme Court immediately to take up whether delays associated with executions make them unconstitutional. "Where a delay, measured in decades, reflects the State's own failure to comply with the Constitution's demands," he writes, "the claim that time has rendered the execution inhuman is a particularly strong one." Justice John Paul Stevens, before his retirement, agreed, asking in his dissent from a certiorari denial in *Lackey v. Texas* "whether executing a prisoner who has already spent some 17 years on death row violates the Eighth Amendment's prohibition against cruel and unusual punishment." "Such a delay, if it ever occurred," Stevens wrote, "certainly would have been rare in 1789, and thus the practice of the Framers would not justify a denial of petitioner's claim." Justice Breyer also dissented from the Court's failure even to consider a Florida case, calling the claim of an inmate who spent more than twenty-three years on death row "a serious one." Such delay, Breyer wrote, "is unusual—whether one takes as a measuring rod current practice or the practice in this country and in England at the time our Constitution was written." And it might be "especially cruel," he wrote, because the inmate "faced the threat of death for nearly a generation," with the delay caused by "the State's own faulty procedures and not because of frivolous appeals." "It is difficult to deny," Justice Breyer explained, "the suffering inherent in a prolonged wait for execution—a matter which courts and individual judges have long recognized." "More than a century ago," Breyer noted in dissent in yet another Florida case, "this Court described as 'horrible' the 'feelings' that accompany uncertainty about whether, or when, the execution will take place."[11]

Before retiring, Justice Stevens, joined by Justice Breyer, also dissented from the denial of certiorari in yet another death penalty case, *Johnson v. Bredesen*. In that case, Stevens reported that the petitioner Cecil Johnson Jr. had been "confined to a solitary cell awaiting his execution for nearly 29 years." Concluding that "Johnson bears little, if any, responsibility for this delay," Stevens noted that Johnson, convicted in 1981 for three murders committed in the course of a robbery, still maintained his innocence and that no physical evidence tied Johnson to the crime. As Stevens wrote: "In 1992 a change in state law gave Johnson access, for the first time, to substantial evidence undermining key eyewitness testimony against him. This evidence calls into question the persuasive force of the eyewitness' testimony, and, consequently, whether

Johnson's conviction was infected with constitutional error." Delay itself, Stevens emphasized, subjects inmates to "decades of especially severe, dehumanizing conditions of confinement," adding that delay furthers neither retribution nor deterrence. "Because I remain steadfast in my view 'that executing defendants after such delays is unacceptably cruel,'" Stevens concluded, "I would grant the stay application and the petition for certiorari." His final appeal denied, Johnson, a fifty-three-year-old African American, was executed by the State of Tennessee and pronounced dead on December 2, 2009, at 1:34 a.m.[12]

While extended stays are now commonplace, creating a backlog of permanent resident–inmates languishing in limbo on death row cell blocks, the number of death sentences handed out by American juries has fallen precipitously. From 1993 to 2000, more than two hundred death sentences were handed out each year, with the number actually exceeding three hundred in 1994, 1995, 1996, and 1998. But the annual number fell to 159 in 2001, to 152 in 2003, and to 139 in 2005. In the last five years, the number of death sentences has remained at slightly more than one hundred per year, with 123 executions in 2006, 120 in 2007, 119 in 2008, and 112 each in 2009 and 2010. Since the 1990s, the number of death sentences imposed in the United States has thus dropped dramatically—yet another sign of Americans' growing preference for life-without-parole sentences and their reticence to resort to executions. As a cornerstone of Anglo-American law, juries—"drawn from the body of the people," to use the 1788 words of the "Federal Farmer"—have long played a key role in capital cases. Not only do juries sit in judgment at the guilt/innocence phase of capital trials, but they typically have the final say during the penalty phase of such trials. As a by-product, the Supreme Court itself has been able to gauge public sentiment on a particular punishment by examining jury verdicts. Those who end up on death row today as a result of such jury determinations are, of course, exactly the same kind of tormented, mentally ill inmates who have been sent there for decades.[13]

Under the Supreme Court's own Eighth Amendment jurisprudence, jurors routinely play a critical role in measuring the public's appetite for executions. "[O]ne of the most important functions any jury can perform," the Supreme Court ruled in 1968 in *Witherspoon v. Illinois,* "is to maintain a link between contemporary community values and the penal system—a link without which the determination of punishment would hardly reflect 'the evolving standards of decency that mark the progress of a maturing society.'" The Founding Fathers themselves held the jury in the highest esteem, with Patrick Henry once saying that "trial by jury" is so beloved "[b]ecause it prevents the hand of oppression from cutting yours off." "It gives me comfort," Henry said, "that as long as I have existence my neighbors will protect me." Indeed, under the Supreme Court's existing case law, juries—at least in an indirect way—play a critical role in deciding the Eighth Amendment's future, while also serving as an additional check on government power. Because states typically commit capital sentencing decisions to juries, the U.S. Supreme Court has repeatedly cited jury verdicts as one of the best indicators of the prevailing "standards of decency." With the Court paying such close attention to jury verdicts in evaluating the constitutionality of capital punishment, fewer death sentences naturally translate into an increased likelihood that the Court will one day strike down death penalty laws altogether.[14]

The decline in death sentences reflects the American public's growing ambivalence, as reflected in polls, toward the death penalty itself. In a 2006 Gallup Poll, when offered a choice, 48 percent of survey respondents chose life without parole over death sentences; in contrast, only 47 percent of respondents chose the death penalty. That marked the first time in twenty years that the death penalty came in second place. A 2007 poll also found that 87 percent of Americans believe innocent people have been executed, and that 58 percent of respondents were supportive of imposing a moratorium on executions. A more recent poll taken in 2009 found that while 65 percent of Americans indicate their support for the death penalty for murder, only 45 percent did so when life without parole was offered as an alternative. "This is the lowest level of support for capital punishment reported in polling data in more than fifty years," explains John Blume, a professor at Cornell Law School. Yet another poll, conducted in 2010, found that a clear majority of voters—61 percent— favored a punishment other than death for murder. The most preferred alternative: life with no possibility of parole, with restitution to the victim's family.[15]

The reason for the drop-off in support for capital punishment is clear. According to A Crisis of Confidence, a recent Death Penalty Information Center report: "People are deeply concerned about the risk of executing the innocent, about the fairness of the process, and about the inability of capital punishment to accomplish its basic purposes." And they should be. Twenty-six states have seen at least one death row exoneration since 1973, with many witnessing far more. James Liebman, a professor at Columbia Law School, did a massive study of 4,578 capital cases and found that from 1973 to 1995 the error rate in those cases was an astonishing 68 percent. In other words, more than two thirds of convictions or sentences in death penalty cases were overturned. Though many cases were retried, the study, published in 2000, showed that it took on average more than seven years for potentially fatal errors to be corrected. Tellingly, the poll commissioned for the Death Penalty Information Center's 2007 report about people's misgivings about capital punishment found that nearly 40 percent of Americans believe they would be disqualified from serving on a capital jury because of their moral objections to the death penalty.[16]

While the Supreme Court insists jury verdicts should reflect the "conscience of the community," the Court's own case law permits "death-qualified" juries. During jury selection, prospective jurors are questioned, often at length, about their views and opinions, with staunch death penalty opponents then systematically excluded from jury service. The Court has held that "[c]apital defendants have the right to be sentenced by an impartial jury" and that "those whose scruples against the death penalty would not substantially impair the performance of their duties" cannot be excluded from capital juries. Still, the Court ruled in *Witherspoon* that jurors can be excluded if they would refuse to "consider" all possible punishments "provided by state law"; if they were "irrevocably committed, before the trial has begun, to vote against the penalty of death"; if they would "automatically" vote against the imposition of the death penalty; or if "their attitude toward the death penalty would prevent them from making an impartial decision as to the defendant's guilt." In *Uttecht v. Brown,* a 2007 case, the Supreme Court specifically held that it owed deference to trial court findings as to the exclusion of prospective jurors. As a result, scores of Americans who oppose executions—including many women, Catholics, and minorities, who in disproportionate numbers find capital punishment morally repugnant—never sit in judgment in capital cases. As Justice John Paul Stevens pointed out in his dissent in that case: "[m]illions of Americans oppose the death penalty" and the death-qualification process is unfair because "[a] cross section of virtually every community in the country includes citizens who firmly believe the death penalty is unjust but who nevertheless are qualified to serve as jurors in capital cases."[17]

The expressed rationale for "death-qualifying" juries is so jurors conscientiously carry out their sworn duty to apply the law. Thus, in *Wainwright v. Witt,* the Court held that a juror may be excluded for cause if the juror's views would "prevent or substantially impair" the performance of the juror's duties. It is the trial judge's duty to determine whether a given challenge to a prospective juror is proper, with the Court stating in *Uttecht* that "the State has a strong interest in having jurors who are able to apply capital punishment within the framework state law prescribes" and that a juror who is "substantially impaired in his or her ability to impose the death penalty under the state-law framework" can be excused for cause. The death penalty, however, is not even relevant to the guilt/innocence phase of the trial, and studies consistently show that death-qualified juries are more conviction-prone. Because death-qualified juries are less skeptical of evidence, the already considerable risk of errors and miscarriages of justice is inflated further. Equally troubling, by allowing "death-qualified" juries, the Court predetermines—and skews—the so-called "objective" data it considers so critical in making Eighth Amendment judgments. With capital juries routinely required to reach unanimous verdicts, death-qualified juries lead to more death sentences at the penalty phase of trials than one would otherwise expect to see. This is because any potential holdouts—and it takes only one—are culled from jury pools in advance. "Litigation involving both challenges for cause and peremptory challenges," Justice Stevens once wrote, "has persuaded me that the process of obtaining a 'death qualified jury' is really a procedure that has the purpose and effect of obtaining a jury that is biased in favor of conviction." "The prosecutorial concern that death verdicts would rarely be returned by 12 randomly selected jurors," he concluded, "should be viewed as objective evidence supporting the conclusion that the penalty is excessive."[18]

Though the death penalty is more often than not directed at some of society's most mentally ill members, it remains popular in the South, especially in Texas. But even in the Lone Star State, where polls have consistently shown high levels of support for capital punishment, things are changing. In 2007, the *Dallas Morning News,* unable to reconcile the death penalty's imperfections and its irreversibility, changed its position and now advocates abolition. "We do not believe that any legal system devised by inherently flawed human beings can determine with moral certainty the guilt of every defendant convicted of murder," the editorial board wrote. A series of wrongful convictions is responsible for much of the change in outlook, with a serious investigation launched in 2010 into whether Texas wrongfully executed the inmate Cameron Willingham. Convicted of killing his three daughters in a 1991 house fire thought to be a case of arson, Willingham, an unemployed mechanic, went to his death insisting that he was innocent. The case brought national attention after several fire experts concluded the original arson investigation relied on outdated techniques and unreliable forensic evidence. In 2008, after one of what is now more than ten exonerations of death row inmates in Texas, Dallas County District Attorney Craig Watkins announced his office would review nearly forty death penalty convictions for potential errors and, if necessary, halt executions.[19]

The prospect of human error in capital cases is in fact well documented. Miscarriages of justice and instances of lawyer incompetence are literally too numerous to recount, and even DNA evidence has been subject to manipulation. As Rachel King, counsel for the Subcommittee on Crime, Terrorism and Homeland Security for the Committee on the Judiciary of the House of Representatives, explains in her 2007 article *No Due Process:* "The most shocking examples of laboratory dereliction came out of Harris County, Texas, where the laboratory had allegedly been providing false DNA evidence for the last twenty-five years." "Considering that about 35% of all executions in the United States during the modern era came out of Texas and that the overwhelming majority of Texas executions have come out of Harris County," King writes, "these lab failures indicate a major failure in the criminal justice system." The head of that DNA lab, King pointed out, had been dismissed from a PhD program, failed algebra and geometry, and never even taken statistics. Other lab workers, including one who had most recently been cleaning elephant cages at a city zoo, had been unqualified too. In 2010, Harris County trial judge Kevin Fine, citing society's "evolving standards," unexpectedly declared the Texas death penalty unconstitutional because of the risk of innocent people being executed. Though Judge Fine, under fire from the district attorney's office and labeled a judicial activist by the Texas Attorney General, later re-scinded his order, his ruling at least for a time brought the issue to the fore. When discussing a due process claim, Judge Fine in his initial bench rul-ing bluntly stated that "we execute innocent people," rhetorically pondering "whether we, as a society, knowing that we execute innocent persons, desire to continue to ignore that reality?" When Judge Fine tried to hold a hearing in December 2010 to examine the risk of innocent people being executed, the Texas Court of Criminal Appeals—acting on its own motion—ordered that the hearing be halted.[20]

Though the advent of DNA evidence has conclusively shown that miscar-riages of justice occur, the death penalty has since its inception been rife with legal and factual errors, incompetent attorneys, juror bias, and mistaken con-victions. In Alabama, 10 percent of death row inmates were represented by trial lawyers later disbarred or disciplined, and that figure is even slightly higher in Louisiana, at nearly 13 percent. Likewise, almost one quarter of Kentucky's death row inmates had attorneys who were subsequently disbarred or suspended. In Alabama, a black man named Walter McMillian was sen-tenced to death for murder after a perfunctory one-and-a-half-day trial. Reject-ing the testimony of a half-dozen black witnesses who testified that McMillian was at a fish fry at the time of the murder, jurors instead accepted the testimony of a murderer who testified falsely against McMillian. Convicted of murdering a white woman, McMillian—known in his rural community to have had an interracial affair—spent nearly six years on death row before he was exoner-ated in 1993 after a tape recording surfaced in which the prosecutor's star witness told police that McMillian had nothing to do with the crime. Kirk Bloodsworth and Ronald Williamson, freed from Maryland and Oklahoma death rows, each spent nine years in prison for murder-rapes they did not commit. Bloodsworth, convicted of raping a nine-year-old girl on the basis of faulty eyewitness identifications, was a former marine, and Williamson, repre-sented by a lawyer with no capital trial experience, was a black man with an IQ of 69 who gave a false confession. All one needs to do is to read the facts of such cases and the lengthy procedural histories that accompany each one to realize how broken America's death penalty machine really is.[21]

The recent curtailment of habeas corpus rights, coupled with the unre-liability of eyewitness testimony and the sheer complexity of capital litigation, only ensures that potentially fatal errors will continue. The frontal assault on habeas corpus—a procedural right the Founding Fathers saw as so fundamen-tal it was included in the Constitution as originally drafted in 1787—began with a series of decades-old U.S. Supreme Court cases restricting the avail-ability of that venerable, centuries-old remedy. Though such rulings turned habeas corpus cases into procedural morasses focused more on "federalism" and "finality" than fairness, the gutting of habeas corpus continued apace with the passage of the Antiterrorism and Effective Death Penalty Act of 1996, passed by Congress in the wake of the Oklahoma City bombing. That act contains a short, one-year statute of limitations, makes it more onerous to file habeas corpus petitions, and requires federal courts to give greater deference to state courts, all in an effort to speed up executions. Though miscarriages of justice often take years to correct, death row inmates, who are not even guaranteed lawyers, let alone effective lawyers, in postconviction proceedings, now face higher hurdles and significant time pressure to lodge their claims, with an even lower expectation of obtaining meaningful habeas corpus review.[22]

Death penalty cases are themselves extraordinarily complex. The law is complicated, the legal issues are varied, and the factual disputes that arise, especially over forensic and mental health issues, necessarily require costly experts to be retained and consulted by prosecutors and defense lawyers alike. The byzantine nature of capital litigation, replete with procedural defaults, finality and exhaustion-of-remedies rules, and now a one-year limitations period for habeas corpus petitions, makes it difficult for even the most seasoned capital litigator to master all the applicable statutes, rules, and precedents. And even one mistake—perhaps not even one made by the death row inmate— can be fatal to a lawyer's client. For example, in *Coleman v. Thompson,* the Supreme Court refused even to consider the merits of a death row inmate's claims after his lawyer filed the notice of appeal three days late. Death row inmates' claims are in fact frequently denied on purely procedural grounds or on the basis of complex legal doctrines such as the *Teague v. Lane* "nonretroactivity" principle. *Teague* held that in certain circumstances a "new" constitutional rule of criminal procedure would not be applied "retroactively" in cases on collateral review. As a result of that decision, an inmate seeking habeas corpus relief often may not rely upon a rule of law announced in a U.S. Supreme Court decision handed down after his or her conviction becomes final upon the completion of any direct appeal. While inmates still appealing their cases on direct review are allowed to invoke a "new" rule of constitutional law, those who have completed their direct appeals are not allowed to do so. In the last few decades, law professor Franklin Zimring points out, "the Court has fashioned a Frankenstein's monster out of death penalty cases."[23]

Capital litigation—with endless traps for the unwary—is difficult enough for the best trained and most experienced lawyers to navigate, let alone for unrepresented, mentally ill inmates with little education and low IQ scores. Death row inmates, often represented as they are by poorly paid or unqualified court-appointed lawyers at trial, may actually lose whatever legal representation they had, once their direct appeals are exhausted. While the Supreme Court unanimously held in 1963 in *Gideon v. Wainwright* that state courts are required by the Sixth Amendment to provide counsel in criminal trials to indigent defendants, no such right is recognized for those in postconviction proceedings. This is so even though death row inmates, under the exhaustion-of-remedies rule, must first lodge any claims they have in state court before bringing them to federal court. Over half of the two hundred people on Alabama's death row were represented at trial by court-appointed lawyers whose compensation for out-of-court preparation was capped at a meager one thousand dollars, and scores of American death row inmates—likely hundreds—currently do not have any lawyer at all. In Mississippi, Willie Russell, who tested in the range of mental retardation in school, once came within forty-five minutes of being executed without a lawyer. Obviously, if no lawyer is located to handle a death row inmate's case, that case will typically not be examined carefully, from either a factual or a legal standpoint, by anyone else. Not surprisingly, poorly educated Mississippi death row inmates who were once administered the Law School Admission Test (LSAT) as part of a study of their intellectual functioning scored abysmally on that exam. On the multiple-choice questions, the inmates taking the exam should have gotten at least 20 percent correct just by answering at random; the mean raw score, however, was 19.2 percent, meaning they did less well than even chance itself would dictate. Such low scores are hard even to fathom until one knows that only four of the inmates had graduated from high school, over 84 percent fell below the seventh-grade level for reading comprehension, and roughly 27 percent fell within the IQ range for potential mental retardation.[24]

Though the Constitution itself guarantees habeas corpus rights, the Supreme Court, bizarrely enough, takes the position that death row inmates have no right to counsel after their direct appeals are done. "There is no constitutional right to an attorney in state post-conviction proceedings," the Court ruled in 1991 in *Coleman,* citing two of its earlier cases, *Pennsylvania v. Finley* and *Murray v. Giarratano.* While criminal defendants have a right to counsel at trial and on their direct appeals, they are essentially on their own after that, dependent on the willingness of often hostile legislative bodies to authorize funds for counsel or, in many cases, on strictly volunteer, pro bono attorneys, if attorneys can be recruited at all. In many Southern states, large numbers of death row inmates are actually represented by out-of-state attorneys located in New England or the Midwest. A Minnesota-based organization called The Advocates for Human Rights has itself recruited more than a hundred volunteer lawyers and paralegals to handle cases for death row inmates in other states. Of course, death row inmates, who are confined to their cells and largely uneducated, have no practical or realistic ability either to learn the requirements of the law or to vindicate their habeas corpus rights without a lawyer. For death row inmates, habeas corpus rights are only as good as the time, commitment, and skills of their attorneys, and if no lawyer can be found, all an inmate can really do is hope against hope that one will be found before execution day arrives. Illinois inmate Anthony Porter, a black man with an IQ of 50 who spent sixteen years on death row, once came within forty-eight hours of being executed. For Porter, it took a dedicated group of Northwestern University *journalism students* to help exonerate him.[25]

That so many errors are caught, some say, shows that the criminal justice system is "working." But that is cold comfort to the wrongfully convicted and certainly does not guarantee that other serious mistakes are not slipping through the cracks. Indeed, in James Liebman's national study of death sentences imposed from 1973 to 1995, 82 percent of the capital judgments that were reversed and retried resulted in a sentence less than death, with 7 percent of the reversals leading to "not guilty" determinations on retrial. Thus, miscarriages of justice, legal and factual errors, misidentifications, and acts of prosecutorial or juror misconduct are hardly theoretical, pie-in-the-sky problems. In fact, the abysmal quality of defense counsel in so many capital trials—replete with inadequately trained, drunk, or sleeping lawyers—is nothing short of scandalous. Calvin Burdine, sentenced to death in Texas in 1983 after his lawyer fell asleep multiple times at trial, was resentenced to three life sentences only in 2003, with Burdine once coming within minutes of being executed. At least three people in Houston, attorney Stephen Bright points out, "were represented by lawyers who slept during their capital trials while supposedly defending them." Other defendants have been sentenced to death after being represented by lawyers who made racial slurs about their own clients, who failed to investigate key evidence, who did not present any mitigating evidence at the penalty phase, who had practiced law for less than a year, or who did not read or understand the applicable law. The quality of representation in capital cases is not even close to that envisioned by the American Bar Association, making it inevitable that even more innocent people will land on death row in the years ahead. One study found that from 1989 to 2003 there were 205 exonerations of defendants convicted of murder—a figure that does not exactly instill confidence in the justice system's ability to make error-free judgments in life-and-death matters. The Innocence Project, a nonprofit legal clinic started in 1992, reports that there have been 266 postconviction DNA exonerations in the United States and that 17 of those exonerated served time on death row. Among the exonerated were 158 African Americans, 80 Caucasians, and 21 Latinos, men and women with names, families, and lives shattered by their wrongful convictions.[26]

The Supreme Court's Approach

The U.S. Supreme Court has for decades given the green light to executions. On more than one occasion, the Court has indicated that the death penalty itself is not unconstitutional. For example, in *Trop v. Dulles,* the Court stated in dicta: "Whatever the arguments may be against capital punishment, both on moral grounds and in terms of accomplishing the purposes of punishment—and they are forceful—the death penalty has been employed throughout our history, and, in a day when it is still widely accepted, it cannot be said to violate the constitutional concept of cruelty." In *Gregg v. Georgia,* the Court also stated that "[t]he Court on a number of occasions has both assumed and asserted the constitutionality of capital punishment," though the Court, in upholding Georgia's death penalty law, acknowledged that until *Furman* it had not "confronted squarely" the claim that capital punishment is itself unconstitutional. The *Baze* decision, which set off a new round of American executions, also reaffirmed that the current members of the Court do not view the death penalty as unconstitutional. In *Baze,* the Court upheld Kentucky's three-drug lethal injection protocol, though the debate over botched executions—as well as the risk of inflicting excruciating pain if protocols are improperly administered—led two states, Ohio and Washington, to move to one-drug protocols. A severe shortage of lethal injection drugs was later revealed, with death penalty states bending importation rules and scrambling to find a supply even as foreign manufacturers halted production or refused to ship them. Whether executions are carried out by three drugs or one, of course, does not change the end result: death.[27]

The death penalty, though still in use in some places, has generated increasing controversy nationwide, even among Supreme Court Justices voting to uphold it. Justice Ruth Bader Ginsburg expressed her support for a moratorium on executions in April 2001, saying that she has "yet to see a death penalty case among the dozens coming to the Supreme Court on eve-of-execution stay applications in which the defendant was well-represented at trial." In a Minnesota speech in July of that same year, Justice Sandra Day O'Connor also said there are "serious questions" about whether the death penalty is administered fairly. She added that Minnesotans "must breathe a big sigh of relief every day" because the state no longer has capital punishment. In *Ring v. Arizona*, Justice Stephen Breyer also wrote of "the continued difficulty of justifying capital punishment in terms of its ability to deter crime," saying "[s]tudies of deterrence are, at most, inconclusive." Noting divided opinion as to whether capital punishment is, as currently administered, "cruel and unusual," Justice Breyer emphasized that "the inadequacy of representation in capital cases" is "a fact that aggravates" the death penalty's "other failings." While on the bench, Justice Stevens also noted that the "recent development of reliable scientific evidentiary methods has made it possible to establish conclusively that a disturbing number of persons who had been sentenced to death were actually innocent."[28]

Indeed, the Supreme Court's decision in *Baze* drew two dissenters. Justice Ginsburg, joined by Justice David Souter, opined that Kentucky's protocol "lacks basic safeguards used by other States to confirm that an inmate is unconscious before injection of the second and third drugs." According to the dissent: "Kentucky's protocol does not specify the rate at which sodium thiopental should be injected. The executioner, who does not have any medical training, pushes the drug 'by feel' through five feet of tubing." "In practice sessions, unlike in an actual execution," the dissenters wrote, "there is no resistance on the catheter, thus the executioner's training may lead him to push the drugs too fast." Justice Stevens—writing with candor and passion, though concurring in the result—also roundly criticized the way in which death penalty laws are maintained and enforced. America's decision to retain capital punishment, he emphasized, is "the product of habit and inattention rather than an acceptable deliberative process," adding that "the imposition of the death penalty represents 'the pointless and needless extinction of life.'" Kentucky, he noted, barred veterinarians from using neuromuscular paralytic agents such as pancuronium bromide for animal euthanasia, with Stevens writing pointedly: "It is unseemly—to say the least—that Kentucky may well kill petitioners using a drug that it would not permit to be used on their pets." Citing juror studies and polls showing reduced support for capital punishment when life-without-parole sentences are offered as an alternative, as well as a lack of credible data showing that the death penalty deters crime any better than life sentences, Justice Stevens declared that state-sanctioned executions are "becoming more and more anachronistic."[29]

The Supreme Court has long held that whether a punishment is excessive, or "cruel or unusual," is not judged by the standards that prevailed in pre–Revolutionary War times or when the Bill of Rights was adopted. Instead, the "basic concept" underlying the Eighth Amendment is "human dignity," with the Court holding that the Eighth Amendment "must draw its meaning from the evolving standards of decency that mark the progress of a maturing society." The Court thus looks to the "norms" that "currently prevail," trying to discern whether or not a "national consensus" exists against one kind of punishment or another. But "[c]onsensus is not dispositive," the Court has clarified, stating that, in assessing whether a punishment is disproportionate to the crime, it is "the Court's own understanding and interpretation of the Eighth Amendment's text, history, meaning, and purpose" that must be consulted. The "'standard of extreme cruelty is not merely descriptive, but necessarily embodies a moral judgment,'" the Court has emphasized, explaining that "'[t]he standard itself remains the same, but its applicability must change as the basic mores of society change.'" "Evolving standards of decency," the Court held in 2008, "must embrace and express respect for the dignity of the person, and the punishment of criminals must conform to that rule."[30]

The way in which the Supreme Court makes Eighth Amendment judgments has been articulated in multiple cases. To assess the proportionality of a particular punishment, the Supreme Court has noted that "Eighth Amendment judgments should not be, or appear to be, merely the subjective views of individual Justices," but "should be informed by objective factors to the maximum extent possible." While the Justices explicitly reserve the right to consult their own sense of morality in making these judgments, the Court routinely weighs a host of "objective" criteria before reaching its decisions. "When sentences are reviewed under the Eighth Amendment," the Court says, "courts should be guided by objective factors that our cases have recognized." Over the years, such "objective" criteria have included the gravity of the offense, a penalty's severity, the circumstances of the crime, public attitudes, state practice, legislative acts, and jury verdicts. The Court has also compared the sentences imposed on other criminals in the same jurisdiction or in other jurisdictions. But no one factor or criterion is dispositive in a given case, no penalty is per se permissible, and the Supreme Court—rightfully so, given its special role as the guardian of constitutional rights—has made clear that the "independent judgment" of Justices themselves must be brought to bear in deciding a punishment's constitutionality.[31]

In its rulings, the Supreme Court typically begins by doing a counting exercise, looking at how many states either prohibit or permit a particular punishment. For example, when *Atkins* was decided in 2002, it was noted that thirty states, including twelve abolitionist ones, prohibited the death penalty for mentally retarded offenders, whereas only twenty states permitted that punishment. Likewise, when *Roper* was handed down in 2005, attention was paid to the fact that thirty states prohibited the death penalty for juveniles, whereas only twenty states authorized such a sentence. In *Enmund,* the Court also emphasized that only eight jurisdictions authorized a death sentence solely for participation in a robbery during which an accomplice committed a murder. In *Kennedy*, the Court similarly emphasized that "it is of significance that, in 45 jurisdictions, petitioner could not be executed for child rape of any kind," a number that "surpasses the 30 States in *Atkins* and *Roper* and the 42 States in *Enmund* that prohibited the death penalty under the circumstances those cases considered." In 2010, when the Court, utilizing the Eighth Amendment, outlawed life-without-parole sentences for nonhomicidal juvenile offenders, it made clear that legislation alone would not dictate the Court's judgment. The Court noted as part of its analysis that six jurisdictions did not allow life-without-parole sentences for any juvenile offenders; that seven jurisdictions permitted life-without-parole sentences for juveniles, but only for homicides; that thirty-seven states and the District of Columbia— a clear majority—permitted life-without-parole sentences in some circumstances; and that federal law also allowed for the possibility of life without parole for nonhomicidal juvenile offenders as young as thirteen.[32]

The counting of jurisdictions permitting or prohibiting a specific punishment, all for the purpose of identifying whether a "national consensus" exists, is now nonetheless a routine part of the Eighth Amendment calculus. Such a mechanical count, the Supreme Court has noted, however, is not always, nor should be, the decisive factor. In *Atkins,* after noting that fifteen states had recently barred the execution of the mentally retarded, the Court held that "[i]t is not so much the number of these States that is significant, but the consistency of the direction of change." Likewise, in *Roper*, the Court acknowledged that "the rate of change in reducing the incidence of the juvenile death penalty, or in taking specific steps to abolish it," had been "slower" than in the mental retardation context, but noted that the "less dramatic" change was still "significant" and that "the same consistency of direction of change has been demonstrated." In *Kennedy,* after acknowledging that a handful of states had passed new laws making child rape a capital crime, the Court put it this way: "The evidence of a national consensus with respect to the death penalty for child rapists, as with respect to juveniles, mentally retarded offenders, and vicarious felony murderers, shows divided opinion but, on balance, an opinion against it." And in *Graham,* the Court emphasized that there are measures of consensus other than legislation. "Actual sentencing practices," the Court ruled, "are an important part of the Court's inquiry into consensus." Thus, the fact that a few states, or even a majority of them, permit a particular punishment is not dispositive.[33]

In making Eighth Amendment decisions, the Court looks carefully not only at laws on the books but also at how often a particular punishment is meted out. In *Enmund,* only six defendants between 1954 and 1982 could be identified who had been sentenced to death for felony murder where the defendant did not personally commit the homicidal act. In *Roper,* though just five additional states had outlawed juvenile executions in the preceding fifteen years, the evidence showed that the execution of juvenile offenders was extremely rare. In the previous ten years, only three states, Oklahoma, Texas, and Virginia, had executed juvenile offenders. In *Atkins,* the case addressing mentally retarded offenders, only five states had executed offenders known to have an IQ below 70 between 1989 and 2002; in *Graham,* only 129 juveniles were serving life-without-parole sentences for nonhomicidal offenses, with a majority of them, 77, serving sentences imposed in Florida; and in *Kennedy,* the Court specifically emphasized that "[s]tatistics about the number of executions may inform the consideration whether capital punishment for the crime of child rape is regarded as unacceptable in our society." The Court in *Graham* stated that "only 12 jurisdictions nationwide in fact impose life without parole sentences on juvenile nonhomicide offenders—and most of those impose the sentence quite rarely—while 26 States as well as the District of Columbia do not impose them despite apparent statutory authorization." In *Kennedy,* the Court emphasized that "no individual has been executed for the rape of an adult or child since 1964" and that "no execution for any other non-homicide offense has been conducted since 1963." If the Court finds that laws are not being used, its willingness to strike down a punishment increases.[34]

Over the years, the U.S. Supreme Court, despite its long-standing approval of executions, has consistently held that under the Eighth Amendment prisoners must be protected from harm. In this regard, the Eighth Amendment case law, which forbids abusive practices by governmental officials, is clear. In *Estelle v. Gamble,* the Court specifically held that "deliberate indifference" to prisoners' "serious medical needs" violates the Eighth Amendment because it inflicts "unnecessary and wanton" pain. In *Helling v. McKinney,* the Court likewise held that a prisoner stated a civil rights claim under the Eighth Amendment based on dangerous levels of exposure to secondhand smoke. And in yet another case, *Hope v. Pelzer,* the Court held that Alabama prison officials violated the Eighth Amendment by handcuffing a shirtless inmate to a hitching post, causing sunburned skin and dehydration. The inmate, the Court ruled, was knowingly subjected to "a substantial risk of physical harm, to unnecessary pain caused by the handcuffs and the restricted position of confinement for a 7-hour period, to unnecessary exposure to the heat of the sun, to prolonged thirst and taunting, and to a deprivation of bathroom breaks that created a risk of particular discomfort and humiliation." "The use of the hitching post under these circumstances," the Court held, "violated the 'basic concept underlying the Eighth Amendment'"—that is, "human dignity" and "the dignity of man." Indeed, the Court in *Hope* found that the facts as alleged by the inmate constituted an "obvious" Eighth Amendment violation.[35]

Lower courts, bound by U.S. Supreme Court precedents, have, not surprisingly, long concurred with this general approach to the Eighth Amendment. For example, in *Slakan v. Porter,* a North Carolina inmate was injured when prison guards used high-pressure water hoses, tear gas, and billy clubs to subdue him while he was securely confined in a one-man cell. Following a loud outburst from the prisoner, a prison guard flung a cup of coffee in the inmate's direction, striking the inmate, Charles Slakan, in the face and shoulder. An enraged Slakan then spewed obscenities at the guard, who in turn called for a water hose to quell the verbal disturbance. Ultimately, blasts of water from two separate hoses were directed at Slakan's head and neck, forcing him against the back wall of his cell. Tear gas was also sprayed into the cell every few minutes, forcing Slakan into submission. When guards finally entered the cell, Slakan was struck twice on the head with a billy club and then beaten on the head and body until he lost consciousness. The beating, which resulted in Slakan's receiving sixty-nine stitches and suffering minor contusions and eye irritation, was found in 1984 to have been a "cruel and unusual punishment" in the context of an excessive force case. "The prison guards' heavy-handed use of water hoses, billy clubs, and tear gas against Slakan," it was ruled, "unquestionably crossed the line separating necessary force from brutality." Though guards are allowed to use reasonable force to quell disturbances, the Eighth Amendment does not allow them to use excessive force not warranted by the situation.[36]

Courts have determined that the Eighth Amendment even protects prisoners from *potential* bodily injuries yet to materialize. "That the Eighth Amendment protects against future harm to inmates," the Supreme Court held in *Helling,* "is not a novel proposition." As the Court explained in that case: "We would think that a prison inmate also could successfully complain about demonstrably unsafe drinking water without waiting for an attack of dysentery. Nor can we hold that prison officials may be deliberately indifferent to the exposure of inmates to a serious, communicable disease on the ground that the complaining inmate shows no serious current symptoms." In 1998, the U.S. Court of Appeals for the District of Columbia held that a threat that put a prisoner in imminent fear for his life was sufficient to state a claim for excessive use of force; in 1985, one of its sister courts, the Ninth Circuit, stated that inadequate "ventilation and airflow" violates the Eighth Amendment if it "undermines the health of inmates and the sanitation of the penitentiary"; and, in 1978, the Fourth Circuit reversed the dismissal of a prisoner's federal civil rights lawsuit alleging that a guard threatened to have the prisoner killed because he had a suit pending against the prison. "Our cases," the Supreme Court itself noted in its plurality opinion in *Baze,* "recognize that subjecting individuals to a risk of future harm—not simply actually inflicting pain—can qualify as cruel and unusual punishment." Bizarrely enough, then, the Court zealously protects inmates from injuries and even potential harm but, in the case of executions, then deliberately allows their deaths.[37]

Through various cases, the Eighth Amendment has already been interpreted to bar bodily punishments short of death. Corporal punishments are no longer allowed in American prisons, as exemplified by *Jackson v. Bishop,* an appellate decision declaring flogging unconstitutional. In that case, Justice Harry Blackmun—writing for the U.S. Court of Appeals for the Eighth Circuit, of which he was then a member—stated in 1968: "[W]e have no difficulty in reaching the conclusion that the use of the strap in the penitentiaries of Arkansas is punishment which, in this last third of the 20th century, runs afoul of the Eighth Amendment; that the strap's use, irrespective of any precautionary conditions which may be imposed, offends contemporary concepts of decency and human dignity and precepts of civilization which we profess to possess." "Corporal punishment," Blackmun added, "generates hate toward the keepers who punish and toward the system which permits it." "It is," he said, "degrading to the punisher and to the punished alike." Blackmun further emphasized that only two states still permitted the use of the strap and that, accordingly, it had been "almost uniformly" abolished. Citing *Trop v. Dulles,* Blackmun's opinion seemed to treat "cruel and unusual" punishment as a unitary concept, stating: "We choose to draw no significant distinction between the word 'cruel' and the word 'unusual' in the Eighth Amendment. We would not wish to place ourselves in the position of condoning punishment which is shown to be only 'cruel' but not 'unusual' or vice versa." In other words, even were whipping a relatively common occurrence, the mistreatment of prisoners, Blackmun said, would not be tolerated. In 1977 in *Ingraham v. Wright,* the Supreme Court itself acknowledged that the United States had already witnessed "the general abandonment of corporal punishment as a means of punishing criminal offenders."[38]

The Eighth Amendment, as a general matter, thus bars debasing corporal punishments that even risk injuring or killing an inmate. The Cruel and Unusual Punishments Clause, lower courts have determined, prohibits the use of a strap to whip prisoners, bars handcuffing inmates to fences or cells for long periods, and refuses to tolerate other forms of physical brutality or misconduct. Depriving an inmate of food or necessary medical care, physically abusing a nonresisting prisoner, and severely mistreating an inmate also have been recognized as Eighth Amendment violations. Such violations in fact have been found when a prisoner was forced to live and sleep for two years in a dark cell with roaches and backed-up sewage; when inmates were forced to work inside a prison's sewage pump station without protective clothing; when prison officials refused to provide an inmate food for more than fifty hours; and when a prison guard assaulted a paraplegic inmate with a knife and forced him to sit in his own feces. Other Eighth Amendment violations have been adjudged when mechanical in-cell restraints subjected those restrained to a known risk of heart attack, dehydration, and asphyxiation; when a stun gun was gratuitously used on an inmate who had not physically threatened any officer; when inmates were shot at or around to keep them moving, or were deprived of mattresses, stripped naked, and had fans directed at them while wet; and when inmates were forced to maintain awkward positions for long periods of time or forced to consume milk of magnesia as a form of punishment.[39]

Federal judges have specifically held that verbal threats, if accompanied by extreme psychological harm, can violate the Eighth Amendment too. In *Babcock v. White,* the U.S. Court of Appeals for the Seventh Circuit emphasized that "the Constitution does not countenance psychological torture merely because it fails to inflict physical injury." Similarly, in *Northington v. Jackson,* the Tenth Circuit found that "psychological injury" may constitute pain under the Eighth Amendment's "excessive force standard," when a parole officer held a gun to a prisoner's head while threatening to kill him. In other words, verbal threats to kill an inmate, causing the prisoner to fear for his life, constitute a cognizable Eighth Amendment claim. As Justice Blackmun wrote in his concurring opinion in *Hudson v. McMillian:* "It is not hard to imagine inflictions of psychological harm—without corresponding physical harm—that might prove to be cruel and unusual punishment." "[T]he Eighth Amendment," Blackmun observed, construing prior precedents, "prohibits the unnecessary and wanton infliction of 'pain,' rather than 'injury.'" "'Pain' in its ordinary meaning," he noted, "surely includes a notion of psychological harm." In support of his position, Blackmun cited yet another case, from the Fifth Circuit, in which a prison guard placed a revolver in an inmate's mouth and threatened to blow the prisoner's head off—something the court in *Babcock* termed "the kind of malicious and sadistic behavior" that "offends contemporary standards of decency."[40]

Despite such rulings, the U.S. Supreme Court continues to hold that death sentences, which immediately subject prisoners to a fear of death, are constitutional. Similarly, though executions—the actual punishment—are specifically designed to kill prisoners, the Supreme Court continues to rule that executions are constitutional. In *Baze v. Rees,* the Court confronted head-on the question of whether a lethal injection protocol—involving strapping an inmate to a gurney and then intentionally injecting the inmate with lethal drugs—violates the Eighth Amendment. In that case, Kentucky death row inmates sued state officials, arguing that the state's three-drug lethal injection protocol posed an unacceptable risk of significant pain. Kentucky's law did not specify a particular protocol that had to be followed, but state officials developed one calling for the injection of two grams of sodium thiopental, fifty milligrams of pancuronium bromide, and 240 milliequivalents of potassium chloride. Sodium thiopental is a fast-acting sedative that, if administered properly, induces a deep, coma-like unconsciousness; pancuronium bromide is a paralytic agent that suppresses muscle movements and stops respiration; and potassium chloride induces cardiac arrest. The first drug was intended to ensure that condemned prisoners do not experience any pain associated with the paralysis and cardiac arrest caused by the second and third drugs.[41]

While the Eighth Amendment prohibits "cruel and unusual punishments," not "painful punishments," the legal battle over lethal injection focused on the concept of pain. The death row inmates in *Baze* contended that improper administration of sodium thiopental would cause them to suffer severe pain and that the State of Kentucky had failed to take adequate precautions to protect inmates from excruciatingly painful executions. Part of the inmates' challenge, which had implications for executions all over the country, dealt with the training and preparedness of execution participants. In Kentucky, doctors play no role in executions because a state statute specifically bars physicians from participating in the "conduct of an execution" except to certify the cause of death. Instead, a certified phlebotomist and an emergency medical technician are tasked with performing the venipunctures necessary for the catheters, with other personnel loading the chemicals into the syringes. In order to reduce the risk of the protocol's maladministration, Kentucky requires IV team members to have at least one year of professional experience and to participate along with other team members in at least ten practice sessions per year. The detailed protocol also calls for the IV team—for redundancy's sake—to establish both primary and back-up lines and to prepare two sets of the lethal injection drugs. These measures, scrutinized in *Baze,* sought to ensure that if an insufficient dose of sodium thiopental was initially administered, an additional dose could be given through the back-up line.[42]

The *Baze* case generated multiple opinions, though no attempt was made to reconcile how the Eighth Amendment can—as a matter of logic—simultaneously protect inmates from harm yet authorize their deaths through execution. In a plurality opinion authored by Chief Justice John Roberts, the Supreme Court simply held that Kentucky's protocol was acceptable and that the state's failure to adopt an alternative, allegedly more humane protocol did not render Kentucky's scheme unconstitutional. "[A]n inmate cannot succeed on an Eighth Amendment claim," Chief Justice Roberts wrote, "simply by showing one more step the State could take as a failsafe for other, independently adequate measures." "It is clear," Roberts noted, "that the Constitution does not demand the avoidance of all risk of pain in carrying out executions." Kentucky's death row inmates had proposed an alternative, one-drug protocol that would have dispensed with the use of pancuronium bromide and potassium chloride, but such a protocol at that time had never been adopted or tested by any state for executions. By seeking a barbiturate-only protocol, the inmates in effect had argued for an execution method similar in kind to that routinely used to put animals to sleep. The inmates, in making their arguments, pointed out that twenty-three states actually barred veterinarians from using a neuromuscular paralytic agent such as pancuronium bromide. In denying relief, the U.S. Supreme Court did not focus on the cruelty or unusualness of killing inmates by whatever means. Instead, it merely ruled that the inmates "have not carried their burden of showing that the risk of pain from maladministration of a concededly human lethal injection protocol, and the failure to adopt untried and untested alternatives, constitute cruel and unusual punishment." The risk of improper mixing of chemicals and the risk of improper setting of IVs, the Court held, could not be characterized as "objectively intolerable."[43]

At Death's Door

The heinous crimes committed by the occupants of America's death rows— mostly men, many of whom grew up in extremely violent, abusive households—are unspeakable. These murderers have, in cold blood, killed people, sometimes more than one. And the manner in which they have done so—with semiautomatic assault rifles or sawed-off shotguns, with switchblades or scissors, or with rat poison or their own bare hands—never ceases to shock and offend our collective sensibilities. One need only read judicial opinions in homicide cases, and, in particular, the brutal facts of the crimes, to know the horror of any murder. When Americans read about brutal murders or the gruesome crimes committed by serial killers such as Ted Bundy, John Wayne Gacy, or Jeffrey Dahmer, they recoil in horror. And when on the nightly news they see police tape at a murder scene or the aftermath of violent bloodshed wrought by suicide bombers or other terrorists, they are, more than understandably, angry and irate. If a killer is still alive and is apprehended to face justice, ordinary Americans in large numbers find themselves in the mood for payback, call it retribution, vengeance, or something else. "Revenge is sweet," is an oft-heard refrain, with new brain imaging research suggesting exactly why so much pleasure is derived from retaliating against others for their despicable acts. Using positron-emission tomography technology to measure blood flow in male subjects' brains, researchers found that imposing penalties activates a region of the brain known as the dorsal striatum, a brain region associated with enjoyment and satisfaction. In other words, when something bad happens, people are hardwired to want to exact revenge.[44]

But a more perfect Union—and a less violent society—cannot be achieved by following blind impulses or animalistic urges or instincts. The human desire for vengeance is real, and its power to shape laws, in our time and in much earlier times, cannot be underestimated. At Cingle de la Mola Remigia, on the eastern coast of Spain, four cave paintings dating from 6500 BC depict prehistoric executions, showing the death penalty's longevity and staying power over the centuries. But if Western civilization is to advance, if we are to make our society safer, we must find ways to stop or reduce violence and channel our energies into more productive crime-fighting strategies. Murders are despicable, but so too are executions. Like first-degree murders, executions are, in their own unique way, calculated and premeditated, from the initial capital charging decisions by prosecutors all the way down to the meticulous planning by prison officials of the step-by-step lethal injection protocols. Executions, like homicides, take lives, but a killer's unhinged and murderous rage is perhaps matched only by society's "fry 'em" mentality following the commission of a heinous crime. Without question, murderers must be locked up in maximum-security prisons to protect us, but with the advent of maximum-security prisons and life-without-parole sentences there is no need to kill killers. A government should protect citizens, not commit random acts of cruelty, and only by better understanding the origins and psychology of violence can crimes be more effectively prevented in the future. Just in terms of dollars, death penalty cases on average cost far more than life-without-parole sentences, making more police and prosecutors—and more schoolteachers and social workers—much better investments than executions.[45]

As part of a larger cycle of violence, convicted murderers have themselves often been brutally abused as children, frequently from very young ages. The former death row inmate John Paul Penry, now serving a life-without-parole sentence after a lengthy series of legal battles over his mental capacity, was found to have organic brain damage, an IQ of 54, and the mental capacity of a six-and-a-half-year-old. Penry's mother repeatedly threatened to cut off his genitals and forced him to eat his own feces and drink his own urine, and as a child he was burned, beaten over the head with a belt, deprived of food, and locked in his room for long stretches without access to a toilet. The mentally retarded Mario Marquez—found to have suffered severe brain damage—was mercilessly beaten by his father for being "slow" and then was abandoned by his parents altogether at age twelve. Marquez's father often bound his son's hands and legs, hung him from a pole or tree, beat him with boards, sticks, and fists—and horsewhipped him—until he was unconscious. Before eating his last meal before his execution, Marquez—who raped and strangled his estranged wife and her fourteen-year-old sister, having also once stabbed a fellow inmate with a ballpoint pen—said he wanted to save his apple pie "for later." Another death row inmate, paranoid schizophrenic Charles Walker, had a mother who whipped her son with electrical cords and a dog leash, denied him food, and burned his penis with an iron. Profound child abuse among death row inmates is so common in the literature that it almost qualifies as a cliché. One prior study of fourteen juveniles on death row found that twelve had been brutally abused, with five having been sodomized by older family members. In his book *Base Instincts: What Makes Killers Kill?* neurologist Jonathan Pincus, a leading expert, calls the physical and sexual abuse committed by parents or parental substitutes "pervasive and extreme among the 150 or so murderers I have seen." Frontal lobe dysfunction is common, with clinicians such as Dr. Pincus routinely identifying horrific child abuse and traumatic brain injuries during adolescence. Once studied, the disturbing backgrounds of death row inmates give added force to the poet W. H. Auden's memorable lines: "*I and the public know / What all schoolchildren learn / Those to whom evil is done / Do evil in return.*"[46]

Whether executions themselves deter crime or just brutalize society is a statistically driven debate that rages on, though in many ways it only obscures questions surrounding the morality of executions and impedes the human rights discourse that should be taking place regarding state-sanctioned killing. The modern deterrence debate traces its origins to a 1975 article by economist Isaac Ehrlich claiming that every execution averts eight murders. Ehrlich's flawed study has been thoroughly discredited by social scientists, but the persistent if misguided belief that killing can somehow stop killing has not gone away. This is so even though the United States, which retains the death penalty, has the highest homicide rate of any affluent democracy, nearly four times that of France and the United Kingdom and six times that of Germany, all of which are abolitionist. In truth, FBI data show that, over a twenty-year period, death penalty states' average murder rates—on a per capita basis—were 48 percent to 101 percent higher than those of non–death penalty states. A few academics, throwing fuel on the fire, still make wild, reckless assertions that executions save lives, but their claims are rebutted by the data amassed over time. Proving the deterrent effect of any punishment is of course a tricky business, and that is especially true of one inflicted so infrequently and haphazardly and involving the control of so many variables, such as the characteristics of a particular state's population. Death penalty states' homicide rates, however, have long been—and continue to be—much higher than those of non–death penalty states, with no credible evidence showing that executions deter homicides better than life sentences. "[T]he evidence against capital punishment as an effective deterrent," explain sociologists Ruth Peterson and William Bailey, "is extensive and cannot be dismissed as resulting from theoretical or methodological weaknesses." "[T]he best reading of the accumulated data," add Justin Wolfers and Cass Sunstein, two other well-known academics, "is that they do not establish a deterrent effect of the death penalty." In short, no persuasive proof exists that executions deter homicides any more effectively than a very real and viable substitute: life-without-parole sentences.[47]

The U.S. Supreme Court, viewing deterrence as a rationale for executions, has stated that "[t]he theory of deterrence in capital sentencing is predicated upon the notion that the increased severity of the punishment will inhibit criminal actors from carrying out murderous conduct." Yet murderers are the exact opposite of rational actors; their murderous conduct shows their utter lack of judgment. Neuropsychological studies show, in fact, that the prevalence rate of brain dysfunction among homicide offenders is 94 percent. Poorly educated, hot-headed killers, who often suffer from brain damage or severe mental illnesses, thus can hardly be said to weigh rationally the consequences of their actions, especially when drunk or on drugs, as they frequently are when they commit their crimes. Indeed, the deterrence hypothesis totally breaks down when one considers how the death penalty is administered in practice. Executions are now carried out in private, away from the public eye—a change initiated by nineteenth-century legislators who, history reveals, found executions to be *brutalizing*. Publicity is needed to achieve a deterrent effect, yet news coverage of executions is now hindered by the legal restrictions on TV cameras in execution chambers. Those restrictions have their origins in nineteenth-century laws specifically designed to curtail press coverage of executions, the very thing needed to achieve a deterrent effect, if one were achievable at all. Even if one accepts the convoluted argument that killing can convince others to stop killing, the rarity of executions and the lack of publicity associated with them makes any deterrent effect highly improbable, to say the least. Indeed, only a tiny percentage of murderers are ever sentenced to death, let alone executed. In the United States, more than fifteen thousand murders have taken place every year since 1970, but since that time the annual number of executions has never exceeded one hundred. Because less than one percent of murders ever lead to executions, the deterrence theory is especially implausible. It is thus rather Orwellian to contend that killing criminals somehow "saves" lives. In fact, the vast majority of police chiefs and criminologists, as reflected in surveys, do not believe executions effectively deter murder.[48]

As a class, killers are simply not the kind of people one would expect to be deterred from committing violent crimes. They often kill intimates or loved ones. They are often drug addicts and alcoholics, are poor and mostly uneducated, or suffer from head injuries or brain damage. Many death row inmates have been found to be mentally retarded, homeless, illiterate, suicidal, or to be suffering from profound depression or debilitating diseases such as paranoid schizophrenia, post-traumatic stress disorder (PTSD), or other severe mental illnesses. For example, the recent U.S. Supreme Court case of *Panetti v. Quarterman* dealt with a capital defendant hospitalized in institutions over a dozen times for schizophrenia, schizoaffective disorder, bipolar disorder, depression, psychosis, and bizarre hallucinations. Scott Panetti, who killed his in-laws in 1992, chose to represent himself at trial, a trial in which he wore a cowboy outfit and attempted to subpoena John F. Kennedy, the Pope, and Jesus Christ. In *Panetti,* the Supreme Court, invoking the Eighth Amendment, held only that the prisoner's documented delusions should have been considered when determining whether he was competent to be executed. Though estimates vary, anywhere between 4 and 20 percent of death row inmates may be mentally retarded and as many as 70 percent of such inmates likely suffer from some form of schizophrenia or psychosis. Death row inmates regularly fall below the poverty line, a number can neither read nor write, and many are high school dropouts. Almost 27 percent of Mississippi death row inmates registered verbal IQ scores of 74 or below, putting them in the mild mental retardation range, with less than 10 percent of those inmates graduating from high school.[49]

The life stories of death row inmates are usually as tragic as their childhoods. Convicted murderer Michael Correll, for instance, endured endless child abuse, with evidence of incest in the family and the neglect of his most basic needs. At age seven, a brick wall collapsed on his head, rendering him unconscious, but his parents failed to seek any medical care for several days. Other inmates had drug addicts or alcoholics for caregivers, a parent who died of a heroin overdose, or a mother who drank heavily during pregnancy. Michael Worthington, convicted of burglarizing, raping, and strangling a woman after drinking heavily and using crack cocaine for several days, likewise had a long history of abuse and neglect. His alcoholic mother, sixteen when she became pregnant, was a prostitute who had sex and abused drugs in front of Worthington when he was a child. At one point, Worthington and his mother lived out of a car until it was sold for drug money, and when Worthington checked into a drug rehabilitation program and underwent psychiatric treatment his family members were unsupportive. Worthington's mother also attempted suicide numerous times in her son's presence, while Worthington's absentee father, a heroin addict, was often in jail. The father had virtually no contact with his son until he was an adolescent, when he introduced his son to drugs and taught his son how to burglarize homes. Donald Gunsby, on Florida's death row before evidence of his mental retardation was brought to light by a group of Minnesota lawyers, was raised in former slave quarters in rural Florida, was neglected as a child, had no birth certificate or driver's license, read at a fourth-grade level, and had an IQ of less than 59. One judge, calling Gunsby "delusional" and "a seriously emotionally disturbed man-child," concluded that "Gunsby's mind operates at the level of a child"; another, noting that Gunsby suffered from organic brain damage, ruefully reported that Gunsby "does not know how many months are in a year or in what direction the sun rises."[50]

In a more recent case, that of Texas death row inmate Bruce Webster, the U.S. Court of Appeals for the Fifth Circuit simply refused to consider new evidence that would have established Webster's mental retardation, because of the wording in a procedural provision of the Antiterrorism and Effective Death Penalty Act of 1996. Webster had been sentenced to death in 1996 for his role in the kidnapping and brutal murder of a sixteen-year-old girl, and he had lost his direct appeal challenging the district court's finding that he was not mentally retarded. After the Fifth Circuit affirmed that result, however, newly discovered evidence, in the form of testimony and government and school records, came to light that Webster contended conclusively proved his mental retardation, thus warranting that his death sentence be set aside. Ruling that a provision in federal law allowed Webster to challenge only his conviction and not his actual sentence, the Fifth Circuit refused to set aside Webster's death sentence. Though Circuit Judge Jacques Wiener, an appointee of George H.W. Bush, concurred in the result because of the wording of the statute, he wrote separately to complain of the "absurdity" of the "Kafkaesque result." "Because Webster seeks to demonstrate only that he is constitutionally ineligible for the death penalty—and not that he is factually innocent of the crime—we must sanction his execution," Judge Wiener wrote in April 2010. "If the evidence that Webster attempts to introduce here were ever presented to a judge or jury for consideration on the merits, it is virtually guaranteed that he would be found to be mentally retarded," Wiener said, pointing out that in 1993, prior to Webster's indictment for the murder, three physicians had independently concluded that Webster was mentally retarded in the context of an application for Social Security benefits. Although Webster's counsel had requested such Social Security records long before trial, they were produced only recently and in fact refuted much of the evidence introduced by the government at the penalty phase of Webster's trial. At trial, the government's physicians, all of whom examined Webster after he was incarcerated, suggested that he was malingering and exaggerating his symptoms to qualify for exemption from the death penalty under the controlling precedent of *Atkins v. Virginia*. "Although I concur in the majority's opinion as to the correct statement of the law," Wiener lamented, "I continue to harbor a deep and unsettling conviction that, albeit under Congress's instruction which ties our judicial hands so illogically, we today have no choice but to condone just such an unconstitutional punishment."[51]

Occasionally, an abuse victim's military combat experience leaves that person especially scarred and unable to cope with life's pressures. In the case of George Porter, a decorated Korean War veteran who killed his ex-girlfriend and her lover, the U.S. Supreme Court itself noted that Porter's combat service, for which he received two Purple Hearts and the Combat Infantryman Badge, "unfortunately left him a traumatized, changed man." After noting that Porter was abused as a child and that his father was violent every weekend, with Porter himself a "favorite target," the Court pointed out that Porter's father once beat his pregnant wife so severely that she had to be hospitalized and lost a child. After enlisting in the army at age seventeen to escape his horrendous family life, Porter suffered a gunshot wound to his leg while his division advanced above the 38th parallel to Kunu-ri. His squad, after being in constant contact with the enemy for five days with little or no sleep or food, engaged in fierce hand-to-hand combat with Chinese forces. In a second battle, Porter was wounded again, and his company sustained the heaviest losses of any unit in that battle, with a casualty rate of more than 50 percent. After he went AWOL on returning to the United States, Porter was discharged from the army and began drinking so heavily that he got into fights and did not remember them. He also suffered dreadful nightmares and attempted to climb his bedroom walls with knives at night, prompting Porter's family to remove all knives from the house. Experts later testified that Porter had brain damage that could manifest itself in impulsive, violent behavior, cognitive defects, and substantial difficulty reading or writing, and that his symptoms would "easily" warrant a diagnosis of PTSD.[52]

Whatever the facts of a particular case, horrendous childhood abuse, severe mental illnesses, and tragic home lives are pervasive among death row inmates. In 2009, one Texas death row inmate, twenty-five-year-old Andre Thomas, actually gouged out his only good eye and then ate it. Thomas, who fatally stabbed his estranged wife and her two children in 2005, had known mental health issues and had gouged out his other eye while awaiting trial for the murders. In spite of his self-mutilating behavior, Thomas had been found competent to stand trial after he was placed on Zyprexa, a strong antipsychotic drug, and several psychiatrists and psychologists examined him, with two of them diagnosing him as "malingering." In what it called "an extraordinarily tragic case" because his mental illness had gone untreated before the murders, the Texas Court of Criminal Appeals reported that Thomas had "a severe mental illness"; "suffers from psychotic delusions and perhaps from schizophrenia"; "has a long history of drug and alcohol abuse"; "was frequently truant" and "quit school in the ninth grade"; "had a series of juvenile and adult arrests"; "had been abusing alcohol since age ten and marijuana since age thirteen"; and, "in the month before the murders, had been taking large doses of Coricidin, a cold medicine, for recreational purposes." Thomas's mother Rochelle, the court said, was mentally ill, as were all three of her sons. One of Thomas's brothers had also previously been diagnosed as schizophrenic. In the months before the murders, Thomas's behavior became stranger and stranger. He put duct tape over his mouth and refused to speak; talked about how the dollar bill contains the meaning of life; said he was experiencing déjà vu and heard the voice of God; and spoke in front of others about his auditory and visual hallucinations of God and demons. Despite being jobless and broke, he burned a one-hundred-dollar bill he won gambling, announcing that "Money is the root of all evil!" as he placed it in an ashtray and lit it on fire.[53]

Thomas's behavior, both in and out of prison, can only be described as bizarre. While the Texas Court of Criminal Appeals stated that Thomas "is clearly 'crazy,'" it found that "he is also 'sane' under Texas law." About twenty days before the killings, Thomas took drugs and tried to take his own life by overdosing; and two days before the murders, he drank vodka and took ten Coricidin tablets before stabbing himself. After a neighbor's son took him to a mental health center, he threatened to throw himself in front of a bus if he could not talk to someone, said he would shoot himself if he had a gun, and told the staff: "Life is too much for me to handle. I want to die right now." After making a reference to Star Trek and saying that he stabbed himself to try to "cross over into heaven," an involuntary commitment order was obtained but unfortunately was never implemented. According to Thomas's statement to authorities, in the days leading up to the murders he came to believe that God wanted him to kill his wife Laura because she was "Jezebel." Thomas called his four-year-old son Andre Jr. the "Anti-Christ" and further stated that his wife's thirteen-month-old daughter Leyha "was involved with it also." Thomas had delusional obsessions regarding his wife's cheating on him by having sex with members of his family; said God told him that he needed to stab and kill his wife and the kids using three different knives so as not to "cross contaminate" their blood and "allow the demons inside them to live"; and, when he committed his crime, proceeded to use a different knife on each victim. Following the murders, Thomas carved out the children's hearts and stuffed them in his pockets but mistakenly cut out his wife's lung instead of her heart, putting that in his pocket too. Thomas then stabbed himself in the heart to "assure the death of the demons that had inhabited his wife and the children," though, surprisingly, he did not die, whereupon he walked home, changed clothes, put the hearts into a paper bag, and threw them in the trash. After that, he called Laura's parents and asked for help on a chilling voicemail, saying, "I think I'm in hell. I need help. Somebody needs to come and help me. I need help bad. I'm desperate. I'm afraid to go to sleep. So when you get this message, come by the house, please. Hello?"[54]

After Thomas told his girlfriend and his cousin what he had done, his girlfriend took him to the police station where he confessed. Thomas later told one psychologist that he had been using large quantities of Coricidin in the days and weeks leading up to the murders, telling another psychologist that he and his girlfriend took up to ten pills a day, mixed with alcohol and marijuana, to get "a high." Thomas's mother saw her family's delusions as "gifts" that gave them "superior powers." "God talks to them" and gives them "visions," she said. Thomas himself thought Coricidin "brings perspective to the whole world," calling it a "reality breakthrough drug." After being hospitalized for his chest wound, he was taken to jail and gave a videotaped statement to the police. Thomas explained at one point that he was a "fallen angel" who could "open the gates of Heaven" by stabbing himself in the heart and killing himself. Though the self-inflicted stab wound turned out not to be life-threatening, he did not understand why he did not die and concluded as a result that he was "immortal." While reading his Bible in his cell five days after the murders, Thomas read a verse to the effect that, "If the right eye offends thee, pluck it out," whereupon he did just that. Three psychologists thereafter concluded that he was not then competent to stand trial. After just five weeks of treatment and medication in the Vernon State Hospital, however, Thomas was found to have regained his competency. Only after a jury rejected his insanity defense and sentenced him to death, and Thomas plucked out his left eye, his last one, was he sent to a prison psychiatric facility near Houston. Before the murders, Thomas had suffered from severe depression and twice been evaluated for psychiatric problems while jailed for stabbing his brother, though in that instance Thomas was released without prosecution after it was found he had acted in self-defense. A Dr. Axelrad noted that Thomas "has experienced psychotic behavior and psychotic symptoms, which appear to be strongly associated with the use of drugs and alcohol since his early adolescence."[55]

David Rice, still another mentally ill inmate, suffered abuse, had a troubled childhood, and developed a paranoid delusional disorder, believing he was a "soldier" in a battle against Communism. Convinced that he had a "black box" in his head into which he put unsolvable problems, that a nuclear war was imminent, and that extraterrestrials gave him advice, Rice wanted to build a large underground shelter in Colorado so that he and hundreds of other people could emerge after radiation had dissipated to create a new society. Unemployed, deeply in debt, and believing that a Communist plot was afoot to take over America, Rice—using chloroform to render a couple and their two young boys unconscious before bludgeoning them with a steam iron and using a fillet knife to stab them—murdered an entire family in 1985 on Christmas Eve. Rice believed that he was in a battle with Satan and that Charles Goodmark, one of his victims, was a member of the local Communist Party. Now serving a life sentence, Rice was originally sentenced to death in absentia—that is, outside the jury's presence—because he was too ill to be at the sentencing. In an apparent suicide attempt, Rice had ingested a nicotine drink brewed from cigarettes, something he had a history of doing and had actually done on the day of his arrest. The overdose made Rice unresponsive and required that his stomach be pumped at the hospital while the jury sentenced him to die.[56]

In capital cases, serious mental health issues often raise questions of competency or insanity, or both. In *State v. Perry*, a Louisiana case, Michael Perry was sentenced to die for murdering his mother, father, two cousins, and a nephew in 1983. Twenty-eight at the time of the murders, Perry was still living with his parents due to a long history of mental illness. He had been diagnosed as schizophrenic at age sixteen; had been committed to mental institutions by his parents several times because of psychotic episodes; and, after twice escaping mental facilities, was forced to sleep in a shed behind his parents' house because of his disruptive behavior. As the Louisiana Supreme Court later reported: "Perry's mental illness raised legal issues throughout the criminal proceedings." Likewise, moments after murdering a white police officer, convicted killer Ricky Ray Rector—a black man who had also killed a man at a restaurant—shot himself in the forehead, inflicting severe brain damage. After being sentenced to death despite conflicting evidence regarding his competency, Rector—still suffering the effects of his self-inflicted gunshot wound—was executed by the State of Arkansas. So mentally impaired was Rector that, just an hour before then-Governor Bill Clinton presided over the execution, Rector saw a television newscast about Clinton's alleged affair with Gennifer Flowers and said that he might vote for him. After the execution, prison guards found an untouched slice of pecan pie from Rector's final meal in his cell. While incarcerated, Rector always saved his dessert until bedtime, with his lawyers reporting that he left the pie because he believed he would be returning to his cell and did not know that he was about to die.[57]

Intermittently insane death row inmates occasionally are even forcibly medicated to make them mentally competent to be executed. That is precisely what happened in 2003, when the Eighth Circuit, on a six-to-five vote, approved the forcible medication and subsequent execution of Charles Singleton. Convicted of aggravated robbery and the 1979 murder of Mary Lou York in Hamburg, Arkansas, Singleton had entered York's Grocery at 7:30 p.m., grabbed Mrs. York, and then stabbed her twice in the neck. Mrs. York was rushed to the hospital in an ambulance, but she lost too much blood and died before reaching the emergency room. The aggravated robbery conviction was set aside, but Singleton's capital murder conviction stood up on appeal, with his execution originally slated for 1982. The mentally ill Singleton was initially prescribed medication to alleviate anxiety and depression. Following delays, however, his mental health deteriorated in 1987. He said his cell was possessed by demons and had "demon blood" in it; that his brother would come to his locked prison cell and take him out for walks; and that a prison doctor had planted a device in his right ear to steal his thoughts when he read the Bible. Singleton was diagnosed as probably schizophrenic and was placed on antipsychotic medication that he sometimes took voluntarily and sometimes refused. When off of his medication, his symptoms recurred, he engaged in self-mutilation, and he experienced hallucinations. Singleton lost weight and became paranoid and delusional, stripping off his clothes, speaking unintelligibly and in a strange language, and saying that he was the victim of a voodoo curse, that his food was worms, and that he had already been executed.[58]

Following a series of appeals, Singleton claimed he was incompetent to be executed. His claim was based upon *Ford v. Wainwright,* the Supreme Court case holding that the Eighth Amendment bars the execution of insane prisoners. Alvin Ford was a disturbed and mentally ill prisoner who referred to himself as a religious leader, believed he had appointed members of the Florida Supreme Court, and spoke in a bizarre, alphanumeric code. After he refused his medication and a medical review panel found that he posed a danger to himself and others, Singleton was involuntarily medicated with antipsychotic drugs. But Singleton's legal saga—with judges evaluating his sanity—did not end there. By 1997, observers noted, Singleton's symptoms had worsened. Singleton told the prison staff that he was "on a mission from God" to kill his treating physician and the President, had been "freed by the Eighth Circuit and the U.S. Supreme Court," and was "God and the Supreme Court." Nude and described by the prison staff as "zombie-like," Singleton displayed a vacant stare after tearing up his mattress and flushing it, flooding his cell. At times referring to himself as "the Holy Spirit" and "the Holy Ghost," Singleton said that he was writing a book at God's request, that he and St. John were on a mission to fight homosexuality, and that Sylvester Stallone and Arnold Schwarzenegger were somewhere between this universe and another one, trying to save him. In 2001, Singleton sent a letter directly to the Eighth Circuit declaring that Mrs. York was not dead and that she "is somewhere on this earth waiting for me—her groom." Although the Louisiana case *State v. Perry* had found that the state's constitution forbade forcibly medicating an insane inmate into competency for the purpose of execution, the Eighth Circuit held that neither due process nor the Eighth Amendment precluded that approach. The Eighth Circuit thus rejected the ethical concerns of doctors, who now face the unsettling prospect of treating an inmate not to improve his health but simply to make him eligible for execution. After the U.S. Supreme Court refused to hear his case, Singleton was executed.[59]

The backgrounds of death row inmates, many of whom suffer from strange delusions, hallucinations, or intermittent episodes of insanity, stand in sharp contrast to those of state and federal judges who sit in judgment in capital cases. For example, the nine Justices of the U.S. Supreme Court, who sit atop America's court system, were educated at renowned institutions of higher education, with Ivy League schools and diplomas galore. They received undergraduate degrees at Harvard College, Princeton University, Stanford University, Cornell University, Georgetown University, and Holy Cross College. They studied overseas at the London School of Economics, Oxford University, or the University of Fribourg in Switzerland. Five of the Justices earned law degrees from top-ranked Harvard Law School; three graduated from Yale Law School, its equally prestigious counterpart; and one attended Columbia Law School, another first-tier school. Before joining the nation's highest court, the Justices worked as judicial clerks, as law professors and corporate counsel, and as partners at major law firms. They also served in a variety of high-level positions: as bar leaders or agency heads, as lawyers or special assistants at the U.S. Department of Justice, as judges on the U.S. courts of appeals, and as counselors to U.S. Presidents. Unlike death row inmates, these men and women had tremendous opportunities and, by any measure, have led privileged lives.[60]

It seems incongruous that judges with such respected pedigrees should spend their days donning black robes and deciding whether overwhelmingly poor, uneducated inmates should live or die. Is there not something terribly amiss when such highly educated jurists spend their time parsing the lexicon of death, arguing over "special issues" and "aggravating" and "mitigating" factors, as human lives—already shattered by abuse, poverty, and the isolation of prison life—literally hang in the balance? It goes without saying that murderers are sick, mentally unstable people who have committed vile acts. After all, if not for being socially deviant and mentally disturbed, why else would they have acted the way they have? They certainly deserve to be punished and incarcerated for their crimes, and life-without-parole sentences are plainly necessary to protect society from such violent, highly volatile individuals. But what does it say about American culture—and, for that matter, American law— when our most respected figures, our governors and our state and federal judges, execute death warrants or cause executions to be carried out? And what does it say about our legal culture when four U.S. Supreme Court Justices—the number necessary for a grant of certiorari—agree to hear a case, only to have the Court itself let the execution go forward anyway, because a fifth vote, the one necessary to obtain a stay, cannot be mustered until the appeal can be heard? The death penalty, aggressively pursued in individual cases for years or decades at a time by a handful of mostly Southern prosecutors hungry to put notches on their belts, is, it seems, every bit as calculated as any premeditated killing.[61]

The death penalty, carried out arbitrarily and in a racially discriminatory fashion, raises all kinds of moral and ethical questions given the ready availability of life-without-parole sentences. Should we derive any satisfaction from the fact that deranged people—and no doubt a few innocent ones—are being put to death on our behalf, in our names? Is justice really furthered by killing killers? Or should we take any solace in the fact that we, by executing inmates, are stooping to the level of the killers themselves? And what about the stigma and pain society inflicts on the mothers and fathers and sons and daughters of those we execute? Homicides inflict untold suffering on murder victims' families, but murders cannot be undone. The family members of death row inmates, already dealing with the trauma of their relation's horrendous homicidal act, also experience still more grief and anguish after an execution. Death row inmates have, on average, eight significant family relationships, be they children, parents, spouses, siblings, or extended family members. Not only do capital jurors suffer adverse physical and psychological symptoms from jury duty in death penalty cases, but death row inmates' relatives and friends, stigmatized and depressed by state-sanctioned killings, have developed serious medical problems or even attempted suicide as a result of executions. While jurors suffer stomach and chest pains, headaches, heart palpitations, and depression, the relatives of the condemned suffer from a wide array of ills of their own, including migraine headaches, panic attacks, high blood pressure, uncontrollable crying, nightmares, and sleepless nights. One woman actually died of a heart attack before her son's execution, her daughter remarking that her mother simply could not cope with the impending execution. Given the severe mental anguish and distress caused by executions, perhaps it is time to ponder again the eighteenth-century wisdom of Dr. James McHenry, a close friend of Dr. Benjamin Rush, who once urged mercy for Pennsylvania mutineers. "Our national character," he said, "can never be supported by a sacrifice of national humanity." As McHenry concluded: "I have always thought, and the history of all nations teach me that I am right that *acts of mercy* serve more to dignify and raise the character of a government than *acts of blood*."[62]

The Transformation of American Law

Executions in the United States were once rowdy, public affairs, attended by hundreds or thousands of spectators. Such spectacles were often accompanied by drunkenness, merriment, and the commission of crimes in the very shadow of the gallows. At the 1822 execution of John Lechler in Pennsylvania, pickpockets worked the crowd, and at least fifteen of the twenty thousand spectators were arrested, one for larceny, another for murder, and still others for assault and battery or vagrancy. The widespread belief that such scenes only brutalized society prompted legislators to relocate executions indoors, behind thick prison walls. In moving executions into the controlled environment of prisons, state legislatures, eager to curtail public information about these gruesome spectacles, often simultaneously enacted gag laws restricting newspaper coverage and requiring private, nighttime executions. Such laws—contemporaries sarcastically dubbed Minnesota's the "midnight assassination law"—typically limited attendance to six to twelve "reputable" or "respectable" citizens, barred reporters from attending executions, and even made it a crime to report execution details. So concerned did politicians become about the brutality and demoralizing tendencies of executions that in 1893, one state—Connecticut—passed a private execution law permitting only "adult males" to attend executions. The ritual of American executions, now universally hidden from public view, thus became visible to only a handful of official witnesses and a few handpicked media representatives.[63]

Not only did removing executions from the public eye radically alter America's death penalty debate, but the move to nighttime executions, as well as changes in the method of execution, shaped the debate too. The passage of nighttime execution laws, requiring hangings "before sunrise" or between, for example, midnight and 3:00 a.m., as Delaware law still provides, made clear that legislators wanted to shield the public and the press from executions. Such laws, first passed in the 1880s in the midwestern states of Ohio, Indiana, and

Minnesota, were soon replicated around the country, forcing executions into the dead of night. From 1977 to 1995, more than 80 percent of all American executions took place between the hours of 11:00 p.m. and 7:30 a.m., with over half of all executions taking place between midnight and 1:00 a.m. Though executions in a few states have migrated back to daylight hours to make last-minute appeals more convenient for judges' schedules and court personnel, executions remain cloaked in secrecy and shrouded in darkness. By law or regulation, cameras—capable of capturing gritty, powerful images on film—are excluded from execution chambers, leading to much public apathy when it comes to executions. Unlike in the heyday of public executions, when such spectacles fomented much antigallows activity, the rise of private, nighttime executions made it literally true that Americans for decades were not only uninformed but often fast asleep when executions took place.[64]

The way in which criminals have been punished or executed over the years also shows the public's shifting attitudes toward the death penalty and the intentional infliction of pain. In medieval and colonial times, as well as in England and early America, capital and corporal punishments were the norm for certain crimes. The stocks and the pillory were designed to humiliate and shame offenders, and executions—those civil and religious ceremonies intended to promote order—were gruesome public events that often provoked disorder and crime. Not only were corporal punishments abandoned over time as societal mores changed, but the continual search for more "humane" ways to put inmates to death shows just how uncomfortable people were, and are, with regard to executions. The preferred method of execution in America has shifted from hanging and the firing squad, to electrocution and the gas chamber, to what we have predominantly today: clinical, state-run lethal injection. The vast majority of post-1976 executions have been lethal injections, and all states now authorize lethal injection as the sole or primary method of execution. Though hardly error-free, lethal injection protocols aim to make capital punishment look more like a medical procedure than a killing. A death by chemicals, of course, only masks the horror of executions, which—method, timing, and locale aside—still serve one, and only one, purpose: to kill inmates.[65]

Despite the legal profession's oversight of sporadic executions, medical professionals now largely shun these veiled rituals that predate the Dark Ages. Following the Hippocratic oath to do no harm, the American Medical Association (AMA) considers it an ethical violation for doctors to take part in executions. While death row inmates in some places can, by law, be forcibly medicated to make them competent for execution, the AMA's Council on Ethical and Judicial Affairs specifically advises physicians not to treat death row inmates for the purpose of restoring competency once declarations of incompetence are made. The American Psychological Association, the American Psychiatric Association, the American Nurses Association, the American Public Health Association, the National Association of Emergency Medical Technicians, and the World Medical Association also prohibit member participation in executions. The well-known American lawyer and jurist Benjamin Cardozo, speaking in 1929 to a group of physicians, himself expressed the view that "enlightenment" would come not from lawyers and judges alone, but only through the "combined labors" of many professions, most of all those in his audience that day. Urging doctors to "hold the torch that will explore the dark mystery of crime—the mystery, even darker, of the criminal himself," Cardozo, predicting that his own descendants would regard the punishments of his day "with the same surprise and horror" with which his generation viewed England's bloody code, freely acknowledged that "[t]he law, like medicine, has its record of blunders and blindness and superstitions and even cruelties." Time no doubt will prove that judges and lawyers still have much to learn from those in the healing arts, the doctors, the nurses, and the mental health professionals. "Lethal injection was not anesthesiology's idea," Dr. Orrin F. Guidry, the president of the American Society of Anesthesiologists, said in a strongly worded statement advising members not to get involved in executions. "The legal system," he said, speaking of the problems associated with capital punishment and lethal injections, "has painted itself into this corner and it is not our obligation to get it out." In 2011, death row inmates sued the Food and Drug Administration for failing to monitor the importation of lethal drugs, and the only American producer of sodium thiopental, Illinois-based Hospira Inc., announced that it would stop selling the lethal injection drug. Hospira had planned to manufacture the drug in Italy, but Italian authorities had insisted on a guarantee that the drug would not be used in executions. This series of events contributed to a severe shortage of the drug in Texas and elsewhere.[66]

Physicians, through their testimony and medical judgments, have long shaped the death penalty debate, whether by offering evidence of an inmate's incompetence or insanity, or by refusing to participate in a particular execution. Albert Deutsch, in *The Mentally Ill in America*, devotes a whole chapter to Dr. Benjamin Rush, calling him the "Father of American Psychiatry," and since Rush's time, medical professionals have routinely testified in capital cases. The failure to present such critical testimony is in fact often a major focus of ineffective assistance of counsel claims. In 2006, one inmate, Michael Morales, was just hours away from execution when two anesthesiologists, citing ethical reasons, refused to participate in his lethal injection, leading to its suspension. Though early American physicians were prominent execution attendees, more and more of these professionals are staying away from—and saying no to—executions. A few doctors, motivated by support for capital punishment or a desire to alleviate a painful death, still participate in executions in violation of the AMA's code. But when they do, they—like executioners—take extreme measures to shield their identities. In Florida, doctors hired to monitor and participate in lethal injections wear purple "moon suits" and goggles to conceal their identities from witnesses. Such evasive measures closely resemble the way in which executioners' identities are routinely concealed. Florida executioners still wear black hoods at executions, and under a now-defunct Illinois law, executioners were once paid in cash for their services to shield their identities. In the state of Washington, when Charles Campbell went to the gallows shortly after midnight in 1994, the executioner's identity was masked by blinds, allowing official witnesses to see only his silhouette. And a Missouri law passed in 2007 made it unlawful to reveal an executioner's identity after a doctor revealed that, in some of the fifty-plus lethal injections he had participated in, he gave condemned inmates smaller doses of a sedative than what was called for by the state's protocol because he is dyslexic. The doctor, it was revealed, had been frequently sued for malpractice, with his privileges having been revoked at two hospitals.[67]

While the execution of America's mentally ill offenders continues unabated, there has in actuality long been a consensus in both the medical and legal professions against the execution of the insane, a practice William Blackstone branded as "savage and inhuman." Though mentally retarded offenders may no longer be executed under the auspices of American law, at least if they assert their legal claims at the right time and are allowed to present their evidence, and though our understanding of complex, often unfathomable mental illnesses is still in its formative stages, the consensus against executing the insane dates back centuries, even before America's founding in 1776. "[I]diots and lunatics," Blackstone said, using the terminology of the day, "are not chargeable for their own acts, if committed when under these incapacities: no, not even for treason itself." "Also," Blackstone added, "if a man in his sound memory commits a capital offense, and before arraignment for it, he becomes mad, he ought not to be arraigned for it: because he is not able to plead to it with that advice and caution that he ought. And if, after he has pleaded, the prisoner becomes mad, he shall not be tried: for how can he make his defence?" "If, after he be tried and found guilty, he loses his senses before judgment," Blackstone continued, "judgment shall not be pronounced; and if, after judgment, he becomes of nonsane memory, execution shall be stayed: for peradventure, says the humanity of the English law, had the prisoner been of sound memory, he might have alleged something in stay of judgment or execution." Other leading legal luminaries, including Sir Edward Coke, concurred, viewing the common law in a similar vein. "[B]y intendment of Law the execution of the offender is for example," Coke wrote, "but so it is not when a mad man is executed, but should be a miserable spectacle, both against Law, and of extream inhumanity and cruelty, and can be no example to others."[68]

As the fields of neurology, psychology, and psychiatry progress, and as mental health issues are taken more seriously, it seems only a matter of time before the consensus against executing the insane and the mentally retarded is extended to cover those suffering from severe mental illnesses. The exact number of death row inmates with such mental illnesses is unknown, though it has been estimated by the American Civil Liberties Union that since 1983 more than sixty people diagnosed as mentally ill or mentally retarded have been executed in the United States. Other organizations and scholars estimate the figure of mentally ill or chronically psychotic death row inmates to be substantially higher. A BBC report placed the number at approximately 10 percent, but some clinical studies have found the number to be in the realm of 40 to 70 percent. Indeed, reform is already afoot in the legal and medical professions, as well as in the legislative arena. The American Bar Association, the American Psychological Association, the American Psychiatric Association, and the National Alliance for the Mentally Ill have all called for a stop to the execution of those inmates who are seriously mentally ill. In 2007, North Carolina's legislature considered a bill to prohibit the execution of those with a "severe mental disability," and in 2008, two organizations—Murder Victims' Families for Human Rights and the National Alliance on Mental Illness—launched a national project concerned with the death penalty's intersection with the mentally ill. In 2000, the UN Commission on Human Rights specifically asked all countries that still use the death penalty "not to impose it on a person suffering from any form of mental disorder; not to execute any such person." "Severe mental illness," writes one scholar, "is the next frontier for the Court's new Eighth Amendment jurisprudence."[69]

Today, American law and the law of nations—now known as international law—are vastly different from what they were in colonial times. Though English and American legislatures once used bills of attainder to sentence people to death in the absence of a jury, American law no longer allows that to happen. In fact, many of the Founding Fathers, as reflected in the Constitution's prohibition of that erstwhile legal device, themselves vehemently opposed their use. John Marshall, responding to Patrick Henry's expression of support for bills of attainder, asked: "Can we pretend to the enjoyment of political freedom or security when we are told that a man has been, by an act of Assembly, struck out of existence without being confronted with his accusers and witnesses, without the benefits of the law of the land?" Marshall, who later lodged in Paris during the XYZ Affair with the beautiful Marquise de Villette, a woman raised by Voltaire and whose mansion was an homage to Voltaire, continued: "Where is our safety, when we are told that this act was justifiable because the person was not a Socrates? What has become of the worthy member's maxims? Is this one of them? Shall it be a maxim that a man shall be deprived of life without the benefit of law?" James Madison himself railed against bills of attainder. Quoting Baron de Montesquieu on the evils of giving judicial powers to the legislative branch, Madison wrote in *The Federalist No. 47:* "Again, 'Were the power of judging joined with the legislative, the life and liberty of the subject would be exposed to arbitrary control, for *the judge* would then be *the legislator.*'" In 1788, Edmund Randolph—the man who served as

Virginia's attorney general and as the country's first United States Attorney General—called the bill of attainder in the Josiah Philips case a "horrid" and "striking" example of how a man could be "deprived of his life" from "a mere reliance on general reports" that someone had "committed several crimes." "Was this arbitrary deprivation of life, the dearest gift of God to man," he asked, "consistent with the genius of a republican government?" "Without being confronted with his accusers and witnesses, without the privilege of calling for evidence in his behalf, he was sentenced to death, and was afterwards actually executed," Randolph noted, adding: "I cannot contemplate it without horror."[70]

Truth be told, ordinary citizens have never been entirely at ease with state-sanctioned killing, whether of mentally ill inmates or of others. Over two centuries ago, Beccaria himself recognized the extraordinary ambivalence that ordinary citizens feel toward executions and executioners, those who carry out the public's cry for vengeance. "What are the sentiments of each individual regarding the death penalty?" Beccaria asked. "We may read them," he offered, "in the attitudes of indignation and contempt with which everyone views the hangman, who is, to be sure, an innocent executor of the public will." European executioners sometimes had their houses painted red; their daughters were forbidden to marry outside the profession; and English and American hangmen were recruited from pools of condemned inmates—inmates who got reprieves if they agreed to serve as executioners. Much of the public's unease and discomfort with executioners, it seems clear, arises from the fact that with the advent of penitentiaries, executions are no longer necessary to ensure society's safety. In his diary, John Adams himself recorded in Italian a line from Beccaria's *On Crimes and Punishments: "Le Pene che oltre passano la necessita di conservare il deposito della Salute pubblica, sono ingiuste di lor natura."* The translation: "All punishments that go beyond the requirements of public safety are by their very nature unjust."[71]

While the law's universal disdain for murder has long been reflected in statutes making homicide a criminal offense, the law has—for whatever reason—long tolerated the killing of criminals under the guise of "justifiable homicide." When John Adams defended the accused in the Boston Massacre, he instructed the all-male jury on the law of homicide, manslaughter, and self-defense, telling jurors that if "a sheriff execute a man on the gallows, draws and quarters him, as in case of high treason, and cuts off his head, this is justifiable homicide, it is his duty." It has long been true, as Adams told jurors in 1770, that those who slay someone in self-defense or who carry out a state-sanctioned execution have a justifiable legal defense when they kill. Executioners, however, kill inmates who are strapped down to a gurney and immobilized. Unlike the typical case of self-defense, where some imminent danger to a person necessitates or warrants the use of deadly force, no such danger is present when a bound inmate is executed within the confines of a prison. If the

Cruel and Unusual Punishments Clause protects defenseless inmates from harm, and—as noted—it generally does, why is it that executioners are by law expressly permitted to kill such inmates? The Eighth Amendment already protects inmates from gratuitous beatings, secondhand smoke, and daylong episodes of handcuffing in the hot sun, yet perversely the law still allows bound prisoners to be deliberately killed. If the Eighth Amendment were interpreted in a truly *principled* fashion, surely executions would be outlawed and the centuries-old profession of the executioner would earn its long-deserved retirement.[72]

Judges and lawyers, who keep executioners in business, would be well advised to take a cue from what has already happened in the medical profession. Physicians, who once proudly or squeamishly stood by to pronounce the precise hour and minute of an inmate's death, now regularly excuse themselves from executions. How long, one wonders, will it take for judges, juries, and lawyers also to stop participating in executions? Why, after all, should judges or juries have to approve killings as part of their duties? And why should members of the bar have to advocate that other human beings die as part of their jobs? As a society, we certainly do not hold up executioners—those who deliver the deadly intravenous drugs at lethal injections—as role models for our children. Parents want their children to grow up to be doctors or lawyers, teachers or successful business people, police officers or firefighters, maybe even a President of the United States. Executioners, though, never make the list. Why? Because what executioners do—kill people who are strapped down on prison gurneys—is so undignified, so uncivilized. The death of a deranged criminal may be quickly forgotten, but for the executioners, the faces of the condemned are forever seared in their memories. One never sees governors or federal judges pulling the switch or pushing the buttons that activate lethal injection machines. No, that would be far too unseemly. Instead, legislators, governors, and judges direct wardens and prison guards, whose identities are zealously protected for their own sake, to carry out executions, to do what few people would want to do themselves.[73]

Because we let them, the gears of America's death penalty machine thus slowly grind on, taking lives and upending the lives of those who administer the lethal chemicals. Because executions—however rare—remain legal, they continue to be carried out using deadly equipment designed and supplied by the likes of Fred Leuchter, a Holocaust denier found to have been practicing engineering without a license. It is the men and women tasked with killing killers, meanwhile, who face the real human consequences wrought by death sentences and executions. As a result of their work, they suffer migraine headaches, loss of sleep, recurring nightmares, even debilitating mental breakdowns. Prison officials have resorted to setting up counseling sessions and "stress inoculation" programs for execution participants, and for Utah firing squads, a blank is still put in one of the firing squad guns as a way to help executioners cope in the aftermath of a shooting. Jim Willett, an ex-warden at a death row facility in Huntsville, Texas, called presiding over Joseph Cannon's execution—the first of eighty-nine executions he oversaw—"the most emotionally draining experience I'd ever had." "Sometimes I wonder whether people really understand what goes on down here and the effect it has on us," he said, with one of his former colleagues, Kenneth Dean, noting that some participants turned to drinking to "you know, forget about it."[74]

Whenever and wherever executions take place, executioners must grapple with the morality of what they do. In Uganda, a prison official who oversaw a recent execution vowed never to attend one again, saying he did not sleep for two days after witnessing it and that it was "particularly unnerving" to have to command others to carry it out. As he attested in an affidavit, "my conscience tells me that killing is wrong." "I wondered most," Jim Willett said, "about the mothers who saw their sons being put to death." "Some," he said, "would just wail out crying. It's a sound you'll never hear any place else, an awful sound that sticks with you." Other wardens, too, have expressed their own qualms or deeply felt personal reservations about executions, with many opposing them altogether. A Mississippi warden named Donald Cabana left his job after presiding over executions. "No more. I don't want to do this anymore," he told his wife after overseeing Connie Ray Evans's execution, later saying: "In the end, all of us, I believe, are diminished by using violence when it is not necessary to do so." In yet another instance, Jeanne Woodford, San Quentin's former warden, came to believe that the death penalty should be replaced with an effective alternative: life-without-parole sentences. "To take a life in order to prove how much we value another life does not strengthen our society," she explained, saying capital punishment "devalues our very being and detracts crucial resources from programs that could truly make our communities safer."[75]

CHAPTER SEVEN

The Road to Abolition

Executions and Barbaric Punishments

Murders and retaliatory killings to avenge murders have taken place throughout human history. "Its precise origins," Justice Thurgood Marshall wrote of the death penalty, "are difficult to perceive, but there is some evidence that its roots lie in violent retaliation by members of a tribe or group, or by the tribe or group itself, against persons committing hostile acts toward group members." Capital punishment, one commentator posits, originated as a way to "placate the gods," and evolved later as a way to punish individuals, with many types of offenders being executed in horrific ways over the centuries. As that scholar, Gregg Mayer, writes: "In the time of Moses in the Bible, the death penalty was inflicted for crimes ranging from murder to gathering sticks on the Sabbath. In ancient Greece, Socrates, convicted of corrupting the youth with his teachings, was executed by being forced to drink hemlock." Asian offenders were skinned alive or tied to stakes, smeared with honey, and left for wild animals to eat; Persian offenders were crucified, trampled by elephants, smothered with hot ashes or heavy stones, or buried alive; the pharaohs embalmed criminals alive for giving false testimony; and mass drownings took place during the French Revolution. Early Native American communities also allowed murder victims' families to kill perpetrators, while the Babylonian code of Hammurabi, circa 1750 BC, punished more than twenty offenses with death, including perjury, adultery, theft, harboring runaway slaves, and even faulty home construction.[1]

Over the centuries, death sentences have been handed out for all sorts of things, from serious offenses such as murder and rape to minor ones such as selling bad beer. Even vices—tobacco use or cursing a parent—could in certain places lead to execution. In India, a person could be put to death for killing a cow or spreading false rumors, while a Connecticut code enacted in 1650 began ominously: "Whosoever shall worship any other God than the Lord shall surely be put to death." The Connecticut code, based on verbatim passages from the books of Deuteronomy, Exodus, and Leviticus, forbade blasphemy, sorcery, adultery, and rape. In American colonies such as New Haven, where the Puritans criminalized anything they regarded as perverse, homosexuality was a death-eligible offense and even masturbation was considered a capital crime. The Massachusetts Bay Colony's "Capitall Lawes of New-England," from 1636, also relied explicitly on biblical passages, listing the following capital crimes: idolatry, witchcraft, blasphemy, murder, assault in sudden anger, sodomy, buggery, adultery, statutory rape, rape, manstealing, perjury in a capital case, and rebellion. An Old Testament verse accompanied each codified offense, with judges using such draconian laws, as in Salem, Massachusetts, to punish heresy and witchcraft. England's eighteenth-century "Bloody Code" made nearly every felony a capital crime, so death sentences could be imposed not only for treason and murder but also for disturbing a fish pond, killing or maiming cattle, shooting a rabbit, setting a cornfield on fire, or cutting down trees. After deer hunting laws were changed for the Windsor Forest, England's notorious Black Act even made it a capital crime to blacken one's face.[2]

In Anglo-American law, the methods of execution—handed down from one generation to the next—could be especially violent. Though English subjects were frequently hanged, as was the custom, they were also burned, boiled in oil, disemboweled alive, or drawn and quartered—with human bodies torn apart, limb by limb, with horses. The dead bodies of the condemned might even be publicly dissected, desecrated, or gibbeted, and the condemned's decomposing body left hanging in an iron cage. As in England, offenders in the American colonies were usually hanged but also occasionally disemboweled or drawn and quartered, with the macabre modes of execution matched only by the wide range of offenses punishable by death. Thomas Graunger, a teenager, was executed in the typical way—by hanging—in the Plymouth Colony in 1642 for committing "buggery" with a horse, a cow, two goats, and a turkey. And around the same time, in the colony of New Haven, George Spencer was hanged for bestiality based on nothing more than a recanted confession and the fact that both he and a piglet were found to have a deformed eye. Superstitions were rampant, leading many executions to be conducted on Fridays, with offenders put to death in an assortment of grisly ways. Aside from well-known means of execution such as firing squads and the noose, methods of execution once authorized in America include drowning, pressing to death, crucifixion, and sawing in half. Slaves in particular were subject to especially brutal executions. They might be mutilated or castrated before being hanged or burned, with their heads sometimes severed for display by court order. Not only were vices and socially unacceptable behavior punishable by death, whether by the gallows or otherwise, but a fair number of innocent people no doubt met their untimely deaths at the hands of the state. In seventeenth-century Massachusetts, four Quakers were executed for returning to the colony after having been banished, while in 1643 James Britton and Mary Latham were hanged there for adultery. In the antebellum South, even those distributing antislavery literature were to be whipped or put to death.[3]

The death penalty's administration was ritualized by society, with public executions once the norm. In England, the village of Tyburn was for a time the customary place of execution. Eighteenth-century offenders were drawn by cart for two miles through London's crowded streets en route to their deaths. In America, executions likewise took place in the public square, whether in big cities or small towns. In 1837, at the last public execution in Philadelphia, an estimated twenty thousand people came to see the hanging of nineteen-year-old James Moran from the Bush Hill gallows. And large crowds at public executions were the rule, not the exception. The largest mass hanging in U.S. history, of thirty-eight Dakota Indians in Mankato, Minnesota, drew four thousand spectators in 1862, with fourteen hundred soldiers on hand to watch the men die and to ensure security and decorum. At America's last public execution, on August 14, 1936, in Owensboro, Kentucky, between ten thousand and twenty thousand "jeering" and "festive" spectators, some perched on a telephone pole to get a better view, crowded around the scaffold to see the execution of Rainey Bethea, a twenty-two-year-old black man convicted of murdering a seventy-year-old white woman. Even after executions were moved into prisons or temporary wooden structures adjoining them, county sheriffs—sometimes in violation of the spirit of the law—tried to accommodate more people than allowed by statute by issuing tickets or "deputizing" hundreds of official witnesses.[4]

In the early days of executions, some forms of capital punishment could be downright bizarre. The Minnesota Supreme Court once reported that the penalty for parricide—the murder of one's parents or children—was "scourging the parricide, and then sewing him up in a leathern sack, with a live dog, a cock, a viper, and an ape, and casting him into the sea." In fact, John Adams discussed a variation on this form of punishment that he encountered in 1779 while in Spain. As Adams wrote: "There was lately a Sentence for Parricide. The Law required that the Criminal should be headed up in a hogshead, with an Adder, a Toad, a Dog and a Cat and cast into the Sea." "But I was much pleased to hear," Adams reported, "that Spanish humanity had suggested and Spanish Ingenuity invented a Device to avoid some part of the Cruelty and horror of this punishment." "They had painted those Animals on the Cask," Adams wrote, "and the dead body was put into it, without any living Animals to attend it to its watery Grave." In early America, Asia, and Europe, even animals—believe it or not—faced capital prosecutions. Pigs, dogs, and other animals were arrested, assigned defense counsel, put on trial, and then, upon conviction, ceremoniously executed, often in public.[5]

Early civilizations also regularly tortured criminal suspects, whether by waterboarding, placing stones on the person's chest, or other means, methods that often in and of themselves led to death. As commentator Stephanie Spencer writes: "Until the mid-eighteenth century, torture was widely used and accepted throughout Europe, in a variety of contexts, including the procurement of testimony and confessions from criminal defendants." The Romans applied red-hot metals and hooks to tear skin, and they also routinely used the rack, a wooden frame mounted on rails and allowing a victim's joints and muscles to be painfully distended. Other forms of torture included leg screws, thumbscrews, the binding of wrists, the use of flammable substances on the soles of feet, rape or other forms of sexual abuse, beatings with fists, the gouging out of eyes, hanging individuals upside down, and sleep deprivation. English subjects who were tried but somehow escaped the death penalty, either through royal pardon or benefit of clergy, could have their genitals or tongues cut off, or be whipped or branded on the forehead or thumb. At common law, a clergyman could not be given a death sentence, and ecclesiastical courts had their own jurisdiction. After a struggle between Henry II and Thomas Becket, lay courts were deemed incompetent to try clergy members for capital offenses. The doctrine of benefit of clergy, as originally conceived, saved clerics from execution, though it evolved—until it was abolished in 1827 in England—to spare first-time offenders or condemned prisoners who could read or memorize scriptures. If an offender could recite Psalm 51, colloquially known as the "neck verse," the offender's life was spared.[6]

The natural human impulse to spare less serious offenders from the gallows led to the imposition of corporal instead of capital punishments and, over time, to the expansion of the doctrine of benefit of clergy. In lieu of a death sentence, a first-time offender convicted of manslaughter might be branded with an "M" for *manslayer*. Offenders were also "burnt in the hand"; branded on the thumb with a "T" for *thief*; or, in colonial New York, branded on the forehead with a "P" for *perjurer*. Eventually, the benefit of clergy privilege, which originated in England before being imported into America, was extended to women and one-time offenders before being abolished by the U.S. Congress in 1790. "This privilege," Thomas Jefferson once explained, "originally allowed to the clergy, is now extended to every man, & even to women." "It is," Jefferson said, "a right of exemption from capital punishment for the first offence in most cases. It is then a pardon by the law." "In other cases," Jefferson noted, "the Executive gives the pardon," though Jefferson himself disliked the idea of pardons, preferring instead that the laws themselves be made less harsh. As Jefferson wrote: "[W]hen laws are made as mild as they should be, both those pardons are absurd. The principle of Beccaria is sound. Let the legislators be merciful but the executors of the law inexorable." In the American colonies, which borrowed heavily from England's harsh penal codes, corporal punishments such as flogging, forced labor, maiming, and whipping, especially of slaves, were common and served as substitutes for death. Such corporal punishments—including gags, stocks, the scarlet letter, and the ducking stool—were designed to cause pain and to humiliate offenders publicly. In Boston, in addition to being punished corporally, offenders were oftentimes sentenced to sit upon the gallows for an hour with ropes around their necks.[7]

The late eighteenth century, when America was forged through revolution, was a time of great upheaval. There were almost constant fears of lawlessness, even as the American and French revolutions dealt crushing blows to monarchies and in turn radically altered those societies. "We are fast verging to anarchy and confusion!" no less a figure than George Washington warned James Madison in 1794. Not only were political cultures transformed during this tumultuous Age of Reason, but U.S. and European societies—taken with new ideas—began questioning long-entrenched policies and punishments, with criminal justice reform suddenly bursting into the spotlight. Americans had carefully read Cesare Beccaria's writings, and they soon began building their own penitentiaries, first in Pennsylvania and then in places such as New York and Virginia. Such reformist ideas thereby shaped the country's founding era and the Bill of Rights, not to mention the public's view of the criminal justice system. Indeed, even in the midst of the Revolutionary War, civic leaders attempted to better care for prisoners, society's lowliest members. Though the organization was short-lived, the Philadelphia Society for Relieving Distressed Prisoners was formed in 1776, the year the Continental Congress issued the Declaration of Independence.[8]

Not until after the war and the adoption of the Constitution, however, did reform efforts really pick up steam. The idea of popular sovereignty, it was recognized, would lead to abuses, especially of criminals, if not restrained by judicial review. Pennsylvania's James Wilson, for example, emphasized the need for judicial independence and attacked the idea of an all-powerful, unicameral legislature, saying it was likely to produce "sudden and violent fits of despotism, injustice, and cruelty." The abuses suffered at the hands of the British, coupled with the writings of Beccaria, Dr. Benjamin Rush, and others, also sensitized Americans to cruel and inhumane practices. Following Philadelphia's penal reform efforts, New Jersey completed its state penitentiary in 1797; New York's first penitentiary was completed in 1799; Virginia and Kentucky followed suit in 1800; Pennsylvania's Eastern State Penitentiary opened in 1829, becoming the first public building to make widespread use of flush toilets and hot water heating; and Maryland and Massachusetts built new penitentiaries in 1829. In the 1830s, as antigallows sentiment intensified, many other states, including Georgia, New Hampshire, Tennessee, and Vermont, also broke ground on new prisons. Because of the Walnut Street Prison's proximity to the events unfolding in Philadelphia in 1787, the Framers necessarily found themselves engaged in discussions about criminal law reform. The Walnut Street Prison was literally across the street from what is now known as Independence Hall, with the Quaker meetinghouse nearby, too.

The Philadelphia Society for Alleviating the Miseries of Public Prisons, of which Benjamin Franklin was a member, was organized by a number of prominent citizens in 1787, the same year the Constitution was hammered out in the City of Brotherly Love.[9]

In the eighteenth century executions were a fact of life in all thirteen colonies, though the frequency of executions varied by locale. The Espy File, a well-known database of U.S. executions, compiles information on executions that have occurred since colonial times. Researched by M. Watt Espy and John Ortiz Smykla, the database catalogs more than fifteen thousand executions that have taken place from 1608 to the present. The Espy File reveals that executions grew exponentially in the late nineteenth and early twentieth centuries, with the post-1850 period witnessing the most executions. The raw data show, however, that a fair number of executions also took place in colonial times and during America's founding era. From the first recorded execution, of George Kendall in Virginia in 1608, to 1791, the year the Eighth Amendment took effect, every jurisdiction witnessed multiple executions: Connecticut, 25; Delaware, 10; Georgia, 15; Maryland, 58; Massachusetts, 193; New Hampshire, 5; New Jersey, 80; New York, 153; North Carolina, 127; Pennsylvania, 192; Rhode Island, 47; South Carolina, 91; and Virginia, 297. The most prevalent method of execution was death by hanging, but shootings, gibbeting, hanging in chains, burnings, and breaking on the wheel also appear sporadically in the historical record. As one would expect, the offenses for which people were executed varied considerably in those early years. On the list are adultery, aiding runaway slaves, arson, attempted murder, attempted rape, bestiality, burglary, concealing birth, counterfeiting, desertion, espionage, forgery, guerilla activity, horse stealing, kidnapping, murder, piracy, poisoning, rape, robbery, slave revolt, sodomy, theft, treason, and witchcraft.[10]

Of the executions that took place, racial prejudice—in particular, a desire to control slave populations—played a central part in a sizable number of those public spectacles. For example, in the 1750s in Massachusetts, there were roughly three thousand blacks, the largest proportion living in Boston and its environs. Though there was less fear of slave revolts in Massachusetts, where much antislavery sentiment was found, sometimes slaves rose up against individual masters, as did Mark and Phillis, with the aid of another slave named Robin, who worked for a doctor. Mark could read and write and was dissatisfied after he, Phillis, and one Phoebe were bought by sea captain John Codman. Wanting to have a different master, the slaves first burned down Captain Codman's shop, hoping to ruin the captain financially and force their sale. But that never happened, so after the shop was rebuilt, the slaves hatched a new plan, to kill the captain. After persuading Robin, a doctor's slave, to steal some arsenic from his master's shop, Mark and his wife Phillis, along with Phoebe, who slept in a garret with them, concocted their murderous plot, which entailed mixing arsenic into Captain Codman's food and drink. After Phoebe turned state's evidence, Mark and Phillis were publicly executed in 1755. Mark was hanged, and Phillis was strangled and then burned alive at the stake. Mark's body was "hung in chains" on Charlestown Common, where it hung for twenty years in a rusty cage, the black, rotting body shriveling up into a grotesque mummy. It was such a familiar sight to those living in the area that, on his famous midnight ride to Lexington, Paul Revere, after passing Charlestown Neck, took special note of the place "where Mark was hung in chains."[11]

A recent doctoral thesis written by historian Gabriele Gottlieb analyzed a snapshot of early American executions. It looked specifically at the frequency of state-sponsored killings from 1750 to 1800 in three major cities: Boston, Philadelphia, and Charleston. Boston, a hub of commerce and the focal point of trade with England, Spain, and the West Indies, had a Puritan legacy; Philadelphia, another large port, was home to scores of merchants and artisans, with an especially large Quaker population; and Charleston, the southernmost city, had the highest percentage of forced labor, with slaves making up a large portion of the workforce. Gottlieb found that capital punishment was not used routinely in any of these urban centers but was "applied most systematically" at "moments of a real or perceived social crisis." In the 1750s, for example, South Carolina slaveholders faced a wave of poisonings by slaves, prompting the death penalty to be applied more frequently. Likewise, social and economic instability in the mid- to late-1780s influenced the application of the death penalty, with executions peaking in the years 1788 and 1789. The Judiciary Act of 1789, passed by the First Congress, set up the structure of the federal courts, gave U.S. district courts exclusive jurisdiction over federal crimes, and conferred local control over capital cases, providing that "in cases punishable with death, the trial shall be had in the county where the offence was committed." Capital trials inevitably drew a lot of public attention, and sermons, newspaper articles, broadsides, and pamphlets about executions served to convey moral lessons or further to disseminate news about those well-attended public events. "The lessons of the execution day," Gottlieb writes, "were geared toward building community cohesion and order by reinforcing principles of social discipline and morality." As Gottlieb emphasizes: "Each participant—the ministers and civil officials, the condemned, and the crowd—had 'assigned' roles to play in this theater of death."[12]

So conceived, execution day thus sought to further the existing social order, with civic leaders—governors, sheriffs, and pastors—cast in leading dramatic roles. In his book *Rites of Execution,* historian Louis Masur describes the elaborate civil and religious rituals associated with eighteenth-century executions. "As a civil ceremony," Masur explains, "the execution exhibited the authority of the state. It sought to bolster order and encourage conformity to a republican code of social values." "As a religious ceremony," Masur writes, "ministers used hanging day to remind the crowd of its own mortality and to demonstrate that God alone could redeem the sinful." Public executions, however, also attracted unsavory crowds and proved to be debasing, inciting much anti–death penalty sentiment in the process. Robert Rantoul Jr., who along with his father fought the Massachusetts death penalty, was influenced early in his career by Beccaria and once cited a survey finding that 164 of 167 condemned inmates had attended a public execution. In *The Death Penalty: An American History,* UCLA law professor Stuart Banner traces the widespread opposition to these spectacles and to the punishment of death itself. "Colonial Americans," Banner writes, "pondered the death penalty and the purposes it served, just as Americans do today." "But because of the institutional structure and prevailing religious beliefs of their time," Banner explains, capital punishment survived, serving—in his words—"a broader set of purposes" than it does today. Early Americans, Banner recounts, punished property crimes and even sodomy capitally, and the fear of slave revolts—then the mother of all fears—spurred death penalty laws targeted at blacks, particularly in the South. As Banner explains: "Execution rates for slaves far exceeded those for southern whites. In North Carolina, for instance, at least one hundred slaves were executed in the quarter-century between 1748 and 1772, well more than the number of whites executed during the colony's entire history, a period spanning over a century."[13]

America's Early Abolition Movement

In pre- and post-Revolutionary America, Beccaria's ideas inspired the Founding Fathers, men who risked everything, including their lives, to form a new republic. Receptive to an Enlightenment agenda after their successful revolution and suffering years of abuse at the hands of the English Crown, these well-educated men took concrete steps to overhaul America's justice system. In England, more than two hundred crimes were punishable by death in 1791, the year the Eighth Amendment came into force. But in America, a less severe approach prevailed. While American legislators initially resisted the calls of Benjamin Rush and Thomas Jefferson to end or curtail capital punishment, significant reform occurred in the 1790s and early 1800s. In 1794, after William Bradford became a convert to the cause, Pennsylvania abolished capital punishment for all crimes except first-degree murder. And in 1796, New York, led by advocates such as Thomas Eddy, Philip Schuyler, and Ambrose Spencer, changed its criminal laws too, outlawing death sentences for all crimes except treason and murder. George Clinton—New York's first governor and the country's fourth Vice President, serving under both Jefferson and Madison—had an especially notable shift in attitude. A lawyer and military commander, Clinton, in the eyes of one observer, had in war been "as cruel and arbitrary as the Grand Turk." "[T]his emissary of rebellion" reportedly had "tried, condemned, imprisoned, and punished the Loyalists most unmercifully," so that "by his orders" victims had been "tarred and feathered" and "whipped" with "every kind of cruelty, death not excepted." By 1795, in his final address to the state legislature in Albany, Clinton was advocating a much different approach. At that time, he sought to substitute hard labor and confinement for the death penalty for most crimes, asking legislators to turn away from the "cruelty of despotic governments" and revise the state's criminal code to bring punishments more in line with "the mild genius of our constitution."[14]

In the 1820s, Edward Livingston, a politician who saw the death penalty as unnecessary, drew worldwide attention by boldly proposing its total abolition in a draft Louisiana penal code. A former New York City mayor and U.S. attorney for the district of New York, as well as a lawyer who became the secretary of state and Andrew Jackson's minister to France, Livingston proposed replacing capital punishment with imprisonment in penitentiaries. His report, seeking to eliminate "cruel or disproportioned punishments," stated that men had been condemned to die "under the most cruel torture" and that some executions "were attended with butchery that would disgust a savage." A member of a prominent New York family that counted among its members Philip Livingston, a signer of the Declaration of Independence, Edward Livingston—whose brother Robert, a lawyer who helped draft the Declaration, administered George Washington's oath of office in 1789, and served as Jefferson's minister at the court of Napoleon, negotiating the Louisiana Purchase—ended his legislative report with the biblical command "Thou shalt not kill." Although Louisiana failed to adopt the proposed code, Edward Livingston mailed thousands of copies around the country and the world, tirelessly campaigning to end capital punishment.[15]

By the 1830s and 1840s, America's abolition movement had intensified even further. William Cullen Bryant of the *New York Post* and Horace Greeley of the *New York Tribune* became influential abolitionist speakers; a legislative committee in Maine, citing Beccaria, recommended abolishing capital punishment entirely in 1836; and the following year, the Maine legislature passed a new law requiring condemned inmates to remain at the state prison for one year from the date of sentencing before any execution could take place. In addition, it was stipulated that Maine's governor had to sign any execution warrant, with governors then agonizing over whether to sign such warrants. The Maine law led to a de facto moratorium on executions in that state, with the first execution at Maine's state prison not occurring until 1864. Charles Spear, a member of the Massachusetts anti–death penalty movement, founded the weekly paper the *Hangman* for agitation purposes, and the New York State Society, an active antigallows group, formed a national organization in 1845. That organization elected George Dallas, James Polk's Vice President, as its president, and in the organization's first year Dallas spoke to abolitionists from across the country at a convention held in Philadelphia. Other sympathizers included William H. Seward and former Vice President Richard M. Johnson of Kentucky, with politicians such as John Quincy Adams also committing to the reform movement. By the 1850s, antigallows societies also existed in places as diverse as Alabama, Indiana, Iowa, Louisiana, Ohio, Pennsylvania, and Tennessee. American newspapers and periodicals—the primary media outlets of the era—devoted countless column inches to the death penalty debate.[16]

The progress of the anti–death penalty movement in such a short span of time was remarkable. The 1845 letter of John Quincy Adams in support of the Philadelphia Society for the Abolition of Capital Punishment shows just how far the abolitionist movement had come. Adams, in Boston but in ill health, expressed his regret at being unable to attend the Philadelphia meeting of "the friends of the Abolition of Capital Punishment." *"Gladly would I co-operate with any Society whose object should be to promote the abolition of every form, by which the life of man can be voluntarily taken by his fellow creature man,"* Adams wrote. "If there be any case which, in the intercourse of human society, can possibly justify this act," Adams noted, "it is that sanctioned by the community for the punishment of enormous crimes." A staunch opponent of slavery who just four years earlier had argued the *Amistad* case before the U.S. Supreme Court, Adams, who foresaw reform ahead, looked to posterity to eliminate all forms of violence. "In the progress of the human race towards that improved condition of their existence to which our religion teaches us that they are destined," Adams explained, "the total abolition of all violent extinction of the life of man by the will and act of his brother, is among the blessed promises of futurity." "War, slavery, murder, and homicide in any form," Adams wrote, "are evils, I fondly hope to disappear, hereafter, from the annals of the human race." "Every step in this progress that can be made during the remnant of my own life," Adams continued, "will be hailed by me with inexpressible delight; and altho' the revocation of that sentence of the Almighty, that 'whoso sheddeth man's blood, by man shall his own blood be shed,' would in my prayers to heaven, be the last accomplishment of the perfectability of man upon earth, I would gladly contribute to it, even in advance of some other forms of homicide more odious in themselves, but perhaps more deeply rooted in the infirmities of man's nature." *"I do, therefore,"* Adams concluded, *"heartily wish and pray for the success of your efforts to promote the abolition of Capital Punishment,"* and if you can shape the laws of the land to a disclaimer of the right of government itself to take from any human being the life granted him by his Creator, I would welcome it as the harbinger of a brighter day, when no individual of the race of man shall ever los[e] his life by the act of another."[17]

By then, America already had a reputation for using executions much less than its European counterparts. In *Democracy in America,* the French writer Alexis de Tocqueville contrasted the "mildness" of America's criminal laws with the "terrible powers" of European societies. As Tocqueville wrote: "In no country is criminal justice administered with more mildness than in the United States. Whilst the English seem disposed carefully to retain the bloody traces of the Middle Ages in their penal legislation, the Americans have almost expunged capital punishment from their codes." "North America is," he wrote in 1840, "the only country upon earth in which the life of no one citizen has been taken for a political offence in the course of the last fifty years." Tocqueville, whose parents were imprisoned by Robespierre and whose father only narrowly escaped execution in France in 1793, first came to America in 1831 with his friend and coworker Gustave de Beaumont to observe America's penal system on behalf of the French government. Tocqueville, who tragically experienced members of his mother's family being guillotined by authorities during the French Revolution, paid visits to American prisons, including Sing Sing and Eastern State Penitentiary in Philadelphia. Noting that Americans are "extremely open to compassion," Tocqueville observed: "in America, no one hesitates to inflict a penalty from which humanity does not recoil." As he explained in discussing the concept of impeachment and the U.S. Constitution's system regarding the removal of public officials from office: "To condemn a political opponent to death, in order to deprive him of his power, is to commit what all the world would execrate as a horrible assassination; but to declare that opponent unworthy to exercise that authority, and to deprive him of it, leaving him uninjured in life and limb, may seem to be the fair issue of the struggle." Though Tocqueville wrote that "the physical condition of the blacks is less severe" in the United States than in any "single European colony in the New World," he had this to say of America and its unequal treatment of blacks, no doubt driven by then-prevailing racism and a continuing fear of slave rebellions: "yet the slaves still endure frightful misery there, and are constantly exposed to very cruel punishments." "Thus," he concluded, "the same man who is full of humanity towards his fellow-creatures, when they are at the same time his equals, becomes insensible to their afflictions as soon as that equality ceases."[18]

Though the death penalty had been curtailed in many places, it took longer for American states to abolish the death penalty entirely. By the 1840s, antigallows societies were active in Massachusetts and New York, but success first came from far away in the Upper Midwest. In 1846, Michigan became the first American state—indeed, the first English-speaking jurisdiction—to abolish capital punishment for murder. As it was, executions had been infrequent in Michigan, a jurisdiction initially governed by the Northwest Ordinance, which had itself expressly prohibited "cruel or unusual punishments." Inspired by the ideas of Beccaria, Benjamin Rush, and others, Michigan legislators passed a law providing for life imprisonment for murder, a law that took effect on March 1, 1847, and thus outlawed capital punishment. Two other states, Rhode Island and Wisconsin, did the same in the 1850s, with societies for the abolition of capital punishment steadily growing in number nationwide. In Rhode Island, swept up in a populist movement known as the Dorr Rebellion, the 1852 abolition of capital punishment was preceded by the issuance of a forty-three-page legislative report concluding that "the spirit of the age in which we live, the sublime principles of Christianity, as well as the ends of justice, demand the abolition of death as a penalty for crime." Wisconsin, led by anti–death penalty activist Marvin Bovee, a farmer and state legislator turned penal reformer, did away with capital punishment the next year. Bovee called capital punishment "a dark spot resting on us Christians," writing in a local newspaper that "[a] life once taken can never be restored."[19]

In those days, lynchings were still a grim reality of American life, though they too had many detractors, with a vigorous antilynching movement—led by the NAACP—emerging in later decades. In 1838, long before the NAACP's formation, a young Abraham Lincoln, in a speech in Springfield, Illinois, shortly after he became a lawyer, himself decried "savage mobs" and the "horrors" of lynchings. Noting that lynchings had taken place "from New England to Louisiana," Lincoln specifically brought up the lynching of some gamblers, a "mulatto man" in St. Louis, and "negroes" in Mississippi "suspected of conspiring to raise an insurrection." "Abstractly considered," Lincoln said of the gamblers, their hanging at Vicksburg would ordinarily have been "of but little consequence," because they constituted "a portion of the population, that is worse than useless." As to the man seized on the streets of St. Louis, dragged to the suburbs, chained to a tree, and burned to death, "had he not died as he did," Lincoln said, referring to that "horror-striking scene," "he must have died by the sentence of the law, in a very short time afterwards" for "the perpetration of an outrageous murder, upon one of the most worthy and respectable citizens of the city." But when men take the law into their own hands, Lincoln warned, "they should recollect, that, in the confusion usually attending such transactions, they will be as likely to hang or burn some one, who is neither a gambler nor a murderer" as "one who is." Opposing "the increasing disregard for law which pervades the country," he lamented that so many lynchings had taken place in Mississippi that "dead men were seen literally dangling from the boughs of trees upon every road side; and in numbers almost sufficient, to rival the native Spanish moss of the country, as a drapery of the forest." Urging "a strict observance of all the laws" and "*a reverence for the constitution and laws,*" Lincoln invoked the Declaration of Independence and "the patriots of seventy-six" as he pleaded with his audience: "Let every American, every lover of liberty, every well wisher to his posterity, swear by the blood of the Revolution, never to violate in the least particular, the laws of the country; and never to tolerate their violation by others."[20]

Despite Lincoln's personal aversion to violence, America's antilynching and antigallows agitation came to an abrupt halt after the country inaugurated its sixteenth President and the Civil War broke out. The country was consumed by the onset of the war, which claimed more than six hundred thousand lives, and little else was or could have been on citizens' minds. The war required Lincoln's constant attention, and he gave it, frequently walking over to the telegraph office to issue orders to his commanders. Lincoln himself recognized that during wartime "blood grows hot" and is spilt by men motivated by "[r]evenge and retaliation." Under immense pressure to quell the rebellion, even from his closest friends, Lincoln suspended the writ of habeas corpus, calling for the arrest of those guilty of disloyal practices. William Herndon, his old law partner, as well as Lincoln's generals in the field, pushed the President to use executions, especially as the war dragged on and desertions became rampant. "Does he suppose he can crush—squelch out this huge rebellion by pop guns filled with rose water," Herndon chided his friend, adding: "He ought to hang somebody and get up a name for will or decision—for character. Let him hang some Child or woman, if he has not Courage to hang a *man*." Almost inevitably, the Civil War delayed the progress of criminal justice reform, with antigallows efforts not resuming until after the war. Marvin Bovee even delayed the publication of his anti–death penalty manifesto *Christ and the Gallows* until 1869, saying that to have presented such a work during the Civil War "would have been 'ill-timed,' to say the least."[21]

As commander in chief, President Lincoln was forced to make many life-and-death decisions during the war, with regard to both the battlefield and individual capital cases. He ended up authorizing executions for some murderers, rapists, and deserters, but he often did so only reluctantly, regularly disregarding his generals' death penalty recommendations when he felt executions would do no good or serve no purpose. When Judge Advocate General Joseph Holt urged more military executions, Lincoln replied, "I don't think I can do it." "They say," Lincoln once remarked, "that I destroy discipline and am cruel to the Army when I will not let them shoot a soldier now and then. But I cannot see it. If God wanted me to see it, he would let me know it, and until he does, I shall go on pardoning and being cruel to the end." "I don't believe it will make a man any better to shoot him," Lincoln famously said, frequently spending his precious time poring over clemency papers. "Get out of the way," he told one friend, "tomorrow is butcher day and I must go through these papers and see if I cannot find some excuse to let these poor men off." Near the end of his life, Lincoln told Secretary of War Edwin Stanton, "[B]lood can not restore blood, and government should not act for revenge." In January 1864, Lincoln even commuted an Ohio soldier's death sentence to hard labor for the war's duration, "not on any merit in the case," which Lincoln described as a "really bad one," but simply "to evade the butchering business." On April 14, 1864, just a year before he was shot at Ford's Theatre, Lincoln pardoned yet another deserter. "Well," Lincoln famously observed, "I think this boy can do more good above ground than under ground."[22]

In the wake of the Civil War's horrendous bloodshed, it took considerable time for the abolitionist movement to regain its footing. Once it did, though, things moved fairly rapidly, at least until economic hard times hit and another war broke out. No state abolished capital punishment during the Civil War, and only Iowa, Maine, and Colorado banned executions after the end of the war and before the turn of the century. Congress, however, reduced the number of capital crimes to five in 1897, and in the Progressive Era, ten states—among them Kansas, Missouri, South Dakota, and Washington—abolished the death penalty. But widespread societal fears brought on by a fear of crime soon overcame that momentum, with all but two of those states, Minnesota and North Dakota, soon reinstating capital punishment. America's entry into World War I and the country's hard economic times, culminating in the Great Depression, dealt yet another severe blow to the antigallows movement, making criminal law reform excruciatingly difficult. The country's focus on the war and people's struggle to find work and to support their families ultimately deflated the abolitionist cause. As Bryan Vila and Cynthia Morris explain in their book *Capital Punishment in the United States*: "During the period from 1918 to 1959, opponents of the death penalty such as Clarence Darrow and the wardens of Sing Sing and San Quentin fought an uphill battle against strong and consistent support for capital punishment." The gradual, state-by-state privatization of executions from the 1830s to the 1930s also no doubt contributed to a reduced public consciousness of them, leading to further public apathy.[23]

The end of World War II saw yet another resurgence of the anti–death penalty movement, though the end of public executions gave the debate far less urgency in the public's mind. From 1958 to 1965, four more states—Delaware, Oregon, Iowa, and West Virginia—abandoned capital punishment, executions became less frequent, and, to many in the media and in the courts, the death penalty's death knell seemed imminent. Oregon's abolition had come through a public referendum, and public opinion was turning against capital punishment. Whereas a Gallup Poll in 1953 showed support for capital punishment at 68 percent, the level of support fell to a record low of 41 percent by 1966. Other developments in the 1950s and turbulent 1960s, including abolition in a number of foreign countries, also pointed to the death penalty's demise. The territories of Alaska and Hawaii abolished capital punishment in 1957; the first edition of Hugo Adam Bedau's influential book *The Death Penalty in America* hit shelves in 1964; and in 1966, the polls—in a reversal—showed that more people opposed the death penalty than favored it. In 1968, the year in which United States Attorney General Ramsey Clark asked Congress to abolish the federal death penalty, no executions took place and the U.S. Supreme Court itself observed that death penalty proponents were a "distinct and dwindling minority." The number of executions had fallen precipitously in a matter of years and then came to a complete standstill as the NAACP, a handful of lawyers, and the crusading law professor Anthony Amsterdam led a litigation effort that culminated with the Supreme Court's landmark decision in *Furman v. Georgia*.[24]

Modern death penalty jurisprudence traces its origins to *Furman,* the case that declared the nation's death penalty laws unconstitutional. In *Furman,* at stake was the fate of three black defendants: a convicted murderer and two men sentenced to death for raping white women. By a five-to-four vote, the Supreme Court set aside all three death sentences, though the rationales for the Court's judgment varied considerably, with all nine Justices issuing their own individual opinions. In a terse one-paragraph per curiam ruling, the majority held simply that "the imposition and carrying out of the death penalty in these cases constitute cruel and unusual punishment in violation of the Eighth and Fourteenth Amendments." The Eighth Amendment's Cruel and Unusual Punishments Clause gave textual support for the Court's ruling, with the Fourteenth Amendment allowing the Eighth Amendment to be applied to the three state-court judgments at issue. After reversing the judgments and cursorily remanding the cases, the Court punctuated its decision with every winning lawyer's favorite words: "So ordered." Coming as it did in the midst of the Vietnam War and all the societal upheaval that that war brought about, the momentous ruling—what the *New Republic* called "one of the biggest surprises" of the Court's history—shocked many Americans. Murderers and rapists are reviled, unsavory people who have inflicted incalculable harm on the community; the *Furman* ruling came just a year after the Court's controversial decision upholding busing as a legitimate tool to integrate public schools; and the effect of *Furman* was to set aside every U.S. death sentence, more than five hundred in all, clearing America's death row. Because of *Furman* and a similar decision in 1972 by the California Supreme Court, the death sentences of murderers, rapists, and criminal masterminds such as Charles Manson were thus commuted to life sentences.[25]

Only two Justices in *Furman* believed executions were unconstitutional per se, making the Justices' separate opinions of special importance. In contrast to the Court's short per curiam opinion, the concurring and dissenting opinions in *Furman*—reflecting Americans' own conflicted views on capital punishment—took up more than two hundred pages, a record length, and were full of back-and-forth sparring. Justice William O. Douglas said death penalty statutes were "pregnant with discrimination" and "unconstitutional in their operation." It violates the Eighth Amendment, he wrote, to apply the death penalty "selectively to minorities." Justice William Brennan, one of the fiercest opponents of executions ever to sit on the Court, concluded that "the Cruel and Unusual Punishments Clause prohibits the infliction of uncivilized and inhuman punishments." "A punishment is 'cruel and unusual,'" Brennan wrote, "if it does not comport with human dignity." Calling the "calculated killing of a human being" by the state "uniquely degrading to human dignity," he said that the death penalty was a rarity and unnecessary, and that it "smacks of little more than a lottery system." "[I]t is certainly doubtful," Brennan concluded, "that the infliction of death by the State does in fact strengthen the community's moral code; if the deliberate extinguishment of human life has any effect at all, it more likely tends to lower our respect for human life and brutalize our values."[26]

Justice Potter Stewart, for his part, called capital punishment "unique in its total irrevocability" and felt death sentences were cruel and unusual "in the same way that being struck by lightning is cruel and unusual." "For, of all the people convicted of rapes and murders in 1967 and 1968, many just as reprehensible as these," Justice Stewart wrote, "the petitioners are among a capriciously selected random handful upon whom the sentence of death has in fact been imposed." "[I]f any basis can be discerned for the selection of these few to be sentenced to die," he noted, "it is the constitutionally impermissible basis of race." "I simply conclude," Stewart wrote, "that the Eighth and Fourteenth Amendments cannot tolerate the infliction of a sentence of death under legal systems that permit this unique penalty to be so wantonly and so freakishly imposed." For Justice Byron White, death sentences were so infrequently imposed that they became "pointless and needless," with White concluding that "the threat of execution is too attenuated to be of substantial service to criminal justice." The death penalty, he said, "is exacted with great infrequency even for the most atrocious crimes," adding that "there is no meaningful basis for distinguishing the few cases in which it is imposed from the many cases in which it is not." The Fourteenth Amendment, which played a central role in *Furman*, had long before injected a "due process" requirement into state-court proceedings. In the 1860s, the Fourteenth Amendment had also specifically elevated the Declaration of Independence's equality principle into binding law by guaranteeing "the equal protection of the laws." In so doing, the Fourteenth Amendment's protections went far beyond what the Founding Fathers' Fifth Amendment and its parallel Due Process Clause had done. Whereas the Fifth Amendment only applied—as originally conceived—to the federal government, the Fourteenth Amendment would now limit state power.[27]

Justice Thurgood Marshall, who as an NAACP advocate argued *Brown v. Board of Education* before the U.S. Supreme Court, saw the question in *Furman* as "not whether we condone rape or murder, for surely we do not; it is whether capital punishment is 'a punishment no longer consistent with our own self-respect' and, therefore, violative of the Eighth Amendment." "The criminal acts with which we are confronted are ugly, vicious, reprehensible acts," Marshall wrote, adding that "[t]heir sheer brutality cannot and should not be minimized." But to Marshall, "[t]he 'cruel and unusual' language limits the avenues through which vengeance can be channeled." "Were this not so," he wrote, "the language would be empty and a return to the rack and other tortures would be possible in a given case." Finding death sentences to be imposed in a discriminatory manner, mostly upon "the poor" and "the ignorant," Marshall found evidence that innocent people had been executed, calling the death penalty "an excessive and unnecessary punishment." Marshall, who with Justice Brennan relentlessly contended that the death penalty is unconstitutional per se, aired his views in his lengthy opinion. "[T]he Eighth Amendment," he wrote, "is our insulation from our baser selves," adding that "whether or not a punishment is cruel and unusual depends, not on whether its mere mention 'shocks the conscience and sense of justice of the people,' but on whether people who were fully informed as to the purposes of the penalty and its liabilities would find the penalty shocking, unjust and unacceptable." "Assuming knowledge of all the facts presently available regarding capital punishment," Marshall wrote, "the average citizen would, in my opinion, find it shocking to his conscience and sense of justice." "The point has now been reached," he opined, "at which deference to the legislatures is tantamount to abdication of our judicial roles as factfinders, judges and ultimate arbiters of the Constitution."[28]

Marshall, who in his days as a practicing lawyer had seen one of his own clients sentenced to death and later executed at a Maryland penitentiary, opined that "a penalty that was permissible at one time in our Nation's history is not necessarily permissible today." In southern Maryland, Marshall had represented James Gross, charged with the 1934 murder of a man who ran a barbecue stand in Prince Georges County, and had argued unsuccessfully that his client had just driven a car while two other men shot the store owner. Almost four decades later, Marshall—as a judge—would write that capital punishment "violates the Eighth Amendment because it is morally unacceptable to the people of the United States at this time in their history." For Marshall, public opinion polls were not decisive. Instead, he focused on whether people, if fully informed, would find the death penalty unjust and unacceptable. "So few people have been executed in the past decade," Marshall explained, "that capital punishment is a subject only rarely brought to the attention of the average American." Accurate information, he believed, would convince Americans that the death penalty was "unwise" and "immoral." Marshall concluded: "In striking down capital punishment, this Court does not malign our system of government. On the contrary, it pays homage to it. Only in a free society could right triumph in difficult times, and could civilization record its magnificent advancement. In recognizing the humanity of our fellow beings, we pay ourselves the highest tribute."[29]

On the flip side, the dissenters in *Furman* saw the majority's judgment as an affront to legislative judgments. Chief Justice Warren Burger found "no authority suggesting that the Eighth Amendment was intended to purge the law of its retributive element," and concluded that "the constitutional prohibition against 'cruel and unusual punishments' cannot be construed to bar the imposition of the punishment of death." He lamented that only one year earlier, in *McGautha v. California,* the Court had upheld the prevailing sentencing scheme in capital cases, finding it "impossible to say that committing to the untrammeled discretion of the jury the power to pronounce life or death in capital cases is offensive to anything in the Constitution." For Burger, jurors were "the keystone in our system of criminal justice," and he thought it "remarkable" that "it should now be suggested that we take the most sensitive and important of all decisions away from them." Burger in fact saw the rarity of death sentences as a positive development, not as a constitutional infirmity. "The very infrequency of death penalties imposed by jurors attests their cautious and discriminating reservation of that penalty for the most extreme cases," Burger wrote.[30]

The other dissenters echoed Burger's sentiments. Justice Lewis Powell saw the majority ruling as "the very sort of judgment that the legislative branch is competent to make and for which the judiciary is ill-equipped," and Justice William Rehnquist wrote that the task of judging "must surely be approached with the deepest humility and genuine deference to legislative judgment." Although Justice Harry Blackmun personally rejoiced at the Court's result, he too found himself unable to accept the result "as a matter of history, of law, or of constitutional pronouncement." He agreed that the Cruel and Unusual Punishments Clause "must draw its meaning from the evolving standards of decency that mark the progress of a maturing society," but he took umbrage at "the suddenness of the Court's perception of progress in the human attitude since decisions of only a short while ago." "We should not," he concluded, "allow our personal preferences as to the wisdom of legislative and congressional action, or our distaste for such action, to guide our judicial decision in cases such as these." Blackmun, though, took time to give a lengthy explanation of his personal opposition to capital punishment. Foreshadowing his later rejection of capital punishment as a matter of constitutional law, Blackmun forcefully wrote:

Cases such as these provide for me an excruciating agony of the spirit. I yield to no one in the depth of my distaste, antipathy, and, indeed, abhorrence, for the death penalty, with all its aspects of physical distress and fear and of moral judgment exercised by finite minds. That distaste is buttressed by a belief that capital punishment serves no useful purpose that can be demonstrated. For me, it violates childhood's training and life's experiences, and is not compatible with the philosophical convictions I have been able to develop. It is antagonistic to any sense of "reverence for life." Were I a legislator, I would vote against the death penalty for the policy reasons argued by counsel for the respective petitioners and expressed and adopted in the several opinions filed by the Justices who vote to reverse these judgments.[31]

The Aftermath of *Furman*

The *Furman* decision, though closely divided, was widely seen as a death sentence for the death penalty. When the first English-language biography of Cesare Beccaria was published in Philadelphia in 1973, the well-known University of Chicago criminologist Norval Morris wrote the foreword, referring to America's death penalty in the past tense. "Beccaria was, of course, one of the leading early opponents of capital punishment," Morris wrote, confidently proclaiming: "The final vindication by the Supreme Court of his view of the social inutility of this punishment, and of its unconstitutionality, confirmed the quality of Beccaria's perceptive vision." Even many of the Justices themselves privately predicted that America would never witness another execution. But state legislatures around the country did not see it that way, and thirty-five states quickly reenacted death penalty laws, all in response to the Court's *Furman* decision, a case that decided the fate of three black men. Public support for capital punishment skyrocketed in the aftermath of *Furman*; Richard Nixon's Solicitor General Robert Bork eagerly expressed his support for death sentences; and Alabama lieutenant governor Jere Beasley suggested that the Supreme Court "had lost contact with the real world." Public opinion, it was clear, had turned once more, putting the Court's ruling front and center in the continuing public controversy over executions. The harsh reaction to the Court's decision ultimately led to yet another round of high-profile, high-stakes litigation before the nation's highest court.[32]

As Americans prepared for bicentennial picnics and celebrations, the U.S. Supreme Court bowed to public pressure and reversed course on capital punishment, handing down its decision in *Gregg v. Georgia* on July 2, 1976. In that case, the Supreme Court defined a "cruel" punishment as one "so totally without penological justification that it results in the gratuitous infliction of suffering." Though mandatory death penalty laws were struck down on that same day in cases originating out of Louisiana and North Carolina, *Gregg* and two other simultaneously issued rulings, *Jurek v. Texas* and *Proffitt v. Florida,* upheld death penalty statutes that guided, or channeled, the sentencer's discretion. Georgia's new law, requiring jurors to find at least one "aggravating circumstance" before imposing a death sentence, was found to be constitutional, and *Jurek* and *Proffitt* approved death penalty laws in Texas and Florida. The Court in *Gregg* specifically ruled that "the concerns expressed in *Furman* that the penalty of death not be imposed in an arbitrary or capricious manner can be met by a carefully drafted statute that ensures that the sentencing authority is given adequate information and guidance." "No longer can a jury wantonly and freakishly impose the death sentence; it is always circumscribed by the legislative guidelines," the Court ruled, finding that "a large proportion of American society" continued to regard executions "as an appropriate and necessary criminal sanction."[33]

Apart from the recent Eighth Amendment challenge to lethal injection, *McCleskey v. Kemp* was the last major systemic challenge to the death penalty to be heard by the U.S. Supreme Court. In that case, an African American named Warren McCleskey argued that Georgia's capital punishment regime was administered in a racially discriminatory fashion. Invoking the Eighth and Fourteenth Amendments, McCleskey contended that a complex statistical study showed that a grave risk existed that racial bias impermissibly entered into Georgia's capital sentencing determinations. Data collected by Professor David Baldus and others indicated that defendants charged with killing whites received the death penalty in 11 percent of cases, but defendants charged with killing blacks received that penalty in just 1 percent of cases. Even more troubling were the statistics for interracial murders and, in particular, black-on-white homicides. The Court, however, rejected reliance on data showing that blacks who killed whites were sentenced to death "at nearly 22 *times* the rate of blacks who kill blacks, and more than 7 *times* the rate of whites who kill blacks." The majority opinion held that, troubling statistics notwithstanding, McCleskey had to prove discriminatory motive *in his case,* blandly noting that "[a]t most, the Baldus study indicates a discrepancy that appears to correlate with race." Racial disparities in sentencing, the Court stated with bald resignation, "are an inevitable part of our criminal justice system." Years later, Justice Lewis Powell, the author of *McCleskey* and the deciding vote in that five-to-four decision, actually expressed regret at his vote in the case. After retiring, he voiced serious concerns to a group of the American Bar Association about the way in which "the system malfunctions." He ended his speech by pondering if "Congress and the state legislatures should take a serious look at whether the retention of a punishment that is being enforced only haphazardly is in the public interest."[34]

The *Gregg* and *McCleskey* cases, which dashed abolitionist hopes for intervention by the U.S. Supreme Court, forced death penalty opponents to open new fronts. Capital litigation continued unabated in death row inmates' cases, as it always has, but abolitionists—following those decisions—had to shift their focus and find other, more receptive outlets to press their cause. Many Americans, as well as human rights organizations such as Amnesty International and The National Coalition to Abolish the Death Penalty, are actively involved in the abolitionist movement, although much credit for reinvigorating that movement goes to two people: Sister Helen Prejean and Justice Harry Blackmun. Sister Prejean's 1993 book *Dead Man Walking* became an instant *New York Times* bestseller and was made into an Academy Award–winning motion picture, and her many public appearances kick-started the debate once more, inspiring a whole new generation of abolitionist leaders. Justice Blackmun, then a sitting member of the U.S. Supreme Court, followed up in a very public way, roundly condemning the death penalty in a 1994 judicial opinion. In his now-famous dissent in *Callins v. Collins,* Blackmun put it succinctly: "From this day forward, I no longer shall tinker with the machinery of death." "For more than 20 years," Blackmun wrote, "I have endeavored—indeed, I have struggled—along with a majority of this Court, to develop procedural and substantive rules that would lend more than the mere appearance of fairness to the death penalty endeavor." "Rather than continue to coddle the Court's delusion that the desired level of fairness has been achieved and the need for regulation eviscerated," Blackmun said, "I feel morally and intellectually obligated simply to concede that the death penalty experiment has failed."[35]

Blackmun's dissenting opinion was premised on the notion that it is impossible to administer the death penalty in a manner consistent with constitutional principles. "To be fair," Blackmun wrote, invoking the Court's prior holding in *Lockett v. Ohio,* "a capital sentencing scheme must treat each person convicted of a capital offense with that 'degree of respect due the uniqueness of the individual.' " On the other hand, he wrote, "[r]easonable consistency" requires that "the death penalty be inflicted evenhandedly, in accordance with reason and objective standards, rather than by whim, caprice, or prejudice." "Experience has taught us," Justice Blackmun explained, "that the constitutional goal of eliminating arbitrariness and discrimination from the administration of death can never be achieved without compromising an equally essential component of fundamental fairness—individualized sentencing." Noting that *Furman* had declared that "the death penalty must be imposed fairly, and with reasonable consistency, or not at all," Blackmun said that "despite the effort of the States and courts to devise legal formulas and procedural rules to meet this daunting challenge, the death penalty remains fraught with arbitrariness, discrimination, caprice, and mistake." "It is tempting, when faced with conflicting constitutional commands," Blackmun opined, "to sacrifice one for the other or to assume that an acceptable balance between them already has been struck." But in the death penalty context, he wrote, "such jurisprudential maneuvers are wholly inappropriate." Saying that "[t]he path the Court has chosen lessens us all," Blackmun concluded "that the decision whether a human being should live or die is so inherently subjective—rife with all of life's understandings, experiences, prejudices, and passions—that it inevitably defies the rationality and consistency required by the Constitution."[36]

As a result of such articulate voices, the abolition movement has only intensified in the last two decades. The American Bar Association, after studying the issue, stepped into the fray in 1997, calling for a moratorium on executions, and that set off yet another round of questions and introspection about America's death penalty. From there, anti–death penalty efforts swelled even further. In 1999 alone, bills to abolish the death penalty were considered in twelve states; in 2000, Illinois governor George Ryan imposed a statewide moratorium on executions before commuting the death sentences of all of the state's 150-plus death row inmates; and in that same year, New Hampshire's legislature voted for abolition, though that state's governor later vetoed the bill. As the twenty-first century began, at least one thousand grassroots organizations were pushing for a moratorium on executions, and in 2007, the State of New Jersey, led by Governor Jon Corzine, abolished capital punishment entirely. Indeed, the American Law Institute, the source of the Model Penal Code, disavowed its fifty-year-old framework for capital sentencing procedures in 2009, the same year that New Mexico, under Governor Bill Richardson's leadership, did away with capital punishment. In 2010, Kansas, which had already twice abolished and twice reinstated capital punishment, failed to abolish the death penalty for a third time by just a single vote, and Justice John Paul Stevens—newly retired—called his 1976 vote to uphold the death penalty "incorrect" and "the one vote I would change." Stevens later called another death penalty precedent, *Tison v. Arizona,* an "unfortunate decision," and wrote in a review of David Garland's *Peculiar Institution: America's Death Penalty in an Age of Abolition,* that the book "will persuade many readers that the death penalty is unwise and unjustified." In an interview on *60 Minutes,* Stevens advocated life-without-parole sentences in lieu of executions and emphasized that the death penalty should be done away with entirely. With a spate of death row exonerations having laid bare the criminal justice system's fallibility, more lawyers and judges—including multiple U.S. Supreme Court Justices—have grown more willing than ever to question or condemn the death penalty's continued use.[37]

The World's Abolition Movement

The U.S. death penalty debate is part of a larger movement to abolish capital punishment—a movement that goes back centuries. Death sentences have been debated for hundreds of years, with the first recorded parliamentary debate over executions occurring in 427 BC in Athens, Greece. Though executions were once common events throughout the world, death sentences are now being utilized less and less, and for fewer offenses. While fifty-eight countries retained the death penalty in 2009, only eighteen countries were known to have carried out executions that year. Saudi Arabia still beheads people; death sentences under Islamic law, or shari'a, remain common in places such as Iran, Nigeria, and Sudan, with men and women still being stoned to death; and China, the world's execution leader, still executes hundreds of people every year, reportedly using mobile execution vehicles to facilitate the harvest of organs for sale on the black market. While China refuses to divulge figures on its use of executions, the vast majority of worldwide executions occurred in Asia, the Middle East, and North Africa. Of the world's 714 known executions in 2009 (excluding those that took place in China, for which numbers are unavailable), more than six hundred took place in just seven Middle Eastern countries. Under Islamic law, many acts—including apostasy, converting to Christianity, and homosexuality—are punishable by death, with some countries still lopping off the hands of thieves or stoning to death women convicted of adultery. Under Iran's Islamic legal code, condemned men are buried in sand up to their waists, and women up to their necks, and pelted with stones until they die or manage to escape. According to Amnesty International's report, Iran conducted at least 388 executions; Iraq, 120; Saudi Arabia, 68; Yemen, 30; Syria, 8; Egypt, 5; and Libya, 4. In terms of death sentences (as opposed to actual executions), Amnesty International reports that in 2009 at least 2,001 people were sentenced to death in fifty-six countries.[38]

The death penalty is not yet universally shunned. At least twenty-three countries carried out executions in 2010, and at the end of that year, at least 17,833 people were under death sentences worldwide, though no official statistics exist for key countries such as China, Egypt, Iran, Malaysia, Sudan, Thailand, or Vietnam. Globally, however, capital punishment is falling out of favor. In 2009, not a single execution took place in Europe or countries making up the former Soviet Union, and no executions were reported that year in places such as Afghanistan, Indonesia, Mongolia, or Pakistan, the first time those countries have been execution-free in recent times. According to Amnesty International, at least 2,390 executions took place in 2008, with at least 1,252 in 2007, 1,591 in 2006, and 2,148 in 2005—numbers that all far exceed 2009 estimates. In 2010, at least 527 executions were carried out, though that figure did not include "the thousands of executions" believed to have been carried out in China that year. Only twenty-five countries carried out executions in 2006 and 2008; only twenty-four countries did so in 2007; and figures show that more than 90 percent of all known executions take place in just six nations: China, Iran, Iraq, Pakistan, Sudan, and the United States. Not only did 2009 and 2010 see a dramatic downward trend in executions, but in those years the United States became the only country in the Americas to carry out an execution. In October 2009, the European Union (EU), seeing executions as clear human rights violations, even formally asked the United States to "heed domestic and international calls to bring an end to the death penalty." The EU, calling attention to America's increasing isolation in the world community, specifically called on America to "admit" that capital punishment "has been a failed experiment with a very high cost in human suffering and inestimable damage to the country's standing and image in the world as a beacon for human rights and democratic values."[39]

As is clear from United Nations (UN), European, and other global anti–death penalty activity, the death penalty is increasingly condemned by the international community. In 1971, the UN General Assembly adopted a resolution asserting that "the main objective to be pursued is that of progressively restricting the number of offenses for which capital punishment may be imposed," with the aim of "abolishing this punishment in all countries." In 1999, the African Commission on Human and Peoples' Rights, a regional body, also adopted a resolution urging African countries to place a moratorium on executions and to "reflect on the possibility of abolishing the death penalty." A global network of activists, using the Internet and petition drives, has in fact long pushed for a halt to executions. In 2002, UN Secretary-General Kofi Annan, a 2001 Nobel Peace Prize recipient, added his own voice to the debate, expressing his support for a moratorium on executions even as he received a petition signed by 3.2 million people. "The forfeiture of life," he declared, "is too absolute, too irreversible, for one human being to inflict it on another, even when backed by legal process." "And I believe," he added, "that future generations, throughout the world, will come to agree." The UN, after a false start, ultimately followed suit. Although a moratorium resolution presented at the UN in 2004 failed to pass by eight votes, the UN General Assembly passed a resolution in 2007 calling upon member states that retain the death penalty "[t]o establish a moratorium on executions with a view to abolishing the death penalty." In 2008, yet another resolution calling for a global moratorium on executions passed by the lopsided vote of 106 to 46 (with 34 abstentions).[40]

The refusal of U.S. courts to see the death penalty as a human rights issue has also drawn major criticism elsewhere. Important U.S. allies such as Canada, England, Italy, and France have all, acting individually, categorically refused to extradite people to the United States in the absence of assurances that the death sentence will not be sought. France even refused to cooperate in the Zacarias Moussaoui terrorism investigation, thereby hindering U.S. law enforcement efforts, once the U.S. government decided to seek Moussaoui's execution. The United States has also been sternly rebuked by the International Court of Justice (ICJ) for its handling of foreign nationals arrested for capital crimes. Article 36 of the Vienna Convention on Consular Relations requires that governments notify detainees from foreign countries of their right to consular assistance. The failure to do so for dozens of foreigners who ended up on American death rows led Paraguay, Germany, and Mexico to file actions before the ICJ in cases concerning these foreign nationals. The ICJ, or the World Court, as it is commonly known, expressly determined that the United States violated international law in its handling of foreign nationals sent to death row. Because American courts have sentenced more than one hundred foreign nationals to die, the United States, by executing such offenders, has drawn the ire of many countries, strained diplomatic relations in the process, and lost much respect in the international community.[41]

Since a wave of postwar idealism led to the UN's creation in 1945, wars have still been fought around the globe, though much has changed since that time in terms of the public's awareness of human rights issues. Before World War II, international law did not systematically address human rights issues and was almost totally silent on the issue of the death penalty. Sovereign states treated their citizens as they pleased, with Nazi courts and dictators such as Stalin— responsible for at least a million executions—routinely imposing death sentences. The atrocities of Hitler and the Holocaust, however, changed all that, sparking worldwide calls for an end to government impunity and the recognition of basic human rights. The UN Charter, requiring states to promote human rights, was signed in San Francisco on June 26, 1945, and the postwar Universal Declaration of Human Rights, adopted in 1948, raised further awareness of fundamental rights, proudly proclaiming: "Everyone has the right to life, liberty and security of the person." That landmark declaration, in effect tracking the Declaration of Independence's articulation of the right to life, was shepherded through the UN by Eleanor Roosevelt. In her work, the popular First Lady successfully moved to delete any reference to the death penalty in that document because of the "movement underway in some states to wipe out the death penalty completely." Roosevelt herself had long condemned lynchings, calling them unlawful and unacceptable, and had worked behind the scenes—albeit unsuccessfully—for a federal antilynching bill.[42]

The right to life, so eloquently described by Thomas Jefferson in the Declaration of Independence as an "unalienable" right, has thus only grown in stature since Jefferson's time. Along with the Universal Declaration of Human Rights, courts and other instruments of international law have sought to end the culture of state impunity and to safeguard the right to life. The Geneva conventions include protections for prisoners of war and civilians relative to the death penalty's imposition, explicitly protecting offenders who are under eighteen, pregnant, or mothers with dependent infants. The U.S. Supreme Court, while still allowing executions, has called the right to life "fundamental," with America itself recognizing the "right to life" in the context of international law. In 1966, the UN General Assembly adopted a binding treaty called the International Covenant on Civil and Political Rights that specifically reiterates that "[e]very human being has the inherent right to life" and provides that "[n]o one shall be arbitrarily deprived of his life." The United States ratified that treaty, which also prohibits "torture" and "cruel, inhuman or degrading treatment or punishment" and bars the execution of pregnant women and those committing crimes when under the age of eighteen. Although the United States entered reservations to the treaty, seeking to retain its ability to execute such offenders, other countries later expanded their commitment by signing an optional protocol to it. The optional protocol was specifically aimed at the death penalty's abolition.[43]

More targeted treaties—both at the international and regional levels—have also sought to protect "the right to life." The Inter-American human rights system protects it, with the American Convention on Human Rights barring the death penalty for political offenses, pregnant women, juvenile offenders, and those over seventy years of age. Article 4(2) states that "[i]n countries that have not abolished the death penalty, it may be imposed only for the most serious crimes," while Article 4(3) states that "[t]he death penalty shall not be reestablished in states that have abolished it." Though the United States has never ratified that treaty, it is a signatory to the American Declaration of the

Rights and Duties of Man, which protects "the right to life" and against "cruel, infamous or unusual punishment." For countries that have ratified the American Convention on Human Rights, an Additional Protocol to it—effective as of 1991—now categorically forbids the death penalty in times of peace. The UN Convention on the Rights of the Child, having come into force in 1990 and ratified by every country save the United States and Somalia, also expressly forbids capital punishment for juvenile offenders. Article 37 of that treaty reads: "No child shall be subjected to torture or other cruel, inhuman or degrading treatment or punishment. Neither capital punishment nor life imprisonment shall be imposed for offences committed by persons below 18 years of age." This treaty, which highlights how out of step the United States has become in the world's eyes, no doubt played a role, however subtle, in the U.S. Supreme Court's decision to bar the practice of executing juvenile offenders. Indeed, in *Roper,* the Supreme Court went out of its way to note that its Eighth Amendment ruling found "confirmation" in the fact that "the United States is the only country in the world that continues to give official sanction to the juvenile death penalty." "It is proper we acknowledge the overwhelming weight of international opinion against the juvenile death penalty," the Court concluded.[44]

The international community, through treaties and regional human rights systems, is undeniably moving steadily away from capital punishment. Indeed, international tribunals formed to prosecute genocide, crimes against humanity, and war crimes—the world's most serious and grave offenses—no longer allow death sentences. Article 77 of the Rome Statute of the International Criminal Court, which came into force in 2002, made "life imprisonment" the maximum penalty. Other ad hoc tribunals of international justice, including those for Rwanda, the former Yugoslavia, and Sierra Leone, did not allow the imposition of the death penalty either. This means that the world's worst human rights offenders—including men such as Slobodan Milosevic, whose trial in The Hague came to an abrupt end after he was found dead in his cell—no longer face capital charges. All of Europe, in fact, is now a death penalty–free zone, with its adoption of human rights instruments over the years progressively outlawing executions. Since 1953, the European Convention on Human Rights has protected "[e]veryone's right to life," with that treaty—now regularly invoked in extradition proceedings—also providing that "[n]o one shall be subjected to torture or to inhuman or degrading treatment or punishment." Protocol No. 6 to the European Convention, in force as of 1985, abolished the death penalty except in time of war or imminent threat of war, with Protocol No. 13—adopted in 2003 and quickly ratified by forty countries—now unequivocally barring the punishment of death even in wartime. Other allies also vehemently oppose U.S. policy. For instance, Australia's Extradition Act was invoked before Australia agreed in 2010 to extradite Gabe Watson, the so-called "Honeymoon Killer," to the United States. An Alabama man convicted of manslaughter in Australia in connection with the death of his new wife while they were scuba diving near the Great Barrier Reef, Watson faced murder charges in Alabama but his deportation was delayed until a pledge not to seek the death penalty was obtained.[45]

The death penalty's rapid global decline can be traced to the work of non-governmental organizations (NGOs) and activists and to advancements in the field of international human rights law. In Europe, the situs of the abolitionist movement's greatest success, it has been noted that "[f]undamentally important was the message that had been conveyed: a *principled* opposition to the death penalty as a violation of fundamental human rights." Both the European Union and its human rights arm, the Council of Europe, have publicly declared that "[t]he death penalty has no legitimate place in the penal systems of modern civilized societies," and that "its application may well be compared with torture and be seen as inhuman and degrading punishment." The clear connection between the death penalty and torture—two topics that Beccaria wrote about extensively in *On Crimes and Punishments*—is in fact long overdue. Execution protocols may be structured to alleviate the risk of pain at the moment of an inmate's death, but even then there is always an undeniable risk of human error. In September 2009, for example, a fifty-three-year-old African American inmate, Romell Broom, was to be executed, but the IV team seeking to administer the lethal injection failed to find a useable vein and gave up after two hours. According to his lawyer, Broom winced in pain as the execution team tried repeatedly but unsuccessfully to locate a vein. In another case, *Nelson v. Campbell,* the U.S. Supreme Court itself heard a claim by an Alabama death row inmate alleging that the use of a "cut-down" procedure, requiring an incision into his arm or leg to access his severely compromised veins, constituted cruel and unusual punishment. Along with botched executions and the ever-present prospect of *physical* pain during their administration, there is also, of course, the sheer *psychological* terror associated with death sentences and executions. Being sentenced to death, which places the defendant in fear of being executed at the hands of the state, should in fact be seen as a species of torture, to say nothing of what it is actually like to live under a death sentence not just for days or weeks, but for years or decades at a time.[46]

Cruel and Unusual Punishments

Should the U.S. Constitution's Cruel and Unusual Punishments Clause be read to bar executions? This question has perplexed lawyers and judges for decades, with the U.S. Supreme Court deciding the question both ways at different times. The Court said "yes" in *Furman,* but then "no" in *Gregg.* Though the Court, using the Eighth Amendment, has barred the execution of a number of categories of offenders, not since *Furman* has it seriously considered whether executions themselves are unconstitutional. Because *Furman* and *Gregg* were decided in the 1970s, and much has transpired since then, it seems especially fitting to reconsider once more whether the Eighth Amendment should bar all executions. In effect, did the Court get it right in *Furman,* but then wrong in *Gregg*? A "punishment"—what Samuel Johnson's 1773 *A Dictionary of the English Language* defined as "[a]ny infliction imposed in vengeance of a crime"—relates to the act of punishing one who has committed a crime. Executions are clearly "punishments," so, in terms of the Eighth Amendment text, which the Framers left us to consider, just one fundamental question arises: Are executions "cruel and unusual"? As the final arbiter of what the Constitution means, the Supreme Court plainly has the power to decide this question, which, if broken down further, might be subdivided into two parts: Are executions "cruel"? And, are executions "unusual"? The only legitimate debate should center not on whether the Court can decide these issues, but on how it should decide them and what the ultimate result should be. While some Justices favor an "originalist" approach to the question at hand, others hold far different views, though all the Justices—who sit atop an independent branch of government, the judiciary—take solemn oaths to uphold the Constitution.[47]

Some, such as Justice Antonin Scalia, say that the Constitution's text precludes the Court from ever declaring the death penalty unconstitutional. Citing the Fifth and Fourteenth Amendments and early American death penalty laws, they invoke the Framers' approval of capital punishment, contending that a constitutional amendment would be needed to abolish it. Such arguments center on capital crimes enacted by the First Congress and the language of prior amendments to the Constitution itself. The Fifth Amendment, they note, references "capital" crimes, providing: "No person shall be held to answer for a *capital,* or otherwise infamous crime, unless on a presentment or indictment of a Grand Jury, except in cases arising in the land or naval forces, or in the Militia, when in actual service in time of War or public danger." Indeed, the Fifth Amendment contemplates both corporal and capital punishments, reading: "nor shall any person be subject for the same offence to be twice put in jeopardy of *life or limb* . . . nor be deprived of *life,* liberty, or property, without due process of law." The Fourteenth Amendment, ratified on July 9, 1868, and used by the U.S. Supreme Court to apply the Eighth Amendment against the States, likewise contemplates the taking of life. It provides, in a manner similar to the Fifth Amendment, that "nor shall any State deprive any person of *life,* liberty, or property, without due process of law." At the other end of the spectrum from Justice Scalia are former members of the Court such as Justices Brennan and Marshall, who have argued that executions are unconstitutional as a matter of law.[48]

Although the U.S. Bill of Rights contains references to "capital," "life," and "life or limb," any Eighth Amendment inquiry with regard to executions cannot end there. After all, the prohibition on "cruel and unusual punishments" is absolute, and nowhere does the Bill of Rights—put in place to *safeguard* rights—ever mandate death as a punishment. The Fifth Amendment's Due Process Clause, like other American legal provisions, has its origins in English law, serving *to prohibit* the arbitrary deprivation of one's property, life, or other rights. The phrase "due process of law" comes from the statutes of King Edward III, and from a country, England, that no longer even uses capital punishment. "[N]o Man of what estate or condition that he be," the relevant English provision read, "should be put out of his land or tenements, nor taken, nor imprisoned, nor disinherited, nor put to death, without being brought to answer by due process of Law." In the Magna Carta, an even earlier protection against the arbitrary deprivation of life, King John promised that "no free man shall be taken, or imprisoned, or disseized, or outlawed, or banished, or in anywise destroyed . . . save by the lawful judgment of his peers, or the law of the land," with Edward III proclaiming that "the Great Charter . . . be kept and maintained." In 1855, the U.S. Supreme Court—the final arbiter of the meaning of American law—determined that the words "due process of law," also used by the New York legislature in early 1787, were intended to convey the same meaning as the words "the law of the land" in the Magna Carta. For Justice Scalia to turn constitutional protections intended as a shield to *protect life* into an ever-foreboding weapon—a Sword of Damocles perpetually authorizing state-sanctioned killing—makes no sense whatsoever.[49]

The words "punish" and "Punishment" do appear in the Constitution, but capital punishment is actually not associated with those references. The U.S. Senate is given "the sole Power to try all Impeachments," but that power only extends to removal "from Office," with Article I, Section 3 noting only that "the Party convicted shall nevertheless be liable and subject to Indictment, Trial, Judgment and *Punishment, according to Law.*" The Eighth Amendment, of course, is itself an important component of U.S. law, and no law that violates the Eighth Amendment can withstand constitutional scrutiny. The Constitution's other references to the concept of punishment also leave the actual punishment to be imposed unstated. Article I, Section 5 simply gives each body of Congress the power to "determine the Rules of its Proceedings, *punish* its Members for disorderly Behaviour, and, with the Concurrence of two thirds, expel a Member," while Article I, Section 8 speaks of the power of Congress "To provide for the *Punishment* of counterfeiting the Securities and current Coin of the United States" and "To define and *punish* Piracies and Felonies committed on the high Seas, and Offenses against the Law of Nations." Though Article III, Section 3 also states that "[t]he Congress shall have Power to declare the *Punishment* of Treason," the power to "provide," "define," or "declare" a punishment does not mean that Congress has the ability to authorize a punishment that is inconsistent with the Eighth Amendment prohibition.[50]

At Virginia's ratifying convention, Patrick Henry made this exact point in urging the adoption of a cruel and unusual punishments clause. "Congress, from their general powers, may fully go into the business of human legislation," he said in 1788, noting that members of Congress "may legislate in criminal cases from treason to the lowest offence, petty larceny." "They may define crimes and prescribe punishments," Henry emphasized as he explained his concerns. "In the definition of crimes," Henry offered, "I trust they will be directed by what wise representatives ought to be governed by." "But when we come to punishments," he made clear, pointing to Virginia's prohibition on cruel and unusual punishments, "no latitude ought to be left, nor dependence put on the virtue of representatives." In other words, judges—*not* legislators—were to decide which punishments crossed the line and ran into the prohibited territory of "cruel and unusual punishments." No one, in fact, has been executed for treason in many decades, making the death penalty extremely "unusual" even for that most serious offense. Indeed, in Article III, Section 3—the provision addressing "Treason against the United States"—death is not ever mandated in the text.[51]

On its face, the Eighth Amendment applies to all "cruel and unusual punishments," without regard to the particular crime to be punished, whether treason, murder, or some other offense. Although the Constitution gives Congress the power to "punish" or "declare the Punishment" for certain offenses, the Eighth Amendment—which restricts judicial, executive, and legislative actions—unequivocally prohibits *all* "cruel and unusual punishments." Any punishment—whether death or a corporal one, or whether for treason or a lesser offense—is capable of being adjudged a "cruel and unusual" punishment so long as it qualifies as such. And historically speaking, the Eighth Amendment's broad prohibition on "cruel and unusual punishments"—with no exception listed for executions—appears to be no accident. Though the Eighth Amendment wording had origins elsewhere, James Madison carefully considered which rights to include in the U.S. Bill of Rights and whether to include exceptions to such constitutional rights. "Supposing a bill of rights to be proper," Madison wrote Jefferson in October 1788, "the articles which ought to compose it, admit of much discussion," with Madison then emphasizing: "I am inclined to think that *absolute* restrictions in cases that are doubtful, or where emergencies may overrule them, ought to be avoided."[52]

The Constitution, for example, qualifies "[t]he Privilege of the Writ of Habeas Corpus" by stating that the privilege can be "suspended" when "in Cases of Rebellion or Invasion the public Safety may require it." The power to suspend the writ of habeas corpus, a right called "essential to freedom" at the Massachusetts ratifying convention, was in fact vigorously debated in the ensuing ratification debate. Likewise, the Fifth Amendment contains an express exception, making the grand jury requirement inapplicable "in cases arising in the land or naval forces, or in the Militia, when in actual service in time of War or public danger." In sharp contrast, the Eighth Amendment's guarantee against "cruel and unusual punishments" is absolute, making all such punishments, of whatever kind, subject to scrutiny under it.[53]

The Constitution's special treason provisions, put in place to protect the rights of the accused as well as those of family members, illustrate the point. Article III, Section 3 first narrowly defines the crime: "Treason against the United States, shall consist only in levying War against them, or in adhering to their Enemies, giving them Aid and Comfort." That section thus limits who might be subjected to a prosecution for treason. Along with requiring a "Confession in open Court" or "the Testimony of two Witnesses to the same overt Act" for a treason conviction, Article III, Section 3 further provides that "no Attainder of Treason shall work Corruption of Blood, or Forfeiture except during the Life of the Person attainted." Thus, the Constitution not only imposes extraordinary evidentiary protections for those accused of treason, but it also serves—by preventing "Corruption of Blood," a common-law concept—to protect the inheritance rights of family members of anyone actually convicted of treason. Although the Constitution states that Congress "shall have Power to declare the Punishment of Treason," that language must be read in conjunction with the Eighth Amendment's Cruel and Unusual Punishments Clause. When that is done, the result is clear: while Congress has the power to declare the punishment, it cannot pass any law that imposes a "cruel and unusual" punishment. The Thirteenth Amendment, notably, also later spoke of "punishment," providing that "[n]either slavery nor involuntary servitude, except as a punishment for crime whereof the party shall have been duly convicted, shall exist within the United States, or any place subject to their jurisdiction." Again, however, the "punishment for crime" is left unspecified—and would, of course, even for convicted criminals, be subject to the Eighth Amendment proscription that no "cruel and unusual" punishment be imposed.[54]

The Cruel and Unusual Punishments Clause has been read in different ways over the centuries. That is no doubt because *cruel* and *unusual*—as with most words—are subject to interpretation. The word *cruel*, the first word in the clause, plainly has a subjective quality to it that makes it amenable to more than one construction. Though dictionaries meticulously define words and courts pride themselves on reading binding legal documents in a reasonable manner, what is cruel to one person may not be cruel—or as cruel—to another. The *Oxford English Dictionary,* not surprisingly, defines *cruel* in multiple ways, making the word capable of different uses in varying contexts. For example, under the subentry "Of actions," which seems a fitting place to start, *cruel* is defined as "[p]roceeding from or showing indifference to or pleasure in another's distress." Under the subheading "Of conditions, circumstances," by contrast, it means "[c]ausing or characterized by great suffering; extremely painful or distressing." The word *unusual*, the other term modifying *punishments*, is similarly subjective, though it, like *cruel*, also has commonly understood meanings. In regular parlance and as defined in standard English dictionaries, the word *unusual* simply means "not usual," "not common," or "rare." American courts routinely use *unusual* to mean something that is "out of the ordinary," "uncommon," "deviating from the norm," "strange," "exceptional," "being unlike others," or "not in accordance with usage, custom, or habit." Justice Scalia, citing *Webster's* dictionaries, has himself said that *unusual* means "such as [does not] occu[r] in ordinary practice," "[s]uch as is [not] in common use."[55]

In considering the word *cruel*, the death penalty fits that description. Death sentences intentionally inflict severe mental distress, and executions—whether painful or painless—result in the end of a person's life. Though *cruel* has multiple meanings, the term is hardly devoid of meaning, and judges, like anyone else, can readily decide what *cruel* means and what so qualifies. The concrete, easily understood dictionary definitions of *cruel* show that it pertains to attitudes or activities that show indifference to others; that cause another distress, pain, or suffering; or that take pleasure in another's mistreatment. The death penalty, once used to kill slaves and religious dissenters and used throughout history against offenders of all stripes to exact retribution or revenge in spite of the pain and distress it causes, should thus be classified as *cruel* within the meaning of the Eighth Amendment. Indeed, many of the Founding Fathers used the word *cruel* to describe American penal practices, sometimes capital punishment itself. James Madison—who scrivened the Cruel and Unusual Punishments Clause with just slight modifications from its English and Virginian counterparts—used that very word as he spoke of the potential of substituting "penitentiary discipline" for "the cruel inflictions so disgraceful to penal codes." Just as an Eighth Amendment violation was found in *Trop v. Dulles*, in which the loss of a deserter's U.S. citizenship was found to be cruel and unusual because it resulted in statelessness, an executed person has, to use the language from *Trop*, "lost the right to have rights."[56]

The very nature of executions—the intentional taking of life—makes them cruel, especially now that maximum-security prisons are available to house such offenders for the rest of their natural lives. Ironically, in the 1989 case of *DeShaney v. Winnebago County Department of Social Services,* the Supreme Court has already specifically held that the Eighth Amendment requires that the government provide for a prisoner's "basic human needs—*e.g.,* food, clothing, shelter, medical care, and reasonable safety." Courts have also found that the Eighth Amendment requires psychological or psychiatric treatment of inmates under certain circumstances, and even before *DeShaney,* the Supreme Court itself recognized that prisoners have basic human rights. In the 1978 case of *Hutto v. Finney,* for instance, the Court held that when inmates were crowded into cells and exposed to infectious diseases such as hepatitis and venereal disease, the Eighth Amendment required a remedy. Death, of course, is a fate far worse than contracting a sexually transmitted disease or not receiving adequate medical attention or mental health treatment in the case of an illness.[57]

As the first and primary focus of Eighth Amendment jurisprudence, the word *cruel* is thus already used to describe a wide array of degrading or inhumane practices. In *Hudson v. McMillian,* yet another case, the U.S. Supreme Court held that a prisoner had an Eighth Amendment claim when prison guards punched and kicked him. Other American courts have used *cruel,* too, to describe whipping prisoners with a strap, depriving them of adequate food, or serving them a contaminated meal. Indeed, Eighth Amendment violations have been found where an inmate's jaw was broken without provocation; a prisoner was forced to live and sleep for two years in an unlit cell with backed-up sewage and roaches; prison officials compelled inmates to work in a sewage lift-pump station without protective clothing and equipment; and a guard assaulted a paraplegic inmate with a knife and forced him to sit in his own feces. In one case, the unsanitary jail conditions involved a lack of flush toilets, sinks, or running water, as well as forcing inmates—confined to their cells for between seventeen and twenty-four hours per day—to eat and sleep next to buckets containing their own urine and feces. Those conditions, a Massachusetts court held, "constitute cruel and unusual punishment in violation of the Eighth Amendment." If it is cruel—and it is—to starve an inmate or to beat up a prisoner without provocation, it surely is cruel to sentence someone to death, let the inmate await execution for years or decades at a time, and then tie down and deliberately inject the securely bound inmate with lethal chemicals for the express purpose of taking that inmate's life.[58]

The word *cruel,* when reasonably construed, certainly connotes far more than barbaric or painful modes of execution—what prior cases suggest as the applicable legal standard. As a textual matter, the Eighth Amendment prohibits "cruel and unusual" punishments, not merely "antiquated," "obsolete," or "physically painful" ones. The prohibition on "cruel and unusual punishments" thus does much more than bar torturous executions such as those carried out in bygone eras through burning at the stake, boiling in oil, or breaking on the wheel. To be sure, horrendously painful executions are unconstitutional, but so too are "cruel and unusual" ones, no matter the mode of execution. Botched executions frequently occur, and their regularity establishes at the very least the risk of a physically painful death. In 2009, University of Colorado professor Michael Radelet readily documented more than forty examples of post-1980 botched executions, a list that is by no means exhaustive. They include electrocutions in which inmates' legs and heads caught on fire, charring the bodies and filling the execution chambers with smoke; lethal injections in which technicians could not locate suitable veins for more than a half hour or needed the inmate's help to find one; and other executions in which intravenous needles were inserted improperly, tubing kinked, drugs solidified, or a syringe came out, spraying deadly chemicals across the room. This pattern of botched executions, which cannot be dismissed as a series of isolated incidents in light of their frequency, highlights the ever-present risk of human error and excruciating physical pain that can—and often does—accompany executions.[59]

But even without the risk of *physical* pain, the death penalty must still be considered cruel. The concept of cruelty encompasses much more than an inmate's painful death on a gurney, something easily shown just by examining existing Eighth Amendment cases barring corporal punishments and striking down punishments deemed disproportionate to the crime. Just as corporal punishments are demeaning and cruel, death sentences, all by themselves, inflict enormous *psychological* harm—physic pain that has been aptly likened to torture and that can, as Justice Blackmun once noted, constitute "cruel and unusual punishment." "Psychological pain," Blackmun wrote, "often may be clinically diagnosed and quantified through well-established methods, as in the ordinary tort context where damages for pain and suffering are regularly awarded." *Webster's* itself defines *torture* as "anguish of body or mind," and capital punishment, given its physical and mental effects, should clearly be seen as a species of torture, a finding that at least some American courts have been prepared to make. For example, in 1972, just prior to the *Furman* decision, the California Supreme Court ruled in *People v. Anderson*: "The cruelty of capital punishment lies not only in the execution itself and the pain incident thereto, but also in the dehumanizing effects of the lengthy imprisonment prior to execution during which the judicial and administrative procedures essential to due process of law are carried out." "Penologists and medical experts agree," the California court wrote in that case, "that the process of carrying out a verdict of death is often so degrading and brutalizing to the human spirit as to constitute psychological torture." The death penalty should thus readily be classified as a form of torture, a concept already long associated with the intentional infliction of agony or severe pain to obtain confessions or other information. One of the definitions listed for *torture* in *Webster's* is "get revenge," an apt description of society's use of executions. At bottom, society's death penalty laws seem to say this, and nothing more, to killers: you killed, so you will be killed; you were cruel to another, so we, in turn, will be cruel to you.[60]

If executions are cruel, and they certainly fit that description, the death penalty's constitutionality hinges on whether they are *unusual*, a word that invites consideration of whether they are commonly employed or out of the ordinary. In prior Eighth Amendment cases, the term *unusual* has often been ignored or shunted aside, with the phrase "cruel and unusual" seemingly viewed as a unitary concept focused on inhumane treatment. In other words, distinctions between *cruel* and *unusual* have not always been drawn. Sometimes, judges just summarily characterize a particular punishment as "cruel and unusual," with little discussion of the rationale behind the characterization. At other times, if a punishment is found to be *cruel*, it is also assumed to be *unusual*. For example, in the plurality opinion in *Trop v. Dulles*, Chief Justice Earl Warren wrote: "Whether the word 'unusual' has any qualitative meaning different from 'cruel' is not clear. On the few occasions this Court has had to consider the meaning of the phrase, precise distinctions between cruelty and unusualness do not seem to have been drawn." Citing three prior cases, *Weems v. United States, O'Neil v. Vermont,* and *Wilkerson v. Utah,* Warren wrote: "These cases indicate that the Court simply examines the particular punishment involved in light of the basic prohibition against inhuman treatment, without regard to any subtleties of meaning that might be latent in the word 'unusual.'" While substantial evidence shows that the Framers themselves paid little attention to the difference between "cruel and unusual" and "cruel or unusual" punishments, the text of the Constitution requires that "unusual" not be given short shrift, particularly as it follows the conjunctive "and" and not the disjunctive "or."[61]

The phrase "unusual punishments" was actually used on multiple occasions, though in varying ways, at Virginia's ratifying convention. In asserting that the Constitution left the states no control of their militias, William Grayson, an Anti-Federalist from Prince William County, said this in reference to "unusual punishments":

> Were this Government well organized, he would not object to giving it power over the militia. But as it appeared to him to be without checks, and to tend to the formation of an Aristocratic body, he could not agree to it. Thus organized, his imagination did not reach so far as to know where this power should be lodged. He conceived the State Governments to be at the mercy of the generality. He wished to be open to conviction, but he could see no case where the States could command the militia.—He did not believe that it corresponded with the intentions of those who formed it, as it was altogether without an equilibrium. He humbly apprehended that the power of providing for organizing and disciplining the militia, enabled the Government to make laws for regulating them, and inflicting punishments for disobedience, neglect, &c— Whether it would be the spirit of the generality to lay unusual punishments, he knew not, but he thought they had the power, if they thought proper to exercise it.

"I object to the want of checks, and a line of discrimination between the State Governments and the generality," Grayson said.[62]

In the debate, George Mason also rose and specifically spoke of "ignominious" and "unusual" punishments. Worried that "the militia of the future day" might not consist of "all classes" but might be "confined to the lower and middle classes of the people, granting exclusion to the higher classes of the people," Mason argued: "If we should ever see that day, the most ignominious punishments and heavy fines may be expected." As Mason told his colleagues, contrasting Virginia's system—with its protection against cruel and unusual punishments—with what might, if ratification occurred, become a national one:

Under such a full and equal representation as ours, there can be no ignominious punishments inflicted. But under this national, or rather consolidated Government, the case will be different. The representation being so small, and inadequate, they will have no fellow-feeling for the people. They may discriminate people in their own predicament, and exempt from militia duty all the officers and lowest creatures of the national Government. If there were a more particular definition of their powers, and a clause exempting the militia from martial law, except when in actual service, and from fines and punishments of an unusual nature, then we might expect that the militia would be what they are.

"[E]xemption of the highest classes of the people from militia service," Mason said, "would justify apprehensions of severe and ignominious punishments."[63]

Patrick Henry also spoke with concern of the infliction of an "unusual punishment." After saying that the history of England shows that "they have blocks and gibbets," Henry made clear he was not necessarily bothered by those particular punishments, though he despised cruelty. As Henry stated: "The violators of the public interest have been tried, justly and impartially, and perished by those necessary instruments of justice." Instead, Henry expressed special concern over inhumane "torture." Henry made his point by way of a series of questions: "When a person shall be treated in the most horrid manner, and most cruelly and inhumanly tortured, will the security of territorial rights"—that is, states' rights—"grant him redress?" "Suppose," he said, "an unusual punishment in consequence of an arrest similar to that of the Russian Ambassador—can it be said to be contrary to the State rights?" Henry continued: "I might go on in this discrimination, but it is too obvious that the security of territory is no security of individual safety. I ask, how are the State rights, individual rights, and national rights secured?" "Not as in England," Henry argued, "[f]or the authority quoted from Blackstone, would, if stated right, prove in a thousand instances, that if the King of England attempted to take away the rights of individuals, the law would stand against him.—The acts of Parliament would stand in his way—The Bill, and Declaration of Rights would be against him." "The rights of the people cannot be destroyed even by the paramount operation of the law of nations, as the case of the Russian Ambassador evinces," Henry said, arguing that more safeguards were needed and that "[t]he common law is fortified by the Bill of Rights." "If you look for a similar security in the paper on your table, you look in vain," he said of the proposed constitution. "That paper is defective without such a Declaration of Rights.—It is unbounded without such restrictions."[64]

Henry specifically highlighted the familiar case of the Russian ambassador, referenced by William Blackstone, to illustrate how problematic it would be to fail to bar "unusual" punishments in the federal constitution. In the late 1700s,

Blackstone made clear, ambassadors had immunity from criminal prosecution under the law of nations. If an ambassador violated the law of a host country, the ambassador could be sent home but could not be prosecuted. Worried that treaties entered into by the national government might lead to the violation of individual rights, Henry contended that an individual's rights would be unprotected against the U.S. government's treaty power due to the lack of a federal bill of rights. Citing the case in which the Russian czar had demanded that Queen Anne summarily execute an officer who had improperly arrested the Russian ambassador, Henry remarked: "A treaty may be made giving away your rights, and inflicting unusual punishments on its violators." "If the Constitution be paramount," he queried, "how are the Constitutions and laws of the States to stand?" "Their operation will be totally controuled by it," Henry responded to his own question, emphasizing that "[t]he rights of persons are exposed as it stands now."[65]

In short, Patrick Henry spoke of a well-known case in which the death penalty might have been inflicted as constituting an "unusual" punishment. "Recollect the case of the Russian ambassador," Henry emphasized, pointing out that the ambassador "was arrested contrary to the rights of his master." As Henry argued: "The Russian emperor demanded the man at whose instance his ambassador was arrested, to be given up to him, to be put to instant death. What did the Queen say? She wrote to him, that that was something paramount to what she could do:—that it exceeded her power to comply with his demand, because it was contrary to the constitution and laws." Fairly construed, Henry's speech thus seems to say that England's own prohibition on "cruel and unusual punishments" would have barred the ambassador's execution. "Can the English Monarch make a treaty which shall subvert the common law of England, and the constitution? Dare he make a treaty that shall violate Magna Charta, or the Bill of Rights? Dare he do any thing derogatory to the honor, or subversive of the great privileges of his people?" Henry asked. "No, Sir," he said. "If he did it would be nugatory, and the attempt would endanger his existence." "But how is it here?" Henry inquired, turning back once more to the proposed constitution being debated. "Treaties are binding, notwithstanding our laws and constitutions," he pointed out, with Henry fearing that "the case of the Russian ambassador" might "happen here." "The president," Henry worried, "can settle it by a treaty, have the man arrested, and punished according to the Russian manner."[66]

To combat this line of argument, those favoring ratification of the Constitution tried to dispel Henry's concerns about "unusual punishments." Governor Edmund Randolph replied with an outright denial, saying that the federal government's treaty power could not result in the taking of life. "[N]either the life, nor property of any citizen, nor the particular right of any state," he said, "can be affected by a treaty." His colleague George Nicholas said, "the English history respecting the Russian ambassador" simply "does not apply to this part of the Constitution." As Nicholas argued: "The arrest of that ambassador was an offence against the law of nations. There was no tribunal to punish it before." Madison, too, spoke up. "As to the case of the Russian Ambassador," he said, "I shall say nothing." "It is," Madison argued, referring to Henry and his approach, "as inapplicable as many other quotations made by the Gentleman." "I conceive," Madison added, "that as far as the Bill of Rights in the States, do not express any thing foreign to the nature of such things, and express fundamental principles essential to liberty, and those privileges which are declared necessary to all free people, these rights are not encroached on by this Government." Madison argued that Henry's fears over the proposed federal constitution were "groundless." The bar on "unusual" punishments, of course, eventually made its way into the Constitution.[67]

The law professor John Stinneford argues that "unusual" was a term of art, and that its original Eighth Amendment meaning referred to government practices contrary to "long usage" or "immemorial usage." "The opposite of a practice that enjoyed 'long usage,'" he writes, was an "innovation" or an "unusual" practice contrary to long-standing common-law precedent. From time to time, the Founding Fathers did use such terminology, making it part of the fabric of eighteenth-century legal discourse. For example, James Wilson, a principal drafter of the Constitution, wrote that "long customs, approved by the consent of those who use them, acquire the qualities of a law." " 'Long use and custom,'" Wilson said, "is assigned as the criterion of law, 'taken by the people at their free liberty, and by their own consent.'" "And this criterion," Wilson added, "is surely sufficient to satisfy the principle: for consent is certainly proved by long, though it be not immemorial usage." Richard Henry Lee likewise thought American rights were built upon "natural law, the British constitution, the charters of the several colonies, and 'immemorial usage,'" while Sir Edward Coke was of the view that customs "are defined to be a Law ... which being established by long use, and the consent of our Ancestors, hath been, and is daily practiced." Blackstone—that oracle of English law— also wrote that "the first ground and chief corner-stone of the laws of England" was "general immemorial custom, or common law, from time to time declared in the decisions of the courts of justice." Customs that had "binding power, and the force of laws," he explained, were ones enjoying "long and immemorial usage" and "universal reception throughout the kingdom."[68]

While Stinneford concedes that *unusual* also meant "rare," "uncommon," and "out of the ordinary" in the seventeenth and eighteenth centuries, he argues that *unusual* should not be read, as it typically has been, in an ordinary way. After brushing aside as aberrational the statements of Representatives Livermore and Smith in the First Congress as to the vagueness of the Eighth Amendment protection, Stinneford argues that the term *unusual* was used in Virginia's ratifying convention "to signify the Antifederalists' concern that the federal government would not be bound by the constraints of the common law and might exercise new and tyrannical powers." He further points to some early precedents associating the "cruel and unusual punishments" prohibition with violations of common-law principles, including the 1828 case of *Commonwealth v. Wyatt*. In that case, the General Court of Virginia upheld a statute that gave judges discretion to order the whipping of those convicted of involvement in illegal gaming operations. "The punishment of offenses by stripes is certainly odious, but cannot be said to be *unusual*," the court ruled in *Wyatt*, emphasizing that the statutory discretion was "of the same character with the discretion always exercised by Common Law Courts to inflict fine and imprisonment, and subject to be restrained by the same considerations." As Stinneford concludes: "The word 'unusual' in the Cruel and Unusual Punishments Clause was meant to be a check on the federal government's ability to innovate in punishment. This is the only plausible meaning of the word as used in the Eighth Amendment." "Indeed," Stinneford writes, "the Framers shared with Coke the opinion that innovation in punishment often led to torture and barbarity."[69]

In a portion of his *Northwestern University Law Review* article addressing "Long Usage and the Death Penalty," Stinneford argues that "[t]o the extent that the death penalty has been continuously imposed for a given crime—murder, for example—over a very long period of time, then it could not properly be found to be unusual." "But to the extent," he clarifies, "that capital punishment has fallen out of usage for a given crime—such as burglary or counterfeiting—any attempt to revive such a punishment would be unusual, and at least arguably cruel." In his attempt to locate what he calls the "original meaning" of "unusual," Stinneford contends that there were only three ways a punishment could ever cease to be authorized by the common law and thus become "unusual." As Stinneford writes: "The punishment could fall completely out of usage for a long period of time; it could be used in England, but not America (and thus never attain 'usual' status on this side of the Atlantic); or it could be disallowed by legislative reform." "Should any of these three events occur," Stinneford notes, "a punishment formerly authorized by the common law would become unusual and would lose its presumption of reasonableness and validity."[70]

Though provocative, Professor Stinneford's arguments are ultimately unconvincing. To be sure, the United States, like England, has a common-law system, which evolved out of what Blackstone called "customs." The Founding Fathers, however, had divergent conceptions of English and American common law, to say nothing of the disparate views of those voting to ratify the U.S. Bill of Rights. The Constitution itself, Madison noted in 1796, "was nothing more than the draught of a plan, nothing but a dead letter, until life and validity were breathed into it, by the voice of the people, speaking through the several state conventions." In his work on the revisal of Virginia's laws, Jefferson expressed the view that "the Common Law" was "not to be meddled with," though he added the massive clawback, "except where Alterations are necessary." As Jefferson explained in an 1809 letter about the Virginia committee's revisal efforts: "We concluded not to meddle with the common law, *i.e.,* the law preceding the existence of the statutes, further than to accommodate it to our new principles and circumstances; but to take up the whole body of statutes and Virginia laws, to leave out everything obsolete or improper, insert what was wanting, and reduce the whole within as moderate a compass as it would bear, and to the plain language of common sense, divested of the verbiage, the barbarous tautologies and redundancies which render the British statutes unintelligible." Though both Jefferson and Madison studied and often showed respect for the common law, with Madison saying "the Constitution is predicated on the existence of the Common law," they certainly had concerns with various aspects of it. Jefferson, for instance, opposed the prosecution of nonstatutory, federal common-law crimes and noted that the common law was "to be altered by ourselves occasionally" and "adapted to our new situation." Indeed, Jefferson himself, writing in 1788 about the French just before the Eighth Amendment's approval, said that abolishing "torture" and reforming "the criminal code" would "do eternal honor" to the administration of the law.[71]

Professor Stinneford's "long usage" approach to the Eighth Amendment, which would apparently leave the death penalty in place for murder even though corporal punishments short of death are already barred by it, also overlooks some important additional facts. First, the phrase "long usage" is clearly *not* the phrase the Founding Fathers chose to include in the Constitution for future generations to interpret for themselves. Second, American society no longer relies on common-law punishments. Instead, death sentences are now authorized by statute, with most states having abolished common-law crimes altogether. The common-law, "long usage" terminology Stinneford seeks to revive thus originated in an antiquated criminal law framework long abandoned by American society. Third, it is simply impossible to equate eighteenth-century death penalty laws with criminal laws in the twenty-first century. The mandatory death penalty—even for murder—has itself long fallen into disuse, meaning today's laws differ in dramatic ways from what they looked like in the Framers' world—a world that treated blacks as inferior beings and that did not require, certainly, the "equal protection of the laws." The latter constitutional guarantee must, when fairly construed, affect the Supreme Court's determination of what is considered "unusual" because discrimination is now expressly forbidden not by some common-law principle, but by the Constitution itself.[72]

It is true, to be sure, that the death penalty in one form or another has been employed in the United States for a very long time. However, the way in which it has been carried out, in terms of the categories of offenders subject to it and the amount of process given to criminal defendants, has changed in fundamental ways since the Framers' time. Even the methods of execution—the actual means used to kill inmates—have changed in substantial ways. In light of that reality, it makes the most sense for the U.S. Supreme Court to continue to interpret the word *unusual* in its ordinary, everyday way, as it long has. This is especially so since the Court is construing the Constitution itself. Indeed, even were the term *unusual* found to be synonymous with "long usage," that old common-law principle would itself be subject to reevaluation based on logic and reason and all the changed circumstances that must of necessity influence modern-day judges' evaluation of death penalty laws. Interpreting the Eighth Amendment to allow executions would itself run contrary to the now well-settled principle that inmates are, as a general matter, to be *protected* from harm.[73]

The common-law tradition in fact embraces change, as it has since the country's founding. Another prominent Virginian, St. George Tucker—who wrote *View of the Constitution of the United States,* the first systematic, post-ratification commentary on the Constitution—actually pointed out that the English common law was adopted only in part by the American colonies. The American Revolution itself, of course, had been fought to end British rule. As Tucker wrote: "[W]hen the American states declared themselves independent of the crown of Great-Britain, each state from that moment became sovereign, and independent, not only of Great-Britain, but of all other powers, whatsoever. . . . From that moment there was no common law amongst them but the general law of nations, to which all civilized nations conform." Though Tucker noted that some early state constitutions declared that English common law would remain in force until altered, he emphasized that states regularly departed from the English common law. Tucker illustrated his point by writing that a provision of Pennsylvania's constitution called for the reform of the penal laws and for punishments to be made less sanguinary and more proportionate. "If the common law be revived," Tucker explained, "this article is a mere nullity." The ideals of American revolutionaries were thus frequently at odds with English law. Joseph Hopkinson, an attorney for Samuel Chase during his impeachment trial, freely acknowledged that the "Common Law is but another name for common sense, tested and systematically arranged by long experience." "It is one of its excellencies," he said, "that it is capable of change, of modification, of adapting itself to new situations and varying times." Americans, as a historical matter, rejected Britain's monarchy and deliberately chose to form a system of government frequently at odds with English principles and traditions.[74]

The Framers, had they so chosen, could easily have used the "long usage" or "immemorial usage" phraseology, defined *unusual* in a more definitive fashion, or otherwise qualified how they wanted it to be read. They did not. Instead, they deliberately selected *unusual*, a word used in the past by lawyers and nonlawyers alike and having a subjective meaning, giving posterity—and, in particular, future generations of judges—added flexibility when they are called upon to construe it. American judges have quite reasonably interpreted the word *unusual* in its ordinary, everyday sense, an approach that makes the Constitution itself consistent with how Americans themselves understand that word. Any arguments about the "original meaning" of *unusual* simply fail to take into account the adaptive nature of the common law, the Fourteenth Amendment's transformative properties, and the fact that eighteenth-century law bears little resemblance to twenty-first-century jurisprudence. Indeed, Patrick Henry equated "cruel and unusual punishments" with "torture," a concept that has evolved over the centuries along with the common law itself. For the Founding Fathers, it mainly meant Stuart-regime excesses and inquisitional, Star Chamber–type proceedings to force defendants to take oaths, confess, or incriminate themselves in brutal interrogations. But for modern-day Americans, the term *torture*, now part of the lexicon of international human rights law, has a much broader meaning and usage.[75]

There are still other reasons for not embracing a "long usage" approach, not the least of which is that the Constitution was changed substantially in the post–Civil War era. Not only did the Fourteenth Amendment's ratification enshrine the concept of "equal protection" within American law, but today's conception of "due process"—a phrase used in both the Bill of Rights and the Fourteenth Amendment—differs materially from the Framers' understanding of that phrase. After Josiah Philips—the subject of Jefferson's bill of attainder—was arrested, he was indicted on May 9, 1778, pled not guilty later that day, and was tried before a jury *on the very same day*. After being sentenced to death a week later for the crime of robbery, he and some of his accomplices were hanged near Williamsburg later that same year. By contrast, the U.S. Supreme Court has already held that the Due Process Clause guarantees certain protections to those facing capital charges. As just one example, the Supreme Court held in *Simmons v. South Carolina* that capital defendants have a due process right to require that their sentencing juries be informed of their ineligibility for parole if convicted. Because maximum-security prisons now exist across the country to house violent offenders, killing inmates is not necessary, a fact that must be considered—in addition to all the others—in evaluating whether executions are "cruel and unusual punishments."[76]

The common law itself was never intended to remain static. James Wilson believed it was "progressive" in nature and reached "higher and higher degrees of perfection, resulting from the accumulated wisdom of ages." While William Blackstone boasted that, under English law, "torture is unknown" and "penalties less uncertain and arbitrary," his conception of torture is quite different from the one that prevails today. The common law, which once made a wide array of offenses capital in nature, is actually far less important now than statutes as a *source* of the criminal law. The Model Penal Code itself, notes one scholar, "is now vying to replace the various criminal codes that virtually all states have adopted in place of the common law." As legal systems and the common law have evolved, so too has scholars' and jurists' understanding of the Eighth Amendment, as is inevitable. Whereas Blackstone pointed to the "cruel and unusual punishments" provision to emphasize that judges' "discretion" in sentencing was "regulated by law," St. George Tucker, one of George Wythe's protégés, felt it most appropriate to consider the Eighth Amendment's protections alongside those of the Fifth and Sixth Amendments because the subjects of those three provisions "are so immediately connected with each other" that he intentionally chose "not to separate them." Invoking common-law maxims, Tucker emphasized that the Fifth Amendment, which he so closely associated with the Eighth Amendment, is "a liberal exposition, and confirmation of the principles of that important chapter of Magna Carta, which declares '*Nullus liber Homo aliquo modo destruatur nisi per legale judicium parium suorum,*' which words, *aliquo modo destruatur,* according to Sir Edward Coke, include a prohibition not only of killing and maiming, but also of torturing, and of every oppression by color of legal authority."[77]

Of course, today's statutes—including ones such as 18 U.S.C. § 2340, explicitly forbidding torture—are much different in character from what they were in the founding era. Not only did the Fourteenth Amendment's ratification make the concept of "equal protection" part of the fabric of American law, but today's conception of "due process," as one would expect, differs substantially from the understanding of that phrase in either 1791 or 1868. While criminal defendants in earlier times were not always given lawyers, the Supreme Court determined decades ago that "due process" requires the appointment of counsel and that trial and appellate lawyers must not render "ineffective assistance" to their clients. "The right to a fair trial, guaranteed to state criminal defendants by the Due Process Clause of the Fourteenth Amendment," the Court has held, "imposes on States certain duties," including turning over exculpatory evidence, letting jurors know if a life-without-parole sentence is available as an alternative to a death sentence, and ensuring that "justice shall be done" in all criminal prosecutions.[78]

When assessing whether executions are "cruel and unusual punishments," the Justices cannot ignore the Fourteenth Amendment in their evaluation of death sentences. In addition to requiring "the equal protection of the laws," the Fourteenth Amendment makes other constitutional rights, including due process, applicable to the states. When the Bill of Rights was ratified in 1791, slavery itself was still firmly entrenched in American life, slave codes punishing blacks more harshly than whites remained in place, and the notion of equal rights—either for minorities or women—was just a pipe dream. The Constitution explicitly protected the slave trade until 1808 and counted slaves as only "three fifths" persons for purposes of apportioning representation. The notorious *Dred Scott* case was handed down in 1857 prior to the Fourteenth Amendment's ratification, with American courts before that time never even pausing to consider—let alone caring—whether death sentences or executions were racially discriminatory in application. After the Fourteenth Amendment's approval, however, that all changed, especially once the U.S. Bill of Rights was held to be applicable to the states by virtue of the Fourteenth Amendment's Due Process Clause. "Once applied against states," law professor Akhil Amar writes of the Cruel and Unusual Punishments Clause, "the clause might have more judicially enforceable bite against state legislatures." "When judged against a national baseline, perhaps a single state legislature, or the legislatures of an entire region," Amar explains, "might indeed be 'unusual' and out of sync with general national sentiment and national morality."[79]

By making the Eighth Amendment applicable to the states, the Fourteenth Amendment expanded the scope of the Cruel and Unusual Punishments Clause and, in the process, changed the dynamic and fundamental nature of the protection. Though conceptions of cruelty have changed significantly over time, the Fourteenth Amendment in effect changed the Eighth Amendment calculus. In 1791, the Eighth Amendment could only be used to challenge an act of Congress. While the meaning of *unusual* has not changed since that time, prior to the Fourteenth Amendment's ratification the presence of "unusual" in the Eighth Amendment required courts to do no more than assess whether a punishment passed by Congress was out of the ordinary or perhaps at odds with traditional Anglo-American practices. The Fourteenth Amendment, however, gave anyone, anywhere in the country, the right to challenge any state or federal law as inflicting a cruel and unusual punishment. While every generation is bound to have different conceptions of what is "cruel," following the Fourteenth Amendment's adoption, the interpretation of "unusual" became more complicated than it was in 1791, with that word taking on greater significance than ever before. Instead of gauging the unusualness of punishments authorized by just one legislative body, the U.S. Congress, the Fourteenth Amendment—the law of the land as of 1868—prohibited all government officials, in all states, from imposing "cruel and unusual punishments." Particularly because the Fourteenth Amendment requires compliance with due process and equal protection principles, the presence of "unusual" in the Eighth Amendment thus raised new considerations, and a host of questions. What does "unusual" mean in the post–Fourteenth Amendment era? How is "unusual" to be read? Are death sentences or executions produced by arbitrary or discriminatory procedures "unusual"? And within what time frame is "unusual" to be judged? Should it be 1791, 1868, or the present day? And within what geographic area? A locality or a state? The nation? Or the rest of the world?[80]

Because the U.S. Supreme Court has properly given "unusual" its regular, ordinary meaning, any "cruel" punishment should also be classified as "unusual" if it is irregular or only rarely or uncommonly inflicted. Though there are many ways to assess what qualifies as "unusual," death sentences and executions—at this point in American history—would seem to fit that description if the term is reasonably construed or applied. Of the thousands of U.S.

murders that take place every year, only a hundred or so defendants are sentenced to death annually, and only a random handful of those—based largely on race, geography, or socioeconomic status—are ever executed. Most importantly, death sentences are no longer mandatory; they are discretionary, with American juries—even "death-qualified" ones—seldom agreeing to impose death sentences. It is common—or usual—for murderers to be imprisoned for life, often without the possibility of parole. As of 2005, almost 10 percent of U.S. prisoners—roughly 132,000 people—were serving life sentences, with approximately 37,000 of those inmates having no chance of parole. However, it is now extremely uncommon, indeed rare, for killers to be sentenced to death, let alone to be executed. The unusualness of American executions is further shown by the fact that most of them take place in the South and are meted out as if the criminal justice system were some kind of state-run lottery, casino, or game of Russian roulette.[81]

If only a handful of states still carry out executions, is it not "unusual" to allow executions in those states when executions are hardly ever carried out elsewhere? Because the Constitution applies nationwide, it certainly makes no sense to assess whether executions are "unusual" just by looking at, for example, the practice in Texas, or even the practices in a single region. American laws must comport with due process and equal protection, with the former doctrine targeting arbitrary government actions and the latter concept aimed at ensuring that similarly situated persons, including offenders, are treated in a like manner. If all convicted murderers were lined up and less than one percent of those murderers were selected for execution by lot, surely that would be unconstitutional. Yet the actual method of selecting those to be executed in America's criminal justice system—rife as it is with forensic and attorney errors, misapplications of the law, arbitrary results, and racial bias—often seems to produce equally random, invidious, and irrational judgments. For example, Michael Richard's execution in 2007 at the "Walls Unit" in Huntsville, Texas, went forward simply because Sharon Keller, the chief judge of the Texas Court of Criminal Appeals, refused to allow defense lawyers to file their papers with the clerk's office a few minutes after the office normally closed for the day. A series of computer crashes had delayed the delivery of the filing, with Keller's words—"We close at five"—sealing the inmate's fate, the merits of any appeal or stay request notwithstanding. Because race still plays such a decisive role in determining who lives and who dies, and because offenders in only some parts of the country are being sporadically executed, due process and equal protection principles are regularly being violated. Indeed, American courts have long recognized a Fourteenth Amendment protection against the "arbitrary" abuse of government power. The fact that the death penalty—different in kind from any other type of criminal sanction—is capriciously imposed, racially discriminatory, and heavily concentrated in just one region, the South, makes it not only unusual but unusual in the extreme.[82]

As far as the death penalty is concerned, the U.S. Supreme Court should no longer tolerate such arbitrary and discriminatory results, which run afoul of important constitutional principles. During Virginia's ratification debate, Edmund Pendleton, the convention's president, noted that the "Judiciary" was "necessary in order to arrest the Executive arm, prevent arbitrary punishments, and give a fair trial, that the innocent may be guarded, and the guilty brought to justice." In noting that "appeals" are "proper and necessary in all free Governments," Pendleton described "appellate jurisdiction" as "undoubtedly proper" to "prevent injustice by correcting the erroneous decisions of local subordinate tribunals" and to "introduce uniformity in decisions." The lottery-like quality of death row appeals, the outcomes of which are all too often based on procedural niceties or the incompetence of counsel, makes a mockery of the words that adorn the Supreme Court building itself: "EQUAL JUSTICE UNDER LAW."[83]

The Supreme Court, despite its hasty retreat from its 1972 ruling in *Furman*, has continued to show its disdain for arbitrary punishments and for "due process" and "equal protection" violations. In *Ohio Adult Parole Authority v. Woodard,* the Court held that even an executive's clemency power—traditionally associated with presidential or gubernatorial prerogative—would itself be subject to a due process inquiry in spite of the separation-of-powers doctrine. While no due process violation was found in that particular case, a majority of the Court specifically held that the Fourteenth Amendment requires that at least minimal due process be afforded to capital inmates in clemency proceedings. As Justice Sandra Day O'Connor wrote in her concurrence in the case: "Judicial intervention might, for example, be warranted in the face of a scheme whereby a state official flipped a coin to determine whether to grant clemency, or in a case where the State arbitrarily denied a prisoner any access to its clemency process." In a separate opinion, Justice Stevens likewise wrote that "no one would contend that a governor could ignore the commands of the Equal Protection Clause and use race, religion or political affiliation as a standard for granting and denying clemency." American judges and juries do not flip coins to decide which defendants will live or die in capital cases, but the results actually produced by the system have a drawn-by-lot quality to them. There is arbitrariness, as well as scores of mistakes, death-qualified juries, racial bias, and frequent reversals and retrials, often brought on by the poor quality of defense counsel. The Court, looking to Eighth and Fourteenth Amendment principles, should forthrightly recognize that the operation of U.S. death penalty laws violates those deeply ingrained principles of law: due process and equal protection.[84]

While the U.S. Supreme Court's Eighth Amendment jurisprudence now attempts to divine the "evolving standards of decency" of a maturing American society, the inquiry as to the constitutionality of executions should be far simpler. The Supreme Court Justices should begin by determining whether executions are "cruel" and then proceed to assess whether executions are "unusual." A determination as to the death penalty's cruelty and unusualness should hinge on the meaning of *cruel* and *unusual* and not on any standard or test that in essence attempts to gauge public sentiment as a way to rationalize a legal determination. An explicit determination by the Court that executions are "cruel" would, in and of itself, force the Justices more squarely to confront whether executions have become "unusual." Of course, whether executions are "unusual" depends in large part on their frequency and the manner in which they are imposed, which does require an evaluation by the Court of *modern practice*. Though this might be seen as gauging the public's "evolving standards of decency," it is really just an adjudicatory, fact-finding method to determine if executions have become "unusual," as that word is commonly understood. The Court's task is to interpret *unusual*, not to make its judgments on the basis of the shifting winds of public opinion.[85]

The "evolving standards of decency" test, as currently applied by the Supreme Court, might be seen as akin to what the Court has long done to assess whether crimes are "infamous" within the meaning of the Fifth Amendment's Grand Jury Clause. As the Supreme Court explained in 1885 in *Ex parte Wilson*: "What punishments shall be considered as infamous may be affected by the changes of public opinion from one age to another." "In former times," the Court said, "being put in the stocks was not considered as necessarily infamous." "But at the present day," the Court said in its late-nineteenth-century opinion, "either stocks or whipping might be thought an infamous punishment." While *Ex parte Wilson* explicitly referenced the notion of "public opinion," what the Court was really trying to do in that case was to assess what people thought in 1885 about what then constituted an "infamous" punishment. In any case, it would seem that the key from the Court's perspective is to gauge the *meaning* of the word in question—be it "cruel," "unusual," or "infamous"—against the present-day facts, not to have the Court reflexively follow polling data and fail to use its own judgment in the application of the terms in the Constitution to particular factual situations. If the facts show that a punishment is both "cruel" and "unusual," it should be invalidated along with any law providing for its infliction.[86]

Another area of constitutional law in which the Court has rather awkwardly looked to "community standards" is in the realm of First Amendment law and the concept of obscenity. In that legal context, using "community standards" to regulate permissible speech—particularly in the Internet era in which we live—makes little sense either. Free speech rights should not be tied to public opinion or to the popularity of the speech itself, just as the right to be free from "cruel and unusual punishments" should not depend on what a legislative body says on that subject. Just as one city council in Kansas or Nebraska should not be able to dictate what gets posted on the World Wide Web, the State of Texas—or just a few states, largely in the South—should not be permitted to dictate how the Supreme Court reads and interprets the Eighth and Fourteenth Amendments. If the Justices find executions both "cruel" and "unusual," and they should, that should be the end of the story— period. Any punishment that is "cruel and unusual" is unconstitutional, and the fact that some Southern prosecutors and members of the general public still vocally support or want to use that punishment does not make that punishment any less so.[87]

To those such as Justice Scalia, who say that language in the Constitution makes executions forever constitutional, that argument makes no sense. The Constitution and the Bill of Rights structure America's government and *protect* individual rights, they do not aim affirmatively to deprive individuals of their property, their liberty, or, alas, their lives. Not only did the Constitution as originally conceived guarantee the right to habeas corpus and the right to trial by jury in criminal cases, but it explicitly prohibited ex post facto laws and bills of attainder, the latter having been used for centuries to kill people without holding any trial whatsoever. After the Constitution ensured those rights, the Bill of Rights then added substantially to that list. And the list is impressive. The First Amendment protects the freedoms of religion, speech, and the press and the right of people to assemble and petition for redress of grievances. The Second Amendment protects "the right of the people to keep and bear Arms," and the Fourth Amendment protects against "unreasonable searches and seizures." The Fifth Amendment confers all-important due process rights, requires grand jury indictments for certain crimes, and guards against double jeopardy, self-incrimination, and takings without just compensation. The Sixth Amendment—another key provision—guarantees speedy and public trials before impartial juries, the assistance of counsel, and confrontation and other process rights, such as the ability to know the nature of accusations and to have compulsory process for obtaining witnesses. The Seventh Amendment further guarantees the right to trial by jury in civil cases, and the Ninth and Tenth Amendments speak of rights "retained by the people" or "reserved to the States . . . or to the people."[88]

The Eighth Amendment, like all the others, is an integral part of the Bill of Rights that cannot be ignored by judges or legislators. Thus, if a fine is "excessive" or a punishment is found to be "cruel and unusual," it violates the Eighth Amendment and is unconstitutional. The Eighth Amendment plainly does *not* say that only punishments deemed cruel and unusual in 1791 are prohibited. On the contrary, the Eighth Amendment absolutely bars "cruel and unusual punishments" of all kinds and does not reference any point in time for assessing a punishment's constitutionality. If the Framers had wanted to prohibit only those punishments they themselves considered "cruel and unusual" in 1791, they could have said so. They did not, choosing instead to employ "excessive," "cruel," and "unusual," familiar words that any judge in any era can interpret perfectly well and with relatively little difficulty. Early American jurists actually had no trouble describing various acts as "cruel" or "unusual" in their judicial opinions, even employing the phrases "cruel or unusual" or "cruel and unusual" to refer to homicidal or other violent acts. For example, a nineteenth-century New York case noted that a second-degree manslaughter offense had been committed in a "cruel and unusual" way, while a Georgia case from the same time period referred to a deadly beating as being done in a "cruel and unusual" manner. New generations of judges can just as easily construe "cruel" and "unusual" for themselves, something that the U.S. Supreme Court, utilizing its own "evolving standards of decency" test as a kind of gloss on the actual Eighth Amendment language, has itself long recognized.[89]

Though judges are—and will always remain—the guardians of Americans' constitutional rights, even state legislatures and the Congress have not had difficulty using "cruel," "cruel or unusual," or "cruel and unusual" terminology in legislation. In fact, early American laws used such language to gauge whether slaves had been mistreated. South Carolina's 1740 legal code recited in its preamble that "cruelty is not only highly unbecoming those who profess themselves *Christian*, but is odious in the eyes of all men who have any sense of virtue or humanity." That code provided for a fine of seven hundred pounds for "any person whosoever shall willfully murder his own slave, or the slaves of any other person." Alabama laws also once forbade killing slaves "by cruel, barbarous or inhuman whipping or beating, or by any cruel or inhuman treatment," with one Alabama law declaring that "no cruel or unusual punishment shall be inflicted on a slave." An 1822 Mississippi law similarly provided "[t]hat no cruel or unusual punishment shall be inflicted on any slave in this State." That law allowed "any master or other person" who inflicted a "cruel or unusual punishment" to be fined up to five hundred dollars, though one commentator, Albert Barnes, pointed out that it is "exceedingly difficult to convict a master of wrong done to a slave" because "no slave can be a witness." As Barnes wrote in 1857: "[W]hat horrid crimes and wrongs may be done by a master before he shall reach the point in punishment that he will himself regard as 'cruel,' or beyond that which is 'unusual' in slaveholding communities!" The penal codes of slave states routinely inflicted much harsher punishments on blacks than on whites, with states such as Georgia, Kentucky, Mississippi, South Carolina, and Virginia making many more offenses punishable capitally for slaves than for whites.[90]

Even in the Deep South, however, there came to be limits, though all-white juries often refused to convict those who assaulted blacks, slaves themselves were forbidden to testify, and blacks were not afforded grand jury or jury trial rights. Laws from before the Civil War thus commonly prohibited any "cruel" or "unusual" punishments. South Carolina's 1740 statute—one of the earliest efforts—explicitly prohibited the "cruel punishment" of slaves. It imposed fines on anyone who "willfully" killed or castrated a slave or "cut out the tongue," "put out the eye," or "cruelly" scalded, burned, or deprived any slave "of any limb or member." That prohibition, however, glaringly exempted what were then common methods of discipline, with the statute expressly allowing "flogging," "putting in irons," "beating with a horse-whip" or "cow-skin," or "striking with a whip, leather thong, switch or small stick." Louisiana's "Black Code" contained similar exemptions in its less-than-absolute prohibition on the "cruel punishment" of slaves, with one provision of that state's law giving a real sense of the era: "The slave is entirely subject to the will of his master, who may correct and chastise him, though not with *unusual rigor*, nor so as to maim or mutilate him, or to expose him to the danger of loss of life, or to cause his death." Such laws were invoked in a handful of cases, with references in judicial opinions to how slaves were "wantonly and cruelly whipped to death" or chastised with "unusual and excessive rigor." One slave's postmortem examination revealed that the slave had been whipped so badly that, from his neck to his heels, the stripes were so close that a witness could not put his fingers between them. Only in that extreme circumstance did the witness— a Southern planter—describe the slave's punishment as "unusually severe." While Louisiana's law made the "cruel punishment" of a slave only punishable by fine, a North Carolina law from 1774—not repealed until 1798—gave judges a choice. It made the killing of any slave, however "cruel," punishable either by imprisonment or by payment of a slave's value.[91]

History shows that such "cruel" or "unusual" treatment laws were largely intended to protect the rights of slaveholders and not necessarily to protect the slaves themselves. In 1853, the writer William Goodell pointed out that Louisiana's law was principally aimed at "the protection of slave *property*, rather than the preventing of *suffering* by the slave." Goodell made this observation on the "unusual rigor" statutory language: "Such a law, instead of *correcting* prevailing usages, receives its definition *from* them. That which is '*usual*' is *authorized*, whatever it may be, short of maiming, mutilation, and murder. And the more rigorous, severe, and cruel may be the prevailing usages of a community, the more rigorous, severe, and cruel they are expressly authorized to be." As Goodell editorialized: "If it is '*usual*' to 'chastise' a slave by inflicting on him a hundred lashes, it is *lawful* to do so. If it is '*usual*' to add five hundred lashes more, it is equally *lawful*!" He lamented that "the current *usages* of the fraternity of slaveholders" were "proclaimed, by the Civil Code of Louisiana, to constitute *the law*." Goodell, an antislavery activist, added that "no satisfaction or remuneration is awarded to the *slave*," and that "it is only an '*unusual*' punishment that is forbidden!" "The masters and overseers," he emphasized, "have only to repeat their excessive punishments so frequently that they become '*usual*,' and the statute does not apply to them!"[92]

Such legal prohibitions on "cruel" and "unusual" treatment also found their way into federal statutory law as those words became catchphrases for mistreatment and abuse. An act of Congress from 1835 thus made it unlawful for "any master or other officer of any American ship or vessel on the high seas" to "inflict" upon any "crew" member "of such ship or vessel" any "cruel and unusual punishment." That law, Justice Joseph Story later found, was "intended to protect every individual composing the ship's crew, in the ordinary acceptation of the term, from an abuse of power by those placed in higher authority." A grand jury charge from 1853 noted that under that law the master or officer of a U.S. vessel could be found guilty of the offense if he, without justifiable cause and for purposes of "malice, hatred, or revenge," "should beat, wound, or imprison one of the crew, or withhold from him suitable food and nourishment, or inflict on him some cruel or unusual punishment." A master's beating of a mariner for "disobedience of orders," "insolent language," and "personal violence," U.S. Supreme Court Justice Brockholst Livingston ruled in 1808, "was not unusual" in its "mode of punishment." The law, Jefferson's appointee and Madison's classmate at Princeton held in a Connecticut circuit court case, recognized "the right of the master, during the voyage, to correct a mariner for disobedience to any reasonable commands, and for insolence and other offenses." "Without it," Livingston ruled, "it would be impossible to navigate our vessels."[93]

Indeed, current federal laws already equate the phrases "cruel or unusual" and "cruel and unusual" with torture and corporal punishments *less than death*. For example, one statute, 10 U.S.C. § 855, not only prohibits "[t]he use of irons, single or double, except for the purpose of safe custody" but also provides that "[p]unishment by flogging, or by branding, marking, or tattooing on the body, *or any other cruel or unusual punishment,* may not be adjudged by any court-martial or inflicted upon any person" subject to the Uniform Code of Military Justice. That section has already been interpreted to bar striking an accused in his groin and genitals and yanking up his pants and underwear in the course of a frisking; maliciously applying force to an inmate's testicles under the pretense of conducting a frisking or "pat down"; and sexually harassing, humiliating, and assaulting an accused at a confinement facility for hours for the purpose of causing both physical and psychological harm. Likewise, 22 U.S.C. § 6912 requires that a U.S. commission "monitor the acts of the People's Republic of China" to check "compliance with or violation of human rights," including "the right to be free from torture *and other forms of cruel or unusual punishment.*" Another statute, 18 U.S.C. § 2191, similarly provides that an officer of a U.S. vessel on the high seas who "flogs, beats, wounds, or without justifiable cause, imprisons any of the crew of such vessel, or withholds from them suitable food and nourishment, or inflicts upon them any corporal *or other cruel and unusual punishment,*" is subject to fine or imprisonment. Still other federal statutes prohibit Guam, the Virgin Islands, and Indian tribes from inflicting "cruel and unusual punishments."[94]

If corporal punishments are already considered "cruel and unusual," it is hardly a stretch to say that judges should find executions "cruel and unusual," too. The Fifth Amendment contains the word "capital" and uses the phrases "in jeopardy of life or limb," and the Fifth and Fourteenth Amendments also provide that no person shall be deprived of "life" without "due process of law." None of that language, however, should be seen as an impediment to a Supreme Court declaration that executions are unconstitutional. The death penalty and corporal punishments were once ubiquitous in American life, so it is hardly surprising that the U.S. Bill of Rights explicitly protected against the arbitrary taking of "life" or "limb." While Massachusetts, reflecting a cultural shift that placed more emphasis on human dignity, abandoned whipping, branding, the stocks, and the pillory in the 1804–05 legislative session and stopped tattooing recidivists in prison in 1829, corporal punishments were retained in the slaveholding South for a longer period of time.[95]

Indeed, when one considers the adoption of the Fifth and Fourteenth Amendments, it would have been shocking had the Bill of Rights *not* guaranteed such individual rights. After all, a man's life—or perhaps his hand, arm, or ears—might have been at stake. When the Fourteenth Amendment was ratified in 1868, the death penalty was then also still a fact of life, again making totally understandable the inclusion of the protection against the taking of life without due process. Both the Constitution and the Bill of Rights, as well as the Fourteenth Amendment, protect individual *rights*; they do not forever enshrine the death penalty in American law. Indeed, the Eighth Amendment plainly does not say that its prohibition against "cruel and unusual punishments" applies only to select punishments. Similarly, the Constitution itself never says murderers or other criminals *shall* be punished by death or that capital punishment *shall* be deemed constitutional *in perpetuity*, regardless of how society may evolve and change. At the Constitutional Convention, Madison himself pointed out that "[i]n framing a system which we wish to last for ages, we should not lose sight of the changes which ages will produce."[96]

Justice Scalia asserts that "the text and tradition of the Constitution" establish "beyond doubt" that "the death penalty is not one of the 'cruel and unusual punishments' prohibited by the Eighth Amendment." In response to Justice Blackmun's dissent in *Callins v. Collins,* Scalia chided Blackmun for his changed views on capital punishment, pointing once more—as he so often does—to the word "capital" in the Fifth Amendment and its provision that no person is to be "deprived of life" without "due process of law." For Justice Scalia, the Eighth Amendment's "original meaning" is what he seeks. For example, in his dissent in *Atkins v. Virginia,* the case outlawing the execution of the mentally retarded, he contended that the majority's opinion found "no support in the text or history of the Eighth Amendment." "The Court," he emphasized, "makes no pretense that execution of the mildly mentally retarded would have been considered 'cruel and unusual' in 1791." "Only the *severely* or *profoundly* mentally retarded, commonly known as 'idiots,' enjoyed any special status under the law at that time," Scalia wrote. The Fourteenth Amendment, Scalia has said elsewhere, also "explicitly" contemplates the death penalty's use, with its "due process" language—concerning the deprivation of "life"—mirroring that of its predecessor, the Fifth Amendment.[97]

Justice Scalia's originalist stance, however, disregards the substantial historical evidence that the Framers crafted the Constitution not just for their generation, but for generations to come. His narrow focus on criminal law practices in 1791 also ignores the fact that the Cruel and Unusual Punishments Clause is phrased in *general terms* and that the Fourteenth Amendment—all by itself—transformed the Constitution that he and the other Justices are bound to interpret. What the Founding Fathers had to say about the death penalty makes for fascinating reading, but the Constitution they gave us ultimately puts in the hands of *living* judges the power to decide—according to its plain text—what constitutes a "cruel and unusual" punishment. Indeed, Justice Scalia's targeted focus on the practices of bygone eras, as well as what he terms the "original meaning" of the text, gives short shrift *to the text itself*. Scalia's approach to constitutional interpretation also neglects to consider the *purpose* of the Bill of Rights and the subsequent individual rights added by the Fourteenth Amendment in 1868, long after the founding era.[98]

The Constitution protects many rights using general language, with the Fourteenth Amendment, for example, broadly and unequivocally guaranteeing to "any person" the "equal protection of the laws." For Scalia, this straightforward language, which makes no distinction between women and men, would nonetheless, as he reads it, not protect women's rights. As Scalia told an interviewer for *California Lawyer* in 2011 when answering a question about the Fourteenth Amendment: "Certainly the Constitution does not require discrimination on the basis of sex. The only issue is whether it prohibits it. It doesn't. Nobody ever thought that that's what it meant. Nobody ever voted for that." Justice Scalia thus apparently takes the position that because the Framers of the Fourteenth Amendment lived at a time when women did not yet have the right to vote, the Fourteenth Amendment—despite its plain and inclusive language—somehow excludes women from its scope in the modern era. Such a reading of the Constitution not only ignores *the text* but also is terribly misguided, to say the least. Just as the U.S. Supreme Court interprets the Equal Protection Clause, as it long has, to protect women against discrimination (as its plain text in fact dictates), the Court should read and apply the *words* of the Cruel and Unusual Punishments Clause, not look to eighteenth- or nineteenth-century practices to try to divine the "original meaning" or the Framers' intent. That is especially so since the Framers themselves recognized that future generations would want—and would have a right—to govern themselves.[99]

A Courtside Seat

Since *Furman,* the U.S. Supreme Court has shown no willingness to declare all executions unconstitutional. It is, however, the Justices—like it or not—

who bear the responsibility of deciding whether executions qualify as "cruel and unusual punishments." Though anti–death penalty agitation will continue before American legislatures, as it has for centuries now, the time has come for the U.S. Supreme Court to embrace its assigned role and to reevaluate its Eighth Amendment case law with regard to executions. Right now, Eighth Amendment precedents are riddled with inconsistencies and are wholly unprincipled and irreconcilable—a situation brought about entirely by the Court's position on executions. The University of Chicago scholar Bernard Harcourt has predicted that a shift in public attitudes toward capital punishment, along with legal and political pressure from the international community, will lead the Supreme Court to impose a constitutional ban on capital punishment by 2050 at the latest. "[R]ecent trends in the United States and within the larger international community," he writes, "suggest that the country is headed toward abolition of capital punishment." "[B]y the mid-twenty-first century," Harcourt speculates, "capital punishment will have the same status as torture within the larger international community: an outlier practice, prohibited by international agreements and customary international law, practiced illicitly by rogue nations." Although that prediction may be realistic, if the Cruel and Unusual Punishments Clause is to be read in a reasonable and principled manner, executions, like corporal punishments, must be barred by the Supreme Court without further delay.[100]

Because the death penalty qualifies as a cruel and unusual punishment, the Supreme Court should not hesitate to declare executions unconstitutional. Not only are federal judges obligated by law to interpret the U.S. Constitution, they are particularly well-suited to the task because they are insulated, to the maximum extent possible, from political pressure. While legislators and state-court judges are elected and can be voted out of office, the Constitution, to ensure judicial independence, guarantees federal judges a "Compensation, which shall not be diminished during their Continuance in Office," and they receive appointments "during good Behavior." In practical terms, that means federal judges have life tenure. This serves to protect—better than anything else would—what Alexander Hamilton in *The Federalist No. 78* called the "complete independence of the courts of justice." As Hamilton emphasized: "no legislative act . . . contrary to the constitution can be valid." "Laws are a dead letter," he wrote, "without courts to expound and define their true meaning and operation."[101]

While state-court judges in California, Tennessee, and Texas have lost elections after pro–death penalty advertising campaigns were waged against them, the guarantees of compensation and life tenure for federal judges exist, the Supreme Court has declared, "not to benefit judges," but "as a limitation imposed in the public interest." Such guarantees are critical, in the Court's words, "to secure an independence of mind and spirit necessary if judges are 'to maintain that nice adjustment between individual rights and governmental powers which constitutes political liberty.'" As the legendary Chief Justice John Marshall once said, a judge may be called upon to decide "between the Government and the man whom that Government is prosecuting: between the most powerful individual in the community, and the poorest and most unpopular." Observing that a judge's decision may affect an individual's "property, his reputation, his life, his all," Marshall called on judges to exercise their duties with "the utmost fairness," adding that a judge, to be guided by "his conscience," must be "perfectly and completely independent." The 1804 impeachment of U.S. Supreme Court Justice Samuel Chase and the U.S. Senate's refusal to convict him at his high-profile trial the following year "assured," in Chief Justice William Rehnquist's words, "the independence of federal judges from congressional oversight" of their judicial decisions. Chase, a Federalist who came under attack from Republicans interested in seizing control of the federal judiciary, had been impeached for allegedly being "arbitrary, oppressive, and unjust" and for letting his partisan leanings affect his rulings. In short, the Supreme Court, not legislative bodies, defines the contours of the Constitution and has the final say as to what it means.[102]

The Framers themselves gave American courts a critical role to play in protecting citizens' constitutional rights. John Adams, for example, long emphasized the importance of an independent judiciary, writing: "It is essential to the preservation of the rights of every individual, his life, liberty, property, and character, that there be an impartial interpretation of the laws." "It is the right of every citizen," he noted, "to be tried by judges as free, impartial and independent as the lot of humanity will admit." In discussing how to protect a republic from despotism, John Dickinson referred to "[t]he genius" and "the masterly hand of a Beccaria," and said that "the judges ought, in a well regulated state, to be equally independent of the executive and legislative powers." The "chief danger" to English subjects, Dickinson once wrote of the mother country, "arose from the arbitrary *designs of the crown*." Dickinson himself was leery of "judges totally dependent on *that crown*" to give effect to "the laws of life and death." "Brutus," an Anti-Federalist writing in 1788 to "the Citizens of the State of New York," acknowledged that the new constitution would render judges "totally independent, both of the people and the legislature," adding that "the judges under this constitution will control the legislature" and that "[n]o errors they may commit can be corrected by any power above them." "The opinions of the supreme court, whatever they may be," he wrote, "will have the force of law; because there is no power provided in the constitution, that can correct their errors, or control their adjudications." "The only causes for which they can be displaced," Brutus said of the members of the nation's highest court, "is, convictions of treason, bribery, and high crimes and misdemeanors."[103]

Before the adoption of the U.S. Bill of Rights, Thomas Jefferson specifically told James Madison that "in the arguments in favor of a declaration of rights you omit one which has great weight with me, the legal check which it puts into the hands of the judiciary." "[T]his is a body, which if rendered independent, & kept strictly to their own department," Jefferson said, "merits great confidence for their learning & integrity." "[I]n fact," Jefferson told Madison, "what degree of confidence would be too much for a body composed of such men as Wythe Blair & Pendleton?" Those three jurists were among Virginia's most respected elder statesmen. George Wythe signed the Declaration of Independence and served as a member of the Federal Convention; John Blair, Virginia's chief justice, was a signer of the Constitution and a member of the committee that in 1776 drafted Virginia's constitution and declaration of rights; and Edmund Pendleton of Caroline County presided over the state supreme court of appeals and the state's ratification convention. "The moral sense, or conscience," Jefferson once said, "is as much a part of a man as his leg or arm," remarking of the Virginia House of Delegates that "173 despots would surely be as oppressive as one." Though Jefferson later came to despise the federal courts, James Madison and John Adams both trumpeted an independent judiciary as indispensable for checking majority rule and popular excesses. Their views, which were consistent with Jefferson's earlier views, prevailed in Philadelphia. In a 1789 letter to John Jay, the country's first Chief Justice, George Washington himself called the judicial branch "that department which must be considered as the keystone of our political fabric."[104]

The power of judicial review, a concept the Framers understood when they debated the Constitution's framework in the summer of 1787, is central to the proper functioning of America's criminal justice system. Along with juries, venerated by the Founding Fathers as an institutional check on power, judicial review constitutes a formidable built-in check on abusive, majoritarian power and ensures, as Chief Justice John Marshall wrote in *Marbury v. Madison,* that the Constitution is enforced as "written." "The doctrine of judicial review," writes historian Bernard Schwartz, was "put forward by James Otis and Patrick Henry even before the Revolution." "By the time of the federal Convention of 1787 (and certainly by the time Madison drew up his draft of the Bill of Rights)," Schwartz writes, "it was generally assumed that the federal constitutional provisions which were being written would be enforced by the courts." "Cases in at least eight states between 1780 and 1787," he notes, "involved direct assertions of the power of judicial review." Those cases include New Jersey's *Holmes v. Walton* (1780); *Commonwealth v. Caton* (1782), a Virginia case in which George Wythe—Thomas Jefferson's mentor—authored one of the opinions; the Rhode Island case of *Trevett v. Weeden* (1786); and a North Carolina case, *Boyard v. Singleton* (1787), in which James Iredell, later one of the original Justices of the U.S. Supreme Court, played a key role. In *Boyard,* the North Carolina court, upholding the right to a jury trial, decided that "the Constitution" constituted "the fundamental law of the land" and thus "abrogated" and held "without any effect" a legislative act. "[I]f the legislature could take away this right, and require him to stand condemned in his property without a trial," the court concluded, "it might with as much authority require his life to be taken . . . without a trial by jury, and that he should stand condemned to die, without the formality of any trial at all."[105]

The separation-of-powers doctrine gave distinct responsibilities to the legislative, executive, and judicial branches, ending once and for all the tyranny of monarchical government. The layers of checks and balances built into the U.S. system, from the veto power to the power of judicial review, were all designed to ensure that too much power is never vested in any one branch of government or in an oppressive majority to the exclusion of the rights of the few, even the unpopular or the despised. To guarantee the rule of law and to ensure that the system works as envisioned, written documents—the U.S. Constitution and the Bill of Rights—were adopted and then ratified by the American people. In *The Federalist No. 44,* for example, Madison explained why the U.S. Constitution included prohibitions on bills of attainder and ex post facto laws, even though they were already "expressly prohibited by the declarations prefixed to some of the state constitutions." "Our own experience has taught us," Madison explained, "that additional fences against these dangers ought not to be omitted." "The sober people of America," he said, "are weary of the fluctuating policy which has directed the public councils." Unlike English law, with its unwritten constitution alterable at will by the British Parliament, the U.S. Constitution is America's premier and highest authority, something neither Congress nor state legislatures can override. As Alexander Hamilton emphasized in *The Federalist No. 81*: "[t]he constitution ought to be the standard of construction for the laws, and that wherever there is an evident opposition, the laws ought to give place to the constitution." And that, of course, is exactly what the Constitution is, with its Supremacy Clause making "[t]his Constitution, and the Laws of the United States *which shall be made in Pursuance thereof* . . . the supreme Law of the Land."[106]

At the heart of the separation-of-powers doctrine sits an independent judiciary, not one that kowtows to popular will or caprice. If judges are beholden to public opinion or legislative will, they are no longer exercising independent judgment and their role is compromised. That is why the Constitution, in Article III, takes such careful precautions to ensure judicial independence. Federal judges are subject only to impeachment. Their compensation—what they need to support themselves and their families—can never be diminished during their time in office, so their judgment is never compromised. James Wilson, in one of his law lectures, saw judicial independence as indispensable for court proceedings—above all else—to be "free from the remotest influence, direct or indirect, of either of the other two powers." Indeed, the Founding Fathers created the U.S. Supreme Court, an Article III institution, to interpret the laws and to resolve any disputes over the Constitution's text. In *The Federalist No. 78,* Alexander Hamilton wrote that judges are the "guardians of the

Constitution," stating that "the complete independence of the courts of justice is peculiarly essential" to our form of government. The "courts of justice," he explained, have a "duty" to "declare all acts contrary to the manifest tenor of the Constitution void." "Without this," he noted, "all the reservations of particular rights or privileges would amount to nothing." James Madison also envisioned a fiercely independent judiciary to protect constitutional rights. "[I]ndependent tribunals of justice," he said, "will consider themselves . . . the guardians of those rights; they will be an impenetrable bulwark against every assumption of power in the legislative or executive." As the Supreme Court itself wrote in 1803 in *Marbury v. Madison*: "It is, emphatically, the province and duty of the judicial department to say what the law is."[107]

If the U.S. Supreme Court read the Eighth Amendment to bar executions, it would not be acting contrary to the spirit or the letter of the Constitution or, for that matter, the original intent of the Founding Fathers. The Framers intentionally used general language in the Eighth Amendment so that future generations could decide for themselves if a particular punishment is "cruel and unusual." While serving on the Committee of Detail at the Constitutional Convention, Virginia's Edmund Randolph articulated two principles that guided the committee's work: "1. To insert essential principles only; lest the operations of government should [be] clogged by rendering those provisions permanent and unalterable, which ought to be accommodated to times and events" and "2. To use simple and precise language, and general propositions, according to the example of the constitutions of the several states." "We should consider," James Wilson emphasized to the delegates in the debate over the Constitution itself, "that we are providing a Constitution for future generations and not merely for the circumstances of the moment." Likewise, in 1787, "Brutus"—an Anti-Federalist writing for a New York audience—emphasized that the Constitution was "intended to stand for ages" and was being "designed not for yourselves alone, but for generations yet unborn," necessitating that the "principles" of "the social compact" be stated "clearly and precisely." It is hardly surprising, then, that the Framers phrased the prohibition on "cruel and unusual punishments" in general terms, so that their children and their children's children would have maximum flexibility to make their own judgments as to particular punishments. After all, the Framers' own society was one in great flux, with mixed views—even then—as to what qualified as a "cruel" or "unusual" punishment.[108]

Simply put, a Supreme Court ruling that executions are "cruel and unusual" would be fully consistent with—and would honor—the text of the U.S. Constitution. Although some argue that a Court ruling to that effect would usurp the role of Congress and state legislatures, "the very purpose of a Bill of Rights," as Justice Robert Jackson once said, "was to withdraw certain subjects from the vicissitudes of political controversy, to place them beyond the reach of majorities and officials and to establish them as legal principles to be applied by the courts." "One's right to life, liberty, and property, to free speech, a free press, freedom of worship and assembly, and other fundamental rights," Jackson noted, "may not be submitted to vote: they depend on the outcome of no elections." The Court itself has already described the Eighth Amendment's purpose as being to proscribe "torture." In the context of coerced confessions, the Court had called "forms of physical and psychological torture" both "revolting" and "offensive to a civilized system of justice." In another area of the law, the Court has in fact emphasized that "the police power of a state . . . may be exerted in such circumstances, or by regulations so arbitrary and oppressive in particular cases, as to justify the interference of the courts to prevent wrong and oppression."[109]

Indeed, the Declaration of Independence, which Madison called "the fundamental act of Union," speaks of the "unalienable" right to "Life." While the philosopher and Presbyterian minister Francis Hutcheson called unalienable rights "essential limitations in all governments," judges and scholars have long debated the significance of the Declaration of Independence's rights clause and its role, if any, in constitutional interpretation. The Declaration of Independence publicly severed the American states from the British Crown, and early American courts—giving it legal significance—used it to mark America's founding and to decide citizenship questions. Individuals born in America after its issuance were, as a rule, Americans, while individuals born before its issuance could elect, through their words or actions, to become Americans or remain British subjects. Although Madison said that the "merit" of the Declaration of Independence consists in its "lucid communication of human rights" and the Declaration has become a much-revered symbol of American identity, modern American courts have generally refused to construe its rights clause as conferring binding legal rights. Justice Scalia, for example, has said that the Declaration of Independence "is not a legal prescription conferring power upon the courts." On the other hand, a growing number of scholars, aware of its historical significance, assert that the Declaration of Independence should be taken more seriously. Some contend that the Declaration's rights clause should be read in conjunction with the Ninth Amendment, which declares that "[t]he enumeration in the Constitution, of certain rights, shall not be construed to deny or disparage others retained by the people." Others likewise emphasize that the Declaration's rights clause should be read in conjunction with the Fourteenth Amendment's Privileges or Immunities Clause. The U.S. Supreme Court, which through the decades has regularly cited the Declaration and the values espoused in it, has in its own rulings described "life, liberty, and the pursuit of happiness" as "natural" or "fundamental rights."[110]

The Founding Fathers approved the aspirational words of the rights clause of the Declaration of Independence even though slavery and capital punishment were still in use. It certainly seems plausible that they approved those lofty and unequivocal words—the ones proclaiming the "unalienable Rights" to "Life, Liberty, and the pursuit of Happiness"—with the understanding that the institution of slavery, as well as the punishment of death, were one day destined to be abolished. Indeed, when the U.S. Constitution was drafted, the Framers scrupulously avoided the use of the word *slavery*, an institution that had already been condemned by many leading political figures. Instead, they spoke in code, referencing "the whole Number of free Persons" versus "three fifths of all other Persons," and stating that "[t]he Migration or Importation of such Persons as any of the States now existing shall think proper to admit, shall not be prohibited by the Congress prior to the Year one thousand eight hundred and eight." Just as the abolition of human bondage gave real meaning to the "unalienable" right to "Liberty" espoused in the Declaration of Independence, the death penalty's abolition would validate—and make meaningful—the "unalienable" right to "Life." Jefferson himself intended the Declaration "to be an expression of the American mind," and in his speeches and writings, Abraham Lincoln, who revered the Founding Fathers and saved the Union they created, saw the Declaration as forming the very foundation of American values. "I have never had a feeling politically that did not spring from the sentiments embodied in the Declaration of Independence," Lincoln said, remarking that the signers had declared the rights in it so that "the enforcement" of them "might follow as fast as the circumstances should permit." As the Supreme Court itself once noted, "it is always safe to read the letter of the Constitution in the spirit of the Declaration of Independence."[111]

It should be obvious to anyone that the law today differs dramatically from what it looked like in the late eighteenth century. Not only did the Fourteenth Amendment not exist at that time, but America's death penalty was administered far differently in 1791 than it is in the modern era. When states ratified the U.S. Bill of Rights, executions could not—unlike now—fairly be described as "unusual." Though execution rates varied by locale, executions—fueled by social unrest, fear of slave riots, and high anxiety about crime—were taking place in all parts of the country. Twenty-three people were executed in Boston in the second half of the eighteenth century; ninety-nine people were executed in Philadelphia during that same period; and in Charleston, South Carolina, ninety executions took place from 1750 to 1800. In that fifty-year period, in a far less populous time, the thirteen North American colonies and their subsequently created sovereign states witnessed at least 1,352 executions. But more significant than those numbers or the geographic diversity of executions, the death penalty was then *mandatory,* making it the *standard*—or *usual*—punishment for crimes such as murder. In other words, if an offender was convicted, the automatic punishment, by statute or custom, was death. As the Supreme Court explained in *Woodson v. North Carolina*: "At the time the Eighth Amendment was adopted in 1791, the States uniformly followed the common-law practice of making death the exclusive and mandatory sentence for certain specified offenses."[112]

Not long after the country's founding, however, Americans began questioning and rebelling against the draconian criminal codes imported from England that made death sentences mandatory. Early American juries, expressing tremendous discontent with such harsh death penalty laws, frequently disregarded their oaths and refused to convict defendants—no matter what the crime—when death sentences would automatically follow guilty verdicts. The concerns of tough-minded prosecutors, as well as low conviction rates in capital cases, eventually led American states to curtail the number of capital offenses. Indeed, in the nineteenth century, there was a push to eliminate mandatory death sentences. Because juries had refused to convict defendants in a substantial number of first-degree murder cases, the public discontent with executions was palpable. In lieu of statutes declaring that convicts "shall" suffer death, legislatures passed laws giving judges or jurors *discretion* to impose death sentences. The first states to repeal mandatory death penalty laws were Tennessee in 1838, Alabama in 1841, and Louisiana in 1846, but the movement took off from there. By the turn of the century, twenty-three states and the U.S. government had made death sentences discretionary for first-degree murder and other capital offenses. Fourteen other states followed suit in the next two decades so that, by the end of World War I, all but eight states, Hawaii, and the District of Columbia had either adopted discretionary sentencing schemes or abolished the death penalty altogether. By 1972, the year of *Furman,* every single state still authorizing capital punishment had abandoned mandatory death sentences—a clear sign of the public's contempt for them.[113]

This change in public sentiment led the Supreme Court, in its 1976 decision in *Woodson,* to strike down mandatory executions as Eighth and Fourteenth Amendment violations. The Justices saw mandatory executions as a departure from society's "contemporary standards"; as "unduly harsh and unworkably rigid"; as merely replacing "unguided and unchecked jury discretion" with another thorny problem, the risk of jury nullification; and as unlawfully preventing the sentencer from considering the offender's individual circumstances. "[T]he fundamental respect for humanity underlying the Eighth Amendment," the Court ruled in *Sumner v. Shuman,* a 1987 case striking down a mandatory death penalty statute, "requires that the defendant be able to present any relevant mitigating evidence that could justify a lesser sentence." Prior to *Furman,* juries and judges were routinely given the unbridled discretion to make sentencing decisions, though the decision maker and the default punishment might change over time. A Minnesota law passed in 1868, for example, made life sentences the standard punishment for murderers unless jurors specifically prescribed the death penalty. An 1883 law, by contrast, repealed the 1868 law, making death the punishment for first-degree murderers unless "exceptional circumstances" warranted a life sentence. Under Minnesota's new law, trial judges, as opposed to jurors, determined if such circumstances were present. Today, death penalty statutes overwhelmingly make juries responsible for sentencing decisions, with jurors asked to weigh aggravating versus mitigating factors in making their decisions. In the few states that still allow judges to override jury recommendations, studies have shown that elected judges, fearful of being labeled soft on crime, often disregard jury recommendations of mercy and impose death sentences as their reelection bids draw near.[114]

This reality shows the Founding Fathers' wisdom in creating the federal judiciary. Federal judges—much more than elected state-court judges—are insulated from public pressure and thus can better protect constitutional rights. Just as giving federal judges appointments for life proved to be a wise decision, the public's sage abandonment of automatic death sentences led to more convictions while simultaneously having meaningful consequences for the Eighth Amendment itself. Once the country moved away from mandatory executions, the likelihood of "unusual" executions increased exponentially. With mandatory executions, every offender actually convicted of a capital crime suffered death, at least in the event that the President or a state's governor failed to commute the sentence or grant a reprieve. But once judges and juries had the choice of imposing a death sentence or a sentence less than death, it became inevitable that similarly situated offenders—whether due to race, geography, poverty, or some other factor—would not be treated alike. Though giving jurors discretion to impose or reject death sentences may have dealt with the recurring problem of jury nullification, the imposition of death sentences became hopelessly arbitrary. Some offenders received death sentences, but many others did not, with the outcome in cases depending largely on the whim or caprice of the presiding judge or the twelve people sitting in the jury box. The worst offenders sometimes did not receive death sentences while less culpable offenders did, and, more often than not, whether criminal defendants got life or death sentences depended on the quality of defense counsel, the availability of local prosecutorial resources to bring capital charges in the first place, or the impermissible factor of race. Because of blatant racial prejudice or more subtle, unconscious bias, the defendant's race and the victim's race have regularly played a decisive role in capital trials in America. The desire of state-court judges to be reelected in Death Belt states such as Florida and Texas has actually led many of those judges serially to impose death sentences or to affirm death verdicts, with the rights of the accused frequently disregarded.[115]

For some, "originalism," the quest to get inside the Founding Fathers' heads, is the be-all and end-all, the legal equivalent of the Holy Grail. But the Framers, it must be remembered, lived in an entirely different age, one with carriages, not cars, and one that would be as foreign to us as our society would be to them. Even Justice Scalia, one of originalism's best-known disciples, has expressed the view in a lecture that originalism "is not, and had perhaps never been, the sole method of constitutional exegesis." Conceding that originalism is "not without its warts" and that "it is often exceedingly difficult to plumb the original understanding of an ancient text," Scalia posed a hypothetical worthy of consideration. "What if some state," Scalia asked, cognizant of the fact that flogging and other corporal punishments were once prevalent, "should enact a law providing public lashing, or branding of the right hand, as punishment for certain criminal offenses?" Scalia, who frequently votes to uphold death sentences, then said this regarding such corporal punishments: "Even if it could be demonstrated unequivocally that these were not cruel and unusual measures in 1791, and even though no prior Supreme Court decision has specifically disapproved them, I doubt whether any federal judge—even among the many who consider themselves originalists—would sustain them against an Eighth Amendment challenge." "It may well be," Scalia said, "that this cannot legitimately be reconciled with originalist philosophy." "Even so," he conceded, "I am confident that public flogging and handbranding would not be sustained by our courts, and any espousal of originalism as a practical theory of exegesis must somehow come to terms with that reality."[116]

Expressing his preference for originalism, Scalia has criticized constitutional law scholars such as Lawrence Tribe and Ronald Dworkin for their "nonoriginalist" views. "Most if not all nonoriginalists," Scalia told the audience, "would strike down the death penalty, though it continues to be widely adopted in both state and federal legislation." Yet Scalia, who noted that the "main danger in judicial interpretation of the Constitution" is that "judges will mistake their own predilections for the law," readily conceded that he himself might prove to be a "faint-hearted originalist." "I cannot imagine myself, any more than any other federal judge," he noted, "upholding a statute that imposes the punishment of flogging." Though Scalia expresses disdain for such corporal punishments, he continues to categorize capital punishment as clearly permissible because—in his words—the death penalty "is referred to in the Constitution itself." Speculating on the Framers' intent and saying that the purpose of "constitutional guarantees" is "to prevent the law from reflecting certain changes in original values," Scalia fleshed out his views: "Perhaps the mere words 'cruel and unusual' suggest an evolutionary intent more than other provisions of the Constitution, but that is far from clear; and I know of no historical evidence for that meaning." "I take the need for theoretical legitimacy seriously," Scalia said, noting that "even if one assumes" that "the Constitution was originally meant to expound evolving rather than permanent values," no basis exists "for believing that supervision of the evolution would have been committed to the courts."[117]

But Scalia's views are flawed. There *is* historical evidence that the Founding Fathers intended to leave the interpretation of the Constitution—and the Eighth Amendment, in particular—to future generations of judges. And there is substantial *textual evidence,* too. In the Constitution, the Framers deliberately gave independence to judges; in writing and approving the Eighth

Amendment, they also chose general, absolute language—"cruel and unusual punishments"—to express their sentiments; and when objections were made that the language was too vague, they approved the language nonetheless. As Samuel Livermore logically concluded when the First Congress debated what became the Eighth Amendment, "[i]t lies with the court to determine" its meaning. Though Representative Livermore felt that the Cruel and Unusual Punishments Clause reflected "humanity," he explicitly expressed concern that the clause might, in the future, limit a legislature's authority to hang a man, whip someone, or cut off a villain's ears. Livermore's concerns obviously failed to carry the day, and, in spite of those expressly stated concerns and with full awareness that judges would later be called upon to construe that general language, the Eighth Amendment was adopted and later ratified by the people. The Eighth Amendment broadly—indeed, without exception—prohibits "cruel and unusual punishments," leading to the inescapable conclusion that the death penalty too must be fully scrutinized under the Cruel and Unusual Punishments Clause.[118]

Although the Constitution was, as the Supreme Court itself once wrote, "intended to endure for ages to come," some Framers did believe its provisions would acquire a "fixed" meaning through subsequent interpretations of the text. Alexander Hamilton believed—to use the jargon of his day—that judicial interpretations would "fix" the meaning of contested language. James Madison and other founders likewise believed that the meaning of constitutional provisions might later be "ascertained," "settled," or "fixed." It was "foreseen at the birth of the Constitution," Madison said, "that it might require a regular course of practice to liquidate and settle the meaning" of its provisions. As Madison wrote in *The Federalist No. 37*: "All new laws, though penned with the greatest technical skill, and passed on the fullest and most mature deliberation, are considered as more or less obscure and equivocal, until their meaning be liquidated and ascertained by a series of particular discussions and adjudications." Thus, Madison hoped for a time when the Constitution's "meaning on all great points" would be "settled by precedents," with Madison taking the view that once the meaning of a word was "fixed," it should endure.[119]

The idea of "fixing" meaning is a centuries-old concept. "In the eighteenth century," writes University of Virginia law professor Caleb Nelson, "the notion of 'fixing' meaning was a topic of considerable controversy, attracting attention from Jonathan Swift, Samuel Johnson, and other literary giants." Efforts were made in France and England—Johnson's *A Dictionary of the English Language*, published in 1755, was one such effort—to define words so that their meaning could be "fixed." In 1712, Jonathan Swift even published a pamphlet in which he worried that "the perpetual Variations of our Speech" would prevent future generations from understanding and appreciating works written in his time. Works "will be read with Pleasure but a very few years," he lamented, noting that "in an Age or two," they "shall hardly be understood without an Interpreter." As a result of his belief, Swift urged that "some Method should be thought on for ascertaining and fixing our Language for ever, after such Alterations are made in it as shall be thought requisite." "For I am of Opinion," Swift wrote, "that it is better a Language should not be wholly perfect, than that it should be perpetually changing." In 1747, Samuel Johnson, the century's foremost lexicographer, indicated in his plan for an English dictionary that "one great end of this undertaking is to fix the English language." Dr. Johnson, however, recognized that changes in the language were inevitable, a proposition with which Thomas Jefferson wholeheartedly agreed. Jefferson announced that he was a "zealous" friend to "Neology" and ridiculed "the preposterous idea of fixing the language."[120]

Living languages, of course, evolve over time. Though Madison himself was desirous of "fixing" the meaning of words, he too viewed it as an "unattainable" ideal, telling one correspondent that "[a]ll languages . . . are liable to changes" and that some of the causes of the changes are "inseparable from the nature of man and the progress of society." In the Eighth Amendment context, the meanings of "cruel" and "unusual"—as revealed by dictionaries from the founding era—have, it turns out, not changed appreciably since that time. In 1773, Samuel Johnson defined "cruel" to mean "[p]leased with hurting others; inhuman; hard-hearted; void of pity; wanting compassion; savage; barbarous; unrelenting," and in *A Dictionary of the English Language*—his dictionary published in the mid-1750s—he defined "unusual" as "Not common; not frequent; rare." In 1828, also using terminology any modern-day American would still recognize, Noah Webster defined "cruel," a central focus of the Eighth Amendment, as "[d]isposed to give pain to others, in body or mind; willing or pleased to torment, vex or afflict; inhuman; destitute of pity, compassion or kindness." Thus, it is only *society's view* of what should be classified as "cruel and unusual" that has undergone a material change, with the Supreme Court's own "evolving standards of decency" test reflecting the change in societal sensibilities since the eighteenth century.[121]

Though judicial precedents were designed to "fix" meaning, they have never been seen as sacrosanct, even by the Founding Fathers. Like many Framers, Madison—consistent with Blackstone and the common-law approach—had enormous respect for precedents. The fact that the U.S. Supreme Court has long upheld executions, though, does not mean that they are forever immune to legal challenge. To be sure, the U.S. Supreme Court frequently adheres to precedents. There is a whole legal doctrine—stare decisis—devoted to that very idea. Eventually, though, bad precedents—the *Dred Scott* case and *Plessy v. Ferguson* come readily to mind—are overruled as American society advances and societal norms evolve. The American public and the Supreme Court itself come to see that such precedents are neither well reasoned nor consistent with the language of, or the values expressed in, the Declaration of Independence or the Constitution and its Fourteenth Amendment. *Plessy v.*

Ferguson notoriously articulated the separate-but-equal doctrine, a doctrine overruled in the Supreme Court's landmark decision in *Brown v. Board of Education.* The *Dred Scott* case was overturned by the Fourteenth Amendment itself.[122]

While the U.S. Supreme Court often invokes the doctrine of stare decisis, counseling adherence to precedent, it has long rejected the notion that the first decision it issues on a point of law will forever remain the law of the land. The Framers themselves recognized the problem of the dead attempting to govern the living; they sometimes saw the application of stare decisis as unjustified; and they even used sunset provisions in their laws so that dead-hand problems would not arise. In other instances, they deliberately crafted language that would readily accommodate the passage of time. In other words, they foresaw the need for dynamic flexibility based on future societal changes, and in drafting the Constitution they built in such flexibility through their careful choice of words. "[A]s I hope we are considering a Government for a perpetual duration," Madison declared, "we ought to provide for every future contingency." "[W]hen we are preparing a Government for perpetuity," Madison said at Virginia's ratification convention, "we ought to found it on permanent principles and not on those of a temporary nature."[123]

Though the Framers said little about the Eighth Amendment itself, the notion of that provision acquiring a permanent, "fixed" meaning based on 1787 or 1791 practices makes no sense. That is because "cruel" and "unusual" set forth normative principles that afford flexibility of interpretation. "Constitutions," Alexander Hamilton said in 1788, "should consist only of general provisions: the reason is, that they must necessarily be permanent, and that they cannot calculate for the possible change of things." The word *cruel* itself is nothing less than an expression of a moral standard, one that each successive generation of judges can apply in the context of individual cases as they arise. "To say that members of the founding generation envisioned a Constitution with a fixed 'meaning,'" notes Caleb Nelson, "is not to say that they expected all future interpreters to apply each provision of the Constitution exactly as members of the founding generation applied it." Indeed, the idea that today's U.S. Supreme Court should read the Cruel and Unusual Punishments Clause in exactly the same way that the Framers did in 1791 is completely undermined by the ratification of a new, transformative provision—the Fourteenth Amendment—that none of them lived to see.[124]

The Way Forward

Since its ratification, courts have long wrestled with how to interpret the Eighth Amendment. For example, in *People v. Morris,* the Michigan Supreme Court noted "[t]he difficulty in determining what is meant by 'cruel and unusual punishments,' as used in our Constitution." In upholding a sentence for stealing a horse, that 1890 ruling emphasized that "[t]he crime of horse-stealing has generally been regarded from the earliest times as involving a greater degree of criminality than the larceny of other property." "When, in England, concessions against cruel and unusual punishments were first wrested from the crown," the court pointed out, "slight offenses were visited with the most extreme punishment, and no protest was made against it." "But our concern," the court noted, "is to ascertain how this language is to be understood *in the constitutional sense.*" Noting that Thomas Cooley, a Michigan jurist, had written that "[p]robably any punishment declared by statute for an offense which was punishable in the same way at the common law could not be regarded as cruel or unusual, *in the constitutional sense,*" the Michigan Supreme Court grappled with how to make sense of the words. In doing so, it did not focus on the everyday, dictionary definitions of "cruel" or "unusual," but instead turned to Justice Cooley's treatise for guidance. "We may well doubt," that treatise offered, "the right to establish the whipping-post and the pillory in states where they were never recognized as instruments of punishments, or in states whose constitutions, revised since public opinion had banished them, have forbidden cruel and unusual punishments." "In such states," it continued, "the public sentiment must be regarded as having condemned them as cruel, and any punishment which, if ever employed at all, has become altogether obsolete, must certainly be looked upon as unusual."[125]

The U.S. Supreme Court, at times, has likewise spoken of the phrase "cruel and unusual" in its "constitutional sense." In *Louisiana ex rel. Francis v. Resweber,* Willie Francis, described as "a colored citizen of Louisiana," was convicted of murder and sentenced to die by electrocution. On May 3, 1946, he was put in the electric chair, but because of some mechanical difficulty, his death did not result once the switch was thrown. Consequently, he was removed from the chair—still very much alive—and returned to his cell. Intent on killing Francis, Louisiana's governor subsequently issued a new death warrant, calling for the execution to take place on May 9, just six days later. In the interim, however, Francis claimed that were he executed, his Eighth Amendment rights would be violated "because he had once gone through the difficult preparation for execution and had once received through his body a current of electricity intended to cause death." Rejecting that argument, the Supreme Court found that "nothing" that took place amounted "to cruel and unusual punishment *in the constitutional sense.*" In so ruling, the Court brushed aside the petitioner's argument about having already endured "the psychological strain" of preparing to die, noting only that "[t]he traditional humanity of modern Anglo-American law forbids the infliction of unnecessary pain in the execution of the death sentence." "Even the fact that petitioner has already been subjected to a current of electricity," the Court ruled, "does not make his subsequent execution any more cruel *in the constitutional sense* than any other execution." "The cruelty against which the Constitution protects a convicted man is cruelty inherent in the method of punishment, not the necessary suffering involved in any method employed to extinguish life humanely," the Court declared, calling the first execution attempt nothing more than an "unforeseen accident." "There is no purpose to inflict unnecessary pain nor any unnecessary pain involved in the proposed execution," the Court held, writing: "The situation of the unfortunate victim of this accident is just as though he had suffered the identical amount of mental anguish and physical pain in any other occurrence, such as, for example, a fire in the cell block."[126]

Yet the Eighth Amendment does not bar "barbaric punishments," "painful punishments," or "obsolete punishments," it bars "cruel and unusual punishments." And there is no reason to believe that the words "cruel" and "unusual" were meant to be read in a *constitutional sense* that differs from the plain text. Alexander Hamilton explained that the Constitution's words were to be given their "grammatical" and "popular" meaning, saying that "arguments drawn from extrinsic circumstances, regarding the intention of the convention, must be rejected" and that "whatever may have been the intention of the framers of a constitution," that intention "is to be sought for in the instrument itself." "The enlightened patriots who framed our Constitution, and the people who adopted it, must be understood to have employed words in their natural sense, and to have intended what they have said," the U.S. Supreme Court itself held in 1824, confirming Hamilton's view. Indeed, the Constitutional Convention of 1787 was conducted in secret, and the Founding Fathers' individual views were purposely withheld from the public, not only at the Convention itself but long thereafter. No one was allowed to make a copy of any entry in the convention journal being kept by Major William Jackson without the presiding officer's permission, and no one but the delegates could even access the journal. "[N]othing spoken in the House," Madison put in his own notes, could be "printed, or otherwise published or communicated without leave." Congress itself sealed the records of its debates until 1818, with James Madison—the man who chose the Eighth Amendment language—saying that "[a]s a guide in expounding and applying the provisions of the Constitution, the debates and incidental decisions of the [Philadelphia] Convention can have no authoritative character." "[A]fter all," Madison said, "whatever veneration might be entertained for the body of men who formed our Constitution, the sense of that body could never be regarded as the Oracular guide in expounding the Constitution." It thus makes little sense to conclude that the Framers, who wanted the Constitution to speak for itself, intended "cruel" and "unusual" to mean one thing in ordinary parlance and another in the Eighth Amendment. What is considered "cruel and unusual" may differ from one generation to the next, but it is implausible to argue that the Founding Fathers wanted future generations to interpret the phrase "cruel and unusual punishments" in exactly the same way that they would have in the late eighteenth century.[127]

Justice William Brennan, who contended for decades that the death penalty is unconstitutional, once aptly noted that the Eighth Amendment does not say that what is considered to be "cruel and unusual" is "to be static over time." In contrast to the Constitution's very specific dictate that no one may serve as President until attaining the age of thirty-five, Justice Brennan explained, the Founding Fathers consciously chose the less definitive and more abstract "cruel and unusual punishments" language. "The Framers," he emphasized, "surely understood that judging would not be easy or straightforward: no doubt that is why they took such great pains to ensure the independence of judges by providing life tenure and protecting against diminution of judges' compensation." What is "cruel and unusual," Brennan argued, cannot be "frozen in time" because that would run afoul of "the Framers' vision— which was to leave to future judges and future generations the right to decide for themselves what constitutes 'cruel and unusual' punishment." "Those who would have the Eighth Amendment read today to bar only what was considered cruel and unusual in 1791," Brennan wrote, "would, it seems to me, do violence to what they purport to embrace, namely the intent of the Framers." If the Framers had intended to forbid only the use of "racks and gibbets," he said, then the clause might easily have been so worded. "Were not these men capable of communicating specific mandates when that was their intention and desire?" Brennan pointed out, concluding, "I think they were." "I want to emphasize just one more time," Brennan said, "that what I am urging is respect for what I believe the Framers insisted of judges: namely, to accept the responsibility and burden and challenge of working with the majestic generalities of their magnificent Constitution."[128]

Ideally, the standards and mores of Americans will evolve to the point where death sentences are abhorred just as much as lynchings are now. Until that happens, however, the lofty language about the "right to life" in the Universal Declaration of Human Rights—as well as the Declaration of Independence's recitation of the "unalienable" right to life—will be mere words, a goal to be sought after, not a reality achieved. Wouldn't it be nice to see those high-minded words matched with deeds, to see that inspiring language become fully operational? If executions, after centuries of struggle, were no more, it would at long last fulfill the dreams of those Enlightenment thinkers and human rights proponents who either fought for the death penalty's abolition or foresaw the end of executions. John Adams—who predicted the American Revolution would be "an Astonishment to vulgar Minds all over the World, in this and in future Generations"—himself recognized that the people, unrestrained, "have been as unjust, tyrannical, brutal, barbarous, and cruel, as any king or senate possessed of uncontrollable power." While the U.S. Supreme Court's "evolving standards of decency" language, first articulated in *Trop v. Dulles*, is lofty phraseology, that language is not in the Constitution itself and has not been interpreted in a manner to do away with executions. By refocusing on the Eighth Amendment's text and by judging whether executions are "cruel and unusual," the Court would be honoring, not disregarding, the Founding Fathers' vision. Indeed, as long as the Supreme Court continues to defer to popular sentiment and legislative enactments, it will be abdicating its judicial independence and the Eighth Amendment will be toothless.[129]

If history is any indication, American executions are destined to disappear, whether through court order or otherwise. The main principle underlying the Eighth Amendment is, as the U.S. Supreme Court has repeatedly said, respect for "humanity" and "human dignity." "If there is a significantly less severe punishment adequate to achieve the purposes for which the punishment is inflicted," Justice William Brennan once opined, "the punishment inflicted is unnecessary and therefore excessive." Finding that "[t]he calculated killing of a human being by the State involves, by its very nature, a denial of the executed person's humanity," Justice Brennan, in his *Furman* concurrence, determined that "the deliberate extinguishment of human life by the State is uniquely degrading to human dignity." Although members of the Supreme Court have taken the position that the Eighth Amendment bars only "unnecessary and wanton" inflictions of pain "totally without penological justification," the Eighth Amendment—with its focus on "cruel and unusual punishments"—says no such thing. Indeed, the Supreme Court has acknowledged that retribution, one of the rationales commonly offered for capital punishment, can sometimes "contradict the law's own ends." "When the law punishes by death," a majority of the Court emphasized in 2008, "it risks its own sudden descent into brutality, transgressing the constitutional commitment to decency and restraint." In an age of life-without-parole sentences and maximum-security prisons, the inescapable reality is that death sentences and executions are unnecessary, cruel, inhumane, and debasing—the polar opposite of a dignified, rational system of punishment. In his 1793 essay *An Enquiry How Far the Punishment of Death Is Necessary in Pennsylvania*, William Bradford, America's second attorney general and Madison's close friend, himself emphasized that every punishment "which is not absolutely necessary" is "a cruel and tyrannical act."[130]

The "retributivist" argument was presented most starkly by the Prussian philosopher Immanuel Kant. In 1785, Kant published *Grundlegung zur Metaphysik der Sitten*, first translated into English in 1798 as *Groundwork of the Metaphysics of Morals*. *Die Metaphysik der Sitten*, the sequel to his 1785 book, was the German name of Kant's 1797 book *The Metaphysics of Morals*. Kant saw executions as "a categorical imperative." "There is," in the case of murder, he stated, "no juridical substitute or surrogate, that can be given or taken for the satisfaction of Justice." "There is," he wrote, "no Likeness or proportion between Life, however painful, and Death; and therefore there is no Equality between the Crime of Murder and the retaliation of it but what is judicially accomplished by the execution of the Criminal." "Only the Law of retribution (*jus talionis*) can determine exactly the kind and degree of punishment," he added. "Even if a civil society were to dissolve itself by common agreement," Kant offered, "the last murderer remaining in prison must first be executed, so that everyone will duly receive what his actions are worth." Though Jefferson and others came to abhor the lex talionis principle, Kant fervently believed that capital punishment was "indispensable to redeem, or restore, the human dignity of the executed." Kant, of course, had a much different conception of dignity than we have today, as highlighted by society's total rejection of mandatory death sentences.[131]

In assessing the abolition movement's prospects for success, it is perhaps instructive to recall another hard-fought crusade, the antilynching movement, against another horrific practice, lynch mobs. Until the NAACP launched a movement to stop them, extrajudicial lynchings in America were common, described by one commentator as "an established custom" in early American life. Such lawless spectacles, often fueled by racism and later by organized white supremacist groups such as the Ku Klux Klan, once pockmarked the American landscape, frequently taking place before unruly mobs. Lynch mobs and other acts of "frontier justice," often targeting blacks, grabbed newspaper headlines in the South, West, and even as far north as Duluth, Minnesota, well into the twentieth century. There were 4,743 lynchings nationwide from 1882 to 1968, and between 1892 and 1940, more than three thousand people in the United States—roughly twenty-six hundred of whom were black—were lynch mob victims. As prominent Americans including Frederick Douglass, Ida B. Wells, and W. E. B. DuBois vocally opposed lynchings, other Americans joined the cause, and the antilynching movement gained traction. Though the movement did not succeed in getting a federal antilynching law passed, several state laws were enacted, with lynchings gradually dwindling and then disappearing entirely in the 1950s. Stephen Bright, the president of the Southern Center for Human Rights, has in fact aptly called the death penalty "a direct descendent of lynching and other forms of racial violence and racial oppression in America."[132]

The national campaign against dueling—another anachronistic practice—also provides more than glimmers of hope for the anti–death penalty movement. "Trial by combat," fought with a club-like baton, was part of England's legal system after the time of William the Conqueror, and early America certainly saw its share of duels, especially among aristocrats and social elites. The common law forbade dueling, but changing public sentiments—accelerated by Alexander Hamilton's untimely death in 1804 at the hands of Aaron Burr—led to the passage of statutes and constitutional provisions more explicitly outlawing the practice. In 1775, the Continental Congress itself adopted a ban on dueling; a law to suppress dueling in the District of Columbia cleared Congress in 1839; and an array of antidueling laws were enacted by state legislatures in eighteenth- and nineteenth-century America. Duelists were barred from elective office or from practicing law or medicine, faced stiff fines, or could be prosecuted for manslaughter, even murder. By 1868, twenty-two states had specific clauses in their constitutions that discouraged or penalized dueling. Legislatures even criminalized the conduct of "seconds," the men who arranged the duels and thus aided and abetted them. Duels still occurred after the passage of such laws, but changing social norms—and the enforcement of antidueling laws—soon spelled the demise of these "affairs of honor." A Tennessee attorney was actually disbarred for killing someone in a duel in 1829; duels declined after the Civil War; and dueling disappeared in Virginia, where the practice once flourished, in the 1880s. By 1909, the Court of Appeals of Kentucky was calling dueling a "barbarous practice," and by the 1920s every Southern state had adopted laws or constitutional provisions to punish duelists.[133]

The last chapter of America's abolition movement has yet to be written, with much anti–death penalty activity still to come. Although the Bush administration fervently backed capital prosecutions, and capital prosecutions are still being brought sporadically, the abolitionist movement in the United States and around the world is very much alive. The National Coalition to Abolish the Death Penalty does advocacy work and puts out alerts, and dozens of affiliates and other national and state organizations, including the Campaign to End the Death Penalty and The Moratorium Campaign, are also working to end capital punishment. The American Civil Liberties Union (ACLU) is seeking a national moratorium on executions; Murder Victims' Families for Reconciliation, comprised of family members of homicide victims, opposes capital punishment; the Innocence Project continues to rack up exonerations; and Amnesty International regularly opposes executions and tracks death penalty developments. Yet another nonprofit, the Washington, D.C.–based Death Penalty Information Center, maintains a comprehensive Web site providing the latest information on death penalty issues. All of these entities are harnessing the power of the Internet and combating injustice and capital punishment with the most potent tool of all: the facts.[134]

Already, the nation's highest court bars the execution of various categories of offenders, among them juveniles, the insane, the mentally retarded, and those who have not taken life. Even after the U.S. Supreme Court's approval of lethal injection in *Baze,* the Eighth Amendment—the cleanest, though certainly not the only way to end U.S. executions—may yet prove instrumental in the death penalty's demise. As death sentences and executions continue to dwindle, the Justices, even applying their own "evolving standards of decency" test, might feel compelled to strike down the death penalty altogether. As fewer states authorize death sentences and fewer juries impose them, American executions—"unusual" already—will become only more so over time. Certainly, the fact that executions have been conducted for centuries, passed down from one generation to the next, does not impede a judicial finding that they are now unconstitutional. As Justice Oliver Wendell Holmes Jr. once wrote: "It is revolting to have no better reason for a rule of law than that so it was laid down in the time of Henry IV. It is still more revolting if the grounds upon which it was laid down have vanished long since, and the rule simply persists from blind imitation of the past." The study of history, Holmes noted, is an important part of the study of law, but it must be part of the study only because "without it we cannot know the precise scope of rules which it is our business to know." History, he said, is simply the "first step" toward an "enlightened" skepticism, "toward a deliberate reconsideration of the worth of those rules." "We must," Holmes said, "beware of the pitfall of antiquarianism, and must remember that for our purposes our only interest in the past is for the light it throws upon the present."[135]

The Supreme Court's reasoning in *Graham v. Florida,* which struck down life-without-parole sentences for juvenile offenders who did not kill, may even provide the road map for a future ruling declaring executions unconstitutional even for those who do kill. In that case, the Court held that the Eighth and Fourteenth Amendments barred the imposition of life-without-parole sentences on juvenile offenders who did not commit homicides even though federal law, thirty-seven states, and the District of Columbia permitted life-without-parole sentences for juvenile, nonhomicidal offenders in some circumstances. "[A]n examination of actual sentencing practices in jurisdictions where the sentence in question is permitted by statute," the Court ruled, "discloses a consensus against its use." The Court noted that in the United States only 123 juvenile offenders were serving life-without-parole sentences for nonhomicidal offenses, and that a majority of those—seventy-seven—were imposed in just one state: Florida. The Court added that "only 11 jurisdictions nationwide in fact impose life without parole sentences on juvenile nonhomicide offenders—and most of those do so quite rarely—while 26 States, the District of Columbia, and the Federal Government do not impose them despite apparent statutory authorization." The willingness of the Court to strike down a punishment that is no longer actively used but that remains on the books in many places could foreshadow a ruling by the Court that ends America's death penalty once and for all. The parallels between the rarity and geographic disparity of executions and life-without-parole sentences for juvenile offenders are indeed remarkable.[136]

A focus on the Eighth Amendment's actual language, meanwhile, leads inexorably to the factual and legal conclusion that executions are "cruel and unusual punishments." Executions are brutal and inhumane, arbitrary and racially discriminatory, and are only rarely carried out, making them unconstitutional. Just as America's criminal justice system does not authorize the rape of rapists, it should no longer authorize the killing of killers. In colonial Virginia, 240 people were bound over for grand jury action in capital cases in the nine years preceding the outbreak of the American Revolution, and punishments for crime ranged from drawing and quartering and hanging in chains to whipping, with slaves often receiving such draconian sentences.

The concept of human dignity, however, has progressed a great deal since Jefferson's time, when it was thought to be a legitimate exercise of state power to maim offenders by, for example, cutting off their ears or boring holes through their noses. Because the federal government and many states still authorize capital punishment, a categorical ruling declaring the death penalty to be unconstitutional may not be forthcoming anytime soon, particularly given the known proclivities of the current Justices of the U.S. Supreme Court. But the future is hard to predict, and it is certainly within the realm of possibility that the Supreme Court will one day put the death penalty out of its misery by unequivocally declaring all executions unconstitutional. That day, when it comes, will be—in the words of Justice William Brennan—"a great day for our country, for it will be a great day for our Constitution."[137]

Conclusion

In 1786, the year before the signing of the U.S. Constitution, Dr. Benjamin Rush described how too many people had come to "confound the terms of *the American revolution* with those of *the late American war.*" "The American war," Rush said of the conflict that ended in 1783, "is over: but this is far from being the case with the American revolution." Observing that only "the first act of the great drama is closed," Rush wrote: "It remains yet to establish and perfect our new forms of government; and to prepare the principles, morals, and manners of our citizens, for these forms of government, after they are established and brought to perfection." "We have changed our forms of government," Rush reiterated to Dr. Richard Price, one of Benjamin Franklin's friends, "but it remains yet to effect a revolution in our principles, opinions, and manners so as to accommodate them to the forms of government we have adopted." "THE REVOLUTION IS NOT OVER!" Rush proclaimed in an address to the American people, calling on all patriots and heroes of the Revolutionary War—all "friends to mankind"—to step forward and serve their country once more. Rush called for the education of America's youth in a federal university, saying that only a plan of "general education" would "render the American Revolution a blessing to mankind." As Rush told Price: "Let the law of nature and nations, the common law of our country, the different systems of government, history, and everything else connected with the advancement of republican knowledge and principles, be taught by able professors in this university."[1]

Dr. Rush, an Enlightenment figure, understood that human progress would not come easily or overnight. Writing to James Madison in 1790 and enclosing a pamphlet to show that men were "growing wiser upon the subject of the penal laws," Rush added a lengthy postscript to his letter. There, Rush wrote of the importance of planting "seeds of truth," even if he did not live long enough to see the benefits of his labors. "Truths," he wrote, "resemble trees—some ripen in a short time, while others require half a century or more to bring them to perfection." Noting that such seeds had to be planted "by *somebody*," Rush recalled that "[t]he seeds of the present humane and enlightened policy upon the subject of the slavery" in Pennsylvania had been "sown" nearly "20 years ago." "To oppose popular prejudices or to propose plans of human happiness that cannot be perfected in the course of the single life," Rush explained, was a worthy goal even if it "subjects a man to the imputation of being a speculator." "We lose the attainment of great objects by not attempting them," Rush lamented, adding, "The seeds of truth differ from the seeds of plants in one particular. None of them are *ever lost*. Like matter, they are indestructible in their very nature. They produce fruit in other ages or countries."[2]

The seeds of the death penalty's abolition were planted in the Enlightenment by the Italian philosopher Cesare Beccaria. Those seeds sprouted in America under the watchful eye of Benjamin Rush and his friend William Bradford, and were further cultivated by Founding Fathers such as Benjamin Franklin, James Wilson, Thomas Jefferson, and James Madison. Beccaria authored *On Crimes and Punishments* in the 1760s, nearly 250 years ago, but his vision remained unfulfilled in his lifetime—and it was left to future generations to pick up the torch where he left off. In America, many of the country's founders—intrigued by Beccaria's ideas—came to oppose executions, if not altogether, then at least for certain categories of offenders. They narrowed the death penalty's use, often expressing deep ambivalence about executions, though they too were unable to slay the death penalty beast. Instead, in drafting the Constitution and the Bill of Rights, they deliberately left to generations yet unborn the ability—indeed, the responsibility—to decide for themselves what constitutes a "cruel and unusual" punishment. The Founding Fathers recognized those words would be subject to interpretation in future eras that they could not fathom or foresee, yet they never attempted to constrain future generations. On the contrary, they purposely used common, everyday language to craft the absolute prohibition. In other words, the choice we face today—whether to retain capital punishment or to abolish it—was one our forefathers intended for us to make unrestrained by eighteenth-century mores. The Constitution itself gives the Justices of the U.S. Supreme Court the power to determine what constitutes a "cruel and unusual" punishment.

When pondering what comes next in the centuries-old death penalty debate, Americans should recall the American Revolution while not deluding themselves as to their own role—in our time—in authorizing executions. "The Revolution," John Adams said, "was in the minds and hearts of the people" and "was effected before the war commenced." "This radical change in the principles, opinions, sentiments, and affections of the people was the real American Revolution," he noted. If death penalty laws were taken off the books, inmates would cease to die at the hands of the state in our country, a republic founded more than two centuries ago when penitentiaries were just being conceived.

The twenty-first century, it must be remembered, is a much different time from the eighteenth century, when the risk of anarchy was palpable, the U.S.-British relationship was consumed by war and retaliation, and Benjamin Franklin—setting forth the dire choices facing the Founding Fathers, who faced many dangers in their lifetimes—published his famous "Join, or Die" cartoon depicting a snake severed into separate segments representing the different American colonies. Though history is instructive when it comes to constitutional interpretation, it remains just that, and Americans should no longer use history to turn a blind eye to what is happening in the bowels of our nation's prisons or to what is at stake from a moral standpoint when it comes to executions. After all, it is our nation's citizenry, the living, who, as their own governors, bear the collective responsibility for those days and times when prison officials, behind closed doors, load up and deliver syringes full of deadly chemicals to inmates strapped down on gurneys. Executioners may do the dirty work, perhaps reluctantly and often in conflict with their own consciences, but they do so only in accordance with statutes, death warrants, and court orders. Because the people's representatives pass those laws and issue those directives, it is not the laws or the pieces of paper that kill. Instead, it is we as American citizens who, through our authorized agents, the executioners, bear the shared responsibility for such killings. As George Bernard Shaw, Great Britain's Nobel Laureate in literature, once remarked, "Criminals do not die by the hands of the law. They die by the hands of other men."[3]

In the eighteenth century, the Founding Fathers foresaw a future—for themselves and for future generations—when Americans not only would govern themselves but also would live in an enlightened, prosperous, and civilized society where cruel and barbarous conditions would not be tolerated. The Founding Fathers, who began their struggle for human rights by signing the Declaration of Independence, knew they would need to fight to realize their vision, but it was one they knew was worth fighting for. Key to that vision was and remains an informed citizenry, as James Madison so eloquently articulated generations ago: "A popular Government, without popular information, or the means of acquiring it, is but a Prologue to a Farce or a Tragedy; or perhaps both. Knowledge will forever govern ignorance; And a people who mean to be their own Governors, must arm themselves with the power which knowledge gives." The quest for "Justice" and "a more perfect Union"—one dominated less by violence and more by knowledge and reason—is contemplated in the U.S. Constitution, with its preamble expressly seeking to "secure the Blessings of Liberty to ourselves and our Posterity." The Declaration of Independence, as the basis of the American Revolution, itself invoked the principles of liberty and equality, as well as the "unalienable" right to "Life," even though slavery and executions remained a gruesome, commonplace reality.[4]

Though the Constitution, as originally drafted, did not protect against cruelty, America's founders soon added the Eighth Amendment to remedy that deficiency. The Bill of Rights guaranteed all Americans certain basic freedoms, and the Eighth Amendment, especially once it was applied against the states via the Fourteenth Amendment, served as a special protection against governmental abuses of power. While the quest for human rights and a less cruel society has taken time, Americans have gradually made strides to perfect the Union and in doing so have given more meaningful expression to the values set forth in the Declaration of Independence. Not until 1791, four years after the Constitution was originally conceived, was the Cruel and Unusual Punishments Clause added; not until 1865 was slavery abolished via the Thirteenth Amendment; not until 1868 did the Fourteenth Amendment guarantee the equal protection of the laws; and not until the ratification of the Fifteenth Amendment in 1870 and the Nineteenth Amendment in 1920 did minorities and women gain the right to vote. The institution of slavery was at last abolished, though it took another war, the Civil War, to end it, even as Americans also came to stop using forms of corporal punishments such as whipping to punish offenders. Many of the Framers themselves owned slaves, and women and African Americans once had few if any legal rights. But the abolition of slavery, the women's suffrage movement, and the Fourteenth Amendment's prohibition on discrimination all materially advanced the values articulated in the Declaration of Independence, just as the death penalty's abolition would do, if that too should come to pass.[5]

Until recently, progress toward abolition has been slow, sometimes excruciatingly so. Yet the anti–death penalty movement, like a storm in ocean waters, is now gathering renewed momentum and strength, not only with rapidity in the international community, but also, if only in more subtle ways, in American communities. The UN Secretary-General has noted "a considerable shift towards the abolition of the death penalty both *de jure* and in practice," and that trend has accelerated as new studies and scientific tools such as DNA evidence have exposed the law's fallibility. With both American death sentences and executions down in numbers, making them rare, the latest public opinion polls show Americans are increasingly ambivalent about capital punishment. Even the U.S. Supreme Court, which still sanctions executions, at least for the most serious offenders, has clearly indicated that any further expansion of America's death penalty would be intolerable. "Evolving standards of decency that mark the progress of a maturing society," the Court emphasized in 2008, "counsel us to be most hesitant before interpreting the Eighth Amendment to allow the extension of the death penalty, a hesitation that has special force where no life was taken in the commission of the crime." The Court may still allow executions, but it appears that it will not allow a turning back of the clock.[6]

In *The Tipping Point*, best-selling author Malcolm Gladwell describes dramatic moments "when everything can change all at once." The question that arises in the capital punishment context is whether Americans are on the cusp of just such a moment. Will there be an event, or perhaps a series of events, that leads to that magical point of no return and the death penalty's abolition? Will Americans witness a future wrongful execution? Will a prior execution be identified as having taken the life of an innocent person? Or will juries just stop sentencing people to death to such an extent that any death sentence that is handed out looks like a freakish outlier? Anything might happen, though one thing remains clear: in retaining capital punishment, America has, through its deadly silence and inaction, chosen a path that requires the continued employment of executioners. That lessens us all by the justice system's resort to violence, the very thing that we condemn in killers. "For me," Justice William Brennan once observed, "arguments about the 'humanity' and 'dignity' of *any* method of officially sponsored executions are a constitutional contradiction in terms." All executions are "cruel and unusual punishments," Brennan and Justice Thurgood Marshall observed again and again in their relentless dissents, words all Americans and the present Justices of the U.S. Supreme Court should take to heart and, in the case of the Court, commit to paper in a future judgment regarding the death penalty.[7]

American history, animated by the Founding Fathers' voices and descriptions of their lives and times, is speckled with the blood of extrajudicial lynchings, the lashing of slaves, and state-sanctioned executions, but also contains much to inspire. "We are fighting for the dignity and happiness of human nature," Benjamin Franklin proclaimed, with Thomas Paine saying that "[w]e have it in our power to begin the world over again." Though some founders such as Dr. Benjamin Rush categorically opposed capital punishment and other forms of violence, many others saw whippings and the death penalty as standard punishments for certain crimes. That the Framers accepted capital and corporal punishments is made clear by laws passed by the First Congress and provisions in the Bill of Rights that contemplate their infliction. That historical reality, however, provides no guidance to twenty-first-century Americans in answering the fundamental Eighth Amendment question: are executions "cruel and unusual punishments" and thus unconstitutional in *our* time? The Founding Fathers lived in an age that witnessed the building of America's first penitentiaries, making the notion of long-term incarceration and life-without-parole sentences a novel one. Indeed, in March 1787, just before the Constitution was signed, eighteen prisoners—in what was then a common occurrence—broke through the walls of the less-than-secure building in which they were confined and escaped from prison, endangering the community. Today, however, Supermax and other maximum-security prisons exist to house securely the world's most violent offenders, whether terrorists, murderers, or rapists.[8]

Although the Bill of Rights contains the words "capital," "life," and "limb," those words are found in constitutional guarantees for individuals and do not constitute an archaic penal code. Indeed, one must recall that people in the founding era also envisioned punishing people by cutting off ears, limbs, and even genitals, something no jurist today, even Justice Scalia, would argue is constitutionally permissible. In that sense, the Fifth Amendment protection against the taking away of a "limb" has already been rendered a nullity, in effect trumped by the Eighth Amendment's unequivocal prohibition against "cruel and unusual punishments." Because it is now considered "cruel and unusual" to lop off criminals' body parts, no criminal or court need be concerned any longer about that reference to "limb," which is simply a vestige of a bygone era. If the state can no longer cut off body parts, as even the well-known originalist Robert Bork once conceded should not be done, why should the state be perpetually authorized to take life under the guise of constitutional protections? The Bill of Rights was plainly designed to *protect* individual rights, not to end lives. The ratification of the Fourteenth Amendment in 1868 now itself ensures that the "equal protection" and "due process" rights of all people are protected.[9]

As the abolition movement that Beccaria began braces for its 250th anniversary, abolitionists must continue to agitate and seek to reframe the death penalty debate. As the deterrence debate rages on, abolitionists must convince Americans that they are not soft on crime by advocating life-without-parole sentences for society's worst offenders. As the moral and philosophical debate continues, abolitionists must also convince the public that the death penalty is fundamentally a human rights issue, that the death penalty's abolition must be seen both in that context and in the context of Martin Luther King Jr.'s nonviolence movement. And as legal arguments about the Eighth Amendment are made, abolitionists must fight on in the legislative arena, exposing wrongful convictions and mounting challenges to the arbitrary and discriminatory nature of death sentences, as well as the discriminatory exclusion of death penalty opponents from juries. Because juries make real decisions in real cases, they provide a unique window into the societal standards to which the Supreme Court's own Eighth Amendment jurisprudence attaches so much importance. Citizen-jurors do not have the luxury of answering a series of abstract questions about the death penalty posed by a pollster on the telephone. Instead, they are asked by judges to make gut-wrenching, life-and-death decisions in concrete cases, to decide whether a man or a woman, with a mother, father, and maybe even children already stigmatized by the offender's act, should live or die. Polls move up and down, whether because of a horrific crime or a series of DNA exonerations, but capital jurors confront head-on the most serious moral questions imaginable when filling out a verdict form. A snapshot of jury verdicts from randomly selected juries, especially ones not death-qualified as the Supreme Court currently permits, would reveal an even more sharply divided public when it comes to executions.[10]

The United States has yet to abolish capital punishment, but it seems only a matter of time before the American death penalty goes the way of the stocks, the pillory, and the whipping post. Perhaps a single event such as the execution of an innocent man or woman will trigger abolition, or perhaps the moratorium movement will take firmer hold so that U.S. executions simply wither away—state by state, or even county by county—as lynchings did decades ago. As it is, many U.S. locales no longer use capital punishment, either because of weighty moral concerns or for practical public policy reasons such as the high cost of death penalty prosecutions or the lack of lawyers to represent death row inmates. Executions are already largely a Southern phenomenon, and even in the South, where they are most frequent, the chances of a criminal's being executed are extremely small and dwindling even further with each passing year. The Eighth Amendment, with its absolute prohibition on "cruel and unusual punishments," contains no exception for death penalty laws, and executions—the evidence shows—qualify as both "cruel" and "unusual." As such, the Eighth Amendment should be used by the U.S. Supreme Court without further delay to end America's death penalty lottery and to put capital punishment out of its misery. Ironically, Dr. Benjamin Rush expressed similar hopes for the death penalty's demise over 220 years ago. In 1787, in an address to the Society for Promoting Political Enquiries, Rush remarked: "I can only hope that the time is not far away when gallows, pillory, scaffold, flogging and wheel will, in the history of punishment, be regarded as the marks of the barbarity of centuries."[11]

America's death penalty can be stopped in one of three ways: through legislation, the courts, or simple disuse. Right now, America's criminal justice system seems to be following all three paths, albeit to varying degrees. Capital punishment is being abolished or curtailed, though slowly, state by state and county by county, through legislative action or prosecutorial decision making; annually, fewer death sentences are being handed down and fewer executions are being carried out; and state and federal judges, led by the U.S. Supreme Court, continue to strike down individual death sentences on an ad hoc basis and, more systematically, for certain classes of offenders. Given this trajectory and what is already known about the death penalty's administration (not even to mention the legal and scientific developments that are yet to come), the Supreme Court—using the Eighth Amendment—may well, and certainly should, declare *all* executions unconstitutional. That may not happen soon, especially given the current composition of the U.S. Supreme Court and its known proclivity toward allowing death sentences. However, if the death penalty's use continues to decline, leaving only a handful of states or counties that continue to inflict it, even the present Court might one day feel compelled to outlaw executions altogether, finding them too cruel, too unusual, and too arbitrary and discriminatory to remain legal. America's death penalty, as one scholar suggests, may also just "fade slowly" away, going out "with a whimper and not a bang." Whatever the scenario, Father Time and human progress seem destined eventually to claim capital punishment, just as lynchings and duels passed from the scene.[12]

While some contend that a U.S. Supreme Court ruling declaring executions unconstitutional would improperly usurp legislative power, the power to decide what qualifies as a cruel and unusual punishment plainly lies in the Supreme Court's hands. Indeed, an independent judiciary not controlled by the executive or legislative branches was one of the reasons the American Revolutionary War was fought in the first place. In *Thoughts on Government*, written in 1776, the patriot John Adams himself harped on the need for separation of powers, writing "that the judicial power ought to be distinct from both the legislative and executive" and "independent" of both so that "it may be a check upon both, as both should be checks upon that." "The Judges," he said, writing at a time when women were still excluded from the legal profession, "should always be men of learning and experience in the laws, of exemplary morals, great patience, calmness, coolness and attention. Their minds should not be distracted with jarring interests; they should not be dependent upon any man or body of men." James Wilson, a fellow patriot in Pennsylvania, also remarked that judges should be "completely independent" and "would be in a bad situation if made to depend on every gust of faction which might prevail in the two branches of our Govt." And the legendary Chief Justice John Marshall called an "an ignorant, a corrupt, or a dependent Judiciary" the "greatest scourge . . . ever inflicted." "Those who founded the Republic," the Supreme Court itself has stated, "recognized the importance of these constitutional principles."[13]

International law is now trending heavily toward abolition, and the swiftly moving current of change has already swept many nations into the abolitionist column. America's death penalty will no doubt eventually collapse under the heavy weight of all of its intractable problems and faults. It is certainly cruel, and it has become unusual—and will become even more so as it is used less and less in the future. Not only are executions "cruel and unusual" in the ordinary sense of those words, but America's death penalty as applied in practice is doubly so. As it has been for centuries, capital punishment continues to be plagued by a bevy of problems: incompetent lawyers, wrongful convictions, evidentiary errors, faulty jury instructions, and racial bias, to name just a few. Over thirty-five years after *Furman*, America's death penalty is thus still as arbitrary and capricious as ever. Who gets the death penalty is often more a function of poverty, race, geography, or the quality of defense counsel than a function of the heinous nature of the crime or anything having to do with logic or rationality. And nearly 250 years after the publication of Beccaria's seminal work *On Crimes and Punishments*, the death penalty is still rife with wrongful death sentences and widespread racial discrimination. All of these facts raise constitutional concerns and claims, especially when the Eighth Amendment is read, as it must be, in the context of other individual rights such as due process and equal protection. By executing people, America now stands shamefully and strikingly in the dubious company of totalitarian regimes and some of the worst human rights offenders, including the People's Republic of China, a country that has used executions for over five thousand years to crack down on political dissidents and to terrorize its citizens.[14]

I have no doubt that a day will come—if not in this generation, then perhaps in the next—when the death penalty will be abolished in the United States and will be held to violate the U.S. Constitution and the precepts of international law. The climb will be steep because capital punishment is so deeply ingrained in American life and because the urge for revenge—to see a killer's life cut short—runs so deep. As Benjamin Cardozo, who sought the death penalty's demise, told a group of New York physicians back in 1928: "The thirst for vengeance is a very real, even if a hideous, thing; and states may not ignore it till humanity has been raised to greater heights than any that have yet been scaled in all the long ages of struggle and ascent." Those heights were not reached during the Enlightenment, the Revolutionary War, or the twentieth century, and for now at least they remain a somewhat distant summit in the annals of American law. But the Eighth Amendment stands as a beacon in the darkness and a bulwark against cruelty, and it must be remembered that the world community, including the United States, has already ratified UN conventions barring genocide, slavery, torture, and other forms of cruel and degrading punishments. The death penalty's abolition, whether achieved legislatively or via the Cruel and Unusual Punishments Clause, would represent yet another step in the direction of a more civilized and humane world, a step that would please Enlightenment thinkers, if only from the grave. Already, modern-day Italians, the descendants of Beccaria's fellow citizens, are lighting up the Coliseum in Rome, once the venue of horrific killings, to honor countries banning or halting executions.[15]

As Americans recall the publication of *On Crimes and Punishments*, Beccaria's words, which were taken to heart by so many of America's Founding Fathers, are just as relevant today as they were almost 250 years ago. The future is impossible to predict, but as abolitionists everywhere look back—and simultaneously look ahead—there is much reason to hope and to continue to agitate even though America's last execution is still over the horizon. The world's anti–death penalty movement continues apace as it has for nearly two and a half centuries, and progress, if sometimes painfully slow, is still being made. News stories about capital punishment have proliferated exponentially in just the past few years; there is a growing awareness of the criminal justice system's fallibility; and the U.S. Supreme Court—utilizing the Eighth and Fourteenth Amendments—has already recognized the cruelty and inhumanity of capital punishment for certain categories of offenders. As more and more Americans begin to see the cruel and debasing nature of executions, there is every reason to believe that America's death penalty—whether at the hands of the American public or the U.S. Supreme Court itself—may finally be in its death throes. I can only say that, when the United States of America finally musters the humanity, fortitude, and courage to do away with state-sanctioned killing, it will be a fitting sight indeed to behold the Roman Coliseum all lit up once more, in bright golden light, no doubt in Beccaria's honor.[16]

NOTES

Sources appearing in the bibliography are abbreviated throughout the endnotes. For such sources, only author or editor surname and, as needed, shortened titles appear in these notes. The bibliography should be consulted for more information and full citations.

Because source material on the Founding Fathers is so voluminous, making it impractical to include all such material in the print edition of the book, extended notes prepared by the author are being made available online. These electronic notes, available on the *Cruel and Unusual* book detail page at UPNE.com, supplement the notes printed here. The "e-notes," which may be cited as such, contain additional material relating to the subject of the book as well as extra citations and references. Any endnote for which an e-note is available contains a notation to that effect, and to make the e-notes as user friendly as possible they appear online, organized by chapter, using the same endnote numbers with which they are associated here. In the endnotes that follow, as well as in the e-notes, the following abbreviations are used in citations to letters:

AA Abigail Adams
AH Alexander Hamilton
BF Benjamin Franklin
BR Benjamin Rush
GM George Mason
GW George Washington
JA John Adams
JD John Dickinson
JH John Hancock
JJ John Jay
JM James Madison
JQA John Quincy Adams
PH Patrick Henry
RHL Richard Henry Lee
SA Samuel Adams
TJ Thomas Jefferson
WB William Bradford

Introduction (pages 1-11)

1. Graham v. Collins, 506 U.S. 461, 479–80 (1993) (Thomas, J., concurring); Furman v. Georgia, 408 U.S. 238, 417 (1972); Furman v. Georgia, 403 U.S. 952 (1971); Jackson v. Georgia, 403 U.S. 952 (1971); Branch v. Texas, 403 U.S. 952 (1971); Furman v. Georgia, 404 U.S. 812 (1971); Jackson v. Georgia, 404 U.S. 812 (1971); Branch v. Texas, 404 U.S. 812 (1971); Rudolph v. Alabama, 375 U.S. 889, 889–91 & n.1 (1963) (Goldberg, J., dissenting); Furman v. State, 167 S.E.2d 628, 628–29 (Ga. 1969); Jackson v. State, 171 S.E.2d 501, 503 (Ga. 1969); Branch v. State, 447 S.W.2d 932, 933 (Tex.

Ct. Crim. App. 1969); Zimring & Hawkins, 33–34; Scott W. Howe, *The Failed Case for Eighth Amendment Regulation of the Capital Sentencing Trial,* 146 U. Pa. L. Rev. 795, 845 & n.192 (1998); Meltsner, 3–19 (discussing the NAACP's role in capital litigation).

2. U.S. Const., amends. VIII & XIV; *Furman,* 408 U.S. at 309 (Stewart, J., concurring); *Furman,* 167 S.E.2d at 628–29; *Jackson,* 171 S.E.2d at 503; *Branch,* 447 S.W.2d at 933; Paul Finkelman, Encyclopedia of American Civil Liberties 60 (2006); Bessler, Kiss of Death, 55–56; Gallup, *Death Penalty,* visited Jan. 29, 2011, http://www.gallup.com/poll/1606/death-penalty.aspx (depicting Gallup poll results on the death penalty since the 1930s).

3. Chernow, Washington, 111, 213, 487, 639, 799; Rita K. Lomio, *Working Against the Past: The Function of American History of Race Relations and Capital Punishment in Supreme Court Opinions,* 9 J.L. & Soc'y 163, 166–67 (2008); Brief for NAACP et al. as Amici Curiae Supporting Petitioners at 7–10, Furman v. Georgia, 408 U.S. 238 (1971) (Nos. 68–5027, 69–5030, 69–5003, and 69–5031), 1971 WL 134376.

4. Brief for NAACP et al. as Amici Curiae Supporting Petitioners at 6, 11–12, 14–15, Furman v. Georgia, 408 U.S. 238 (1971) (Nos. 68–5027, 69–5030, 69–5003, and 69–5031), 1971 WL 134376.

5. Id. at 5–6, 17–18; Mamie Till-Mobley & Christopher Benson, Death of Innocence: The Story of the Hate Crime that Changed America xii, 118, 129, 136 (2003); David Lewis, King: A Biography 59, 133 (1978).

6. The Oyez Project, *Recording of Oral Argument in* Furman v. Georgia, visited Jan. 29, 2011, http://www.oyez.org.

7. Id.; McGautha v. California, 402 U.S. 183 (1971); Trop v. Dulles, 356 U.S. 86, 101 (1958).

8. *Furman,* 408 U.S. at 239–40; Michael Mello, *Executing Rapists: A Reluctant Essay on the Ethics of Legal Scholarship,* 4 Wm. & Mary J. Women & L. 129, 181 (1997).

9. Bessler, Death in the Dark, 133; Gregg v. Georgia, 428 U.S. 153, 158–61, 169, 180–81, 193–97, 205–7 (1976); *Furman,* 408 U.S. at 245, 253, 257 (Douglas, J., concurring); id. at 281, 291, 293, 295 (Brennan, J., concurring); id. at 309–10 (Stewart, J., concurring); id. at 311, 313 (White, J., concurring); id. at 364–65 (Marshall, J., concurring).

10. McCleskey v. Kemp, 481 U.S. 279, 282–320, 325 (1987); Baze v. Rees, 128 S. Ct. 1520, 1552 (Scalia, J., concurring); id. at 1556 (Thomas, J., concurring); Amnesty International, *Abolitionist and Retentionist Countries,* visited Jan. 29, 2011, http://www.amnesty.org/en/death-penalty/abolitionist-and-retentionist-countries; Death Penalty Info. Ctr., *Searchable Execution Database,* visited Jan. 29, 2011, http://deathpenaltyinfo.org/executions (listing dates of U.S. executions and showing the brief moratorium on executions prior to *Baze*).

11. Bessler, Death in the Dark, 137–45; Illinois Coalition to Abolish the Death Penalty, *20 Exonerations/10 Years of Moratorium,* 2010 Annual Report, 5; Monica Davey, "Illinois Bill Eliminating Death Row Is Approved," N.Y. Times, Jan. 11, 2011; John Schwartz & Emma G. Fitzsimmons, "Illinois Governor Signs Capital Punishment Ban," N.Y. Times, Mar. 10, 2011, A18.

12. Ford v. Wainwright, 477 U.S. 399, 401 (1986); Atkins v. Virginia, 536 U.S. 304, 314–15 (2002); Roper v. Simmons, 543 U.S. 551, 578 (2005); Hudson v. McMillian, 503 U.S. 1, 9 (1992); Wilkins v. Gaddy, 130 S. Ct. 1175, 1178 (2010); Death Penalty Info. Ctr., *Recent Legislative Activity,* visited Jan. 29, 2011, http://www.deathpenaltyinfo.org/recent-legislative-activity.

13. Paula C. Johnson, *At the Intersection of Injustice: Experiences of African American Women in Crime and Sentencing*, 4 Am. U. J. Gender & L. 1, 11 (1995); Gutterman, 1517. For information on Thomas Jefferson's 1781 reprieve of Billy, a slave convicted of treason, consult e-note.

14. Peter M. Carlson & Judith Simon Garrett, Prison and Jail Administration: Practice and Theory 8 (2d ed. 2007); Gutterman, 1517–18; *see also* e-note (regarding eighteenth-century execution practices in Spain).

15. Grundfest, 210.

16. Chernow, Alexander Hamilton, 167.

17. The Federalist No. 78 (Alexander Hamilton).

18. Joint Resolution of Congress (Sept. 25, 1789).

19. Death Penalty Info. Ctr., Facts about the Death Penalty (Jan. 26, 2011); Jackson v. Bishop, 404 F.2d 571, 579 (8th Cir. 1968) (finding the use of the strap in penal institutions an Eighth Amendment violation); Gordon v. Faber, 800 F. Supp. 797, 800 (N.D. Iowa 1992) (finding an Eighth Amendment violation when inmates were exposed to harsh winter conditions, including sub-freezing temperatures, without proper winter clothing); Rogers v. Commonwealth, 5 Serg. & Rawle 463, 1820 WL 1790 *2 (Pa. 1819) ("On assaults committed with very atrocious designs on the person, as with intention to murder, ravish or commit the unnatural crime, it has been usual to inflict, at the common law, the punishment of the pillory, or other ignominious corporal punishments."); id. at 3 ("Whipping or the pillory is the usual punishment of one convicted of infamous crimes."); *The Originalist*, California Lawyer (Jan. 2011), visited Jan. 29, 2011, http://www.callawyer.com/story.cfm?eid=913358&evid=1; *see also* e-note (discussing the distinction between "original meaning" and "original intent" and citing additional authorities showing the abandonment of corporal punishments such as whipping).

1. In Cold Blood (pages 12–30)

1. Roper v. Simmons, Case No. 03–633, 2004 WL 903158 (U.S. Supreme Court, Appellate Brief, Apr. 20, 2004) *3; State v. Simmons, 944 S.W.2d 165, 169–70, 177–78 (Mo. 1997).

2. Roper v. Simmons, Case No. 03–633, 2004 WL 903158 (U.S. Supreme Court, Appellate Brief, Apr. 20, 2004) *3–4; *Simmons*, 944 S.W.2d at 169–70, 177–78; Simmons v. Bowersox, 235 F.3d 1124, 1128–29 (8th Cir.), *cert. denied,* 534 U.S. 924 (2001).

3. Roper v. Simmons, Case No. 03–633, 2004 WL 903158 (U.S. Supreme Court, Appellate Brief, Apr. 20, 2004) *4; *Simmons*, 944 S.W.2d at 170; *Bowersox*, 235 F.3d at 1129.

4. Roper v. Simmons, Case No. 03–633, 2004 WL 903158 (U.S. Supreme Court, Appellate Brief, Apr. 20, 2004) *4–5; *Simmons*, 944 S.W.2d at 170, 173, 180; *Bowersox*, 235 F.3d at 1127–29.

5. Roper v. Simmons, Case No. 03–633, 2004 WL 903158 (U.S. Supreme Court, Appellate Brief, Apr. 20, 2004) *4–5; *Simmons*, 944 S.W.2d at 170, 173, 185; *Bowersox*, 235 F.3d at 1127.

6. *Simmons*, 944 S.W.2d at 185–86; Roper v. Simmons, 543 U.S. 551, 558 (2005).

7. *Simmons*, 944 S.W.2d at 169, 171–72, 175–76, 183–86; *see also* e-note (discussing charges against Tessmer).

8. *Simmons*, 944 S.W.2d at 169, 171–72, 175–76, 183–85; *Bowersox*, 235 F.3d at 1133–34.

9. *Simmons*, 944 S.W.2d at 171–76; *Bowersox*, 235 F.3d at 1127.

10. *Roper,* 112 S.W.3d at 399–400; Thompson v. Oklahoma, 487 U.S. 815 (1988).

11. Roper v. Simmons, Case No. 03–633, 2004 WL 903158 (U.S. Supreme Court, Appellate Brief, Apr. 20, 2004) *6–7 (*citing* Stanford v. Kentucky, 492 U.S. 361 (1989)); *Simmons,* 944 S.W.2d at 176; *Roper,* 112 S.W.3d at 418–21 (Price, J., dissenting).

12. Roper v. Simmons, Case No. 03–633, 2004 WL 903158 (U.S. Supreme Court, Appellate Brief, Apr. 20, 2004) *3; *Roper,* 543 U.S. at 555–56, 560; *see also* e-note (citing U.S. Supreme Court opinions discussing "dignity," "decency," "civilized standards" and "humanity").

13. *Roper,* 543 U.S. at 564.

14. Id. at 565.

15. Id.

16. Id. at 566.

17. Id. at 568–69.

18. Id. at 575, 577; *Trop,* 356 U.S. at 102–3.

19. *Roper,* 543 U.S. at 578.

20. Id. at 587 (Stevens, J., concurring); Marbury v. Madison, 5 U.S. (1 Cranch) 137 (1803); *see also* e-note (discussing *Dr. Bonham's Case* and American judicial opinions prior to *Marbury v. Madison* legitimizing the concept of judicial review).

21. *Roper,* 543 U.S. at 588, 607 (O'Connor, J., dissenting).

22. Id. at 604–5.

23. Id. at 608 (Scalia, J., dissenting); *see also* e-note (discussing the citation of international and foreign law and the controversy surrounding it).

24. *Roper,* 543 U.S. at 608–9 (Scalia, J., dissenting).

25. Id. at 616.

26. Id. at 622, 624, 627.

27. Id. at 628–29.

28. *Atkins,* 536 U.S. at 337–38, 352–53 (Scalia, J., dissenting).

29. Arizona v. Gant, 129 S. Ct. 1710, 1722 (2009) (*citing* Lawrence v. Texas, 539 U.S. 558, 577 (2003)); Pearson v. Callahan, 129 S. Ct. 808, 816 (2009); Blodgett v. Holden, 275 U.S. 142, 147–48 (1927) (Holmes, J., concurring).

30. U.S. Const., amend. V; An Act for the Punishment of Certain Crimes Against the United States, 1 Stat. 112, 1st Cong., 2d Sess. (Apr. 30, 1790); Antonin Scalia, *Response, in* A Matter of Interpretation 145–46 (1998); Baze v. Rees, 128 S. Ct. 1520, 1552 (2008) (Scalia, J., concurring); id. at 1556 (Thomas, J., concurring); *see also* e-note (containing additional citations and discussing Pelatiah Webster's statement that the Constitutional Convention did not seek to make "a code of laws").

31. *Atkins,* 536 U.S. at 337, 353 (Scalia, J., dissenting); *Walton,* 497 U.S. at 657 (Scalia, J., concurring in part); *see also* e-note (citing cases in which the Eighth and Fourteenth Amendments were used to regulate aspects of capital trials).

32. Northern Pipeline Constr. Co. v. Marathon Pipe Line Co., 458 U.S. 50, 59 (1982); TJ to George Hay (June 20, 1807); Amar, Bill of Rights, 130.

33. Brennan, *Constitution of the United States,* 438; Rehnquist, 401–2.

34. Strauss, 112; Cass R. Sunstein, A Constitution of Many Minds: Why the Founding Document Doesn't Mean What It Meant Before (2009) (reviewed in Wash. Lawyer, July/Aug. 2009, at 43, 45); Rehnquist, 405.

35. Rehnquist, 402; *see also* e-note (containing citations pertaining to various theories of constitutional interpretation).

36. U.S. Const., amends. V & XIV; Strauss, 11, 27; TJ to JM (Sept. 6, 1789); *see also* e-note (comparing different approaches to Eighth Amendment interpretation).

2. On Crimes and Punishments (pages 31–65)

1. Maestro, 20, 43 & n.10; Robert Darnton, The Business of Enlightenment: A Publishing History of the *Encyclopédie 1775–1800*, at 315 (1979); Cesare Beccaria, An Essay on Crimes and Punishments 6 (Adolph Caso, ed., 1983); Bellamy, xxxi; Vila & Morris, 4; Masur, 52; Thomas, xxix; Paolucci, x; *see also* e-note (regarding Beccaria's treatise and various editions and translations of it).

2. Thomas, 17, 26, 51–52, 55; Schabas, Abolition of the Death Penalty in International Law, 5; Bedau, *Interpreting the Eighth Amendment*, 805. The term *abolitionist* is commonly used to refer to opponents of slavery or to opponents of capital punishment. It is used throughout this book to refer to anti–death penalty advocates.

3. Thomas, 26, 51, 55–56, 61; Brennan, *Natural Rights and the Constitution*, 971–74.

4. Thomas, 32–34; Lippman, 281–82; Christoph Burchard, *Torture in the Jurisprudence of the Ad Hoc Tribunals*, 6 J. Int'l Crim. Just. 159, 160 (2008); *see also* e-note (discussing concept of "infamy" and "infamous" crimes).

5. Thomas, xxi, 3, 34; Bellamy, xxxiii, 1; Hunt, 31, 76–77; Günter Frankenberg, *Torture and Taboo: An Essay Comparing Paradigms of Organized Cruelty*, 56 Am. J. Comp. L. 403, 413 (2008); Parker B. Potter Jr., *Antipodal Invective: A Field Guide to Kangaroos in American Courtrooms*, 39 Akron L. Rev. 73, 83 (2006); Margaret Jane Radin, *The Jurisprudence of Death: Evolving Standards for the Cruel and Unusual Punishments Clause*, 128 U. Pa. L. Rev. 989, 1031 (1978); "Medieval Torture," 2 Lapham's Quarterly 2:165 (Spring 2009); *see also* e-note (describing medieval forms of torture including the Pear of Anguish, the rack, and the Judas Chair).

6. Frankenberg, 408; Maestro, 18–19, 126–27, 134, 136; Thomas, 173 nn.10–11; Heikki Pihlajamäki, *The Painful Question: The Fate of Judicial Torture in Early Modern Sweden*, 25 Law & Hist. Rev. 557, 574 (2007); Isaac A. Linnartz, *The Siren Song of Interrogational Torture: Evaluating the U.S. Implementation of the U.N. Convention Against Torture*, 57 Duke L.J. 1485, 1491–93 (2008); *see also* e-note (noting the shift in public attitudes toward torture and punishment after the publication of Beccaria's book, as well as Beccaria's influence on Joseph von Sonnenfels, an Austrian lawyer who published *On the Abolition of Torture* in 1775).

7. Thomas, 52, 57.

8. Bellamy, x; Thomas, xvi–xviii, xxi, xl–xli; Maestro, 5–6, 8–9.

9. Thomas, xviii, xxii–xxiii, xix, xxv–xxvi, 30, 32–37, 166 n.36; Maestro, 6, 20, 47–50; Paolucci, xiv; *Special Collections Focus: New Acquisitions*, Legal Miscellanea: A Newsletter for the Friends of the Jacob Burns Law Library (Autumn 2004), 1.

10. Thomas, 32–37, 51, 55–57.

11. Montesquieu, xi, xiv, xxvii–xxviii, xxix–xxx, 86, 89, 93, 191, 259, 564; *see also* id. at 84–85, 489 (referring to "cruel" penalties and "cruel punishments"); id. at 91 ("[i]n China robbers who are cruel are cut to bits, the others are not").

12. Montesquieu, xi, xiv, xxvii–xxviii, xxix–xxx, 86, 89, 93, 191, 259, 564; *see also* e-note (discussing the views of Charles Carroll, the only Roman Catholic signer of the Declaration of Independence).

13. Thomas, 11, 26, 52–54.

14. Mercer, 86; Thomas, xlvi, 10–11, 53–54.

15. Thomas, 21–22, 26, 52; *see also* e-note (further delineating Beccaria's views).

16. Thomas, xvii, xxix, 153–55, 178–79 n.1; Opinion of the Undersigned Members of the Committee Charged with the Reform of the Criminal System in Austrian Lombardy for Matters Pertaining to Capital Punishment (1792), *reprinted in* Thomas, 153–59; *see also* e-note (describing the relationship of Scotti and Risi to Beccaria).

17. Thomas, 18, 39–41, 80, 84, 155, 159.

18. Id. at xxiii–xxiv, xxvi–xxix, 113, 176 n.6; Bellamy, xxxvii; Maestro, 35–39, 68–71, 128–29; Paolucci, x–xi; Schwartz & Wishingrad, 812; Thomas Banchoff & Robert Wuthnow, eds., Religion and the Global Politics of Human Rights 288 (2011); *see also* e-note (additional citations for Beccaria's influence on Voltaire, who read Beccaria's book in Italian in 1765).

19. Thomas, x, 100, 114–15, 128–29, 132; Immanuel Kant, The Philosophy of Law: An Exposition of the Fundamental Principles of Jurisprudence as the Science of Right (W. Hastie, trans., 1887); Marci A. Hamilton & Rachel Steamer, *The Religious Origins of Disestablishment Principles,* 81 Notre Dame L. Rev. 1755, 1759 (2006); Ishay, 88; *see also* e-note (further delineating Kant's views).

20. Kastenberg, 55–58; Jupiter, 468 & n.157; Pauley, 127; Craig A. Stern & Gregory M. Jones, *The Coherence of Natural Inalienable Rights,* 76 UMKC L. Rev. 939, 949 (2008).

21. Adams recorded the famous meeting between Voltaire and Benjamin Franklin two days later, only a month before Voltaire died. *See* e-note (containing citations and noting that Benjamin Franklin had admired Voltaire's writings as early as 1764).

22. Unger, Last Founding Father, 120; Davidson, 152–57; Ishay, 87; Kastenberg, 60–61 & n.89; Redman, 31–32, 36, 501–8.

23. Kastenberg, 59, 62–63, 66–68 & nn.46, 138; Hunt, 70–75 & 240 nn.2–3.

24. Davidson, 155–57; 2 Martha Walker Freer, History of the Reign of Henry IV: King of France and Navarre 274 (2004); H. C. Barnard, Education and the French Revolution 39 (1969).

25. Thomas, 2, 50, 57.

26. Megivern, Death Penalty, 20–21, 35, 47–48; Bessler, *Revisiting Beccaria's Vision,* 220 n.163 (citing sources); *see also* e-note (noting opposition to the death penalty from English Friends and Pennsylvania Quakers).

27. Thomas, 52, 174 n.15; Evgenii V. Anisimov, Five Empresses: Court Life in Eighteenth-Century Russia 227 (2008); Robert Nisbet Bain, The Daughter of Peter the Great: A History of Russian Diplomacy, and of the Russian Court under the Empress Elizabeth Petrovna, 1741–1762, at 135 (1899); Bessler, *Revisiting Beccaria's Vision,* 199 & n.33; Cyril Bryner, *The Issue of Capital Punishment in the Reign of Elizabeth Petrovna,* 49 Russian Rev. 386 (1990).

28. Gary P. Gershman, Death Penalty on Trial: A Handbook with Cases, Laws, and Documents 19 (2005); R. C. Van Caenegem, Legal History: A European Perspective 47 (1991); Reginald Allen Brown, The Normans and the Norman Conquest 200 (1969); George Slocombe, William the Conqueror 242 (1961); Hunt, 241 n.5; Millett, 551.

29. Kenneth W. Morgan, ed., Path of the Buddha: Buddhism Interpreted by Buddhists 368 (2006); Hermann Kulke & Dietmar Rothermund, A History of India 86 (3d rev. ed. 2002); Leonhard Schmitz, A Manual of Ancient History, from the Remotest Times to the Overthrow of the Western Empire, A.D. 476, at 52 (1859); Hong Lu & Terance D. Miethe, China's Death Penalty: History, Law and Contemporary Practices 27, 199 (2007); 1 Demetrius Charles Boulger, History of China 238 (1898); Petra

Schmidt, Capital Punishment in Japan 10–11 (2002); Bessler, *Revisiting Beccaria's Vision*, 199 & nn.29–32; Amnesty International, When the State Kills: The Death Penalty vs. Human Rights 72 (1989).

30. Nicholas Terpstra, The Art of Executing Well: Rituals of Execution in Renaissance Italy (2008); Mercer, 86–87; Wolfgang Behringer, Witchcraft Persecutions in Bavaria: Popular Magic, Religious Zealotry and Reason of State in Early Modern Europe 13, 33, 115–354 (2003); A Hangman's Diary: Being the Journal of Master Franz Schmidt, Public Executioner of Nuremberg, 1573–1617, at 49–50, 52 (Albrecht Keller ed., 1928); Hunt, 77; *see also* e-note (discussing an Icelandic drowning pool used to execute women until 1838).

31. Thomas, 57; Richard A. Bauman, Crime and Punishment in Ancient Rome 7 (1996); *see also* e-note (discussing Roman emperors and the Coliseum in Rome).

32. Thomas, xxix; Maestro, 122, 124, 135–36, 153–55; Fisher, 1278; Pauley, 131; Laurence A. Grayer, *A Paradox: Death Penalty Flourishes in U.S. While Declining Worldwide,* 23 Denv. J. Int'l L. & Pol'y 555, 557 (1995); Carlo Calisse, A History of Italian Law 471–74 (2001); Daye v. State, 769 A.2d 630, 637 (Vt. 2000); *see also* e-note (discussing Joseph II's relationship to Empress Maria Theresa and Marie Antoinette, as well as Dr. Guillotin's views on a beheading machine and his service on a panel of scientists with Benjamin Franklin).

33. Decl. of Rts. (Oct. 14, 1774); Rutland, 26–29.

34. Conley & Kaminski, 351; Bessler, *Revisiting Beccaria's Vision,* 284–85 & nn.668–80; Lepore, 82; *see also* e-note (containing additional citations and discussing the influence of Enlightenment thinkers—including Barlemaqui, Beccaria, Locke, Montesquieu, and Vattel—on the Founding Fathers).

35. Hunt, 72–74; Schabas, Abolition of the Death Penalty in International Law, 5; Devereaux, 123 & n.63; Kastenberg, 50–51, 58, 61–62; Maestro, 18–19, 44–45; Brands, 564–65; United States v. Blake, 89 F. Supp.2d 328, 343 (E.D.N.Y. 2000); *see also* e-note (discussing Robespierre's 1791 comments on public executions).

36. Bessler, *Revisiting Beccaria's Vision,* 205–6 & nn.65–74; Jeremy Bentham, An Introduction to the Principles of Morals and Legislation 168 (J. H. Burns & H. L. A. Hart, eds., 1970) (1789); Jeremy Bentham, The Theory of Legislation 201 (N. M. Tripathi Private Ltd. 1975) (1802); James E. Crimmins, On Bentham 51–57 (2004); H. L. A. Hart, "Bentham and Beccaria," *in* Essays on Bentham: Studies in Jurisprudence and Political Theory 40 (1982).

37. Alan Watson, *The Structure of Blackstone's Commentaries,* 97 Yale L.J. 795, 816 (1988); Francis Bowes Sayre, *Criminal Responsibility for the Acts of Another,* 43 Harv. L. Rev. 689, 699 (1930); Daniel R. Coquillette, *The Legal Education of a Patriot: Josiah Quincy Jr.'s Law Commonplace* (1763), 39 Ariz. St. L.J. 317, 327–28 (2007); 4 Blackstone, 12; Loving v. United States, 517 U.S. 748, 761 (1996).

38. Maestro, 130; 4 Blackstone, 10, 17–18; A Complete and Universal English Dictionary (1792); *see also* e-note (citing state constitutions that used the word "sanguinary," and citing authorities defining "sanguinary" punishments as ones that are "arbitrary," "bloody," or "cruel").

39. Cesare Beccaria, An Essay on Crimes and Punishments 9 (Adolph Caso, ed., 1983); Adams' Argument for the Defense (Dec. 3–4, 1770); Bessler, *Revisiting Beccaria's Vision,* 207–8 & nn.80–85; Masur, 175 n.10; Bigel, 40; Banner, 91; *see also* e-note (citing the digital edition of the Adams Papers and instances in which Beccaria's

name was invoked in the ratification debates over the U.S. Constitution, as well as noting that Americans questioned the propriety of capital punishment in the 1760s and in the decades that followed).

40. Nancy Isenberg, Fallen Founder: The Life of Aaron Burr 102–5, 372–75 (2008).

41. 26 Syrett, 238; Public Correspondence and Public Papers of Aaron Burr 72, 74 (Mary-Jo Kline & Joanne Wood Ryan, eds., 1983); Jeremy Bentham, Panopticon: or the Inspection-House (1787), *reprinted in* The Panopticon Writings (1995); *see also* e-note (noting that some Founding Fathers handled murder cases as defense lawyers).

42. Charles Page Smith, James Wilson: Founding Father, 1742–1798, at 31 (2009); Bessler, *Revisiting Beccaria's Vision,* 209 & nn.87–89; *see also* e-note (discussing James Wilson's role at the Constitutional Convention).

43. Bessler, *Revisiting Beccaria's Vision,* 226 & n.215, 258 n.459, 263 & nn.489–94; Aitken, 64–65; Brent Tarter & Wythe Holt, *The Apparent Political Selection of Federal Grand Juries in Virginia,* 49 Am. J. Legal Hist. 257, 260–64 (2007); Susan W. Brenner, *The Voice of the Community: A Case for Grand Jury Independence,* 3 Va. J. Soc. Pol'y & L. 67, 68–71 (1995); *see also* e-note (citation discussing the purpose of grand juries).

44. Bessler, *Revisiting Beccaria's Vision,* 263–64 & nn.492–98; Roger A. Fairfax, Jr., *Grand Jury Discretion and Constitutional Design,* 93 Cornell L. Rev. 703, 721–24 (2008); Rappleye, 191–96; *see also* e-note (discussing the deadly attack on James Wilson's home).

45. 2 James DeWitt Andrews, ed., The Works of James Wilson 348 (1896); Bessler, *Revisiting Beccaria's Vision,* 263–64 & nn.492–98; Bowen, 64, 276–77; Homer T. Rosenberger, *James Wilson's Theories of Punishment,* 43 Pa. Mag. of His. & Biography 45, 55, 58, 61 (1949).

46. 1, 2 Butterfield, 316, 416–17, 463, 479–82, 490–91, 496, 526–27, 570, 581, 584, 620–21, 628, 799, 874–75, 922–23, 1090–91, 1102, 1114, 1126; The Selected Writings of Benjamin Rush 41, 46, 97 (Dagobert D. Runes, ed., 2007); Christopher Hitchens, Thomas Jefferson 39 (2005); Rush, *Enquiry,* 15; Maestro, 140–41; Douglas, 159; Joan Fitzpatrick & Alice Miller, *International Standards on the Death Penalty: Shifting Discourse,* 19 Brook. J. Int'l L. 273, 336 n.289 (1993); Hugo Adam Bedau, *Bentham's Utilitarian Critique of the Death Penalty,* 74 J. Crim. L. & Criminology 1033, 1033–36 (1983) (describing Bentham's writings against capital punishment, including his 1775 book *The Rationale of Punishment*).

47. Ketcham, 27; 3 Conway, 123–24, 127; Unger, John Hancock, 329 & 358 n.36; Bessler, *Revisiting Beccaria's Vision,* 210–11 & nn.96–103.

48. Maier, American Scripture, 7–17; TJ to John Garland Jefferson (June 11, 1790); TJ to John Norvell (June 11, 1807); Schwartz & Wishingrad, 817; Randy E. Barnett & Don B. Kates, *Under Fire: The New Consensus on the Second Amendment,* 45 Emory L.J. 1139, 1215 (1996); Spak, 55–56; Pauley, 131; Jupiter, 476 n.191; *see also* e-note (discussing John Norvell's career, Vattel's views on punishment, and Jefferson's commonplace book and his letters recommending Beccaria, Locke, Montesquieu, and Vattel).

49. Thomas, 14–15, 41–42, 156–57; The Innocence Project, *Eyewitness Misidentification,* visited Jan. 31, 2011, http://www.innocenceproject.org/understand/Eyewitness-Misidentification.php ("Eyewitness misidentification is the single greatest cause of wrongful convictions nationwide, playing a role in more than 75% of convictions overturned through DNA testing.").

50. Thomas, 10, 50, 55; *see also* e-note (noting other references to "cruel" or "cruelty" in Beccaria's treatise).

51. Adrienne Koch & William Peden, eds., The Life and Selected Writings of Thomas Jefferson 241 (1998); 1 J. A. Leo Lemay, The Life of Benjamin Franklin: Journalist, 1706–1730, at 427–28 (2005); Adolph Caso, We the People: Formative Documents of America's Democracy 239 (2001); Brant, 464 ("*On Crimes and Punishments* helped shape our Fifth and Eighth Amendments"); Schwartz & Wishingrad, 813, 829–30; Rumann, 674; Liberty Fund, Inc., "Founding Father's Library," The Forum at The Online Library of Liberty, visited Jan. 31, 2011, http://oll.libertyfund.org/index.php ?option=com_staticxt&Itemid=29; *see also* e-note (noting the influence of European writers on the Founding Fathers and the founders' frequent citation of the Bible, in addition to discussing books that Madison recommended in 1783 for use by Congress).

52. Labunski, 29; Mayer, 347; Stahr, 379; Spak, 55–56; JJ to John Murray (Apr. 15, 1818); Mannheimer, 823; *see also* e-note (noting that most Framers tolerated the death penalty's use and further delineating the views of John Adams and John Langdon on executions).

53. David J. Vaughan, Give Me Liberty: The Uncompromising Statesmanship of Patrick Henry 111, 175–76, 205 (1997); JJ to Gouverneur Morris (Apr. 29, 1778); Stahr, 345; J. C. A. Stagg, ed., The Papers of James Madison, Digital Edition (Univ. of Virginia Press, Rotunda, 2010), visited Feb. 2, 2011, http://rotunda.upress.virginia.edu/ founders/JSMN-01-08-02-0130; id. n.2 (referencing Henry's letter to the mayor of Richmond); *see also* e-note (discussing James Monroe's views on capital punishment and New York's curtailment of capital crimes).

54. 2 Hall & Hall, ch. I ("Of the Nature of Crimes; and the Necessity and Proportion of Punishments"); id., ch. IV ("Of Crimes Against the Right of Individuals to Personal Safety"); David L. Holmes, The Faiths of the Founding Fathers 161–62 (2006); Aitken, 73; William Ewald, *James Wilson and the Drafting of the Constitution,* 10 U. Pa. J. Const. L. 901, 913–14 & n.28 (2008); Natalie Wexler, *In the Beginning: The First Three Chief Justices,* 154 U. Pa. L. Rev. 1373, 1379 (2006); The Friend: A Religious and Literary Journal, vol. 80, no. 13 (1906); Binder, 119 (noting Wilson and others promoted the law dividing murder into degrees); *see also* e-note (discussing Sabacos, the Ethiopian king, and Benjamin Rush's views on Pennsylvania's 1776 constitution).

55. Maier, Ratification, 405–6; 2 Mildred Crow Sargent, William Few, A Founding Father: A Biographical Perspective of Early American History 893, 898, 1055 (2006); Marshall De Lancey Haywood, Governor William Tryon, and His Administration in the Province of North Carolina, 1765–1771, at 9–10, 88, 104–7, 115, 133–36, 160 (1908); Pierce Butler to Colonel Gunn (Aug. 31, 1791); *see also* e-note (discussing Charles Pinckney's views on capital punishment and the execution of Regulators in North Carolina).

56. Chernow, Washington, 255, 427, 726; Kauffman, 136–37; Lyle Saxon, Lafitte the Pirate 194–96 (1989); Gottlieb, Theater of Death, 226; Journals of the Continental Congress 1774–1789, vol. 25, at 565–66 (1922) (reprinting 1783 journal entries); *see also* e-note (discussing executive clemency; James Madison's many pardons of condemned men, including William Hull; pardons issued by Congress, including those for a 1783 mutiny, before the Constitution's ratification; and John Adams's pardon of rioters and his refusal to execute those involved in Fries Rebellion).

57. Chernow, Washington, 718–22; Hogeland, 7, 20, 22–23, 104–5, 131, 143–44, 238; Unger, Lion of Liberty, 263; Preyer, 68–69.

58. JA to James McHenry (Sept. 18, 1799); JA to James McHenry (June 5, 1799); JA to Samuel Dexter (July 30, 1800); Samuel Dexter to JA (Aug. 7, 1800); JA to

Samuel Dexter (Aug. 16, 1800); Papers of the War Department, Unsigned Presidential Endorsement of Capital Punishment for Andrew Anderson and Court Martial of Samuel Ewing, visited Jan. 31, 2011, http://wardepartmentpapers.org/document.php?id= 37293 & http://wardepartmentpapers.org/document.php?id=40151.

59. John Adams autobiography, part 1, "John Adams," through 1776, sheet 20 of 53 [electronic edition], Massachusetts Historical Society, *Adams Family Papers: An Electronic Archive*, visited Feb. 27, 2011, http://www.masshist.org/digitaladams/; Banner, 88; *see also* e-note (discussing the Adams letters seized by the British, and the acceptance of death as a punishment for treason and rebellion in the founding era).

60. Charles Francis Adams, ed., Familiar Letters of John and His Wife Abigail Adams During the Revolution 247, 391 (1876); Chernow, Washington, 169; *see also* e-note (discussing correspondence between John and Abigail Adams relating to capital punishment).

61. "U" to the Boston Gazette (Aug. 1, 1763), Papers of John Adams (1977).

62. Chernow, Alexander Hamilton, 447; AA to JA (Jan. 12, 1794); AA to JA (Mar. 25, 1797); AA to JA (Mar. 31, 1797).

63. Chernow, Washington, 173; Gelles, 160; Charles W. Akers, Abigail Adams: An American Woman 195 (1980); AA to Elizabeth Cranch (Sept. 2, 1785). ("[T]here must be some essential defect in the Government and Morals of a people," Abigail Adams added in her letter to her niece, "when punishments lose their efficacy and crimes abound.").

64. Masur, 52; 2 Diary of John Quincy Adams 159–60 (1981); Josiah Quincy, Memoir of the Life of John Quincy Adams 20–21 (2010).

65. 7 Charles Francis Adams, ed., Memoirs of John Quincy Adams Comprising Portions of His Diary from 1795 to 1848, at 29 (1875); 8 Charles Francis Adams, ed., Memoirs of John Quincy Adams Comprising Portions of His Diary from 1795 to 1848, at 285 (1876); JQA to JA (Feb. 12, 1795); *see also* e-note (discussing John Quincy Adams's report to Congress in 1829 regarding the federal death penalty).

66. Sarah Joseph, *Committee Against Torture: Recent Jurisprudence,* 6 Hum. Rts. L. Rev. 571 (2006); Amnesty International, *Abolitionist and Retentionist Countries* and *Abolish the Death Penalty,* visited Apr. 28, 2011, http://www.amnesty.org/en/death-penalty/abolitionist-and-retentionist-countries#retentionist and http://www.amnesty .org/en/death-penalty; Kyodo News, "Chiba Urges Death Penalty Debate," Japan Times (Sept. 18, 2009); Death Penalty Worldwide, *Japan,* visited Apr. 28, 2011, http:// www.deathpenaltyworldwide.org. Amnesty International lists all "Abolitionist" and "Retentionist" countries, breaking down the abolitionist countries into three categories: "Abolitionist for all Crimes," "Abolitionist for Ordinary Crimes only," and "Abolitionist in Practice." Nations that are abolitionist for "ordinary crimes" retain the death penalty for crimes such as those committed in wartime or under military law. *See* Ursula Bentele, *Race and Capital Punishment in the United States and Africa,* 19 Brook. J. Int'l L. 235, 240 n.15 (1993).

67. Sangmin Bae, When the State No Longer Kills: International Human Rights Norms and Abolition of Capital Punishment 24–27 (2007); State v. Makwanyane, Case No. CCT/3/94 (judgment of 6 June 1995), ¶¶ 8, 26, 146; William E. Nelson, Marbury v. Madison, *Democracy, and the Rule of Law,* 71 Tenn. L. Rev. 217, 227 (2004); Scott M. Malzahn, *State Sponsorship and Support of International Terrorism: Customary Norms of State Responsibility,* 26 Hast. Int'l & Comp. L. Rev. 83, 86 (2002); *see also* e-note

(discussing the abolition of the death penalty in Great Britain, Canada, and Mexico, and in Europe generally).

68. Gates v. Collier, 501 F.2d 1291, 1306 (5th Cir. 1974); Jackson v. Bishop, 404 F.2d 571, 579 (8th Cir. 1968); *see also* e-note (discussing George Washington's views on corporal punishment and his orders that soldiers be flogged).

3. The Abolitionists (pages 66-96)

1. Barton, 180; *see also* e-note (listing biographical sources on Benjamin Rush and discussing Rush's advice to John Adams on the ineffectiveness of military executions).

2. Barton, 176–78; Mease, 179; Gottlieb, Theater of Death, 104–5; *see also* e-note (discussing the Walnut Street Prison, the proximity of Rush's house to it, Philadelphia's prison society, and early American opposition to capital punishment).

3. Kann, 123; John Howard, An Account of the Principal Lazarettos in Europe 169 n.* (1789); Fisher, 1236; Calvert, 149; Post, 39; Notice of Bidding for the Erection of a Prison, Virginia Gazette (Jan. 31, 1771); Robert J. Turnbull, A Visit to the Philadelphia Prison (1796), *reprinted in* 2 Crimmins; Note, *The Eighth Amendment, Proportionality, and the Changing Meaning of "Punishments,"* 122 Harv. L. Rev. 960, 967–68 (2009); *see also* e-note (discussing the influence of the Quakers and George and Martha Washington's support of an organization formed to aid those in prison).

4. John Howard, The State of the Prisons in England and Wales (1777); Friedman, Crime and Punishment in American History, 78; Calvert, 148–49; Colvin, 55; Kann, 131; Hindus, 162–65, 202–4; Rodriguez, 68; Devereaux, 127–28; Fisher, 1239, 1267–68; Randall McGowen, "The Well-Ordered Prison," *in* The Oxford History of the Prison 87 (1995); Act of Apr. 5, 1790, ch. 1516, 1790 Pa. Laws 511; Negley K. Teeters, The Cradle of the Penitentiary: The Walnut Street Jail at Philadelphia 1773–1835 (1955); *see also* e-note (discussing the building of penitentiaries in Pennsylvania, Virginia, and New York).

5. Wilf, 138–43; The Life of Hon. Nathaniel Chipman, LL.D. 230 (1846).

6. Rush, *Enquiry,* 3–4, 8–9, 14, 18, *reprinted in* Reform of Criminal Law in Pennsylvania (1972); *see also* e-note (discussing Rush's essays and comparing Rush's and Beccaria's views on public punishments).

7. Rush, *Enquiry,* 9–12, 18; *see also* e-note (discussing Rush's views on corporal punishments and the use of "mock executions" in the founding era).

8. Rush, *Enquiry,* 14–15.

9. William Paley, Principles of Moral and Political Philosophy, ch. IX, at 431–32, 440 (1785), *reprinted in* 2 Crimmins; Jeremy Bentham, Principles of Penal Law, Bk. II, chs. XI–XII (1775), *reprinted in* 2 Crimmins; *see also* Michel de Montaigne, Essays, Book II, "On Cruelty" 174 (1958).

10. BR to William Gordon (Dec. 10, 1778); BR to the Trustees of Dickinson College (Oct. 21, 1786); Address of BR to the Ministers of the Gospel of All Denominations (June 21, 1788); BR to TJ (May 5, 1803); BR to TJ (Aug. 22, 1800); TJ to BR (Apr. 21, 1803); "Syllabus of an Estimate of the Merit of the Doctrines of Jesus, compared with those of others," *reprinted in* 9 Ford; *see also* e-note (discussing Rush's sentiments on newspapers and public executions, eighteenth-century views of executions, and the publicizing of executions in the founding era).

11. Rush, *Enquiry,* 15–16; Maier, American Scripture, 76; *see also* e-note (discussing Rush's views on equality and the use of jails).

12. Calvert, 6, 14; Sydney George Fisher, The Quaker Colonies, a Chronicle of the Proprietors of the Delaware 49 (2006); Mease, 160; BR to JD (Apr. 5, 1787); Gottlieb, Theater of Death, 194 n.494; *see also* e-note (discussing John Dickinson's views, the relationship between Dickinson and Rush, and the sentiments of others, including Thomas Jefferson, relative to Pennsylvania's "wheelbarrow law").

13. Barton, 179; Robert R. Sullivan, *The Birth of the Prison: The Case of Benjamin Rush,* 31 Eighteenth-Century Studies 333 (1998); BR to Julia Rush (Aug. 22, 1787); BR to Julia Rush (Aug. 22, 1793).

14. Alexander Biddle, ed., Old Family Letters Relating to the Yellow Fever, Series B (1892); Chernow, Alexander Hamilton, 449; BR to RHL (Jan. 14, 1777); BR to JA (Dec. 15, 1807); BR to JA (July 26, 1809); BR to JA (Apr. 26, 1810); BR to JA (July 26, 1809); BR to JA (July 4, 1810); BR to TJ (Jan. 2, 1811); *see also* e-note (discussing eighteenth-century duels and Richard Rush's duel with a member of the Philadelphia bar).

15. Rush, *Considerations, 2–3, reprinted in* Reform of Criminal Law in Pennsylvania (1972); Schwartz & Wishingrad, 823; *see also* e-note (discussing Rush's essays).

16. Rush, *Considerations, 4–8; see also* e-note (discussing references to God and the Bible in the founding era and Ethan Allen's views on cruelty and punishment).

17. Rush, *Considerations, 9; see also* e-note (discussing Rush's appeals to posterity and his contempt for antiquated practices).

18. The Founding Fathers: The Essential Guide to the Men Who Made America 190 (2007); Michael Meranze, Laboratories of Virtue: Punishment, Revolution, and Authority in Philadelphia, 1760–1835, at 143 & n.29 (1996); Gottlieb, Theater of Death, 194 & n.497; Wilf, 150; BR to John Howard (Oct. 14, 1789); BR to Jeremy Belknap (Oct. 13, 1789); BR to John Coakley Lettsom (Aug. 16, 1788); BR to John Coakley Lettsom (May 18, 1787); BR to John Coakley Lettsom (Nov. 15, 1783); Barton, 135; *see also* e-note (discussing the activities of the Philadelphia Society for Alleviating the Miseries of Public Prisons and Rush's respect for John Howard's reform work).

19. BR to John Howard (Oct. 14, 1789); BR to Jeremy Belknap (Oct. 13, 1789); BR to Jeremy Belknap (Aug. 19, 1788).

20. Rush, *Considerations, 10;* BR to Jeremy Belknap (Oct. 7, 1788); *see also* e-note (discussing Rush's opposition to slavery, capital punishment, and war, as well as his correspondence with John Adams on "sanguinary" punishments).

21. Rush, *Considerations, 10–14; see also* e-note (discussing Rush's views on "solitude" to treat madness).

22. Rush, *Considerations, 10, 15–19;* Thomas, 84.

23. BR to Enos Hitchcock (Apr. 24, 1789); *see also* e-note (discussing Rush's views on corporal punishments).

24. Barton, 178; Binder, 119; Rush, *Essays, 164;* Brian Angelini, *Trinidad and Tobago's Controversial Death Penalty Law: A Note on* Hilaire, Constantine and Benjamin v. Trinidad & Tobago, 10 S.W. J.L. & Trade Am. 361, 384 (2004) (referring to William Bradford's proposed language for dividing murder into degrees and its influence on federal and state legislation).

25. Rush, *Essays, 164–66; see also* e-note (noting the common-law distinction between murder and manslaughter).

26. Rush, *Essays,* 166–71.

27. Id. at 172–75.

28. Id. at 175–76, 178.

29. Id. at 179.

30. Id. at 181–82; Okun, 38, 99; *see also* e-note (describing Thomas Jefferson's dealings with Caleb Lownes).

31. Colvin, 57; BR to Noah Webster (Dec. 29, 1789); BR to Elizabeth Graeme Ferguson (Jan. 18, 1793); BR to Humane Society of Massachusetts (Mar. 9, 1793); BR to Thomas Eddy (Oct. 19, 1803); Wanger, 757–58; Holly Boyer, *Home Sweet Hell: An Analysis of the Eighth Amendment's "Cruel and Unusual Punishment" Clause as Applied to Supermax Prisons,* 32 Sw. U. L. Rev. 317, 326 (2003); Edwin G. Burrows & Mike Wallace, Gotham: A History of New York City to 1898, at 366 (1999); *see also* e-note (discussing eighteenth-century penal reforms in Pennsylvania, New York, and other states).

32. Kann, 108; BR to Thomas Eddy (Oct. 19, 1803); *see also* e-note (discussing the 1809 legislative message of Pennsylvania governor Simon Snyder recommending that life imprisonment be substituted for the death penalty).

33. Rush, *Medical Inquiries,* 7, 9–28, 41, 94–95, 127–28, 178, 363–64.

34. Benjamin Rush, "On the Study of Medical Jurisprudence," Sixteen Introductory Lectures 363, 369–70, 384–85 (1811); F. W. Hunt, *Derangements of the Human Mind in Their Relation to Physical Diseases,* 11 N. Am. J. of Homoeopathy 321, 334 (1863); Susanna L. Blumenthal, *The Mind of a Moral Agent: Scottish Common Sense and the Problem of Responsibility in Nineteenth-Century American Law,* 26 Law & Hist. Rev. 99 (2008); *see also* e-note (discussing death sentences imposed in the wake of the Whiskey Rebellion, and John Adams's pardon of David Bradford).

35. Rush, Sixteen Introductory Lectures, 388, 393–95; *see also* e-note (discussing influences on Rush and the fact that suicide was once considered a criminal act).

36. BR to JA (July 11, 1806); *see also* e-note (discussing the close friendship of James Madison and William Bradford).

37. Louis Alexander Biddle, ed., A Memorial Containing Travels Through Life or Sundry Incidents in the Life of Dr. Benjamin Rush 150 (1905) (containing Rush's writings); Okun, 37; BR to JA (Apr. 5, 1808).

38. Bradford, *Enquiry,* 1, 3–4, 6; *see also* e-note (discussing Montesquieu's disdain for severe punishments and the repeated invocation of Montesquieu by the Founding Fathers).

39. Bradford, *Enquiry,* 5–7, 13.

40. Id. at 4–5.

41. Id. at 6, 9.

42. Id. at 14–16; Vila & Morris, 10–11; *see also* e-note (contrasting Pennsylvania and Massachusetts law, discussing William Penn's persecution in England, and explaining why Pennsylvania Quakers were reluctant to resort to executions).

43. Bradford, *Enquiry,* 16–19; *see also* e-note (discussing William Penn, Pennsylvania's founder and first governor, and Benjamin Rush's ancestors and religious beliefs).

44. Bradford, *Enquiry,* 20; An Act Amending the Penal Laws of this State, ch. MCCXLI, 1786 Pa. Stat., *reprinted in* Pa. Stat. ch. MCCXLI vol. XII at 280–90 (Mitchell & Flanders 1810); *see also* e-note (discussing Montesquieu's views on the need for proportionality in punishment).

45. Bradford, *Enquiry,* 20–21; *see also* e-note (discussing "crimes against nature").

46. Bradford, *Enquiry,* 21–26.

47. Id. at 26–33.

48. Id. at 35.

49. Id. at 35–36.

50. Antoine de Baecque, Glory and Terror: Seven Deaths Under the French Revolution 87 (Charlotte Mandell, trans. 2003); James R. Arnold, The Aftermath of the French Revolution 4, 7–8, 42 (2009); Kann, 93; BR to David Ramsay (Nov. 5, 1778); BR to Charles Lee (Oct. 24, 1779); BR to JA (Jan. 22, 1789); BR to John Coakley Lettsom (Apr. 26, 1793); Gouverneur Morris to TJ (Jan. 25, 1793); *see also* e-note (discussing Richard Henry Lee's sentiments on Louis XVI's execution).

51. BR to PH (Jan. 12, 1778); BR to JD (July 15, 1788); BR to JM (Feb. 27, 1790); BR to TJ (Mar. 1, 1796); BR to JD (Oct. 11, 1797); BR to JM (Dec. 5, 1801); BR to JA (July 9, 1807); 2 Butterfield, 861 n.1; BR to Richard Price (May 25, 1786); BR to TJ (Oct. 6, 1800); *see also* e-note (discussing Rush's February 1790 letter to James Madison and the pamphlet likely enclosed with it, as well as Rush's May 1796 letter to Thomas Jefferson).

52. J. H. Powell, Richard Rush: Republican Diplomat 6, 51, 69, 98 (1942); BR to JA (Feb. 4, 1811); BR to TJ (Dec. 17, 1811); 3 Frank M. Eastman, ed., Courts and Lawyers of Pennsylvania: A History, 1623–1923, at 777 (1922); Charles Alan Wright & Kenneth W. Graham Jr., 30 Federal Practice and Procedure *Evid.* § 6355 (2010) (text at n.246).

53. BR to JA (Aug. 8, 1777); BR to JA (Oct. 17, 1809); BR to TJ (Jan. 2, 1811); BR to JA (Dec. 16, 1811); BR to TJ (Dec. 17, 1811); BR to JA (Feb. 12, 1812); BR to JA (Feb. 17, 1812); BR to TJ (Mar. 3, 1812); TJ to BR (Apr. 8, 1813); *see also* e-note (discussing Rush's repeated invocations of Frederick II, the king of Prussia, and the two editions of Beccaria's *On Crimes and Punishments* in the library of John Adams).

54. Bowen, 246–47; BR to David Ramsay (Nov. 5, 1778); BR to David Ramsay (Mar. or Apr. 1788); *see also* e-note (discussing Frederick and Peter Muhlenberg's communications with Rush in 1789 concerning constitutional amendments).

55. George Jellinek, The Declaration of the Rights of Man and Citizens: A Contribution to Modern Constitutional History 27 (Max Farrand, trans. 2009); Pincus, 3–5, 14, 91–92, 104, 106, 110–11, 115–16, 155, 163, 184, 198, 226, 229, 257–62, 285, 292–93, 478; *see also* e-note (discussing Lord Chancellor George Jeffreys).

56. Maier, American Scripture, 52, 54; Amar, Bill of Rights, 87; *see also* id. at 279 ("that 1689 clause was written to restrain lawless and bloody judges like George Jeffreys").

57. BR to David Ramsay (Mar. or Apr. 1788); The Federalist No. 51 (James Madison); *see also* e-note (discussing the 1788 opposition of "The Impartial Examiner" to abuses of power and "cruel and violent" acts).

58. Labunski, 10, 104; Appleby, 126–299, 215, 349; Seminole Tribe of Florida v. Florida, 517 U.S. 44, 132–36 & n.32 (1996) (Souter, J., dissenting); *see also* e-note (discussing the views of Joseph Story and John Marshall on the English common law).

59. Labunski, 10, 104.

4. America's Founding Fathers (pages 97-161)

1. Mayer, 75–78, 94; Brands, 362, 364–66, 369, 371, 377, 424, 465, 479–80, 503, 510; Gelles, 26–27, 30–33, 40, 46, 51, 55, 84; Stoll, 24, 26, 100–101, 263; Chernow, Alexander Hamilton, 54–55, 57, 62, 65; Unger, John Hancock, 89–90, 95, 100; Unger, Lion of Liberty, 44–45, 47; Bernstein, xiv; Gottlieb, Theater of Death, 59, 61–62; *see also* e-note (discussing the displaying of effigies in Philadelphia).

2. Bernstein, xiv–xv; Articles of Confederation, arts. I, II, III, XIII (Nov. 15, 1777; effective Mar. 1, 1781); Decl. and Resolves of the First Cont. Cong. (Oct. 14, 1774); *see*

also e-note (discussing Jean-Jacques Rousseau, the concept of natural rights, and the American colonists' invocation of them).

3. Lancaster, 150; Unger, John Hancock, 246–47; L. Carroll Judson, A Biography of the Signers of the Declaration of Independence 159–62 (1839); RHL to SA (Feb. 4, 1775); RHL to PH (Apr. 20, 1776); RHL to PH (Nov. 15, 1778); *see also* e-note (discussing Richard Henry Lee's criticism of "Tory excesses in the realm of punishment" and George Washington's lament over the execution of Abraham Patten, an American spy).

4. 3 Harry Alonzo Cushing, The Writings of Samuel Adams 359–60 (1907); 2 John Marshall, The Life of George Washington 260–61 (1804); Maass, 6; *see also* e-note (discussing the execution of James Molesworth and the comments of John Adams about it).

5. Maass, 5–7, 15–19.

6. Brands, 216.

7. Phil Webster, 1776 Faith: The Christian Worldview of the Signers of the Declaration of Independence 62–63 (2009); Daniel Manuel & Peter Marshall, The Light and the Glory: 1492–1793, at 470–71 (2009); Larson, 1443, 1481; Rappleye, 163; Alfred William Savary, Lydia Adelia Savary Allen, & Samuel Smiles, A Genealogical and Biographical Record of the Savery Families (Savory and Savary) xviii (1893); *see also* e-note (noting the danger of execution faced by American revolutionaries).

8. Mayer, 286–87; Decl. of Independence (July 4, 1776); BR to Charles Lee (July 23, 1776); BR to Walter Jones (July 30, 1776). In Jefferson's listing of "unalienable Rights," he used the phrase "preservation of life" instead of "Life" in his original draft. Library of Congress, *Declaring Independence: Drafting the Documents*, visited Feb. 6, 2011, http://www.loc.gov/exhibits/declara/ruffdrft.html.

9. BR to JA (July 20, 1811); Larson, 3; *see also* e-note (referencing other gallows humor from John Adams).

10. Brands, 512; Gelles, 86; Decl. of Independence (July 4, 1776); *see also* e-note (discussing the British government's efforts to punish the leaders of the American Revolution).

11. Chernow, Washington, 236; Gelles, 84–85; Hunt, 117–18; Lewis Henry Boutell, The Life of Roger Sherman (1896); A Biographical Sketch of Robert R. Livingston 2 (Univ. of Mich. Univ. Lib., 2005); Bernstein, xiv; Maier, American Scripture, 6–13. The word "inalienable" became "unalienable" in the course of printing the Declaration of Independence. Id. at 144. The terms "inalienable" and "unalienable" are used interchangeably in multiple state constitutions with no apparent difference in meaning between the two terms.

12. Brands, 7, 511–12; Chernow, Washington, 236; Walter Isaacson, "Benjamin Franklin Joins the Revolution," Smithsonian.com (Aug. 1, 2003).

13. The Founding Fathers: The Essential Guide to the Men Who Made America 176 (2007); Keane, 98–102; Appleby, iii–iv, xii, xviii, xxv, 5; Kaye, Thomas Paine and the Promise of America, 21; *see also* e-note (describing how Thomas Paine grew up near the site of a gallows and came to oppose capital punishment).

14. Brands, 509–10; Gelles, 74; BR to James Cheetham (July 17, 1809); BR to JA (Aug. 14, 1809); Chernow, Alexander Hamilton, 70; Keane, 101–9, 112, 120; Appleby, xxiv–xxv.

15. Appleby, 13, 20, 29, 37, 44, 55, 65–66.

16. Id. at 73, 89, 92; 2 Conway 180; Steelwater, 24; *see also* e-note (noting that measures pertaining to currency and banks generated inflammatory language among the founders, including references by Thomas Jefferson to "treason").

17. Appleby, xiii, xvii–xviii, 107–8, 110; Lancaster, 24.

18. Appleby, 110–11, 114, 122–23; City of London, *Temple Bar*, visited Apr. 17, 2011, http://www.cityoflondon.gov.uk.

19. Appleby, 123–24, 269; *see also* e-note (containing a description by John Adams of London in 1780).

20. Larson, 25–26, 68; Schiff, 403; Marie Kimball, Jefferson: The Scene of Europe 1784 to 1789, at 295 (2007); TJ to JJ (July 19, 1789).

21. Hunt, 129; Autobiography of Thomas Jefferson (1821).

22. Miller, 15, 26–27; *see also* e-note (containing descriptions of the French Revolution by Thomas Jefferson and Gouverneur Morris).

23. 3 Conway, 123–24; David Freeman Hawke, Paine 273–75 (1992).

24. 3 Conway, 125–27; 2 Moncure D. Conway & William Cobbett, The Life of Thomas Paine: With a History of His Literary, Political and Religious Career in America, France and England 19–20 (2006); Craig Nelson, Thomas Paine: Enlightenment, Revolution, and the Birth of Modern Nations 242–43 (2006); Clifford D. Connor, Jean Paul Marat: Scientist and Revolutionary 11, 227, 236 (1997); Geoffrey Robertson, *Ending Impunity: How International Criminal Law Can Put Tyrants on Trial,* 38 Cornell Int'l L.J. 649, 652 (2005); Keane, 368; Jack Fruchtman Jr., The Political Philosophy of Thomas Paine 2, 5, 9–10, 21, 24, 26–27, 29 (2009).

25. Chernow, Alexander Hamilton, 432–34, 439, 459, 463; McCullough, 190, 443–44; Ketcham, 341; Andrew Lipscomb, ed., 9 The Writings of Thomas Jefferson 284–85 (1903); Jacob E. Cooke, Tench Coxe and the Early Republic 155 (1978); *see also* e-note (discussing Tench Coxe).

26. Appleby, iii–iv, xiii–xiv, xxxi–xxxii, 308, 360–63; Kaye, Thomas Paine, 71, 78–80, 84–85; Thomas Paine: Collected Writings 220 (2009); John P. Frank, Book Review, 61 Yale L.J. 1227, 1229 (1952); Thomas Clio Rickman, The Life and Writings of Thomas Paine 261–62 (1908).

27. Unger, Last Founding Father, 2, 4, 28, 30, 115–17; R. B. Bernstein, *Rediscovering Thomas Paine,* 39 N.Y.L. Sch. L. Rev. 873, 889 (1994); The Thomas Paine Reader 15–16 (1987); Chernow, Alexander Hamilton, 432; *see also* e-note (discussing Robespierre's shifting views on executions and his own death by the guillotine).

28. Bernstein, xv; Chernow, Alexander Hamilton, 157; Articles of Confederation, arts. IV, VI, VIII, IX (Nov. 15, 1777; effective Mar. 1, 1781).

29. Brands, 670–72; Gelles, 195; Chernow, Alexander Hamilton, 224–25; Unger, Lion of Liberty, 178; Jaired Stallard, *Abuse of the Pardon Power: A Legal and Economic Perspective,* 1 DePaul Bus. & Com. L.J. 103, 106 & n.24 (2002).

30. Chernow, Alexander Hamilton, 228–29, 239–41; Chernow, Washington, 530–31; Bowen, 50; Gouverneur Morris, A Diary of the French Revolution 316, 376 (2008); *see also* e-note (discussing the execution of John Bly and Charles Rose in the aftermath of Shays' Rebellion and the pardon or commutation of sentences of other men associated with it).

31. U.S. Const., art. I, § 8; Chernow, Washington, 514, 713; Eugene Kontorovich, *The "Define and Punish" Clause and the Limits of Universal Jurisdiction,* 103 Nw. U. L. Rev. 149, 160–76 (2009); Beth Stephens, *Federalism and Foreign Affairs: Congress's Power to "Define and Punish . . . Offenses Against the Law of Nations,"* 42 Wm. & Mary L. Rev. 447, 462–77 (2000); Timothy H. Goodman, *"Leaving the Corsair's Name to Other Times": How to Enforce the Law of Sea Piracy in the 21st Century Through Regional International Agreements,* 31 Case W. Res. J. Int'l L. 139, 145 (1999); Brandon L. Bige-

low, *The Commerce Clause and Criminal Law,* 41 B.C. L. Rev. 913, 931 (2000); The Federalist No. 42 (James Madison); *see also* e-note (discussing the dispute as to whether the federal government had jurisdiction of certain offenses, including Thomas Jefferson's views on the subject).

32. Railway Labor Executives' Ass'n v. Gibbons, 455 U.S. 457, 472 (1982); Bowen, 221–23; 2 Records of the Federal Convention of 1787, at 489 (Max Farrand, ed., 1911); Kauffman, 47–48; Frederick P. Corbit, *The Founding Fathers' Influence on Bankruptcy Law,* 26 Am. Bankr. Inst. J. 50, 50 n.4 (2007); Randolph J. Haines, *The Uniformity Power: Why Bankruptcy Is Different,* 77 Am. Bankr. L.J. 129, 153 (2003); Little, 361 n.52; *see also* e-note (noting debates over treason and other criminal law issues, George Mason's opposition to the President's pardoning power, and the fact that James Wilson and Robert Morris served time in prison as debtors).

33. Debate in Virginia Ratifying Convention (June 18, 1788); *see also* e-note (discussing George Mason's objections to the Constitution).

34. U.S. Const., art. I, §§ 9–10 & art. III, §§ 2–3; Amar, America's Constitution, 233–38, 250, 253; Thomas Baggott, Cultivating Effective Lawyer-Juror Relationships: Understanding the Process 1 (1999); Unified Judicial System, *Juror Questionnaire,* visited Feb. 6, 2011, http://ujsjurors.sd.gov; *see also* e-note (discussing the debate over the definition of treason).

35. *Brown,* 381 U.S. at 445; Collins v. Youngblood, 497 U.S. 37, 45, 48 (1990); Peyton v. Rowe, 391 U.S. 54, 58 (1968); Duncan v. State, 152 U.S. 377, 382 (1894); Fletcher v. Peck, 3 L.Ed. 162 (1810); In re Extradition Request of McMullen, 989 F.2d 603, 604–5 & n.1 (2d Cir.), *cert. denied,* 510 U.S. 913 (1993); Justice James Iredell, "Charge to the Grand Jury of the Circuit Court for the District of New York" (Apr. 6, 1795); Reynolds, 187; *see also* e-note (discussing the concept of *attainder*—the consequence of a death sentence under English common law—and the use of *bills of attainder*).

36. U.S. Const., art. II, § 2, art. III, §§ 2–3, & art. IV, § 2; Joseph Wheelan, Jefferson's Vendetta, The Pursuit of Aaron Burr and the Judiciary (2006); Buckner F. Melton Jr., Aaron Burr: Conspiracy to Treason (2001); United States v. Burr, 25 F. Cas. 187 (D. Va. 1807); Schick v. Reed, 419 U.S. 256 (1974); United States v. Smith, 953 F.2d 1060, 1065 (7th Cir. 1992); Williams v. United States, Civ. No. 80–2249, 1981 WL 1938 at *1 (S.D. W. Va. Sept., 23, 1981); Gregg v. Georgia, 428 U.S. 153, 199 n.50 (1976) (opinion of Stewart, Powell, and Stevens, JJ.); Brands, 688; *see also* e-note (containing additional citations and discussing the President's power to grant reprieves or conditional commutations, even for death sentences).

37. Northwest Ordinance of 1787 (July 13, 1787), Arts. II and VI; Furman v. Georgia, 408 U.S. 238, 244 (1972) (Douglas, J., concurring); Duffey, 929–30, 937; Thomas Jefferson, Notes on the State of Virginia (1784); *see also* e-note (discussing Nathan Dane's background, the Northwest Ordinance, and its predecessor, the Ordinance of 1784).

38. James Morton Smith, The Republic of Letters: The Correspondence Between Thomas Jefferson and James Madison 622–23 (1995); David Reiss, *Jefferson and Madison as Icons in Judicial History: A Study of Religion Clause Jurisprudence,* 61 Md. L. Rev. 94, 136 (2002); 3 Documentary History of the First Federal Congress, 1789–1791: House of Representatives Journal 84, 110 (Linda Grant De Pauw, ed., 1977); John Witte Jr., Religion and the American Constitutional Experiment: Essential Rights and Liberties 76 (2000); *Furman,* 408 U.S. at 262 (Brennan, J., concurring).

39. U.S. Const., amend. XIII, § 1; Chernow, Washington, 113, 623; Strauss, 112;

State v. Hershberger, 462 N.W.2d 393, 399 (Minn. 1990) (Simonett, J., concurring); State v. Combs, 504 N.W.2d 248, 251–52 (Minn. App. 1993); People v. Lorentzen, 194 N.W.2d 827, 829 n.3 (Mich. 1972); People v. Bullock, 485 N.W.2d 866, 872 (Mich. 1992); W. Sherman Rogers, *The Black Quest for Economic Liberty: Legal, Historical, and Related Considerations,* 48 How. L.J. 1, 32 (2004); *see also* e-note (discussing Virginia's 1748 fugitive-slave law and the comments of "Phileleutheros" on the unequal treatment of "white people" and "Africans" in the founding era).

40. A Citizen of Philadelphia [Pelatiah Webster], Remarks on the Address of Sixteen Members of the Assembly of Pennsylvania (Oct. 12, 1787); Larry D. Kramer, *Madison's Audience,* 112 Harv. L. Rev. 611, 668 (1999); Book Review, *The Origin and Growth of the American Constitution,* 25 Harv. L. Rev. 747 (1912); Book Review, *Science of Jurisprudence,* 18 Yale L.J. 290 (1909); Hannis Taylor, *Pelatiah Webster,* 17 Yale L.J. 73 (1907).

41. Giuseppe Caracciolo di Brienza to TJ (Nov. 26, 1801); Barbara B. Oberg & J. Jefferson Looney, eds., The Papers of Thomas Jefferson, Digital Edition (Univ. of Virginia Press, Rotunda, 2008), visited Feb. 2, 2011, http://rotunda.upress.virginia.edu/founders/TSJN-01-35-02-0553.

42. John Adams, "A Dissertation on the Canon and the Feudal Law," no. 4 (Oct. 21, 1765); 1 Robert Joseph Taylor, ed., Papers of John Adams 103 (1977).

43. Judiciary Act of 1789 (Sept. 24, 1789), 1 Stat. 73, §§ 1, 9, 14, 29; Little, 360; Paul Taylor, *Congress's Power to Regulate the Federal Judiciary: What the First Congress and the First Federal Courts Can Teach Today's Congress and Courts,* 39 Pepp. L. Rev. 847, 851 (2010); *see also* e-note (discussing the efforts of the First Congress to define federal crimes and the concept of federal common-law crimes advanced by some, including Oliver Ellsworth).

44. Chernow, Washington, 601; Labunski, 133, 174; Act of Apr. 30, 1790, 1 Stat. 112–19; Banner, 62–64; *see also* e-note (noting amendments by Congress to the Articles of War in 1789 and 1806; the passage of a federal law in 1790 allowing the pillory's use for perjury and the postmortem dissection of murderers; James Madison's advocacy of legislation in 1785 providing for the pillory's use in Virginia; England's use of executions and "transportation" in the eighteenth century; and the substantial threat of anarchy and lawlessness posed by acts of treason, rebellion, and piracy in America's early years).

45. Little, 363–64; The George Washington University, *Birth of the Nation: The First Federal Congress 1789-1791,* visited Feb. 1, 2011, http://www.gwu.edu/~ffcp/exhibit/p1/members/; Gales & Seaton's History 1571–72 (Apr. 6, 1790); *see also* e-note (discussing the dissection of the bodies of those executed).

46. Little, 363–64; The George Washington University, *Birth of the Nation: The First Federal Congress 1789-1791,* visited Feb. 1, 2011, http://www.gwu.edu/~ffcp/exhibit/p1/members/; Gales & Seaton's History 1573–74 (Apr. 5, 1790).

47. Banner, 88; Brands, 503; Maestro, 130–31, 133, 137; BF to Benjamin Vaughan (Mar. 14, 1785); Schwartz & Wishingrad, 822; *see also* e-note (discussing penal reform in England, Samuel Romilly's contact with Thomas Jefferson and John Adams, and Romilly's views on the cruelty of death sentences for crimes other than murder).

48. Brands, 350–53; BR to BF (Oct. 22, 1766); BF to BR and Jonathan Potts (Dec. 20, 1766); BR to BF (May 1, 1773); BF to BR (July 14, 1773); *see also* e-note (discussing Pennsylvania's constitution).

49. Kastenberg, 67; BF to Benjamin Vaughan (Mar. 14, 1785); Adams' Argument for the Defense (Dec. 3–4, 1770), C. James Taylor, ed., The Adams Papers, Digital Edition

(Univ. of Virginia Press, Rotunda, 2008), visited Feb. 2, 2011, http://rotunda.upress
.virginia.edu/founders/ADMS-05-03-02-0001-0004-0016 (quoting English and
Roman maxims similar to the one expressed by Benjamin Franklin, with John Adams
noting that "even the judges in the Courts of Inquisition"—who with their "racks, burnings and scourges, examine criminals"—preserved the principle "that it is better the
guilty should escape punishment, than the innocent suffer"); *see also* e-note (discussing
Benjamin Franklin's views and correspondence).

50. Brands, 8, 16, 20–21, 60, 69, 97–98, 150–51, 316–17, 446, 661; Schiff, 399; 1
J. A. Leo Lemay, The Life of Benjamin Franklin: Journalist, 1706–1730, at 427–28
(2006); Bowen, 34; Lawrence Herman, *The Unexplored Relationship Between the Privilege Against Compulsory Self-Incrimination and the Involuntary Confession Rule (Part
I), 53 Ohio St. L.J. 101, 163 (1992).

51. Chernow, Washington, 65, 73; GW to John Ashby (Dec. 28, 1755); GW to John
Stanwix (July 15, 1757); GW to John Stanwix (July 30, 1757); GW to Robert Dinwiddie (Aug. 3, 1757); Masur, 58 ("Under Washington's orders scores of men from both the
continental and British armies faced the gallows."); *see also* e-note (containing additional
citations and discussing corporal and capital punishments for soldiers and deserters in
the founding era).

52. Brands, 503; Banner, 91; Kirchmeier, *Another Place Beyond Here*, 6 n.26; Gottlieb, Theater of Death, 181–82; GW to Benedict Arnold (Sept. 14, 1775); GW to
William Heath (Nov. 5, 1780); *see also* e-note (discussing the execution of spies in the
founding era, the concept of retaliatory punishments, George Washington's approval of
executions, as well as containing additional citations).

53. Chernow, Washington, 228, 248; GW to Lewis Nicola (Feb. 5, 1780); GW to
Cont. Cong., July 15, 1776; GW to Lt. Col. Samuel Blachley (Jan. 8, 1777); GW to
William Livingston (Apr. 26, 1778); GW to Lewis Nicola (Feb. 5, 1780); *see also* e-note
(discussing George Washington's views of Native Americans and his disdain for the
"cruel treatment" of prisoners).

54. William Howe to GW (Feb. 21, 1778).

55. Report on Retaliation against British (entered Oct. 1, 1781; read Dec. 3, 1781) &
Motion for Reprisal for Detention of Henry Laurens, J. C. A. Stagg, ed., The Papers of
James Madison Digital Edition (Univ. of Virginia Press, Rotunda, 2010), visited
Feb. 2, 2011, http://rotunda.upress.virginia.edu/founders/JSMN-01-03-02-0133 &
JSMN-01-03-02-0161; Biographical Directory of the U.S. Congress, *Henry Laurens
(1724-1792)*, visited Feb. 11, 2011, http://bioguide.congress.gov/scripts/biodisplay
.pl?index=L000121; *see also* e-note (discussing British "cruelties" during the Revolu-
tionary War and the American rejection of "retaliation").

56. Chernow, Washington, 255, 287, 352, 389–90; Charles Patrick Neimeyer, The
Revolutionary War 46 (2007); GW to Preudhomme de Borre (Aug. 3, 1777); *see also*
e-note (describing Washington's order that a soldier be pardoned just minutes before his
execution, Washington's regret over a Tory's execution, and Washington's approval of
other executions to serve as "Examples").

57. GW to Cont. Cong. Conf. Comm. (Jan. 29, 1778).

58. Bessler, *Revisiting Beccaria's Vision*, 229 n.226; GW to Henry Laurens (Aug. 31,
1778); *see also* e-note (discussing Lafayette's advice to Washington on military
punishments).

59. Thomas Bird to GW (June 5, 1790); David Sewall to GW (June 5, 1790); GW to

JJ (June 13, 1790); JJ to GW (June 13, 1790), Theodore J. Crackel, ed., The Papers of George Washington, Digital Edition (Univ. of Virginia Press, Rotunda, 2008), visited Feb. 2, 2011, http://rotunda.upress.virginia.edu/founders/GEWN-05-05-02-0299.

60. George Washington, Proclamation of Pardons in Western Pennsylvania (July 10, 1795); GW to Brig. Gen. James Clinton (Dec. 31, 1778); National Archives, RG 46, Fourth Cong., Records of Legislative Proceedings, President's Messages; Neil A. Hamilton, Rebels and Renegades: A Chronology of Social and Political Dissent in the United States 62 (2002); 7 Henry Cabot Lodge, ed., The Works of Alexander Hamilton 352 (1904).

61. Chernow, Alexander Hamilton, 4, 7, 75–76; Chernow, Washington, 232–33; Lancaster, 323; Roger P. Alford, Roper v. Simmons *and Our Constitution in International Equipoise,* 53 UCLA L. Rev. 1, 11 n.48 (2005); *see also* e-note (discussing the cases of Thomas Hickey, Joseph Perkins, and Richard Hunt, along with the views of John Adams and Alexander Hamilton).

62. 2 Steve Sheppard, ed., The Selected Writings of Sir Edward Coke 574, 944, 952, 955, 957, 992–94, 1033, 1041–43 (2003); Raleigh Trevelyan, Sir Walter Raleigh 328, 372, 377, 412 (2002); Antonia Fraser, Faith and Treason: The Story of the Gunpowder Plot xv, 221 (1997); *see also* e-note (discussing the writings of Sir Edward Coke and Jefferson's reading of them).

63. Chernow, Alexander Hamilton, 48–49, 60, 71–72, 168–69, 189–90, 196–99, 206; Chernow, Washington, 233; Humphry William Woolrych, The Life of the Right Honourable Sir Edward Coke 74, 86–87 (1826); *see also* e-note (discussing admiralty cases in which John Adams saved his clients from hanging, and noting Alexander Hamilton's distaste for Governor George Clinton's punitive postwar policies).

64. The Federalist No. 74 (Alexander Hamilton); AH to Secretary of War (July 29, 1799).

65. Chernow, Alexander Hamilton, 143–44; Chernow, Washington, 378–87; *see also* e-note (discussing Alexander Hamilton's and James Madison's reactions to the hanging of André, and George Washington's desire summarily to execute Benedict Arnold).

66. JA to James McHenry (June 19, 1799); JA to James McHenry (July 13, 1799); JA to James McHenry (July 19, 1799); *see also* e-note (discussing the concern of President John Adams for the proper conduct of court-martial proceedings).

67. Steiner, 381–82; 23 Syrett, 56, 65, 151–52, 181–83, 286–87, 293–94; AH to Secretary of War (July 29, 1799); Chernow, Alexander Hamilton, 92; AH to Washington Morton (Apr. 23, 1799); *see also* e-note (discussing the controversial decision of President John Adams to extradite a seaman to Great Britain, whereupon the British navy took the man to Jamaica and tried and hanged him).

68. Chernow, Washington, 160, 426–27; Masur, 56–58; *see also* e-note (describing the reactions of Congress and James Madison to the death of Joshua Huddy).

69. Chernow, Washington, 203, 426–27; Masur, 56–58; Edwin G. Burrows, Forgotten Patriots: The Untold Story of American Prisoners During the Revolutionary War 180–88 (2008); JM to Edmund Randolph (docketed by Randolph on Aug. 27, 1782), J. C. A. Stagg, ed., The Papers of James Madison, Digital Edition (Univ. of Virginia Press, Rotunda, 2010), visited Feb. 2, 2011, http://rotunda.upress.virginia.edu/founders/JSMN-01-05-02-0037; *see also* e-note (discussing other views of Captain Asgill).

70. Chernow, Alexander Hamilton, 1, 116–17, 164, 491–92, 539–41, 650–55, 682–91,

696–97, 700–708; Preyer, 66; *see also* e-note (discussing the Burr-Hamilton duel and the antidueling campaign that followed).

71. TJ to Maria Cosway (Oct. 12, 1786); Maier, American Scripture, 99–100.

72. Ellis, American Sphinx, 55, 65; 2 Ford, 7–8 & n.1; Maier, American Scripture, 48, 103; Wills, 3, 17; *see also* e-note (discussing George Wythe and his students Thomas Jefferson, John Marshall, and St. George Tucker).

73. 2 Ford, 8 n.1; Marshall Wingfield, A History of Caroline County, Virginia 200 (1924).

74. Masur, 72; 1 Boyd, 490; 2 Ford, 13, 17, 169; *see also* e-note (citations to drafts of Thomas Jefferson).

75. Broadwater, 104; Aitken & Aitken, 54–55; TJ to George Wythe (Nov. 1, 1778); 2 Ford, 394; Dubber & Farmer, 129, 134–35; Maestro, 141; Randall, 298; *see also* e-note (discussing Jefferson's continuing interest in Beccaria's book, his association with George Wythe, and Jefferson's role in drafting a new code of laws for Virginia).

76. Maestro, 142; Thomas, 39, 86; William G. Merkel, *Jefferson's Failed Anti-Slavery Proviso of 1784 and the Nascence of Free Soil Constitutionalism,* 38 Seton Hall L. Rev. 555, 560 n.18 (2008); Douglas, 157; Blinka, 89–91; 2 Ford, 396–98, 401–4; Randall, 299; Thomas Jefferson, Autobiography Draft Fragment, Jan. 6–July 27, 1821 (entry for Feb. 6); *see also* e-note (discussing the influence of Bentham's writings on Jefferson's bill).

77. "Observations on the Article Etats-Unis Prepared for the Encyclopedie" (June 22, 1786); 4 Paul Leicester Ford, ed., The Writings of Thomas Jefferson 138 n.1 (1894).

78. 2 Ford, 403; Crompton, 277–78, 285, 287; Elvia Rosales Arriola, *Sexual Identity and the Constitution: Homosexual Persons as a Discrete and Insular Minority,* 14 Women's Rts. L. Rep. 263, 288 n.243 (1992); Christopher Bopst, *Rape Shield Laws and Prior False Accusations of Rape: The Need for Meaningful Legislative Reform,* 24 J. Legis. 125, 126 n.7 (1998) (quoting 9 Boyd) (letter to JM); TJ to JM (Dec. 16, 1786); Broadwater, 278; Randall, 299.

79. Randall, 298, 300; 2 Ford, 395; Crompton, 277, 279; TJ to Edmund Pendleton (Aug. 26, 1776); 1 Boyd, 490 (reprinting letter from Edmund Pendleton that Jefferson was responding to, with Pendleton's letter referencing Jefferson's efforts at "reformation as to our criminal system of laws"); *see also* e-note (discussing Jefferson's writings on torture, Virginia practices, and his proposed penal code).

80. 2 Ford, 393–94, 411 & n.4, 414.

81. Id. at 395 & n.2, 397–400 & n.4, 404–5 & n.2, 407 & n.1, 408 & n.2; Preyer, 57 n.13.

82. Banner, 96; TJ to George Wythe (Nov. 1, 1778); Thomas Jefferson, Autobiography Draft Fragment, Jan. 6–July 27, 1821; Preyer, 57 n.16; *see also* e-note (discussing society's rejection of Kant's views and William Blackstone's writings).

83. Report on Cedars Cartel (June 17, 1776); *see also* e-note (discussing Thomas Jefferson's views on retaliation and the law of nations).

84. Levy, 72–78; Thomas Jefferson, "Bill to Attaint Josiah Phillips" (May 28, 1778); "An act to attaint Josiah Philips and others," Session of May 4, 1778, ch. 12, 9 Laws of Virginia 463 (Hening 1821); Blinka, 95; 2 Ford, 149 (Jefferson's draft bill); *see also* e-note (discussing military law, the Articles of War and prisoners of war, and Thomas Jefferson's and Patrick Henry's views pertaining to the Josiah Philips bill of attainder).

85. Thomas Jefferson, Autobiography Draft Fragment, Jan. 6–July 27, 1821; TJ to Albert Gallatin (Sept. 9, 1808); Garry Wills, James Madison 52–54 (2002).

86. Maier, American Scripture, xvii, 125, 188; TJ to Roger Weightman (June 24, 1826).

87. TJ to Edmund Pendleton (Aug. 26, 1776).

88. 10 Ford, 58–63; Hunt, 16, 220–21; Marcello Maestro, *Lafayette as a Reformer of Penal Laws*, 39 J. Hist. Ideas 503, 503 (1978); James Thuo Gathii, *Commerce, Conquest, and Wartime Confiscation*, 31 Brook. J. Int'l L. 709, 718 n.46 (2006); Roger P. Alford, *In Search of a Theory for Constitutional Comparativism*, 52 UCLA L. Rev. 639, 656 (2005); Michael A. Cokley, *Whatever Happened to that Old Saying "Thou Shall Not Kill?": A Plea for the Abolition of the Death Penalty*, 2 Loy. J. Pub. Int. L. 67 (2001); 2 B. Sarrans, Memoirs of General Lafayette and of the French Revolution of 1830, at 56–59 (1833); 1 The Writings of Thomas Jefferson 67 (1903); Thomas Jefferson, Autobiography Draft Fragment, Jan. 6–July 27, 1821 (Feb. 6 entry); Mackey, 98 (indicating Lafayette uttered those words on August 17, 1830); *see also* e-note (discussing Lafayette, the abolition of torture in France, the French Declaration of the Rights of Man and of the Citizen, and Virginia's 1796 penal reform bill championed by George Keith Taylor).

89. 1 Albert Ellery Bergh, ed., The Writings of Thomas Jefferson 257–58 (1907); Masur, 86; Preyer, 76–77; James Rood Robertson, Petitions of the Early Inhabitants of Kentucky to the General Assembly of Virginia, 1769 to 1792, at 99 (1998); *see also* e-note (discussing the 1783 Virginia law making the issuance of fraudulent tobacco certificates punishable by death, the opening of the Virginia penitentiary in 1800, Thomas Jefferson's involvement in suggesting plans for its construction, and George Keith Taylor's desire to "imitate and adopt" Pennsylvania's system).

90. TJ to Skelton Jones (July 28, 1809).

91. Larson, 190–92; Dunn, 154–55; James Monroe to JM (Sept. 9, 1800); Scot French, The Rebellious Slave: Nat Turner in American Memory 15–16 (2004) (reprinting letter from James Thomson Callender to TJ).

92. Larson, 193; Dunn, 155; Unger, Last Founding Father, 140; Douglas R. Egerton, Gabriel's Rebellion: The Virginia Slave Conspiracies of 1800 and 1802, at 82–84 (1993); James Monroe to TJ (Sept. 15, 1800), Barbara B. Oberg & J. Jefferson Looney, eds., The Papers of Thomas Jefferson, Digital Edition (Univ. of Virginia Press, Rotunda, 2008), visited Feb. 2, 2011, http://rotunda.upress.virginia.edu/founders/TSJN-01-32-02-0094.

93. Account of Richmond Trials, Barbara B. Oberg & J. Jefferson Looney, eds., The Papers of Thomas Jefferson, Digital Edition (Univ. of Virginia Press, Rotunda, 2008), visited Feb. 2, 2011, http://rotunda.upress.virginia.edu/founders/TSJN-01-32-02-0109.

94. Fawn M. Brodie, Thomas Jefferson: An Intimate History 342 (1974); Larson, 197–98; Dunn, 156; Unger, Last Founding Father, 141–42; Harry Ammon, James Monroe: The Quest for National Identity 188, 198, 200–201 (1990); Thomas Jefferson's Monticello, *The Plantation and Agriculture*, visited Feb. 6, 2011, http://www.monticello.org/site/plantation-and-slavery/plantation-agriculture; *see also* e-note (discussing a slave revolt in Virginia and alternate punishments considered for slaves and Native Americans).

95. James Madison, Speeches of June 16, 1788 ("Power over the Militia") and June 20, 1788 ("Power of Judiciary"); John P. Kaminski, Gaspare J. Saladino, Richard Leffler, Charles H. Schoenleber, & Margaret A. Hogan, eds., The Documentary History

of the Ratification of the Constitution, Digital Edition (Univ. of Virginia Press, Rotunda, 2009), visited Feb. 2, 2011, http://rotunda.upress.virginia.edu/founders/RNCN-02-10 -02-0002-0005-0001 (Virginia ratification debate); RHL to GW (Oct. 12, 1781) (advocating "a well-conceived law for the speedy capital punishment of such offenders" to "lessen greatly, if not to suppress, a practice extremely injurious to those who live near the water").

96. JM to WB (Jan. 24, 1774); WB to JM (Mar. 4, 1774); Reynolds v. United States, 98 U.S. 145, 165 (1878); John Brown Dillon & Ben Douglass, Oddities of Colonial Legislation in America 21 (1879); E. Christopher Reyes, In His Name 236 (2010); Michael W. McConnell, *Establishment and Disestablishment at the Founding: Part I: Establishment of Religion,* 44 Wm. & Mary L. Rev. 2105, 2163–66 (2003); Donald L. Drakeman, Reynolds v. United States: *The Historical Construction of Constitutional Reality,* 21 Const. Comment. 697, 705–9 (2004); Marvin Olasky, *The White House Faith-Based Initiative: What's Going Right, What's Going Wrong,* 16 Notre Dame J.L. Ethics & Pub. Pol'y 355, 356 (2002); Douglas Laycock, *Religious Liberty as Liberty,* 7 J. Contemp. Legal Issues 313, 345 (1996); *see also* e-note (discussing the death penalty's long history in Virginia).

97. JM to WB (Sept. 25, 1773); WB to JM (Nov. 5, 1773); JM to WB (Dec. 1, 1773); JM to WB (Jan. 24, 1774); Mary Sarah Bilder, *James Madison, Law Student and Demi-Lawyer,* 28 Law & Hist. Rev. 389, 393–404 (2010); Amelia J. Uelmen, *Can a Religious Person Be a Big Firm Litigator,* 26 Ford. Urb. L.J. 1069, 1087 (1999); Laura Underkuffler-Freund, *The Separation of the Religious and the Secular: A Foundational Challenge to First Amendment Theory,* 36 Wm. & Mary L. Rev. 837, 875–76 (1995); *see also* e-note (discussing JM-WB correspondence).

98. Austin v. United States, 509 U.S. 602, 609 (1993); Ingraham v. Wright, 430 U.S. 651 (1977); 1 W. & M., 2d Sess., ch. 2, 3 Stat. at Large 441 (1689); Claus, *Antidiscrimination Eighth Amendment,* 127–28; *see also* e-note (discussing the Rhode Island and North Carolina ratification conventions).

99. U.S. Const., art. V; Banner, 88; Ketcham, 12; Jack N. Rakove, *Two Foxes in the Forest of History,* 11 Yale J.L. & Human. 191, 192 (1991); BR to JM (Feb. 18, 1790); BR to JM (Feb. 27, 1790); JM to BR (Mar. 7, 1790); *see also* e-note (discussing materials Rush sent to James Madison).

100. Banner, 95–96; King, 952; JM to James Monroe (Dec. 9, 1785); JM to TJ (Feb. 15, 1787); JM to Thomas S. Grimke (Jan. 15, 1828); Preyer, 73; Caleb Foote, *The Coming Constitutional Crisis in Bail: I,* 113 U. Pa. L. Rev. 959, 977 (1965); 2 Ford, 408.

101. Observations on the "Draught of a Constitution for Virginia" (1788); Ketcham, 162; JM to James Monroe (Dec. 17, 1785); *see also* e-note (discussing correspondence of Madison and Jefferson on the Virginia bill for proportionate punishments and the French Revolution).

102. James Madison: Writings, 1772–1836, at 488 (1999); Ketcham, 608 & 723 n.53 (citing James Madison's message of Dec. 3, 1816); G. F. H. Crockett to JM (Sept. 24, 1823); *see also* e-note (pertaining to G. F. H. Crockett's address to Kentucky's legislature).

103. JM to G. F. H. Crockett (Nov. 6, 1823). Madison's letter to Crockett further stated, "I must ask the favor of you to make no possible use of this letter," with Madison adding that his letter was "meant merely" as a "friendly" reply, with Madison closing by sending his "good wishes" to his correspondent.

104. Banner, 138; JM to Edward Livingston (July 10, 1822).

105. JM to Roberts Vaux (June 22, 1827); James J. McCadden, Education in Pennsylvania, 1801–1835, and Its Debts to Roberts Vaux 114, 121–23 (1937); JM to Thomas J. Wharton (May 5, 1828); Calendar of the Correspondence of James Madison 129 (1894); 2 James Kent, Commentaries on American Law 420 (6th ed. 1848); 2 John Fanning Watson, Annals of Philadelphia and Pennsylvania in Olden Time 501 (2009); George Washington Smith, A Defence of the System of Solitary Confinement of Prisoners Adopted by the State of Pennsylvania 3 (1833).

106. JM to Thomas J. Wharton (Aug. 1827).

107. Silas M. Stilwell to JM (Sept. 14, 1831); Howard Malcom to JM (June 3, 1830); JM to Silas M. Stilwell (Sept. 28, 1831); David McAdam, The Act to Abolish Imprisonment for Debt and to Punish Fraudulent Debtors, Commonly Called "the Stilwell Act," with Forms and References to the Judicial Decisions Thereunder 1–17 (2009) (1880).

108. Silas M. Stilwell to JM (May 19, 1832); *see also* e-note (discussing Stilwell's New York bill to abolish capital punishment).

5. The Eighth Amendment (pages 162–221)

1. Bowen, 47; Unger, Lion of Liberty, 192; U.S. Const., art. 1, § 8, cl. 18; 2 Schwartz, 443–47; Cogan, 619–20; 5 Storing, 247–49; Reply to Wilson's Speech: "Centinel" [Samuel Bryan] II, *in* 1 The Debate on the Constitution: Federalist and Antifederalist Speeches, Articles, and Letters During the Struggle over Ratification 77, 79 (1993); *see also* e-note (discussing the identity of "Centinel" and describing the dissenting views of members of Pennsylvania's ratifying convention).

2. Cogan, 621; 2 Storing, 375; 3 Storing, 129; 5 Storing, 185; Anti-Federalist Papers: The Impartial Examiner, Virginia Independent Chronicle (Mar. 5, 1788); *see also* e-note (discussing the views of "Brutus" and the likely identity of "Brutus" and "Philadelphiensis").

3. Friedman, 24; Berkin, 158–59; Cogan, 622–23; Claus, *Antidiscrimination Eighth Amendment,* 132; Nelson, 544 n.119; Jack Balderson Jr., *Temporal Units of Prosecution and Continuous Acts: Judicial and Constitutional Limits,* 36 San Diego L. Rev. 195, 219 (1999); Philip A. Hamburger, *The Constitution's Accommodation of Social Change,* 88 Mich. L. Rev. 239, 314 n.284 (1989); *see also* e-note (discussing the 1788 views of "Marcus" for why a "cruel and unusual punishments" clause was believed to be unnecessary).

4. Chernow, Alexander Hamilton, 260; Mayer, 428–29, 450–51; 3 Robert A. Rutland, ed., The Papers of George Mason 1725–1792, at 981 (1970).

5. Labunski, 7–9; Rakove, 558; U.S. Const., art. VI, cl. 2; GM to John Lamb (June 9, 1788); *see also* e-note (discussing the refusal of George Mason and Elbridge Gerry to sign the Constitution).

6. Labunski, 60; JM to TJ (Oct. 17, 1788); *see also* e-note (discussing Jefferson's advocacy of a U.S. Bill of Rights).

7. Mayer, 434, 451–52; Chernow, Alexander Hamilton, 246–47; Labunski, 59, 62–63, 232–34; Rappleye, 460; James Madison, Notes for Speech on Constitutional Amendments, June 8, 1789, in 12 Madison Papers 193–94 (C. Hobson & R. Rutland, eds., 1979).

8. RHL to Dr. William Shippen Jr. (Oct. 2, 1787); *see also* e-note (discussing Richard Henry Lee's efforts to amend the Constitution).

9. Labunski, 109, 113–14; Virginia Ratifying Convention, Proposed Amendments to the Constitution (June 27, 1788); *see also* e-note (discussing Wythe's report).

10. Maier, Ratification, 214–15; 2 Schwartz, 385–86, 400; Stephen L. Schechter, ed., Roots of the Republic: American Founding Documents Interpreted 254 (1990); Eugene W. Hickok Jr., The Bill of Rights: Original Meaning and Current Understanding 48 (1991); *Furman,* 408 U.S. at 243–44 (Douglas, J., concurring); Rutland, 104; Rakove, 171; Ordinance of 1787: The Northwest Territorial Government (July 13, 1787), art. II ("All fines shall be moderate; and no cruel or unusual punishments shall be inflicted."); *see also* e-note (discussing Madison's involvement in various bills of rights).

11. Levy, 239; Maier, Ratification, 56, 66–67; McGaughy, 191–93; RHL to GM (Oct. 1, 1787); RHL to Edmund Randolph (Oct. 16, 1787); *see also* e-note (discussing Richard Henry Lee's activities and support for a "cruel and unusual punishments" clause).

12. Veit, Bowling, & Bickford, 14–18, 21–22; A Declaration of Rights and Form of Ratification, Poughkeepsie Country J., July 29, 1788, John P. Kaminski, Gaspare J. Saladino, Richard Leffler, Charles H. Schoenleber, & Margaret A. Hogan, eds., The Documentary History of the Ratification of the Constitution, Digital Edition (Univ. of Virginia Press, Rotunda, 2009), visited Feb. 2, 2011, http://rotunda.upress.virginia.edu/founders/RNCN-03-18-02-0084-0002 (containing the New York Convention's order signed by its president, George Clinton, on July 26, 1788).

13. Veit, Bowling, & Bickford, 67, 73, 77–78, 83, 87 n.10, 104, 116, 176, 240, 250; id. at 266–67 (in Roger Sherman's Proposed Committee Report of July 1789, the seventh proposed amendment reads "Excessive bail shall not be required, nor excessive fines imposed, nor cruel & unusual punishments be inflicted in any case."); *see also* e-note (discussing George Washington's Inaugural Address in 1789 and his distribution of proposed constitutional amendments).

14. Veit, Bowling, & Bickford, 11–12, 29–31, 37–40, 45–49, 85, 109, 118; Mayer, 455–57, 460; Labunski, 269–70 (Amendments Reported by the House Select Committee on July 28, 1789); id. at 272–80 (listing amendments proposed by Congress in 1789); *see also* e-note (discussing Madison's preference for incorporating amendments into the text of the Constitution).

15. Veit, Bowling, & Bickford, 77–82; Labunski, 169, 187, 194, 201–2; Speech of James Madison (June 8, 1789); *see also* e-note (discussing Noah Webster's opposition to Madison's efforts to amend the Constitution and his dislike of the idea of forbidding "unusual" punishments).

16. Veit, Bowling, & Bickford, 77, 80, 281–82, 284, 310; Labunski, 188–89, 198.

17. *Furman,* 408 U.S. at 316 (Marshall, J., concurring); *Solem,* 463 U.S. at 284–85; Levy, 232; Rumann, 668–69 & nn.53, 147, 268; Magna Carta (1215), §§ 20–22, 55; *Wheeler,* 175 P.3d 438, 442 & n.2; The Avalon Project, English Bill of Rights (1689), visited Feb. 7, 2011, http://avalon.law.yale.edu/17th_century/england.asp; An Act Declareing the Rights and Liberties of the Subject and Setleing the Succession of the Crowne, 1 W. & M., ch. 2; The Frame of Government of Pennsylvania (Apr. 25, 1682), cl. XVIII; *see also* e-note (discussing amercements and the English monarch's use of the rack by special royal warrant).

18. The University of Chicago, *The Founders' Constitution,* William Blackstone, Commentaries on the Laws of England (Univ. of Chicago Press, 1979), visited Feb. 8, 2011, http://press-pubs.uchicago.edu/founders/documents/amendVIIIs4.html.

19. Id.; *see also* e-note (quoting JA to Mercy Warren).

20. Vila & Morris, 7–9 (reprinting the Body of Liberties); Conley & Kaminski, 71–72; 1 Schwartz, 72–84; Rumann, 667–68; Hanover College, The Massachusetts Body of Liberties (1641), visited Feb. 8, 2011, http://history.hanover.edu/texts/masslib .html#ms; *see also* e-note (discussing torturous interrogations, colonists who emigrated to Massachusetts Bay in 1630, and early American legal codes including the Body of Liberties drafted by Nathaniel Ward).

21. English Bill of Rights, 1 W. & M., 2d sess., ch. 2 (1689) (quoted in *Solem,* 463 U.S. at 285); *Harmelin,* 501 U.S. at 967–68; Ingraham v. Wright, 430 U.S. 651, 664–65 & n.33 (1977); Richard L. Perry & John C. Cooper, eds., Sources of Our Liberties 245–47 (1959); Levy, 234; Maier, American Scripture, 52–53; Pierce, 781; Ryan, 575–76; *Trop,* 356 U.S. at 100 (plurality opinion); In re Kemmler, 136 U.S. 436, 446 (1890); *Solem,* 463 U.S. at 285–86; *Furman,* 408 U.S. at 242 (Douglas, J., concurring); *see also* e-note (discussing John Dickinson, the abuses of Chief Justice Jeffreys, and the origins of the English prohibition of "cruel and unusual punishments").

22. Cogan, 624–25; Levy, 236; Pincus, 152–53, 184; Stinneford, 1760–61.

23. Hunt, 21; Pincus, 184; Stinneford, 1759–62; Ben Trachtenberg, *Coconspirators, "Coventurers," and the Exception Swallowing the Hearsay Rule,* 61 Hastings L.J. 581, 592–93 (2010); Trial of Titus Oates, 10 Howell's State Trials 1079, 1316 (K.B. 1685); Ryan, 577; *Harmelin,* 501 U.S. at 968–75; Granucci, 853–60; Brennan, *Supreme Court's Excessive Deference,* 553; Pierce, 781–83; Parr, 43–44; *see also* e-note (containing information on Alexander Leighton, a Puritan clergyman whipped and pilloried in 1630).

24. Amar, Bill of Rights, 279; Dubber & Farmer, 116; Kukla, 134; Stinneford, 1762; Trial of Titus Oates, 10 Howell's State Trials 1079, 1314 (K.B. 1685); *see also* e-note (discussing the English Bill of Rights, Titus Oates, and the rarity of particularly cruel punishments in colonial America compared to England).

25. Va. Decl. of Rts., § 9 (June 12, 1776); Maier, Ratification, 40–41; Kaye, 16; *Harmelin,* 501 U.S. at 966; *Solem,* 463 U.S. at 285 n.10; *Furman,* 408 U.S. at 319–20 (Marshall, J., concurring); Conley & Kaminski, 337; Granucci, 840; Massey, 1242; *see also* e-note (discussing the concerns of Anti-Federalists over the lack of a bill of rights and common-law protections in the Constitution, George Mason's drafting of the Virginia Declaration of Rights, the use of the terms "privileges" and "immunities" in the Articles of Confederation and the U.S. Constitution, and Robert Bork's testimony regarding the Fourteenth Amendment).

26. Hunt, 15, 23–26; Gerber, 29, 41–42, 52; Maier, American Scripture, 125–27, 133–34, 166; Helen Hill, George Mason: Constitutionalist 141–42, 144 (1938); Joshua E. Baker, *Quieting the Clang:* Hathcock *as a Model of the State-Based Protection of Property Which* Kelo *Demands,* 14 Wm. & Mary Bill Rts. J. 351, 355–56 (2005); James L. Wright & M. Matthew Williams, *Remember the Alamo: The Seventh Amendment of the United States Constitution, the Doctrine of Incorporation, and State Caps on Jury Awards,* 45 S. Tex. L. Rev. 449, 504 (2004); *see also* e-note (discussing John Locke, Sir Edward Coke, and William Blackstone).

27. Va. Decl. of Rts. (June 12, 1776); Thomas Jefferson, Autobiography Draft Fragment, Jan. 6–July 27, 1821 ("When we proceeded to the distribution of the work, Mr. Mason excused himself as, being no lawyer, he felt himself unqualified for the work, and he resigned soon after."); Claus, *Antidiscrimination Eighth Amendment,* 129; *see also* e-note (noting the views of law professor Laurence Claus on the founders' perception of the "cruel and unusual punishments" language).

28. Md. Decl. of Rts. §§ XIV, XXII (Aug. 14, 1776); Del. Decl. of Rts. § 16 (Sept. 11, 1776); *see also* e-note (discussing bills of attainder and bills of pains and penalties).

29. Pa. Const., §§ 29, 38–39 (Sept. 28, 1776); *see also* e-note (discussing the role of James Wilson in drafting Pennsylvania's constitution of 1790).

30. N.C. Decl. of Rts. (Dec. 14, 1776); S.C. Const., art. XL (Mar. 19, 1778); Mass. Const., pt. I, arts. I, XXVI, XXIX, & XXX (Mar. 2, 1780); Stoll, 210–13; Ronald J. Peters Jr., The Massachusetts Constitution of 1780: A Social Compact (1978); Marsha L. Baum & Christian G. Fritz, *American Constitution-Making: The Neglected State Constitutional Sources,* 27 Hastings Constitutional L. Q. 199, 208 & n.40 (2000) (quoting JA to BR (Sept. 10, 1779)); Alexander J. Cella, *The People of Massachusetts, a New Republic, and the Constitution of 1780: The Evolution of Principles of Popular Control of Political Authority, 1774-1780,* 14 Suffolk Univ. L. Rev. 975 (1980); John Adams, Novanglus Papers, Boston Gazette, no. 7 (1774); *see also* e-note (discussing the use of the term *magistrate* in the founding era, the role of John Adams in drafting the Massachusetts Constitution of 1780, and early state constitutions and bills of rights that did not adopt any "cruel and unusual" or "cruel or unusual" language).

31. N.H. Bill of Rts., pt. I, arts. XV, XVIII, & XXXIII (1783); N.Y. Bill of Rts., § 8 (Jan. 26, 1787).

32. 1 Elliott, 194; Calabresi & Agudo, 83; Ky. Const. of 1792, art. XII, § 15; State v. Wooddell, 1 Del. Cas. 482, 1797 WL 692 *1 (Del. Quar. Sess. 1797) (referencing a law that blacks "shall not give evidence against any white person").

33. Sullivan & Frase, 154–55; Stinneford, 1798–99 & nn.367–69 (noting that "cruel and unusual" punishments were forbidden by Virginia in 1776 and New York in 1787; that "cruel or unusual" punishments were forbidden by Delaware (1776), Maryland (1776), Massachusetts (1780), New Hampshire (1783), and North Carolina (1776); and that "cruel punishments" were forbidden by Pennsylvania and South Carolina in 1790); *see also* e-note (discussing state constitutions explicitly requiring that punishments be proportioned to the offense; noting that Delaware and Kentucky enacted constitutions in 1792 that prohibited "cruel punishments"; and describing a commentator's view, criticized by some, that the phrases "cruel and unusual" and "cruel or unusual" were understood to capture the same meaning).

34. Miller, 13; Bessler, *Revisiting Beccaria's Vision,* 266 nn.511–21 (citing Franklin's letters and writings); State v. Norris, 2 N.C. 429, 1796 WL 327 *5 (N.C. Super. L. & Eq. 1796) (it is reported in the case report that a "Solicitor-General" referred to a "beating in a cruel or unusual manner"); Commonwealth v. Tilton, 8 Metcalf 232, 234, 1844 WL 4263 *3 (Mass. 1844) (referring to the sport of cockfighting as "barbarous and cruel"); *see also* e-note (discussing the seventeenth-century usage of *cruel,* George Washington's use of "cruel and humiliating punishments," the use of *cruel* in the founding era, and its use by John and Abigail Adams in their letters to one another).

35. State v. Norris, 2 N.C. 429, 1796 WL 327 *1, 3–5 (N.C. Super. L. & Eq. 1796).

36. Id. at *3–4.

37. Id. at *6–7.

38. JM to Henry Lee (Nov. 23, 1786); JM to TJ (Dec. 4, 1786); Annual Message of JM (Dec. 5, 1815); Committee of the Whole (June 16), *reprinted in* 3 The Writings of James Madison (1900); Convention Notes (July 26 and Aug. 8, 1787), *reprinted in* 4 The Writings of James Madison (1900); Speech in the First Congress (Apr. 9, 1789), *reprinted in* 5 The Writings of James Madison (1900); JM to James Monroe (Jan. 5, 1804); Second Inaugural Address of JM and Message of JM (Sept. 20, 1814), *reprinted*

in 8 The Writings of James Madison (1900); *see also* e-note (discussing the execution and ear-cropping of George Mason's slaves and Alexander Hamilton's use of the word *cruel* in advocating for exceptions to the Alien and Sedition Acts).

39. John P. Kaminski, Gaspare J. Saladino, Richard Leffler, Charles H. Schoenleber, & Margaret A. Hogan, eds., The Documentary History of the Ratification of the Constitution, Digital Edition (Univ. of Virginia Press, Rotunda, 2009) (citing Ratification by the States, Volume X: Virginia, No. 3); C. James Taylor, ed., The Adams Papers, Digital Edition (Univ. of Virginia Press, Rotunda, 2008), visited Feb. 2, 2011, http://rotunda .upress.virginia.edu/founders/ADMS-06-02-02-0072-0005.

40. Cogan, 620. Near the end of his life, Edmund Randolph wrote in an essay that Virginia's prohibition "against excessive bail and excessive fines, was borrowed from England with additional reprobation of cruel and unusual punishments." 2 Schwartz, 246–49.

41. Debate in Virginia Ratifying Convention (June 17, 1788).

42. Decl. of Independence (July 4, 1776); JM to WB (July 1, 1774); JM to Joseph Jones (Dec. 5, 1780); JM to Edmund Randolph (Oct. 22, 1782); JM to TJ (Aug. 20, 1784); Speech in the Virginia Convention (June 5, 1788) & Speech in the First Congress (Feb. 18, 1790), *reprinted in* 5 The Writings of James Madison (1900); Fourth Annual Message (Nov. 4, 1812) & Fifth Annual Message (Dec. 7, 1813), *reprinted in* 8 The Writings of James Madison (1900); JM to Henry Lee (Feb. 1827); Report on the Resolutions (House of Delegates, Session of 1799–1800), *reprinted in* 6 The Writings of James Madison (1900); JM to TJ (Mar. 15, 1800); JM to Wilson C. Nicholas (July 10, 1801); *see also* e-note (discussing early American references to "unusual severity" in relation to punishments).

43. 1 Annals of Cong. 754 (1789); Veit, Bowling, & Bickford, 187; *Weems,* 217 U.S. at 368 ("The provision received very little debate in Congress."); *Furman,* 408 U.S. at 244 (Douglas, J., concurring); *Furman,* 408 U.S. at 258, 262 (Brennan, J., concurring); *see also* e-note (discussing the reaction of Representatives Livermore and Smith to James Madison's proposed amendments, and quoting another source discussing Rep. Livermore's objection to the Cruel and Unusual Punishments Clause because of his view that "taking away life," which he thought was "sometimes necessary," "may be thought cruel").

44. *Furman,* 408 U.S. at 258–59 (citing 2 J. Elliot's Debates 111 (2d ed. 1876)); Mannheimer, 834; Roger W. Kirst, *Does* Crawford *Provide a Stable Foundation for Confrontation Doctrine?,* 71 Brook. L. Rev. 35, 79–81 (2005).

45. *Furman,* 408 U.S. at 259–60 & n.2 (Brennan, J., concurring); Granucci, 840, 841 & n.10; 3 Elliot's Debates, 412 (June 16, 1788); Chernow, Alexander Hamilton, 244; Unger, Lion of Liberty, 89, 113. Connecticut's Declaration of Rights of 1650 forbade "Cruel and Barbarous" punishments. Conley & Kaminski, 106–7; *see also* e-note (discussing the Sixth Amendment's Confrontation Clause and the difference between "civil law" and "common law" approaches).

46. 3 Elliot's Debates, 431 (June 16, 1788); Cogan, 619–20; Granucci, 841–42; Debate in Virginia Ratifying Convention (June 14 and 16, 1788); John P. Kaminski, Gaspare J. Saladino, Richard Leffler, Charles H. Schoenleber, & Margaret A. Hogan, eds., The Documentary History of the Ratification of the Constitution, Digital Edition (Univ. of Virginia Press, Rotunda, 2009), visited Feb. 2, 2011, http://rotunda .upress.virginia.edu/founders/RNCN-02-10-02-0002-0005-0001; *see also* e-note (discussing the creation of a ten-mile square federal district and the views of the editor of

George Mason's papers on the prohibition against cruel and unusual punishments in the Virginia Declaration of Rights).

47. Singer v. United States, 380 U.S. 24, 27 (1965); State v. Gainer, 3 N.C. 140, 1801 WL 710 *1 (N.C. Super. L. & Eq.), 2 Hayw. (NC) 140 (1801); Aldridge v. Commonwealth, 2 Va. Cas. 447, 447–50 (Va. 1824); *see also* e-note (discussing early American judicial opinions on the concept of cruelty and the 1787 views of "John Humble" on the subject of executions and corporal punishments).

48. Dunaway v. Commonwealth, 663 S.E.2d 117 (Va. App. 2008); Hart v. Commonwealth, 109 S.E. 582, 586–87 (Va. 1921); Sullivan & Frase, 149.

49. United States v. Travers, 2 Wheel. Crim. Cas. 490 (D. Mass. 1814).

50. 2 Joseph Story, Commentaries on the Constitution of the United States 651 (5th ed. 1994); Joseph Story and the *Encyclopedia Americana* 47–51 (2006) (reprinting the text of the 1844 edition of the *Encyclopedia Americana*).

51. 6 Nathan Dane, Digest of American Law 631–32, 635–37, 715 (1823); Alan Rogers, *"A Sacred Duty": Court Appointed Attorneys in Massachusetts Capital Cases, 1780-1980*, 41 Am. J. Legal Hist. 440, 442–43 (1998); *see also* e-note (discussing an 1812 law prohibiting the use of corporal punishment by whipping militia soldiers serving with the U.S. Army, and the abandonment by the U.S. Army of whipping in favor of "cobbing," striking the buttocks with a flat instrument).

52. James Kent, Commentaries on American Law 12–14 (1836).

53. Rodney P. Carlisle, ed., Life in America: The Colonial and Revolutionary Era 150 (2010); James v. Commonwealth, 12 Serg. & Rawle 220, 1825 WL 1899 *1, 10, 13 (Pa. 1825); United States v. Gallagher, 2 Paine 447, 25 F. Cas. 1241, 1241 (D. N.Y. 1832); *see also* e-note (discussing the *James* decision).

54. U.S. Const., amend. VIII; Ronald Dworkin, Life's Dominion: An Argument About Abortion, Euthanasia, and Individual Freedom 127 (1993).

55. Ingraham v. Wright, 430 U.S. 651, 664 (1977); Austin v. United States, 509 U.S. 602, 609 (1993); Browning-Ferris Industries of Vermont, Inc. v. Kelco Disposal, Inc., 492 U.S. 257, 262 (1989); *see also* e-note (citing additional authorities and case law).

56. Considerations on a Convention with Spain (Mar. 22, 1792), Barbara B. Oberg & J. Jefferson Looney, eds., The Papers of Thomas Jefferson, Digital Edition (Univ. of Virginia Press, Rotunda, 2008), visited Feb. 2, 2011, http://rotunda.upress.virginia .edu/founders/TSJN-01-23-02-0275; *see also* e-note (discussing Thomas Jefferson's proposed extradition convention with Spain).

57. *Austin*, 509 U.S. at 604, 622; United States v. Salerno, 481 U.S. 739, 752–55 (1987); Stack v. Boyle, 342 U.S. 1, 4–5 (1951); *Bajakajian*, 524 U.S. at 327, 334; United States v. Beaman, 631 F.2d 85, 86 (6th Cir. 1980); United States v. James, 674 F.2d 886 (11th Cir. 1982); Evans v. Foster, 1 N.H. 374, 1819 WL 470 *3 (N.H. Super. Ct. 1819); *see also* e-note (citing authorities showing that persons facing murder charges do not have a constitutional right to bail).

58. Coyne & Entzeroth, 433; Stinneford, 1740; Penry v. Lynaugh, 492 U.S. 302 (1989); Atkins v. Virginia, 536 U.S. 304 (2002); Roper v. Simmons, 543 U.S. 551 (2005); Stanford v. Kentucky, 492 U.S. 361 (1989); Payne v. Tennessee, 501 U.S. 808 (1991); Booth v. Maryland, 482 U.S. 496 (1987); South Carolina v. Gathers, 490 U.S. 805 (1989).

59. *Payne*, 501 U.S. 808 (Marshall, J., dissenting); *Kennedy*, 128 S. Ct. at 2659.

60. Weems v. United States, 217 U.S. 349, 357–58, 367, 371–73, 382 (1910); Unger,

Lion of Liberty, 170, 297 n.14; Vaughan, 175–76; *see also* e-note (discussing *Weems* and the nature of the Eighth Amendment's protection).

61. *Solem,* 463 U.S. at 287; id. at 307 (Burger, C.J., dissenting); *Weems,* 217 U.S. at 373; *see also* e-note (discussing *Weems* and Justice William Brennan's views).

62. Thomas Jefferson actually had a theory that any constitution should be revised every nineteen to twenty years. *See* e-note (discussing Jefferson's theory).

63. U.S. Const., art. I, § 8; David J. Siepp, *Our Law, Their Law, History, and the Citation of Foreign Law,* 86 B.U. L. Rev. 1417, 1429 (2006); Koh, 1100; Trop v. Dulles, 356 U.S. 82, 87–88, 100–102 (1958); *see also* e-note (authorities noting international law influences on U.S. death penalty decisions and the influence of the "Law of Nations" on the Framers themselves).

64. *Robinson,* 370 U.S. at 666–67; *Solem,* 463 U.S. at 296–97 & n.22, 303; Harmelin v. Michigan, 501 U.S. 957 (1991); Ewing v. California, 538 U.S. 11 (2003); *see also* e-note (discussing *Solem* and other U.S. Supreme Court decisions in the Eighth Amendment context regarding life sentences or the treatment of prisoners).

65. Ford v. Wainwright, 477 U.S. 399, 409–10 (1986); Atkins v. Virginia, 536 U.S. 304 (2002); Roper v. Simmons, 543 U.S. 551 (2005); Enmund v. Florida, 458 U.S. 782, 783–86, 794, 801 (1986); *Kennedy,* 128 S. Ct. at 2650 (discussing *Enmund*); Jones v. Commonwealth, 5 Va. 555, 1799 WL 260 *2 (Va. 1799); *see also* e-note (discussing other U.S. Supreme Court cases, including those concerning the *Enmund* culpability requirement).

66. Coker v. Georgia, 433 U.S. 584, 592, 595–96, 598 (1977); Kennedy v. Louisiana, 128 S. Ct. 2641, 2646, 2659 (2008); Supreme Court of the United States Blog, *Final Brief on* Kennedy v. Louisiana, visited Feb. 9, 2011, http://www.scotusblog.com/2008/09/final-brief-on-kennedy-v-louisiana/; *see also* e-note (discussing a motion for rehearing in the *Kennedy* case).

67. Caldwell v. Mississippi, 472 U.S. 320 (1985); *Woodson,* 428 U.S. at 304; Lockett v. Ohio, 438 U.S. 586, 604–5 (1978) (plurality opinion); Eddings v. Oklahoma, 455 U.S. 104, 110–12 (1982); *see also* e-note (containing additional citations and discussing the conflict between Supreme Court decisions mandating that defendants be treated in an individualized fashion and the principle that like defendants be treated in a like manner).

68. Wilkerson v. Utah, 99 U.S. 130, 134 (1878); In re Kemmler, 136 U.S. 436, 447–49 (1890); Holden v. Minnesota, 137 U.S. 483 (1890), *called into doubt by* California First Amendment Coalition v. Woodford, 299 F.3d 868, 875 n.3 (9th Cir. 2002); McElvaine v. Brush, 142 U.S. 155, 158–60 (1891); Louisiana ex rel. Francis v. Resweber, 329 U.S. 459, 463 (1947); *Baze,* 128 S. Ct. at 1531 (plurality opinion); Bryan v. Moore, 528 U.S. 1133 (2000); Bessler, Death in the Dark, 41, 56–59, 84, 88–89; *see also* e-note (discussing the Supreme Court's ruling in *Holden*).

69. Gregg v. Georgia, 428 U.S. 153 (1976); Jurek v. Texas, 428 U.S. 262 (1976); Proffitt v. Florida, 428 U.S. 242 (1976); Roberts v. Louisiana, 431 U.S. 633 (1977); Roberts v. Louisiana, 428 U.S. 325 (1976); Woodson v. North Carolina, 428 U.S. 280 (1976).

70. Godfrey v. Georgia, 446 U.S. 420 (1980); Maryland v. Cartwright, 486 U.S. 356 (1988); Arave v. Creech, 507 U.S. 463 (1993); id. at 482–84 (Blackmun, J., dissenting); *see also* e-note (citing U.S. Supreme Court cases that have rejected Eighth and Fourteenth Amendment claims).

71. *In re Kemmler,* 136 U.S. at 446–47; *Wilkerson,* 99 U.S. at 136; Graham v. Florida, 130 S. Ct. 2011 (2010); *see also* e-note (discussing *In re Kemmler* and early American

legal commentary by James Bayard and Benjamin Oliver on the Eighth Amendment regarding the modes of punishment).

72. *Kennedy,* 128 S. Ct. at 2649–50 (citing *Weems* with approval); Coker v. Georgia, 433 U.S. 584, 592 (1977); *Solem,* 463 U.S. at 284; *see also* e-note (containing additional authorities).

73. *Graham,* 130 S. Ct. at 2021–22.

74. Amar, America's Constitution, 386; Dred Scott v. Sandford, 60 U.S. 393 (1857), *abrogated by constitutional amendment,* U.S. Const., amends. XIII & XIV; Saenz v. Roe, 526 U.S. 489, 502 n.15 (1999); U.S. Const., amend. XV.

75. Amar, Bill of Rights, 171, 182, 279–80; Epps, 232; Michael Kent Curtis, *John A. Bingham and the Story of American Liberty: The Lost Cause Meets the Lost Clause,* 36 Akron L. Rev. 617, 637–38, 650–51 (2003); U.S. Const., amend. XIV; McDonald v. City of Chicago, 130 S. Ct. 3020, 3033 n.9 (2010); Cong. Globe, 42d Cong., 1st Sess. App. at 84 (Mar. 31, 1871) (Rep. Bingham); Cong. Globe, 39th Cong., 1st Sess. 2765–66 (1866); *see also* e-note (discussing *The Amistad* and *The Antelope* cases and the "great cruelty" and "extreme cruelty" with which slaves were treated).

76. Barron v. Baltimore, 32 U.S. (7 Pet.) 243, 247 (1833); Ex parte Watkins, 32 U.S. (7 Pet.) 568 (1833); Pervear v. Commonwealth, 72 U.S. (5 Wall.) 475, 480 & n.6 (1866); Withers v. Buckley, 61 U.S. 84, 91 (1857); Ex parte Spies, 123 U.S. 131, 166 (1887); Brown v. State of New Jersey, 175 U.S. 172 (1899); Barker v. People, 3 Cow. 686 (N.Y. Sup. Ct. 1824); *see also* e-note (discussing the Supreme Court's 1868 decision in *Twitchell v. Commonwealth*).

77. Alexander Hamilton, Remarks on an Act for Regulating Elections, N.Y. Assembly (Feb. 6, 1787); Hurtado v. People of the State of California, 110 U.S. 516, 535 (1884); County of Sacramento v. Lewis, 523 U.S. 833, 845–46 (1998); Collins v. City of Harker Heights, Tex., 503 U.S. 115, 125 (1992); Daniels v. Williams, 474 U.S. 327, 331 (1986); Patterson v. New York, 432 U.S. 197, 202 (1977); Lawrence v. Texas, 539 U.S. 558, 564 (2003); Griswold v. Connecticut, 381 U.S. 479 (1965); Brinkerhoff-Faris Trust & Savings Co. v. Hill, 281 U.S. 673, 680 (1930); Pacific Mutual Life Ins. Co. v. Haslip, 499 U.S. 1, 28 (1991) (Scalia, J., concurring); Solesbee v. Balkcom, 339 U.S. 9, 16 (1950) (Frankfurter, J., dissenting); Raoul Berger, *Liberty and the Constitution,* 29 Ga. L. Rev. 585, 586–87 (1995); *see also* e-note (discussing the 1788 comments of "Brutus" using the word "unusual," as well as the Supreme Court's decisions in *Solesbee v. Balkcom* and *Ford v. Wainwright*).

78. Slaughter-House Cases, 83 U.S. (16 Wall.) 36, 72–79 (1872); Epps, 232; Vila & Morris, 65.

79. Twining v. New Jersey, 211 U.S. 78 (1908), *overruled,* Malloy v. Hogan, 378 U.S. 1, 6 (1964) ("We hold today that the Fifth Amendment's exception from compulsory self-incrimination is also protected by the Fourteenth Amendment against abridgment by the States."); Chicago, Burlington & Quincy R.R. Co. v. Chicago, 166 U.S. 226, 241 (1897); O'Neil v. Vermont, 144 U.S. 323, 332 (1892); In re Kemmler, 136 U.S. at 447–49; McElvaine v. Brush, 142 U.S. 155, 158–59 (1891); *see also* e-note (discussing the Privileges or Immunities Clause and the Supreme Court's recent refusal to overrule *Slaughter-House Cases*).

80. Robinson v. California, 370 U.S. 660, 666 (1962); *Resweber,* 329 U.S. at 462–63 (plurality opinion); Spaziano v. Florida, 468 U.S. 447, 468 n.1 (1984) (Stevens, J., concurring in part and dissenting in part) ("The Eighth Amendment is incorporated in the Due Process Clause of the Fourteenth Amendment."); Maxwell v. Bugbee, 250 U.S. 525,

538 (1919); Bullard v. Valentine, 592 F. Supp. 774, 775–76 (D. Tenn. 1984); State v. Sieyes, 225 P.3d 995, 1001 (Wash. 2010).

81. Eastern Enterprises v. Apfel, 524 U.S. 498, 537 (1998); Wolff v. McDonnell, 418 U.S. 539, 558 (1974); Graham v. Conner, 490 U.S. 386, 393–94 (1989); United States v. Lanier, 520 U.S. 259, 272 n.7 (1997); *see also* e-note (discussing the bill of attainder of Josiah Philips).

82. Deck v. Missouri, 544 U.S. 622, 629 (2005); Vacco v. Quill, 521 U.S. 793, 799 (1997); Batson v. Kentucky, 476 U.S. 79, 82–83, 89 (1986); *see also* e-note (discussing *Strauder v. West Virginia* and the *O'Neil* case).

83. *Robinson*, 370 U.S. at 661 n.1, 666–67; Barker v. People, 3 Cow. 686, 701 (N.Y. Sup. Ct. 1824); Epps, 268.

84. Whitten v. Georgia, 47 Ga. 297, 297–301 (1872); *see also* e-note (discussing the castration of slaves and black rapists).

85. In re Birdsong, 39 F. 599, 599–603 (S.D. Ga. 1889); *see also* e-note (discussing common-law restrictions on jailers).

86. *In re Birdsong*, 39 F. at 599–603; *see also* e-note (containing further discussion of *In re Birdsong*).

87. In re McDonald, 33 P. 18, 21 (Wyo. 1893); Minnesota v. Borgstrom, 72 N.W. 799, 803 (Minn. 1897), *overruled on other grounds,* State v. Sailor, 153 N.W. 271, 272–73 (Minn. 1915); *see also* e-note (discussing the writings of Thomas Cooley and authorities cited by him).

88. In re Kemmler, 7 N.Y.S. 145, 148–52 (N.Y. County Ct. 1889); *see also* e-note (discussing a 1910 *Harvard Law Review* article).

89. *In re Kemmler,* 7 N.Y.S. at 149–52; Va. Comm'n on Constitutional Government, Nor Cruel and Unusual Punishments Inflicted: A Few Observations on the Meaning of the Eighth Amendment 12 (1965) (citing 10 How. St. Tri. Colo. 1316, 1317); Frederick Howard Wines, Punishment and Reformation 51 (1983).

90. State v. Becker, 51 N.W. 1018, 1022 (S.D. 1892), *overruled,* State v. Phipps, 318 N.W.2d 128, 132 (S.D. 1982).

91. State v. Stubblefield, 58 S.W. 337, 361–63 (Mo. 1900); Hobbs v. State, 32 N.E. 1019, 1020–21 (Ind. 1893).

92. In the Matter of Bayard, 25 Hun. 546, 63 How. Pr. 73 (N.Y. 1881) (citing *Stephens' English Const.,* 33; *Cooley's Const. Lim.,* 329; *Story on Const.,* § 1903; *Cooley's Prin. Const. Law,* 296).

93. State v. Driver, 78 N.C. 423 (1878) (citing 11 State Trials 1354); *see also* e-note (discussing the *Driver* ruling).

94. *Driver,* 78 N.C. at 427 (citing 3 Story, Com. on Const. § 1896); *see also* e-note (discussing *Driver*).

95. Kow v. Nunan, 12 F. Cas. 252, 253 (D. Cal. 1879).

96. Id. at 253–57.

97. Claus, *Antidiscrimination Eighth Amendment,* 121–22, 135–36; *see also* e-note (discussing the cases of Titus Oates and Samuel Johnson and prior references to "cruel and illegal" proceedings).

98. Ely v. Thompson, 10 Ky. (3 A.K. Marsh) 70 (1820); Claus, *Antidiscrimination Eighth Amendment,* 121, 152–53.

99. Claus, *Antidiscrimination Eighth Amendment,* 121; *Furman,* 408 U.S. at 242 (Douglas, J., concurring); *In re Kemmler,* 136 U.S. at 448–49.

100. Wahl, 3, 8–9 (citing State v. Mann, 2 Dev. 263, 266 (N.C. 1829)); Act of 1740,

P. L. 173, § 45; State v. Boozer, 36 S.C.L. 21, 1850 WL 2829 (S.C. App. 1850); State v. Wilson, 25 S.C.L. 163, 1840 WL 2007 (S.C. App. L. 1840).

101. Andrew Fede, People Without Rights: An Interpretation of the Fundamentals of the Law of Slavery in the U.S. South (1992); Howe, 1005; Wahl, 6 n.19 (noting that six states "fined those who subjected slaves to cruel or unusual punishment"); Scott v. Mississippi, 31 Miss. 473, 1856 WL 2627 *4 (Miss. Err. & App. 1856).

102. Mann v. Trabue, 1 Mo. 709, 1827 WL 1987 *1 (Mo. 1827); State v. Maner, 20 S.C.L. 453 *1–3 (S.C. App. 1834); Kelly v. State, 11 Miss. 518, 1844 WL 2092 *5–7 (Miss. Err. & App. 1844); Trotter v. McCall, 26 Miss. 410, 1853 WL 3700 *1–3 (Miss. Err. & App. 1853).

103. Kelly, Timanus & Co. v. Andrew Wallace, Trustee, 6 Fla. 690, 1856 WL 1530 *7 (Fla. 1856); Lamar v. Williams, 39 Miss. 342, 1860 WL 3160 *1–2 (Miss. Err. & App. 1860); Oliver v. State, 39 Miss. 526, 1860 WL 3176 *1, 3, 9–10 (Miss. Err. & App. 1860).

104. Farmer v. Brennan, 511 U.S. 825, 828–32 (1994); Rhodes, 452 U.S. at 347; id. at 353–54, 359 (Brennan, J., concurring); see also e-note (discussing Farmer and citing another case on conditions in American prisons).

105. Sullivan & Frase, 146–49; Cummings v. Harrison, No. 4:07cv428, 2010 WL 503079 at *7 (N.D. Fla. 2010); Hudson v. McMillian, 503 U.S. 1, 9 (1992); Helling v. McKinney, 509 U.S. 25, 31 (1993); DeShaney v. Winnebago County Dept. of Social Servs., 489 U.S. 189, 199–200 (1989); George v. King, 837 F.2d 705, 707 (5th Cir. 1988); Green v. Ferrell, 801 F.2d 765, 770–71 (5th Cir. 1986); Rust v. Grammer, 858 F.2d 411, 412 (8th Cir. 1988); Harrison v. Stallings, 898 F.2d 145, 1990 WL 27233 (4th Cir.), cert. denied, 498 U.S. 832 (1990); Peterkin v. Jeffes, 855 F.2d 1021, 1027 (3d Cir. 1988); see also e-note (citing other cases).

106. Hudson, 503 U.S. at 4, 6–7, 9 (citing Whitley v. Albers, 475 U.S. 312 (1986)); see also e-note (discussing Hudson and authorities holding that de minimis harm or uses of force against inmates fall outside the Eighth Amendment's prohibition against "cruel and unusual punishments").

107. Farmer, 511 U.S. at 828–47; Whitley, 475 U.S. at 319–21; see also e-note (discussing the standard for Eighth Amendment claims).

6. Capital Punishment in America (pages 222–264)

1. Death Penalty Info. Ctr., Facts About the Death Penalty (Apr. 12, 2011); Death Penalty Info. Ctr., Federal Laws Providing for the Death Penalty, visited Feb. 7, 2011, http://www.deathpenaltyinfo.org/federal-laws-providing-death-penalty; Tirschwell & Hertzberg, 75 n.132; see also e-note (listing the states that authorize and do not authorize the death penalty).

2. Death Penalty Info. Ctr., Facts About the Death Penalty (Jan. 26, 2011); Death Penalty Info. Ctr., Federal Death Row Prisoners, visited Feb. 7, 2011, http://www .deathpenaltyinfo.org/federal-death-row-prisoners; see also e-note (discussing federal death penalty prosecutions).

3. Ogletree & Sarat, 72, 162; Death Penalty Info. Ctr., Searchable Execution Database, visited Feb. 7, 2011, http://www.deathpenaltyinfo.org/executions; Southern Methodist University, Texas Execution Statistics, visited Feb. 7, 2011, http://people .smu.edu/rhalperi/texascounty.html; Wikipedia, List of Counties in Texas, visited Feb. 7, 2011, http://en.wikipedia.org/wiki/List_of_counties_in_Texas.

4. Death Penalty Info. Ctr., Women and the Death Penalty, visited Feb. 7, 2011, http://www.deathpenaltyinfo.org/women-and-death-penalty.

5. Id.; Richard C. Dieter, The Death Penalty in Black and White: Who Lives, Who Dies, Who Decides (1998); Miller-El v. Dretke, 545 U.S. 231, 236 (2005); U.S. General Accounting Office, Death Penalty Sentencing: Research Indicates Pattern of Racial Disparities (1990); *see also* e-note (citations to studies showing racial discrimination in capital sentencing).

6. *Death Row Futility,* L.A. Times, Feb. 23, 2009; Knight v. Florida, 528 U.S. 990, 995 (1999) (Breyer, J., dissenting); Margaret Vandiver & David J. Giacopassi, *Geriatric Executions: Growing Old and Dying on Death Row,* 46 Crim. L. Bull. (Summer 2010); Philip J. Cook, *Potential Savings from Abolition of the Death Penalty in North Carolina,* 11 Am. L. & Econ. Rev. 498, 504 (2009); Cal. Comm'n on the Fair Administration of Justice, Report and Recommendations on the Administration of the Death Penalty in California 7, 22, 26–27 (June 30, 2008).

7. Chapman v. Commonwealth, 265 S.W.3d 156, 160 (Ky. 2007); Stephen Skaff, Chapman v. Commonwealth: *Death Row Volunteers, Competency, and "Suicide by Court,"* 53 St. Louis U. L.J. 1353, 1353, 1355, 1364–65 (2009); Ogletree & Sarat, 28; Bessler, Death in the Dark, 149; Bessler, *Revisiting Beccaria's Vision,* 303 & n.813.

8. McElvaine v. Brush, 142 U.S. 155, 158–59 (1891); In re Medley, 134 U.S. 160, 167–68 (1890); *see also* e-note (discussing Eighth Amendment concerns regarding solitary confinement in cells kept in darkness 24 hours a day).

9. District Attorney for Suffolk Dist. v. Watson, 411 N.E.2d 1274, 1290–91 & n.5 (Mass. 1980) (Liacos, J., concurring); Solesbee v. Balkcom, 339 U.S. 9, 14 (1950) (Frankfurter, J., dissenting); Aarons, 162–81; Florida Dept. of Corrections, *Death Row Fact Sheet,* visited Feb. 7, 2011, http://www.dc.state.fl.us/oth/deathrow/; *see also* e-note (discussing the size of death row inmates' cells in Arizona and Texas).

10. Dan Crocker, *Extended Stays: Does Lengthy Imprisonment on Death Row Undermine the Goals of Capital Punishment?,* 1 J. Gender Race & Just. 555, 569–72, 574 (1998); Jeremy Root, *Cruel and Unusual Punishment: A Reconsideration of the* Lackey *Claim,* 27 N.Y.U. Rev. L. & Soc. Change 281, 282 (2002); Aarons, 203–4; Pratt and Morgan v. Attorney General for Jamaica, 3 SLR 995, 2 AC 1, 4 All ER 769 (Privy Council 1993) (en banc); Soering v. United Kingdom, 161 Eur. Ct. H.R. (ser. A) (1989); Chahal v. United Kingdom, 1996-V Eur. Ct. H.R. 1831; Sher Singh v. State of Punjab, A.I.R. 1983 S.C. 465; Catholic Comm'n for Justice and Peace in Zimbabwe v. Attorney-General, [1993] 1 Zimb. L.R. 239, 240, 269(S) (Aug. 4, 1999); Kigula and Others v. Attorney Gen., 2006 S. Ct. Const. App. No. 03, at 56–57 (Uganda 2009); Vathesswaran v. State of Tamil Nadu, (India 1983) 2 S.C.R. 348; Triveniben v. State of Gujaret, (India 1989), 1 S.C.J. 383, 410; Mehta v. Union of India, (India 1989) 3 S.C.R. 774, 777.

11. Lackey v. Texas, 514 U.S. 1045, 1045–46 (1995) (Stevens, J., respecting denial of cert.); Elledge v. Florida, 525 U.S. 944 (1998) (Breyer, J., dissenting from denial of cert.); Ring v. Arizona, 536 U.S. 584, 617 (2002) (Breyer, J., concurring); Knight v. Florida, 528 U.S. 990, 994 (1999) (Breyer, J., dissenting from denial of cert.).

12. Johnson v. Bredesen, 130 S. Ct. 541 (2009) (Stevens, J., statement respecting denial of cert.); Death Penalty News, *Tennessee Executes Cecil C. Johnson Jr.,* visited Feb. 7, 2011, http://deathpenaltynews.blogspot.com/2009/12/tennessee-executes-cecil-c-johnson-jr.html; *see also* e-note (discussing another case in which Justice Stevens issued a statement respecting the denial of certiorari).

13. Amar, Bill of Rights, 94–95; Death Penalty Info. Ctr., Facts About the Death Penalty (Apr. 28, 2011).

14. Unger, Lion of Liberty, 217; Witherspoon v. Illinois, 391 U.S. 510, 519 n.15

(1968) (quoting Trop v. Dulles, 356 U.S. 86, 101 (1958)); Ring v. Arizona, 536 U.S. 584, 608 n.6 (2002); Enmund v. Florida, 458 U.S. 782, 797 (1982); Atkins v. Virginia, 536 U.S. 304, 324 (2002) (Rehnquist, J., dissenting); *see also* e-note (citing statistics showing that the rate of death sentences has declined in recent years).

15. Richard Dieter, A Crisis of Confidence: Americans' Doubts About the Death Penalty 5, 7, 10, 15 (2007); Death Penalty Info. Ctr., Facts About the Death Penalty (Sept. 28, 2010); Death Penalty Info. Ctr., Facts About the Death Penalty (Apr. 12, 2011).

16. Bessler, Kiss of Death, 89; Ogletree & Sarat, 28; Richard Dieter, A Crisis of Confidence: Americans' Doubts About the Death Penalty 5, 7, 10, 15 (2007); *see also* e-note (discussing the results of a poll conducted for the Death Penalty Information Center).

17. *Witherspoon,* 391 U.S. at 522 & 523 n.21; Uttecht v. Brown, 127 S. Ct. 2218, 2224–25, 2231 (2007); id. at 2238 (Stevens, J., dissenting); *see also* e-note (discussing the evolution of the Supreme Court's "death-qualification" standard).

18. *Baze,* 128 U.S. at 1150 (Stevens, J., concurring); *Buchanan,* 483 U.S. at 420; *Witherspoon,* 391 U.S. at 519; Wainwright v. Witt, 469 U.S. 412, 420–31 (1985) (citing Adams v. Texas, 448 U.S. 38, 45 (1980)); Cochran, 1444; *see also* e-note (containing additional citations and discussing *Morgan v. Illinois*).

19. Dave Montgomery, "Judge to Open Court of Inquiry in Willingham Arson Case," Fort Worth Star-Telegram, Sept. 28, 2010; Jennifer Emily & Steve McGonigle, Dallas Morn. News, Sept. 16, 2008.

20. Death Penalty Info. Ctr., A Crisis of Confidence: Americans' Doubts About the Death Penalty 14 (2007); Death Penalty Info. Ctr., Facts about the Death Penalty (Sept. 28, 2010); King, No Due Process, 239; Richard Connelly, *Texas High Court Halts Hearing on Death Penalty*, visited Feb. 7, 2011, http://blogs.houstonpress.com/hairballs/2010/12/death_penalty_hearing_halted.php; FOX 26 News, *Judge Explains His Death Penalty Ruling*, visited Feb. 7, 2011, http://www.myfoxhouston.com/dpp/news/local/100305-judge-death-penalty-ruling-apx; Associated Press, *Texas Judge Rescinds Order Declaring Death Penalty Unconstitutional*, visited Feb. 7, 2011, http://www.dallasnews.com/sharedcontent/dws/dn/latestnews/ stories/030910dntexdeath .18fb33eec.html.

21. Bessler, Kiss of Death, 73; Michael L. Perlin, *"The Executioner's Face Is Always Well-Hidden": The Role of Counsel and the Courts in Determining Who Dies,* 41 N.Y.L. Sch. L. Rev. 201, 204 (1996).

22. Pub. L. 104–132, 110 Stat. 1214; 28 U.S.C. § 2244(d)(1); 28 U.S.C. § 2254(d); Barry Friedman, *Failed Enterprise: The Supreme Court's Habeas Reform,* 83 Cal. L. Rev. 485, 486 (1995); James S. Liebman & Randy Hertz, Federal Habeas Corpus Practice and Procedure § 3.2 (5th ed. 2005) (providing an overview of AEDPA's provisions); *see also* e-note (discussing death row exonerations).

23. Coleman v. Thompson, 501 U.S. 722 (1991); Danforth v. Minnesota, 128 S. Ct. 1029, 1032 (2008); Zimring, 68; *see also* e-note (discussing *Teague v. Lane* and its progeny, as well as the application of *Teague* and the nonretroactivity principle in death penalty cases).

24. Gideon v. Wainwright, 372 U.S. 335 (1963); Rae K. Inafuku, Coleman v. Thompson—*Sacrificing Fundamental Rights in Deference to the States: The Supreme Court's 1991 Interpretation of the Writ of Habeas Corpus,* 34 Santa Clara L. Rev. 625, 652 (1994); Donald P. Lay, *The Writ of Habeas Corpus: A Complex Procedure for a Simple Process,* 77 Minn. L. Rev. 1015 (1993); Smith & Starns, 58, 67–76; Equal Justice

Initiative, *Inadequate Counsel*, visited Feb. 7, 2011, http://www.eji.org/eji/death penalty/inadequatecounsel; Teague v. Lane, 489 U.S. 288 (1989) (plurality).

25. Bessler, Kiss of Death, 74; Murray v. Giarratano, 492 U.S. 1 (1989) (plurality opinion); *Coleman*, 501 U.S. at 752; The Advocates for Human Rights, *Death Penalty*, visited Feb. 7, 2011, http://www.theadvocatesforhumanrights.org/Death_Penalty _Project.html; *see also* e-note (discussing death row inmates' lack of mental capacity).

26. Bessler, Kiss of Death, 75–77; Ogletree & Sarat, 27; Kirchmeier, *Drinks, Drugs and Drowsiness*, 425; Bright, *Death Penalty and the Society We Want*, 375; McFarland v. Scott, 512 U.S. 1256, 1259 (1994) (Blackmun, J., dissenting); Samuel R. Gross, Kristen Jacoby, Daniel J. Matheson, Nicholas Montgomery, & Sujata Patil, *Exonerations in the United States, 1989 through 2003*, 95 J. Crim. L. & Criminology 523 (2005); Innocence Project, *Facts on Post-Conviction DNA Exonerations*, visited Feb. 11, 2011, http:// www.innocenceproject.org/Content/Facts_on_PostConviction_DNA_Exonerations .php; James S. Liebman, Jeffrey Fagan, & Valerie West, A Broken System: Error Rates in Capital Cases, 1973–1995 (2000); James S. Liebman, et al., *Capital Attrition: Error Rates in Capital Cases, 1973-1995*, 78 Tex. L. Rev. 1839 (2000); *see also* e-note (citations regarding the ABA's capital defense representation guidelines and supplementary guidelines for the mitigation function of defense teams).

27. R. Bonner, "Indian Company Ends Sale of Lethal-Injection Drug to the U.S.," The Atlantic, Apr. 7, 2011; Death Penalty Info. Ctr., *Washington Becomes Second State to Adopt One-Drug Protocol*, visited Feb. 7, 2011, http://www.deathpenaltyinfo.org/ washington-becomes-second-state-adopt-one-drug-protocol; *Baze*, 128 S. Ct. at 1529, 1537 (plurality opinion); *Coker*, 433 U.S. at 591; *Gregg*, 428 U.S. at 168–69; *Trop*, 356 U.S. at 99.

28. Ruth Bader Ginsburg, *In Pursuit of the Public Good: Access to Justice in the United States*, 7 Wash. U. J.L. & Pol'y 1, 10 (2001); Kirchmeier, *Another Place Beyond Here*, 30; Craig M. Cooley, *Mapping the Monster's Mental Health and Social History: Why Capital Defense Attorneys and Public Defender Death Penalty Units Require the Services of Mitigation Specialists*, 30 Okla. City U. L. Rev. 23, 29 n.25 (2005); Ring v. Arizona, 536 U.S. 584, 614–16 (2002) (Breyer, J., concurring). Federal judges in the lower courts have also begun to speak out against the death penalty. Kirchmeier, *Another Place Beyond Here*, 34.

29. *Baze*, 128 S. Ct. at 1567, 1572 (Ginsburg, J., dissenting); id. at 1543, 1546–48, 1551 (Stevens, J., concurring).

30. *Kennedy*, 128 S. Ct. at 2649–50; *Atkins*, 536 U.S. at 311; *Trop*, 356 U.S. at 100–101; *see also* e-note (containing additional citations).

31. *Coker*, 433 U.S. at 592, 597; *Kennedy*, 128 S. Ct. at 2650, 2658; *Solem*, 463 U.S. at 290–91 & n.17; *Atkins*, 536 U.S. at 312, 321 ("proportionality review" should be informed by objective factors "to the maximum extent possible"); *Thompson*, 487 U.S. at 822 & n.7 (plurality opinion); id. at 852 (O'Connor, J., concurring); *Roper*, 543 U.S. at 564; *see also* e-note (discussing sources of "objective evidence of contemporary values" invoked by the Supreme Court).

32. *Graham*, 130 S. Ct. at 2023; *Kennedy*, 128 S. Ct. at 2653; *Roper*, 543 U.S. at 564 ("The beginning point is a review of objective indicia of consensus, as expressed in particular by the enactments of legislatures that have addressed the question.").

33. *Graham*, 130 S. Ct. at 2023; *Roper*, 543 U.S. at 565–66; *Kennedy*, 128 S. Ct. at 2653, 2656; *Atkins*, 536 U.S. at 314–15; *see also* e-note (discussing the *Atkins* ruling).

34. *Enmund*, 458 U.S. at 794; *Atkins*, 536 U.S. at 316; *Kennedy*, 128 S. Ct. at 2657;

Graham, 130 S. Ct. at 2023–24; *Roper,* 543 U.S. at 564–65; *see also* e-note (discussing *Roper* and *Kennedy*).

35. Estelle v. Gamble, 429 U.S. 97, 104 (1976); Helling v. McKinney, 509 U.S. 25, 35 (1993); Hope v. Pelzer, 536 U.S. 730, 733–35 & n.2, 738, 745 (2002); *see also* e-note (citing additional authorities pertaining to prisoners' exposure to secondhand smoke).

36. Slakan v. Porter, 737 F.2d 368, 370–72 (4th Cir. 1984), *cert. denied,* 470 U.S. 1035 (1985).

37. *Helling,* 509 U.S. at 33; *Baze,* 128 S. Ct. at 1530 (plurality opinion); Chandler v. District of Columbia Dept. of Corrections, 145 F.3d 1355, 1360–61 (D.C. Cir. 1998); Hoptowit v. Spellman, 753 F.2d 779, 784 (9th Cir. 1985); Hudspeth v. Figgins, 584 F.2d 1345, 1348 (4th Cir. 1978), *cert. denied,* 441 U.S. 913 (1979).

38. *Jackson,* 404 F.2d at 579–80; Ingraham v. Wright, 430 U.S. 651 (1977); *see also* e-note (discussing the Supreme Court's interpretation of *unusual* and its decision in *Ingraham*).

39. Gates v. Collier, 501 F.2d 1291, 1301, 1306 (5th Cir. 1974); Ort v. White, 813 F.2d 318, 324 (11th Cir. 1987); McCord v. Maggio, 927 F.2d 844, 848 (5th Cir. 1991); Bailey v. Turner, 736 F.2d 963, 973 (4th Cir. 1984); *Slakan,* 737 F.2d at 372; Landman v. Royster, 333 F. Supp. 621, 649 (E.D. Va. 1971), *op. supplemented,* 354 F. Supp. 1302 (E.D. Va. 1973); Fruit v. Norris, 905 F.2d 1147, 1150 (8th Cir. 1990); Hickey v. Reeder, 12 F.3d 754, 758–59 (8th Cir. 1993); Parrish v. Johnson, 800 F.2d 600, 605 (6th Cir. 1986); Hadix v. Caruso, 461 F. Supp.2d 574, 595 (W.D. Mich. 2006); Jackson v. Bishop, 404 F.2d 571, 572 (8th Cir. 1968) (Blackmun, J.); Comer v. Stewart, 230 F. Supp.2d 1016, 1057 (D. Ariz. 2002); Leland v. Edge, No. 4:06cv568, 2008 WL 4790342 (N.D. Fla.) (Oct. 22, 2008); Cooper v. Sheriff, Lubbock, Tex., 929 F.2d 1078, 1083 (5th Cir. 1991); Dearman v. Woodson, 429 F.2d 1288, 1289–90 (10th Cir. 1970).

40. Hudson v. McMillian, 503 U.S. 1, 16 (1992) (Blackmun, J., concurring) (citing Wisniewski v. Kennard, 901 F.2d 1276, 1277 (5th Cir.), *cert. denied,* 498 U.S. 926 (1990)); Northington v. Jackson, 973 F.2d 1518, 1522–24 (10th Cir. 1992); Cummings v. Harrison, No. 4:07cv428, 2010 WL 503079 at *8 (N.D. Fla. 2010); *see also* e-note (citing other authorities).

41. *Baze,* 128 S. Ct. at 1526–28, 1533; *see also* e-note (discussing the origins of lethal injection and lethal injection protocols).

42. Ky. Rev. Stat. Ann. § 431.220(3); *Baze,* 128 S. Ct. at 1528, 1533–34; *see also* e-note (defining a "phlebotomist").

43. *Baze,* 128 S. Ct. at 1526, 1529, 1531–38; *see also* e-note (discussing *Baze,* Kentucky's three-drug protocol, and a *Lancet* study on executed inmates).

44. John C. Williams, *What Constitutes Murder by Torture,* 83 A.L.R.3d 1222 (1978); John Roach, *Brain Study Shows Why Revenge Is Sweet,* Nat'l Geographic News, Aug. 27, 2004.

45. Mercer, 13; *see also* e-note (discussing the high cost of executions in comparison to life sentences).

46. Bessler, *Revisiting Beccaria's Vision,* 300–301 & nn.792–93, 795–801 (citing cases and studies); Thompson, 1528 & nn.101, 105; Sara Rimer, "Mentally Retarded Man Facing Texas Execution Draws Wide Attention," N.Y. Times, Nov. 12, 2000, at A34; Penry v. Lynaugh, 492 U.S. 302, 307–8 (1989), *overruled,* Atkins v. Virginia, 536 U.S. 304 (2002).

47. Ogletree & Sarat, 22; Cass R. Sunstein & Justin Wolfers, "A Death Penalty Puzzle: The Murky Evidence for and Against Deterrence," Wash. Post, June 30, 2008,

at A11; Charles Fried, *Reflections on Crime and Punishment,* 30 Suffolk U. L. Rev. 681, 694 n.36 (1997); Lepore, 79–80; Bessler, *America's Death Penalty,* 14; Isaac Ehrlich, *The Deterrent Effect of Capital Punishment: A Question of Life and Death,* 65 Am. Econ. Rev. 397, 398 (1975); Isaac Ehrlich, *Capital Punishment and Deterrence: Some Further Thoughts and Additional Evidence,* 85 J. Pol. Econ. 741 (1977); Death Penalty Info. Ctr., *Deterrence,* visited Feb. 7, 2011, http://www.deathpenaltyinfo.org/deterrence-states-without-death-penalty-have-had-consistently-lower-murder-rates; Fagan, Zimring, & Geller, 1804 nn.6–7, 1859 (finding that "studies claiming a relationship between death penalty policy and homicide rates suffer from an important and avoidable aggregation error: they examine the relationship between death penalty variables and total non-negligent homicide rates, despite the fact that three-fourths of all such killings do not meet the statutory criteria to be eligible for the death penalty"); *see also* e-note (citing additional scholarship on the deterrence debate).

48. Bessler, Death in the Dark, 41–44; King, *No Due Process,* 228; Richard E. Redding, *The Brain-Disordered Defendant: Neuroscience and Legal Insanity in the Twenty-First Century,* 56 Am. U. L. Rev. 51, 57 (2006); Craig Haney, *The Social Context of Capital Murder: Social Histories and the Logic of Mitigation,* 35 Santa Clara L. Rev. 547, 566, 585 (1995); Michael J. Perry, *Is Capital Punishment Unconstitutional? And Even If We Think It Is, Should We Want the Supreme Court to So Rule?,* 41 Ga. L. Rev. 867, 894 (2007); *Atkins,* 536 U.S. at 320; Death Penalty Info. Ctr., Facts About the Death Penalty (Aug. 30, 2010); The Disaster Center, *United States Crime Rates 1960–2009,* visited Feb. 7, 2011, http://www.disastercenter.com/crime/uscrime.htm; *see also* e-note (citing studies concluding that there is no evidence that the death penalty deters crime more effectively than life-without-parole sentences or that it may actually have a brutalizing effect, causing even more homicides).

49. Bessler, *Revisiting Beccaria's Vision,* 301–3 & nn.802–11 (citing studies and cases); Ray Sebastian Pantle, *Blacker Than Death Row: How Current Equal Protection Analysis Fails Minorities Facing Capital Punishment,* 35 Cap. U. L. Rev. 811, 825 (2007); Laura M. Argys & H. Naci Mocan, *Who Shall Live and Who Shall Die? An Analysis of Prisoners on Death Row in the United States,* 33 J. Legal Stud. 255, 267 (2004); John M. Fabian, *Death Penalty Mitigation and the Role of the Forensic Psychologist,* 27 Law & Psychol. Rev. 73, 109 n.258 (2003); Lauren E. Perry, *Hiding Behind Precedent: Why* Panetti v. Quarterman *Will Create Confusion for Incompetent Death Row Inmates,* 86 N.C. L. Rev. 1068, 1068 (2008); Panetti v. Quarterman, 127 S. Ct. 2842, 2847, 2860, 2862 (2007).

50. Correll v. Ryan, 539 F.3d 938, 952 (9th Cir. 2008), *cert. denied,* 129 S. Ct. 903 (2009); Haliym v. Mitchell, 492 F.3d 680, 712–14 (6th Cir. 2007); Washington v. Roper, 619 F. Supp.2d 661, 665–67 (E.D. Mo. 2009), *aff'd in part and rev'd in part,* 2001 WL 31529 *2–3, 11 (8th Cir., Jan. 6, 2011); Bessler, Kiss of Death, 92–93.

51. In re Webster, 605 F.3d 256, 257 (5th Cir.), *cert. denied,* 131 S. Ct. 794 (2010); id. at 259–60 (Wiener, J., concurring).

52. Porter v. McCollum, 130 S. Ct. 447, 448–55 (2009).

53. Ex parte Thomas, No. WR-69859–01, 2009 WL 693606 *1–2 (Tex. Ct. Crim. App., Mar. 18, 2009) (Cochran, J., concurring).

54. Id. at *2, 6.

55. Id. at *1–4.

56. Rice v. Wood, 77 F.3d 1138, 1139, 1140 (9th Cir.), *cert. denied,* 519 U.S. 873 (1996); In re Rice, 828 P.2d 1086, 1090 (Wash.), *cert. denied,* 506 U.S. 958 (1992); State v. Rice,

757 P.2d 889, 892, 897, 900 (Wash. 1988); Jeanine Girgenti, *Bridging the Gap Between Law and Psychology: The Deific Decree*, 3 Rutgers J.L. & Religion 10 (2001).

57. Smith v. Armontrout, 604 F. Supp. 840, 841 (W.D. Mo. 1984); State v. Perry, 610 So.2d 746, 748 (La. 1992); Rector v. Lockhart, 727 F. Supp. 1285, 1286 (E.D. Ark. 1990), *aff'd*, 923 F.2d 570 (8th Cir. 1991); Bessler, Death in the Dark, 137–38.

58. Singleton v. Norris, 319 F.3d 1018, 1020–21, 1025 (8th Cir.), *cert. denied*, 540 U.S. 832 (2003); id. at 1030–31 (Heaney, J., dissenting); Bessler, *Revisiting Beccaria's Vision*, 304 n.816; Angela M. Kimber, *Psychotic Journeys of the Green Mile*, 22 T.M. Cooley L. Rev. 27, 27–28 & n.11 (2005) (discussing conflicting legal rulings over whether death row inmates can be forcibly medicated to render them competent to be executed); Staley v. State, 233 S.W.3d 337 (Tex. Ct. Crim. App. 2007) (discussing death row inmate's appeal from order compelling him to take antipsychotic medication).

59. *Singleton*, 319 F.3d at 1020–21, 1025 (8th Cir. 2003); id. at 1031–35 (Heaney, J., dissenting); *see also* e-note (discussing Gerald Heaney's dissent in *Singleton*).

60. Bessler, *Revisiting Beccaria's Vision*, 304; *see also* e-note (citing studies estimating the number of death row inmates with mental illnesses or intermittent insanity).

61. Bessler, *Revisiting Beccaria's Vision*, 304–5 & nn.818–21.

62. Id. at 305–6 & nn.822–25; King, *No Due Process*, 197–98, 209, 212–13, 216, 218, 242.

63. Bessler, Death in the Dark, 37–39, 42–44; Bessler, *Revisiting Beccaria's Vision*, 290 & nn.724–31.

64. Bessler, *Revisiting Beccaria's Vision*, 290–91 & nn.732–36.

65. Id. at 291–92.

66. Id. at 299 & nn.789–90; Ellen Kreitzberg & David Richter, *But Can It Be Fixed? A Look at Constitutional Challenges to Lethal Injection Executions*, 47 Santa Clara L. Rev. 445, 501–2 (2007); Leigh B. Bienen, *Anomalies: Ritual and Language in Lethal Injection Regulations*, 35 Fordham Urb. L.J. 857, 861 (2008); Benjamin Cardozo, *What Medicine Can Do for Law*, 5 Bull. N.Y. Acad. Med. 581, 593–94, 606 (July 1929); Aimee Logan, *Who Says So? Defining Cruel and Unusual Punishment by Science, Sentiment, and Consensus*, 35 Hast. Const. L.Q. 195, 217–18 (2008); Eileen P. Ryan & Sarah B. Berson, *Mental Illness and the Death Penalty*, 25 St. Louis U. Pub. L. Rev. 351, 352 (2006); Nathan Koppel, "Inmates Sue FDA Over Lethal-Drug Imports," Wall St. J., Feb. 2, 2011; Brandi Grissom, "A Drug Used in Executions Becomes Very Hard to Get," N.Y. Times, Feb. 5, 2011; *see also* e-note (describing Dr. Benjamin Rush's prediction in 1793 that a law would pass in Pennsylvania "in a few weeks to abolish capital punishment in *all cases* whatever").

67. Herbert Aptheker, The American Revolution, 1763–1783, at 244 (1960); Deborah W. Denno, *The Lethal Injection Quandary: How Medicine Has Dismantled the Death Penalty*, 76 Fordham L. Rev. 49, 123 (2007); Mary-Beth Moylan & Linda E. Carter, *Clemency in California Capital Cases*, 14 Berkeley J. Crim. L. 37, 66 (2009); Michael Mello, *Alvin Ford's Delusions—and Our Own: Executing the Insane*, 45 Crim. L. Bull., no. 6 (Winter 2009); Death Penalty Info. Ctr., *Florida Doctors Wear 'Moon Suits' to Hide Participation in Lethal Injections*, visited Feb. 7, 2011, http://www.deathpenalty info.org/executions-news-and-developments-2007; Bessler, *Kiss of Death*, 110; Adam Liptak, "After Flawed Executions, States Resort to Secrecy," N.Y. Times, July 30, 2007; Cullen v. Pinholster, 131 S. Ct. 1388 (2011).

68. Ford v. Wainwright, 477 U.S. 399, 406–7 (1986); Helen Shin, *Is the Death of the Death Penalty Near? The Impact of Atkins and Roper on the Future of Capital*

Punishment for Mentally Ill Defendants, 76 Fordham L. Rev. 465 (2007); Ronald S. Honberg, *The Injustice of Imposing the Death Penalty on People with Severe Mental Illnesses*, 54 Cath. U. L. Rev. 1153 (2005); Richard C. Dieter, *The Path to an Eighth Amendment Analysis of Mental Illness and Capital Punishment*, 54 Cath. U. L. Rev. 1117, 1121 (2005) (predicting that "eventually state and federal legislation will emerge to provide the Court with an objective basis for sparing the mentally ill from the death penalty"); *see also* e-note (discussing a law enacted in Henry VIII's reign).

69. Eileen P. Ryan & Sarah B. Berson, *Mental Illness and the Death Penalty*, 25 St. Louis U. Pub. L. Rev. 351, 352 (2006); Christopher Slobogin, *Mental Illness and the Death Penalty*, 1 Cal. Crim. L. Rev. 3 n.7 (2000); Rhonda K. Jenkins, *Fit to Die: Drug-Induced Competency for the Purpose of Execution*, 20 So. Ill. U. L.J. 149, 149 (1995); Dominic Rupprecht, *Compelling Choice: Forcibly Medicating Death Row Inmates to Determine Whether They Wish to Pursue Collateral Relief*, 114 Penn. St. L. Rev. 333, 334 & n.115 (2009); Bruce J. Winick, *The Supreme Court's Evolving Death Penalty Jurisprudence: Severe Mental Illness as the Next Frontier*, 50 B.C. L. Rev. 785, 789, 856 (2009); Amnesty International, The Death Penalty Disregards Mental Illness (2006); Senate Bill 1075, N.C. General Assembly, 2007 Sess. (citing the opposition from various associations in "Whereas" clauses); Death Penalty Info. Ctr., *Murder Victims' Families for Human Rights and the National Alliance on Mental Illness to Launch National Project*, visited Feb. 7, 2011, http://www.deathpenaltyinfo.org/murder-victims'-families-human-rights-and-national-alliance-mental-illness-launch-national-project; Barua, 4; John E. Theuman, *Propriety of Carrying Out Death Sentences Against Mentally Ill Individuals*, 111 A.L.R.5th 491 (2003).

70. Levy, 74–75; Sloan & McKean, 41; Jean Edward Smith, John Marshall: Definer of a Nation 215–18 (1996); *Four Fugitive Cases from the Realm of American Constitutional Law*, 49 Am. L. Rev. 818, 821 (1915); The Federalist No. 44 (James Madison).

71. Bessler, Death in the Dark, 150; John Adams Diary Entry for July 20 (London), C. James Taylor, ed., The Adams Papers, Digital Edition (Univ. of Virginia Press, Rotunda, 2008), visited Feb. 2, 2011, http://rotunda.upress.virginia.edu/founders/ADMS-01-03-02-0005-0004-0005.

72. Adams' Argument for the Defense (Dec. 3–4, 1770); Allen v. United States, 150 U.S. 551, 557 (1893) ("The law of self-defense is a law of proportions as well as a law of necessity, and it is only danger that is deadly in its character that you can exercise a deadly act against."); Gilmore v. Taylor, 508 U.S. 333, 359 (1993) (Blackmun, J., dissenting) ("self-defense converts what is otherwise murder into justifiable homicide"; "the person who kills in self-defense, instead of being guilty of murder, is guilty of no offense at all").

73. Bessler, Kiss of Death, 110; Bessler, *Revisiting Beccaria's Vision*, 299 & nn.787–88; Cottrol, 1649.

74. Bessler, Kiss of Death, 102–3, 111.

75. Id. at 102–3, 132; Bessler, *Revisiting Beccaria's Vision*, 298–99 & nn.782–86.

7. The Road to Abolition (pages 265-338)

1. Bessler, Legacy of Violence, 2; Michael P. Scharf & Ahran Kang, *Errors and Missteps: Key Lessons the Iraqi Special Tribunal Can Learn from the ICTY, ICTR, and SCSL*, 38 Cornell Int'l L.J. 911, 915 (2005); Gregg Mayer, *The Poet and Death: Literary Reflections on Capital Punishment Through the Sonnets of William Wordsworth*, 21 St. John's J. Legal Comment. 727, 728 n.8 (2007); University of Evansville, *Hammurabi's*

Code of Laws, visited Feb. 7, 2011, http://eawc.evansville.edu/anthology/hammurabi
.htm; *Furman*, 408 U.S. at 333 (Marshall, J., concurring). A few American states—in
what might be thought of as part of society's deep-seated desire for revenge—actually
allow murder victims' families to hire and pay private attorneys to prosecute capital
murder defendants. Bessler, *Public Interest and the Unconstitutionality of Private Prosecutors,* 513 & n.9.

2. Tocqueville, 21; Hogeland, 34; Arthur W. Campbell, Law of Sentencing § 1.2 (3d
ed. 2004); David Hackett Fischer, Albion's Seed: Four British Folkways in America 91–
92 (1991); E. P. Thompson, Whigs and Hunters: The Origin of the Black Act 22
(1975); Harry Potter, Hanging in Judgment: Religion and the Death Penalty in England
from the Bloody Code to Abolition (1993); James G. Hodge Jr. & Gabriel B. Eber,
Tobacco Control Legislation: Tools for Public Health Improvement, 32 J.L. Med. & Ethics
516, 516 (2004); Rudolph J. Gerber, *Death Is Not Worth It,* 28 Ariz. St. L.J. 335, 336
(1996); Richard D. Lamm, *Privacy and Public Policy,* 79 Denv. U. L. Rev. 532, 532
(2002); Fisher, 1238; Hirsch, 1296 n.90; Douglas, 155 & n.93; Millett, 585; *Furman,*
408 U.S. at 335 (Marshall, J., concurring); *see also* e-note (describing a 1611 compilation
of laws for the Jamestown Colony, England's "Bloody Code," and Draco's criminal
code).

3. Amar, Bill of Rights, 161, 279; Banner, 6; Bessler, Death in the Dark, 33; Scott,
155–57; Laurence, 28–69, 220–30; John P. Rutledge, *The Definitive Inhumanity of
Capital Punishment,* 20 Whittier L. Rev. 283, 288–89 (1998); Seth Kotch & Robert P.
Mosteller, *The Racial Justice Act and the Long Struggle with Race and the Death Penalty
in North Carolina,* 88 N.C. L. Rev. 2031, 2047 n.56 (2010); *Baze,* 128 S. Ct. at 1557
(Thomas, J., concurring); Hayden, 251; Gilreath, 565–66; Anthony V. Baker, *Slavery
and Tushnet and Mann, Oh Why? Finding "Big Law" in Small Places,* 26 Quinnipiac L.
Rev. 691, 700 n.39 (2008); Cottrol, 1654; Kastenberg, 63; Andrew E. Taslitz, *Slaves No
More!: The Implications of the Informed Citizen Ideal for Discovery Before Fourth Amendment Suppression Hearings,* 15 Ga. St. U. L. Rev. 709, 739 (1999); Tom Donnelly, *A
Popular Approach to Popular Constitutionalism: The First Amendment, Civic Education,
and Constitutional Change,* 28 Quinnipiac L. Rev. 321, 328 (2010); Austin Community
College, *Massachusetts Sex Ways: Puritan Ideas of Flesh and the Spirit,* visited Feb. 7,
2011, http://www.austincc.edu/jdikes/Sex%20Ways%20ALL.pdf; *see also* e-note (discussing Thomas Jefferson's desire for religious tolerance).

4. Bessler, Death in the Dark, 23, 32–33, 107–9; Mary Lethert Wingerd, North
Country: The Making of Minnesota 326 (2010); Madow, 495.

5. Jen Girgen, *The Historical and Contemporary Prosecution and Punishment of Animals,* 9 Animal L. 97, 98–115, 122–27 (2003); Edward P. Evans, The Criminal Prosecu-
tion and Capital Punishment of Animals (1987); Paul Schiff Berman, *Rats, Pigs, and
Statues on Trial: The Creation of Cultural Narratives in the Prosecution of Animals and
Inanimate Objects,* 69 N.Y.U. L. Rev. 288 (1994); State of Minnesota v. Bilansky, 3
Minn. 246, 1859 WL 3085 *3 (1859); Massachusetts Historical Society, John Adams
autobiography, part 3, "Peace," 1779–1780, sheet 6 of 18 [electronic edition], *Adams
Family Papers: An Electronic Archive,* visited Feb. 7, 2011, http://www.masshist.org/
digitaladams/; *see also* e-note (discussing a 1779 diary entry of John Adams).

6. People v. Woods, 11 Cal. Rptr.2d 231, 239 (Cal. App. 1992); Lewis v. Huntleigh
Healthcare, LLC, No. CCV095028365, 2009 WL 4851479 *1 n.1 (Conn. Super. Nov. 19,
2009); Lippman, 275, 277, 281, 291–92, 305–6; Hayden, 251; Fisher, 1238–39, 1266
n.151; Stephanie J. Spencer, A and Others v. Secretary: *The Use of Torture Evidence*

Against Criminal Defendants, 21 Temp. Int'l & Comp. L.J. 205, 206 (2007); Joachim Herrmann, *Implementing the Prohibition of Torture on Three Levels: The United Nations, the Council of Europe, and Germany,* 31 Hast. Int'l & Comp. L. Rev. 437, 438 (2008); Aaron R. Jackson, *The White House Counsel Torture Memo: The Final Product of a Flawed System,* 42 Cal. W. L. Rev. 149, 150 (2005); *Requiem for* Miranda: *The Rehnquist Court's Voluntariness Doctrine in Historical Perspective,* 67 Wash. U. L.Q. 59, 71 & n.47 (1998); Dawn E. Johnson, *Faithfully Executing the Laws: Internal Legal Constraints on Executive Power,* 54 UCLA L. Rev. 1559, 1571 (2007); *see also* e-note (discussing waterboarding).

7. James Q. Whitman, Harsh Justice: Criminal Punishment and the Widening Divide Between America and Europe 175 (2003); Robert J. McWhirter, "Baby, Don't Be Cruel," 46 Ariz. Att'y 13, 26 n.88 (2009); Fisher, 1239 & n.15; Gottlieb, Theater of Death, 155–57; Observations on the Article États-Unis Prepared for the Encyclopédie, in 5 Ford; Meskell, 841–42; Alexandra Bak-Boychuk, *Liar Laws: How MPC § 241.3 and State Unsworn Falsification Statutes Fix the Flaws in the False Statements Act (18 U.S.C. § 1001),* 78 Temp. L. Rev. 453, 468 (2005); *see also* e-note (discussing corporal punishments authorized in North Carolina in 1786, the fact that Indians and slaves were sometimes burned to death, and the Boston Massacre trials resulting in two defendants being branded on their thumbs).

8. GW to JM (Nov. 5, 1786); Grundfest, at 210–11; *see also* e-note (discussing George Washington's concerns and the state of affairs in 1793).

9. Cochran, 1406 n.36; Okun, xxi; Wilmarth, 154; James M. Binnall, *Respecting Beasts: The Dehumanizing Quality of the Modern Prison and an Unusual Model for Penal Reform,* 17 J.L. & Pol'y 161, 171 n.68 (2008); *see also* e-note (discussing Madison's correspondence with Boston lawyer Perez Morton on the subject of Virginia penal reform).

10. Death Penalty Info. Ctr., *Executions in the U.S. 1608-2002: The Espy File,* visited Feb. 7, 2011, http://www.deathpenaltyinfo.org/executions-us-1608-2002-espy-file; University Libraries—University at Albany, *National Death Penalty Archive,* visited Feb. 7, 2011, http://library.albany.edu/speccoll/ndpa.htm (describing the Espy File).

11. Banner, 12; Esther Forbes, Paul Revere and the World He Lived In 37–39 (1999); David Hackett Fischer, Paul Revere's Ride 10, 106 (1995).

12. Gottlieb, Theater of Death, iv, 2–6, 15, 21, 23–24, 35–36, 40, 46–50, 56–57, 64, 68, 70, 73–74; Daniel A. Cohen, Pillars of Salt, Monuments of Grace: New England Crime Literature and the Origins of American Popular Culture, 1674–1860 (1993); Daniel W. Williams, Pillars of Salt: An Anthology of Early American Crime Narratives 23, 186 (1993); Daniel A. Cohen, *In the Defense of the Gallows: Justifications of Capital Punishment in New England Execution Sermons, 1674-1825,* 40 Am. Q. 147–64 (June 1988); Judiciary Act of 1789, 1 Stat. 73 (approved Sept. 24, 1789), §§ 9, 29; *see also* e-note (discussing the Judiciary Act of 1789).

13. Banner, 5–9; Masur, 27; Alan Rogers, Murder and the Death Penalty in Massachusetts 80–82 (2008).

14. Kaminski, 14, 18–19, 248, 266; *see also* e-note (discussing George Clinton's postwar policies).

15. Harmelin v. Michigan, 501 U.S. 957, 975 (1991); Thomas, xxix; Davis, 25; *Special Collections Focus: New Acquisitions,* Legal Miscellanea: A Newsletter for the Friends of the Jacob Burns Law Library (Autumn 2004), 2; Banner, 138; Levi, 135–36; Philip English Mackey, *Edward Livingston and the Origins of the Movement to Abolish Capital Punishment in America,* 16 La. Hist. 145, 146, 148, 154, 159–66 (1975); Edward Living-

ston, *Report made by Edward Livingston to the Honourable the Senate and House of Representatives of the State of Louisiana in General Assembly convened* (1822) & *Introductory Report to the Code of Crimes and Punishments* (1824), *reprinted in* 3 Crimmins; Mary S. Van Deusen, *The Livingston Branch*, visited Feb. 7, 2011, http://www.iment .com/maida/familytree/livingston/livingston.htm; *see also* e-note (describing abolitionist efforts in Pennsylvania and New York and by reformers in England such as Samuel Romilly).

16. *Furman,* 408 U.S. at 337 (Marshall, J., concurring); Bessler, Death in the Dark, 44; Samuel Walker, Popular Justice: A History of American Criminal Justice 75 (1980); Vila & Morris, 31–35; Mackey, Voices Against Death, xxii–xxv; Douglas, 160; Filler, 129; Post, 44, 48–50; Levi, 137; *see also* e-note (citing other authorities and discussing abolitionist efforts in Maine).

17. The Universalist Union, Jan. 3, 1846 (reprinting letter dated Nov. 7, 1845).

18. Tocqueville, xv–xvi, 82, 540–41; Cottrol, 1654; James Wood, *Tocqueville in America,* New Yorker, May 17, 2010, at 105. Benjamin Rush's son Richard, a diplomat, actually developed a close friendship with Tocqueville. Powell, 264, 271.

19. Bessler, Death in the Dark, 44; Vila & Morris, 45; *Furman,* 408 U.S. at 338 (Marshall, J., concurring); William Wirt Blume, *Criminal Procedure on the American Frontier: A Study of the Statutes and Court Records of Michigan Territory 1805–1825,* 57 Mich. L. Rev. 195, 242–44 (1958); Eugene G. Wanger, *Michigan and Capital Punishment,* 81 Mich. Const. Hist. 38 (2002); Eugene G. Wanger, *Historical Reflections on Michigan's Abolition of the Death Penalty,* 13 T.M. Cooley L. Rev. 755 (1996); Patrick T. Conley, *Death Knell for the Death Penalty: The Gordon Murder Trial and Rhode Island's Abolition of Capital Punishment,* 34 R.I. Bar J. 11 (1986); Philip English Mackey, *"The Result May Be Glorious"—Anti-Gallows Movement in Rhode Island 1838–1852,* 33 R.I. Hist. 19 (1974); Carrie Cropley, *The Case of John McCaffary,* 35 Wis. Mag. Hist. 281 (1952); Elwood R. McIntyre, *A Farmer Halts the Hangman: The Story of Marvin Bovee,* 42 Wis. Mag. Hist. 3 (1958); *see also* e-note (discussing Michigan's law).

20. Abraham Lincoln, Address Before the Young Men's Lyceum of Springfield, Illinois (Jan. 27, 1838).

21. Bessler, Legacy of Violence, 26, 44, 51; Marvin H. Bovee, Christ and the Gallows; or, Reasons for the Abolition of Capital Punishment (1869).

22. Bessler, Death in the Dark, 45–46; Bessler, Legacy of Violence, 55–56, 64; Filler, 124; Lisa Rein & Jennifer Buske, "Good Tale Slain by Stroke of Pen," Wash. Post, Jan. 25, 2011, at A1.

23. Bessler, Death in the Dark, 41–67; Bessler, Legacy of Violence, 161; Vila & Morris, 76; Kirchmeier, *Another Place Beyond Here,* 10; Bedau, 9; John F. Galliher, Larry W. Koch, David Patrick Keys, & Teresa J. Guess, America Without the Death Penalty: States Leading the Way (2005); John Galliher, Gregory Ray, & Brent Cook, *Abolition and Reinstatement of Capital Punishment During the Progressive Era and Early 20th Century,* 83 J. Crim. L. & Criminology 538 (1992); "An Act to Reduce the Cases in Which the Death Penalty May Be Inflicted," Act of Jan. 15, 1897, ch. 29, 29 Stat. 487 (1898); *see also* e-note (discussing a report of the House Judiciary Committee issued in 1897 noting the propensity of nineteenth-century jurors to refuse to convict individuals of capital crimes, and discussing the effect of war on the abolitionist movement).

24. Furman v. Georgia, 408 U.S. 238 (1972); Friedman, Will of the People, 286; Witherspoon v. Illinois, 391 U.S. 510, 520 (1968); Kirchmeier, *Another Place Beyond*

Here, 11–12; *see also* e-note (discussing the NAACP's role and the decline of executions, coupled with anti–death penalty efforts, in the lead-up to *Furman*).

25. Bessler, Death in the Dark, 131; Friedman, Will of the People, 285; Swann v. Charlotte-Mecklenburg Board of Education, 402 U.S. 1 (1971); Coyne & Entzeroth, 148; *Furman,* 408 U.S. at 239–40; Nicci Lovre-Laughlin, *Lethal Decisions: Examining the Role of Prosecutorial Discretion in Capital Cases in South Dakota and the Federal Justice System,* 50 S.D. L. Rev. 550, 555 n.44 (2005); *see also* e-note (discussing the California Supreme Court's 1972 decision in *People v. Anderson*).

26. *Furman,* 408 U.S. at 245, 256–57 (Douglas, J., concurring); id. at 270, 290–91, 293, 303–4 (Brennan, J., concurring); *see also* e-note (discussing the backgrounds of the petitioners in *Furman*).

27. *Furman,* 408 U.S. at 306, 309–10, 313 (Stewart, J., concurring); id. at 312–13 (White, J., concurring); *see also* e-note (citing other authorities).

28. *Furman,* 408 U.S. at 315, 345, 358–59, 361, 365–66 (Marshall, J., concurring); Williams, 214–16, 350–51, 359; Michael Mello, Against the Death Penalty: The Relentless Dissents of Justices Brennan and Marshall (1996); Bigel, 13; *see also* e-note (discussing "the Marshall hypothesis").

29. *Furman,* 408 U.S. at 329, 360–62 & n.145, 362, 369, 371 (Marshall, J., concurring); Williams, 65–66; *see also* e-note (discussing Marshall's experience defending capital cases).

30. *Furman,* 408 U.S. at 245–47 (Douglas, J., concurring); id. at 375, 394, 402 (Burger, C.J., dissenting); McGautha v. California, 402 U.S. 183, 199–200, 207 (1971); *see also* e-note (discussing Chief Justice Warren Burger's opinion and the Supreme Court's decision in *McGautha*).

31. *Furman,* 408 U.S. at 418 (Powell, J., dissenting); id. at 468 (Rehnquist, J., dissenting); id. at 404–6, 410–11, 414 (Blackmun, J., dissenting).

32. Bessler, Death in the Dark, 133; David Von Drehle, Among the Lowest of the Dead: Inside Death Row 162 (1996); Friedman, Will of the People, 287; Norval Morris, "Foreword," *in* Maestro, vii–x.

33. Gregg v. Georgia, 428 U.S. 153, 164–65, 179–80, 183, 195, 206–7 (1976) (plurality opinion); Woodson v. North Carolina, 428 U.S. 280 (1976); Roberts v. Louisiana, 428 U.S. 325 (1976); Jurek v. Texas, 428 U.S. 262 (1976); Proffitt v. Florida, 428 U.S. 242 (1976); Hudson v. McMillian, 503 U.S. 1, 5 (1992) ("the unnecessary and wanton infliction of pain . . . constitutes cruel and unusual punishment"); *see also* e-note (discussing *Gregg*).

34. McCleskey v. Kemp, 481 U.S. 279, 312 (1987); id. at 327 (Brennan, J., dissenting); Bright, *Discrimination, Death and Denial,* 474.

35. Helen Prejean, Dead Man Walking: An Eyewitness Account of the Death Penalty in the United States (1996); Kirchmeier, *Another Place Beyond Here,* 5, 22–23, 28 & nn.164–65; Callins v. Collins, 510 U.S. 1141, 1145 (1994) (Blackmun, J., dissenting from denial of cert.); Lewis F. Powell Jr., *Capital Punishment,* 102 Harv. L. Rev. 1035, 1045–46 (1989).

36. *Callins,* 510 U.S. at 1143–45, 1159 (Blackmun, J., dissenting from denial of cert.).

37. Thompson, 1515; Adcock, 8; Hugo Adam Bedau, The Death Penalty in America: Current Controversies 9 (1997); John Paul Stevens, *On the Death Sentence,* N.Y. Rev. of Books, Nov. 23, 2010; CBS News, *Justice John Paul Stevens Opens Up,* visited Feb. 7, 2011, http://www.cbsnews.com/stories/2010/11/23/60minutes/main7082572.shtml; Midwest Democracy Project, *Live Blogging from KS Death Penalty Debate: Bill 20-20*

Vote, visited Feb. 7, 2011, http://midwestdemocracyproject.org/blogs/entries/live-blogging-from-ks-death-penalty-debate-bill-fails-on-20-20-vote/; Barry Scheck, *Innocence, Race, and the Death Penalty,* 50 How. L.J. 445 (2007); Bruce P. Smith, *The History of Wrongful Execution,* 56 Hast. L.J. 1185 (2005); Death Penalty Info. Ctr., *Legislative Activity—New Jersey,* visited Feb. 7, 2011, http://www.deathpenaltyinfo.org/article.php?did=2208; Nina Totenberg, National Public Radio, *Justice Stevens: Life on the High Court,* visited Feb. 7, 2011, http://www.npr.org/templates/story/story.php?storyId=130332059; Kirchmeier, *Another Place Beyond Here,* 3–5, 44.

38. Amnesty International, Death Sentences and Executions 2009 (2010); Amnesty International, Death Sentences and Executions 2010 (2011); Thucydides, The History of the Peloponnesian War 25–50 (3d ed. 1972); Thomas Erdbrink, "Iran Stones 2 Men to Death; 3rd Flees," Wash. Post, Jan. 14, 2009, at A14; Chenwi, 48–49, 140–41; Jennifer F. Cohen, *Islamic Law in Iran: Can It Protect the International Legal Right of Freedom of Religion and Belief?,* 9 Chi. J. Int'l L. 247, 260 (2008); Nicola Browne, Seema Kandelia, Rupa Reddy, & Peter Hodgkinson, *Capital Punishment and Mental Health Issues: Global Examples,* 25 St. Louis U. Pub. L. Rev. 383, 391 (2006).

39. Lilian Chenwi, Towards the Abolition of the Death Penalty in Africa: A Human Rights Perspective vii, 7–8, 24 (2007); Amnesty International, Death Sentences and Executions 2009 (2010); Adcock, 6; Rachel Saloom, *Is Beheading Permissible under Islamic Law? Comparing Terrorist Jihad and the Saudi Arabian Death Penalty,* 10 UCLA J. Int'l L. & Foreign Aff. 221, 244–45 (2005); Bowden, 51, 53; Calum MacLeod, "China Makes Ultimate Punishment Mobile," USA Today, June 15, 2006; Amnesty International, *Breakthrough UN Resolution on Global Moratorium on Executions,* visited Feb. 7, 2011, http://www.amnesty.org/en/news-and-updates/news/breakthrough-un-resolution-global-moratorium-executions-20071115.

40. G.A. Res. 2857 (XXVI), U.N. GAOR, 26th Sess., Supp. No. 29, at 94, U.N. Doc. A/8429 (1971); U.N. General Assembly Resolution 62/149, A/RES/62/149 (Dec. 18, 2007); Kirchmeier, *Another Place Beyond Here,* 69; Koh, 1131; Schabas, Abolition of the Death Penalty in International Law, 357–58.

41. Bessler, *Revisiting Beccaria's Vision,* 253–54 & nn.422–27; *see also* e-note (discussing the aftermath of the ICJ's *Avena* decision and the execution of Jose Ernesto Medellín).

42. Bessler, *Revisiting Beccaria's Vision,* 245–46 & nn.355–60; *see also* e-note (discussing the Universal Declaration of Human Rights and international humanitarian law).

43. Bessler, *Revisiting Beccaria's Vision,* 246–47 & nn.361–63; Ford v. Wainwright, 477 U.S. 399, 409 (1986) ("fundamental right to life"); Schabas, Abolition of the Death Penalty in International Law, 23, 180; 999 U.N.T.S. 302 (1976); International Covenant on Civil and Political Rights ("ICCPR"), arts. 6(1), 6(5) & 7; *see also* e-note (discussing the U.S. ratification of the ICCPR in 1992, in addition to reservations to it and the Convention Against Torture and Other Forms of Cruel, Inhuman or Degrading Treatment or Punishment).

44. Bessler, *Revisiting Beccaria's Vision,* 250–51 & nn.389–95; *Roper,* 543 U.S. at 575–78; Am. Decl. of the Rights and Duties of Man, O.A.S., Res. XXX, arts. I & XXVI, adopted by the Ninth International Conference of American States (1948).

45. Bessler, *Revisiting Beccaria's Vision,* 248–49 & nn.378–86; ABC News, *Gabe Watson Charged with Wife's Scuba-Diving Murder After Return to U.S.,* visited Feb. 7, 2011, http://abcnews.go.com/US/honeymoon-killer-gabe-watson-charged-wifes-

scuba-diving/story?id=12247798&page=1; MSNBC.com News Service, *Australia Deports American "Honeymoon Killer,"* Nov. 24, 2010.

46. Amnesty International, Death Sentences and Executions 2009 (2010); Schabas, Death Penalty as Cruel Treatment and Torture; Nelson v. Campbell, 541 U.S. 637 (2004); People v. Anderson, 493 P.2d 880, 894 (Cal. 1972), *cert. denied,* 406 U.S. 958 (1972); *see also* e-note (citing Justice Brennan's opinions regarding "the inevitable long wait between the imposition of sentence and the actual infliction of death" and "the 'physical and mental suffering' inherent in *any* method of execution").

47. 2 Samuel Johnson, A Dictionary of the English Language (London: W. Strahan, 1773); Thomas K. Landry, *"Punishment" and the Eighth Amendment,* 57 Ohio St. L.J. 1607, 1624 & n.103 (1996); *see also* e-note (discussing the oath of judicial officers).

48. U.S. Const., amends. V & XIV; *Gregg,* 428 U.S. at 177–78 (plurality opinion); Walton v. Arizona, 497 U.S. 639, 669–71 (1990) (Scalia, J., concurring); Callins v. Collins, 510 U.S. 1141, 1141 (Scalia, J., concurring); Banner, 78; *see also* e-note (discussing the Fifth Amendment's grand jury requirement and the Founding Fathers' use of the phrase "life or limb").

49. Maier, Ratification, 379, 391, 449; Edward S. Corwin, *The Doctrine of Due Process of Law Before the Civil War,* 24 Harv. L. Rev. 366, 368 (1910); W. J. Brockelbank, *The Role of Due Process in American Constitutional Law,* 39 Cornell L. Q. 561, 561–62 (1954); Den v. The Hoboken Land & Improvement Co., 59 U.S. 272 (1855).

50. U.S. Const., art. 1, §§ 3, 5, & 8 & art. III, § 3.

51. Debate in Virginia Ratifying Convention (June 16, 1788); James G. Wilson, *Chaining the Leviathan: The Unconstitutionality of Executing Those Convicted of Treason,* 45 U. Pitt. L. Rev. 99, 156 (1983); *see also* e-note (discussing the debate at Virginia's ratifying convention, including the remarks of George Nicholas as well as those of Patrick Henry on the lack of a cruel and unusual punishments clause in the Constitution).

52. JM to TJ (Oct. 17, 1788); U.S. Const., art. I, § 8.

53. U.S. Const., art. I, § 9 & amend. V; Maier, Ratification, 189.

54. U.S. Const., art. III, § 3 & amend. XIII, § 1; *see also* e-note (noting James Wilson's support for the pardoning power in the case of treason).

55. Oxford English Dictionary 78 (2d ed. 1989); Stinneford, 1744 n.32; Harmelin v. Michigan, 501 U.S. 957, 976 (1991) (citing Webster's American Dictionary (1828); Webster's Second International Dictionary 2807 (1954)); *see also* e-note (containing other citations and discussing definitions of *cruel* and *unusual,* as well as John Adams's use of the word *cruel*).

56. JM to Thomas J. Wharton (May 5, 1828); Trop v. Dulles, 356 U.S. 86, 87–91 & n.4, 101–2 (1958).

57. DeShaney v. Winnebago County Dept. of Social Servs., 489 U.S. 189, 199–200 (1989); Hutto v. Finney, 437 U.S. 678, 682 (1978); Bowring v. Godwin, 551 F.2d 44, 47–48 (4th Cir. 1977); Domino v. Texas Dep't of Crim. Justice, 239 F.3d 752, 754 (5th Cir. 2001).

58. Hudson v. McMillian, 503 U.S. 1, 4 (1992); McCord v. Maggio, 927 F.2d 844, 848 (5th Cir. 1991); Cooper v. Sheriff, Lubbock County, Tex., 929 F.2d 1078, 1083 (5th Cir. 1991); Fruit v. Norris, 905 F.2d 1147, 1150 (8th Cir. 1990); Parrish v. Johnson, 800 F.2d 600, 605 (6th Cir. 1986); Jackson v. Bishop, 404 F.2d 571, 579–80 (8th Cir. 1968); Leland v. Edge, No. 4:06cv568, 2008 WL 4790342 (N.D. Fla., Oct. 22, 2008); Madrid v. Gomez, 889 F. Supp. 1146, 1164 n.2 (N.D. Cal. 1995); Bailey v. Turner, 736 F.2d 963, 973 (4th Cir. 1984); Ferguson v. Dier-Zimmel, 809 F. Supp. 668, 669 (E.D. Wis.

1992); Michaud v. Sheriff of Essex County, 458 N.E.2d 702, 708 (Sup. Jud. Ct. Mass. 1983). *But see* State v. Cannon, 190 A.2d 514 (Del. 1963) ("[W]e are of the opinion that the Eighth and Fourteenth Amendments to the Federal Constitution do not invalidate the statutes of the State of Delaware imposing the punishment of whipping for certain crimes."); Foote v. Maryland, 59 Md. 264, 1883 WL 4110 *1 (Md. Ct. App. 1883) ("The terms 'cruel and unusual pains and penalties,' and 'cruel or unusual punishment,' have been incorporated in each successive Constitution in this State from 1776 to the present time. That the punishment of whipping was not considered a 'cruel or unusual punishment,' and, therefore, coming within the prohibition of the Constitution, is most conclusively shown by the fact that the punishment by whipping was recognized by the statute law of the State under all these Constitutions.").

59. Michael L. Radelet, Some Examples of Post-Furman Botched Executions (Oct. 1, 2010), *at* Death Penalty Info. Ctr., visited Feb. 7, 2011, http://www.deathpenaltyinfo .org/some-examples-post-furman-botched-executions; Deborah W. Denno, *The Lethal Injection Quandary: How Medicine Has Dismantled the Death Penalty,* 76 Fordham L. Rev. 49, 104 (2007) (discussing a study published in a British medical journal in 2005 that reported that the level of sodium thiopental used in lethal injections might be insufficient, particularly in light of the heightened anxiety of inmates and the potential of poorly trained executioners).

60. Hudson v. McMillian, 503 U.S. 1, 16 (1992) (Blackmun, J., concurring); *Anderson,* 493 P.2d at 894; Bowden, 51, 53; Webster's Ninth New Collegiate Dictionary 1246 (1985); *see also* e-note (discussing the definition of "torture" in the Convention Against Torture as including severe "physical" or "mental" pain or suffering but currently excluding "pain or suffering arising only from, inherent in or incidental to lawful sanctions").

61. Trop v. Dulles, 356 U.S. 86, 100 n.32 (1958).

62. Debate in Virginia Ratifying Convention (June 14, 1788); Jean Edward Smith, John Marshall: Definer of a Nation 134 (1998).

63. Debate in Virginia Ratifying Convention (June 14, 1788); *see also* e-note (discussing George Mason's objection to the Constitution's Necessary and Proper Clause and the 1788 criticism of that objection by "An Impartial Citizen").

64. Debate in Virginia Ratifying Convention (June 19, 1788); *see also* e-note (noting Patrick Henry's remarks at Virginia's ratifying convention).

65. Virginia Ratifying Convention (June 18, 1788); Curtis A. Bradley, *The Alien Tort Statute and Article III,* 42 Va. J. Int'l L. 587, 637 (2002); David M. Golove, *Treaty-Making and the Nation: The Historical Foundations of the Nationalist Conception of the Treaty Power,* 98 Mich. L. Rev. 1075 (2000); *see also* e-note (discussing the controversy surrounding the arrest of the Russian Ambassador in 1708).

66. Virginia Ratifying Convention (June 18, 1788); *see also* e-note (Thomas Jefferson's account of the "Stanhope Affair" and remarks about the case of the Russian ambassador).

67. Debate in Virginia Ratifying Convention (June 18–19, 1788).

68. Stinneford, 1739 nn.211 & 213, 1769, 1787, 1795; *see also* e-note (discussing Madison's use of the "long use" terminology, George Mason's views on the common law, and the use by the "Federal Farmer" of the phrases "long custom" and "immemorial usage").

69. Stinneford, 1745, 1764, 1767–68, 1770–72, 1809–11.

70. Id. at 1814, 1821–22.

71. William R. Casto, The Supreme Court in the Early Republic: The Chief Justice-ships of John Jay and Oliver Ellsworth 162 (1995); Maier, Ratification, xvii; Meyler, 567–68, 573–75, 578 & n.94; TJ to William Carmichael (Aug. 12, 1788); TJ to Skelton Jones (July 28, 1809); *see also* e-note (discussing the Sedition Act, the controversy over federal common-law crimes, and Justice Scalia's view of the Cruel and Unusual Punishments Clause).

72. Gregory C. Lisby, *No Place in the Law: The Ignominy of Criminal Libel in American Jurisprudence,* 9 Comm. L. & Pol'y 433, 478 (2004) ("[M]ost criminal law today is statutory law rather than common law. Most states have thus abolished common law crimes.").

73. *See* State v. Olson, 435 N.W.2d 530, 535 (Minn. 1989) ("the common law, which constantly evolves with the changing needs of society, may appropriately reevaluate the traditional definition" of "death" in light of "advances of science"); *see also* e-note (discussing the concepts of "long usage" and "unalienable rights").

74. St. George Tucker, View of the Constitution of the United States with Selected Writings (Clyde N. Wilson, ed., 1999) (1803) ("Of the Cognizance of Crimes and Misdemeanors"; "Of the Unwritten, or Common Law of England").

75. Debate in Virginia Ratifying Convention (June 16, 1788); Akhil Reed Amar & Renee B. Lettow, *Fifth Amendment First Principles: The Self-Incrimination Clause,* 93 Mich. L. Rev. 857, 865 & n.20 (1995); *Furman,* 408 U.S. at 260 n.2 (Brennan, J., concurring); State v. Martin, 944 A.2d 867, 886 (Vt. 2007); Julianne Harper, *Defining Torture: Bridging the Gap Between Rhetoric and Reality,* 49 Santa Clara L. Rev. 893 (2009); *see also* e-note (discussing the Torture Victim Protection Act, regulations implementing the Convention Against Torture, and the classification by American judges of horrific acts *short of death* as constituting "torture").

76. Blinka, 72, 95, 98; Eicholz, 75; Stinneford, 1745, 1764, 1767–68, 1770–72; Wilmarth, 161–63, 185–87; Simmons v. South Carolina, 512 U.S. 154 (1994); *see also* e-note (discussing English and American common law and the rejection of some English common-law precedents even in the founding era).

77. Wilmarth, 161–63, 185–87; St. George Tucker, View of the Constitution of the United States with Selected Writings 242–43 (Clyde N. Wilson, ed., 1999) (1803); Mark D. Rosen, *What Has Happened to the Common Law? Recent American Codifications, and Their Impact on Judicial Practice and the Law's Subsequent Development,* 1994 Wis. L. Rev. 1119, 1123 n.7.

78. Cone v. Bell, 129 S. Ct. 1769, 1772 (2009); Banks v. Dretke, 540 U.S. 668, 691 (2004); Kelly v. South Carolina, 534 U.S. 246, 248 (2002); Brady v. Maryland, 373 U.S. 83, 87 (1963); Eicholz, 75; Stinneford, 1790–91; Evitts v. Lucey, 469 U.S. 387 (1985); Strickland v. Washington, 466 U.S. 668 (1984); United States v. Cronic, 466 U.S. 648 (1984); Cuyler v. Sullivan, 446 U.S. 335 (1980); Douglas v. California, 372 U.S. 353 (1963); Gideon v. Wainwright, 372 U.S. 335 (1963); *see also* e-note (discussing the Constitution and appeals by criminal defendants).

79. Amar, Bill of Rights, 171, 279–80; Collins v. Johnston, 237 U.S. 502, 510–11 (1915); *see also* e-note (discussing George Mason's views on the slave trade).

80. U.S. Const., amend. XIV.

81. Death Penalty Info. Ctr., Facts about the Death Penalty (Jan. 26, 2011); Ogletree & Sarat, 169.

82. Hilary Hylton, *A Texas Judge on Trial: Closed to a Death-Row Appeal?,* visited Feb. 7, 2011, http://www.time.com/time/nation/article/0,8599,1915814,00.html;

David R. Dow, "The Last Lethal Injection?" Wash. Post, Nov. 1, 2007; In re Kemmler, 136 U.S. 436, 448–49 (1890); Village of Euclid v. Ambler Realty Co., 272 U.S. 365, 395 (1926) (a municipal zoning ordinance would survive a substantive due process challenge only if it was not "clearly arbitrary and unreasonable, having no substantial relation to the public health, safety, morals, or general welfare"); *see also* e-note (containing additional citations and discussing substantive due process and its relationship to the Eighth Amendment).

83. Debate in Virginia Ratifying Convention (June 18, 1788), *in* Jonathan Elliot, ed., The Debates in the Several State Conventions on the Adoption of the Federal Constitution 517–19 (1836).

84. Ohio Adult Parole Authority v. Woodard, 523 U.S. 272 (1998); id. at 292 (Stevens, J., concurring in part and dissenting in part); *see also* e-note (discussing the *Woodard* decision).

85. Graham v. Florida, 130 S. Ct. 2011, 2021 (2010) ("To determine whether a punishment is cruel and unusual, courts must look beyond historical conceptions to 'the evolving standards of decency that mark the progress of a maturing society.'").

86. Ex parte Wilson, 114 U.S. 417, 427–28 (1885); *see also* e-note (citations discussing "infamous" punishments, the abandonment of corporal punishments, and the grand jury requirement).

87. F.C.C. v. Pacifica Foundation, 438 U.S. 726, 729–31, 744–45 (1978) (ruling that the Federal Communications Commission had the power to regulate a radio broadcast— of George Carlin's "Filthy Words" monologue—as "indecent" because "their content is so offensive to contemporary moral standards"); Roth v. United States, 354 U.S. 476, 479 n.1, 482–85 & nn.10–13, 489 (1957) (upholding the constitutionality of a federal and state obscenity statute and articulating this test for obscenity: "whether to the average person, applying contemporary community standards, the dominant theme of the material taken as a whole appeals to prurient interest"); Miller v. California, 413 U.S. 15, 24 (1973) (saying that "contemporary community standards" are to be judged by the trier of fact in an obscenity case); *see also* e-note (containing additional citations regarding the use of "community standards" in the context of the First Amendment).

88. U.S. Const., art. I, § 9 & art. III, § 2; U.S. Const., amends. I–X.

89. Bessler, *Revisiting Beccaria's Vision,* 309–10 n.846; *Thompson,* 487 U.S. at 821 (plurality opinion) (citing *Trop,* 356 U.S. at 101 [plurality opinion]):

> The authors of the Eighth Amendment drafted a categorical prohibition against the infliction of cruel and unusual punishments, but they made no attempt to define the contours of that category. They delegated that task to future generations of judges who have been guided by the "evolving standards of decency that mark the progress of a maturing society."

90. Goodell, 178–79; Stroud, 62, 64–65; Barnes, 174; United States v. Gallagher, 2 Paine 447, 25 F. Cas. 1241, 1241 (D. N.Y. 1832) (citing Alabama's law).

91. 1 Elliott, 188–90, 193 (1850); Stroud, 34, 66–67; Thomas D. Russell, *A New Image of the Slave Auction: An Empirical Look at the Role of Law in Slave States and a Conceptual Reevaluation of Slave Property,* 18 Cardozo L. Rev. 473, 489–90, 493–94 (1996); Miller v. Stewart, 12 La. Ann. 170, 1857 WL 4826 *1–2 (La. 1857); Poydras v. Mourain, 9 La. 492, 1836 WL 869 *5 (La. 1836); Markham v. Close, 2 La. 581, 1831 WL 877 *1–4 (La. 1831).

92. Goodell, 161–62, 165.

93. Turnipseed v. State, 6 Ala. 664, 1844 WL 301 *1 (Ala. 1844); State v. Wilson, 25 S.C.L. 163, 1840 WL 2007 *1 (S.C. App. L. 1840) (referencing 1740 law); Markham v. Close, 2 La. 581, 1831 WL 877 (La. 1831) (discussing the "16th section of the Black Code"); United States v. Winn, 28 F. Cas. 732, 732 (C.C. Mass. 1838) (referencing "the act of March 3, 1835, § 3 [4 Stat. 776]") (Story, J.); Scott v. State of Mississippi, 31 Miss. 473 (1856); Charge to Grand Jury, 30 F. Cas. 981, 981 (Curtis, Circuit Justice, C.C.D.R.I. 1853) (No. 18,249); Michaelson v. Denison, 3 Day 294, 17 F. Cas. 258, 258–59 (D. Conn. 1808); The Oyez Project at IIT Chicago-Kent College of Law, *Brockholst Livingston*, visited Apr. 18, 2011, http://www.oyez.org/justices/brockholst_livingston; William Winslow Crosskey, Politics and the Constitution in the History of the United States 775–76 (1978); *see also* e-note (discussing *United States v. Collins* and the use of the phrase "cruel or unusual" in trade legislation enacted before the adoption of the U.S. Bill of Rights).

94. Bessler, *Revisiting Beccaria's Vision,* 310 n.847; United States v. Bright, 63 M.J. 683 (Army Ct. Crim. App. 2006), *review denied* 64 M.J. 395 (U.S. Armed Forces Jan. 22, 2007); United States v. Kinsch, 54 M.J. 641 (Army Ct. Crim. App. 2000), *abrogated by* United States v. Bright, 63 M.J. 683 (Army Ct. Crim. App. 2006); United States v. Towns, 52 M.J. 830 (A.F. Ct. Crim. App. 2000), *review granted in part,* 54 M.J. 320 (U.S. Armed Forces 2000), *aff'd,* 55 M.J. 361 (U.S. Armed Forces 2001).

95. Louis A. Knafla, *The Theory and Practice of Incarceration in the Colonial and Federal Periods,* 5 Crim. L.F. 729, 731 (1994); *see also* e-note (citing other authorities).

96. Ralph Ketcham, ed., The Anti-Federalist Papers and the Constitutional Convention Debates 90 (1986); Hindus, 100–102; *see also* e-note (discussing Justice Brennan's concurrence in *Furman*).

97. Callins v. Collins, 510 U.S. 1141, 1141 (1994) (Scalia, J., concurring); Atkins v. Virginia, 536 U.S. 304, 337, 340, 348 (Scalia, J., dissenting); Antonin Scalia, A Matter of Interpretation: Federal Courts and the Law 46 (1997).

98. "The Originalist," California Lawyer (Jan. 2011), visited Feb. 7, 2011, http://www.callawyer.com/story.cfm?eid=913358&evid=1.

99. Id.; *see also* e-note (quoting the Fourteenth Amendment, which protects "any person," and discussing the majority view of the U.S. Supreme Court—which has prevailed for four decades now—that the Fourteenth Amendment *does* protect women's rights).

100. Ogletree & Sarat, 72, 92, 350.

101. U.S. Const., art. III, § 1; The Federalist No. 78 (Alexander Hamilton).

102. United States v. Hatter, 532 U.S. 557, 568–69 (2001); Proceedings and Debates of the Virginia State Convention of 1829–1830, at 616 (1830); Articles of Impeachment for Samuel Chase (Nov. 30, 1804); Bessler, Death in the Dark, 12; Chernow, 255, 259; Kaufmann, 134–40, 142; John Blume & Theodore Eisenberg, *Judicial Politics, Death Penalty Appeals, and Case Selection: An Empirical Study,* 72 S. Cal. L. Rev. 465, 471 (1999); Bright & Keenan, 760–63; United States v. Will, 449 U.S. 200, 217–18 (1980); Northern Pipeline Const. Co. v. Marathon Pipe Line Co., 458 U.S. 50, 59 (1982); *see also* e-note (discussing Samuel Chase's impeachment trial and the practice of judges enjoying tenure on good behavior).

103. 1 The Political Writings of John Dickinson 228–31, 350–51 (1801); Ralph Ketcham, ed., The Anti-Federalist Papers and the Constitutional Convention Debates 269, 293, 295–96, 299, 305 (1986); *see also* e-note (discussing the 1788 views of "Brutus" on

the independence of the Supreme Court and its power to declare void those laws that are inconsistent with the Constitution).

104. Chernow, Washington, 601; Ellis, 265–68, 330–33; Wood, 106–7; Sloan & McKean, 168; Veit, Bowling, & Bickford, 218 & n.1, 310; Pennekamp v. State of Florida, 328 U.S. 331, 355 (1946) (Frankfurter, J., concurring); *see also* e-note (discussing the importance of an independent judiciary and the power of courts to declare laws unconstitutional).

105. 2 Schwartz, The Roots of the Bill of Rights, 403–31; Wilmarth, 118 & n.22, 131–32; *see also* e-note (discussing James Iredell's essay).

106. U.S. Const., art. VI (emphasis added); United States v. Brown, 381 U.S. 437, 444 n.18 (1965); St. George Tucker, Blackstone's Commentaries with Notes of Reference to the Constitution and Laws, of the Federal Government of the United States and of the Commonwealth of Virginia 353 (1803) ("In England the judiciary may be overwhelmed by a combination between the executive and the legislature. In America (according to the true theory of our constitution,) it is rendered absolutely independent of, and superior to the attempts of both, to control, or crush it."); Friedman, Will of the People, 34; *see also* id. at 16 ("Judicial review would indeed be a puzzling addition to the American system of government if all the Supreme Court did was mirror transient public opinion. The value of judicial review in the modern era is that it does something more than that.").

107. U.S. Const., art. III, § 1; Helen E. Veit et al., eds., Creating the Bill of Rights: The Documentary Record from the First Federal Congress 83–84 (1991) (quoting 1 Annals of Cong. 439 (Joseph Gales, ed., 1789)); The Federalist No. 78 (Alexander Hamilton); Marbury v. Madison, 1 Cranch 137, 177, 2 L.Ed 60 (1803); O'Donoghue v. United States, 289 U.S. 516, 530 (1933); Bradley v. Fisher, 80 U.S. 335, 349 n.16 (1871) ("judges who are appointed to administer the law should be permitted to administer it under the protection of the law, independently and freely, without favor and without fear"); *see also* e-note (discussing the Compensation Clause and its importance to an independent judiciary).

108. "Brutus," New York J. (Nov. 1, 1787); John R. Vile, *The Critical Role of Committees at the U.S. Constitutional Convention of 1787*, 48 Am. J. Legal Hist. 147, 164 (2006); *see also* e-note (citing case law as to the Constitution's "general language" and discussing Ronald Dworkin's view of the words of the U.S. Bill of Rights as creating "a breathtakingly abstract, principled constitution").

109. Gerber, To Secure These Rights, 5–7; Bowen, 88; Brown v. Mississippi, 297 U.S. 278, 286 (1936); Miller v. Fenton, 474 U.S. 104, 109 (1985); Estelle v. Gamble, 429 U.S. 97, 102 (1976); Chambers v. Florida, 309 U.S. 227, 236–37 (1940); Jacobson v. Commonwealth of Massachusetts, 197 U.S. 11, 38 (1905); Seth F. Kreimer, *Rejecting Uncontrolled Authority over the Body: The Decencies of Civilized Conduct, the Past and the Future of Unenumerated Rights*, 9 U. Pa. J. Const. L. 423 (2007) (citing other cases).

110. Gerber, To Secure These Rights, 142, 144, 157; Garry Wills, Inventing America: Jefferson's Declaration of Independence 213–17, 229–31 (1979); Clarence Thomas, *Toward a 'Plain Reading' of the Constitution: The Declaration of Independence in Constitutional Interpretation*, 30 How. L.J. 983, 985–87, 994–95 (1987); Clarence Thomas, *The Higher Law Background of the Privileges or Immunities Clause of the Fourteenth Amendment*, 12 Harv. J.L. & Pub. Pol'y 63, 65 (1989); Craig A. Stern & Gregory M. Jones, *The Coherence of Natural Inalienable Rights*, 76 UMKC L. Rev. 939 nn. 249, 257

(2008); Cosgrove, 108, 117, 125–26, 138–39; Troxel v. Granville, 530 U.S. 57, 91 (2000) (Scalia, J., dissenting); *see also* e-note (discussing the debate over the role of the Declaration of Independence in interpreting the Constitution).

111. U.S. Const., art. 1, §§ 2 & 8; Maier, American Scripture, xvii, 125; Abraham Lincoln, Address at Independence Hall (Feb. 22, 1861); Gulf, C. & S.F. Ry. Co. v. Ellis, 165 U.S. 150, 159–60 (1897); *see also* e-note (discussing Lincoln's invocation of the Declaration of Independence).

112. Gottlieb, Theater of Death, 98–127, 187–89, 211 & n.556, 216–22, 227–35; Woodson v. North Carolina, 428 U.S. 280, 289 (1976) (plurality opinion).

113. Hindus, 94–95, 98, 104–5; Roberts v. Louisiana, 428 U.S. 325, 335 (1976) (plurality opinion); *Furman,* 408 U.S. at 402 (Burger, C.J., dissenting); *see also* e-note (noting that the common law at one time treated all homicides as capital offenses with mandatory death sentences).

114. *Woodson,* 428 U.S. at 288–93 & n.25, 301–4 (plurality opinion); Sumner v. Shuman, 483 U.S. 66, 85 (1987); Bessler, Legacy of Violence, 95–105; Kritzer, 464; Fred B. Burnside, *Dying to Get Elected: A Challenge to the Jury Override,* 1999 Wis. L. Rev. 1017, 1039; Michael L. Radelet, *Rejecting the Jury: The Imposition of the Death Penalty in Florida,* 18 U.C. Davis L. Rev. 1409 (1985); Mike Mello & Ruthann Robson, *Judge Over Jury: Florida's Practice of Imposing Death Over Life in Capital Cases,* 13 Fla. St. U. L. Rev. 31 (1985); *see also* e-note (discussing the role of juries in death penalty cases).

115. Bright & Keenan, 759; Stephen B. Bright, *Elected Judges and the Death Penalty in Texas: Why Full Habeas Corpus Review by Independent Judges Is Indispensable to Protecting Constitutional Rights,* 78 Tex. L. Rev. 1806 (2000).

116. Scalia, *Originalism,* 852, 856, 861–62; Steve Bachmann, *Starting Again with the Mayflower . . . England's Civil War and America's Bill of Rights,* 20 Quinnipiac L. Rev. 193, 254–55 (2000); *see also* e-note (discussing the movement away from corporal punishments).

117. Scalia, *Originalism,* 853–54, 862–63.

118. *Furman,* 408 U.S. at 244; 1 Annals of Cong. 754, 782–83 (1789); *see also* e-note (discussing the implications of the Fourteenth Amendment's ratification for the Cruel and Unusual Punishments Clause).

119. McCulloch v. Maryland, 17 U.S. (4 Wheat) 316, 415 (1819); Raoul Berger, *"Original Intention" in Historical Perspective,* 54 Geo. Wash. L. Rev. 296, 330 (1986); The Federalist No. 37 (James Madison); G. Brinton Lucas, *Structural Exceptionalism and Comparative Constitutional Law,* 96 Va. L. Rev. 1965, 1992 (2010); Nelson, 535 & n.40; Henry Paul Monaghan, *Supremacy Clause Textualism,* 110 Colum. L. Rev. 731, 785 (2010); JM to Charles J. Ingersoll (June 25, 1831); JM to Samuel Johnston (June 21, 1789); JM to Spencer Roane (Sept. 2, 1819); TJ to Skelton Jones (July 28, 1809); *see also* e-note (discussing Jeremy Bentham's correspondence with James Madison).

120. Nelson, 530–34; Samuel Johnson, A Dictionary of the English Language (2007) (1755).

121. JM to Converse Sherman (Mar. 10, 1826); Baze v. Rees, 553 U.S. 35, 97 (2008) (Thomas, J., dissenting) (*citing* 1 S. Johnson, A Dictionary of the English Language 459 (1773) & 1 N. Webster, An American Dictionary of the English Language 52 (1828)); *see also* e-note (discussing the founders' divergent views as to whether the Constitution should be read in a technical way—as a lawyer might understand it—or as a document accessible to the average layperson).

122. U.S. Const., amend. XIV; Dred Scott v. Sandford, 60 U.S. 393 (1857); Plessy v. Ferguson, 163 U.S. 537 (1896), *overruled,* Brown v. Board of Education, 347 U.S. 483, 492 (1954) ("We cannot turn the clock back to 1868 when the Amendment was adopted, or even to 1896 when *Plessy v. Ferguson* was written."); JM to Charles Jared Ingersoll (June 25, 1831); Bader, 9; *see also* e-note (discussing respect for precedents, though not absolute, in the founding era).

123. Nelson, 540–42 & n.113; Kurt T. Lash, *Originalism, Popular Sovereignty, and Reverse Stare Decisis,* 93 Va. L. Rev. 1437, 1149 (2007); *see also* e-note (noting that the Founding Fathers did not follow a strict adherence to the theory of *stare decisis* and that the U.S. Supreme Court has overruled more than a hundred of its own decisions).

124. Nelson, 544–47 & n.114; *see also* e-note (noting the debate between Justice Scalia and Ronald Dworkin over the proper interpretation of the Eighth Amendment).

125. People v. Morris, 45 N.W. 591, 591–92 (Mich. 1890) (citing Const. Lim.) (4th ed. 408)) (emphasis added).

126. Louisiana ex rel. Francis v. Resweber, 329 U.S. 459, 460–64 (1947) (emphasis added).

127. Berkin, 64; Christopher Collier & James Lincoln Collier, Decision in Philadelphia: The Constitutional Convention of 1787, at 109–113 (1986); Jack N. Rakove, ed., Interpreting the Constitution: The Debate over Original Intent 69, 82–83 (1990); Gibbons v. Ogden, 22 U.S. 1, 188 (1824); Cosgrove, 133.

128. Brennan, *Constitutional Adjudication and the Death Penalty,* 325–26; Brennan, *Supreme Court's Excessive Deference,* 575–76; *see also* Brennan, *Neither Victims Nor Executioners,* 6 ("[T]he fact that the Framers did not view the death penalty as 'cruel and unusual' cannot settle the matter. The resort to this position is nothing less than an abdication of the judicial responsibility of interpreting the Constitution.").

129. Universal Decl. of Hum. Rts. (Dec. 10, 1948), art. 3; Decl. of Independence (July 4, 1776), ¶ 2; Sharon M. Harris, Executing Race: Early American Women's Narratives of Race, Society, and the Law 66 (2005); Stinneford, 1749; Gilreath, 563; Wood, 179, 188; *see also* e-note (discussing *Weems v. United States* and the 1788 views of the "Federal Farmer" that "one supreme court" would resolve "all great questions in law").

130. Rhodes v. Chapman, 452 U.S. 337, 346 (1981); *Furman,* 408 U.S. at 271, 273, 279, 290–91 (Brennan, J., concurring); *Kennedy,* 128 S. Ct. at 2650; *see also* e-note (Supreme Court opinions emphasizing respect for "human dignity" and "humanity").

131. Immanuel Kant, Groundwork of the Metaphysics of Morals (H. J. Paton, trans., 1785), *in* The Moral Law (1948); Immanuel Kant, The Metaphysics of Morals 142–43 (Mary Gregor, trans. 1991) (1797); Immanuel Kant, The Philosophy of Law: An Exposition of the Fundamental Principles of Jurisprudence as the Science of Right 196, 198 (W. Hastie, trans. 1887) (1796–97); Immanuel Kant, The Metaphysical Elements of Justice 100–108 (John Ladd, trans. 1965) (1797); Ernest van den Haag, "The Death Penalty Once More," *in* Bedau, 445, 452; Edwin M. Orchard, Guide to the Law and Legal Literature of Germany, Library of Congress, 27 (1912) (referencing translations of *Grundlegung zur Metaphysik der Sitten* in 1798, 1836, and 1873); Hong Kong Baptist University, *Exhaustive Bibliography of English Translations of Kant,* visited Feb. 5, 2011, http://www.hkbu.edu.hk/~ppp/fne/bibl.html; *see also* e-note (discussing Kant's writings on capital punishment and their translation into English after the Constitution and the U.S. Bill of Rights were ratified).

132. Bessler, *Revisiting Beccaria's Vision,* 314–15 & nn.872–80; Kirchmeier, *Another*

Place Beyond Here, 89–90; Bright, *Discrimination, Death and Denial,* 439; *Furman,* 408 U.S. at 272–73 (Brennan, J., concurring).

133. Ward v. Commonwealth, 116 S.W. 786, 787 (Ky. App. 1909); Wells, 1805–11, 1813–47; Calabresi & Agudo, 102; Alison L. LaCroix, *To Gain the Whole World and Lose His Own Soul: Nineteenth-Century American Dueling as Public Law and Private Code,* 33 Hofstra L. Rev. 501, 502–69 (2004); Edward L. Rubin, *Trial by Battle, Trial by Argument,* 56 Ark. L. Rev. 261, 262–71 (2003); Richard O. Zerbe Jr., *Justice and the Evolution of the Common Law,* 3 J.L. Econ. & Pol'y 81, 109–10 (2006); Daryl J. Levinson, *Collective Sanctions,* 58 Stan. L. Rev. 345, 383–84 (2003); *see also* e-note (describing how dueling was once widely accepted in many parts of the world but was later opposed).

134. National Coalition to Abolish the Death Penalty, visited Feb. 7, 2011, http://www.ncadp.org/; Campaign to End the Death Penalty, visited Feb. 7, 2011, http://nodeathpenalty.org/; The Moratorium Campaign, visited Feb. 7, 2011, http://www.moratoriumcampaign.org/; Murder Victims' Families for Reconciliation, visited Feb. 7, 2011, http://www.mvfr.org/. The Moratorium Campaign was founded by Sister Helen Prejean, author of *Dead Man Walking.* Several international organizations, including Amnesty International, Hands Off Cain, and Human Rights Watch, are also actively pushing for the death penalty's abolition.

135. Oliver Wendell Holmes, *The Path of the Law,* 10 Harv. L. Rev. 457, 469, 474 (1897).

136. Graham v. Florida, 130 S. Ct. 2011, 2023–24 (2010).

137. Brennan, *Constitutional Adjudication and the Death Penalty,* 331; Preyer, 61–64, 67; *Solem,* 463 U.S. at 299–300 ("we compare the sentences imposed for commission of the same crime in other jurisdictions"; "[i]t appears that Helm was treated more severely than he would have been in any other State"); *see also* e-note (noting that courts have thus far declined to bar the execution of the mentally ill and have rejected challenges to the death penalty's constitutionality based on the risk of executing the innocent).

Conclusion (pages 339–348)

1. Benjamin Rush, Address to the People of the United States (June 3, 1786); BR to Richard Price (May 25, 1786); Butterfield, 372 n.1.

2. BR to JM (Feb. 27, 1790); *see also* e-note (discussing Benjamin Rush's letter to John Adams).

3. Lewis D. Eigen & Jonathan P. Siegel, Dictionary of Political Quotations 63 (1993); Lancaster, 37, 55; *see also* e-note (discussing George Bernard Shaw's views).

4. Decl. of Independence (July 4, 1776); Bessler, Death in the Dark, 211.

5. U.S. Const., amend. XIII (ratified Dec. 6, 1865), amend. XIV (ratified July 9, 1868), amend. XV (ratified Feb. 3, 1870), & amend. XIX (ratified Aug. 18, 1920); *see also* e-note (discussing John Adams's view of the Declaration of Independence).

6. Kennedy v. Louisiana, 128 S. Ct. at 2641, 2658–59 (2008); Capital Punishment and Implementation of the Safeguards Guaranteeing the Protection of the Rights of Those Facing the Death Penalty: Report of the Secretary-General, U.N. ESCOR, at 12, U.N. Doc. E/1995/78 (1995); Schabas, *War Crimes, Crimes Against Humanity and the Death Penalty,* 733 ("There can be no more dramatic evidence of the progress and evolution of human rights norms than in the fact that the first international war crimes tribunals, created in the aftermath of the Second World War, made widespread use of the

death penalty and that their successors, created by the Security Council in 1993 and 1994, prohibit it.").

7. Malcolm Gladwell, The Tipping Point: How Little Things Can Make a Big Difference 9 (2000); Glass v. Louisiana, 471 U.S. 1080, 1093–94 (1985) (Brennan, J., dissenting from denial of cert.).

8. Kaye, 50; Schiff, 64; Gottlieb, Theater of Death, 198–99.

9. Peter Irons & Stephanie Guitton, eds., May It Please the Court 234 (1993); Ronald Dworkin, *Bork's Jurisprudence,* 57 U. Chi. L. Rev. 657, 668–73 (1990) (reviewing Robert H. Bork, The Tempting of America: The Political Seduction of the Law (1990)); Lain, 12 ("The Constitution's text clearly assumes the death penalty's legitimacy, and the Framers did as well. At the time the Eighth Amendment was adopted, the death penalty was mandatory for most felonies and prevalent in every state. Executions were common; even twelve-year-old children were not immune."); Bessler, *Revisiting Beccaria's Vision,* 307–8 nn.834–35 (quoting Robert Bork's statement at oral argument that a barbaric practice would be "so out of step with modern morality and modern jurisprudence that the state cannot return to it," and citing other sources for the proposition that it would be unconstitutional to remove an offender's "limb"); *see also* e-note (noting that a number of U.S. Supreme Court Justices have already indicated that corporal punishments such as branding, ear-cropping, and the use of the pillory would no longer be constitutional).

10. John J. Ansbro, Martin Luther King, Jr.: Nonviolent Strategies and Tactics for Social Change (2007); Adam M. Clark, *An Investigation of Death Qualification as a Violation of the Rights of Jurors,* 24 Buff. Pub. Int. L.J. 1, 3, 38 (2006) (arguing that "the process of death-qualifying a jury is a serious violation of the rights of potential jurors" and "is obviously tilted against the viewpoints of death penalty abolitionists"); Katherine Corry Eastman, *The Progress of Our Maturing Society: An Analysis of State-Sanctioned Violence,* 39 Washburn L.J. 526, 533 (2000) (rejecting the view that state-sanctioned killing is "legitimate violence" because an execution "is not an immediate response to a threat of harm" but is, instead, "a contemplated act, thought out over a period of years"; "[t]hus, this act of killing appears to be an expression of illegitimate control rather than an act of self-preservation").

11. Foucault, 10; Andrew Ditchfield, *Challenging the Intrastate Disparities in the Application of Capital Punishment Statutes,* 95 Geo. L.J. 801, 803–4 (2007) ("geography, which is a powerful predictor of whether a capital crime will be charged as such, is the sort of arbitrary factor mentioned in *Furman v. Georgia*" that leads to wanton and freakish imposition of death sentences violative of the Eighth Amendment).

12. Victor Streib, Death Penalty in a Nutshell 300 (2008).

13. John Adams, Thoughts on Government (April 1776), *reprinted in* Rakove, 84; 2 M. Farrand, Records of the Federal Convention of 1787, at 429 (1911); Proceedings and Debates of the Virginia State Convention of 1829–1830, at 619 (1830); United States v. Hatter, 532 U.S. 557, 568–69 (2001).

14. Bright, *Counsel for the Poor,* 1835; Bright, *Death by Lottery,* 679; Lawrence C. Marshall, *The Innocence Revolution and the Death Penalty,* 1 Ohio St. J. Crim. L. 573, 575–81 (2004); Samuel R. Gross & Robert Mauro, Death and Discrimination: Racial Disparities in Capital Sentencing (1989); Anthony G. Amsterdam, *Race and the Death Penalty Before and After* McCleskey, 39 Colum. Hum. Rts. L. Rev. 34 (2007); Theodore M. Shaw, *Maintaining Hope in the Struggle Against the Constitutional Tolerance of Racial Discrimination,* 39 Colum. Hum. Rts. L. Rev. 59 (2007); David C. Baldus,

George Woodsworth, David Zuckerman, Neil Weiner, & Barbara Broffitt, *Racial Discrimination and the Death Penalty in the Post*-Furman *Era: An Empirical and Legal Overview, with Recent Findings from Philadelphia,* 83 Cornell L. Rev. 1638 (1998); Jeremy T. Monthy, *Internal Perspectives on Chinese Human Rights Reform: The Death Penalty in the PRC,* 33 Tex. Int'l L.J. 189, 190–95 (1998); Stephen B. Davis, *The Death Penalty and Legal Reform in the PRC,* 1 J. Chinese L. 303, 305–12 (1987); Qiang Fang & Roger des Forges, *Were Chinese Rulers Above the Law? Toward a Theory of the Rule of Law in China From Early Times to 1949 CE,* 44 Stan. J. Int'l L. 101, 116, 125, 129, 140 (2008); Liam P. Deeney, *The Abolition of the Death Penalty in International Law,* 23 Suffolk Transnat'l L. Rev. 803, 812–13 (2000); Poindexter v. Greenhow, 114 U.S. 270, 286 (1885) (noting that one "part of the constitution" must "be construed and applied in harmony with all the provisions of that instrument").

15. Benjamin Cardozo, *What Medicine Can Do for Law,* 5 Bull. N.Y. Acad. Med. 581, 581, 590 (July 1929); Allen E. Shoenberger, *The European View of American Justice,* 36 Loy. U. Chi. L.J. 603, 603 (2005); Peter Fitzpatrick, *Life, Death and the Law—and Why Capital Punishment Is Legally Insupportable,* 47 Clev. St. L. Rev. 483, 490–91 (1999); Gayle Young, CNN.com, *On Italy's Passionate Opposition to Death Penalty,* Feb. 24, 2000, visited Feb. 11, 2011, http://www.cnn.com/SPECIALS/views/y/2000/02/young.italydeath.feb24/; William A. Schabas, *International Law and Abolition of the Death Penalty,* 55 Wash. & Lee L. Rev. 797, 799 (1998) ("While it is still premature to declare the death penalty prohibited by customary international law, it is clear that we are somewhere in the midst of such a process, indeed considerably close to the goal"); Robert F. Drinan, S.J., *Will Religious Teachings and International Law End Capital Punishment?,* 29 St. Mary's L.J. 957, 968 (1998) ("The resistance by the United States to accede to world law is uniquely visible and dramatic in American's retention of the death penalty in defiance of the decisive change in all of the nations most respected by Americans").

16. Kirchmeier, *Another Place Beyond Here,* 3 ("Since 1981, the number of news stories about the death penalty has almost doubled every five years."). Stuart Banner's *The Death Penalty: An American History,* which chronicles the macabre practice of capital punishment, is just one of many books devoted to the subject to have come out in recent years. The sheer number of books and articles being written about the death penalty confirms just how controversial executions have become in American life. That histories of capital punishment are already being written strongly suggests that American executions may soon *be* history, relegated to nothing more than dark, barbaric chapters in world history, as they should be.

BIBLIOGRAPHY

Books

Akhil Reed Amar, America's Constitution: A Biography (New York: Random House, 2005).

Akhil Reed Amar, The Bill of Rights: Creation and Reconstruction (New Haven, CT: Yale University Press, 1998).

Joyce Appleby, ed., Thomas Paine, Common Sense and Other Writings (New York: Barnes & Noble Books, 2005).

Stuart Banner, The Death Penalty: An American History (Cambridge, MA: Harvard University Press, 2002).

Albert Barnes, An Inquiry into the Scriptural Views of Slavery (New York: John A. Gray, 1857).

Mary-Margaret H. Barr, Voltaire in America 1774–1880 (Baltimore: Johns Hopkins University Press, 1941).

David Barton, Benjamin Rush: Signer of the Declaration of Independence (Aledo, TX: WallBuilders, 1999).

Hugo Adam Bedau, The Death Penalty in America: Current Controversies (Oxford: Oxford University Press, 1997).

Richard Bellamy, ed., Cesare Beccaria, On Crimes and Punishments and Other Writings, trans. Richard Davies (Cambridge: Cambridge University Press, 1995).

Carol Berkin, A Brilliant Solution: Inventing the American Constitution (Orlando: Harcourt, 2002).

Larry Charles Berkson, The Concept of Cruel and Unusual Punishment (Lexington, MA: Lexington Books, 1975).

R. B. Bernstein, The Founding Fathers Reconsidered (Oxford: Oxford University Press, 2009).

John D. Bessler, Death in the Dark: Midnight Executions in America (Boston: Northeastern University Press, 1997).

John D. Bessler, Kiss of Death: America's Love Affair with the Death Penalty (Boston: Northeastern University Press, 2003).

John D. Bessler, Legacy of Violence: Lynch Mobs and Executions in Minnesota (Minneapolis: University of Minnesota Press, 2003).

William Blackstone, Commentaries on the Laws of England (Oxford: Clarendon Press, 1765–69).

Catherine Drinker Bowen, Miracle at Philadelphia: The Story of the Constitutional Convention May to September 1787 (Boston: Back Bay Books, 1966).

Julian P. Boyd, ed., The Papers of Thomas Jefferson (Princeton, NJ: Princeton University Press, 1950).

H. W. Brands, The First American: The Life and Times of Benjamin Franklin (New York: Anchor Books, 2002).

Irving Brant, The Bill of Rights: Its Origin and Meaning (Indianapolis: Bobbs-Merrill, 1965).

Jeff Broadwater, George Mason: Forgotten Founder (Chapel Hill: University of North Carolina Press, 2006).

L. H. Butterfield, ed., Benjamin Rush, Letters (Princeton, NJ: Princeton University Press, 1951).

Jane E. Calvert, Quaker Constitutionalism and the Political Thought of John Dickinson (Cambridge: Cambridge University Press, 2009).

Lilian Chenwi, Towards the Abolition of the Death Penalty in Africa: A Human Rights Perspective (Pretoria: Pretoria University Law Press, 2007).

Ron Chernow, Alexander Hamilton (New York: Penguin Press, 2004).

Ron Chernow, Washington: A Life (New York: Penguin Press, 2010).

Neil H. Cogan, ed., The Complete Bill of Rights: The Drafts, Debates, Sources, and Origins (Oxford: Oxford University Press, 1997).

Mark Colvin, Penitentiaries, Reformatories, and Chain Gangs: Social Theory and the History of Punishment in Nineteenth-Century America (New York: St. Martin's Press, 1997).

Patrick T. Conley and John P. Kaminski, eds., The Bill of Rights and the States: The Colonial and Revolutionary Origins of American Liberties (Madison, WI: Madison House Publishers, 1992).

Moncure Daniel Conway, ed., The Writings of Thomas Paine (New York: G. P. Putnam's Sons, 1894–96).

Randall Coyne and Lyn Entzeroth, Capital Punishment and the Judicial Process (Durham, NC: Carolina Academic Press, 3d ed., 2006).

James E. Crimmins, ed., The Death Penalty: Debates in Britain and the U.S., 1725–1868 (London: Continuum International, 2004).

Nathan Dane, Digest of American Law (Boston: Cummings, Hilliard & Co., 1823).

Ian Davidson, Voltaire in Exile (New York: Grove Press, 2004).

Markus D. Dubber and Lindsay Farmer, eds., Modern Histories of Crime and Punishment (Stanford, CA: Stanford University Press, 2007).

Susan Dunn, Jefferson's Second Revolution: The Election of 1800 and the Triumph of Republicanism (New York: Houghton Mifflin Co., 2004).

Ronald Dworkin, Life's Dominion: An Argument About Abortion, Euthanasia, and Individual Freedom (New York: Vintage Books, 1993).

Hans L. Eicholz, Harmonizing Sentiments: The Declaration of Independence and the Jeffersonian Idea of Self-Government (New York: Peter Lang, 2001).

Charles Elliott, Sinfulness of American Slavery (Cincinnati: L. Swormstedt & J. H. Power, 1850).

Joseph J. Ellis, American Sphinx: The Character of Thomas Jefferson (New York: Vintage Books, 1998).

Joseph J. Ellis, Founding Brothers: The Revolutionary Generation (New York: Vintage Books, 2000).

Garrett Epps, Democracy Reborn: The Fourteenth Amendment and the Fight for Equal Rights in Post–Civil War America (New York: Henry Holt and Co., 2006).

Paul Leicester Ford, ed., The Works of Thomas Jefferson (New York: G. P. Putnam's Sons, 1904–5).

Michel Foucault, Discipline and Punish: The Birth of the Prison, trans. Alan Sheridan (New York: Vintage Books, 1995).

Barry Friedman, The Will of the People: How Public Opinion Has Influenced the Supreme Court and Shaped the Meaning of the Constitution (New York: Farrar, Straus and Giroux, 2009).

Lawrence Friedman, Crime and Punishment in American History (New York: Basic Books, 1994).

Edith B. Gelles, Abigail and John: Portrait of a Marriage (New York: William Morrow, 2009).

Scott Douglas Gerber, The Declaration of Independence: Origins and Impact (Washington, D.C.: CQ Press, 2002).

Scott Douglas Gerber, To Secure These Rights: The Declaration of Independence and Constitutional Interpretation (New York: New York University Press, 1995).

William Goodell, The American Slave Code in Theory and Practice: Its Distinctive Features Shown by Its Statutes, Judicial Decisions, and Illustrative Facts (New York: American and Foreign Anti-Slavery Society, 3d ed., 1853).

Jerry Grundfest, George Clymer: Philadelphia Revolutionary, 1739–1813 (New York: Beaufort Books, 1982).

Kermit L. Hall and Mark David Hall, eds., Collected Works of James Wilson (Indianapolis: Liberty Fund Inc., 2009).

David Freeman Hawke, Benjamin Rush: Revolutionary Gadfly (New York: Irvington Publishers, 1971).

Michael Stephen Hindus, Prison and Plantation: Crime, Justice, and Authority in Massachusetts and South Carolina, 1767–1878 (Chapel Hill: University of North Carolina Press, 1980).

William Hogeland, The Whiskey Rebellion: George Washington, Alexander Hamilton, and the Frontier Rebels Who Challenged America's Newfound Sovereignty (New York: Simon & Schuster, 2006).

Lynn Hunt, Inventing Human Rights: A History (New York: W. W. Norton & Co., 2007).

Micheline R. Ishay, The History of Human Rights: From Ancient Times to the Globalization Era (Berkeley: University of California Press, 2004).

John P. Kaminski, George Clinton: Yeoman Politician of the New Republic (Madison, WI: Madison House Publishers, 1993).

Mark E. Kann, Punishment, Prisons, and Patriarchy: Liberty and Power in the Early American Republic (New York: New York University Press, 2005).

Bill Kauffman, Forgotten Founder, Drunken Prophet: The Life of Luther Martin (Wilmington, DE: Intercollegiate Studies Institute, 2008).

Harvey J. Kaye, Thomas Paine: Firebrand of the Revolution (Oxford: Oxford University Press, 2000).

Harvey J. Kaye, Thomas Paine and the Promise of America (New York: Hill and Wang, 2005).

John Keane, Tom Paine: A Political Life (New York: Grove Press, 2003).

Ralph Ketcham, James Madison: A Biography (Charlottesville: University Press of Virginia, 1990).

Jon Kukla, ed., The Bill of Rights: A Lively Heritage (Richmond: Library of Virginia, 1987).

Richard Labunski, James Madison and the Struggle for the Bill of Rights (Oxford: Oxford University Press, 2006).

Bruce Lancaster, The American Revolution (New York: First Mariner Books, 2001).

Edward J. Larson, A Magnificent Catastrophe: The Tumultuous Election of 1800, America's First Presidential Campaign (New York: Free Press, 2007).

John Laurence, A History of Capital Punishment (New York: The Citadel Press, 1960).

Leonard W. Levy, Origins of the Bill of Rights (New Haven, CT: Yale University Press, 1999).

Philip English Mackey, ed., Voices Against Death: American Opposition to Capital Punishment, 1787–1975 (New York: Burt Franklin, 1976).

Marcello Maestro, Cesare Beccaria and the Origins of Penal Reform (Philadelphia: Temple University Press, 1973).

Pauline Maier, American Scripture: Making the Declaration of Independence (New York: Vintage Books, 1998).

Pauline Maier, Ratification: The People Debate the Constitution, 1787–1788 (New York: Simon & Schuster, 2010).

Pauline Maier, ed., The Declaration of Independence and the Constitution of the United States (New York: Bantam Dell, 1998).

Louis P. Masur, Rites of Execution: Capital Punishment and the Transformation of American Culture, 1776–1865 (Oxford: Oxford University Press, 1989).

Henry Mayer, A Son of Thunder: Patrick Henry and the American Republic (New York: Grove Press, 2001).

David McCullough, John Adams (New York: Simon & Schuster, 2001).

J. Kent McGaughy, Richard Henry Lee of Virginia: A Portrait of an American Revolutionary (Lanham, MD: Rowman & Littlefield Publishers, 2003).

James Mease, The Picture of Philadelphia (Philadelphia: B. & T. Kite, 1811).

James J. Megivern, The Death Penalty: An Historical and Theological Survey (Mahwah, NJ: Paulist Press, 1997).

Michael Meltsner, Cruel and Unusual: The Supreme Court and Capital Punishment (New York: Random House, 1973).

Jeremy Mercer, When the Guillotine Fell: The Bloody Beginning and Horrifying End to France's River of Blood, 1791–1977 (New York: St. Martin's Press, 2008).

Melanie Randolph Miller, Envoy to the Terror: Gouverneur Morris and the French Revolution (Dulles, VA: Potomac Books, 2005).

Charles-Louis de Secondat Montesquieu, The Spirit of the Laws, trans. Anne M. Cohler, Basia Carolyn Miller, and Harold Samuel Stone (Cambridge: Cambridge University Press, 1989).

Charles J. Ogletree Jr. and Austin Sarat, The Road to Abolition? The Future of Capital Punishment in the United States (New York: New York University Press, 2009).

Peter Okun, Crime and the Nation: Prison Reform and Popular Fiction in Philadelphia, 1786–1800 (New York: Routledge, 2002).

Henry Paolucci, trans., Cesare Beccaria, On Crimes and Punishments (Indianapolis: Bobbs-Merrill, 1963).

Steve Pincus, 1688: The First Modern Revolution (New Haven, CT: Yale University Press, 2009).

John H. Powell, Richard Rush, Republican Diplomat 1780–1859 (Philadelphia: University of Pennsylvania Press, 1942).

Jack N. Rakove, ed., Founding America: Documents from the Revolution to the Bill of Rights (New York: Barnes & Noble Books, 2006).

Willard Sterne Randall, Thomas Jefferson: A Life (New York: Henry Holt & Co., 1994).

Charles Rappleye, Robert Morris: Financier of the American Revolution (New York: Simon & Schuster, 2010).

Ben Ray Redman, ed., The Portable Voltaire (New York: Penguin Books, 1977).

Benjamin Rush, Medical Inquiries and Observations upon the Diseases of the Mind (Philadelphia: Grigg and Elliot, 5th ed., 1835).

Robert Allen Rutland, The Birth of the Bill of Rights, 1776–1791 (Chapel Hill: University of North Carolina Press, 1955).

William A. Schabas, The Abolition of the Death Penalty in International Law (Cambridge: Cambridge University Press, 3d ed., 2002).

William A. Schabas, The Death Penalty as Cruel Treatment and Torture: Capital Punishment Challenged in the World's Courts (Boston: Northeastern University Press, 1996).

Stacy Schiff, A Great Improvisation: Franklin, France, and the Birth of America (New York: Henry Holt and Co., 2005).

Bernard Schwartz, ed., The Roots of the Bill of Rights: An Illustrated Sourcebook of American Freedom (New York: Chelsea House Publishers, 1980).

George Ryley Scott, The History of Capital Punishment (London: Torchstream Books, 1950).

Cliff Sloan and David McKean, The Great Decision: Jefferson, Adams, Marshall, and the Battle for the Supreme Court (New York: Public Affairs Books, 2009).

Walter Stahr, John Jay: Founding Father (New York: Hambledon, 2005).

Eliza Steelwater, The Hangman's Knot: Lynching, Legal Execution, and America's Struggle with the Death Penalty (Boulder, CO: Westview Press, 2003).

Bernard C. Steiner, Life and Correspondence of James McHenry: Secretary of War Under Washington and Adams (Cleveland: Burrows Brothers Co., 1907).

Charles J. Stille, The Life and Times of John Dickinson, 1732–1808 (Charleston, S.C.: Nabu Press, 2010).

Ira Stoll, Samuel Adams: A Life (New York: Free Press, 2008).

Herbert J. Storing, ed., The Complete Anti-Federalist (Chicago: University of Chicago Press, 1981).

Joseph Story, Commentaries on the Constitution of the United States, ed. Melville M. Bigelow (Buffalo, N.Y.: William S. Hein & Co., 5th ed., 1994).

David A. Strauss, The Living Constitution (Oxford: Oxford University Press, 2010).

George M. Stroud, Stroud's Slave Laws: A Sketch of the Laws Relating to Slavery in the Several States of the United States of America (Baltimore: Inprint Editions, 2005) (2d ed., 1856).

E. Thomas Sullivan and Richard S. Frase, Proportionality Principles in American Law: Controlling Excessive Government Actions (Oxford: Oxford University Press, 2009).

Harold C. Syrett, ed., The Papers of Alexander Hamilton (New York: Columbia University Press, 1964.–87).

Aaron Thomas, ed., Cesare Beccaria, On Crimes and Punishments and Other Writings, trans. Aaron Thomas and Jeremy Parzen (Toronto: University of Toronto Press, 2008).

Alexis de Tocqueville, Democracy in America, trans. Henry Reeve (Clark, NJ: The Lawbook Exchange, Ltd., 2003).

Harlow Giles Unger, John Hancock: Merchant King and American Patriot (Edison, NJ: Castle Books, 2005).

Harlow Giles Unger, The Last Founding Father: James Monroe and a Nation's Call to Greatness (Philadelphia: Da Capo Press, 2009).

Harlow Giles Unger, Lion of Liberty: Patrick Henry and the Call to a New Nation (Philadelphia: Da Capo Press, 2010).

David J. Vaughan, Give Me Liberty: The Uncompromising Statesmanship of Patrick Henry (Nashville, TN: Cumberland House Publishing, 2002).

Helen E. Veit, Kenneth R. Bowling, and Charlene Bangs Bickford, eds., Creating the Bill of Rights: The Documentary Record from the First Federal Congress (Baltimore: Johns Hopkins University Press, 1991).

Bryan Vila and Cynthia Morris, eds., Capital Punishment in the United States: A Documentary History (Westport, CT: Greenwood Press, 1997).

Steven Wilf, Law's Imagined Republic: Popular Politics and Criminal Justice in Revolutionary America (Cambridge: Cambridge University Press, 2010).

Juan Williams, Thurgood Marshall: American Revolutionary (New York: Three Rivers Press, 1998).

Garry Wills, Inventing America: Jefferson's Declaration of Independence (New York: Mariner Books, 2002).

Gordon S. Wood, Revolutionary Characters: What Made the Founders Different (New York: Penguin Books, 2006).

Franklin E. Zimring, The Contradictions of American Capital Punishment (Oxford: Oxford University Press, 2004).

Franklin E. Zimring and Gordon Hawkins, Capital Punishment and the American Agenda (Cambridge: Cambridge University Press, 1986).

Articles

Dwight Aarons, *Can Inordinate Delay Between a Death Sentence and Execution Constitute Cruel and Unusual Punishment?*, 29 Seton Hall L. Rev. 147 (1998).

Thomas Adcock, *A History of the Death Penalty in America,* 36 Cornell L. Forum 6 (Spring 2010).

Robert Aitken, *James Wilson: A Lost American Founder,* 29 Litigation 61 (Summer 2003).

Robert Aitken and Marilyn Aitken, *The Life and Death of George Wythe: "I am Murdered,"* 31 Litigation 53 (Summer 2005).

Akhil Reed Amar, *Intratextualism,* 112 Harv. L. Rev. 747 (1999).

Vidisha Barua, *"Synthetic Sanity": A Way Around the Eighth Amendment?,* 44 Crim. L. Bulletin 4 (2008).

Hugo Adam Bedau, *Interpreting the Eighth Amendment: Principled vs. Populist Strategies,* 13 T.M. Cooley L. Rev. 789 (1996).

John D. Bessler, *America's Death Penalty: Just Another Form of Violence,* 82 Phi Kappa Phi Forum 13 (Winter 2002).

John D. Bessler, *The Public Interest and the Unconstitutionality of Private Prosecutors,* 47 Ark. L. Rev. 511 (1994).

John D. Bessler, *Revisiting Beccaria's Vision: The Enlightenment, America's Death Penalty, and the Abolition Movement,* 4 Nw. J.L. & Soc. Pol'y 195 (2009).

John D. Bessler, *Televised Executions and the Constitution: Recognizing a First Amendment Right of Access to State Executions,* 45 Fed. Comm. L.J. 355 (1993).

Alan I. Bigel, *Justices William J. Brennan, Jr. and Thurgood Marshall on Capital*

Punishment: Its Constitutionality, Morality, Deterrent Effect, and Interpretation by the Court, 8 Notre Dame J.L. Ethics & Pub. Pol'y 11 (1994).

Guyora Binder, *The Origins of American Felony Murder Rules,* 57 Stan. L. Rev. 59 (2004).

Daniel D. Blinka, *Jefferson and Juries: The Problem of Law, Reason, and Politics in the New Republic,* 47 Am. J. Legal Hist. 35 (2005).

John H. Blume, *Killing the Willing: "Volunteers," Suicide and Competency,* 103 Mich. L. Rev. 939 (2005).

Mark Bowden, *The Dark Art of Interrogation,* Atlantic Monthly 51 (Oct. 2003).

James J. Brennan, *The Supreme Court's Excessive Deference to Legislative Bodies Under Eighth Amendment Sentencing Review,* 94 J. Crim. L. & Criminology 551 (2004).

Terry Brennan, *Natural Rights and the Constitution: The Original "Original Intent,"* 15 Harv. J.L. & Pub. Pol'y 965 (1992).

William J. Brennan Jr., *The Constitution of the United States: Contemporary Ratification,* 27 S. Tex. L. Rev. 433 (1986).

William J. Brennan Jr., *Constitutional Adjudication and the Death Penalty: A View from the Court,* 100 Harv. L. Rev. 313 (1986).

William J. Brennan Jr., *Neither Victims Nor Executioners,* 8 Notre Dame J.L. Ethics & Pub. Pol'y 1 (1994).

Stephen Bright, *Counsel for the Poor: The Death Sentence Not for the Worst Crime but for the Worst Lawyer,* 103 Yale L.J. 1835 (1994).

Stephen Bright, *Death by Lottery—Procedural Bar of Constitutional Claims in Capital Cases Due to Inadequate Representation of Indigent Defendants,* 92 W. Va. L. Rev. 679 (1990).

Stephen Bright, *The Death Penalty and the Society We Want,* 6 Pierce L. Rev. 369 (2008).

Stephen Bright, *Discrimination, Death and Denial: The Tolerance of Racial Discrimination in Infliction of the Death Penalty,* 35 Santa Clara L. Rev. 433 (1995).

Stephen B. Bright and Patrick J. Keenan, *Judges and the Politics of Death: Deciding Between the Bill of Rights and the Next Election in Capital Cases,* 73 Boston Univ. L. Rev. 759 (1995).

Steven G. Calabresi and Sarah E. Agudo, *Individual Rights Under State Constitutions When the Fourteenth Amendment Was Ratified in 1868: What Rights Are Deeply Rooted in American History and Tradition?,* 87 Tex. L. Rev. 8 (2008).

Laurence Claus, *The Antidiscrimination Eighth Amendment,* 28 Harv. J.L. & Pub. Pol'y 119 (2004).

Laurence Claus, *Methodology, Proportionality, Equality: Which Moral Question Does the Eighth Amendment Pose?,* 31 Harv. J.L. & Pub. Pol'y 35 (2008).

Jill M. Cochran, *Courting Death: 30 Years Since* Furman, *Is the Death Penalty Any Less Discriminatory? Looking at the Problem of Jury Discretion in Capital Sentencing,* 38 Val. U. L. Rev. 1399 (2004).

Charles H. Cosgrove, *The Declaration of Independence in Constitutional Interpretation: A Selective History and Analysis,* 32 U. Rich. L. Rev. 107 (1998).

Robert J. Cottrol, *Finality with Ambivalence: The American Death Penalty's Uneasy History,* 56 Stan. L. Rev. 1641 (2004).

Louis Crompton, *Homosexuals and the Death Penalty in Colonial America,* 1 J. of Homosexuality 277 (1976).

David Brion Davis, *The Movement to Abolish Capital Punishment in America, 1787–1861,* 63 Am. Hist. Rev. 23 (Oct. 1957).

Simon Devereaux, *Imposing the Royal Pardon: Execution, Transportation, and Convict Resistance in London, 1789,* 25 Law. & Hist. Rev. 101 (2007).

Davison M. Douglas, *God and the Executioner: The Influence of Western Religion on the Death Penalty,* 9 Wm. & Mary Bill Rts. J. 137 (2000).

Denis P. Duffey, *The Northwest Ordinance as a Constitutional Document,* 95 Colum. L. Rev. 929 (1995).

Ronald Dworkin, *Bork's Jurisprudence,* 57 U. Chi. L. Rev. 657 (1990).

Jeffrey Fagan, Franklin E. Zimring, and Amanda Geller, *Capital Punishment and Capital Murder: Market Share and the Deterrent Effects of the Death Penalty,* 84 Tex. L. Rev. 1803 (2006).

Louis Filler, *Movements to Abolish the Death Penalty in the United States,* 284 Annals Am. Acad. Pol. & Soc. Sci. 124 (1952).

George Fisher, *The Birth of the Prison Retold,* 104 Yale L.J. 1235 (1995).

Shannon D. Gilreath, *Cruel and Unusual Punishment and the Eighth Amendment as a Mandate for Human Dignity: Another Look at Original Intent,* 25 T. Jefferson L. Rev. 559 (2003).

Michael K. Gottlieb, *Executions and Torture: The Consequences of Overriding Professional Ethics,* 6 Yale J. Health Pol'y, L. & Ethics 351 (2006).

Anthony Granucci, *"Nor Cruel and Unusual Punishments Inflicted": The Original Meaning,* 57 Calif. L. Rev. 839 (1969).

Melvin Gutterman, *"Failure to Communicate": The Reel Prison Experience,* 55 SMU L. Rev. 1515 (2002).

Daniel W. Halston, *The Meaning of the Massachusetts 'Open Courts' Clause and Its Relevance to the Current Court Crisis,* 88 Mass. L. Rev. 122 (2004).

Jessica Powley Hayden, *The Ties that Bind: The Constitution, Structural Restraints, and Government Action Overseas,* 96 Geo. L.J. 237 (2007).

Adam J. Hirsch, *From Early Pillory to Penitentiary: The Rise of Criminal Incarceration in Early Massachusetts,* 80 Mich. L. Rev. 1179 (1982).

Wythe Holt, *George Wythe: Early Modern Judge,* 58 Ala. L. Rev. 1009 (2007).

Scott W. Howe, *Slavery as Punishment: Original Public Meaning, Cruel and Unusual Punishment, and the Neglected Clause in the Thirteenth Amendment,* 51 Ariz. L. Rev. 983 (2009).

Stephen H. Jupiter, *Constitution Notwithstanding: The Political Illegitimacy of the Death Penalty in American Democracy,* 23 Fordham Urb. L.J. 437 (1996).

Joshua E. Kastenberg, *An Enlightened Addition to the Original Meaning: Voltaire and the Eighth Amendment's Prohibition Against Cruel and Unusual Punishment,* 5 Temp. Pol. & Civ. Rts. L. Rev. 49 (1995).

Nancy J. King, *The Origins of Felony Jury Sentencing in the United States,* 78 Chi.-Kent L. Rev. 937 (2003).

Rachel King, *No Due Process: How the Death Penalty Violates the Constitutional Rights of the Family Members of Death Row Prisoners,* 16 Pub. Int. L.J. 195 (2007).

Jeffrey L. Kirchmeier, *Another Place Beyond Here: The Death Penalty Moratorium Movement in the United States,* 73 U. Colo. L. Rev. 1 (2002).

Jeffrey L. Kirchmeier, *Drinks, Drugs and Drowsiness: The Constitutional Right to Effective Assistance of Counsel and the* Strickland *Prejudice Requirement,* 75 Neb. L. Rev. 425 (1996).

Harold Hongju Koh, *Paying "Decent Respect" to World Opinion on the Death Penalty*, 35 U.C. Davis L. Rev. 1085 (2002).

Herbert M. Kritzer, *Law Is the Mere Continuation of Politics by Different Means: American Judicial Selection in the Twenty-First Century*, 56 DePaul L. Rev. 423 (2007).

Corinna Barrett Lain, Furman *Fundamentals*, 82 Wash. L. Rev. 1 (2007).

Carlton F. W. Larson, *The Revolutionary American Jury: A Case Study of the 1778-1779 Philadelphia Treason Trials*, 61 SMU L. Rev. 1441 (2008).

Jill Lepore, *Rap Sheet: Why Is American History So Murderous?*, The New Yorker, Nov. 9, 2009.

Nicholas Levi, *Veil of Secrecy: Public Executions, Limitations on Reporting Capital Punishment, and the Content-Based Nature of Private Execution Laws*, 55 Fed. Comm. L.J. 131 (2002).

Matthew Lippman, *The Development and Drafting of the United Nations Convention Against Torture and Other Cruel, Inhuman or Degrading Treatment or Punishment*, 17 B.C. Int'l & Comp. L. Rev. 275 (1994).

Rory K. Little, *The Federal Death Penalty: History and Some Thoughts About the Department of Justice's Role*, 26 Fordham Urb. L.J. 347 (1999).

John R. Maass, *"From Principles of Humanity and Virtue": Moderation and the Revolutionary Settlement in North Carolina*, 2 J. Backcountry Studies 1 (2007).

Michael Madow, *Forbidden Spectacle: Executions, the Public and the Press in Nineteenth Century New York*, 43 Buff. L. Rev. 461 (1995).

Pauline Maier, *The Strange History of "All Men Are Created Equal,"* 56 Wash. & Lee L. Rev. 873 (1999).

Michael J. Zydney Mannheimer, *When the Federal Death Penalty Is "Cruel and Unusual,"* 74 U. Cin. L. Rev. 819 (2006).

Calvin R. Massey, *The Excessive Fines Clause and Punitive Damages: Some Lessons from History*, 40 Vand. L. Rev. 1233 (1987).

James J. Megivern, *Our National Shame: The Death Penalty and the Disuse of Clemency*, 28 Cap. U. L. Rev. 595 (2000).

Matthew W. Meskell, *The History of Prisons in the United States from 1777 to 1877*, 51 Stan. L. Rev. 839 (1999).

Bernadette Meyler, *Towards a Common Law Originalism*, 59 Stan. L. Rev. 551 (2006).

Frederick C. Millett, *Will the United States Follow England (and the Rest of the World) in Abandoning Capital Punishment?* 6 Pierce L. Rev. 547 (2008).

Caleb Nelson, *Originalism and Interpretive Conventions*, 70 U. Chi. L. Rev. 519 (2003).

Stephen T. Parr, *Symmetric Proportionality: A New Perspective on the Cruel and Unusual Punishment Clause*, 68 Tenn. L. Rev. 42 (2000).

Matthew A. Pauley, *The Jurisprudence of Crime and Punishment from Plato to Hegel*, 39 Am. J. Juris. 97 (1994).

Ray S. Pierce, *Now You Can't Do That: Disproportionate Prison Sentences as Cruel and Unusual Punishment*, 24 U. Ark. Little Rock L. Rev. 775 (2002).

Albert Post, *Early Efforts to Abolish Capital Punishment in Pennsylvania*, 68 Pa. Mag. Hist. & Biography 38 (1944).

Kathryn Preyer, *Crime, the Criminal Law and Reform in Post-Revolutionary Virginia*, 1 Law & Hist. Rev. 53 (1983).

William H. Rehnquist, *The Notion of a Living Constitution*, 29 Harv. J.L. & Pub. Pol'y 401 (2006).

Jacob Reynolds, *The Rule of Law and the Origins of the Bill of Attainder Clause,* 18 St. Thomas L. Rev. 177 (2005).

Sara A. Rodriguez, *The Impotence of Being Earnest: Status of the United Nations Standard Minimum Rules for the Treatment of Prisoners in Europe and the United States,* 33 New Eng. J. on Crim. & Civ. Confinement 61 (2007).

Celia Rumann, *Tortured History: Finding Our Way Back to the Lost Origins of the Eighth Amendment,* 31 Pepp. L. Rev. 661 (2004).

Meghan J. Ryan, *Does the Eighth Amendment Punishments Clause Prohibit Only Punishments that Are Both Cruel and Unusual?,* 87 Wash. U. L. Rev. 567 (2010).

Antonin Scalia, *Originalism: The Lesser Evil,* 57 U. Cin. L. Rev. 849 (1989).

William A. Schabas, *War Crimes, Crimes Against Humanity and the Death Penalty,* 60 Alb. L. Rev. 733 (1997).

Deborah A. Schwartz and Jay Wishingrad, *The Eighth Amendment, Beccaria, and the Enlightenment: An Historical Justification for the* Weems v. United States *Excessive Punishment Doctrine,* 24 Buff. L. Rev. 783 (1975).

Douglas L. Simon, *Making Sense of Cruel and Unusual Punishment: A New Approach to Reconciling Military and Civilian Eighth Amendment Law,* 184 Mil. L. Rev. 66 (2005).

Michael I. Spak, *It's Time to Put the Military's Death Penalty to Sleep,* 49 Clev. St. L. Rev. 41 (2001).

Tom Stacy, *Cleaning Up the Eighth Amendment Mess,* 14 Wm. & Mary Bill Rts. J. 475 (2005).

Clive A. Stafford Smith and Remy Voisin Starns, *Folly by Fiat: Pretending that Death Row Inmates Can Represent Themselves in State Capital Post-Conviction Proceedings,* 45 Loy. L. Rev. 55 (1999).

John F. Stinneford, *The Original Meaning of "Unusual": The Eighth Amendment as a Bar to Cruel Innovation,* 102 Nw. U. L. Rev. 1739 (2008).

Kara Thompson, *The ABA's Resolution Calling for a Moratorium on Executions: What Jurisdictions Can Do to Ensure that the Death Penalty Is Imposed Responsibly,* 40 Ariz. L. Rev. 1515 (1998).

Eric A. Tirschwell and Theodore Hertzberg, *Politics and Prosecution: A Historical Perspective on Shifting Federal Standards for Pursuing the Death Penalty in Non-Death Penalty States,* 12 U. Pa. J. Const. L. 57 (2009).

Jenny Bourne Wahl, *Legal Constraints on Slave Masters: The Problem of Social Cost,* 41 Am. J. Legal Hist. 1 (1997).

Eugene G. Wanger, *Historical Reflections on Michigan's Abolition of the Death Penalty,* 13 T.M. Cooley L. Rev. 755 (1996).

C. A. Harwell Wells, *The End of the Affair? Anti-Dueling Laws and Social Norms in Antebellum America,* 54 Vand. L. Rev. 1805 (2001).

Arthur E. Wilmarth Jr., *Elusive Foundation: John Marshall, James Wilson, and the Problem of Reconciling Popular Sovereignty and Natural Law Jurisprudence in the New Federal Republic,* 72 Geo. Wash. L. Rev. 113 (2003).

Essays, Pamphlets, and Theses

William Bradford, An Enquiry How Far the Punishment of Death Is Necessary in Pennsylvania (1793) ["Bradford, *Enquiry*"].

Gabriele Gottlieb, Theater of Death: Capital Punishment in Early America, 1750–1800 (PhD thesis, University of Pittsburgh, 2005).

Benjamin Rush, Considerations on the Injustice and Impolicy of Punishing Murder by Death (1792) ["Rush, *Considerations*"].

Benjamin Rush, An Enquiry into the Effects of Public Punishments upon Criminals, and Upon Society (1787) ["Rush, *Enquiry*"].

Benjamin Rush, Essays, Literary, Moral and Philosophical (1806) ["Rush, *Essays*"].

INDEX

abolition: antigallows societies, 273–75; in foreign countries, 9, 43–46, 64, 247, 278, 287, 291, 346; incremental, 26; movement, 6, 9, 31, 34, 64, 66, 69, 79, 81–82, 149, 192, 258, 269, 273–76, 277–78, 284–91, 318, 335–36, 340, 342–48; organizations, 284, 286; in peacetime, 64, 290; in U.S., 6, 222, 273–75, 277–78, 324, 347; in wartime, 290; worldwide, 64, 286–91. *See also specific countries, organizations, and states*

Academy of Fists, 34

accomplice liability, 199, 239

Açoka (king), 45

Adams, Abigail, 61–62, 111, 114

Adams, Betsy, 99

Adams, John, 51, 133–34, 139; on American Revolution, 333; and Beccaria, 50, 93; and Benjamin Rush, 53, 57, 66, 73–74, 85, 91–93, 102, 180; on death penalty, 9, 56, 62–63, 262; and Declaration of Independence, 103; as diplomat, 113; on duels, 138; on French Revolution, 111–12; on independent judiciary, 179, 319–20, 346; on juries, 117; and Massachusetts constitution, 177, 179–80; on natural law, 121, 179; pardons of, 59–60, 136–37; on punishment of parricides, 267; on rebellion, 114; on revenge, 61–62; on tyranny, 50; use of "cruel"/"cruelty," 60–61, 120–21, 184, 333; and Voltaire, 41

Adams, John Quincy, 50, 63–64, 92, 273–74

Adams, Samuel, 99, 105, 168, 179

Adams, Thomas, 50

adultery, as capital crime, 80, 89, 173, 265–67, 270, 287

Advocates for Human Rights, 235

Afghanistan, executions in, 64, 287

Africa, 131, 198; executions in, 64, 286–88; transportation to, 144. *See also* Barbary states; North Africa

African Americans: on death row, 224; exclusion from juries, 224; execution of, 3, 156, 229, 284; exoneration of, 236; lynching of, 3, 335; right to vote, 204, 342; treatment of, 275, 304, 307. *See also* racial discrimination; slave trade; slavery; slaves

African Commission on Human and Peoples' Rights, 287

Age of Reason, The, 108

"aggravating" factors/circumstances, 5, 133, 201–2, 222, 256, 283, 326

aiding runaway slaves, as capital crime, 270

Alabama, 283, 290–91; abolition efforts in, 274; death penalty law, 325; death row inmates, 224, 235; executions in, 223; exoneration in, 233; lawyers disciplined in, 233; treatment of slaves in, 217, 313

Alaska, abolition in, 278

Albania, abolition in, 64

alcohol (ab)use, 248–49, 251–53

Aldgate, 175

Aldridge, John, 188

Alien and Sedition Acts, 59

Amandagamani (king), 45

Amar, Akhil, 94–95, 118, 176, 308

amercements, 171, 214

American Bar Association, 236, 261, 284–85

American Civil Liberties Union, 261, 336

American Convention on Human Rights, 289–90

American Declaration of the Rights and Duties of Man, 289–90

American Medical Association, 258–59
American Museum, 74, 77
American Nurses Association, 258
American Philosophical Society, 66
American Psychiatric Association, 258, 261
American Psychological Association, 258, 261
American Public Health Association, 258
American Revolution, 33, 61, 79, 91, 97–100, 108, 110, 139, 165, 269, 276, 305, 320, 333, 337, 339–41
American Society of Anesthesiologists, 259
Amistad, The, 274
Amnesty International, 284, 287, 336
Amsterdam, Anthony, 1, 3–4
Amsterdam, mob in, 91
anarchy: fear/risk of, 114, 269, 341; state/times of, 38, 139
Anderson, Andrew, 60
André, John, 135–36
Angola, abolition in, 64
animal(s): euthanasia, 238, 245; prosecution/execution of, 267; use in executions, 211, 265
Annan, Kofi, 288
Annan, Robert, 77
Anne (queen), 88, 301
antidueling laws/movement, 208, 335–36
Anti-Federalists, 162, 176, 186, 299, 319, 322
antigallows movement. *See* abolition
antilynching laws/movement, 2, 276, 289, 335
antipsychotic medications, 251, 254–55
antislavery: literature, distribution of, 267; sentiment/societies, 2, 81, 270, 274
Antiterrorism and Effective Death Penalty Act of 1996, 233, 250
Antoinette, Marie (queen), 62, 147
apostasy, as capital crime, 286
appeal(s), 228, 310; abandonment of, 225; direct, 234–35. *See also* errors; habeas corpus
Arave v. Creech, 202
arbitrariness: and Bill of Rights, 316; and

due process, 205, 207, 215–16, 293, 309–10; and Eighth Amendment, 215; and English law, 94, 173, 293, 319; and executions, 5, 283, 285, 308, 310, 326, 337, 344–46; James Madison on, 261; judicial disdain of, 55, 216, 283, 285, 310, 323. *See also* death sentences; Due Process Clause(s); execution(s)
Arizona: death row inmates, 224–25
Arkansas: corporal punishments in, 242; death row inmates, 224; murder in, 254
Arnold, Benedict, 127, 135–36, 146
Arouet, François-Marie. *See* Voltaire
Arsenault, Henry, 227
arson: abolition for, 88; as capital crime, 2, 88, 90, 270
Art of Virtue, The, 126
Articles of Confederation, 98, 113, 118, 167
Articles of War, 56, 126, 130–31, 136, 146
Asgill, Charles, 137–38
Asia, 198, 267; executions in, 265, 286
asphyxiation, risk of, 243
assault, 193; as capital crime, 266; as "cruel or unusual punishment," 315; as Eighth Amendment violation, 219–20, 243, 263, 297
Athens, Greece, 286
Atkins v. Virginia, 7, 16–19, 25–26, 195, 199, 239–40, 250, 316
attainder: concept of, 173; references in Constitution, 164, 295, 312. *See also* bills of attainder; Bill of Attainder Clause(s)
attempted murder, as capital crime, 270
attempted rape, as capital crime, 270
attorneys. *See* counsel, defense; prosecutors
Auburn Prison, 82
Auden, W. H., 247
Austin v. United States, 194–95
Australia, refusal to extradite, 290
Austria(n): abolition in, 46; penal laws/reform, 33, 38, 55; rulers, 33–34, 38–39
Azerbaijan, abolition in, 64

Babcock v. White, 243
Babylon, 265. *See also* Code of Hammurabi

Bache, Richard, 105

Bacon, Francis, 33

bail: and Constitution, 193–95, 214; excessive, 94–95, 155, 162–63, 166–69, 171, 174, 176, 178–80, 184, 186, 195, 213, 215, 376; and Judiciary Act of 1789, 121–22; limitations on, 56, 118, 121, 179; and Northwest Ordinance, 118; set by judges, 195. *See also* Bail Clause

Bail Clause, 194

Bailey, William, 247

Baldus, David, 284

Baldus study, 6, 284

Baltimore, MD, 120

banishment, 7–8, 42, 172, 267, 293. *See also* exile; transportation

Bankruptcy Clause, 115

bankruptcy, punishment of, 115

Banner, Stuart, 272, 404

Baratarian pirates, 59

Barbary states, 115, 125

Barker v. People, 208

Barnes, Albert, 313

Barr, Mary-Margaret, 47

Barron v. Baltimore, 205

Bastille prison, 107, 109

Batson v. Kentucky, 207

Bavaria, 45

Bayard, Isadore, 212

Baze v. Rees, 6, 201, 223, 237, 242, 244–45, 336

Beale, Robert, 171–72

bearing false witness, as capital crime, 173

Beasley, Dorothy, 4

Beasley, Jere, 283

beating(s): as "cruel"/"unusual," 181, 219–20, 243, 263, 297, 313, 315; as "not unusual," 315; of prisoners, 44, 220–21; of slaves, 217, 314; as torture, 268

Beaumont, Gustave de, 275

Beccaria, Cesare, 8–9, 64, 68, 75, 78, 80, 88, 347–48; background of, 31, 34–35, 43, 46; censorship/criticism of, 35, 39; on cruelty, 55–56; death of, 79; on death penalty, 31–32, 34–39, 42–43, 157, 262, 291, 340, 344; on deterrence, 34, 36–39, 43, 55; on executioners, 262; on infamy, 32–33, 47; influence of, 46–57, 63, 66, 69, 82, 93, 131, 141–42, 145, 156, 190–91, 269, 272–73, 275, 283, 319; on jury trials, 35; on life sentences, 43; on natural law, 31; nephew of, 89; on pardons, 77–78, 268; on proportionality, 31, 37, 39; on rebellion, 71; on torture, 32–36, 42, 56, 157, 291; and U.S. Supreme Court, 196; and Voltaire, 41–43, 48; writings of, 35, 43–46, 55–56, 262. See also *On Crimes and Punishments*

Becket, Thomas, 268

Bedau, Hugo Adam, 278

beheading, 41, 44–46, 62, 172, 174, 176, 262. *See also* guillotine

Belknap, Jeremy, 76–77

Bell, Robert, 105

benefit of clergy: abolition of, 157, 268; doctrine of, 122, 268

Benjamin, Charlie, 12–14

Bentham, Jeremy, 48, 50–51, 70–71

bestiality: as capital crime, 173, 266, 270; crime of, 143, 181

Bethea, Rainey, 267

Bexar County, TX, 224

Bible, 66, 71, 74, 77–78, 80, 92, 134, 173, 253–54, 265–66, 268, 273

bigamy, as capital crime, 154

Bigelow, Brandon, 115

Bill for Proportioning Crimes and Punishments, 54, 141–45, 149, 156–57

Bill of Attainder Clause(s), 116–17, 170

Bill of Rights, 8–10, 156, 186, 212, 226, 269, 294, 306, 320; adoption of, 8, 27, 29–30, 96, 168, 320; applicability to states, 10, 28, 197, 203–7, 308; as contemplating executions, 343–44; as "fundamental" law, 214; general language of, 28, 188, 340; introduction of, 119, 170–71; opposition to, 93, 95–96, 163–65; as "paper" check, 170–71; as protecting rights, 292, 312, 316–17, 342–44; purpose of, 316–17, 322; ratification of, 8, 10, 38, 52, 68, 108, 170, 176, 303, 307, 324; relationship to Constitution, 169–70; support for, 162, 164–65, 168, 185, 187; text of, 292. *See also specific amendments* bills of attainder: prohibition of, 116, 147, 164, 170, 261, 312, 316, 321; use of, 117, 146–47, 261–62, 306. *See also* Bill of Attainder Clause(s)

bills of rights: distinguished from constitutions, 185; and natural rights, 184, 188; to protect citizens, 163, 166, 168; purpose of, 188; and torture, 188. *See also* Bill of Rights; *specific jurisdictions*

billy clubs, use of, 241

binding of wrists, 268

Bingham, John, 204

bipolar disorder, 248

Bird, Thomas, 131–32

Black Act, 266

black codes. *See* slave codes

blackening face, as capital crime, 266

Blackmun, Harry, 200, 242–43, 282, 284–85, 298, 316

blacks. *See* African Americans; racial discrimination

Blackstone, William, 48, 53, 105, 210, 300–3, 306–7; on attainder, 173; background of, 48–49; on bail, 195; and Beccaria, 48–49; on corporal punishments, 172; on "cruel and unusual punishments," 173; on cruelty, 49, 172; on death penalty, 49, 172; on "idiots"/ "lunatics," 260; influence of, 56, 133, 141, 155; on natural law, 177; on precedent, 329; on punishments, 48–49, 172–73; on sanguinary laws, 214

Blair, John, 320

Blake, William, 112

blasphemy, as capital crime, 173, 266

blinding, as punishment, 44

Bloodsworth, Kirk, 233

Bloody Assizes, 94, 174, 176

"Bloody Code," 68, 157, 259, 266. *See also* England

blowing from cannon's mouth, 211

Blume, John, 230

"Body of Liberties," 173

boiling to death, 211; in lead/water, 32, 211; in oil, 45, 210–11, 266, 297

Booth v. Maryland, 196

boring through nose, 143, 338

Bork, Robert, 283, 344

Boston Gazette, 120

Boston Massacre, 50, 97, 262

Boston, MA, 76–77, 160, 177, 179, 269, 274; executions in, 271, 324; mobs in, 62, 97; slaves in, 270–71; Tories in, 99

Boston Tea Party, 97

Bovee, Marvin, 276–77

Boyard v. Singleton, 320

Bracton, Henry de, 150

Bradford, William: abolition efforts of, 54, 79, 82, 84–91, 272, 334, 340; background of, 84–85; and Beccaria, 54, 86, 88; and Benjamin Rush, 85; and James Madison, 54, 84, 154–55, 185

brain-damaged offenders, 246–49, 254. *See also* mentally ill/retarded offenders

Branch, Elmer, 1–2

branding, 44, 46, 54, 83, 142, 172, 191, 268, 315–16, 327

Brandywine, battle of, 113

breaking on the wheel, 42–43, 46, 55, 202, 211–12, 270, 297

Brennan, William, 1, 27, 200, 219–20, 279–81, 292, 332–34, 338, 343

Breyer, Stephen, 17, 228, 237

Bright, Stephen, 236, 335

British Army, 126, 128, 135; executions by, 126

British constitution, 121, 302

British Navy, 129

British Parliament, 20, 45, 93–94, 97, 101, 107, 121, 155, 166, 171, 174–76, 211, 300, 321; House of Commons, 94, 155, 176; House of Lords, 94, 175

British prisons, 68

Britton, James, 267

Brooks, Christie, 12

Broom, Romell, 291

Brown, Charles, 82

Brown v. Board of Education, 280, 330

Bruce, David, 31

brutalization effect, of executions, 32, 69, 74, 79, 247–48, 257, 280

"Brutus," 162, 319, 322

Bryan, Samuel, 162

Bryan, William Cullen, 273

Buddhism, 43, 45

"buggery": abolition for, 143; as capital crime, 88, 266; castration for, 149. *See also* sodomy

Bundy, Ted, 245

Bunker Hill, battle of, 98

Burdine, Calvin, 236

Burger, Warren, 197, 281–82

burglary: abolition for, 88–89, 124, 143, 303; as capital crime, 67, 88–89, 120, 145, 208, 270; execution for, 67, 191

Burke, Edmund, 107

Burke, Thomas, 100

Burlamaqui, Jacques, 104

Burning: alive, 46, 172, 271; feet/hands, 83, 145, 268; of slaves, 217, 314; to death, 2, 40–42, 134, 174, 209–11, 266, 270; at the stake, 41–42, 156, 202, 212, 271, 297. *See also* branding

Burr, Aaron, 50–51, 118, 138–39, 149, 335

burying alive, 49, 145, 211, 265

Bush, George H. W., 250

Bush, George W., 336

Butler, Pierce, 58

Cabana, Donald, 264

cadena temporal, punishment of, 197

Calas, Jean, 41–42, 48

Caldwell v. Mississippi, 200

California, 214, 318; death row inmates, 224–25; and execution delays, 225, 227; executions in, 225; Supreme Court, 279, 298

Callins v. Collins, 200, 284–85, 316

Cambodia, abolition in, 64

Cambridge University, 173

cameras, barred at executions, 248, 258

Campaign to End the Death Penalty, 336

Campbell, Charles, 260

Campbell, Henry, 126

Canada, 47, 127, 194; abolition in, 64; refusal to extradite, 288

Cannon, Joseph, 264

capital cases, error rate in, 230, 232, 236

capital crimes, 52, 90, 163; in 1790, 26, 122, 292; throughout history, 81, 154, 173, 265–66, 278; under federal law, 222–23. *See also specific crimes and jurisdictions*

capital litigation/prosecutions, 226, 284, 336; complexity of, 233–34

capital punishment. *See* death penalty; death sentence(s); execution(s)

capital sentencing, 26, 230, 248, 271, 284–85; and Model Penal Code, 290. *See also* death sentence(s); judges; juries; juror(s)

capital statutes. *See* capital crimes; *specific jurisdictions*

Caracciolo di Brienza, Giuseppe, 120

cardiac arrest: inducement of, 244; risk of, 243

Cardozo, Benjamin, 259, 347

carjacking, 222

Carlyle, Abraham, 101–2

castration: punishment of, 44, 142–44, 149, 208, 268, 344; of slaves, 217, 266, 313–14

Catherine I (empress), 44

Catherine II (empress), 39, 78. *See also* Russia

Catholics, 34, 40–42, 94; exclusion from juries, 231; execution of, 174–75

Caucasians. *See* whites

causing leak in ship, as capital crime, 45

cave paintings, 246

Cedars, The, 146

"Centinel," 162

Chahal v. United Kingdom, 227

chain gangs, 69, 72–73

chains: hanging in, 189, 208, 270–71, 337; use of, 46, 120, 126, 197, 209

Chapman, Marco, 225

Charles I (king), 94, 121

Charles II (king), 94, 174

Charleston, SC, 31, 271; executions in, 271, 324

Charlottesville, VA, 67

Chase, Samuel, 59, 305, 319

checks and balances, 321

Cheetham, James, 105

Chernow, Ron, 115, 120, 138

Chiba, Keiko, 64

child abuse/neglect, 15, 246–47, 249, 250–51

child rape, 199, 239–40. *See also* rape

children. *See* juveniles

China: abolition efforts in, 45; death sentences in, 287; executions in, 20, 64, 286–87, 347; monitoring of, 315; punishments in, 142

Chipman, Nathaniel, 69

Christ and the Gallows, 277

Christianity, 61, 154, 178, 209–10, 214, 276, 286, 313; Dr. Rush's views on, 67, 71–72, 80–81, 83; Jefferson's views on, 71

Christians, and opposition to executions, 34, 43–44, 276. *See also* religious persecution

Chrysostom, John (archbishop), 44

Cingle de la Mola Remigia, 246

civil forfeitures, 195

civil law, versus common law, 187

civil rights lawsuits, 241–42

Civil War, 28, 203–4, 219, 276–78, 306, 313, 342

Clark, Ramsey, 278

Claus, Laurence, 178, 215

Clay, Henry, 167

clemency, executive, 59, 78, 120, 310; commutations/pardons approved, 18, 57, 59–60, 128, 132–33, 153, 197, 277; petitions, 131, 277; power to pardon/reprieve, 157, 268, 310, 326; and slaves, 152. *See also* pardons; President(s); reprieves

Clinton, Bill, 254

Clinton, George, 50–51, 272–73

Cloots, Anacharsis, 112

clothing, duty to provide, 219, 296

Clymer, George, 79

Cocke, Frances, 104

Code of Hammurabi, 265

Codman, John, 270

Coke, Edward, 133–34, 141, 209, 260, 302–3, 307

Coker v. Georgia, 199

Coleman, Edward, 175

Coleman v. Thompson, 234–35

College of New Jersey, 66, 93, 154

College of Philadelphia, 51, 66

College of William and Mary, 140

colonial charters/laws, 47, 87–88, 302

Colorado: abolition in, 278; executions in, 223; solitary confinement in, 226

Colosseum (Rome), 347–48

Columbia, abolition in, 64

Columbia Law School, 230, 255

Comity Clause. *See* Privileges and Immunities Clause

Commentaries on American Law, 192

Commentaries on the Constitution of the United States, 190

Commentaries on the Laws of England, 48–49, 105, 133, 155, 172–73

common law: adaptability/evolution of, 21, 305–6; attainder, 173; capital crimes, 145; and "Corruption of Blood," 295; courts, 303; crimes, 304; and "customs," 302–3; on duels, 335; of England, 92, 95–96, 134, 201, 209, 268, 301–5; and federal crimes, 304; as fortified by Bill of Rights, 300; founders' views of, 150, 168, 177, 302–6; and "long"/"immemorial" usage, 302–6; maxims, 25, 125, 191, 261, 307; punishments, 191, 210–11, 213, 304, 331; rights, 177, 215; and state-law crimes, 304; and treason, 115; in U.S., 21, 201, 339; use of precedent, 328–30; versus civil law, 187

Common Sense, 98, 105, 112

Commonwealth v. Caton, 320

Commonwealth v. Wyatt, 303

community standards, 311. *See also* "evolving standards of decency"; Eighth Amendment; First Amendment

commutation(s). *See* clemency, executive

Compensation Clause, 318, 333

competency, 225, 253–54, 258

concealing birth, as capital crime, 270

conditions of confinement, 67–68, 226–27; and Eighth Amendment, 194, 219–21, 226, 228–29, 242–43, 297. *See also* death row

Confederation Congress, 98, 113

confession(s): coerced, 68, 306, 323; false, 35, 51; and torture, 32, 35, 172, 174, 187–88, 298; and Treason Clause, 118, 295

Congress, 114, 116, 138, 164, 166, 169, 250, 270, 284, 321–22; and duels, 335; First, 56, 116, 118–19, 121, 123, 155,

165, 167–70, 184, 186, 234, 271, 292, 302, 321, 328, 332, 343; and juvenile offenders, 19; laws of, 26, 122, 222–23; members of, 222; messages to, 132, 158; pardons of, 59; powers of, 10, 162–63, 187, 293–95; restrained by Eighth Amendment, 176, 184, 308; rules of, 293; and slavery, 324; use of "unusual," 313–15. *See also* Confederation Congress; Continental Congress

conjuration, punishment of, 134, 144

Connecticut, 47, 103, 115, 121–22, 130, 266, 315; death penalty debate in, 47; executions in, 223, 270; penal codes, 143–44, 265–66; prison in, 68, 129; private execution law, 257; and Stamp Act, 97

Connor, John, 131

Constitution, 5–11, 23–25, 27–29, 36, 47, 65–66, 92, 113, 115–19, 162–70, 176–77, 186, 204–5, 207, 212, 215, 219, 227, 270, 285, 291–92, 302–3, 305, 311–12, 318–20, 327–29, 338, 347; adoption of, 96, 118, 269, 339, 343; Article I, 115–16, 164, 170, 293, 306, 316–17, 320–22; Article II, 59, 117; Article III, 116–18, 293–95, 321; Article IV, 118; Article V, 156; and bills of attainder, 261, 321; and common law, 304; drafting/design of, 115, 197, 302, 324, 340–41; and evidentiary protections, 295; and ex post facto laws, 321; as fundamental law, 10, 320–21; and future generations, 197, 340; general language of, 27, 197, 306, 317, 330, 332–33, 340; and habeas corpus, 233, 235; and impeachment, 10, 275; and interpretative theories, 28–29; as majoritarian check, 10; objections to, 116, 164, 169, 187–88; and popular meaning, 332; preamble, 341; and "privileges"/"immunities," 206; process for amending, 156; proposed amendments to, 166–68; as protecting rights, 117, 156, 316–17; ratification debate, 162, 167, 184; ratification of, 51, 68, 93, 116, 119, 121, 131, 155, 166, 176, 184, 321; references to "punish"/"punishment,"

293–95; signers of, 51, 58, 72, 136, 320; and slave trade, 307; supremacy of, 164–65; text of, 115–18; and "unusual," 298–99, 309; and use of precedents, 328–30. *See also* Bill of Rights; Constitutional Convention; *individual amendments, clauses, and states*

Constitutional Convention, 58, 66, 85, 118, 162–68, 184, 316, 320, 322; attendees of, 9, 115; Committee of Detail, 322; Committee of Style and Arrangement, 114–15; debate at, 115, 118, 184; need for, 114; secrecy of, 114, 162, 332

constitutional interpretation: and Declaration of Independence, 323–24; and Justice Scalia's views, 22–26, 28, 316–17, 323, 326–27; theories of, 27–29. *See also specific theories*

Continental Army, 59, 66, 98–99, 102–3, 114, 127, 130, 133, 146, 149

Continental Congress, 51, 53–54, 56, 66, 79, 97–98, 100–103, 105, 118, 127–31, 139–41, 167–68, 269, 335; and Declaration of Independence (1776), 105, 184; and Declaration of Rights (1774), 47; Letter to the Inhabitants of Quebec (1774), 47

Convention on the Rights of the Child, 20, 23, 290

conversion to Christianity, as capital crime, 286

Cooley, Thomas, 210, 331

Cornell Law School, 230

Cornell University, 255

Cornwallis, Charles (lord), 129

corporal punishments, 7–8, 10–11, 36, 48–49, 55, 59, 65, 78, 120, 122, 144, 172, 175, 193, 197, 216, 268, 292, 318, 341, 343; abandonment of, 242, 258, 342; abolition of, 191; as common/"usual," 120, 316; as "cruel"/"unusual," 241–43, 315; as degrading, 242; and Eighth Amendment, 194, 242–43, 294, 297–98, 304, 315, 327; to shame/humiliate, 258, 268; and U.S. law, 315. *See also* ducking stool; ear cropping; limb(s), deprivation of; pillory; whipping corpses: desecration of, 33; public dissection of, 122, 145, 172, 266. *See also* gibbeting

correctional officers: attitudes toward executions, 263–64; murder of, 222; and use of force, 241–43. *See also* wardens

Correll, Michael, 249

"Corruption of Blood," 164, 295

Corzine, Jon, 286

cosmopolitanism, 28

Cosway, Maria, 139

Council of Europe, 291

counsel, defense: and ABA standards, 236; appointment of, 51, 122, 167, 191, 234–35, 307; disbarred/disciplined, 233; drunk, 236; incompetence of, 29, 232–34, 236–37, 309–10, 346; and ineffective assistance, 7, 259, 307; right to, 312; sleeping at trial, 236

counterfeiting: abolition for, 150, 303; as capital crime, 50, 57, 67, 88, 90, 122–23, 145, 270; executions for, 67; and U.S. Constitution, 115, 293

courts. *See* federal courts; United States; *individual states*

courts-martial proceedings, 59–60, 99, 127, 131, 133, 136, 198

Coxe, Tench, 112

Cranch, Elizabeth, 62

Crew, Thomas, 156

"crime against nature": abolition for, 88–89; as capital crime, 89; and corporal punishments, 193; punishment of, 143–44

crimes. *See specific crimes*

crimes against humanity, 290

criminologists, views of, 248

Crockett, G. F. H., 158–59, 371

Cromwell, Oliver, 94

Crook, Shirley, 13–14, 16

Crook, Steven, 13–14

crucifixion, 2, 202, 211, 265–66

Cruden, Alexander, 92

"cruel": meaning of, 29, 176, 181, 212, 295–96, 311, 329; as moral standard, 238, 330; relationship to "unusual," 181, 308; as subjective, 295, 330;

"treatment," 181, 217–18; use by founders, 52–53, 61, 86, 101, 108–9, 111, 122, 124–25, 130–31, 135–36, 146, 159–60, 181, 183–84, 186, 296, 299, 312, 322; use by jurists, 181–82, 188, 216, 296–97, 312–13; use in statutes/legislation, 173, 181, 217, 313–15. *See also* punishment(s)

"cruel and unusual": "pains and penalties," 178; relationship to slavery, 216–19; "treatment," 217–18; use in case law, 182–83, 190, 217–18, 313; use in legislation/statutes, 181, 204, 315. *See also* punishment(s)

"cruel and unusual punishments": bar against, 2, 8, 17, 20, 65, 118, 170, 181, 184, 192, 211, 244, 281, 292, 294, 308, 328, 397; and common law, 303; concern about, 162–64, 166, 168, 170, 293–94; corporal punishments as, 10–11, 197, 242, 294, 297–98, 304, 318, 327; death sentences as, 227, 296, 308, 318, 334; and English law, 8, 155, 174–76, 215, 301, 331; exclusion of blacks from protection of, 188–89; executions as, 10–11, 32, 200, 211, 228–29, 270, 273, 291, 296–98, 306–9, 311–12, 318, 322, 324, 326, 334, 336–37, 343–46; and federal legislation, 204; and Fourteenth Amendment, 204, 207, 307–8; as fundamental/sacred protection, 164, 184–85, 197; as general/vague language, 163–64, 193–94, 302, 317, 322, 328, 330; and Indian tribes, 315; and judges' role, 161, 294, 311–12, 322–23, 332–33, 397; and modes/methods of execution, 193–94, 209, 211; and "privileges"/"immunities," 204; in state constitutions/declarations, 119, 176–78, 180–81, 188, 210; and torture, 188, 306; under state law, 204, 331; as unitary concept, 180–81, 242, 298–99; use in statutes, 181, 315. *See also* Cruel and Unusual Punishments Clause; Eighth Amendment; English Bill of Rights; *specific states and cases*

Cruel and Unusual Punishments Clause, 3, 7–8, 10, 28–29, 96, 155, 160, 184–

85, 187, 192–95, 197, 199, 202, 207–8, 213, 219–20, 263, 279, 282, 291, 295–96, 303, 308, 317–18, 342, 347; as "constitutional boilerplate," 176, 178; in "constitutional" sense, 210, 331–32; and "unusual," 298–99; and use of common/general terms, 161, 317. *See also* Eighth Amendment; English Bill of Rights; "evolving standards of decency"; *specific cases*

"cruel or unusual": use in case law, 181–83, 217, 313; use in legislation/statutes, 181, 204, 217, 315

"cruel or unusual punishments": concern about, 163; in Northwest Ordinance, 118–19, 167, 275; in state constitutions/declarations, 119, 169, 178–81, 227; use in statutes, 181, 217–18, 313, 315

"cruel punishments": references to, 55, 67, 87, 163, 184, 190, 218, 275; in state constitutions, 87, 180–81, 211, 215–16; in state statutes, 218, 314, 317

cruelty: acts of, 128, 172, 246; concept/consideration of, 25, 55–56, 83, 100, 120, 136, 181, 185, 190–91, 236, 238, 260, 298, 308, 331–32, 341

Cuba, executions in, 64

Cuneo, Daniel, 15

cutting down trees, as capital crime, 266

cutting off ears. *See* ear cropping

cutting off hair, 214

cutting off hand(s), 145, 172, 210, 286–87

cutting off lip(s), 142

cutting off nose(s), 49, 142

cutting out heart, 108

cutting out tongue, 142, 217, 313

Dade Code, 154

Dahmer, Jeffrey, 245

Dallas County, TX, 224, 232

Dallas, George, 273

Dallas Morning News, 232

Damien, execution of, 108

Damiens, François, 45

Dane, Nathan, 118, 167, 191–92

Darrow, Clarence, 278

de Borre, Preudhomme, 129

de la Madelaine, Louis Philipon, 42

de La Barre, Jean-François, 41–42

de La Rouchefoucauld, Duc, 109, 111

de Launay, Bernard-René, 109

de Meusnier, Monsieur, 142

de non sane memorie, 134

deadly force, use of, 262

Dean, Kenneth, 264

death penalty: arbitrary nature of, 5, 256, 346; categorical restrictions on, 21, 199, 203, 290; as constitutional, 7, 202, 211, 243, 281–82; cost of, 234, 246, 345; as cruel, 4–5, 10, 35–36, 237, 279–81, 296–98, 303, 346–47; as discriminatory, 216, 256, 280–81, 284, 307–9; and geographic disparities, 3, 223, 309, 337; as human rights issue, 288; in 1791, 26, 29; irrevocability of, 38, 48, 55, 71, 232, 280, 288; origins of, 265; as standard punishment, 258, 343; as torture, 298, 318; as unconstitutional, 55, 279–81, 284–85, 332–33; as unusual, 3, 5, 10, 237, 279–81, 294, 309, 346. *See also* abolition; capital statutes; death sentence(s); execution(s); *specific jurisdictions*

Death Penalty Information Center, 230, 336

death row: conditions on, 226–27; lengths of stay on, 225–27; racial composition of, 224–25; size of, 224. *See also specific jurisdictions*

death row inmates: and brain damage, 246–49, 251, 254; characteristics of, 235, 245–55; and child abuse/neglect, 246–47, 249–51; crimes of, 245; current number of, 11; death by natural causes, 224–25; and depression, 225, 248, 253–55; elderly, 289; family members of, 256–57; forcible medication of, 254–55; hallucinations of, 249, 251, 254–55; head injuries of, 247–48; and incest, 249; indigency of, 234; and insanity, 254–55, 260–61; lack of education, 235, 248–49, 251, 256; male vs. female, 224; mental illness/retardation of, 195, 225, 232, 234–35, 247–56, 260–62; and poverty, 4, 249, 256, 346; pre-*Furman,* 1; pregnant, 289; and self-mutilation, 251, 253–54; and sexual abuse, 247; substance abuse of, 225, 248–49, 251–53; suicide (attempts) by, 225–26, 253; in U.S., 4, 224–25; unrepresented, 234–35; volunteering for execution, 225. *See also* counsel, defense; habeas corpus; innocence

"death row phenomenon," 227

death sentence(s): annual number of, 229; arbitrary nature of, 5, 55, 280, 283, 326, 344; and common law, 201, 304; commutation of, 153, 279, 285; as cruel, 227, 296, 318, 334; declining number of, 64, 229–30, 286, 309, 342, 345; delays in carrying out, 53, 224–29; discretionary, 4, 55, 309, 325; as discriminatory, 284, 307–8, 344; eligibility for, 7, 19; and error rate, 230, 236; individualized, 200; as inflicting severe mental distress, 226–27, 257, 296; mandatory, 25–26, 58, 173, 304, 309, 324–26; as rare, 5, 248; as torturous, 227, 291, 298; in U.S., 248, 309; as unnecessary, 334; as unusual, 227, 308, 318; worldwide, 286–87. *See also* death penalty; *names of specific people*

death warrants, 256, 273

debtors: imprisonment/punishment of, 68, 160; prosecution of, 113–14. *See also* bankruptcy

Decemviri, twelve tablets of, 190

Deck v. Missouri, 207

Declaration of Independence: drafting of, 31, 54, 102–4, 139; issuance of, 98, 102, 104, 127, 144, 178, 184, 269, 305; Lincoln's reverence for, 276, 324; and natural law, 177–78; rights clause of, 177, 289, 323–24, 333; signers of, 51, 53, 59, 79, 97, 101–2, 140, 273, 320, 341; text of, 54, 102–4, 185, 341; translation of, 111; values/principles of, 92, 148, 280, 324, 330, 342

declarations of rights, 108; as paper/ parchment barriers, 165, 170–71, 188; state law, 164, 168–70, 178–80, 321; violations of, 165. *See also specific jurisdictions*

deference: concept of, 27; to legislation, 24, 27, 30, 189, 210, 281–82, 334; to state courts, 234

dehydration, of inmates, 241, 243

Dei delitti e delle pene, 31, 35, 43. See also *On Crimes and Punishments*

Delaware: abolition in, 278; bill of rights, 169, 178; executions in, 270; nighttime execution law, 257

Democracy in America, 274

Democratic Republic of Congo, executions in, 20, 64

desecration of corpses. *See* corpses

desertion: as capital crime, 67, 130, 133, 270; executions for, 67, 126–27, 270, 277; pardons for, 59, 63; punishment of, 60, 126–27, 136, 198

DeShaney v. Winnebago County Department of Social Services, 296

destruction of property, as capital crime, 222

deterrence, 1, 202, 229; debate, 26, 34, 36–39, 43, 55, 63, 86–87, 91, 125, 127, 179, 186, 192, 247, 344; research/ studies on, 237–38, 247–48

Deutsch, Albert, 259

Dickinson College, 71

Dickinson, Harry, 94

Dickinson, John, 72–73, 92, 101, 319

dictionaries: defining "cruel," 295–96, 329; defining "punishment," 292; defining "unusual," 295–96, 329; to "fix" language, 328–29

Dictionnaire Philosophique, 41

Dillwyn, Susanna, 72

Dillwyn, William, 72

Dinwiddie, Robert, 127

Discourse on Political Economy, 40–41

discretionary sentencing: death sentences, 4–5, 325–26; fines/terms of imprisonment, 173

discrimination. *See* minorities; racial discrimination

disembowelment, 172, 174, 210, 266

disfigurement, 142, 172, 313, 343–44. *See also* maiming

dismemberment, 172–73, 211, 266, 313–14

disproportionality: concept of, 202–3;

between crimes/punishments, 1–2, 17–18, 20–21, 57, 123–24, 189–90, 194–96, 198–99, 202–3, 213, 238, 273, 298

dissection. *See* public dissection

District of Columbia. *See* Washington, D.C.

disturbing fish pond, as capital crime, 266

DNA evidence, 55, 232–33, 342; exonerations, 236, 344; lab failure, 232

doctors. *See* physicians

domestic violence, 213

Dorr Rebellion, 275

double jeopardy, 169, 312

Double Jeopardy Clause, 292, 316

Douglas, William, 1, 216, 279

Douglass, Frederick, 335

Draco, 69

drawing and quartering, 43, 46, 109, 172, 174, 176, 189, 208–9, 262, 266, 337

Dred Scott v. Sandford, 203, 307, 329–30

Drinker, Elizabeth, 102

drive by shooting, 222

Driver, Giles, 213

drowning, death by, 210, 265–66

drug (ab)use, 248–49, 251–53

drug kingpins, 199, 222

Dubber, Markus, 176

DuBois, W. E. B., 335

ducking, punishment of, 144

ducking stool, 172, 192–93, 269

due process, 2, 4, 29, 169, 197, 207, 255, 280, 292–93, 306–10, 312, 316, 344, 346; as barring arbitrariness, 205, 207, 309; as concept, 205–6; in English law, 205, 293; as ensuring fairness, 205; and innocence claims, 233; substantive, 205, 207; in U.S. law, 204–5, 207, 293

Due Process Clause(s), 4, 7, 28–29, 205–7, 280, 292–93, 306–8; applicability to states, 307; as articulating moral/fairness principles, 205–6, 307. *See also* Fifth Amendment; Fourteenth Amendment

duels/dueling, 36, 42, 45, 73–74, 83, 138–39, 335–36, 345

Duffy, Clinton, 227

Duke of Monmouth, 94, 174

dungeons, 56, 68, 120, 171

Dworkin, Ronald, 193, 327

ear cropping, 49, 54, 83, 85, 142, 172, 175, 186, 210, 328, 338, 343

Eastern State Penitentiary, 8, 269, 275

ecclesiastical courts, 172, 174–75, 268

ecclesiastical offenses, 171

Eddy, Thomas, 82–83, 272

Eden, William, 48

Edict of the Grand Duke of Tuscany, 76

Edward III (king), 293

Edwards, Ignatious, 127

effigies, burning/hanging of, 97, 112

Egypt, 57; death sentences/executions in, 287

Ehrlich, Isaac, 247

Eighth Amendment, 1–10, 15–30, 55, 65, 96, 155, 171, 180–81, 185, 191, 193–94, 199–200, 217, 222, 279–82, 284, 295–96, 302, 307, 310, 312, 329–34, 342–47; as absolute prohibition, 8, 64–65, 184, 294, 312, 316, 328, 344–45; and accomplice liability, 199, 240; adoption of, 119, 185–86, 324; applicability to states, 8, 28–29, 194, 204–8, 279, 308, 342; and arbitrary punishments, 201, 207, 215–16, 308, 316, 345–46; and assaults/beatings, 219–20, 243, 263, 297; and "barbaric" punishments, 202, 332; as barring corporal punishments, 197, 242–43, 297–98, 304, 315, 327; as barring executions, 7, 24, 64, 199–200, 228–29, 279, 291–92, 309, 312, 316–18, 336, 337–38, 343, 345; as barring statelessness/"status" crimes, 198; as barring torture, 187–88, 202, 243, 323; and child rape, 199, 239–40; and common law, 302–7; and competency for execution, 249; and "consistency in determining who receives a death sentence," 200; and "consistency of the direction of change," 19, 239–40; and "constitutional sense," 210, 331–32; and "contemporary standards," 7, 220, 243, 325; and counting of states, 18, 23, 26–27, 239; and death row phenomenon, 226, 228–29; debates surrounding, 8, 162–71, 184–88; and discriminatory punishments, 214–16, 279, 284, 308; and "disproportionate" punishments, 202–3, 298; and distrust of abuse/power, 196–97, 192; and "dramatic shift" in "legislative landscape," 199; and "evolving standards of decency," 1, 4, 7, 17–18, 21–23, 25, 207, 229, 232, 238, 282, 310–11, 313, 329, 333, 336, 342, 397; and "excessive" sanctions, 17, 202–3; and executions, 291–93, 318, 322, 336; and federal government, 194, 205–6, 208; and felony murder, 240; and forcible medication, 254–55; and human dignity, 17, 198, 238, 241–42, 279, 334, 343; and "independent judgment," 18, 21, 23, 25, 27, 29, 203, 239; and individualized sentencing, 200, 285; and "inhuman"/"inhumane" treatment, 298–99; and insane, 7, 199, 254, 336; and "international consensus," 22; and international/foreign law, 22–24, 290; introduction of, 119; judicial reversals, 195–96; and judicial role/responsibility, 195, 327–28; and jury instructions, 201–2; and jury verdicts, 27, 229–30, 239, 344; and juvenile offenders, 7, 16–26, 199, 202–3, 239–40, 336–37; and legislative acts, 203, 239; legislative history of, 186–88; and less culpable offenders, 19, 199; and lethal injection, 6, 26, 201, 223, 244–45, 284, 336; and life/life-without-parole sentences, 198, 202–3, 240, 337; and "long usage," 302–7; and mandatory sentences, 201, 324–25; and mental illness/retardation, 7, 16, 18–19, 195, 199, 239–40, 254–55, 260, 316, 336; and modes of execution/punishment, 198, 200–202, 209, 211; and "national consensus," 16, 18, 21–24, 26–27, 203, 238–40; and non-homicidal offenders, 199, 203, 239–40, 337; as not static, 7, 27, 198, 333; "objective" factors/indicators, 17–19, 203, 231–32, 238–39, 285; origins of, 20, 171–72, 174, 176–77, 210, 294; and pain, 26, 241–42, 245, 297, 329, 332, 334; and potential bodily harm, 341–42; and proportionality, 17, 202–3; as protecting inmates, 219–21, 240–43, 296–97, 305; and psychiatric/psychological care, 296; and psychological harm, 243, 291; and public attitudes, 239; purpose of, 194, 197, 203, 323; and "rate of change," 18, 239; ratification of, 2, 174, 180, 182, 189, 270, 272; and rape, 199; scope of, 184; and secondhand smoke, 241, 263; and solitary confinement, 201; and state practice, 203, 239–40; text of, 2, 65, 193, 196; and torture, 202, 214, 243, 323; as unprincipled, 196, 318; and verbal threats, 243; as "warning," 196, 213–14; and whipping, 242, 297. *See also* Cruel and Unusual Punishments Clause; Bail Clause; Excessive Fines Clause; *specific cases*

elderly inmates, on death row, 289
electric chair, 202, 210, 216, 331
electrocution(s), 202; botched, 297, 331; constitutionality of, 200–202, 216; as execution method, 193, 210, 212, 258
Elizabeth (queen), 40, 134
Elizabeth of Moscovy, 34
Elliott, Charles, 180–81
Ellsworth, Oliver, 121
Ely, Rhody, 215–16
Ely v. Thompson, 215
embalming alive, 265
embezzlement, execution for, 126
emergency medical technicians, 244, 258
enchantment, punishment of, 144
Encyclopedia Americana, 190
Encyclopédie Politique, 142
England, 34, 40, 58, 62, 70, 73, 87, 92, 100–101, 106, 111–12, 129, 173, 175, 194, 196, 271, 300, 303, 325, 328, 335; abolition in, 20, 44, 293; and benefit of clergy, 268; and bills of attainder, 261; capital crimes in, 52, 68, 81, 115, 123–24, 133–34, 144–45, 154, 212, 268, 272, 302; and corporal punishments, 268; Court of Common Pleas, 134; and

"cruel and unusual punishments," 163, 172; executions in, 49, 64, 69, 176, 267; felonies in, 87, 134, 145; Inns of Court, 154; and modes of execution/punishment, 108, 176; refusal to extradite, 227, 288; and solitary confinement, 150. *See also* "Bloody Code"; Glorious Revolution of 1688

English Bill of Rights, 8, 20, 93–95, 107, 155, 166, 171–72, 173–78, 180, 188, 212, 215–16, 296, 300–301

English constitution, 106; principles of, 47, 93; as unwritten, 321

English Declaration of Rights, 94, 174, 215, 300; use of "ought," 155, 215. *See also* English Bill of Rights; Glorious Revolution of 1688

English law: and bankruptcy, 115; common-law rights/tradition, 92, 134, 177, 193, 301–5; and counsel, 51; cruelty of, 49, 57, 68–70, 172–73, 192, 212, 266; and death sentences, 172–73; and due process, 293; and insanity, 260; and torture, 306; use of, 134. *See also* "Bloody Code"; British Parliament

Enlightenment, 9, 34, 48, 64, 66, 103, 272, 333, 340, 347

Enmund, Earl, 199

Enmund v. Florida, 199, 239–40

Enquiry How Far the Punishment of Death Is Necessary in Pennsylvania, 85–91, 334

equal protection, 2, 29, 200, 207, 214, 216, 280, 304, 306–10, 317, 342, 344, 346. *See also* Fourteenth Amendment

Equal Protection Clause, 3, 7, 28–29, 215, 310; purpose of, 204, 207; text of, 204, 317

equality, principle of, 275, 280, 307

errors in capital cases, 29, 70–71, 230, 232–33, 235, 285, 309–10, 346. *See also* innocence; wrongful convictions

espionage: as capital crime, 222, 270; crime of, 199. *See also* treason

"Espy File," 270

Espy, M. Watt, 270

Estelle v. Gamble, 240

Estridge, Thomas, 100

Europe, 40, 198, 267; abolition in, 64, 287, 290–91; army discipline in, 63, 133; executions/punishments in, 8, 45, 143, 172; homicide rates in, 247; monarchs in, 33, 35, 77; penal reform in, 74, 77–78; refusals to extradite, 288; and torture, 33, 44–45, 268. *See also specific countries and monarchs*

European Convention for the Protection of Human Rights, 227, 290

European Court of Human Rights, 227

European Union, 287, 291

Evans, Connie Ray, 264

"evolving standards of decency," 1, 4, 7, 17–18, 21–23, 25, 207, 229, 232, 238, 282, 310–11, 313, 329, 333, 336, 342, 397. *See also* Eighth Amendment

Ewing, Samuel, 60

Ewing v. California, 198

Ex parte Wilson, 311

Ex Post Facto Clause(s), 116, 170, 226

ex post facto laws, 116–17, 164, 170, 200, 312, 321

"excessive": bail/fines, 94–95, 155, 162–63, 166–69, 171, 173–74, 176, 178–80, 184, 186, 195, 213, 215, 376; punishment, 194, 199, 334; as subjective, 194. *See also* Bail Clause; Excessive Fines Clause

Excessive Bail Clause. *See* Bail Clause

Excessive Fines Clause, 194–95

excessive force: and Eighth Amendment, 7, 219–21, 241–43; use of, 7, 219, 241–42

executioners: anonymity of, 259–60, 263; attitudes toward executions, 43, 263–64, 341; and executions, 263; instructions to, 53; lowly status of, 69, 262–63; payment of, 40, 343; profession of, 262–63; training/preparedness of, 237–38, 244; unease toward, 262–64

execution(s): ambivalence toward, 9, 62, 262, 340; annual number of, 223; arbitrary nature of, 5, 308–10, 326, 337, 345–46; attendance at, 257, 267; botched, 237, 291, 297; as brutalizing, 32, 69, 74, 79, 247–48, 257, 280; cam-

eras excluded from, 248; as civil ceremony, 271; in colonial times, 126–27, 226, 270–72; as constitutional, 237, 243–44, 291; as cruel, 32, 211, 228–29, 273, 296–98, 306, 311–12, 322, 334, 337, 343, 345–46; day, purpose of, 271–72; declining number of, 64, 223, 278, 288, 342, 345; as degrading, 334; delay in carrying out, 53, 224–29; as discriminatory, 3, 307–9, 337, 345; distribution in U.S., 223; in early America, 226, 258, 270–72, 324; federal, 223; filming of, 6; in foreign countries, 286–87; and geographic disparities, 3, 223, 337; in medieval times, 64; of mentally ill/retarded, 7, 16, 18–19, 25–26, 42, 195, 199, 232, 239–40, 250, 254–56, 260–61, 316; methods/modes of, 37, 43, 46, 176, 193, 198, 211, 266, 297, 304–5; news coverage of, 68, 71, 200, 248, 257, 273–74, 347; nighttime, 200, 257–58; prehistoric, 246; private, 6, 200, 248, 257–58, 278; and psychological terror, 243, 291, 298, 323, 331; public, 37, 40, 70, 152, 257–58, 267, 271–72, 278; as punishments, 292; rarity of, 223, 248, 263, 309, 337; and relatives of condemned, 256–57; as religious ceremony, 271; of religious minorities, 40, 296; and risk of physical pain, 291, 297–98; since 1976, 1, 223; of slaves, 7–8, 152–53, 156, 188–89, 266, 270–72, 296; in South, 3–4, 219, 272, 223, 311, 345; summary, 108; timing of, 142, 174, 226, 258; as tortuous, 273, 291, 298, 318; as unconstitutional, 7, 24, 64, 200, 228–29, 279, 291–92, 309, 312, 316–18, 336, 337–38, 343, 345; in U.S., 64, 223, 270–72, 287, 324; as unnecessary, 85–91, 334; as unusual, 228, 306, 308–9, 311–12, 322, 324, 326, 336–37, 343, 345–46; use by monarchs, 33, 40, 49, 77–78; of "volunteers," 225; worldwide, 64, 286–87. *See also specific jurisdictions; names of specific people*
executive branch: and Eighth Amendment constraints, 294; official, murder

of, 222. *See also* President(s); United States
executive clemency. *See* clemency, executive
exhaustion of remedies, 234
exile, as punishment, 7, 40, 49, 194. *See also* banishment; transportation
exonerations, 6, 232–33, 235, 237, 286; DNA, 236, 344; number of, 230, 236. *See also* innocence
explosives, transportation of, 222
extradition, refusals to allow, 227, 288, 290. *See also specific countries*
eyewitness identifications/testimony, 228, 233, 236

Facchinei, Ferdinando, 39
Faneuil Hall, 179
Farmer v. Brennan, 219–21
faulty home construction, as capital crime, 265
Federal Bureau of Investigation (FBI), 247
federal courts, 194, 271, 288, 320, 326; and deference to state courts, 234; establishment of, 121–22, 271. *See also* Supreme Court; United States
federal death penalty, 222–23. *See also* United States
Federal Death Penalty Act of 1994, 19
federal government. *See* United States
federalism, 201, 233
Federalists, 51, 163–65
"Federal Farmer," 229
federal judges, 113, 121, 222, 243, 255–56, 263, 345, 384; and compensation, 318, 321; independence of, 8, 318–19; and impeachment, 10, 321; as insulated from political pressure, 318, 326; life-tenured, 6, 10, 318, 326, 333
Federalist Papers, 10, 164–65, 198; *No. 37, 328; No. 42,* 115; *No. 44,* 116, 321; *No. 47,* 261; *No. 74,* 135; *No. 78,* 10, 22, 318, 321; *No. 81,* 321
felonies: as capital crimes, 2, 26, 53, 57, 88, 100, 145, 191, 197; in colonies, 87, 143; in England, 87, 134, 144–45; punishment of, 191; and U.S. Consti-

tution, 115, 153, 293. *See also specific crimes*

felony murder, 25, 240

Few, James, 58

Few, William, 58

Fifth Amendment, 26, 47–48, 205, 207, 280, 307, 311, 316–17; provisions/text of, 29, 47–48, 292–93, 312, 316, 344

Fifteenth Amendment, 204, 342

finality, principle of, 30, 71, 233–34

Fine, Kevin, 232–33

fine(s): for "cruel and unusual punishment," 315; discretionary, 173, 303; disproportionate, 171; for dueling, 335; excessive, 94–95, 155, 162–63, 166–69, 171, 173–74, 176, 178–80, 184, 186, 213–15, 312, 376; for harming slaves, 217, 313–14; "heavy," 299–300; moderate, 171, 179; and Northwest Ordinance, 118; as punishment, 36, 210; and U.S. Constitution, 193–94, 212. *See also* Excessive Fines Clause

firing squad(s): constitutionality of, 200, 202, 211; as execution method, 60, 127, 129, 191, 221, 258, 266, 270; use of blanks, 263

Firmian, Carlo, 39

First Amendment, 311–12

First Congress. *See* Congress

Fitzsimons, Thomas, 123

"fixing" meaning, 328–30

flogging, 60, 65, 126, 242, 268, 314–15, 327, 345. *See also* whipping

Florida: death penalty law, 201, 283; death row inmates, 224–25, 228; death sentences in, 326; executioners, 260; executions in, 223, 259–60; life sentences in, 240, 337; Supreme Court, 218, 254

Flowers, Gennifer, 254

Fluegge, Judith, 15–16

food: deprivation of, 61, 220, 243, 297, 315; duty to provide, 219–20, 296; inspectors, killing of, 222

Food and Drug Administration, 259

forced labor, 38, 46, 268, 271. *See also* slavery

Ford, Alvin, 254

Ford v. Wainwright, 7, 199, 254

foreign law: citation of, 22–24; use by founders, 198

foreign nationals, on death row, 288

forfeiture of property, 295; as punishment, 143, 145, 191, 195, 198

forgery, 99, 180; abolition for, 88; as capital crime, 50, 57, 122–23, 208, 210, 270; executions for, 126, 270; in Great Britain, 123

Forster, George, 146

Founding Fathers. *See individual founders*

Fourteenth Amendment, 1–5, 10, 15–17, 181, 201–2, 205, 219, 279–80, 312, 316, 324–25, 337, 347; applicability of, 206–7; as barring arbitrariness, 215–16, 309–10; as barring discrimination, 28, 204, 206, 214–16, 317, 342; and Bill of Rights, 204–5; as ensuring equality, 207, 217, 306–7, 310; intent of, 206; "privileges"/"immunities," 206–7, 323; as protecting rights, 316–17; ratification of, 8, 96, 203–4, 207–8, 292, 306–8, 316, 344; and right to fair trial, 307; text of, 2, 29, 204, 292, 316–17; as transformative, 28–29, 306, 317, 330, 342; values of, 330; and women's rights, 317. *See also* Due Process Clause(s); Equal Protection Clause

Fourth Amendment, 312

Framers. *See individual framers*

France, 34, 41–43, 47, 62, 92, 108–13, 139, 150, 174, 273, 275, 328; as abolitionist, 247; capital crimes in, 45; executions in, 108; homicide rate in, 247; and modes of execution, 108; penal code in, 40; refusal to extradite, 288; torture in, 187. *See also* French Revolution; Paris, France

Francis, Willie, 201, 331

Frankfurter, Felix, 205

Franklin, Benjamin, 66, 77, 85, 91, 105, 113–14, 137, 339–41; and Beccaria, 53; and Benjamin Rush, 124, 126; at Constitutional Convention, 125–26; on death penalty, 8–9, 123–25; and Declaration of Independence, 103–4; on dignity, 343; on duels, 138; house of,

53, 69; on lynchings, 124; and militia discipline, 127; and penal reform, 125, 269; and Pennsylvania constitution, 177, 179; on torture, 56, 126; on transportation, 101; on treason, 118; use of "cruel," 124–25, 181; use of "unusual," 182; and Voltaire, 41, 48, 125

Franklin, William, 137

Frase, Richard, 189

Frederick II (king), 33, 93

freedom of assembly, 323

freedom of press, 164, 204, 323

freedom of religion/worship, 154–55, 323

freedom of speech, 204, 311, 323

Freeman's Journal, 162

French Declaration of the Rights of Man and of the Citizen, 108–9, 149

French National Assembly, 54, 108–10

French National Convention, 110, 112

French Revolution, 38, 46, 64, 107–12, 147, 151, 265, 269, 275

Fridays, executions on, 226, 266

Friedman, Lawrence, 68

Friends (English), 43. *See also* Quakers

Fries, John, 59

Fries's Rebellion, 59

frisking, 315

Full faith and credit, 113

Furman v. Georgia, 3–5, 8, 26, 55, 199, 201–2, 216, 224, 237, 278–83, 285, 291–92, 298, 310, 317, 325, 334; backlash to, 5, 10, 201, 283

Furman, William, 1–3

future generations: consideration of, 8, 29, 107, 288, 317, 322, 333, 340–41; and U.S. Constitution, 197, 304–6, 327, 332, 340, 397; and use of language, 328–29. *See also* posterity

Gabriel's Rebellion, 151–53, 188

Gacy, John Wayne, 245

gags, use of, 268

Galileo, 35

Gallatin, Albert, 148

Galloway, Joseph, 99

gallows. *See* hanging(s)

Garland, David, 286

gas chamber, 258

gathering sticks, as capital crime, 265

Gelles, Edith, 103

Geneva Conventions, 289

genocide, 290, 347; as capital crime, 222

George III (king), 98, 187

Georgetown University, 255

Georgia: "cruel or unusual punishments" clause, 209; death penalty laws, 5, 199, 201, 237, 283–84; death row inmates, 224; death sentences in, 5–6, 224, 284; defendants in, 4–6, 58, 224, 313; executions in, 223, 270; penitentiary in, 269; Supreme Court, 201, 208; treatment of slaves in, 313

German(y): as abolitionist, 247; executions in, 45; and foreign nationals, 288; homicide rate in, 247; penal code, 78; torture in, 187

Gerry, Elbridge, 103, 168

Giannone, Pietro, 35

gibbeting, 45, 69, 78, 123, 130, 142, 186, 189, 266, 270, 300, 333

Gideon v. Wainwright, 234

Gilmore, Gary, 225

Ginsburg, Ruth Bader, 17, 20–21, 237

Gladwell, Malcolm, 342

Glorious Revolution of 1688, 8, 93, 106

Godfrey v. Georgia, 201–2

Goldberg, Arthur, 3

Goodell, William, 314

Goodman, Timothy, 115

Goodmark, Charles, 253

Gottlieb, Gabriele, 271

gouging of eyes, 217, 268, 313–14

government officials, murder of, 222

government property, destruction of, 222

governors, 256, 263, 271, 273, 310, 326, 341. *See also* clemency, executive; *specific governors*

Graham v. Connor, 207

Graham v. Florida, 202–3, 240, 337

grand juries: charges/indictments, 52, 67–68, 101, 168, 314–15, 337; to check power, 52–53; requirement of, 47, 292, 294, 312–13; and treason trials, 101

Grand Jury Clause, 47, 292, 295, 311

Graunger, Thomas, 266

Grayson, William, 299

Great Britain, 20, 101, 105; capital crimes in, 81, 123, 164, 177; common law of, 92, 95–96; and English colonies, 87–88; executions in, 69; prisoners in, 129; and relevance to Eighth Amendment analysis, 20; rights in, 177. *See also* England

Great Depression, 278

Greece, 265

Greeley, Horace, 273

Greene, Nathanael, 100, 105

Greenleaf, Thomas, 162

Gregg v. Georgia, 5, 201, 236, 283–84, 291–92

Gregory I (pope), 43–44

Grenville, George, 97

Griffitts, Samuel, 84

Gross, James, 281

Grotius, Hugo, 104

Guam, 315

guerilla activity, as capital crime, 270

Guidry, Orrin, 259

Guillotin, Dr. Joseph-Ignace, 46

guillotine, 91, 111–12, 275. *See also* beheading

Gunn, James, 58

Gunpowder Plot, 134

Gunsby, Donald, 249

Gustavus III, 33

habeas corpus: curtailment of, 233–34, 277; petitions/proceedings, 16–17, 234; privilege/writ of, 47, 56, 93, 116–17, 162, 164, 167, 235, 277, 294, 312. *See also* Suspension Clause

Habeas Corpus Act of 1679, 93

Habsburgs, 33–34, 39

Hague, The, 63, 290

Haiti: abolition in, 64; slave rebellion in, 2

Hale, Nathan, 98, 130

Hall, Josias Carvel, 133

Hamilton, Alexander, 21–22, 73, 82, 111–12, 114; background of, 133–34; on Constitution, 95, 318, 330, 332; on death sentences, 133, 135–38; duel with Aaron Burr, 138, 335; on due process, 205; and dueling, 138–39; and *Federalist Papers,* 10, 22, 164–65, 318,

321–22; on "fixing" meaning, 328; on judicial independence/review, 134, 318, 321–22; on Major André, 135; on natural rights, 134; on Tories, 134–35; on Whiskey Rebellion, 132–33

Hamilton, Eliza, 138

Hamilton, Philip, 138

Hancock, John, 53–54, 103

handcuffing, use of, 220, 241, 243, 262

hanging(s), 51, 67, 85, 100, 102, 120, 126–27, 133–36, 139, 151–53, 206, 267; in chains, 189, 208, 270–71, 306, 337; constitutionality of, 200, 211; as execution method, 46, 57, 108, 122, 142, 145, 172, 186, 191, 193, 208, 212, 258, 266, 270

harboring slaves, as capital crime, 265, 270

Harcourt, Bernard, 318

hard labor, 43, 54, 57, 73, 80, 86, 89–90, 131, 145, 159, 172, 179, 191–92, 197, 205, 273, 277

Hargrove, James, 147

Harlem Heights, battle of, 130

Harmelin v. Michigan, 198

Harris County, TX, 223–24, 232

Harrison, Benjamin, 103

Hart v. Commonwealth, 189

Harvard College, 255

Harvard Law School, 255

Haskell, Elnathon, 109

Hawaii: abolition in, 278; sentencing practices, 325

Hawkins, Kimberly, 14

Hazen, Moses, 137

hearsay, use of, 42

Heath, William, 127

Hecht, Laura, 15–16

Helling v. McKinney, 241

hemlock, 265

Henry I (king), 44

Henry II (king), 268

Henry IV (king), 43, 337

Henry VIII (king), 64

Henry, Patrick, 56, 98–99, 149; and American independence, 91–92, 97; on bills of attainder, 146–47, 261; and Bill of Rights, 164, 185, 300–301; on "cruel and unusual punishments," 162, 187, 293–94, 306; on death penalty, 57, 196–97; on judicial review, 320; on pardons, 196; on torture, 300, 306; on trial by jury, 229; on "unusual" punishments, 300–302; at Virginia ratifying convention, 166, 184, 293–94

heresy, punishment of, 134, 266

Herndon, William, 277

Hessian troops, 128

Hickey, Thomas, 133

High Commission, 171–72

high crimes and misdemeanors, 319

high treason. *See* treason

highway robbery: commission of, 69; execution for, 67, 147

Hippocratic Oath, 258

Hispanics. *See* Latinos

Hitchcock, Enos, 78

hitching post, use of, 241

Hitler, Adolf, 288

Hobbs v. State, 212

Holden v. Minnesota, 200

Holdsworth, William, 49

Holland, 91, 129

Holmes, Abraham, 186

Holmes, Oliver Wendell, 25, 336–37

Holmes v. Walton, 320

Holocaust, 263, 288

Holt, Joseph, 277

Holy Cross College, 255

homicide(s): as "cruel"/"unusual," 224, 313; interracial, 284; "justifiable," 189–90, 262; offenders, 245, 248; and race of victims, 224, 284; rates/ frequency of, 247, 308–9; victims, 246, 256, 336. *See also* murder(s)

homosexuality: abolition for, 143; as capital crime, 143, 266, 286; punishment of, 143

Hope v. Pelzer, 241

Hopkinson, Joseph, 305

horse-stealing: as capital crime, 58, 125, 270; crime of, 157, 188, 331; punishment of, 142–43, 145, 157, 210

Horton, Willie, 6

Hospira Inc., 259

Hospital San Michele, 226

hostage taking, 222

Houston, TX, 223, 236, 253

Howard, Jacob, 204, 206

Howard, John, 48, 68, 76

Howe, Richard (lord), 99

Howe, Scott, 217

Howe, William, 98, 128

Huddy, Joshua, 137

Hudson, Keith, 220

Hudson v. McMillian, 7, 219–21, 243, 297

Hull, William, 59

human dignity, principle of, 17, 21–22, 238, 241–42, 279, 316, 334, 338. *See also* Eighth Amendment

human rights, 9, 22, 30, 64–65, 155–56, 184, 247, 284, 287–91, 296, 306, 315, 323, 333, 341–42, 344, 347

Humane Society of Massachusetts, 82

Hume, David, 56, 104, 141

humiliation of offenders, 241, 258, 269, 315. *See also* corporal punishments

Hunt, Lynn, 45

Hunt, Richard, 60, 136–37

Huntsville, TX, 264, 309

Hutcheson, Francis, 323

Hutto v. Finney, 296

Idaho: death penalty law, 202; executions in, 223; Supreme Court, 202

"idiots," 260, 316

idolatry, as capital crime, 134, 266

Il Caffè, 34–35

Illinois, 3, 118, 276; abolition in, 6, 285; commutations in, 285; executions in, 6; exonerations in, 6, 235; wrongful convictions in, 235

"immemorial" custom/usage, 302, 305

impalement, 211

"Impartial Examiner," 163

impeachment, 10, 275, 293, 305, 319, 321

imprisonment, 49, 78, 191, 210, 298; for "cruel and unusual punishment," 315; as death penalty substitute, 8, 37, 43, 46, 57, 83, 86, 159, 191, 246–48, 264, 273, 307; discretionary terms of, 173; and Eighth Amendment, 194, 198, 212. *See also* life imprisonment; prison(s)

In re Birdsong, 209

In re Kemmler, 200, 202, 206, 210–11, 216
In re McDonald, 210
In the Matter of Bayard, 212–13
inalienable rights, 54, 104, 179, 363. *See also* unalienable rights
incarceration. *See* imprisonment; life imprisonment; prison(s)
incest, 181, 249. *See also* sexual abuse
inchantment, punishment of, 134
Independence Hall, 269. *See also* State House
Index of Forbidden Books, 39
India, 227; abolition in, 45; capital crimes in, 265; and execution delays, 228; Supreme Court of, 228
Indiana, 118; abolition efforts in, 274; nighttime execution law, 257; Supreme Court, 212
Indians. *See* Native Americans
indictments. *See* grand juries
individual rights. *See specific rights*
individualized sentencing, 26, 200, 285
Indonesia, executions in, 287
ineffective assistance of counsel. *See* counsel, defense; Sixth Amendment
"infamous" crimes/punishments, 32–33, 47, 89, 168, 191, 193, 292, 311
infamy, 32–33, 46–47, 69–70, 173
infanticide, executions for, 67
infants, 134. *See also* juveniles
informant, killing of, 222
Ingraham v. Wright, 194, 242
inmates. *See* death row inmates; prisoners
innocence: and executions, 26, 40–42, 44, 55, 230, 256, 266, 281, 343–45; and maxims, 125; and torture, 32, 35, 56; and wrongful convictions, 29, 41–42, 118, 232–33, 236–37, 336, 344, 346. *See also* exonerations
Innocence Project, 336
Inns of Court, 154
inquisitions, 184, 306. *See also* Spanish Inquisition
insane, bar on executing, 7, 19, 199, 254, 260, 336
insanity, 60, 84, 226–27, 252–55, 259–60
Institutes of the Laws of England, 133
international community: abolition vs. retention, 287, 290, 318, 342; and juvenile offenders, 20, 22–23; loss of respect in, 288; and torture, 318; and treaties, 347. *See also* international law; treaties
"international consensus," 22
International Court of Justice, 288
International Covenant on Civil and Political Rights, 24, 289
International Criminal Court, 290
international law, 9, 22–24, 261, 288–91, 346–47; citation of, 22–24; customary, 318; and Eighth Amendment, 198; and foreign nationals, 288; and torture, 33, 318; use by founders, 198; U.S. reservations to, 289. *See also* "Law of Nations"; treaties
International Tribunal for the Former Yugoslavia, 290
interrogations, 14, 36, 48, 306. *See also* self-incrimination
Intolerable Acts, 97
involuntary servitude, 118–19, 203, 295
Iowa, 204; abolition efforts in, 274; abolition in, 278
Iran: death sentences in, 286–87; executions in, 20, 64, 286–87
Iraq, executions in, 64, 287
Iredell, James, 117, 163–64, 320
irons, use of, 56, 68, 196, 209, 314–15
Isenberg, Nancy, 51
Islamic law, 286
Italy, 68, 70; and lethal injection drugs, 259; punishments in, 142; refusal to extradite, 288. *See also* Tuscan(y)

Jackson, Andrew, 273
Jackson, Lucious, 1–2
Jackson, Robert, 322–23
Jackson, William, 332
Jackson v. Bishop, 242
jails, 7; character/condition of, 67–68, 297. *See also* prison(s); Walnut Street Jail
Jamaica, death penalty in, 227–28
James I (king), 154
James II (king), 93–94, 121, 173–75, 212, 215

James, Nancy, 192–93

James v. Commonwealth, 192–93

Japan: abolition efforts in, 45, 64; executions in, 36, 64

javelins, death by, 211

Jay, John, 9, 56–57, 110, 113, 132, 165, 320

Jefferson, John Garland, 54

Jefferson, Thomas, 66, 101, 103, 114, 120, 140, 272–73, 315, 320, 338; admirer of Beccaria, 50, 53–55, 141, 145, 268; background of, 139, 141; on benefit of clergy, 268; and Benjamin Rush, 71, 73–74, 91–93, 149; on Bill of Rights, 96, 165–66; on bills of attainder, 117, 147, 306; on common law, 150, 303–4; on corporal punishments, 144; on death penalty, 8–9, 54, 56, 86, 140–51, 272, 340; and Declaration of Independence, 102–4, 139, 148, 177–78, 289, 324; on duels, 138; on "fixing" meaning, 329; and French Revolution, 108–12; on George Mason, 177; and James Madison, 29, 108, 114, 119, 143, 155–57, 165–66, 183, 294, 319–20; on judicial independence, 27, 319–20; on juries, 117; on lex talionis, 64, 141–42, 335; and natural law, 104, 177; ownership of slaves, 2, 118; on pain, 139; on pardons, 268; pardons of, 59–60; and penal reform, 63, 139–51, 155–57, 178; and prisons, 67, 150; and proportionality, 141–51; religious views of, 71; on slave rebellion, 151–53; and slavery, 144, 153; on solitary confinement, 150; on smuggling, 148; and Thomas Paine, 148; on torture, 56, 141, 304; use of "cruel," 144; use of "excessive," 194; and Voltaire, 41; and Western lands, 118–19; writings of, 98

Jeffreys, George, 94–95, 174–76, 204

John (king), 293

Johnson, Cecil, 228–29

Johnson, Richard M., 273

Johnson, Samuel, 292, 328–29

Johnson, William Samuel, 114–15

Johnson v. Bredesen, 228

John the Baptist, 80

Joint Committee on Reconstruction, 204

Joseph II (emperor), 46

journalists. *See* media representatives

Judas Chair, 33

judges: bail/fine determinations, 186; discretion of, 5, 149, 173, 307; and Eighth Amendment constraints, 184, 294; and elections, 318, 323, 326; as guardians of rights, 27, 294, 313; independence of, 8, 27, 166, 179, 269, 292, 318–22, 327, 333–34, 346; pro–death penalty campaigns against, 6, 319; role in executions, 32, 256, 263; role in interpretation, 28, 312–13, 317, 319–21, 328; and "unusual," 305–6. *See also* federal judges

judicial activism, 10

Judicial Committee of the Privy Council, 227

judicial independence, 8, 27, 166, 179, 269, 292, 318–22, 327, 333–34, 346

judicial review, use of, 10, 117, 134, 269, 320–21; as check on majoritarian power, 320

judicial torture, 33, 42. *See also* torture

judiciary. *See* federal judges; judges; *specific courts*

Judiciary Act of 1789, 121, 271

Jurek v. Texas, 201, 283

juries: as check on power, 320; as conscience of community, 4, 230; conviction-prone, 231–32; death-qualified, 4, 15–16, 230–32, 309–10, 344; and death sentences, 4, 229–30, 263, 325–26, 343; discretion of, 5, 201, 282, 325–26; impartial, 312; practices of, 4; selection of, 15–16, 230–32

juror(s): attitudes toward death penalty, 230; and jury duty, 256; misconduct, 236; murder of, 222; selection of, 15–16, 207, 224; studies, 238

jury instructions, 26, 218, 346

jury nullification, 58, 325–26

jury trial, right to, 47, 117, 162, 167–68, 204, 229, 312–13, 320

jury verdicts: in death penalty cases, 299–30, 344; as Eighth Amendment "objective" indicator, 27, 229–32; unanimity requirement, 222–23

Justices, 222, 338; backgrounds of, 255; responsibility of, 317–18, 333, 340. *See also specific Justices*

"justifiable homicide," 189–90, 262

juveniles: bar on executing, 7, 16–21, 24–25, 199, 289–90, 336; execution of, 7, 16, 18, 22–24, 26, 240; and life-without-parole sentences, 202–3, 240, 337; and non-homicide offenses, 202, 240, 337; study of, 247

Kansas: abolition in, 278, 286; executions in, 223; reinstatement in, 286

Kant, Immanuel, 39, 334–35

Kasson, John, 204

Keller, Sharon, 309

Kelly v. State, 218

Kemmler, William, 211

Kendall, George, 270

Kennedy, Anthony, 17–21, 29

Kennedy v. Louisiana, 199, 239–40

Kent, James, 192

Kentucky, 225, 273; commutation in, 18; constitution, 180, 215–16; Court of Appeals, 215–16, 336; "cruel punishments" clause, 215; death row inmates, 224, 245; executions in, 223, 267; lawyers disciplined in, 233; legislature, 158; lethal injection protocol, 6, 201, 237–38, 244–45; penitentiary in, 269; treatment of blacks in, 313

kidnapping, as capital crime, 222, 270

killers. *See* murderers

killing. *See* executions; homicide(s); murder(s)

killing cattle/cows, as capital crime, 265–66

King, Coretta Scott, 3

King, Martin Luther, 3, 344

King, Rachel, 232

King, Rufus, 115, 138

King's Bench, Court of, 174, 213

King's College, 133

kings, 45, 67, 95, 112, 121, 132, 147–48, 190; "divine right" of, 78. *See also* monarchs; *specific kings*

Knoll, Shane, 14

Knox, Henry, 114, 138

Korean War, 250

Kow v. Nunan, 214

Ku Klux Klan, 335

labor, punishment of, 76, 78, 81, 83, 85, 144, 150, 160. *See also* hard labor; involuntary servitude

Lackey v. Texas, 228

Lafayette, Adrienne, 113

Lafayette, Marquis de, 108–9, 113, 131, 149

Lafitte, Jean, 59

Lancaster, Pennsylvania, 125

Lane, Ira, 84

larceny: abolition for, 88; as capital crime, 208, 210, 212; punishment of, 145, 212

lashes. *See* whipping

Latham, Mary, 267

Latinos: on death row, 224; exonerations of, 236

Laurens, Henry, 129

law enforcement officers: murder of, 222. *See also* police chiefs

"Law of Nations," 115, 134, 146, 198, 261, 293, 300–302, 305

law of nature. *See* natural law

"law of the land," 163, 165, 167, 180, 193, 261, 293, 320–21

Law School Admission Test, 235

Laws of the United States, 92, 164, 321. *See also* United States

lawyers. *See* counsel, defense; prosecutors

Lechler, John, 257

Lee, Charles, 102

Lee, Henry, 183

Lee, Richard Henry, 47, 97–99, 101, 103, 140, 153, 166, 168, 302

Lee, Thomas, 141

Leffingwell, Ebenezer, 130

leg screws, use of, 268

legislation: asserted primacy of, 21, 24, 189, 209, 211; "consistency of the direction of change," 19, 239–40; deference to, 4, 26–27, 210, 281–82; and "evolving standards of decency," 25, 238; and "national consensus," 16, 18, 21–24, 26–27, 203, 238–40; as "objective indicia of consensus," 17–19, 27, 203; and "rate of change," 18, 239

legislators, 29, 263, 318; and Eighth Amendment constraints, 219–20, 294, 308, 312; and public pressure, 6
Leland, John, 154
Leopold II (emperor), 46
Leopold, Peter (grand duke), 39, 46
lethal injection(s), 26, 258–59, 263; botched, 260, 297; legal challenge to, 6, 201, 223, 237, 244–45, 336; protocols, 6, 200–201, 237, 246, 258; risk of maladministration, 245, 291; shortage/importation of drugs, 237, 259
Lettsom, John Coakley, 75–76
Leuchter, Fred, 263
Levy, Leonard, 146, 175
levying war, abolition for, 88
lex talionis, doctrine of, 63, 141–42, 145, 334–35
Lexington, battle of, 105
Library of Congress, 54
Libya, executions in, 64, 287
Liebman, James, 230, 236
"life," deprivation of, 2, 4, 29, 83, 167, 169, 178, 180, 204, 261–62, 289, 292, 312, 316. See also Due Process Clause(s)
life imprisonment, 55, 57, 64, 175, 279, 286, 290, 296, 325; as common/usual punishment, 309; cost of, 246; necessity of, 256; number of sentences imposed, 309; "perpetual"/"permanent" servitude, 36–38, 43, 49, 71, 86–87, 191; without parole, 9, 18, 64, 161, 198, 202–3, 238–40, 246–48, 256, 264, 306–7, 309, 334, 337, 343–44; in U.S., 5, 9, 198, 275, 309
"life or limb," 144–45, 169, 217, 292, 316, 343–44
limb(s), deprivation of, 36, 42, 45, 49, 144, 210, 217, 286–87, 314, 343–44. See also ear cropping; "life or limb"
Lincoln, Abraham, 276–77, 324
Lippencott, Richard, 137–38
Little, Rory, 120
Livermore, Samuel, 186, 302, 328
living constitutionalism, 27–29, 197
Livingston, Brockholst, 315
Livingston, Edward, 149, 159, 273

Livingston, Philip, 273
Livingston, Robert, 103, 273
Lloyd, David, 88
Locke, John, 40, 47, 56, 104, 141, 177, 184
Lockett v. Ohio, 200, 285
Lombardy, 34–35, 38, 46, 55
London, England, 50, 62, 74–75, 105, 123, 126, 137, 139; executions in, 267; mob violence in, 108; pillories in, 175
London School of Economics, 255
"long customs," 302
"long usage," 302–6
looting, executions for, 129
Louis XV (king), 45
Louis XVI (king), 54, 91, 110–12, 138, 147
Louisiana, 206, 220, 273; abolition efforts in, 273–74; "Black Code," 314; death penalty laws, 283, 325; death row inmates, 224, 331; death sentences in, 253; and forcible medication, 255; lawyers disciplined in, 233; lynchings in, 276; penal reform in, 159; Supreme Court, 253; transportation to, 153; treatment of slaves in, 217, 314
Louisiana ex rel. Francis v. Resweber, 201, 207, 331
Lownes, Caleb, 82
"lunatics," 260
Luxembourg Prison, 112
lynch mobs, 3, 335
lynching(s): abhorrence of, 289, 333, 345; in America, 2–3, 124, 223, 276, 289, 335, 343; of blacks, 2–3, 276, 335; of Indians, 124; threat of, 152
Lyons, France, prison at, 150

Machiavelli, Niccolo, 35
Madison, James, 29, 95, 108, 121, 164–65, 189, 269, 272, 315, 371; background of, 154–55; and Beccaria, 56, 156; and Benjamin Rush, 91–92, 156; on Bill of Rights, 27, 96, 119, 156, 161, 165–71, 183, 185, 204, 294, 320; on bills of attainder, 116, 170, 261, 321; on common law, 304; and Constitution, 36, 155, 160, 165–67, 169–70, 185, 302–4, 332; at Constitutional Convention, 114–15, 184, 316; on Convention

debates, 332; on counterfeiting, 115; and "cruel and unusual punishments," 155, 166; on death penalty, 8–9, 138, 156–59, 340; on Declaration of Independence, 323; on ex post facto laws, 116, 170, 321; and *Federalist Papers,* 165, 261, 328; on "fixing" meaning, 328–29; on framing Constitution, 316; on judicial independence, 27, 322; on militia, 153–54; on Northwest Ordinance, 167; ownership of slaves, 2, 156; on pardoning power, 116, 157; pardons of, 59; and penal codes/reform, 63, 86, 155–61, 296, 339; on penitentiary system, 159–60; on "permanent principles," 330; on popular sovereignty, 341; on public dissection, 122; on religious tolerance, 154–55; on retaliation, 128–29; on Russian ambassador, 302; on separation of powers, 261; and Thomas Jefferson, 119, 143, 155–57, 165–66, 183, 294, 319; on treason, 157–58; use of "cruel," 159–60, 183, 185, 296; use of "unusual," 183, 185; and Voltaire, 41; and William Bradford, 54, 84, 154–55, 334

"mad-men," 134, 260

madness, 83–84. *See also* insanity

magistrates: authority of, 98–99, 113; constraints on, 180, 184; cruelty of, 32, 36; discretion of, 51, 173; and executions, 32, 147, 152

Magna Carta, 93, 163, 171–72, 293, 301, 307

maiming, 142, 172, 212, 217, 268, 307, 313–14, 338, 343–44

Maine, 131; abolition in, 273, 278

majoritarian power, abuse of, 111, 321

Malaysia: death sentences in, 287; executions in, 64

Malcom, Howard, 160

malice aforethought, 182, 190

malicious maiming, as capital crime, 88

malicious mayhem, as capital crime, 90

mandatory death sentences, 25–26, 58, 122, 141, 173, 201, 324–26; repeal/abandonment of, 304, 309, 325–26; unconstitutionality of, 201, 283, 325

Mann v. Trabue, 217

manslaughter, 79, 126, 145, 262, 268, 290, 336; as capital crime, 2, 88, 90; as "cruel"/"unusual," 181–83, 313; compared to murder, 181–83, 190, 218

Manson, Charles, 279

"manstealing," as capital crime, 266

Marat, Jean-Paul, 110–12

Marbury v. Madison, 21, 320, 322

"Marcus," 163

Marquez, Mario, 246

Marshall, John, 21, 99, 118, 166, 197, 261, 319–20, 346

Marshall, Thurgood, 196, 200, 265, 280–81, 292, 343

Mary (queen), 40, 94

Mary (queen of Scots), 171

Mary II (queen), 94, 174

Maryland, 122; and Articles of Confederation, 98; constitution, 87; declaration of rights, 169, 178–79; effigy hanged in, 97; executions in, 223, 270, 281; exoneration in, 233; penitentiaries in, 269, 281; and Stamp Act, 97

Mason, George: background of, 177; and Bill of Rights, 154, 162–65, 166–68, 185; on Committee of Revisors, 141, 150; on "cruel" punishments, 184; on "ignominious"/"severe" punishments, 299–300; "Objections to the Constitution," 116, 187–88; on pardoning power, 116; on "unusual" punishments, 299–300; and Virginia Declaration of Rights, 104, 168, 177–78

Mason, Jeremiah, 63

Massachusetts, 54, 98, 103, 113–14, 118, 127, 167, 173, 191, 270–71, 297; abolition efforts in, 273, 275; appointment of counsel in, 192; Bay Colony, 99, 266; bill of rights, 169; capital crimes in, 173, 189, 266; constitution, 167, 177, 179–80, 184; corporal punishments in, 316; "cruel or unusual punishments" clause, 167–68, 227; death penalty in, 227; effigy hanged in, 97; executions in, 270, 324; General Court, 173; laws of, 167, 266; pardoning power in, 116; penitentiary in, 269; ratifying convention, 167–68, 186, 295; Tories in, 99

masturbation, as capital crime, 266

Masur, Louis, 271

Mathews, John, 100

Mayer, Gregg, 265

Maynard v. Cartwright, 201

McCain, John, 199

McCay, Henry, 208

McCleskey, Warren, 6, 284

McCleskey v. Kemp, 5–6, 284

McElvaine, Charles, 226

McElvaine v. Brush, 201, 206

McGautha v. California, 4, 282

McHenry, James, 60, 136, 257

McKean, Thomas, 101–2

McMillian, Walter, 233

McVeigh, Timothy, 223

media representatives: and execution attendance, 200; and news coverage of executions, 68, 71, 200, 248, 257, 273–74, 347. *See also* newspapers; television

medical care: deprivation of, 243; duty to provide, 219–20, 296

Medical Inquiries and Observations upon the Diseases of the Mind, 83

medical professionals, 83, 258–60, 263. *See also* physicians

men: on death row, 11, 224; execution of, 286

mentally ill/retarded offenders, 7, 16, 42, 225, 229, 234–35, 239–40, 246, 248–54, 260–63, 316; execution of, 7, 16, 18–19, 25–26, 42, 195, 199, 232, 239–40, 250, 254–56, 260–61, 316; and U.S. Supreme Court, 7, 16, 18–19, 336. *See also* brain-damaged offenders; death row inmates

Mercer, George, 97

Mercer, Jeremy, 45–46

Mercer, John, 177

mercy, 59, 61, 111, 116, 129, 138, 149, 152, 166, 257. *See also* clemency, executive

method(s) of execution, 26, 43, 46, 176, 211, 266; changing nature of, 258, 304–5; and Eighth Amendment, 6,

193, 200–2, 210–12, 216, 237, 244; and English law, 108, 172, 174, 176; under 1790 law, 122. *See also specific methods*

Mexican-American Legal Defense and Educational Fund, 2

Mexico: abolition in, 64; and foreign nationals, 288

Michigan, 118, 206, 331; abolition in, 119, 275; constitution, 119; Supreme Court, 330–31

Middle Ages, 64, 274

Middle East, executions in, 286–87

"midnight assassination law," 257

Mifflin, Thomas, 52, 85

Milan, Italy, 31, 34–35, 39

military: combat, 250; death row of, 223–24; executions, 223–24, 277; punishments, 141, 191

military law, 49, 64, 126–27, 129–31, 136, 146, 200, 222–23, 315, 358. *See also* Articles of War; courts-martial proceedings

militia(s), 59, 292, 294; desertions from, 126–27; punishment of, 184, 187; state, 84, 102, 151, 153–54, 299–300

Miller, Samuel, 59, 206

Miller-El v. Dretke, 224

Milosevic, Slobodan, 290

Minnesota, 118, 235, 237; abolition in, 278; executions in, 267; lynching in, 335; nighttime execution law, 200, 257–58; private execution law, 200, 257; sentencing practices, 325; Supreme Court, 210, 267

Minnesota v. Borgstrom, 210

minorities: attitudes toward death penalty, 231; on death row, 224; discrimination against, 2–3, 181, 224, 272, 275, 284, 307, 313; exclusion from juries, 224, 231; right to vote, 204, 342. *See also* African Americans; Latinos; racial discrimination

miscarriages of justice, 7, 231–34, 236. *See also* wrongful convictions

misdemeanors, 193, 198

Mississippi: death row inmates, 223, 235, 249; executions in, 264; High Court of

Errors and Appeals, 218; lynchings in, 3, 276; treatment of slaves in, 181, 217–18, 313

Missouri: abolition in, 278; death penalty laws, 17; death row inmates, 224; death sentences in, 7, 15–17; and executioner's identity, 260; executions in, 223; lynching in, 276; murder in, 13–14; Supreme Court, 15–17, 211, 217

Mitchell, John, 59

"mitigating" factors/circumstances, 5, 200–201, 222, 236, 256, 325–26

mock executions, 269

Model Penal Code, 286, 306

modes of execution, 26, 198, 211, 266, 297. *See also* methods of execution; *specific modes*

modes of punishment, 26, 188–89, 191, 202, 209, 211, 214, 315

Molière, 134

monarchs: and "divine right," 78; power to pardon/commute, 117, 132; rejection of, 305; and torture, 172; tyranny/cruelty of, 93, 106, 110, 121, 171, 187, 272, 321, 333; use of executions, 49, 77–78, 110. *See also specific monarchs*

Mongolia, executions in, 287

Monmouth. *See* Duke of Monmouth

Monroe, Elizabeth, 113

Monroe, James, 41, 113, 151–53, 156–57, 167, 184

Montaigne, 41, 70

Montana, executions in, 223

Montesquieu, Charles de, 45, 63, 92; background of, 37; influence on Beccaria, 34, 37; influence on founders, 36, 41, 47, 55, 86, 125, 141, 184, 187; views of, 33, 36–37, 55, 88, 261. See also *Spirit of the Laws*

Monticello, 148, 150, 153

Moomey, Brian, 12–13, 15

Morales, Michael, 259

Moran, James, 267

Moratorium Campaign, The, 336

moratorium(s) on executions, 230, 285–86, 336, 345; de facto, 6; support for, 6, 9, 237, 287–88

Morris, Cynthia, 278

Morris, Gouverneur, 57, 109–10, 115–16, 181, 184

Morris, Norval, 283

Morris, Robert, 52, 76, 165

Morton, Washington, 136

Moses, law of, 74, 80, 89, 123, 142

Mothers with dependent infants, 289

Moussaoui, Zacarias, 288

murder(s), 14, 17, 72, 79, 90, 120, 123, 137, 146, 181, 228, 245–46, 249–54, 256, 258, 265, 267, 276, 280, 285, 325; and abolition efforts, 68, 70, 84, 275; as capital crime, 2, 25–26, 37, 43, 53–54, 57–58, 60, 67–68, 71, 86, 88, 90, 120, 122–24, 141–42, 144–45, 150, 157, 173, 224, 265–66, 270, 272, 336; attempted, 2, 37, 270; "cold-blooded," 202; compared to manslaughter, 181–83, 190, 218; degrees of, 79–81, 123, 149–50, 272; executions for, 3, 248, 277; and federal law, 222; for hire, 222; interracial, 284; and mandatory death sentences, 141; number of, 308–9; premeditated, 53, 58, 88, 190; punishment of, 67, 70, 74, 77, 80, 83, 124, 145, 172, 180, 190–91; rates, 247; and torture, 33, 43. *See also* homicide(s)

Murder Victims' Families for Human Rights, 261

Murder Victims' Families for Reconciliation, 336

murderers, 343; attitudes toward, 62, 245–46, 256, 279–80; backgrounds of, 248; and drug/alcohol (ab)use, 248; execution of, 309; irrationality of, 248; and life sentences, 309; number sentenced to death, 248. *See also* death row inmates

Murray v. Giarratano, 235

mutilation, 40, 44, 46, 54, 172, 212, 217, 266, 314. *See also* maiming

mutiny, as capital crime, 123, 127, 129, 133

NAACP, 1–3, 270, 276, 278, 335

Napoleon (emperor), 44–45, 273

Nash, Leroy, 225

National Alliance for the Mentally Ill, 261

National Alliance on Mental Illness, 261
National Association of Emergency Medical Technicians, 258
National Association for the Advancement of Colored People. *See* NAACP
National Coalition to Abolish the Death Penalty, 284, 336
"national consensus," 16, 18, 21–24, 26–27, 203, 238–40
National Council of Negro Women, 2
National Urban League, 2
Native Americans, 61, 127, 146, 185; and "cruel and unusual punishments," 315; execution of, 267; lynching of, 124
natural law, 104, 128, 146, 302, 339; concept of, 177; founders' embrace of, 31, 47, 56, 98, 121, 139, 177–78
natural rights, 32, 95, 102, 104, 106, 108–9, 134, 163, 168, 177–80, 216, 323
Nazis, 288
Nebraska, executions in, 223
Necessary and Proper Clause, 116, 162
"Negro Act of 1740," 217–18, 313
Nelson, Caleb, 328, 330
Nelson v. Campbell, 291
Nevada, death row inmates, 224
New Hampshire, 186; abolition efforts in, 285; bill of rights, 169; constitution, 86, 180, 184; executions in, 223, 270; penitentiary in, 269; ratification convention, 168; Superior Court of Judicature, 195
New Jersey: abolition in, 286; and common law, 96; dueling in, 137, 139; executions in, 137, 270; and judicial review, 320; penal reform in, 81; penitentiary in, 269; and Stamp Act, 97
New Mexico, abolition in, 286
New Orleans, 206; defense of, 59; duel in, 73
New York, 50, 82, 103, 133, 135, 160–61, 166–67, 192, 273, 313, 319–20; abolition efforts in, 79, 272, 275; Attorney General, 50–51; bill of rights, 180; City, 56, 118, 134, 136, 167–68, 273; constitution, 176; County Court for Cayuga County, 210; and duels, 138; effigy hanged in, 97; and electrocu-

tions, 211; and English law, 96; executions in, 270; legislature, 273, 292; penal reform in, 81, 272–73; prisons in, 82, 192, 269; ratifying convention, 155, 169; and solitary confinement, 201, 226; and Stamp Act, 97; State Society, 273; Supreme Court, 208, 212
New York Journal, 162
New York Post, 273
New York Tribune, 273
Newgate prison, 68, 175
news coverage, of executions, 68, 71, 200, 248, 257, 273–74, 347
newspapers. *See specific newspapers*
Newton, Isaac, 104
Nicaragua, abolition in, 64
Nicholas, George, 188, 301–2
Nicholas I (pope), 43
Nigeria, executions in, 20, 286
nighttime execution laws: passage/purpose of, 257–58; timing of executions under, 258
nighttime executions. *See* execution(s)
Nineteenth Amendment, 342
Ninth Amendment, 312, 323
Nixon, Richard, 283
non-homicidal acts, 239–40, 336–37
"nonoriginalism," 28, 327
nonretroactivity, principle of, 234
nonviolence: movement, 344; principle of, 3
Norfolk and Portsmouth Journal, 164
Norfolk, England, 104
North Africa: and Barbary states, 115; executions in, 286
North America, 47, 98, 275, 324
North Carolina, 100, 216; constitution, 188; "cruel and unusual punishments" clause, 188; death penalty law, 283; death row inmates, 224–25; declaration of rights, 169, 179; executions in, 58, 100, 223, 225, 270, 272; and judicial review, 320–21; murder trial in, 181–83; ratifying convention, 155; and seriously mentally ill, 261; Regulators in, 58; and Stamp Act, 97; Supreme Court, 213; and Tories, 99; treatment of slaves in, 314

North Dakota, abolition in, 278
North Korea, executions in, 64
Northington v. Jackson, 243
Northwest Ordinance, 118–19, 167–68, 191, 275
Northwestern University, 235
Norvell, John, 54
nostrils, tearing of, 44, 142
Notes on the State of Virginia, 56, 118
Nuremberg, Germany, 45

Oates, Titus, 174–76
Obama, Barack, 199
obscenity, concept of, 311
O'Connor, Sandra Day, 21–22, 237, 310
offenders: characteristics of, 200, 203; individualized consideration of, 200. *See also* death row inmates
offenses: against individuals, 199; "against the Law of Nations," 293; against the State, 199; federal, 222. *See also specific crimes*
official witnesses, at executions, 257, 260, 267
Ohio, 118; abolition efforts in, 274; death row inmates, 224; lethal injection protocol, 237; nighttime execution law, 257
Ohio Adult Parole Authority v. Woodard, 310
Oklahoma: City, 223, 233; death penalty law, 201–2; death row inmates, 224; executions in, 18, 223; exoneration in, 233; and juvenile offenders, 240
Okun, Peter, 85
Old Bailey, 123
Olive Branch Petition, 98
Oliver, Andrew, 97
On Crimes and Punishments, 8–9, 31–40, 44–45, 47–48, 50, 55–56, 66, 123, 141, 157, 262, 291, 340, 346–47
O'Neil v. Vermont, 206, 299
opinion polls. *See* public opinion
ordeals by fire, 32
Ordonnance Criminelle of 1670, 40
Oregon: abolition in, 278; death row inmates, 224; executions in, 223

organs, harvesting of, 286
original intent, 27, 322
original meaning, 22, 27, 302–3, 306, 316–17
originalism, 11, 24, 26, 28–29, 292, 316–17, 326–27
Otis, James, 177, 320
Oxford English Dictionary, 295
Oxford University, 49, 171, 255

pain: avoidance/minimization of, 46, 139, 259; concept of, 243–44; and cruelty, 37, 295–96, 329; and Eighth Amendment, 26, 241–42, 297, 329, 332, 334; infliction of, 26, 32, 35, 37, 49, 53, 144, 172, 202, 221, 241–43, 256, 258, 268–69, 296–97, 331–32, 334; physical, 291, 297–98, 329; psychological, 243, 291, 298, 329; risk of, 6, 237, 244–45, 291, 297–98; and torture, 35, 268, 298. *See also* torture
Pain, Joseph, 104
Paine, Thomas, 66, 343; abolitionist views of, 54, 106–8, 110–11; background of, 104–5; on Beccaria, 54; on Bill of Rights, 95; and *Common Sense,* 98, 104–6; on duels, 138; on French Revolution, 107–13; imprisonment of, 112–13; on natural rights, 95; and Thomas Jefferson, 148
"pains and penalties," 179; Maryland's prohibition on, 178–79
Pakistan, executions in, 20, 64, 287
Paley, William, 70
pancuronium bromide, 238, 244–45
Panetti, Scott, 248–49
Panetti v. Quarterman, 248–49
Panopticon, 51
Paraguay, 288
paralysis, inducement of, 244–45
paranoid schizophrenia. *See* schizophrenia
pardoning power. *See* clemency, executive
pardons, 51, 57, 59–60, 78, 84, 89, 116–17, 128, 130–33, 153, 174, 197, 268, 277
Paris, France, 40–41, 56, 62, 91, 108, 110–12, 114, 126, 143, 153, 181, 261; mob violence in, 107–8, 113

Parliament. *See* British Parliament

parole, ineligibility for. *See* life imprisonment

parricides, 42–43, 120, 267

"pat down" search, 315

Payne v. Tennessee, 195–96

Pear of Anguish, 33

Pearson, Charles, 57

peine forte et dure, 188. *See also* pressing to death

penal codes. *See specific jurisdictions*

penal colonies, 68

Pendleton, Edmund, 86, 140–41, 144, 148–50, 184, 310, 320

penitentiaries. *See* prison(s)

Penn, William, 87–88, 90

Pennsylvania, 8, 51, 57, 59, 66, 83–85, 101–2, 105, 115, 120, 122, 126, 154, 346; abolition efforts in, 62, 76, 78–79, 87–89, 193, 257, 272, 274; Attorney General, 54, 79, 84, 92; capital offenses, 88–90; common law, 193; constitution, 87–88, 155, 178–79, 305; Court of Common Pleas, 58; death row inmates, 224; declaration of rights, 169, 179; dividing murder into degrees, 79, 149; effigy hanged in, 97; and English law, 96; executions in, 67, 223, 257, 267, 270, 324; Frame of Government, 171; governor, 85–86, 159; Hospital, 62, 73; legislature, 82, 85–88, 159, 166, 171, 179, 269; penal laws of, 69, 72–73, 86–88; penal reform in, 71, 81–82, 85–87, 89, 124–25, 143, 149–51, 269, 305; prisons in, 8–9, 67–68, 82–83, 269; Quakers in, 8, 76, 149, 271; ratifying convention, 93, 155; religious freedom in, 154; and Stamp Act, 97; Supreme Court, 84, 101, 192–93

Pennsylvania Gazette, 101, 177

Pennsylvania Journal, 79

Pennsylvania v. Finley, 235

Penry, John Paul, 246

Penry v. Lynaugh, 18–19, 195

People v. Anderson, 298

People v. Morris, 210, 330

People's Republic of China. *See* China

perjury: as capital crime, 265–66; and Titus Oates, 174–76

"perpetual" imprisonment/servitude, 36–38, 43, 49, 71, 86–87. *See also* life imprisonment

Perry, Michael, 253–54

Persia, executions in, 265

Pervear v. Commonwealth, 205–6

Peter the Great (emperor), 44

Peters, Richard, 166, 171

Peterson, Ruth, 247

petit treason, 134

Petition of Right of 1628, 93

Petrovna, Elizabeth (empress), 44

petty larceny, 294. *See also* larceny

petty treason, 145

Philadelphia, 31, 51, 92, 99, 103, 125, 136, 271, 283; abolition efforts in, 273; anti-slavery efforts, 2, 81; and Congress, 56–57, 98, 132, 140; and Constitutional Convention, 162, 164–65, 167–68, 187, 269, 320; crime in, 89; death sentences in, 224; executions in, 67, 267, 271, 324; jail/prison in, 8–9, 67–68, 82–83, 89–90, 269, 226, 275; and penal reform, 66, 72–74, 76, 79, 84, 149–51, 159, 269–70; slavery in, 340; treason trials in, 52, 101. *See also* Constitutional Convention; Pennsylvania; Walnut Street Jail/Prison

Philadelphia Bible Society, 66

Philadelphia Medical Society, 66

Philadelphia Mercury, 77

Philadelphia Society for Alleviating the Miseries of Public Prisons, 66, 76, 82, 270

Philadelphia Society for Relieving Distressed Prisoners, 67, 269

Philadelphia Society for the Abolition of Capital Punishment, 274

"Philadelphiensis," 163

Philippines, 197

Philips, Josiah, 146–47, 262, 306

"Philochoras," 77

phlebotomists, 244

physicians: barred as execution participants, 244; ethical concerns of, 255, 258–59; at executions, 259–60, 263;

and legal system, 83, 250, 259; opposing executions, 258–59, 263; shielding identity of, 259–60

pillory: abolition of, 209, 316, 344–45; as infamous punishment, 191; use of, 7, 11, 65, 89, 120, 126, 172, 175–76, 193, 210, 212, 258, 331

Pinckney, Charles, 58, 114

Pincus, Jonathan, 247

piracy: as capital crime, 26, 57, 67, 115, 120, 122, 270; problem of, 115; and U.S. Constitution, 153, 293

pirates: Baratarian, 59; Barbary, 115; pardon of, 59

Pitts, John, 99

Pius, Antoninus, 46

Plessis prison, 113

Plessy v. Ferguson, 329–30

Plunkett, Oliver, 175

Plutarch, 56

poisoning: as capital crime, 2, 142, 270–71; killing by, 142

police chiefs, on deterrence/executions, 248

political offenses, bar on executing for, 289

Polk, James, 273

polls. *See* public opinion

polygamy: as capital crime, 154; punishment of, 143

"Popish Plot," 175

populism, 28. *See also* public opinion

Porcian law, 190

Porter, Anthony, 235

Porter, George, 250–51

Post Traumatic Stress Disorder, 248, 251

postconviction proceedings, 234–35. *See also* habeas corpus

posterity, 95, 101, 305; appeals to, 75, 101, 106, 178, 274, 276, 305, 341; attempts to govern, 107, 177–78; reference in Declaration of Independence, 341. *See also* future generations

potassium chloride, 244–45

Powell, John, 92

Powell, Lewis, 282, 284

precedentialism, 28

pregnant offenders, 289

Prejean, Helen, 284

prejudice, racial. *See* racial discrimination

premeditation, 53, 58, 88, 246. *See also* murder(s)

President(s), 92, 222, 255, 333; approval of death sentences, 131–32, 277; constrained by Eighth Amendment, 184; pardons/commutations issued by, 59–60, 63, 83–84, 132–33, 136–37, 277; power to commute/reprieve, 117–18, 326; power to pardon, 59, 116–18, 132–33, 135, 310; and treaty power, 23. *See also specific presidents*

pressing to death, 188, 266–67

Price, Richard, 339

Price, William Ray, 16–17

Princeton University, 6, 50, 84, 154, 255, 315. *See also* College of New Jersey

Principles of Moral and Political Philosophy, 70

Principles of Natural Law, 104

Principles of Penal Law, 48, 70

prison(s): building of, 7–8, 43, 68–70, 150–51, 192, 269, 343; conditions, 67–68, 219–21, 226–27; guards, 241, 263; history of, 51, 76, 151, 208, 340; and James Madison's views, 296; maximum-security, 9, 161, 246, 296, 306, 334, 343; reform, 68; regulation of, 67; societies, 66–67, 85; use of, 120; wardens, 227, 263–64, 278. *See also* conditions of confinement; excessive force; imprisonment; life imprisonment

prisoners: basic needs of, 219–20, 296; duties owed to, 209, 219–20, 240–43, 296; exposure to diseases, 241–42, 296; treatment of, 76. *See also* death row inmates

prisoners of war, 100; safeguarding, 129; treatment of, 100, 128, 137, 146, 289. *See also* Geneva Conventions

private execution laws: anti-publicity provisions of, 248, 257; constitutionality of, 200; effect/purpose of, 248, 257. *See also specific jurisdictions*

private executions. *See* execution(s)

"privileges"/"immunities," 95, 118, 120, 163, 169, 177, 179–80, 204, 206, 216, 301–2, 322

Privileges and Immunities Clause, 118

Privileges or Immunities Clause, 2, 203–4, 206–7, 323

Privy Council, 171

procedural default, 234

Proffitt v. Florida, 201, 283

Progressive Era, 278

property crimes: as capital crimes, 67, 272; executions for, 67. *See also* burglary; forgery; larceny; robbery; stealing; theft

proportionality, concept of, 17, 31, 39, 49–50, 54, 57, 69, 86–87, 122–23, 125, 130–31, 141–51, 157, 175, 179–80, 189, 195–96, 238, 305; and Eighth Amendment, 202–3

prosecutors: charging decisions, 246, 256, 312; and jury strikes, 207, 224; misconduct of, 236; practices of, 4

Prosser, Thomas, 151

Prussia, 33, 93

public dissection, of corpses, 122, 145, 172, 266

public executions. *See* execution(s)

public opinion: and Bill of Rights, 170; on death penalty, 1, 149, 191–92, 222, 230, 232, 238, 278, 283; on "infamous" punishments, 311; on innocence, 230; international, 290; on jury service, 230; and juvenile offenders, 290; on life-without-parole, 229–30, 238; and Supreme Court, 24–25, 281, 311; on torture, 191; versus judicial independence, 321–23

"Publius," 164

Pufendorf, Samuel, 104

punishment(s): arbitrary, 5, 173, 215–16, 310; "barbaric," 202, 210, 332; "barbarous," 108, 174–76, 187, 189, 202, 313, 376; "barbarous, inhuman, and unchristian," 175; common law, 303–4; "cruel," 55, 67, 87, 163, 180, 184, 190, 211, 215–18, 275, 313–14; "cruel and barbarous," 187, 376; "cruel and ignominious," 184, 187; "cruel and immod-

erate," 67; "cruel and unheard-of," 186, 213; "cruel and unjust," 119; "cruel and unnatural," 193; "cruel and unusual," 2, 8, 10, 20, 65, 118–19, 155, 161–64, 166, 170, 176–78, 180–81, 184, 187–89, 192, 197, 200, 204, 209–11, 215, 244, 281, 291–92, 294, 301, 303, 306–8, 311–12, 315, 322, 328, 331–33, 343–44, 397; "cruel, barbarous and illegal," 175; "cruel, infamous or unusual," 290; "cruel nor unusual," 176; "cruel or disproportioned," 273; "cruel or unusual," 118–19, 163, 167, 169, 178–82, 198, 204, 209–11, 217–18, 227, 238, 275, 313, 315, 331; "cruel, unusual, unnatural and ludicrous," 193; definition of, 292; discriminatory, 215–16, 281, 308, 310, 337, 345; disproportionate, 17, 190, 194, 196, 298; "excessive," 17, 194–95, 199, 202–3, 211, 213, 238, 314, 334; goals of, 202; "grievous," 154; "ignominious," 154, 193, 299–300; "ignominious, cruel, and unusual," 209; "illegal," 155; "illegal and cruel," 174, 215; "infamous," 93, 168, 191, 193, 311; "inhuman"/"degrading," 227–28; "inhumane, barbarous or cruel," 174; modes/methods of, 26, 43, 46, 176, 188–89, 191, 193, 198, 202, 209, 211, 214, 217, 266, 297, 304–5; "odious," 51, 136, 184, 188, 303, 313; private, 6, 69, 81, 200, 248, 257–58, 278; proportionate, 39, 54, 130–31, 141, 143, 146, 148–49, 157, 175, 179, 305; public, 37, 40, 69–70, 72–73, 75–76, 81, 152, 257–58, 267, 271–72, 278; references in U.S. Constitution, 293–95; "sanguinary," 49, 86–87, 92, 108, 135–36, 141, 148, 179, 192, 305; "severe," 38, 60, 154, 163–64; "severe and ignominious," 300; "unusual," 16, 25, 176, 294, 299–306, 314; "unusual and severe," 116, 162–63, 187; "unusually severe," 314; "usual," 11, 84, 193, 204, 218, 303, 314, 324. *See also* "cruel and unusual punishments"; Cruel and Unusual Punishments Clause; "cruel or unusual punishments"; corporal punishments; death penalty; execution(s)

Puritanism, 87, 172–73, 266, 271

Quaker Meeting House, 269

Quakers, 75, 87, 104–5, 111; execution of, 101–2, 266; in Pennsylvania, 8, 67–68, 72, 76, 82, 87–88, 101–2, 105–6, 149, 159, 179, 271; persecution of, 94

Quebec, 127

"Queue Ordinance," 214–15

Quinn, Pat, 6

race, 55, 216, 280, 309, 326; of death row inmates, 224; of defendants/victims, 224; and executive clemency, 310. See also minorities; racial discrimination

racial discrimination, 28–29, 275, 342; against Chinese, 214–15; and "cruel and unusual punishments," 188–89; and death penalty, 2–6, 10, 200, 206, 219, 224, 256, 270, 272, 279, 284–85, 307–10, 326, 346; in jury selection, 207; and lynchings, 2–3. See also Fourteenth Amendment; minorities

rack, use of, 26, 33, 68, 84, 109, 171–72, 186, 189, 210, 268, 280, 333

Radelet, Michael, 297

Raleigh, Walter, 134

Ramsay, David, 93, 95

Randolph, Edmund, 57, 85, 138, 164, 168, 184–85, 261–62, 301, 322

Rantoul, Robert, 272

rape, 1, 4, 143, 240, 268, 337; abolition for, 88; attempted, 2, 270; as capital crime, 2, 67, 88, 90, 265–66, 270; castration for, 142–44, 149; executions for, 3, 67, 277; non-homicidal, 240; prison, 219–20; punishment of, 191, 199, 279; and race, 2, 279; statutory, 266. See also child rape

rapists, 1, 90, 142, 144, 240, 277, 279, 337, 343; bar on executing, 199; race of, 3

ratification debates/conventions, 184, 186–87, 303. See also specific states

Ravaillac, 43

Ray, James Earl, 3

rebellion, 128; attempted, 2; as capital

crime, 2, 46, 59, 71, 173–74, 266; reference in Constitution, 294. See also treason

recidivists, tattooing of, 316

Reconstruction Amendments, 203. See also Fifteenth Amendment; Fourteenth Amendment, Thirteenth Amendment

Rector, Ricky Ray, 254

Redman, Ben Ray, 41

Rees, Daniel, 126

Reflections on the Revolution in France, 107

regicides, 42

Regulators, 58

Rehnquist, William, 22, 27–28, 282, 319

Reign of Terror, 64, 112–13. See also French Revolution

religious persecution, 39–43, 46, 94, 154

reparations, 179, 230

repeat offenders, 198

reprieves, 59, 117–18, 130, 148, 153, 326; for executioners, 262

rescuing from gallows, as capital crime, 122

restitution, 230

retaliation: concept of, 128, 143, 146, 265, 277, 334, 341; law of, 128–29, 135–37

retribution, 3, 202, 229, 245, 281, 296, 334

retroactivity, principle of, 234

revenge: concept of, 61, 68, 153, 182, 190, 245–46, 277, 298; pleasure derived from, 245–46, 296, 347

Revere, Paul, 271

Revolutionary War, 45, 57, 59, 61, 66–67, 71, 73, 88, 100–1, 106, 113, 118, 120, 128, 132, 134, 142, 146, 149, 153, 155, 238, 269, 339, 346–47

Rhode Island, 78, 97, 320; abolition in, 275–76; capital crimes in, 99–100; executions in, 270; ratifying convention, 155

Rhodes v. Chapman, 219–21

Rice, David, 253

Rice, John, 126

Richard, Michael, 309

Richard I (king), 49

Richardson, Bill, 286

Richmond, VA, 57, 151, 153, 196

right to life: in Bill of Rights, 8; in colonial America, 98; in Declaration of Independence, 54, 102, 289, 323–24, 333, 341; as fundamental/sacred, 168, 289, 323; in treaties, 289–90, 333; William Bradford on, 90

right to vote: of minorities, 204, 342; of women, 317, 342

Rights of Man, 106–8, 112

Ring v. Arizona, 237

Risi, Paolo, 38

robbery: abolition for, 88–89, 124, 143; as capital crime, 2, 62, 67, 88–89, 120, 270, 306; executions for, 67

Roberts, John, 101–2

Roberts, John (chief justice), 244–45

Roberts v. Louisiana, 201

Robertson, Edward, 14

Robespierre, Maximilien, 48, 110–13, 275

Robinson v. California, 198, 207–8

Roman Coliseum, 347–48

Roman Inquisition, 39

Roman law, 36, 56, 67, 80, 134, 190

Rome, Italy: punishments in, 43–44, 46, 70; solitary confinement in, 226

Rome Statute, 290

Roosevelt, Eleanor, 289

Roper v. Simmons, 7, 17–22, 24–26, 29, 195, 199, 239–40, 290

Rousseau, Jean-Jacques, 34, 40–41, 177

Rudolph v. Alabama, 1

Ruffin, Thomas, 216

Rule of Law, 276, 321

Rumbold, Richard, 148

Rush, Benjamin, 102, 133, 257, 269; background of, 53, 66, 73, 136; and Beccaria, 53; and Benjamin Franklin, 124, 126; and Christianity, 67, 71–72, 74–75, 83; and *Common Sense,* 105; on corporal punishments, 78, 345; on cruelty, 75, 80, 83–84, 91–92, 96; on death penalty, 8–9, 53–54, 57, 66–72, 74–84, 272, 343, 345; on dueling, 73–74, 83; on incarceration, 53; influence of, 84–86, 91–96, 275; and James Madison, 156; and John Adams, 180; on pardoning power, 77; on penal laws, 72–73, 339–40; on public punishments, 69–70, 72–73, 76; on solitary confinement, 78–79; and Thomas Jefferson, 149; and Thomas Paine, 105; urging pardons, 59, 83–84; and Voltaire, 41, 48; on "wheelbarrow" law, 72–73; writings of, 69–84

Rush, John, 73–74

Rush, Julia, 72–73

Rush, Richard, 92

Russell, Willie, 235

Russia: abolition in, 44, 74; in Empress Elizabeth's reign, 34, 44; executions in, 288; penal laws in, 34, 39, 44, 74, 77; William Howard's death in, 76

Russian ambassador, case of, 300–302

Rutledge, John, 100

Rwanda, abolition in, 64, 290

Ryan, George, 285

Sabacos (king), 57

St. Dominque, 2

St. Louis, MO, 14, 276

St. Paul, 56

Salem, MA, 266

salt, smuggling of, 45

San Francisco, 214, 289

San Quentin, 227, 264, 278

"sanguinary": definition/use of, 49, 61; laws/punishments, 49, 52, 70, 86–88, 92, 110–11, 135–36, 139, 141, 144, 148, 178–80, 192, 214, 305

Santo Domingo, 152

Saudi Arabia, executions in, 20, 64, 286–87

sawing in half, 266

scaffold. *See* hanging(s)

Scalia, Antonin, 6, 11, 22–26, 28–29, 292–93, 296, 312, 316–17, 323, 326–27, 344

scarlet letter, 268

schizoaffective disorder, 248

schizophrenia, 225, 247–48, 251, 253–54

schizotypal personality disorder, 15

Schuyler, Philip, 82, 272

Schwartz, Bernard, 320

Schwarzenegger, Arnold, 255

scolding, 192–93

Scotland, 34

Scotti, Francesco Gallarati, 38

Second Amendment, 312

secondhand smoke, exposure to, 241, 263

Sedgemoor, battle of, 94, 174

Sedgwick, Theodore, 122

sedition, 133. *See also* Alien and Sedition
　　Acts

seditious libel, 112

selective incorporation, doctrine of, 206

self-defense, 216, 262

self-incrimination, 306; protection
　　against, 48, 126, 188

self-mutilation, 251

selling bad beer, as capital crime, 265

sentence(s): individualized, 200, 285. *See
　　also* death sentence(s); imprisonment;
　　life imprisonment

separation of powers: concept of, 321; in
　　Massachusetts, 179, 346; in U.S. Con-
　　stitution, 29, 310, 321; in Virginia, 140

September Massacres, 112

serial killers, 245

setting cornfield on fire, as capital crime,
　　266

Seventh Amendment, 312

Sewall, David, 132

Seward, William H., 273

sexual abuse, 247, 268

sexual harassment, 315

shackles, use of, 43, 196, 207, 220. *See also*
　　irons

Shakespeare, 63

Shari'a law, 286

Shaw, George Bernard, 341

Shays, Daniel, 113

Shays' Rebellion, 113–14

shelter, duty to provide, 219, 296

Sherman, Roger, 103, 115, 122–23, 164

Shippen, Edward, 155

Shippen, William, 63, 84, 166, 168

Shomu (emperor), 45

shooting rabbits, as capital crime, 266

shooting swans, as capital crime, 69

shooting, death by. *See* firing squad(s)

Shuvalov, Peter, 44

Siberia, 44

Sierra Leone, 290

Simmons, Christopher, 7, 12–18

Simmons v. South Carolina, 306

Simsbury, CT, 68, 129

Sinfulness of American Slavery, 180

Singleton, Charles, 254–55

Sing-Sing, 192, 226, 275, 278

Sirvens, 41

Sixth Amendment, 7, 15, 234, 307, 312

skinning alive, 265

Slakan, Charles, 241

Slakan v. Porter, 241

Slaughter-House Cases, 206

slave codes, 2, 216–19, 307, 313

slave riot(s)/rebellion(s), 2, 151–53, 324;
　　as capital crime, 270; fear of, 2, 270–
　　72, 275

slave trade, 2, 81, 120, 307

slavery, 2–3, 37, 49, 53, 77, 118–19, 144,
　　151–53, 180–81, 184, 203, 206, 217–19,
　　307, 323–24, 341; abolition of, 81, 119,
　　295, 342; convention barring, 347; and
　　"cruel"/"unusual" punishments, 216–
　　18; cruelty of, 204; opposition to, 51,
　　66, 105, 120, 124, 274, 340

slaves: bar on testimony of, 56, 181, 313;
　　castration of, 217, 266, 313–14; and
　　Constitution, 307; execution of, 7–8,
　　152–53, 156, 188–89, 266, 270–72,
　　296; ownership of, 2, 203, 313, 316,
　　342; punishment of, 2, 8, 120, 144,
　　152–53, 181, 216–19, 266, 270–72,
　　275; whipping of, 7–8, 188–89, 215–
　　19, 268, 313–14, 337, 343

sleep deprivation, 268

sleeping on duty, punishment for, 127

slitting the nostrils, 172

Smith, William, 127

Smith, William (colonel), 114

Smith, William Loughton (rep.), 186, 302

smuggling: as capital crime, 45, 222;
　　operations, 35; punishment of, 148, 153

Smykla, John Ortiz, 270

social compact: concept of, 116, 166, 168,
　　322; as excluding blacks, 216

Social Contract, The, 34, 40, 177

Society for Promoting Political Enquiries,
　　345

Socrates, 261, 265

sodium thiopental, 237, 244, 259

sodomy: abolition for, 124, 143; as capital crime, 88, 266, 270, 272; castration for, 142–43. *See also* "buggery"

Soering v. United Kingdom, 227

Solem v. Helm, 198

solitary confinement: and Dr. Rush's views, 78–79; and James Madison's views, 160; origins of, 226; prior to execution, 201, 226; use of, 68, 73, 82–83, 86, 150, 159, 191–92, 201, 226

solitude, 76, 78, 81, 85. 90. *See also* solitary confinement

Somalia: executions in, 64; and juvenile offenders, 20, 23, 290

Sonnenfels, Joseph von, 33

Sons of Liberty, 66, 97

sorcery, punishment of, 134, 144, 266

Souter, David, 17, 237

South: corporal punishments in, 316; death penalty in, 4, 6, 159, 219, 232, 309, 311–12; executions in, 3, 223, 272, 309, 345; lynchings in, 3, 223; and slave codes, 2, 216–19, 272, 307, 313. *See also* slaves; slavery; *specific states*

South Africa(n): abolition in, 64; Constitution, 64–65; Constitutional Court, 64

South America, 144

South Carolina, 31, 58, 93, 100, 129, 186; constitution, 179; Court of Appeals, 218; death row inmates, 224; executions in, 223, 270, 324; and Stamp Act, 97; and Tories, 99; treatment of slaves in, 217, 271, 313

South Carolina v. Gathers, 196

South Dakota: abolition in, 278; "cruel punishments" clause, 211; executions in, 223; Supreme Court, 211

Southern Center for Human Rights, 335

Southern Christian Leadership Conference, 2–3

Soviet Union, 287

Spain, 39, 271; abolition of torture, 44; cave paintings in, 246; executions in, 267; and rendition, 194; torture in, 44, 187

Spanish Inquisition, 186

Spear, Charles, 273

"special issues," 256

Spencer, Ambrose, 272

Spencer, George, 266

Spencer, Stephanie, 268

Spirit of the Laws, 33, 36–37, 45, 47, 187

spreading false rumors, as capital crime, 265

spying, executions for, 98, 130, 135–36

Sri Lanka, 45

Stack v. Boyle, 195

Stalin, Joseph, 288

Stallone, Sylvester, 255

Stamp Act of 1765, 97

Stanford, Kevin, 18

Stanford University, 255

Stanford v. Kentucky, 16–19, 195

Stanton, Edwin, 277

Stanwix, John, 126

Star Chamber, 306

stare decisis: doctrine/principle of, 17, 25, 196, 329–30

starvation, as execution method, 2, 56, 211. *See also* food, deprivation of

state constitutions, 87, 98, 163, 181, 205, 305, 321, 323, 363. *See also specific states*

state courts. *See individual states*

State House (PA), 114, 126

state legislators, 6, 10, 257, 284, 322. *See also* legislation

state penitentiaries. *See* prison(s)

State v. Becker, 211

State v. Driver, 213–14

State v. Maner, 217–18

State v. Perry, 253, 255

State v. Stubblefield, 211

statelessness, as punishment, 198, 296

"status" crimes, 194, 198

stealing: as capital crime, 68, 143, 194; fruit, 143; hare, 194. *See also* burglary; horse-stealing; robbery; theft

Stevens, John Paul, 17, 20–21, 228–29, 231, 238, 286, 310

Stewart, Potter, 5, 198, 280

Stilwell, Silas, 160–61

Stinneford, John, 302–4

stocks, use of, 7, 65, 172, 258, 268, 311, 316, 341

Stone, Michael, 122

stoning to death, 111, 286–87

Story, Joseph, 189–91, 196, 213, 315

strangling, as punishment, 172

Strauss, David, 28–29

stress inoculation programs, 263

strict constructionism, 28

stripes. *See* whipping

structuralism, 28

Stuart dynasty, 174, 196, 213, 306

Stuart, James (king), 175

substantive due process. *See* due process

Sudan: death sentences/executions in, 286–87

suicide: "by court," 225; and Eighth Amendment, 220; and murderers, 83, 225–26; punishment of, 33, 42. *See also* corpses, desecration of; death row inmates

Sullivan, Thomas, 189

Summary View of the Rights of British America, A, 98

Sumner v. Shuman, 325

sunburning, of inmate, 241

Sunstein, Cass, 28, 247

superstition: beliefs based on, 42; and executions, 266

Supremacy Clause, 165, 321

Supreme Court, 1, 3–7, 9–11, 16–27, 29–30, 47, 51, 55, 57, 65, 117–18, 121, 163, 181, 189, 193–203, 205–8, 248–50, 254–55, 310–12, 315–16, 319–20, 330–34, 337–38; and abolition, 26, 318; on accomplice liability, 239–40; on beatings/assaults, 220, 297; building, 310; on child rape, 199, 239–40; on competency for execution, 248–49; and corporal punishments, 194, 242, 327; on death penalty, 236–38, 240, 242–43, 278, 286, 334, 342–48; and death row phenomenon, 226, 228–29; and Declaration of Independence, 323–24; on deterrence, 248; and discriminatory juror strikes, 224; on due process, 293, 306–7, 310; and Eighth Amendment, 206–7, 216, 219–21,

228–29, 238–42, 278–84, 290–91, 296, 304–5, 340, 342, 344–48; and "evolving standards of decency," 18, 25, 207, 238, 310–11, 313, 329, 333, 342; and exculpatory evidence, 307; and Fourteenth Amendment, 206–7, 317; and habeas corpus, 233; on insanity, 7, 199, 254, 336; and judicial independence, 27, 318–19, 322; and jury verdicts, 229–32; on juvenile offenders, 7, 17–22, 24–26, 29, 195, 199, 202–3, 239–40, 290, 336–37; and lethal injections, 6, 201, 223, 237, 242, 244–45, 336; on less culpable offenders, 19, 199, 239–40; on life-without-parole, 198, 203, 240, 306–7, 337; and mandatory death sentences, 201, 324–25; on mentally retarded offenders, 7, 16–19, 25–26, 195, 199, 239–40, 250, 316, 333; on "non-retroactivity" principle, 234; on pain, 202, 221, 241, 243, 245, 331–32, 334; on rape, 199, 239–40; and right to counsel, 234–35; on right to life, 289, 323; role/responsibility of, 317–19, 321–22, 327–28; and solitary confinement, 226; and stays of execution, 256; on torture, 198, 202, 323; on "unusual," 304–5, 308 and use of precedents, 329–30. *See also specific cases and Justices*

Suspension Clause, 116, 294

Sweden: abolition in, 74, 78; penal reform in, 74; torture abolished in, 33

Swift, Jonathan, 328–29

Switzerland, 41, 45, 135, 255

Syria, executions in, 287

Takings Clause, 312

Tang Dynasty, 45

Tarrant County, TX, 224

tarring and feathering: of government officials, 59; of Tories/British loyalists, 98, 134, 272

tattooing body, 315. *See also* branding

Taylor, George Keith, 150–51

Teague v. Lane, 234

tear gas, use of, 241

tearing skin, as punishment, 268

television: cameras, 248; coverage of executions, 248

Temple Bar, 108

Ten Commandments, 56

Tennessee, 318; abolition efforts in, 274; death penalty law, 325; death row inmates, 224; dueling in, 336; executions in, 223, 229; penitentiary in, 269

Tennô, Saga (emperor), 45

Tenth Amendment, 312

terrorism, 199, 245

terrorists, 343

Tessmer, John, 12

Texas, 311, 318, 326; Attorney General, 233; Court of Criminal Appeals, 233, 251–52, 309; death penalty law, 201, 283; death row inmates, 224, 232, 249–50; Department of Criminal Justice, 259; executions in, 18, 223–25, 232, 309; exonerations in, 232; and juvenile offenders, 240; treatment of slaves in, 217

textualism, 28

Thailand, death sentences in, 287

theft: abolition efforts for, 40, 70, 123–25, 180; as capital crime, 36–37, 63, 120, 125, 265, 270; punishment of, 89, 105, 123–25

Theresa, Maria (empress), 33, 39. *See also* Austria; Habsburgs

Thetford, England, 105

Thirteenth Amendment, 119, 203, 295, 342

Thomas, Andre, 251–53

Thomas, Clarence, 6, 22, 25

Thompson v. Oklahoma, 16–17

Thoughts on Government, 103, 346

threats: as instilling fear, 242–43; verbal/violent, 242–43

Three-fifths Clause, 307, 324

thumbscrew, use of, 26, 33, 268

Till, Emmett, 3

Tison v. Arizona, 286

tobacco: notes/certificates, 150; smuggling of, 45

Tocqueville, Alexis de, 274–75

Tompkins, Cydnor, 204

Tories: during Revolutionary War, 99;

execution/killing of, 99–100, 129, 137; prosecution/punishment of, 52, 57, 100; tarring and feathering of, 98, 134; treatment of, 60–61, 100

torture: abolition of, 33, 44–46, 64, 141, 304; acts of, 41, 43, 64, 81, 128, 141, 198, 209, 214, 267–68, 281, 303, 307; and Bill of Rights, 187–88; in China, 315; compared to statelessness, 198; and confessions, 32, 35, 172, 174, 187–88, 323; as "cruel," 32, 35–36, 171–72, 184, 188–89, 210, 227, 273, 300, 306, 315; and death row phenomenon, 227–28; death sentences as, 227, 291, 298; definition of, 298, 306; executions as, 202, 227, 273, 318; in Europe, 33–34, 41–42, 44–45, 68, 81, 171–72, 187, 267–68, 306; founders' views of, 9, 53, 56, 128, 141, 184, 187–88, 280–81, 300, 304, 306; and infamy, 32–33; and infliction of pain, 32, 35, 53, 298; and international law, 289–91, 306, 318; and interrogations, 36, 48; judicial, 33, 42; opposition to, 32–33, 42, 126, 157, 187, 191; physical, 243, 297–98, 323; pretrial, 32; and prisoners of war, 146; psychological, 243, 298, 323; by royal prerogative, 172; treaties barring, 227, 289, 347; and U.S. law, 202, 307, 315; and "unusual," 188–89, 306, 315

Tower of London, 94, 129

traditionalism, 28

traitors, 99, 112; drawing and quartering of, 172, 176; execution of, 100, 172; family members of, 164

transportation: British use of, 68, 100–101; of explosives, 222; as punishment, 68, 144, 153

Travers, George, 190

treason: and abolition efforts, 106, 150; acts of, 113, 135, 180, 199, 319; and bills of attainder, 147; British charges of, 101, 129; as capital crime, 26, 54, 57, 86, 88, 90, 99, 101, 116, 122, 134, 141–42, 144–45, 149–50, 157, 262, 266, 270, 272; and common law, 115; and Congress, 122; crime of, 99, 113, 118, 149, 157, 180, 191, 199, 294, 319; death sentences for, 83–84, 141, 145, 172; definition of, 116, 149; and English law, 44, 99, 134, 148, 172, 174, 266; executions for, 142, 147–48; and insanity/madness, 83–84, 260; and torture, 33, 172; trials for, 52, 101, 118, 149, 174; and U.S. Code, 222; and U.S. Constitution, 116–18, 164, 293–95

Treason Clause, 115–18, 293–95

treaties, 9, 24, 165, 289–90, 301, 318; as binding law, 165, 301. *See also specific treaties*

Treatise on the Constitutional Limitation, A, 210

Treaty of Paris, 113

Trevett v. Weeden, 320

trial by jury. *See* jury trial

Tribe, Lawrence, 327

Trop v. Dulles, 4, 20, 198, 236, 242, 296, 298, 333

Tryon, William, 58, 133

Tucker, St. George, 305, 307

Turkey, punishments in, 142

Turnbull, Robert, 67–68

Turner, George, 134

Turner, William, 72, 75

Tuscan(y), 35; abolition in, 38, 46, 53, 70, 74, 78; penal code, 38–39, 46, 76

Tyburn, 175, 267

Uganda: executions in, 64, 228, 264; Supreme Court, 227–28

unalienable rights, 102, 104, 162, 168, 179–80, 289, 323–24, 333, 341, 363. *See also* inalienable rights

Uniform Code of Military Justice, 315

United Kingdom, 20; as abolitionist, 247; and death row phenomenon, 227; homicide rate in, 247. *See also* England; Great Britain

United Nations, 1, 288–89, 347; Charter, 289; Commission on Human Rights, 261; Convention on the Rights of the Child, 20, 23, 290; General Assembly, 287–89; resolutions, 287–88; Secretary General, 288, 342; Universal Declaration of Human Rights, 289, 333

United States: Army, 130, 191, 198, 251, 277; Attorney General, 54, 85, 92, 262, 278, 334; capital crimes in, 122, 222–23, 278; Capitol, 54; Code, 222; Courts of Appeals, 220, 242–43, 249–50, 254–55; Department of Justice, 255; Department of War, 129; district courts, 121, 271; failure to ratify treaty, 20, 23, 289; formation of, 7; General Accounting Office, 224; House of Representatives, 116, 121–22, 159, 170, 184, 232; number of executions in, 223–24, 270; Senate, 23–24, 51, 116, 122, 170, 184, 204, 293, 319; treaty reservations, 24, 289. *See also* Bill of Rights; Confederation Congress; Congress; Constitution; Continental Congress; military; President(s); Supreme Court; *specific jurisdictions*

United States v. Bajakajian, 195

United States v. Salerno, 195

Universal Declaration of Human Rights: right to life, 289, 333; text of, 289

University of Bordeaux, 36

University of Chicago, 283, 318

University of Edinburgh, 66

University of Fribourg, 255

University of Pavia, 34

University of Pennsylvania, 83

"unusual": in Declaration of Independence, 185; and discrimination, 216; meaning of, 4, 29, 176, 181, 212, 295–96, 298–99, 302–3, 305, 308, 311, 329; punishments, 16, 25, 176, 294, 299–306, 314; relationship to "cruel," 181, 308; "rigor," 217, 314; as subjective, 185, 295, 330; use by founders, 181, 185, 299, 306, 312, 322; use by jurists, 312–13; use in legislation, 181, 313–15; versus "illegal," 215

"unusual and cruel treatment," 218

Utah: executions in, 211, 223, 225; stress inoculation programs, 263

Uttecht v. Brown, 231

Valley Forge, 130

Vaughan, Benjamin, 125

Vaughan, David, 57

Vaux, Roberts, 159

Venetian Inquisition, 39

vengeance, 3, 74, 110, 116, 124, 135, 143, 245–46, 262, 280, 292, 347

Venturi, Franco, 44

Vermont, 69; constitution, 87; penitentiary in, 269

Verri, Alessandro, 34

Verri, Pietro, 33–34

Versailles, court of, 138

vices, as death eligible, 265–66

victim impact statements, 195

victim(s) of murder. *See* homicide(s)

Vienna Convention on Consular Relations, 288

Vietnam, death sentences in, 287

Vietnam War, 279

View of the Constitution of the United States, 305

Vila, Bryan, 278

Villette, Marquise de, 261

violence: concept of, 343; cycle/psychology of, 246; forms of, 274

violent crimes. *See* homicide(s); murder(s); rape; terrorism

Virgin Islands, 315

Virginia, 52, 59, 98, 103, 123, 127, 146, 149, 227, 262, 320, 322; abolition efforts in, 86, 139–46, 156–57; capital cases/crimes in, 154, 337; Committee of Revisors, 141, 150, 156, 304; constitution, 54, 98, 140–41, 147, 157, 163, 185, 189, 320; constitutional convention, 154; Court of Appeals, 60; "cruel and unusual punishments" clause, 119, 155, 162–63, 177–78, 187–89, 294, 299; Declaration of Rights, 104, 119, 155, 165, 167–69, 171, 176–78, 185, 187–88, 216–17, 296, 320; dividing murder into degrees, 150; dueling in, 336; effigies hanged in, 97; executions in, 8, 18, 223, 270, 306; General Assembly, 48, 147; General Court, 303; House of Burgesses, 98, 140; House of Delegates, 156, 320; and judicial review, 320; and juvenile offenders, 240; legislature, 86, 150, 154, 156–57, 160, 167; oath of allegiance, 56; penal

reform in, 139–51, 141–51, 156–57, 178, 196, 303–4; prisons in, 150, 269; ratifying convention, 155, 165–67, 168–69, 177, 184, 187–88, 294, 299, 302, 310, 320, 330; Regiment, 126; slave rebellion in, 151–53, 188–89; and slavery, 56, 120; and Stamp Act, 97; Supreme Court, 188, 320; Supreme Court of Appeals, 189, 199; and torture, 188; treatment of slaves in, 8, 188–89, 313

Virginia Independent Chronicle, 163

"volunteers," 225

Voltaire, 78, 92; background of, 40–41, 48; on Beccaria, 33, 39–40, 47–48; influence of, 41–42, 125, 134, 261; views of, 39–43

Wainwright v. Witt, 16, 231

waiver of appeals. *See* "volunteers"

Walker, Charles, 247

Walnut Street Jail, 8, 66, 82, 114, 126

Walnut Street Prison, 68, 83, 226, 269

Waltheof (Earl of Northumbria), 44

Ward, Nathaniel, 173

war(s), 2, 28, 45, 77, 81, 88, 105–6, 112, 203, 219, 274, 276–78, 288, 295, 336, 341–42; rules of, 128. *See also* Articles of War; *specific wars*

war crimes, 290

War of 1812, 54, 59

War of the Austrian Succession, 34

wardens, 227, 263–64, 278

Warren, Earl, 298–99

Warren, Joe, 209

Warren, Thomas, 128

Washington, D.C., 59, 148, 188; abolition in, 222; and dueling, 335; and life-without-parole sentences, 239–40, 337; sentencing practices, 325

Washington (state): abolition in, 278; executioners, 260; executions in, 223, 260; lethal injection protocol, 237

Washington, George, 51, 59, 62, 84, 111, 114, 140, 162–63, 273; and Beccaria, 51, 131; on Bill of Rights, 170–71; as commander, 98, 127, 133, 135, 149; on corporal punishments, 65, 126–27; on cruelty, 61, 130; on death penalty, 9,

126–33; on desertion, 126–27; on importance of judicial branch, 320; on Major André, 135–36; and military discipline, 126–32; ownership of slaves, 2; pardons of, 59, 128, 130–32; on proportionality, 127, 130–31; on retaliation, 129, 137–38; on risk of anarchy, 269; and Voltaire, 41; on war profiteering, 130

Washington, Martha, 51

water hoses, use of, 241

waterboarding, 267

Watkins, Craig, 232

Watson, Gabe, 290–91

Wayne, Anthony, 129

weapons of mass destruction, use of, 222

wearing armor, as capital crime, 45

Webster, Bruce, 249–50

Webster, Noah, 329

Webster, Pelatiah, 120

Weems v. United States, 196–98, 299

Weightman, Roger, 148

Weiner, Jacques, 250

Wells, Ida B., 335

West Indies, 133, 144, 271

West Point, 135

West Virginia, 225; abolition in, 278

Western lands, 118–19, 167. *See also* Northwest Ordinance

Western State Penitentiary, 8

Westminster, 94, 108, 175

Wharton, Thomas, 159–60

"wheelbarrow" law, 72–73, 78

"wheelbarrow" men, 69, 72–73, 120

Whigs, 100, 177

whipping, 59–60; abandonment/abolition of, 65, 83, 85–86, 210, 316, 331, 342, 344; as common/standard punishments, 7, 217, 268, 343; congressional authorization of, 122; as "cruel," 184, 212, 215–16, 218, 242–43, 272–73, 297, 313–14; in Eighth Amendment debate, 186, 327; and English law, 172, 175, 268; and Fourteenth Amendment, 204; as "indignity"/shameful, 54, 69; as "infamous" punishments, 191, 311; as "light punishments," 78; limitations on, 121, 144, 173–74; as military discipline,

127, 130–31; as not "unusual," 303, 314; as "not usual," 193; as "odious," 303; of parricides, 267; of rapists, 90; of slaves/blacks, 7–8, 188–89, 215–19, 268, 313–14, 337, 343; of thieves, 50, 89; as "unusual," 218, 242–43; as "usual," 11, 219, 314

Whiskey Rebellion, 59, 83, 132

White, Alexander, 123

White, Byron, 280

White, Phillip, 137

White, William, 76

whites: on death row, 224; and death sentences/executions, 272, 284; exonerations of, 236

Whitgift, John, 172

Whitley v. Albers, 221

Whitten v. Georgia, 208

Wigle, Philip, 59

Wilf, Steven, 68

Wilkerson v. Utah, 200, 202, 211, 299

Wilkins v. Gaddy, 7

Willett, Jim, 264

William III (king), 94, 174

William of Orange. *See* William III

William the Conqueror, 44, 335

Williamsburg, VA, 140, 150, 306

Williamson, Ronald, 233

Willingham, Cameron, 232

Wilmington, DE, 72

Wilson, Bird, 58

Wilson, James, 9, 51–53, 57–58, 105, 186, 269, 321–22, 340; background of, 51–53; and Beccaria, 51–53; on common law, 306; on cruelty, 52–53; as defense counsel, 101; on judicial independence, 346; on "long use"/"custom," 302

Wirt, William, 149

Wisconsin, 118; abolition in, 275–76

witchcraft: as capital crime, 88–89, 173, 266, 270; in Germany, 45; punishment of, 134, 144, 266

Witherspoon, John, 154

Witherspoon v. Illinois, 229, 231

witness, killing of, 222

Wolfers, Justin, 247

women: and benefit of clergy, 268; burning of, 45, 172, 174; on death row, 11,

224; and dependent infants, 289; exclusion from juries, 231; execution of, 45, 286; and Fourteenth Amendment, 317; pregnant, 289; and rape, 2, 143, 199, 279; stoning of, 286–87

women's suffrage, 317, 342

Woodford, Jeanne, 264

Woodson v. North Carolina, 201, 324–25

World Court. *See* International Court of Justice

World Medical Association, 259

World War I, 278, 325

World War II, 278, 288

Worthington, Michael, 249

Wren, Christopher, 108

wrongful convictions, 29, 41–42, 118, 232–33, 235–37, 336, 344, 346. *See also* errors; innocence

Wyoming: executions in, 223; Supreme Court, 210

Wythe, George, 86, 114, 140–41, 150, 166–67, 183, 307, 320

Xuanzong (emperor), 45

XYZ Affair, 261

Yale Law School, 255

Yale University, 47, 63, 69, 120

Yemen, executions in, 20, 64, 287

York, Mary Lou, 254–55

Yorktown, battle of, 137

Yugoslavia, 290

Zimbabwe Supreme Court, 228

Zimring, Franklin, 234

Zyprexa, 251